Ray Charles
Man and Music

ALSO BY **MICHAEL LYDON**

Rock Folk **1971**

Boogie Lightning **1974**

How to Succeed in Show Business by Really Trying **1985**

Writing and Life **1995**

Ray Charles
Man and Music

MICHAEL **LYDON**

RIVERHEAD BOOKS

A MEMBER OF PENGUIN PUTNAM INC. *NEW YORK 1998*

Riverhead Books
a member of
Penguin Putnam Inc.
375 Hudson Street
New York, NY 10014

Song permissions may be found beginning on page 435.

Library of Congress Cataloging-in-Publication Data

Lydon, Michael.
Ray Charles: man and music / by Michael Lydon.
p. cm.
Includes bibliographical references, discography, and index.
ISBN 1-57322-132-5
1. Charles, Ray, 1930– . 2. Singers—United States—Biography.
I. Title.
ML420.C46L93   1998   98-29602 CIP MN
782.42164'092—dc21
[B]

Printed in the United States of America

1   3   5   7   9   10   8   6   4   2

This book is printed on acid-free paper. ∞

Book design by Mauna Eichner

FOR MY DAUGHTER, **SHUNA LYDON**

Tiger, tiger, burning bright
In the forests of the night

William Blake

Contents

Prologue

Through the seventeenth, eighteenth, and nineteenth centuries, borne in the bodies and souls of millions of settlers and slaves, two great rivers of music, one from Europe, one from Africa, flowed three thousand miles west across the Atlantic. Washing up on the shores of the Americas, the rivers began to blend and commingle. The confluence came to full flood in the twentieth century as music wedded itself to electricity. This charged union gave birth to a new music, the popular music of our time.

These grand events in music history open the broadest view upon the life this book relates.

PART I

YOUTH

**The woodworking shop on South Campus at the
Florida School for the Deaf and Blind, mid-1930s.**

Florida School for the Deaf and Blind

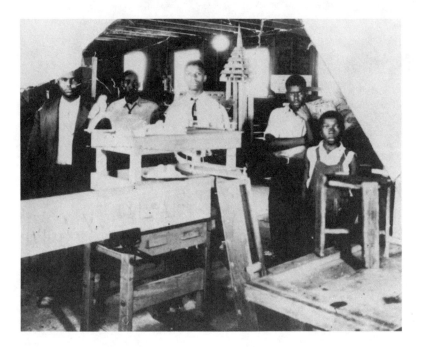

I was born with music inside me.
Like my ribs, my liver, my kidneys,
my heart. Like my blood.

Ray Charles

Greenville
1930–1937

For a hundred miles west of the Atlantic coast, the land of northern Florida lies flat as a floor covered by a thick rug of gray-green vegetation. In fertile fields, venerable live oaks, bearded by Spanish moss, bend grandly to earth. Bright green palmettos bunch cheerfully around slender brown trunks in the piney woods, and creepers tangle everything in flowered variety and profusion. East of the Suwannee River, the land is marshy; lakes and ponds and lazy creeks abound. West of the Suwannee, the land starts a gradual rise, and the old east-west road, U.S. 90, begins to undulate to the rhythm of mountains eroding into plain, a rhythm that accelerates slowly into rolling hills and pastured valleys over the sixty miles to Tallahassee. Atop the first real hill in the rhythm stands the Madison County courthouse. The six windows of its silver cupola survey the territory in all directions like six bright eyes.

In 1776 that territory was a wilderness. Then white settlers brought slaves to fell the virgin forests and to plant cotton and tobacco, wresting the land from the Indians and the Spanish, until in 1821 Spain ceded the whole peninsula to the new United States of America. Sandy Ford, at a ford on the Aucilla River, was the first settlement to spring up in Madison County's western reaches. The second was Station Five, the fifth stop from Tallahassee on the Florida Central and Western Railway.

In 1876 an ambitious settler, Elijah James Hays, bought a huge tract of land sur-rounding Station Five and began using the station to market his plantation's livestock, cotton, tobacco, and timber. Hays owned a general store, a brickyard, and a turpentine still; he sold his cotton direct to W. W. Gordon, exporters in Savannah. Hays' enter-prise drew tradesmen and their families, and the railroad village prospered as Sandy Ford declined. By 1887 the town's Ladies Aid Society had decided that Station Five needed a more genteel name. Mrs. Morgan, a native of Greenville, South Carolina, sug-gested that Greenville sounded nice and refined. Their husbands spit skeptically at the notion that a new name would change rough-and-ready Station Five, but the ladies pre-vailed and Greenville the town became.

Greenville grew with the infant century. In 1912, the town passed a "milestone," as a local history put it: an ordinance forbidding hogs to roam the streets. World War I and the booming twenties provided eager markets for all the lumber, cotton, and cat-tle Greenville could bring to rail, and other milestones followed: the first electric power company in 1923, the first high school graduation in 1926, and the first town well, 195 feet deep, dug in 1927.

Busy North Grand Street, Greenville's main drag, along the east-west railroad track, was still unpaved as the 1930s began. On the station side, porters loaded trains from stacks of freight brought in by mule wagons and gasoline trucks. Ladies and chil-dren stepped off passenger coaches, back from a week's vacation with relatives on the Atlantic coast. On the store side, planters in broad-brimmed hats signed bills with clerks in the shaded interior of Mr. Hays' Bank of Greenville, talking among themselves about the price of cotton and the troubles on Wall Street. In the warehouses, farmers with cotton to sell bargained for harnesses and nails, canvas and candles, while their wives shopped for sundries at Reams' department store. White teenagers spooned at King's pharmacy, dawdling over their Cokes, and little colored boys, barefoot and in ripped overalls, hung on hitching posts and watched the world go by.

Hot humid summer gripped Greenville in September 1930. Through the still air came the puffing of trains, the screech of tenders trundling to and from warehouse de-pots. Smoke rose from the Prince Veneer and Southern Lumber mills, where sweating black men, stripped to the waist, wrapped iron chains around their wrists to tug raw trunks to the screaming blades that sliced tall yellow pine into board feet of lumber and skinned short white pine into orange-crate strips. Greenville's business district extended a few blocks north of North Grand through drab streets lined with barbershops and cafes, a blacksmith and stables, to the Andrews Hotel, the biggest building in town. Be-hind its awninged windows the Porkchop Gang, rural politicians and their landowner cronies, met over bourbon and cigars to plot control of the state legislature, a discreet fifty miles west in Tallahassee. To the south of North Grand, the land rose in a slight hill, where stood the big white Baptist church and the houses of the town's leading white families, unpretentious frame dwellings on streets canopied by spreading oaks.

West of town, North Grand soon wore down to a double wagon track, and songbirds and buzzing bugs drowned out the sawmills. Wild morning glories wrapped green vines and blue trumpets over sagging fence posts. Rickety shacks perched on tiny lots squeezed between forests and farms. Across from the big wooden New Zion Baptist Church, a nameless smaller road turned south across the railroad tracks and past a second wooden church, the modest New Shiloh Missionary Baptist. A half-mile farther a cluster of small houses and shacks stood under tall pines and oaks, a black quarter everybody called Jellyroll.

The name, rightly, had a raffish air. Colored folk who had lived in Greenville for years lived in Blackbottom, the black quarter in town watched over by the white folks on top of the hill. Jellyroll was out from under white eyes, a sandy clearing in the woods where transient workers had thrown up tar-paper shacks when work held through more than one season. Nobody had lived in Jellyroll long, nobody knew where the others had come from or might go next. The men and women of Jellyroll were by and large greenhorns from the plantations, drawn by the promise of cash for menial labor. Living close to Greenville felt more like town than the sharecropper cabins they had left, but Jellyroll was still country. On Sunday the people prayed hard, all week they worked hard, and Saturday night they found a bit of the free and easy at Mr. Pit's Red Wing Cafe.

Wiley Pitman was a jovial brown-skinned man, fat, with a wide grin, and known far beyond Jellyroll as a fine piano player. With his wife, Miz Georgia, he owned the Red Wing, a wooden plank building facing the road from North Grand. The cafe doubled as a small general store where Miz Georgia sold kerosene and matches, flour and salt, cold beer and pig's-foot sandwiches. A few tables filled the middle of the floor, and against one wall stood a jukebox and a piano. Out back stood a boardinghouse where Mr. Pit had rooms for the watermelon pickers who overflowed the place in summertime, and rooms, as one longtime resident put it, "for husbands going with other men's wives." Behind the boardinghouse stood several shacks.

Time has swept those shacks and the Red Wing Cafe into "the limbo of things that disappear," as Dreiser wrote. Decades later, under gray December skies, only the tumbledown boardinghouse remained, a fading specter in a tangled wood of weeds and baby trees. Yet in September 1930, the Red Wing was the lively hub of a village, and the shacks out back housed a family: Margaret Robinson, her grown son Bailey, his wife Mary Jane, and an orphan girl they had adopted, Aretha Williams.

Bailey Robinson and his mother had come to Greenville from Albany, Georgia, a hundred miles to the north, in the 1920s. That much two elderly Jellyroll natives,

Bessie Brown and Mrs. Mary Clemmons, remembered clearly. Neither knew where Mary Jane came from, and the deeper roots of the Robinson family may be lost forever. Jellyroll respected Margaret, called "Muh," as a nice old lady and Bailey as a big, rough man, six feet tall or more and heavily muscular. He worked at a mill pulling logs into the skids; sometimes he laid track for the railroad. Mary Jane, a plain, thickset woman, worked at a mill too, stacking planks, "uneducated but a good person," remembered a neighbor. Aretha was a slip of a girl, lovely to look at, with long wavy black hair. Her mother had died a year or two before. Her father, a man Bailey worked with, couldn't keep her, and Bailey and Mary Jane took her in as their ward. Williams was her surname, but everybody called her Retha Robinson.

That September 1930, the goings-on at the Robinsons' had all Jellyroll gossiping. Little Retha was pregnant, there was no way such a skinny girl could hide it. She wasn't stepping out with anybody as far as anybody knew. Who could the daddy be? Bailey blamed a boy named Jack Wilkerson, because, as Bessie Brown remembered, Jack had gone with the two girls into the fields one day when their mamas sent them out to cut straw for brooms. Bailey told Jack he'd have to marry Retha. But Bessie told her aunt Eliza that Jack and Retha hadn't done anything out in the fields. Instead, a few weeks before, Bailey had taken a few kids for a ride in his car down to Petty Springs. The group had gotten separated in the woods, and when Bessie and her friends came back, they found Bailey lying with Retha. Aunt Eliza spread that word about the quarter, Bailey stopped denying he was the daddy, and Jack was free to go.

Few in Jellyroll had time for high and mighty attitudes, yet to judge by Zora Neale Hurston's *Their Eyes Were Watching God,* set in a West Florida quarter just like Jellyroll, tongues must have wagged about swollen little Retha, just as they wagged over Janie when she came back from her adventure with Tea Cake: "What she doin' coming back here in dem overhalls? Can't she find no dress to put on?—Where's dat blue satin dress she left here in?"

To still such tongues, Margaret and Bailey sent Retha back to relatives in Albany late that summer to have the baby. Toward the end of September she gave birth to a baby boy. No birth certificate exists, but the baby, when grown, always declared his birthday to be September 23, 1930. After a couple of months to get back on her feet, Retha returned to Jellyroll with her son. She named him Ray Charles Robinson.

▐▌▐▌▐▌▐▌▐▌▐▌

Retha came back to Jellyroll with little Ray, RC everybody called him, but there was no going back to how things had been. Bailey and Mary Jane soon separated, and Bailey moved south to Shamrock, another small town, where he took a new wife, Stella, by whom he had several children; he seldom came back to Greenville and had little to do with raising the boy. Retha and Mary Jane remained close—Mary Jane had lost a son, Jabbo, and doted on RC—but Retha, no more than sixteen and with a baby in diapers, was on her own as never before.

"What was life here like in the Depression?" said one Greenville man in his seventies. "Bad." In 1932, Loomis King, the town's leading doctor, took in only $450, much of that in hams or eggs. The Bank of Greenville survived the worst days, but out in Jellyroll, Jim Crow and poverty, like twin pitiless gods, decreed the destinies and daily lives of Retha, RC, and their Jellyroll neighbors. One Christmas the town police shot a black man near Mr. Pit's cafe. "He hadn't done nothing," Mrs. Clemmons remembered. "After it happened, it was like it hadn't happened at all." Dinner in Jellyroll was a dish of homegrown greens; when they had no fuel to fry or boil their sweet potatoes, the people ate them raw. Folding money was as scarce as shoes on children.

To keep abreast in this struggle, physical strength was a must, and Retha, in the memory of all, was weak. No one remembered just what was wrong with her—Mrs. Clemmons blamed it on giving birth so young—but she was "sickly," "walked with a cane," and "had a sore on her leg." She couldn't handle the better-paying mill work as Mary Jane could, nor could she run a laundry business, as many black women did, with white clients on the hill. Retha and RC were among the poorest of the poor in Jellyroll, yet there was little chance they'd starve or be forced to move on. Everybody knew Retha and her story, and they liked her and her bright-eyed boy. The other women sent her their extra washing and ironing. Mary Jane became RC's second mother, glad to watch him when Retha was working or had to lie down, and she loved to buy him sweets at the cafe.

RC grew, a healthy, happy baby. By his first birthday he had a brother, George. No one remembered who George's father was, but all remembered that Mr. Pit and Miz Georgia, who had no children of their own, adopted George to take the added burden off Retha. As soon as RC could run about, little George toddling behind him, the brothers were inseparable, a tiny Tom and Huck playing hide-and-seek in the woods, throwing rocks and stomping on bugs like boys from time immemorial. RC loved to play with matches, lighting them in the blackness of a moonless night and holding them before his face, feeling like he was "lighting up the whole world."

Retha believed in strict discipline, and by the time RC and George were five and four, she had set them to their chores, chopping wood and hauling water. Every Sunday she took them to the New Shiloh Baptist Church back up the road toward Greenville. Founded before the Civil War as a mission to "our black brothers and sisters" from Greenville's white Baptists, the New Shiloh had become a full black church, with fiery preachers stirring the spirits of the faithful to tears and shouts of joy, to songs and beating tambourines, swaying hips and clapping hands. Sometimes Sunday meant chicken for dinner, and every great while, for sure once a year on May 20, the old maypole day colored folk still celebrated, all Jellyroll gathered for parties that lasted deep into the night, feasts when they barbecued whole hogs and goats over open pit fires, and the moonshine flowed free. Other nights Muh tucked the boys into bed and told them stories of the bad old days when hooded white men bearing torches thundered through the quarter, and they fell asleep shivering in fear and wonder.

When still too young for school at Greenville Training, the town's public school for colored children, RC and George began to evidence gifts of particular intelligence. George amazed Jellyroll with his skill at arithmetic, his inventiveness in making toys from bits of wood and baling wire. RC showed a similar curiosity in mechanical things, poking his head between the men as they bent over sputtering Model T engines, tinkering with broken bikes and farm machinery. Most of all, RC began to demonstrate an unusual interest in and aptitude for music.

"Either RC was playing the piano or he was listening to the jukebox"—that is Greenville's universal memory of the young Ray Charles, and the grown man's memory fully agrees. "I was a normal kid, mischievous and into everything," Charles recalled years later, "but I loved music, it was the only thing that could really get my attention." One day when he was about three, RC was playing by the shacks when he heard Mr. Pit break into a driving boogie-woogie on the Red Wing's battered old upright. Magnetized by the clanging chords and rocking beat, RC ran up the alley past the boardinghouse, pushed open the battered screen door, and stared amazed at Mr. Pit's flying fingers. Seeing him, Mr. Pit laughed, swept the boy onto his lap, and let him reach out his hands to the keys, run his fingers up and down over their warm ebony and ivory textures.

From then on whenever RC heard Mr. Pit playing, he'd race into the cafe and, as he remembered years later with gratitude, "the man *always* let me play." Wiley Pitman was no amateur, as Ray Charles recalled him, but a stride pianist who, had he not chosen the simple life in Greenville, could have duked it out with giants like Pete Johnson and Willie "The Lion" Smith. That may be a student's exaggeration, but Mr. Pit did prove to be a superb teacher, showing RC first how to pick out a melody with one finger. "Oh no, son, you don't play like that," he said when RC banged too hard on the keys, but when out of awkward fumblings the boy got a beat going on his own, Mr. Pit encouraged him with noisy shouts of "That's it, sonny, that's it."

Near the piano stood the cafe jukebox, a marvel of flashing lights and moving metal. For a nickel, a mechanical arm would lift a black platter from a drum of records and set it spinning, the steel needle falling into the groove with a scratchy hiss, filling the room with electric sounds magically recorded long ago and far away. RC soon had a special place on a bench beside the jukebox where he sat for hours, his ear pressed up against the speaker. Sometimes when Mary Jane gave him a few coins for candy, they'd end up in the jukebox instead. More often RC didn't have the money to pick his own songs, so he listened to everything anybody played: boogie-woogie piano by Albert Ammons, gutbucket blues by Tampa Red, the big bands of Fletcher Henderson and Duke Ellington.

Work and music, running in the woods, church on Sunday—life flowed on for RC and George, Retha and Mary Jane, with little to mark one day from the next, until one terrible afternoon in 1935. "I can still hear the women shouting for help, the sound of their cries," remembered Mrs. Clemmons' daughter Elesta, then a girl of six or seven. The scene seared itself irrevocably into Ray Charles' mind, leaving a scar that would never fully heal.

The afternoon was hot and sunny. To cool off, the two boys splashed in and out of a big washtub behind the cafe. Retha was inside ironing. George climbed inside the tub, ducking under the water for a shiny penny, shouting and laughing. Suddenly RC realized that George's splashings had a frightening urgency. His baby brother wasn't playing, he was in trouble. For a moment he froze in terror, then he lunged to the tub to try and pull George out. He couldn't; George was kicking and flailing his arms and legs, and RC, only a year older, didn't have the strength. He ran to the shack screaming, "Mama, Mama." Retha dropped her iron and came running. She lifted George from the tub and tried to shake, rub, and breathe life back into him, but it was too late. George had drowned. RC burst into tears, and Retha started wailing in pain. Neighbors came running. All Jellyroll mourned the little boy, and even white Greenville heard about the colored child who had died so sadly.

To have a beloved brother die at any age is a bitter, wrenching blow; to have that brother die while you and he are still infants, to see it happen and be powerless to prevent it, can only be a primal experience that will reverberate through a lifetime. Grief, guilt, anger, fear, loneliness, a bewildered sense of innocence crushed by fate—all must have coursed through RC's little-boy spirit.

A second blow followed on the heels of the first. A few months after George's death, mucus began to ooze from RC's eyes like thick tears, and he woke every morning to find his eyelids stuck shut. Retha bathed off the crusts, but it still took the boy ten minutes to adjust to the light. Over months the breadth of his vision began to shrink, and he found he could see less and less distance into the world. People and things became unfocused blobs. Retha took the boy into Greenville to see Frank McLeod, the doctor who saw the colored people in town. Dr. McLeod peered into RC's eyes with bright lights, prescribed drops and ointments, then sent Retha and the boy on to a clinic in Madison, fourteen miles away, RC's longest trip to date. The clinic doc-

Greenville Training; they didn't know how to teach blind children there. Where could he go to school? How could Retha find out?

For answers to questions of that kind in the South of 1936, colored folks had to go to white folks, and that's what Retha did. She talked to the lady at the post office and to Dr. McLeod, and soon all Greenville knew about the blind boy in Jellyroll and his determined mother. Dr. McLeod told her there was a state school for the deaf and blind in St. Augustine that took a few colored children. Retha didn't read or write well enough to apply to the school, but Mitty King, a Jellyroll neighbor, cooked for the Reams family, who lived on the hill. Mr. Reams owned the big store in town and Miz Ruth was a nice lady. Maybe the Reamses would help.

Reams is still a common name in and around Greenville, twenty-one listings in the 1994 Madison County phone book, all descendants of Albert Reams, a settler contemporary with Isaac Hays and a cofounder of the bank. Mitty King's Reamses—Albert's son Albert Dupree, his wife, the former Ruth Scruggs, and their three children—ranked among Greenville's first families, and the Madison *Enterprise Recorder* respectfully noted their comings and goings. Yet they lived more like plain folks than aristocrats. A.D.'s knack for business made him rich, but he remained a farmer at heart, and Ruth, known affectionately as "Ma Pop," taught Sunday school at Greenville Baptist and kept busy on civic projects sponsored by the Women's Club. "A.D. and Ruth lived the country tradition of helping your neighbor," recalled a neighbor who grew up playing with their children. "They tried to act on what they heard in church."

Retha, with RC by the hand, walked up to the Reamses' white house on the western slope of the hill. Mitty King, smiling encouragement, met them at the kitchen door. In the living room, RC played for the company on Miz Ruth's piano, and Retha told her story one more time. A.D. and his wife were taken with the bright boy and his forceful mother, and, yes, if they could help a blind child get his chance in life, they'd do all they could.

Dr. McLeod told A.D. whom to write to, and soon word came back: the Florida School for the Deaf and Blind did have a department for colored children. The fall 1937 term had begun September 7, but RC could begin school whenever he got there. The state paid room, board, and tuition, plus train fare to and from in the fall and spring. It wouldn't cost Retha a thing. She could put RC on a train, the conductor would keep an eye on him, and a teacher from the school would meet him at the station in St. Augustine.

Retha knew at once that RC would go to the blind school, no doubt about it. This was her son's only hope; she had to make him take it. Little RC, barely seven, knew just as certainly he didn't want to leave Mama and Mary Jane, his playmates Johnnycake and Elesta Mae, all of Jellyroll and Greenville. "Mama," he cried, "don't make me go,

Mama. I wanna stay with you." He ran and hid behind Mary Jane's skirts as she argued on his side against Retha. How could she send RC so far from home, alone among strangers? He'd be better off here where folks knew and loved him.

Retha didn't budge. The morning came, and the little family walked up the road from Jellyroll to town. The locomotive steamed into the train station, eastbound from Tallahassee. RC had never been on a train before, and this one was no more than a black blob to his failing eyes. This was RC Robinson, Retha told the conductor, going to the blind school. The conductor said the boy would be fine. "All aboard!" With a last hug and kiss from Mary Jane, a last "Mind your teachers, son!" from Retha, RC climbed up the metal steps and took a seat on a hard wooden bench in the colored car. The other passengers gave the blind boy a passing glance, then paid him no more mind. RC sat by himself, as unhappy as a little boy can be, and didn't say a word. From Madison County the train ran clickety-clack out of the low hills, east into the rising sun, over the bridge across the Suwannee, and on to the flatlands and the coast.

St. Augustine
1937-1945

When seven-year-old RC Robinson got off the train from Greenville on October 23, 1937, the Florida School for the Deaf and Blind had just passed its fiftieth birthday. Thomas Hines Coleman, a graduate of Gallaudet, then America's only college for the deaf, convinced the Florida legislature in 1882 to approve $20,000 for the state's first school for the deaf and blind. By donating $1000 and five acres on San Marco Avenue a mile north of its famed Spanish fort, St. Augustine, "The Oldest City in America," won the bidding to be home to the school, and the first students began classes in 1885. In fifty years, the five acres had grown to fifteen, yet the campus was still modest: a dozen low wooden dormitories and classroom buildings connected by cinder paths winding between mossy oaks and tall palms—a quiet world far removed from the winter resort's social splash.

A colored teacher met RC at the train and guided him to what everyone called South Campus, a two-story I-shaped building on the south side of a stand of wild bamboo. RC soon learned he better not wander north of the bamboo: Florida D&B was rigidly segregated by race in 1937, and the rest of the fifteen acres, called North Campus, belonged to the white kids and teachers. North Campus had separate buildings for every purpose; South Campus, crowded classrooms for the deaf and blind, boys' and girls' dormitories, auditorium, dining room, laundry, as well as a residence for colored employees, under one roof. This would be RC's second home, and tough training ground, through the next eight years of his life.

Known officially as the Colored Department of the Florida School for the Deaf and Blind, South Campus existed in those days as a school within a school, ninety students compared with 300-plus on the white side. The colored faculty, lower-paid than white teachers and always shorthanded, taught a curriculum geared more to "industrial arts" like broom making than to higher education. The colored staff grew vegetables for the dining rooms on North Campus that came back to the colored kids as the white kids' leftovers. "When a typewriter or a sewing machine got too old or broke on North Campus, they'd send it over to us," a retired music teacher remembered, wincing in pain as he spoke. "We got their old Braille books with the bumps so mashed down the children could hardly read them." North Campus' power kept South Campus tense, the colored faculty and students sharing a seldom expressed fear: "Let's not get out of step with the people over there, they can make trouble for us." Yet veterans of the era also remembered the pride of surviving adversity with their chins up. "We did with what we had," remembered Joe Walker, a blind student a year younger than RC. "And you know what? We enjoyed ourselves too!"

The Colored Department's esprit de corps in the 1930s and 40s began with a dedicated faculty. In the Depression and under Jim Crow, a position at Florida D&B was a good job for a young colored professional, and the school attracted talented teachers who labored on, knowing full well that little future lay ahead for many of their charges. Three couples stood out: the school's first deaf black graduate, Cary White, who aside from teaching drove the school trash truck, and his wife Jennie; Ernest and Opal Lawrence, who both taught music; and Inez Knowles, who began teaching deaf black children in 1924 as Miss Harrison and later married Otis Knowles, a Braille teacher and boys' supervisor.

"These were fine people," remembered Joe Walker. "They gave their all to us." Even spare Mr. Knowles had a gentle side. Little Joe had a hard time learning Braille until one night Mr. Knowles sat with him at dinner. "Who's gonna win the World Series?" Mr. Knowles asked Joe. "The Yankees," he replied. "Why are the Yankees gonna win?" Mr. Knowles asked, and Joe said, "Because they have Joe DiMaggio," and he gave statistics—everybody knew Joe loved sports. "Would you like to meet Joe DiMaggio tomorrow?" said Mr. Knowles. "Sure!" said Joe. He really knew Joe DiMaggio couldn't come to St. Augustine in the middle of the World Series, but he was a kid, and so part of him hoped that just maybe he might. The next day Mr. Knowles gave Joe a Braille book and asked him, "What letter does Joe DiMaggio start with?" "J," said Joe, and Mr. Knowles put his fingers on a J, saying, "Every time you touch this letter, you're shaking hands with Joe DiMaggio. What other player do you like?" "Tommy Henrich," said Joe, and the teacher put his fingers on T and H. "He took me like that through the alphabet," Walker recalled years later, "and that's how I learned Braille."

RC didn't have Joe's trouble learning to read. Mr. Knowles started RC on his Braille primers, *Living on John's Farm* and *The White Rabbit,* and in a few weeks the boy had mastered the basics of reading with his fingertips. Doing well in the classroom, however, couldn't hide the basic fact that RC was miserable his first year on South Campus. Beginning six weeks late made him an instant outsider, and being poor enough to need clothes donated by the state put him at the bottom of the pecking order. The big boys called him "Foots" because he went barefoot, and taunted him as a crybaby when he sobbed for his mama back in Greenville. Their mockery made him cry all the more.

After a wretched fall, RC got more bad news: he couldn't go home for Christmas. Retha didn't have the money, and the state paid for travel only at the end of each year. For two weeks RC wandered the South Campus alone, missing the kids who had teased him up to the moment they left to go home for the holidays. His spirits lightened when the halls were noisy again, but soon his right eye began to throb and ache. The school doctor declared the eye had to be removed and moved RC to a bed at the North Campus infirmary for the operation. The prospect of having an eye cut out of his head terrified the little boy even more than going blind, but he couldn't stand the pain. Out came the eye, and with it RC lost his last vestige of sight. St. Augustine's mild winter became spring as he recuperated, getting back to classes just before the summer break.

In June, after nine long months away, RC stepped off the train in Greenville and ran overjoyed to his mama's arms. In what became a yearly ritual, they walked up the hill to the Reamses' for a visit and a chance for RC to show A.D. and Ruth all he had learned. Out in Jellyroll his pals crowded around. "Every spring the word would spread, 'RC is back, RC is back!' " remembered Elesta Pritchett. "We'd all get together and swap stories. In a few days it'd be like he had never left." Mr. Pit welcomed RC back to the piano and jukebox at the Red Wing Cafe, Mary Jane plied him with treats, and Retha set him back at his chores. Two ladies at the New Shiloh Baptist, Hattie Alexander and Effie Washington, had pianos in their homes, and Sunday afternoons they invited RC and his friend Johnny Williams to play and sing hymns and gospel songs, then served them sandwiches and cake. Soon enough the summer fled, and as he turned eight RC took the train back to school.

RC's second year at D&B was a whole new ballgame. Joe Walker was the new boy that fall, and RC wasted no time dishing out what he had been forced to take the year before. "Ain't you done yet, boy?" he'd ask Joe at breakfast. "Can't you see the people trying to clean up here? When we get outside, I'm gonna whip your ass." At first Joe didn't fight back because his mother had told him, "Whatever you do, son, don't fight." When the boys did tangle, stocky Joe jumped close to get inside tall RC's flailing arms. "The teachers stopped us," Walker remembered, "made us sit together by ourselves, glum and sore, but that's when our friendship began, talking to each other when we had nobody else to talk to. Bit by bit, we started to get in the groove together."

RC also began to get in the groove of school life, a routine that varied little during his St. Augustine years. The sixty boys, blind and deaf, slept in one large open room, the beds lined along the walls. A bell woke them at 5:30 in the morning, and they gathered by four basins to wash their faces, the quick dressers racing downstairs to hang around outside. Breakfast was served at 6:40, and the boys lined up in the hall, the blind along one wall, the deaf along the other. At a signal from a supervisor, the deaf line led the way into the dining room. The boys assembled around the tables and stood there until one of the blind boys asked a blessing over the food.

The food was good for an institution, remembered Paul Behn, a chubby kid a few years younger than RC and Joe. Breakfast was grits and a little butter; cream of wheat or oatmeal on colder days. They had milk every morning, and once a week on Mondays, a glass of orange juice. When the blind boys heard the deaf children pushing their chairs back, it was time to race back upstairs and finish off last night's homework. Some, especially jazz fans like RC and James Kendrick, would turn on the radio, WFOY, St. Augustine, their favorite station.

At five to eight the school bell would ring and they'd go to the chapel, the girls sitting on the left side, the boys on the right. Mrs. Lawrence played, and the blind sang an opening song, "America the Beautiful" or "Be Still My Soul." After the Lord's Prayer, Professor Walter Rembert, principal of the Colored Department, preached from the Bible as the kids dozed off. Classes began at nine o'clock, the lowest grades in a corner of the chapel, fourth-, fifth-, and sixth-graders in one room, upper grades in another. At 12:45 the boys went back upstairs, washed their hands, and lined up again for one o'clock dinner: vegetables and macaroni, potatoes and gravy. For meat they had stew beef, sometimes a sausage.

After dinner the girls took home economics with Mrs. Knowles: crafts, crocheting, or making rugs on frames. The boys got into coveralls and went out to the workshop, where they put together brooms. RC's main job was sewing the band around the broom straw, and he was quick at that. They also put strings on mops and caned chairs that got used on the North Campus or sold to other institutions.

With four o'clock came playtime. Generally the blind kids would play with the blind kids, the deaf with the deaf. They had what everybody called a walking pole, high bars they hung from by their hands, and on which they played tussling games. Best of all, the blind boys developed their own game, Score Ball or Sco Ball, and Paul Behn described with relish how they played it. "We'd get a thick magazine like *The Gospel Trumpet,* and we'd roll it up tight and tie a string around it, that was our ball. We'd hold it out, and using a broom handle for a bat, wham, we'd knock it down to the other fellows. If the ball hit the fence at one end, that was a score for our side, six points. If they knocked it back up this way past the cinder path, it was six points for the other team. How could we see where the ball landed? Here's where we tested our ability to hear. We'd run to where we heard it land, then sweep the ground with the bat until we found it."

The score might be 30 to 24 by five o'clock, when the boys went in, washed, and lined up for a supper of syrup and bread or spaghetti. If the Sco Ball game had been left a tie, the boys would play after supper until study hour in the classrooms downstairs. RC sometimes slept through study hour, curled up on the trunk at the end of his bed—they weren't allowed in bed until bedtime. Just before lights out, Joe Walker sometimes announced a baseball game—this the boys loved. When an afternoon game was on the radio, the Yankees against the Red Sox, for example, Joe would take down the game in Braille shorthand. When Phil Rizzuto came to bat, he'd punch out "Rizz," and if Rizz singled to left, Joe would punch out SLF. Then at night he'd replay the game on a make-believe radio station for the boys gathered around his bed, creating sound effects with bottle lids and belt buckles, ad-libbing his own comments: "It's a beautiful day here at Fenway Park, ladies and gentlemen, and Scooter Rizzuto's gonna lead off for the Yankees, here's the pitch . . ." When stern Mr. White clumped up the steps at nine o'clock, the boys scurried back to their own beds.

Through days like these RC grew from little-boyhood to young manhood, moving year by year into the "big boy" status that had seemed so regal when he first arrived. Boarding school's young-cub competition hardened RC just as Eton and Winchester harden English boys the same age. To run relay races, the blind boys stretched a long wire between two kids, the runners holding on as they dashed back and forth. In RC's first year the big boys fooled little Foots by tying one end of the wire to an iron post. "I grabbed hold of the wire," he remembered as an adult, "and started running fast as I could. I was gonna show those boys who could run barefoot. And wham!" In his second year he learned to retaliate. "I'd tie a piece of wire between two benches. Then I'd settle back and wait till the kid started walking down the sidewalk. I'd take great pleasure in hearing him fall on his face. Yeah, it might take a while, but I'd always pay back these kinds of debts. And I always did it in a way where I wouldn't get hurt."

Mr. Knowles recalled RC as a "mischievous boy," but Joe Walker countered, "RC was the kind of kid who got blamed for stuff he didn't do." Everyone remembered one thing he did do: drive a teacher's Ford around the school with a deaf kid sitting on the hood, banging with his right or left hand to give directions. Finally the car crashed backward into a tree, and a stunned RC got thrown into the back seat. Joe Walker shook him awake and helped him make his getaway.

Like many bright kids, RC learned faster than the rest of the class and goofed off waiting for them to catch up. He got more B's than A's, but Joe Walker emphatically recalled him as "the smartest kid at the school." English came easy to RC but didn't thrill him; math was a challenge, but his best classroom subject as well. He was good with his hands, a chair-caning, broom-making demon in the workshop, and he pulled apart every radio he could get his hands on. In time he learned to type seventy-five words a minute with no mistakes.

During his second year, eight-year-old RC discovered his single grand ambition, to be "a great musician," and he set about achieving it with unflagging determination. Mrs. Lawrence taught him piano, but she frowned on the boogie-woogie he had learned on Mr. Pit's knee, and schooled him instead in the classical European music tradition: harmony, keyboard technique, and the piano works of Bach, Mozart, Beethoven, and Chopin. The romance of the "Moonlight Sonata" and Chopin's nocturnes tugged at RC, but he wasn't sure he liked Bach's running lines; they gave him a nervous, unsettled feeling.

Mrs. Lawrence taught RC to read music in Braille, which includes all the symbols necessary for music notation. Yet reading music in Braille poses difficulties a sighted student doesn't face. To learn a piece, RC and the other blind students needed to play the piano's left-hand part while reading the Braille with their right hand, then switch to playing the right-hand part while reading with their left, and then combine the two into the whole piece. Never able to read the music as they played, they needed "to learn two bars and play the two from memory," as Ray remembered years later. "Then we'd learn maybe ten more bars and play the twelve . . . then learn twenty more and play the thirty-two. The roughest things were the classics. Some of them might have two hundred bars."

Outside the classroom, RC sang in the South Campus chorus and hung out with the jazz cats. Popular music, jazz, and blues were hot topics at D&B, and playing ability a prime source of status. Arguments raged around the dorm radio—who was better, Benny Goodman or Artie Shaw? RC liked Artie Shaw, but if he, a little boy, tried to change the dial, the big boys slapped his hand. Joe Lee Lawrence, Mr. Lawrence's blind younger brother, reigned as South Campus piano king in RC's first years. When Joe Lee sat down to play, the other kids listened awestruck: he was almost as good as Art Tatum! The Colored Department had only one piano the boys could practice on, because the good piano in the auditorium was for special occasions only. Competition for practice time was fierce. Joe Walker remembered that once James Kendrick tried to bully RC out of his practice time. Finally RC said Kendrick could have the piano in fifteen minutes.

"Right away I knew something was wrong. It wasn't like RC to give up so easy. RC came upstairs and James went down to play but came back up in minutes screaming mad, shouting, 'What you done, man?' Then RC opens this sack he had on the bed— it was the keys! He had taken the keys out of the piano! And he says to James, real cool, 'You only said you wanted the *piano.*'"

In time RC became D&B's reigning musician. On Fridays the South Campus Literary Society held auditorium assemblies at which, as at schools everywhere, the kids declaimed "Friends, Romans, countrymen" and read stories and essays. At these RC became the kid who played the piano, accompanied singers, and sang popular songs. "Besame Mucho" was one RC favorite, Lionel Hampton's "Joe-Joe the Devil" was another. Once he did Lil Green's "Romance in the Dark," sexy lyrics and all ("I get such a thrill, when she presses her fingertips to my lips . . . in the dark"). The kids screamed for more, but Mrs. Lawrence was not amused and ordered RC never to perform such tunes again. "Yes, ma'am," he said and obeyed.

Twice a year, at Halloween and George Washington's Birthday, the Colored Department had socials that the school paid for; for a special year-end party, the kids put in their own dimes and quarters for soda and decorations. RC, with James Kendrick on drums, got the kids dancing at many such events. For the Christmas party one year, RC found time in the workshop to rehearse five boys to sing behind him on "Jingle Bell Boogie," his own arrangement. RC Robinson and the Shop Boys stole the show.

After the first lonely Christmas, the staff chipped in for RC's trips home over the holidays, and he continued to go back to Greenville every summer. He learned to ride a bike in Greenville, guiding himself by the sound and feel of the tires on dirt and macadam, veering to the center when roadside grass whipped at his legs. A. D. Reams gave the boy rides on his truck, and sometimes Ruth invited him in to play. "Once he played Nat Cole's 'I Can't See for Looking,'" remembered Patricia Reams, one of Ruth's daughters-in-law, "and because he couldn't see, I thought he wrote it."

RC was the only blind child in Greenville, and there, more than at school, he lived alone in his dark world. He wanted to be a regular kid, to box and wrestle with the other boys, but sometimes the others left him out of their games, and he slipped off by himself into the woods and cried. On the sidewalks of town he heard adults saying, "Someday that boy'll need a cane and a tin cup." Yet Retha had no patience for self-pity in her son. "See what happens to you now," she told him. "It'll be twice as bad when you're an adult." Knowledge is the key, she told him again and again. "You're blind, but you ain't stupid. If you don't know something, people won't fool with you at all." The world is full of "educated fools," she told RC. He'd better develop some "plain horse sense," and realize that if he wanted something, he'd better learn to work for it.

Retha's fierce wisdom sunk deep into RC's soul, becoming in time the bedrock of his character, but as a twelve-year-old, he grew restive under his mama's nagging. Sometimes he stayed over a night or two with Mary Jane; she was more fun than Retha. Some of the kids had started working, and the old Jellyroll gang broke up. When they did get together, they hung around talking and teasing instead of playing their old games. RC still sang for the ladies with Johnnycake Williams, but Johnny had a girlfriend, pretty Beatrice Johnson from Daytona Beach, and they didn't want RC hanging around them all the time. Girls were on RC's mind too, and he made his first awkward moves toward the opposite sex. One afternoon alone with Elesta, he tried to teach her a card game he had learned at school. "Buck Nekkid he called it," she recalled, "but it was nothing but strip poker!"

A couple who had owned a Greenville store like Mr. Pit's before moving to Tallahassee, Henry and Alice Johnson, knew RC well—he had often played the piano at their cafe—and they didn't like what they heard about him bouncing around Jellyroll at loose ends, at home but nearly homeless. In the summers of the war years, they invited RC, just coming into his gangling height, to their little house in Frenchtown, the city's colored section. Another Frenchtown couple, Freddy and Margaret Bryant, also took RC under their wing; he felt cozy enough at their house to call them Kiddy Boo and Dolly. Their daughter Lucille taught him how to ring up sales and make change at the store's jingly cash register.

RC loved Tallahassee. Here he could zoom up and down hills on a motorbike owned by a drugstore delivery boy who lived next door; RC guided himself by listening to the exhaust of another pal riding ahead. Tallahassee was musically exciting too. The Johnsons' social lodge took up a collection to buy RC a clarinet; now he could try playing like Artie Shaw. He sat in with the Florida Agricultural and Mechanical student band, playing with two lively brothers, Julian and Nat Adderley. Most important, he began playing gigs with Lawyer Smith and his Band.

A short, balding guitar player, Lawyer Halliburton Smith led Tallahassee's premier working jazz band for over thirty years. Smith founded the band in the late 30s as the Famce Collegians—most of the players taught or studied at Florida A&M. While working as a baker at Martin and Dalton's cafeteria to make ends meet for his wife Daisy and their seven children, Smith booked the band—sometimes as big as eight pieces—into every kind of gig, weekends at the Cafe DeLuxe and the Red Bird Club, society parties, Elks Hall dances, weddings, high school proms, and roadhouses in a wide radius around the city. Every New Year's Eve at the state capitol atop Tallahassee's tallest hill, they played the Governor's Ball.

To Daisy Smith, RC was an uncouth country boy with no family to speak of, living in Tallahassee virtually as a foster child. Lawyer, however, liked RC and, recognizing the eager kid's talent, put him on gigs as pianist when he could. Those gigs gave thirteen-year-old RC his first taste of life as a professional musician, and he took right away to the smoke and the loose laughter, hanging out with the cats, the music hot and cool. Mostly he played unobtrusively in the rhythm section, tuning in on Lawyer's swinging guitar chords, but sometimes he sang. Unlike the women teachers at D&B who had punished him for singing sexily, women in the clubs liked the big blind boy's bluesy way with a lyric. One rewarded him with his first full sexual experience. Until that night sex for RC, as for most thirteen-year-olds, had been all talk and masturbation. Now the woman, herself still in her teens, took the kid to a gas station next door to the club, into the bathroom, and up onto a wooden platform with a seat and hole that served as a toilet. "She pulled up her dress, leaned against the wall, and rested one foot on that platform," Ray recalled as a grown man. "We were both standing up. . . . I loved it. It was smooth and easy, sweet and hot. Finally I was able to understand what everyone had been bullshittin' 'bout for so long."

D&B could only seem dull by comparison. Mr. Knowles went into the army in 1942; otherwise war in Europe and the Pacific didn't much stir the Colored Department's daily rounds. RC enjoyed his hard-won laurels as a popular big boy, but by the ninth grade he had learned what D&B could teach him. Many afternoons he walked down San Marco Avenue to St. Augustine proper, exploring the city until he knew it nearly as well as he knew Greenville. Musical growth also came more off-campus than on. RC began playing piano for afternoon tea parties and ladies' club socials, genteel gigs approved by the school. He also broadcast live over WFOY, where, Joe Walker recalled, RC once insisted to the conductor of the studio orchestra that one of the violinists was flat. "It got heated, a colored fourteen-year-old standing up to an old white pro, but then he checked it out and RC was right."

At school RC became something of a wiseass. "When the teachers said don't do something," remembered Paul Behn, "RC would keep on *because* they said not to. He'd be happy playing the piano for hours, but to punish him, they'd keep him out of the music room. That made him restless." As much for the thrill of risking expulsion as for the sex, RC figured out a way to crawl through South Campus' dusty attic to the girls' dorm. When all the other boys were asleep, he'd jump up through a trapdoor, feel his way across the rough joists, and jump down to his date on the other side. One night Joe Walker woke up when RC was slipping off and begged to go along.

"Lemme come, RC," Joe whispered, grabbing RC's arm. "I want some of that pussy you been talking about."

"Joe, get back under those covers," RC whispered back, pulling Joe's hand off his arm and pushing him back into bed. "Listen to me," he said, his voice low but intense. "If we get caught, they'll throw us out. Now, I can make a living from music. But nobody's hiring no black radio announcers."

RC padded off to the trapdoor, and Joe stayed in bed. Thinking it over, he sensed depths under the bravado of this precocious boy-man. "RC was not just smart, though he could discuss anything, politics, books, music, but he *knew* things. Listen: we used to play dominoes and card games, betting a few pennies, nickels, and dimes. I didn't have but the dollar my family sent from home, so I'd play slow, thinking over every angle. One day RC took me aside and said, 'The other boys don't like to play with you because you play too slow.' 'I know,' I said, 'but I worry about losing.' And RC said, and I've never forgotten it, 'A jealous man can't work and a scared man can't gamble.' Now I've lived to see the truth of that, but how did RC know it so young?"

Some nights after lights out, the sigh of ocean breezes through the oaks wafting in the windows, the boys lay awake in their bunks talking about what they would be when they grew up. One boy wanted to be a lawyer, another a psychiatrist. Paul Behn was sure he'd go to college and come back and teach at D&B, and Joe Walker said that he'd be on the radio someday. RC always said, "I'm gonna be a great musician."

"And I'll play your records!" Joe would respond, and he'd sit up in bed, grab a pair of balled-up socks as a microphone, and put on his suavest announcer voice. "Good evening, ladies and gentlemen of America, this is Joe Walker of the Columbia Broadcasting Network, and tonight, we're proud to present, direct from the Meadowbrook Club in Overton, New Jersey, *RC Robinson, His Piano and Orchestra!*"

"Yeah, Joe, yeah," RC would whisper. "Say it again, say it again."

The Death of
Retha Robinson
1945

In the faraway world, through the spring of 1945, the Allied armies fought their way deep into Germany to the shattered streets of Berlin. On the first of May the news spread: Hitler was dead. A week later the Nazis surrendered, and the Allies wheeled their bloody war machines to the task of defeating Japan.

On quiet South Campus the din of battle rumbled like distant thunder, too weak to disturb the flow of sunny days. By RC Robinson's own estimation, life was going well. At fourteen and a half he had his growth and stood five feet, eight inches. Blindness had become a long-accepted fact. School was stupid at times, but there was music, friends, nice girls. A new teacher had come to South Campus from the Navy, a noncom who ran a tight ship. When he made RC one of his dorm monitors, RC's behavior instantly improved. "RC handled that job," Paul Behn remembered. "If we were acting up, he'd say, 'Listen, boys, we better not do that,' and we'd stop."

Then out of the blue a call came to South Campus from Greenville. Retha had died; RC must come home right away. Mr. Lawrence and Mr. White found RC and broke the news to him bluntly. The boy felt struck as by a blow to his body. "Nothing had hit me like that," he recalled years later. "Not George drowning. Not going blind. Nothing."

RC took the train home, frozen by a grief bigger than his soul could handle. The grown man told the story of his mother's death many times, and each time his tone, ordinarily jaunty, turned flat and tortured. "I was completely in another world," he wrote in *My Early Years,* and in *Brother Ray.* "For a while I went a little crazy. . . . All my memories of those first days are silhouettes, shadows hanging over me." Thinking and feeling became a bruised and confused sense that life was "rotten" and "unfair," that he would never see Mama again, that she was too young to die and he was too young to be alone. RC wandered about Jellyroll in a trance, a lump in his throat so big he couldn't eat or talk. "I sat alone, silent, not moving a muscle or saying a word. Not crying, not eating, not praying. My mind just drifted somewhere out there in space."

Indomitable, frail Retha Robinson had died at no more than thirty-one. Dr. McLeod told the family and neighbors it was a freak accident, a spoiled sweet potato pie, but it may have been a final bout of the illness that had been tugging her down for so long. While she lay in a funeral parlor coffin, RC remained locked in sadness. Mary Jane tried to comfort him; so did Mr. Pit and Miz Georgia. Mr. and Mrs. Johnson drove over from Tallahassee. No one could reach him. "Folks worried about the boy," remembered Bessie Brown. "He got sicker and sicker, so they sent for Ma Beck."

Rebecca Bea, Ma Beck to colored Greenville, was a respected midwife and medicine woman then in her mid-sixties. Short and stout, the wife of carpenter Sam Bea and the mother of nineteen children, Ma Beck had doctored Retha for years with herbal remedies, had delivered George, and had comforted her and RC when George died. People loved Ma Beck for her wisdom and her goodness. If anybody could talk directly to God, they felt, that person was Ma Beck.

Ma Beck approached the withdrawn boy and sat down beside him. "Son, you know that I knew your mama," she began, "and I know how she tried to raise you. . . . She knew she wasn't always gonna be with you. Didn't she tell you that?"

"Yes, ma'am," said RC. For the first time tears began to flow.

"Your mama spent her whole life preparing you for this here day," Ma Beck went on sternly. "You gotta carry on. That's all there is to it. That's what she'd want. And that's what you gotta do. You gotta carry on, RC."

The sympathy beneath Ma Beck's firm words reached RC, and he collapsed on her bosom sobbing. She put her arms around him and let him cry for hours without saying a word. "I howled like a tiny infant," Ray remembered, "crying for the loss and the grief and the sweet memories that Mama had given me. Ma Beck broke me."

Ray Charles has called the deaths of Retha and his brother George "the two greatest tragedies of my life." His music tells us how deeply they marked him. The healing embrace of Ma Beck also profoundly affected the grown man's music and character. On the threshold of maturity, RC was overwhelmed by sadness, then touched by the love of another human being, the sound of a sympathetic voice. From these experiences as much as any springs the empathy that vibrates in Ray Charles' music. The event engraved itself on the young man's heart, to be worked out in song for the rest of his life.

By the day of the funeral RC had recovered enough to be able to touch Retha's face and say goodbye. A. D. and Ruth Reams came to the service at the New Shiloh Baptist, and a long procession followed the casket past Mr. Pit's to the Pallbearers' cemetery. Like many of her neighbors, Retha never had the money for a church plot, but she had paid the Pallbearers' Society a nickel or dime a month year after year to ensure a decent burial. In decades to come, the Pallbearers' cemetery became a trash dump in the woods, and Retha's grave was forever lost.

RC spent that summer alone. He didn't see much of the Jellyroll gang, and he never spoke to them about his mother's dying. He went over to Tallahassee, rode the motorbike, and played with Lawyer and the band, but all the time he was thinking, thinking, thinking. Carry on, he must carry on. But what did that mean? Without Mama, Greenville wasn't home anymore. Where would he go? Could he really make his living from music, as he had boasted to Joe Walker?

In September, RC took the train back to D&B. More than ever he felt he had outgrown the school, and under the surface, perhaps, he had decided to leave. Only a few weeks into the term, just after his fifteenth birthday, RC provoked the ex–Navy man with a prank, and in response the teacher stripped him of his monitor rank. After days of taking RC's sass, the teacher reported him. Dr. Rembert ordered the boy into his office and told him Florida D&B had given RC Robinson enough second chances; he was expelled. RC replied that they couldn't expel him, that he would quit. The last entry on D&B's official student card for Robinson, R.C., reads "Sent home Oct. 5, 1945. Unsatisfactory pupil."

But RC didn't go home. During the summer Mary Jane had told him about her friend Louise in Jacksonville, a maid who, on her days off, lived upstairs from her sister Lena Mae and Lena Mae's husband, Fred Thompson, a carpenter. The Thompsons had an extra room in their house on West Church Street, and they would be glad to take him in. Jacksonville was a bigger city than St. Augustine or Tallahassee; maybe there he could make some money playing music. RC made up his mind: he would go to Jacksonville, live with the Thompsons, and see what happened next. He said goodbye to Joe and Paul, Mr. and Mrs. Lawrence, and all his friends. Mr. White gave him a lift to the station in the school truck, and RC got on the train, headed fifty miles north to a new and unknown life.

PART II

APPRENTICE

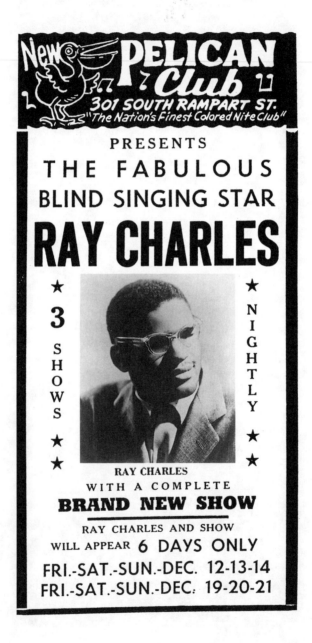

New **PELICAN** Club
301 SOUTH RAMPART ST.
"The Nation's Finest Colored Nite Club"

PRESENTS

THE FABULOUS
BLIND SINGING STAR
RAY CHARLES

★ **3 SHOWS** ★ ★

★ **NIGHTLY** ★ ★

RAY CHARLES

WITH A COMPLETE

BRAND NEW SHOW

RAY CHARLES AND SHOW

WILL APPEAR **6 DAYS ONLY**

FRI.-SAT.-SUN.-DEC. 12-13-14
FRI.-SAT.-SUN.-DEC. 19-20-21

Jacksonville
1945–1946

In October 1945, Jacksonville, Florida, like America and fifteen-year-old Ray Charles Robinson, was crossing a threshold into the postwar era. A deepwater port on the St. Johns River and, at two hundred thousand residents, still the state's biggest city, Jacksonville had boomed in the 20s, gone bust in the 30s, and boomed again during World War II, when eighty-two liberty ships, twelve tankers, and countless smaller craft had been launched from city shipyards. Now the war was over and civic leaders worried that peace might end prosperity. Yet for Americans everywhere, the joy of August did not fade but became transformed into widespread optimism. Returning servicemen got out of uniform, got to work, and got married. Young couples pledged their faith in the future with new babies, new homes, and new cars, and Jacksonville, like many other cities, began a spurt of growth that would double its size in a decade.

The seventy-four thousand Negroes of Jacksonville felt the stirrings of postwar optimism with more skepticism than did white Jacksonville. Good times were better than bad, but Jim Crow still ruled, and all prospects pointed to more of the same old same old. *Crisis,* the magazine of the National Association for the Advancement of Colored People, devoted a 1942 issue to Jacksonville. Beside photographs of the proud homes owned by prominent black families, the president of the local NAACP Youth Council wrote, "In none of its tall office buildings will I find stenographers, clerks, secretaries, and business men of my race. In none of its . . . modern stores do I find Negro sales-girls." A 1948 report by the Jacksonville Social Agency council found "no beach front available to colored." The one park Negroes could use had "neither trees nor benches"; the only paved streets in Negro districts were "streets . . . formerly occupied by white people."

Fred and Lena Mae Thompson lived at 752 West Church Street, a two-story wooden frame house in a neighborhood, west of downtown, of modest dwellings and shaded streets called La Villa. In city directories of the mid-40s, La Villa residents all have a little "(c)" for colored after their names. Fred and Lena had no children of their own, and they gladly took this bright boy into their home. RC responded to their love and soon felt as cozy with them as he had with Kiddy Boo and Dolly in Tallahassee. After dinner, he was welcome to spend evenings in the kitchen. Saturday nights the family gathered around the radio to listen to the Grand Ole Opry, and Sundays they howled together at the antics of Amos and Andy. Lena wanted to buy the boy clothes, Fred to give him an allowance for carfare. RC, however, was determined to earn his keep by becoming a professional musician as soon as possible. Fred said the first step was to join the musicians' union, and he soon walked RC a block north to the union hall on West Ashley Street.

In the mid-1990s weedy vacant lots outnumbered the buildings on West Ashley, and residents of the remaining wrecks hung listlessly about sagging stoops. In 1945, however, the four blocks from Broad to Davis Street were bustling, "Jacksonville's An-swer to Harlem," according to longtime residents. Fred guided RC along sidewalks crowded with people shopping and waiting for the bus; past cafes and beauty parlors, past the Knights of Pythias Hall, the Strand Theatre, Manuel's Tap Room, and the Lenape Billiard Hall. The tall Richmond Hotel stood around the corner on Broad, and on the opposite corner Stanton School, the city's only Negro high school. James Wel-don Johnson had taught at Stanton and had composed the school song, "Lift Every Voice and Sing," a stirring chorale that later become the unofficial "Negro national an-them."

The boss of West Ashley, James "Charlie Edd" Craddock, often stood outside his pawnshop, nodding to passersby. Charlie Edd also owned the Two Spot, "the finest dance palace in the country owned by a Negro," said *Crisis,* and a dozen or more after-hour juke joints. Charlie Edd hired musicians for his clubs, and he sold them band uni-forms at his store. To help them keep their horns out of hock, he did the paperwork and paid the fees to start their own union, Jacksonville Local 632 (colored) of the American Federation of Musicians. In 1945, Local 632, one hundred fifty members strong, had offices in the Clara White Mission, an impressive three-story stucco building at 613 West Ashley. Born a slave, Clara White had founded the mission as a soup kitchen, taking as her motto:

> *Do all the good you can*
> *In all the ways you can*
> *For all the people you can*
> *While you can.*

Carried on by Clara White's daughter Eartha, the mission became a linchpin of the black community through the Depression and war years. The bright windows of a barbershop and the Hollywood Music Store flanked the entrance. Local 632 had its offices on the third floor, but the members often gathered to sit and chat around an old upright piano in a corner of the white-walled mission hall downstairs.

After a couple of trips RC had memorized the height of each curb on his way, the spots where tree roots had cracked the sidewalk, and he got to the mission building every afternoon, telling everyone that he was RC Robinson, piano player and singer, ready and able to take any gig going. The veterans looked at the overgrown blind kid with the big shoulders and restless body, and they grinned. Here was a greenhorn for sure!

Alexander Perry, a tall, slender Gainesville native in his mid-thirties, was a member of Local 632 as 1945 became 1946. Fifty years later and still playing music at his North Jacksonville church, he well remembered RC making his daily trek to the local. "I was just out of the army, playing in Alvin Downing's band at Manuel's Tap Room. Ray Charles was but a boy—blind, but a nice personality."

Perry's life in music resembles the lives of so many black (and white) popular musicians of his era that a sketch of his career depicts a generation. A teenager in the 1920s, Perry followed his two musician brothers "up the country" to New York. After learning music basics in night courses at Juilliard, he played through the 30s and 40s in long-forgotten bands that toured from Asbury Park to Atlantic City, Philadelphia to Pittsburgh, Cleveland to Chicago, and back to New York through Buffalo. "Sometimes we'd get stranded on the road for weeks before the booker could get another tour together," Perry recalled. "Whatever city we were in, we'd go sit on the union hall benches till somebody called for players. Trumpet was my instrument, but I took calls for sax, trombone, piano, and drums too. That way I made do until the booker called again." Getting stranded in Jacksonville brought Perry back to Florida, and he was not the only strandee on 632's benches that winter. "Duke Ellington's band came to the Two Spot," Perry remembered. "So did Louis Armstrong and Jimmy Lunceford. But even Duke might not have a gig to go right on to, and the guys would lay around here two weeks, looking for what they could get. The whole band wouldn't work, but some of them would."

All the musicians of Local 632 could read music—"You had to read to gig," Perry said—and many, like him, had the training necessary to play classical music. The classical world, however, kept its doors closed to black musicians in the 30s and 40s, the precarious successes of Paul Robeson and Marian Anderson proving the "No Negroes" rule by exception. Black composers like William Grant Still wrote concerti, and jazz musicians from time to time played chamber music for fun, but the brief notes on Hazel Scott sheet music published in 1943 speak volumes: "Like many other colored entertainers, Hazel found that the path of least resistance lay in popular music, although her original training groomed her for the concert stage."

Popular music, the day-to-day music of America, was the music Perry and his colleagues played. In popular music, black musicians could get gigs, national record contracts, and radio shows, as well as local jobs. As in Lawyer Smith's Tallahassee and many other cities, Jacksonville's popular musicians tended to be black. Black bands and combos played clubs and bars in the black world, country club balls and society events in the white world. "The white musicians' local had maybe three bands who could play any style, any affair," Perry recalled. "We had twenty!"

At a time when entrenched custom kept Negroes out of most intellectual professions, black musicians could find work in popular music because of the nature of the music itself. From the early nineteenth century onward, in dozens of shades and styles, American popular music had blended African and European elements. The white culture preferred to deny black accomplishment when possible, but in music that wasn't possible. Americans everywhere recognized and enjoyed the Negro contribution to American music. Without being historians, the members of Local 632 and their white and black audiences understood that the music they played and applauded had its roots in slave shouts and spirituals as well as in old English airs, in the banjo and in Bach, in Stephen Foster's "coon songs" like "Camptown Races" and in his sweet songs like "Beautiful Dreamer." Buddy Bolden and Bix Beiderbecke, Bessie Smith and Mae West, Eubie Blake and George Gershwin had blended America's popular music palette into an inextricable mix of black, white, and blues: Louis Armstrong growled Irving Berlin, Billie Holiday sighed Jerome Kern, and Duke Ellington played Duke Ellington, a pastel rainbow unto himself.

This was the music that pulled RC like a magnet, and at the union hall he enrolled in the only school that could teach him how to play it. Being a D&B hotshot with a few Tallahassee gigs under his belt didn't cut much ice with the veterans of Local 632. To gig with them, RC had to prove he knew more music than that.

First, he needed to be able to keep a rock-steady beat at any tempo, fast or slow. Pop music didn't speed up and slow down like classical music; players sank deep into the unchanging backbeat groove, one TWO three FOUR, one TWO three FOUR, that gave the music its African, hand-clap rhythm. A feeling for "blue notes" ran in RC's blood, but he still needed to learn just how to use those aching African tones, bent between major and minor, to give the plainest melody a tragic twist, tint the plainest harmony with the red-purples of a southern sunset.

To cover any gig that might come up, RC also needed a working knowledge of popular music's entire repertoire of songs. Night after night in the clubs, the musicians of Local 632 played, not the extended works of classical music, but short, simple songs, ballads and novelty songs, fast songs and slow songs, songs happy and sad. Like most beginners, RC first learned songs one by one, "Ain't Misbehavin' " and "Night and Day," memorizing each one in a particular key, but that wasn't good enough to play professionally. No one could keep in mind all the pop songs, from "Avalon" to "Yesterdays," that might be requested on any given night. Pros memorized as many as possible, but more important, they learned certain oft-repeated forms that shaped pop songs. In grasping those, they learned, in effect, all the songs at once.

Two forms included nearly all the songs: the blues, twelve African-rooted measures rocking endlessly back and forth from tonic to dominant; and the 32-bar "standard," America's streamlined version of the European art song, often laid out in four sections, AABA. With a feeling for these forms and their most common chord sequences, a pro could fake his way through anything. "We'd get a request," as Perry described the process, "and whoever knew the song would call the chords to the piano player. If you didn't know the song, you could still hear the chords going around, like G minor, C seven, F in 'Honeysuckle Rose,' and you'd catch on. The sax or trumpet would take hot solos, and by the end the crowd would think we knew the damn thing!"

Learning how to jump into pop songs and the blues, to stay on track while the combo improvised its way through the chords—that was RC's work as winter became the spring of 1946. Driven by ambition to not only enter this world but conquer it, he practiced every chance he got. The new kid at the hall, he had to wait his turn at the piano, but as he waited he listened to the older fellows. Some veterans gladly showed RC new chord voicings or left-hand runs; others stopped playing when he was around: the kid stole any lick that wasn't nailed down. Evenings and Sundays, RC played on the parlor pianos of Fred and Lena's friends, but there he felt constrained to entertain. For concentrated study, what really counted were the jam sessions.

Jam sessions were popular music's boot camp, griddle-hot proving grounds that RC, like all raw recruits, had to cross over to gain entry into the fraternity of players. "We used to love to sit up all night jamming," Perry recalled. "Whenever the clubs got out, the best players met anyplace there was a piano. We learned from each other, but I was trying to cut you, and you were trying to cut me."

On gigs, musicians presented a united front to please the public, playing songs in standard keys, "Take the A Train" in C, for example, making the music polished by making it easy to play. Jam sessions, in contrast, were stomp-or-be-stomped combat with one inflexible rule: get your chops together or go home. A wily veteran might suggest starting a ballad like "Body and Soul" in the standard key, D-flat, then advancing through all the keys around the circle of fifths. But not at ballad tempo; for the hell of it, he'd count off up-tempo. Boom, everybody's off and running, the drummer rocketing away, the bass thundering like an elephant on the run, the horns crying like prowling cats. A beginner like RC might be okay through the first chorus, but the second chorus would be in G-flat, and he'd have to remember to switch G-flat to F-sharp in his mind to be ready to play the third chorus in B. The bridge of "Body and Soul" modulates up a half-step, tricky for a flailing novice. If at that moment the drummer switches from swing to a Latin beat, veterans may be able to flow over the abrupt change in rhythm, but the novice will get flipped like a kid in a game of crack the whip, ass into the thornbush. He may stab at some chord, any chord to get back into the song, but it's way off and sounds awful. The tenor sax player rolls his eyes, and the bass player chuckles under his breath, while the kid, cheeks burning, struggles back on track by the time the song reaches the safer waters of D, G, and C.

From many a Jacksonville jam session RC made his way home to Fred and Lena's heartsore and discouraged. Young as he was, he bounced back in a day or two, but the cuts to his pride left permanent scars and taught a permanent lesson: music was war. Duke Ellington called jazz musicians "gladiators," and the elbow-gouging D&B Sco-Ball champ was ready for all comers. Struggling to hold his own, RC began to find his own strengths. He had perfect pitch and could hear the whole combo and each instrument's distinct voice at the same time. Blindness posed no handicap in learning song forms and chord sequences—all musicians visualize the structure of music in the darkness of the mind's eye—and his aptitude for math gave him an advantage. Thinking of a chord sequence as the VI chord going to the II chord to the V meant that it didn't matter what key the combo played the song in—the chords linked up at the same angles in every key.

Soon the vets couldn't throw the kid off no matter what tricks they pulled. RC began getting gigs that paid only two to five dollars each. By accumulation, these gigs become a pro's bread and butter. "We played everywhere in those days," Perry said. "One night a white place where we'd go in through the kitchen and play behind a curtain, the next night a whorehouse where they played cards and drank moonshine." Perry's regular band, Alvin Downing's ensemble, had a six-night-a-week gig at Manuel's

Tap Room, low-paying but steady. When his regular sidemen took more lucrative work, Downing needed substitutes, and RC became one of the pianists he called as needed. Semi-steady work at the Tap Room also meant RC could look for work at clubs higher on Jacksonville's club ladder, and he started hanging out at the Two Spot.

Drummer Henry Washington, a tall man of regal bearing who led the Two Spot's house band, held first rank among Jacksonville musicians. His band had shrunk to ten pieces during the war, but afterward grew back to seventeen pieces. At first RC listened from the door, too young to be in the club legally, but he soon talked his way into Washington's attention, and the leader began to toss him occasional substitute gigs. Nights at the Two Spot with Washington's band were big nights for RC, his first playing inside the classic big band of jazz—five saxes, four trombones, four trumpets, plus piano, guitar, bass, and drums for rhythm. The bold brassy sounds he had heard from Artie Shaw back at D&B, from Harry James on Fred and Lena's radio that afternoon, drenched his ears: wah-wah 'bones, a muted trumpet burning through the saxes like a cigarette through silk, the guitar's ching-ching chords locked in with the shush-snap of the drummer's high-hat cymbal, the band building pulsing riffs to orgasmic climaxes. RC leapt into the swirling music, flipped to be adding his own lick. This was the orchestra of his dreams. You can always make a little band out of a big band, he learned, but only a big band could paint all the sound colors that belonged to popular music. Someday, he decided, he would have a big band of his own.

With the passing of the war, however, the big bands began to pass their prime. The top names, Ellington, Basie, and the Dorsey brothers, continued to tour and record, but territory bands died as popular music's ball bounced in new directions. Tiny Bradshaw, Illinois Jacquet, and Joe Liggins led the postwar bands packing the Two Spot. These leaders stripped the big-band sound down to its essentials, long, loose riffs and honking solos over a dancing beat. T-Bone Walker turned his electric guitar up loud, adding its sleek timbres to the horns-and-rhythm blend. The postwar bands played a music rougher than big-band jazz, with more blues bubbling up beneath its glossy surface. Up in New York *Billboard* magazine began to call the new style "Rhythm and Blues."

Small bands were hot too. Rumors of what Charlie Parker, Dizzy Gillespie, and Thelonious Monk were doing at Minton's in Harlem had drifted down to Jacksonville. Be-bop was a bit too far out for the members of Local 632. Perry and his colleagues liked to stick to a song's basic feeling as they improvised. "The words of a song are as important as the chords when you solo," as Perry put it. "We jazzed the melody, but we based our phrasing on the lyric." Square! said the be-boppers; they broke songs down to their raw harmonic structure and built new songs on the bare bones—Gillespie, for example, remaking the understated "Whispering" into the bravura "Groovin' High."

The new sounds made RC's ears perk up, but he heard the nay-saying of his elders too. Crazy chords and superfast tempos were fun in jam sessions, but ballads and blues went over best on money gigs. Only other musicians gave a damn about frenzied virtuoso solos. The people wanted human feelings presented in plain terms, music that told a story and made them dance.

Three small bands, all black, figured out how to give America just what it wanted that summer and fall of 1946: Louis Jordan and his Tympany Five, the Nat "King" Cole Trio, and Charles Brown and the Three Blazers. All three leaders sang and played an instrument, Cole and Brown the piano, Jordan alto sax, and all three made records that won the hearts of RC, Fred and Lena Mae, and millions more across the country. Louis Jordan was the first to become well known. Born in Brinkley, Arkansas, and a thoroughly schooled big-band veteran, Jordan began releasing novelty jazz 78s on the Decca label in 1941, and became a big enough star that he could say truthfully, "Me and Bing Crosby, we made Decca Records." Louis Jordan's records remain pop masterpieces, witty sketches of black life that gave Amos and Andy jocularity an irresistible jump swing beat. "Choo Choo Ch'Boogie" hit big that year, audiences white and black chuckling as they sang along with the chorus:

> *Choo choo, choo choo ch'boogie*
> *Choo choo, choo choo ch'boogie*
> *Get me right back to the track, Jack!*

Nathaniel Adams Coles, son of a Baptist pastor from Montgomery, Alabama, put together a band in Los Angeles before the war that was even smaller than Jordan's: himself, Johnny Miller on bass, and Oscar Moore, a dazzling electric guitarist. Jazz cats discovered Cole as a superb pianist when the trio played Fifty-second Street in 1941; the public discovered him as a superb singer in 1944 with "Straighten Up and Fly Right," a comedy blues in the Jordan mold that caught the optimism of the war's end. "King" Cole charmed America with a creamy smooth baritone, a suave Fred Astaire–like style, and puckish eyebrows that dabbed his handsome face with humor. Acting suave despite the pain of segregation gave Cole bleeding ulcers and a three-pack-a-day smoking habit, but the public didn't know that. White listeners heard in him the "ideal" Negro (or so they thought), graceful, musical, and deferential; blacks envied and emulated his processed hair, black and shiny as patent leather. By 1946 Cole had had a string of hits on Capitol Records, including "Get Your Kicks on Route 66." In the summer he replaced Bing Crosby on radio's Kraft Music Hall; in the fall he topped the charts with "Christmas Song."

One trio that bobbed up in Cole's wake featured pianist-singer Charles Brown, who, the jazz magazine *Metronome* noted, "closely reproduced every nuance of Nat's voice and piano." Like Cole, Brown broke through in Los Angeles, loved ballads, and admired the precise diction of white singers like Helen O'Connell, but he was also steeped in the slow blues of his native Texas. Brown cut his first hit, "Driftin' Blues," for Aladdin Records, a West Coast independent, in September 1945, and it stayed on the jukeboxes of Jacksonville and the rest of black America for years, the perfect record for long barroom afternoons: "I'm driftin' and driftin', like a ship out on the sea."

Playing one gig and prowling for the next in the now familiar darkness of La Villa, RC heard these small-band sounds everywhere he went, and he, more than most, heard in them opportunity for himself. "Little Nats" and "Little Louis" had sprung up in cities across the country, local leaders who played carbon copies of the national hits. Jacksonville already had its Little Louis: Tiny York, a roly-poly tenor sax player who mugged and danced in front of his quintet. RC couldn't buck York's popularity, and in any case, Jordan's clowning style was too hammy for the still-shy kid. Nobody in town was doing Cole and Brown, however, and their jazz-blues were right up RC's alley. RC idolized Cole and had been imitating him since Greenville. The teenager struggled to fit his piano fills around his voice as the King did, and to get his idol's precise diction, he had to fix his throat and jaw tighter than came naturally. Doing a slow Charles Brown blues was, in contrast, like rolling off a log. If Cole and Brown could make big money doing what they did, RC figured he could do the same and make a little money too.

Henry Washington liked RC's Cole and Brown act and began giving him featured spots to do "Driftin' Blues" or "Route 66" with the rhythm section before disappearing back into the band. For the hardworking black people of Jacksonville, the real Nat "King" Cole lived in a faraway world called Hollywood, but three or four nights a week they had their own "Little Nat" at the Two Spot. People found something cute in the blind boy at the Two Spot who could do Cole so coolly, and then sing so much like Charles Brown that, with your eyes closed, you couldn't tell the difference.

Here was RC's first hint of success, applause at the end of a number, the shouts and laughter rising from the couples at the tables in the dark, whispered good words from other players in the band. Between sets young ladies pressed themselves forward, saying they liked the way he sang. RC felt ready and willing to respond to the women in kind, but being blind made the preliminaries awkward. Sudden attacks of shyness could leave him tongue-tied at just the wrong moment. The older fellows sometimes played matchmaker for the kid, steering a girl RC's way at the end of a gig. Most nights, however, RC went back to Fred and Lena's and slept alone. Daytimes and Sundays he went for walks with Lovey Herman, the girl next door in La Villa, but Lovey was a churchgoing girl, and try as he might, RC couldn't get past hand-holding and a few stolen kisses.

In the fall of 1946, RC turned sixteen. After only a year in Jacksonville, he had broken into the little world of Local 632, become a pro and even put together an act, a meal ticket. A flow of five-dollar and eight-dollar gigs covered his room and board to Fred and Lena and left a little over in his pocket. He began to think of getting a place of his own. Fred and Lena wouldn't hear of it. As long as RC lived in Jacksonville, he had a home at 752 West Church Street.

Tiny York's reputation as a "Little Louis," meanwhile, had spread beyond Jacksonville, and the bouncy singer-saxophonist had pieced together a tour of central Florida around a gig in Orlando. Tiny asked RC to go along as the band pianist with his own featured spot. With RC doing his Cole and Brown bit, Tiny would have all three of the little-band stars covered, and the whole show would make a bigger impression. Ready to try the road, RC said yes in an instant. The band loaded their instruments into Tiny's van and headed south along the coast. Some of the fellows took offense at the kid being a star of the show, and when they took seats, they made RC sit on a soda crate. As the newcomer in the band, RC couldn't fight it, but he didn't like it. The van rolled all afternoon down the dusty two-lane highway, after Daytona slanting southwest deep into the middle of the state. The air grew more humid, more fragrant with flowers. For miles they drove past orange groves, the rows of trees reaching to the horizon, their branches laden with ripening fruit. By nightfall the band had pulled into Orlando.

Orlando
and Tampa
1946-1948

For a few weeks after arriving in Orlando, Tiny York did find work for his orchestra and featured vocalist, but the wave of popularity he hoped for never crested, and when the trickle of gigs ran dry, the band, like so many before it, ran aground. The fellows didn't blame Tiny; he'd tried his best. Everybody was free to go his own way.

Until this moment, RC Robinson had always been attached as a child to people and places, to Retha and Mary Jane in Greenville, to the teachers at D&B, to Fred and Lena in Jacksonville, and to Tiny York as his employee. Now he was unemployed in a city where he knew no one and no one knew him, a hundred and fifty miles from La Villa. Would he go home or would he stay? Tiny and the fellows were headed back to Jacksonville as soon as they could raise gas money. He could ride with them—if he was willing to bounce on the soda crate again. The rankle of that memory, perhaps, tipped the balance. RC decided to stay in Orlando on his own.

That RC chose to rely on himself at sixteen is noteworthy in itself: few reach this turning point so young, fewer still who are blind. It also stands as a first clear example of many such choices to come. From Orlando onward, when faced with dependence one way, independence another, Ray Charles will, with rare consistency, choose independence. Again and again he would move away from people and places previously known, cut himself out of webs of the past when they threaten his freedom in the future. Independence became in time an ingrained habit of the man, an element of his makeup that some found grouchy, others cold-blooded. The darkness he lived in revealed one plain fact: humans live and die one by one, all ultimately alone. With the passing years he became more and more determined to reap what advantage he could from facing that truth without flinching.

Back at his boardinghouse, RC had his clarinet and an extra shirt, and a little silver in his pocket. The landlady said the rent was $3 a week. RC asked her for a few days' credit, and told her he'd find work and pay her back. That would be all right, she said, but don't get too far behind. Then he set off to explore the city he couldn't see.

In the days before booming resorts wrapped the old downtown in tacky motel strips, citrus, not Disney, ruled Orlando, Florida, a city of 55,000 drowsing in the humid heart of the state. In groves for fifty miles around, pickers in leather gauntlets climbed ladders into the thorny trees to gather oranges and grapefruit; trucks carried crates of the fall crop to Orlando to be processed and shipped north. Every dip in the wholesale citrus price got a page-one story in the Orlando *Times;* a fire at the Bardo Products canning plant, Halloween night, 1946, rated a banner headline.

Fifteen thousand black people lived in Orlando in 1946, but the *Times* noted their existence only in scattered crime stories and a weekly ad for a fortune-teller who kept a "Separate Room for Colored." Most lived in West Orlando, a district across the railroad tracks from downtown, its hub a block of modest red and yellow brick buildings along West Church between Division and Terry streets. The Lincoln Theater stood tall at the corner of Church and Division, and in the lobby of Sadler's Hotel next door, Florida Joe kept his barbershop spanking clean. The Atlanta Life Insurance Company had an office at 537 West Church, and A. J. Kleckly had just opened his Knick-Knack Cafe a few doors away.

Across the street from the Knick-Knack stood the Sunshine Club, Orlando's top black nightclub, its squared-off stucco front set back from the sidewalk behind a narrow patio. Patrons entered under an elegant canopy into a large open room with a long bar and a shiny dance floor surrounded by tables and banquettes. Tough-as-nails Fats Fryer managed the club. When waiters apologized for breaking glasses and spilling whiskey, they always got the same growled response: "Sorry, my ass." Joe Anderson led the house band at the Sunshine Club, a polished fifteen-piece big band filled, like Henry Washington's, with stranded players and soldiers just back from the Army bands. Only Acie Price's South Street Casino, a block east off Terry, could compete with the Sunshine Club.

RC approached the Sunshine Club and the Casino looking for gigs, but Anderson and Price had nothing for him right away; he could try again, they said. No work meant no money. In these first months in Orlando RC slipped into dire poverty, poorer than he had ever been as a kid in friendly Jellyroll, poorer than he would let himself become ever again. For days he had little or nothing to eat. He fell at times into stupors of hunger, too woozy to focus his mind. A scrounged can of sardines and a few salt crackers counted as a feast. One day he bought a jar of preserves, but back in his room, as he struggled to twist off the top, it slipped from his hands and smashed into a gooey mass of fruit and broken glass.

In these dark days came word that Bailey Robinson had died. Now RC was truly an orphan. His family became the other kids scuffling on the edge of West Orlando's music scene: Richard Parrish and Billy Bowsman, a trumpeter and alto sax player, a year or two older than RC, and Bill Peeples, studying drums, four years younger. They still lived with their families, and that meant occasional home-cooked meals for RC. When the pals felt flush, they pooled their change to buy a bag of beans and a slice of fatback bacon; when broke, they idled away afternoons playing cards, kid games like hearts and bid whist.

Acie Price threw occasional gigs to Parrish and Bowsman, and when Joe Anderson couldn't get his regular drummer away from the pool table, he'd call Mrs. Peeples to send over little Bill. In time RC began to get a call or two himself. Price put him into combos that played weekend gigs in nearby Kissimmee and De Land, at fish fries at country crossroads, and in tin-roof clubs so small they had only one door. Sometimes the musicians got paid $4 a night, and sometimes nothing. "If the man didn't show up that night, you weren't paid," Ray remembered years later. "If he said he wanted to hire you again, you certainly weren't going to say you wouldn't go because he didn't pay you the last time. You didn't have no money anyway, so you might as well go and take the chance." After one weekend RC had enough money in his pocket to loan Bill Peeples fifty cents. Two days later he was broke, and he stormed up the steps at Mrs. Peeples' house, demanding his money back so noisily that she wouldn't let him in. Bill hid in a bedroom, whispering to his mother to tell RC he wasn't home. Eventually RC stomped off.

RC's fortunes rose in the spring of 1947. Anderson began to call him to play in the Sunshine Club band. After one gig, RC said he had written arrangements for the school band at D&B; maybe he could write something for Joe's outfit. Like most small-city leaders, Anderson depended on stock charts available from New York music publishers, some by anonymous scribes in Tin Pan Alley, some touted as "Sy Oliver's arrangement for Tommy Dorsey." Original charts gave a local band a touch of class, and since RC was willing to write for free, Anderson gave the kid a chance.

Thrilled at the idea of topflight musicians playing his lines and riffs, RC began to arrange for Anderson's band. In writing these first professional charts (none of which has survived), Ray Charles developed an aspect of his talent seldom noticed by the public but as important as the singing and piano playing that made him famous. In his years as an unknown working pro, arranging became a valuable addition to his bag of marketable skills; the signature small-band sound Ray forged in the 1950s sprang from his own bluesy charts.

Writing arrangements for a pop music band meant creating legible charts of a song from intro to coda with key and time signature, repeats, dynamics, and tempo changes all clearly marked. The horns needed note-for-note melodies; the rhythm section was left more to its own devices, piano, bass, and guitar getting lead sheets with sketched chords, the drums lucky to have shorthand indications of breaks and fills. Since RC couldn't scratch out rough drafts of his ideas as most arrangers do, he worked out complete charts in his head, every voice top to bottom, then dictated the parts to another musician, calling out what he wanted each instrument to play: "The trumpet starts on the fourth beat with an eighth-note triplet pick up, B-flat, C, D, then the D ties over the bar to a dotted quarter . . ." and so on for all the instruments, keeping the line he had dictated in mind as he stacked the next line above it. At rehearsals RC improved the charts when they didn't deliver the sound he hoped for, but he never made a mistake in matching up two lines, forgetting the trumpet part when he called out the saxes.

This dictating method, one Charles would use for years, proved RC's uncommon musical ability to all the musicians in town. The charts, moreover, swung on the bandstand. Anderson asked him to keep writing, and RC felt he had stepped into "a whole new arena." As spring became summer, he could sense his abilities and confidence growing. He composed a song, "Confession Blues," and started playing alto sax. When he had a few dollars above the rent, he bought a record player and his first records, shellac 78s so precious that he never dropped one. He listened and relistened to the latest sounds in jazz: Illinois Jacquet and Roy Eldridge on Jazz at the Philharmonic discs, Charlie Parker and Dizzy Gillespie, Ella Fitzgerald and Billie Holiday. He loved Lester Young's tenor sax, Charlie Christian's electric guitar, and Billy Eckstine's big band. Pressing his ear to the speaker in his Orlando room, RC felt a perfect rapport with the star players in the faraway studios—"I could hear what everybody was doing."

Any young man this bright gets noticed. People on West Church Street stopped, amazed, to watch RC ride a bicycle around in circles on the Sunshine Club patio and stride along the crowded sidewalk, never bumping into anybody. He often dashed over to Orange Avenue downtown to buy records at the Southland Music Store and play on the store piano. "RC was a bouncy fellow," A. J. Kleckly remembered, "always a cheerful word for everybody, 'Hey, how you doing, what's up, my friend?'" RC knew every seat and stool in the Knick-Knack Cafe and made his calls from the pay phone. No one ever saw him stumble getting a nickel into the slot. A.J. let RC eat on the cuff. "I'd be paying for his dinner, and he'd be telling me, 'A.J., someday I'm gonna take care of you.' "

In the summer of 1947, RC reached his Orlando high point, only to plunge from it straight to disaster. A gleaming custom-built Orchestra Bus pulled up one evening to the Sunshine Club, and out stepped Lucky Millinder and his sixteen-piece band, on tour from New York. A Decca recording artist riding his latest hit, "Shorty's Got to Go," Lucky Millinder ranked as a class act in 1947, one notch below the biggest stars. Irving Mills managed Millinder and sold his band to bookers who couldn't afford his top acts, Duke Ellington and Cab Calloway. Some called Millinder an "arm-waver," a non-playing leader who relied more on charm and impeccable tailoring than musicality, but the band was a tight, swinging unit, and all the musicians on West Church made sure they got to the Sunshine Club that weekend.

Rumors spread Friday night that Millinder was looking for a new piano player. RC's friends encouraged him to try out for the open spot; they'd help him get past Millinder's road manager, a beefy sourpuss, the only white guy in the outfit. RC didn't need much convincing. Every small-city musician dreamed of hooking up with a national band, and puffed up by his friends' praise, RC believed he was ready. Millinder agreed to audition the local prodigy, and they met in the Saturday-afternoon quiet of the empty club. RC played and sang several songs. Millinder didn't say anything until RC finished and turned to face him. From the darkness came the verdict: "Ain't good enough, kid."

RC found his way out of the club, went off by himself, and cried. Deep in his heart he'd known that he was too green to work in a national band, but he'd let himself be shamed by his own vanity. Worst was the thought that Millinder was right: maybe he wasn't good enough, maybe his dreams would never come true.

Weeks passed. RC's hurt pride simmered like a fire in his gut, forging a new determination and fueling long hours of practice at the piano. Someday that s.o.b. Lucky Millinder would eat his words. The wound healed but left a scar; forty years later Charles was still chewing what he had learned from Millinder's rejection. "Lucky Millinder didn't say, 'You're no good.' He said, 'You're not good *enough*,' " he told a radio interviewer in 1985. "Now I'm older, I know it's not an insult. If you got a certain sound in your band, you've got to find a person who can give you the sound you want. John may be *good*, but maybe he ain't *good enough* to fit into your plans. What Lucky did to me was make me stop kidding myself. I learned you aren't good just because people around you *say* you are good!"

RC climbed back up on his feet through the summer of '47, but after eight months little Orlando had lost its appeal. Work dried up again, and money got tight. When one of his pals said, "Let's go to Tampa," RC packed up his sax and his records, got in the fellow's car, and said, "Okay, let's go to Tampa."

▐▌▐▌▐▌▐▌▐▌

The same fifty years that bombed out Jacksonville's West Ashley and wore Orlando's West Church down to a nub had caused Central Avenue, the old hub of black Tampa, to vanish from the earth. In the 1960s the city razed a broad swath of buildings on both sides of the avenue and carved a smooth parkway through it for cars flowing to and from downtown. The white city fathers called the project "urban renewal"; black residents called it a vengeful body blow to a community that supported Martin Luther King, Jr.

When RC and his footloose friends pulled into Tampa on Highway 92, Central Avenue was jumping. Black longshoremen at Tampa's busy port had organized a union in the 1930s, and their earnings put dollars into the whole black community. Dozens of black-owned businesses lined Central Avenue: the Palace Drugstore, Richard's Photo Studio, and Mason's sundry shop that sold everything "From Ice Cream to Hardware." Patrons stopped at the Palm Dinette for coffee and chili, at Johnny Gray's Restaurant for more elegant dining. At 1310 Central stood the Blue Room Bar and Grill, the avenue's biggest club, owned by Watts Sanderson, the "Mayor of Central Avenue."

RC stayed first in a flophouse, but his greenhorn days in Tampa were briefer and less painful than those in Orlando. He had more experience, more money in his pocket, and for company, his record player and precious 78s. He also had the luck, on an early foray to the Blue Room, to run into Gossie D. McKee, a cheery, light-skinned guitar player with a pencil-line mustache above a friendly grin. Gossie remembered RC from the Two Spot: a year before he had come through Jacksonville with "Harlem in Havana," a revue headed to fairs and rodeos as far north and west as Calgary, Canada. Just back from his second tour, Gossie had a gig in Manzy Harris' band that played the Blue Room's upstairs lounge. Born in Tampa, Gossie knew everybody, and he introduced RC to two sisters, Fredericka and Lydia Simmons, who rented him a room in their house at 813 Short Emery Street, a few doors down from the redbrick Bethel Baptist Church. The older sister, straitlaced Fredericka, owned the house. She taught music lessons and allowed RC to play the piano in the parlor. Younger Lydia was more outgoing; RC talked and laughed with her in the kitchen.

By his birthday in 1947, RC had landed two good gigs. The first, playing piano for Charlie Brantley's Honeydrippers, a seven-piece band modeled on Louis Jordan's Tympany Five. Brantley had a singer, Clarence Jolly, and hired RC only as a pianist, but the pay was decent, the band worked steadily, and RC took the work gladly. "Ray Charles was a clean-cut youngster," remembered Freddie Thompson, one of Brantley's horn players. "Talented, but all the guys were talented. He didn't stand out, he was one of the fellows."

RC stood out on the second gig: playing with a white country band, the Florida Playboys. RC had quickly found his way to Tampa's big music store, the Arthur Smith Music Store on East Tyler, and one day a clerk said his guitar and fiddle band needed a pianist; could RC play country music? Sure, RC said, he had been listening to the Grand Ole Opry all his life. Compared with jazz standards, country songs were a snap, and country music's ambling tempos posed no challenge to a veteran of hell-bent-for-leather jam sessions. One audition convinced the Playboys that RC could play country music with a genuine flavor, and they hired him, no questions asked about race. For several months he gigged with the band, playing current country hits like "Kentucky Waltz" in white honky-tonks in and around Tampa, learning to yodel, and singing "Waiting All for You" as his featured number. Either because, being blind, he was not perceived as a threat, or because he fit in so well musically, white audiences didn't make a fuss about skin color. RC enjoyed both the music and the money playing country-style.

RC's interlude with the Playboys, though brief, planted a seed in Ray Charles' music that would lie dormant for a decade before sprouting. Yet this important event has left barely a trace in any but Charles' own memory. Gossie McKee and Manzy Harris recalled the Playboys as older fellows and good musicians, but neither they nor Ray remembered any names. Newspaper notices in Tampa turned up no other surviving Playboys or anyone who remembered a black piano player in a white country band in the late 40s. The histories of some bands, however, are written on the wind, and the other Playboys may have forgotten the nights with RC in a blur of other nights. Ambitious RC counted those nights as proof of his growing ability to take any gig and do it well, no matter what music was called for. Long before the birth of his own country music, Charles looked back with pride on his stint with the Playboys. On an out-take snippet from a 50s recording session, Ray plays a limpid country lick. The producer chuckles over the studio intercom that he hadn't known Ray could play Nashville, and Ray crows, "Man, didn't you know I gigged with the Florida Playboys!"

The Playboys paid $15 to $20 a night, Charlie Brantley about $10. Added up monthly, the trickle became a stream; in Tampa RC began to earn from music a living he could count on. He opened a savings account, sending every dime he didn't need back to the Bank of Greenville for Mr. Reams to look after. Gigging with the bands and on his own, RC ranged north to Gainesville and south to Sarasota. Joe Lee Lawrence, the pianist from D&B, was making the same rounds, and when the old schoolmates ran into each other, they compared notes and traded songs.

At seventeen, RC had caught the first steady wind of young manhood, and like many another fellow so buoyed up, he soon fell head over heels in love. Mama Eva, a friend of the Simmons sisters, enjoyed opening her parlor to young people for informal socials. One evening at Mama Eva's, RC flirted with a girl named Marion. Marion wasn't interested, but she introduced him to her friend Louise Mitchell, a pretty, petite sixteen-year-old with a wide smile and a nicely rounded figure. The two young people felt a spark of mutual attraction, and soon enough they acted on it in full measure. "Kids," recalled Gossie McKee with a grin. "Louise and RC were teenagers in love."

Louise's parents, well established in Tampa, thought their daughter was too young to take up with anyone, certainly not a blind blues musician whose future was as dubious as his past. RC and Louise didn't care; they lived in a world all their own, making love and fighting and making love again. When the Mitchells tried to force a breakup, the young lovers ran away to Miami by bus. Letters and long stormy phone calls produced a compromise: RC and Louise could live together if they came back to Tampa. RC moved out of the Simmonses' house, and the lovers took a $3-a-week apartment across the Cass Street bridge in West Tampa. They would prove they could make it on their own.

At the Blue Room lounge, meanwhile, Manzy Harris was getting bored playing second fiddle to the name bands in the showroom. Then he got wind of a new nightspot, the Skyhaven Club, in the former officers' mess at Drew Field. The ex–Air Force colonel who managed the club wanted an easygoing pop jazz group like Nat "King" Cole's to entertain his well-to-do white crowd. Manzy quickly booked Gossie to play guitar and another Tampa regular, Otto McQueen, on bass. When he asked RC to front the group as Tampa's "Little Nat," RC was not too lovesick to see his big break. He said yes in a second.

The Skyhaven Club billed the group as "The Manzy Harris Quartet," but Harris soon turned the musical reins over to RC and sat back at the drums, keeping time for whatever songs RC wanted to play. A quartet didn't need charts, but at daily rehearsals, RC drilled the other three in his arrangements of a varied repertoire of blues and ballads, tangos and rumbas. On the bandstand Gossie played his best Oscar Moore licks and sang a bit, but it was RC's dead-on impression of Nat Cole singing "To a Wild Rose" and "It's Only a Paper Moon" that packed the Skyhaven Club weekend after weekend as 1947 became 1948. The Manzy Harris Quartet had made a little success, and RC Robinson become a little star.

With tips, the gig at the Skyhaven Club paid over $30 on good nights. RC's savings account in Greenville grew past the $500 mark, and he still had money to make a major purchase: a wire recorder. Wire recorders hold a quirky place in the history of electric music. Danish inventor Valdemar Poulsen's wire "Telegraphone" won the first patent for electric sound recording in 1899, but the superior fidelity of disc recording relegated wire recorders to use as dictaphones through the 1930s. The war brought technical improvements, and in the late 40s General Electric and Sears marketed wire recorders as the first practical device to record music at home. The 1947 Clarion model, in an "attractive wooden cabinet," sold for $154.50 and could "Record from Radio, Mike or Records" with "No Background Noise, Needle Scratch, Hiss or Crackle." Hourlong spools of wire cost $5.50 and could be "erased 10,000 times." Tape, however, soon proved to be a vastly superior recording medium, and the few Clarions sold got consigned in the 50s to dusty attic shelves. RC may have been the only blind person to buy one: even the sighted found that the wires spun themselves into snarls that engineers cursed as "bird nests." Yet RC loved to tinker with every mechanical device, and several times he got a few fellows together in a room with a piano, set up the recorder, and tried a few songs to hear what he sounded like.

RC later mislaid the recorded spools, yet he has long insisted that a few survived and were released over the years on obscure labels. Mysteries do linger about many early listings in Ray Charles' discography, and fogs particularly thick obscure the origins of four blues songs, "Wondering and Wondering," "Walking and Talking," "Why Did You Go?" and "I Found My Baby There." Some discographies list the four as recorded in Miami in 1951, others say Los Angeles in 1952, yet the tracks are cruder than anything else Charles recorded in the 50s. That crudity and a double Florida connection—they appeared on Florida's Sittin' In With Records, and RC found his baby "down in old St. Pete"—suggest that these could be the wire spools lost in Tampa, the earliest fragments of Ray Charles' work as a recording artist.

All four tracks are slow blues played in the most dolorous fashion by piano, guitar, bass, and barely audible drums. The guitar strums land clumsily off the beat, the bass thuds steady half-notes in a nearly static rhythm, and RC sing-shouts undistinguished lyrics in a droning monotone. For all their flaws, however, the four tracks make riveting music. RC's piano playing is brilliant, flashing chords and discordant runs. For one astonishing chorus he plays wild be-bop lines on piano while moaning the same lines like a saxophone. RC's sophisticated piano hints at modern jazz, but his stately tempos step to the slow-drag of a Dixieland funeral march. As the muffled drums cast a somber shadow and the bass tolls like a bell at midnight, RC sings more like a stern prophet than a lamenting lover. At the Skyhaven Club, RC was crooning cool city blues, but on these early fragments he sank deep into country blues, tapping roots deep enough to sustain a half-century of making records.

The Manzy Harris Quartet continued to pack the Skyhaven Club through the winter of 1948. As far as Manzy and Otto McQueen were concerned, the gig could have lasted forever. They were older than Gossie and RC, family men settled in Tampa. Otto's cousin, Butterfly McQueen, was a movie star in Hollywood, but Otto had no such ambitions, nor was Manzy hoping for more than local success. Gossie felt loyal to Manzy, the leader who had given him his first job, yet touring with Harlem in Havana had touched Gossie with wanderlust. In Calgary, he had met a girl named Connie who was still writing and asking him to come back. As the younger fellows in the group, Gossie and RC were often thrown together, and on breaks Gossie told him tales of the world beyond the Deep South. There were places up north, Gossie said, where nobody cared what color you were. One of these days he was going to buy a bus ticket for someplace, anyplace up north.

Bright-eyed Gossie was not talking just to be talking: He wanted RC to come with him. He had a better chance, he knew, as a sideman than as a soloist, and RC had talent worth attaching himself to. Every night Gossie could see the Skyhaven Club audience respond to RC, see the money coming in at the door and into his own wallet. He and RC already made a good team. They didn't need a bass player or drummer to create the Nat Cole ambience, and if they did, they could pick up those fellows anywhere. "If you came along," Gossie told RC, "I could hustle up good-paying gigs for the two of us anywhere in the United States."

RC listened, tempted. All the music he heard on radio and records came from the big cities up north, and he had never been out of Florida. Manzy often said he'd seen talented kids die on the vine if they didn't leave home. But RC didn't want to leave Louise and their happy house in West Tampa. Louise was his true love; her family would never let her go, and he couldn't stand to go without her. Still, RC was tempted.

Finally Gossie got down to brass tacks. "Listen, RC," he said, "let's get away."

"Where will we go?" replied RC.

"I'll get a map!" said Gossie. He found a map of the United States, and unfolded it on the table and started calling out the names of states and cities. New York and Chicago sounded too big to both of them. RC wanted someplace not too big where they didn't know anybody, as far away from Tampa as they could go.

"Let's go to Great Falls, Montana," said Gossie. Great Falls was close to Connie up in Calgary, but Gossie didn't mention that to RC. RC thought Great Falls sounded too small, and they talked a bit more without coming to any decision. A few weeks later Gossie got a phone call from Connie. She was moving to Vancouver; why didn't Gossie come to Seattle instead? Gossie started playing down Great Falls to RC. "Great Falls is all cowboys," he said. "I think we should go to Seattle. Farther than that and we'll be out in the ocean." Seattle sounded better to RC, but still he hung back from making a decision.

One night at the Skyhaven Club a group of white girls from Cleveland came in. Between sets the quartet usually sat by themselves backstage drinking Cokes and smoking cigarettes; the club's all-white rule didn't allow them to mingle with the patrons. The Ohio girls, heedless of Jim Crow, asked if they could go back and say hello to the band. The ex-colonel who ran the club, a liberal from Los Angeles, said sure, go ahead.

"They were pretty girls," McKee remembered fifty years later. "They said, 'Ooh, we love your music, what's your name?' " The next night when the girls again stopped backstage for a chat, Gossie saw this was the way to get RC to go to Seattle. He screwed up his courage and asked the girls, "Would you all like to go by my place after we get off tonight and play some records?" The girls said yes. "Oowee!" said RC, Louise for the moment forgotten.

After the last set Gossie found a black taxi driver. "I told him to be careful, we were going to pick up these white girls and take them to my place, and that he should come back to pick them up at 4 A.M., no later." The cabbie made the girls get down on the floor of the cab so they wouldn't be seen. At Gossie's they sat and played records and talked, RC becoming bold enough to hold one girl's hand and stroke her hair. The cabbie picked them up, and again they crouched down below the line of the windows.

The next day, the girls left for Cleveland and Gossie sprang the second half of his trap. "You like these pretty girls, but here they gotta hide to see you," he told RC. "In Seattle, there's nothing to worry about. You won't have to slip around to talk to girls like that." His strategy worked.

"When are we going?" RC asked.

"We're gonna start saving the money tonight," said Gossie, and in two weeks they went down to the bus station and bought two one-way tickets to Seattle. Then, with his ticket in his pocket and his clothes and records packed, RC got cold feet. He wanted to stay a few more days, he told Gossie. Seeing his hopes going up in smoke, Gossie thought quickly. "Okay," he said, "I'll go ahead, and I'll take your clothes and records." He knew if he took RC's records, RC would be sure to follow. Okay, said RC, he just wanted a few extra days with Louise.

Gossie got on the bus to Seattle, carrying RC's precious 78s in a box tied up with string. RC's few days with Louise stretched to a week. She clung to him, and he couldn't pull away. One day a driver at a Central Avenue cabstand had a message for him. Gossie had gotten to Seattle, things were going great, come.

RC said good-bye to Louise. As soon as he'd found his feet, he'd send for her, promise. One last kiss, and he got on the bus. The bus rolled north to Tallahassee, nicking the southwest corner of Georgia on the way into Alabama. Through Tennessee, Kentucky, Indiana, and Illinois, RC sat with the other colored travelers in the back of the bus. Deep in his bag was the $500 he had withdrawn from his Greenville savings account, but he lived on crackers and candy bars. That money wasn't to be touched. Nobody, not even Gossie, knew he had it.

After Chicago came a three-night haul across the plains of Iowa and South Dakota, the mountains of Montana and Idaho. People got on the bus, people got off. RC couldn't see the scenery, but as the vast breadth of America whooshed under the wheels of his bus, he could smell early spring mornings on the prairie, crisp frosts high in the Rockies, and the damp breezes of the evergreen forests in Washington on the long last leg to Seattle.

Seattle
1948-1949

The Trailways bus rolled into the terminal at 3rd and Virginia, downtown Seattle, late one rainy night in March 1948. Winds, cold and damp after sunny Tampa, blew up from the Elliot Bay docks, and the sounds of the city—the biggest he had ever been in—surrounded RC. How could he find Gossie? He spoke to the man at the Traveler's Aid desk, and soon a local radio station began announcing that RC Robinson, a blind piano player, was at the bus station waiting for his friend Gossie McKee. RC sat down on a bench, listening to the people walk by. Their clipped, flat accents told him how far he had come. Here everybody waited in one room, white and black.

The colored fellow at the shoeshine stand noticed RC sitting by himself. Figuring he must be the blind kid the guitar player had asked him to look out for, he approached RC and said that Gossie McKee was staying at the Coast Hotel on Jackson Street. RC spent a precious quarter on a cab to the hotel, but again, no Gossie. Another hour and Gossie came panting into the lobby. He'd heard on the radio that RC was at the station, but when he ran over there, the shoeshine fellow said the kid had already left. When RC heard Gossie come in, he jumped out of his seat, and the two hugged in happy reunion. By now dawn had become full morning. Gossie got him a room upstairs, and RC slept all day and into the evening. When he woke up, Gossie took him out to a cafe on Jackson Street, and as RC wolfed down his dinner, Gossie told him his story.

He had gotten to Seattle okay and found dozens of places to play up and down Jackson Street near Twelfth Avenue. At the second club he went into, the Black and Tan, the lady piano player, Melody Jones, was very friendly. He said he was a guitar player from Tampa, scouting for gigs, and she replied, "If you had a piano player, I could give you four or five spots."

"I have a friend who's a marvelous piano player," Gossie said right back. "And he sings just like Nat 'King' Cole."

"You get him," Melody said, "and I'll pass this job on over to you—I'm leaving for a USO tour in Germany." Whenever RC had finished his pie and coffee, they could go meet Melody at the Black and Tan.

The Black and Tan, Seattle's oldest black nightclub, was a basement place only a few doors away at 404 ½ Twelfth Avenue, open to the public and also home of the Colored Waiters, Porters and Cooks Club, whose members strolled up the hill from the King Street and Union stations to relax between trains. RC took Gossie's arm down the steps and into the smoky club. Melody Jones, a well-rounded woman well known in Seattle, stood at the bar. Gossie introduced RC, and when the band took a break, Melody took the mike and told everybody there were newcomers in the house tonight, Gossie McKee and RC Robinson, all the way from Tampa, Florida, give them a big hand. "We stepped up there," Gossie said, the thrill of the moment still alive decades later, "and we went into all the pretty tunes we'd been doing at Drew Field. The people went wild, and this was our very first night! Before we left, Gus West, who ran the Elks Club, came up and offered us a gig. We could hardly believe our ears."

The two kids from Florida landed lucky in a big city booming with postwar prosperity. Peacetime had revived the Pacific Ocean trade, filling Seattle's docks with freighters in from Tokyo and bound for Hong Kong. Shifts worked round the clock at the sprawling Boeing plant south of the city, building passenger planes and a jet bomber bigger than any known during the war, the B-52. America needed those B-52s, the Seattle *Post-Intelligencer* warned in tall headlines, with "RED MIGHT ONLY 48 MILES FROM ALASKA."

Gossie and RC weren't the only southern Negroes finding jobs in postwar Seattle. The migration that fed Chicago's South Side and New York's Harlem also sent streams to Denver, Los Angeles, San Francisco, and Seattle. Old-timers in the community feared that the uncouth manners of these "sharecroppers" might threaten hard-won black respectability, but teenagers like Buddy Catlett, a budding saxophone player in the Garfield High School marching band, thought the migrants brought a welcome splash of color. "My grandparents had come north after the Civil War," Catlett recalled. "I didn't know what being black meant until I met blacks direct from the South. It was a good awakening."

Like young Malcolm Little (later Malcolm X) in Boston, Catlett felt lured by the "walk-up flats, cheap restaurants, poolrooms, bars" around Jackson Street, a world where "Negroes . . . were being their natural selves and not putting on airs," where young "cats" in flashy suits straightened their hair in shiny "conks" and sprinkled their talk with words like "cool" and "hip." When a big band blew up a hurricane, as Malcolm wrote in his *The Autobiography of Malcolm X,* these cats and their chicks let the music play over them with primal force: *"'Wail, man, wail!'"* people would be shouting at the band; and it *would* be wailing, until first one and then another couple just ran out of strength and stumbled off toward the crowd, exhausted and soaked with sweat."

Nightlife on Jackson Street never slept. Down by the docks prostitutes strolled under redbrick warehouse arches. Gamblers and bookies worked the back rooms of the bars, and opium smokers dozed in twilit rooms upstairs. Sailors smuggled in marijuana from Mexico, heroin from the Far East, and benzedrine from Los Angeles. Soldiers came in from Fort Lewis to score the drug of their choice. A few musicians dealt drugs, many indulged. A stick of reefer made the music seem to play itself; a benny could stretch a jam session past dawn and deep into the morning. On a backstage table one night, Buddy Catlett saw a mountain of cocaine he swore looked as high as Mt. Rainier.

The police descended on the Jackson Street joints in occasional staged raids that the *Post-Intelligencer* covered in juicy detail. Otherwise the paper, like the Orlando *Times,* ignored the city's black community and its musical life. Music for the *Post-Intelligencer* was classical and white: concerts by the city's fifty-seven choral societies, chamber music at the University of Washington, the Seattle Symphony conducted by Sir Thomas Beecham. Out of the paper's limited earshot, however, the black music scene buzzed with activity. The clubs Gossie had discovered were but one stratum in a scale that rose up through the Washington Social Club to the Trianon Ballroom and concerts at the Civic Auditorium. Black musicians had their own union, AF of M Local 493, and its 250-odd members played proms, fraternity parties, and country club dances in the suburbs.

"Seattle, Tacoma, Olympia," recalled bassist Traf Hubert, "from Portland to Vancouver, the Northwest was one big scene." Hubert, a white kid from Puyallup, Washington, was one of a half-dozen new faces on that scene the spring RC Robinson got to town. Out at Garfield High Buddy Catlett had met a trumpet player with big ideas, fifteen-year-old Quincy Jones. Quincy's family had just moved to Seattle from Chicago; he wanted to arrange. Floyd Standifer and his high school pals had formed the Hot Club of Eastern Multnomah County. Now he was studying physics at the university and trumpet at jam sessions. Floyd was still wet behind the ears professionally, but Buddy and Quincy played with bands put together by quick-talking Robert A. "Bumps" Blackwell, a vibraphone player at night, butcher by day, and Traf had a midnight-to-four-A.M. gig at the New Chinatown, a tough joint downtown. In one dull predawn stretch, he wandered across the street into the Tuxedo, a dive tougher even than the New Chinatown. The place was empty but for a young black man playing the piano, and Traf sat down to listen.

"I knew in a minute this guy was a fantastic piano player," Hubert remembered. "But I knew all the cats around town, and I had never heard him. So I went up to him and said, who are you? He said he was RC Robinson and had just been in town a few days. I invited him over to the New Chinatown—there was me, Gerald Brashear on sax, Big Dave Henderson on piano, and Jimmie Rodgers on drums. RC blew us away. He played piano, Gerald's tenor sax, and my bass. And he did this wild thing. He said, 'Bud Powell,' and then he played like Bud Powell, hard and fast, and then he named another piano player and another, and he played all their styles, and then he said, 'RC Robinson,' and he played the blues. We were the first to hear him, but we knew right away this RC Robinson was the best pianist in the Northwest. I went down to Tacoma and told everybody to go to Seattle and hear this guy, he's a giant."

▮▮▮▮▮▮▮▮▮▮

Had his career gone no further, Tampa, Orlando, and Jacksonville would have forgotten RC Robinson. But Seattle would never forget the comet that flashed into town in the spring of 1948. Any fears RC had that the big city would overwhelm him disappeared as he, in a small way, overwhelmed the city.

Gossie and RC made an immediate hit with the mom-and-pop crowd at the Elks Club, a handsome building of white-and-green-glazed terra-cotta on Jackson Street. They also made friends with the cook, Georgia Kemp, who owned a house on 20th Street at Madison where she let rooms to musicians. RC took Melody Jones' room when she left for the USO tour, and Gossie took a room downstairs. Georgia Kemp had a grand piano, where they could rehearse, and she cooked them the greens and rice and beans they loved from home. When he heard her coming into the room, RC teased Georgia by singing a few bars of "Georgia on My Mind."

By summer RC felt settled enough to send for Louise, and he rented a house near Georgia's at 1809 24th Avenue, the earliest Ray Charles residence known to survive. A neat wooden frame house on a hillside looking east over Lake Washington, this was the couple's real first home, and they were proud of it. They bought a dining room set and on cold nights cuddled near the kerosene heater. RC soon had the essential geography in mind: a few steps down to the sidewalk, one block up cobbled East Denny Street to the busy intersection of 23rd and Madison. From there he could walk the few blocks to Georgia's and rehearse with Gossie or catch a bus the mile and a half down Madison to Jackson Street.

Georgia Kemp had a friend, Big Louis, who managed the Rocking Chair, a cozy club in an old mansion at 14th and Yesler. When Big Louis saw how RC and Gossie pulled people into the Elks Club, he fired his trio and offered the one-to-five-A.M. gig to them. The Rocking Chair was a step up Seattle's club ladder and a step deeper into the city's shady side. Cardsharps and touts hung out at the Rocking Chair, pimps showed off their best girls, con men worked marks, dealers sold drugs. These rakish late-nighters wanted a sound with more body than the duo could provide; to play the Rocking Chair, RC and Gossie needed a bass player.

Seattle's best bassist in 1948 was, by common consent, twenty-four-year-old Milton S. Garret, pronounced "Jarret," a big lumbering fellow from West Virginia. Milt Garret didn't read much music, but he had a big sound and a big beat and could play bebop and the blues. He was also known, even feared, as a wild man, a big drinker and heroin addict who had been jailed for assault and rape. "Don't you know what he's on?" Gossie's friends warned him, and cautious Gossie suggested they try someone else. But RC had jammed with Garret and liked his freewheeling style, so Gossie said okay, figuring, "Who cares what he does as long as he does his job?"

A trio needed a name. RC was the star, but Gossie handled the business, and they compromised on the McSon Trio, for *Mc*Kee and Robin*son*. Big Louis paid the trio $45 a night, but tips from the pimps and high rollers could more than double that. When a sport strutted in showing off his new zoot suit and fedora, Gossie would announce, "Ladies and gentlemen, the next tune is a request from Mr. So 'n' So," and the sport, flattered and grinning, would drop $20 in the kitty. Wisely, Gossie invested some of the money they earned in the group. Saxophonist Jabo Ward, who had a day job with a mail-order men's clothing company, got him a discount on three matching double-breasted navy blue suits. Gossie put $15 a week into a fifteen-minute pay-to-play spot on radio station KRSC at four o'clock Saturday afternoons. In between songs RC announced Gossie's phone number, and calls began to come in from kids at the university and from clubs in outlying towns. Gossie also asked a photographer to come to the station and take their picture. The results, one of the trio, one a headshot of RC, are the earliest known photographs of Ray Charles.

The photograph of the trio, as Gossie soon realized, was inadequate for publicity purposes, out of focus and dimly lit. Yet there, though many years dead, is Milt Garret, his mouth open and his eyes shut, his left hand stretched high on his G string; Gossie smiling down at his guitar; and RC, his head back singing, his fingers spread wide on the keys of a boxy upright, his knees splayed apart as they would splay apart countless times in years to come. Before Gossie had duplicates printed, a retouch artist painted sunglasses on RC's face because, about this time, Gossie had suggested that RC wear dark glasses in public: some people found his eyeless visage disconcerting. Sunglasses worked as an instant, glamorous solution, and thus was born the Ray Charles mask, the pregnant symbol, known around the world, of a sightless singer who cannot be fully seen.

The headshot of RC turned out too like a snapshot to use as a showbiz glossy. Yet because the sunglass mask descended so soon afterward, the headshot is now a most revealing window. Here is RC Robinson, age eighteen, a handsome young man with an open, friendly face. He does not look blind; his eyes could have just blinked shut. His smile conveys both the shyness and the self-confidence of youth, and he has a youth's thin mustache and trace of beard. The ears are high and prominent, the jaw and neck strong, but overall there is a lightness to the head that suggests a slender figure. The picture could be from any high school yearbook, of a fellow who could be both valedictorian and class cutup, best dancer and best debater, his motto "Baby, the C stands for charm!"

Buddy Catlett and his pals looked up to RC as a big man on campus, still in his teens but living on his own, in a house with a girlfriend and furniture. RC was friendly but kept his privacy. None of the kids got to know Louise, and it was a long time before RC admitted he was an orphan. When Buddy Catlett asked him where his parents were, RC told him, "They're on vacation, but they'll be back." RC bought a Wurlitzer electric piano, and the house on 24th Street became a place where young musicians could hang out and jam. RC's electric piano was the first that Floyd Standifer had seen, and RC attacked it so fiercely that the plastic keys flew off as he played. When Gossie picked up RC for a gig, the kids would keep going, and when he returned, he'd jump back into the music without missing a beat. At midnight Buddy's parents would call to insist he come home, and RC would wail a sexy blues in the background to scandalize the old folks. Sometimes he broke into broad parodies of a gospel-singing southern preacher. "We used to laugh, startled, because it was so unlike his cool jazz singing," Catlett remembered. "He sounded so *real.*"

Fifteen-year-old Quincy Jones idolized RC. Another tall, good-looking young fellow, Quincy had already written charts for Bumps Blackwell's band, but when he tried them out at Friday-night dances at the 23rd Street Y, they sounded square and colorless compared with the hip dissonances he'd heard on be-bop band records. "I couldn't figure out how eight horns—four trumpets and four trombones—could play together at the same time and not play the same note," Jones remembered years later. RC had the answer. "He hit a B-flat-seventh chord in root position and a C-seventh above that, and there it was, the eight-note chord with the Dizzy Gillespie sound. He hit that thing, and the whole world opened up. Everything from then on made sense."

Quincy started coming over for lessons when RC was getting up from the gig the night before. RC showed him charts he was writing on Dizzy's "Emanon," and when he heard Quincy's charts on gigs with Bump's band, he made suggestions that helped Quincy's writing take a big leap forward. The kid's grateful admiration got through the defenses RC kept up with most other musicians, and the two became close friends, big brother and little brother, listening to records and going to each other's gigs. Those days in Seattle were the first in a lifelong friendship. If moving on from friends, lovers, and colleagues is the rule of Ray Charles' life, Quincy Jones stands as its great exception. Through the thick and thin of long careers, the two men have remained close, working together often and coming to each other's aid as needed. Even in Seattle other kids noticed the link between the two. "RC and Quincy had charisma," Buddy Catlett remembered. "They'd come into a room together, you could feel it. We all knew they had what it takes to make it."

Life was not all stardust for RC Robinson. He and Louise were young to be on their own as grown-ups. She was homesick for Tampa, and RC felt the strain of being the sole breadwinner. The couple fought often and noisily. They dreamed of having a baby together, and when Louise had a miscarriage, they were heartbroken together. The McSon Trio continued to do well at the Rocking Chair as the summer of 1948 became fall, but tensions undercut that situation too. After the gigs, RC and Milt headed off to jam sessions with Gerald Brashear and the other be-boppers. Gossie wasn't invited and didn't want to go. You couldn't earn money from be-bop, and he had to be up the next morning to hustle up more work.

Drugs also created tension in the trio. Milt and his buddies were smoking, sniffing, and shooting any drug they could get their hands on. Gossie wanted no part of it, but RC was intrigued. He could feel the silence that fell over fellows gathered in a kitchen corner, he could smell the sweet pot smoke and hear the tinkle of a spoon in the sink. RC knew all the legends about Bird and Billie, how drugs gave their music its poignant edge and beauty, and he kept after the fellows to let him try. They said no at first. He was too young and he was blind; nobody wanted the responsibility of being the first to turn him on. Curious, hungry for experience, RC persisted until somebody said the kid was old enough to make up his own mind and passed RC a joint. He liked marijuana's relaxing effect. A few tokes and he could feel himself sink deeper into the rhythm of the music; lovemaking with Louise became sexier too. He also kept after the fellows about that other thing they were doing. Soon enough, somebody fixed RC up a needleful, showed him how to tie off his left arm, and gave him his first shot of heroin.

Heroin: the word opens a dark motif in the life of Ray Charles. The drug would be integral to Charles' life for the next sixteen years. So too would marijuana, alcohol, and nicotine for many years longer, but these caused him no particular problem. Heroin, however, became a private pleasure for which Charles paid a high price in money, time wasted, and opportunities lost. Heroin humiliated Ray Charles and nearly killed him; the lies and secrets attendant on addiction scarred his character with a sour mistrust of other people. In the mid-60s the law forced Charles to choose between heroin or music, and his struggle with the drug rose in a dramatic crescendo. Yet in 1948 no thunderclouds had gathered over Seattle. Getting stoned was one more experience this cocky kid knew he could handle. A bag of heroin cost about $5, and RC could make one last a week or two. Sometimes they pulled crazy stunts when stoned, like the time Milt let RC drive through downtown rush-hour traffic. Luckily, nobody got hurt.

In November 1948, Jackie McVea, a tenor player from Los Angeles with a big hit, "Open the Door Richard," came to town for a weekend at the Washington Social Club; the McSon Trio had the intermission gig. One night RC asked to play McVea's horn and, while McVea listened amazed, played a burning solo that brought the house down. Back in LA, McVea told everybody about this blind cat in Seattle that somebody should sign up. A few weeks later a brown-skinned bear of a man, with a big smile and enveloping handshake, approached Gossie on a break at the Rocking Chair. He was Jack Lauderdale, he said, president of Down Beat Records from Los Angeles. He had made the trip on McVea's tip, but he told Gossie that he'd just stopped by to gamble in the rooms upstairs. The music was so smooth, he said, that at first he thought it was the jukebox. Maybe they'd like to make a record?

Gossie thought the stranger was putting him on. He had never heard of Down Beat Records. Lowell Fulson was on the label, Lauderdale said, along with Jimmy Witherspoon and Lloyd Glenn. Gossie went back to RC and Milt. "There's this guy saying he's gonna put us on a record," he told RC and Milt. "He must think we're damn fools." RC was too thrilled to be skeptical, and when he and Gossie went back to talk to the man, Lauderdale said he had meant every word. He would pay all expenses, and they could record tomorrow at a small studio right here in Seattle. He didn't have any contract with him, but they could make the record now and discuss all that later.

Here it was, his dream come true, RC Robinson on a record just like the records on Mr. Pit's jukebox. The next day the excited trio met Lauderdale at the small studio downtown. In the control booth a recorder stood ready to cut the sound from the mikes onto big glass transcription discs. Mistakes could not be corrected on the discs and studio time was precious, so they decided to do songs they had down pat. Lauderdale wanted original songs; standards meant paying publisher royalties. They consulted and decided on "I Love You, I Love You," a lighthearted ballad Joe Lee Lawrence had written back at D&B, and RC's song from Orlando, "Confession Blues." They got each song done in one take, and Lauderdale liked both. The singer had something special. But RC Robinson wasn't a name for a marquee, and Ray Robinson was no good because boxer Sugar Ray Robinson had it first. How about Ray Charles, short and to the point? RC didn't care what Lauderdale called him as long as he pressed the record. Lauderdale left for LA with the discs; they'd hear from him soon. Write more songs, he said. If this was a hit, he'd come back and record them again.

New Year's Day 1949 came and went, and the young hopefuls in rainy Seattle heard nothing from sunny LA. In February word came that the record had been released, and soon after the first shiny black 78s came in the mail. On the maroon label a conductor, his baton raised, stood between the words "Down Beat" in cursive script. Smaller print declared this to be Down Beat record number 171, "I Love You, I Love You (I Will Never Let You Go)" the A-side and "Confession Blues" the B-side, both written by R. C. Robinson and performed by the Maxin Trio, G. D. McKee, Guitar; Ray Charles, Piano; Milton Garret, Bass; Vocal: Ray Charles. They noticed the mistakes—Lauderdale must have misunderstood McSon, and Joe Lee had written "I Love You," but so what? By March copies got to the stores, and the trio's status on the local scene soared. "A record on an LA label was a big deal," Floyd Standifer remembered. "We kept asking ourselves, this cat's been here a year, how can he have a record?"

With Down Beat 171, Ray Charles makes a boyish, winning debut on record. "I Love You, I Love You," a ballad, opens with a bluesy discord, but soon settles into a creamy groove, Ray delivering the endearing "I love you, I love you" hook as casually as his idol, King Cole. "Confession Blues" features Ray as Charles Brown, but here, almost unknowingly, he cuts closer to the bone. As Gossie and Milt set up an insinuating riff, Ray sings and repeats the long first line smoothly:

I want to tell you a story of a boy who was once in love,

but when he gets to the even longer third line:

how the girl that I loved argued me out of the happiness I had dreamed of.

he stumbles, and for a moment the unsure kid peeps out of the world-weary bluesman.

Soon the trio had the thrill of hearing the record on local radio and seeing it sell well in Seattle stores. More surprising, the B-side made a little noise nationwide. On April 9, 1949, "Confession Blues" by the "Maxine Trio" entered *Billboard*'s Best Selling Retail Race Records chart at #11. Through the next few weeks, in the company of Paul Williams' "The Hucklebuck" and John Lee Hooker's "Boogie Chillen," "Confession Blues" slipped in and out of the race music chart, peaking in mid-May at #5. Not a big hit, but big enough for Lauderdale to call Gossie and tell him he'd be flying up the second week in June.

"I was in hog heaven," Charles recalled years later of that exuberant spring. He was still RC Robinson to himself, Louise, and everybody else, but on jukeboxes across the country he was vocalist and pianist Ray Charles. He began to write songs for the second session, and so did Gossie, determined to keep up with the burgeoning star. Together they rented a disc recorder from the Sherman Clay music store and made a few scratchy test runs of the new songs.

This time, Lauderdale had a contract with him, a three-page single-spaced document in which Down Beat undertook to record "a minimum of 200 record sides" during the six years G. D. McKee and musicians were exclusive Down Beat artists. Down Beat would pay them union scale for every session, and a 2 percent royalty on 90 percent of all records sold. All but the union scale per session was pure fiction, the promised number of sides laughably high and the low royalty never to be accounted, but on June 11, like many a greenhorn before and since, Gossie signed it as leader of the group. In two days, the trio recorded seven blues and ballads, the liveliest Gossie's "Rocking Chair Blues," a tribute to the club and its colorful characters "Cocktail Shorty" and "Gin Fizz Flo." This time the young players relaxed a bit in the studio and took a few more chances on their solos, Gossie hitting a couple of clunkers, RC playing brilliantly, his voice coolly focused in the center of the sound.

Lauderdale took the discs back to LA, and the trio went back to the Rocking Chair and their other gigs. "Confession Blues" fell off the charts for the last time in July. No word came from Lauderdale through September, and no new records were released. In October the mail brought a letter from Lauderdale with $50 in cash and airplane tickets to Los Angeles. Lauderdale wanted to record more sides with the trio, but there were only two tickets; he was sure he could find a substitute bass player in LA. Gossie and RC talked it over: could they drop Milt? Sure, said RC; the two of them had come from Tampa, after all, and started the duo. Gossie agreed; they had to go with Lauderdale's offer. They told the bad news to Milt, who felt insulted and told them so without effect. RC and Gossie flew down to LA, the first flight for both of them, in mid-November.

The two young men loved LA, sunny and warm like Tampa, but they stayed only two nights and didn't do much but record. At the first session, November 15, Gossie got a surprise: Lauderdale, evidently not satisfied with Gossie's playing, had booked a second guitarist, Mitchell "Tiny" Webb. Gossie knew he was a better rhythm guitarist than soloist, and he chorded along in support as Webb played the solos and filigree fills. Still, it was another sign that Lauderdale was interested not in the trio but in RC, "The Blind Sensation, Ray Charles," as he called him in publicity releases. They cut six good sides, including two slow blues, "How Long Blues" and "Blues Before Sunrise," by Leroy Carr. Ray captured a deep blues feeling in his voice, and the extra guitar filled out the sound; these Swingtime would release right away. (The jazz magazine *Downbeat* had just forced Lauderdale to change the label name to Swing Beat and then Swingtime.)

Lauderdale didn't have return tickets for them or any royalties from "Confession Blues," but he did put money down on a used Chevy they could drive back to Seattle. The car had no heater, and Gossie and RC froze at night as they pushed north through Oregon. When they got back, the trio continued gigging, but the seeds of discontent had been sown. Through the winter of '49 and '50 the Maxin Trio—its name changed to match the record—began to fall apart.

Gossie felt he was losing his leadership, that RC was growing beyond him. Milt no longer trusted either RC or Gossie, and both Gossie and Milt suspected that Lauderdale was talking to RC on the side, urging him to leave the trio and move down to LA by himself. They were right, and RC, or Ray as Lauderdale called him, was listening. When the other two accused him of disloyalty, RC got his back up. Nothing tied him to them or to Seattle, he said. "One of these nights, I'm just going to disappear," he told them. "I'm going to get on a train and I'll be gone."

At the same time, envious criticism stung RC, as it stings any artist growing out of a local scene. The young jazz players who had worshiped him a year before now saw flaws in his pop success. "We dug his be-bop piano playing," Traf Hubert remembered, "but his singing was too commercial, too imitative." Floyd Standifer felt RC was unsure of his musical identity: "It was divided. At jam sessions he sounded like Bud Powell, on gigs like Charles Brown." RC had his answer ready. He liked giving the public what it wanted. Musicians who told audiences, "This is my music. If you like it, cool, if not, fuck it," bothered him. "People give you their bread and are entitled to some kind of musical return on their dollar. I don't mean you got to give them exactly what they want, but you do have to keep them in mind."

Tension in the trio reached a breaking point. RC started asking his jamming and dope buddy Gerald Brashear to play tenor sax with them on gigs. Gossie didn't like it but couldn't stop it. He felt out of step as the one square among three junkies and was afraid that if they got busted for drugs, the police might think he was a user too. RC got so annoyed at timid Gossie one night after a college gig that he dashed out to the Chevy and started to drive off by himself. Gossie had to jump in and pull him away from the wheel. Only Milt's "the hell with it, let's play" attitude held the group together.

RC took the trouble home. The lure of LA tugged at RC's deepest ambitions, but he was scared. Could he take the big step to the big leagues with Louise? Quarrels over anything, nothing, became senseless screaming matches that climaxed with Louise in tears on the phone to her mother. One night RC grabbed the receiver and shouted that if Louise's mother wanted her to come back to Tampa so bad, well, send a ticket and he would put her on the bus. The teenagers made up in a few hours, but Mrs. Mitchell didn't forget. A week later, like a delayed but fatal blow, the ticket arrived in the mail. RC felt bound to his promise; Louise could hold out no longer against her family. They hugged each other and cried their eyes out, but to no use. Their romance was over. She didn't know, and neither did he, that she was pregnant with a baby daughter. RC put her on the bus back to Tampa, and Louise was gone.

Alone, RC fell into a sullen funk, withdrawing deep inside himself as he had the summer after Retha died. Gigs with the trio dwindled. He let go of the house on 24th Avenue and moved to a cheap hotel on Jackson near 12th Street. Junkies and dealers infested the place, and RC stayed stoned for days. Buddy Catlett came to the hotel and found him slumped in a big overstuffed chair, listening to records, scratching himself incessantly, and not saying a word.

In his funk, however, springtime changes stirred, and RC emerged from a dreary winter with a new sense of himself. When he came from Tampa two years before, he had needed Gossie. Now he didn't need anybody. Just short of twenty, he was a man, unencumbered by the past, ready for the future. In May, Lauderdale upped his offer. He would record Ray with a big band and set up a session late in the month. That bait, plus rumors of a coming drug bust at the hotel, provided a final impetus. It was time to go. As he had warned, RC told no one he was leaving. One day he was gone.

When Gossie found out, he felt a sudden relief, "like a heavy weight had been lifted off my back." In a few weeks Gossie left Seattle for his original destination, Great Falls, and did well there, joining Nat's brother Eddie Coles in a music/comedy act, Three Nuts and a Bolt. In time the heat of their breakup cooled, but the two kids from Tampa met only once again, when their paths crossed years later in Philadelphia. Indeed, the youngsters they had been disappeared with their names. In Great Falls, Gossie began to call himself Garcia McKee, and the young man who stepped on the train in Seattle as RC Robinson stepped off the train in Los Angeles as Ray Charles.

I love to dress in style, got a sunny smile,

and keep a pocketful of money for fun,

I love the life I live, with plenty time to give,

a friendly word and favor for everyone.

Los Angeles
1950

That's why, Ray Charles sang on Friday May 26, 1950, "all the girls in town are crazy about me." Ray was singing at the Universal Recording studio on Hollywood Boulevard, backed by an eight-piece band and having the time of his life. The two slow blues Ray cut that afternoon evoke the hard times he had come through ("Everyone's against me, I don't care where I go"), but the session's two lighthearted numbers, "Th' Ego Song," quoted above, and "I'll Do Anything for You," capture his exuberance at arriving in Los Angeles, as starstruck as a sweater girl sipping a soda at Schwab's. Lloyd Glenn, a well-known West Coast pianist and songwriter, produced the session as Lauderdale's artists and repertoire (A&R) man. Sax stars Marshall Royal and Jack McVea were among the sidemen, and Ray was the one getting double scale, $82.50, as leader!

This was the big leagues, and the rookie responded to the lift in musical energy around him by rising effortlessly to meet it. He played piano with a new freedom, and his voice, though still cool, opened up to ride over the Basie-style horns, reaching a devil-may-care climax in "I'll Do Anything for You." The title suggests a love song, but the kicker (". . . but work!") reveals that this guy loves only himself. Each time Ray spoke-sang ". . . but work!" he laughed out loud, and for the first time on record we hear his natural voice, sounding animated and innocently self-delighted. The new voice flashes by too quickly for us to guess how it might develop, but its contrast with the surrounding lines makes plain how carefully RC had constructed his "Nat" voice.

Lauderdale and Glenn picked "Th' Ego Song" and "Late in the Evening" for immediate release as Swingtime 228. The next day Lauderdale put Ray on the train north for a one-nighter with the company's top artist, singer-guitarist Lowell Fulson, a pairing that won a nice plug in the entertainment section of the Los Angeles *Sentinel*:

> GROWING BY LEAPS AND BOUNDS is demand for more blues by LOWELL FULSON (Swing Beat's "Every Day I Have the Blues" star) . . . Following Fulson's veddy, veddy successful dance at the Avodon last week, his 8-piece crew (Featuring RAY CHARLES, blind piano Sensation!) packed 'em in at the Savoy, in Oakland.

Once again Ray Charles Robinson had landed on his feet in a new city. This time, however, the city was too huge to overwhelm. At four million–plus in 1950, Los Angeles would soon zoom past Philadelphia to become the country's second-largest metropolis after New York. As the postwar boom matured into an ongoing era, Los Angeles, more than any other city, set the new American style. Developers transformed Orange County and the San Fernando Valley into vast suburban tracts, and a generation of young families accepted a house, a TV, and a two-tone car in the garage as fulfillment of the American dream. The cars needed freeways to connect the vast horizontal city, and smog became commonplace. That June in Los Angeles, Billy Wilder finished shooting *Sunset Boulevard,* Marilyn Monroe won raves for a bit part in *Asphalt Jungle,* and Richard Nixon was running for reelection to Congress. The 50s had begun.

The Negro community that Ray Charles entered was a small part of Los Angeles but, at 216,000 souls, larger than all of Jacksonville. Central Avenue and 10th Street had been the first heart of black Los Angeles; through the 20s, 30s, and 40s, black Central Avenue lengthened southward, crossing Washington, Adams, Jefferson, and Santa Barbara (now Martin Luther King) Boulevards, while the black community in Watts grew north along the avenue. White neighborhoods still filled a few gaps in 1950, but "Central Avenue" commonly meant a black district half a mile wide and six miles long.

Unlike the little Harlems Ray had lived in before, Central Avenue had the style and sophistication to match the New York original. Among the barbershops and pool halls on Central stood banks, car dealerships, and the offices of three newspapers, the *Eagle,* the *Tribune,* and the *Sentinel.* Gold's department store, at the corner of Washington, sold records for seventy-nine cents, as well as furniture and appliances. The Lincoln

Theatre at 24th combined movies and stage shows; Charles Brown had started there in Bardu Ali's band. A block south stood the Kentucky Club, where Art Tatum and Charlie Parker played, and the 28th Street Y, where Langston Hughes gave readings. At 41st Street stood the redbrick Dunbar Hotel, a Central Avenue landmark where Ethel Waters and Bill "Bojangles" Robinson stayed, as did Ray Charles for a few days when he first arrived. Nearby at Vernon stood the street's classiest restaurant, the Chicken Shack, owned by former Ellington singer Ivie Anderson.

"Sound trucks rolled slowly up and down Central when I was a kid," remembered tenor saxophonist Clifford Solomon. "A pickup with a plywood sign saying, 'This weekend! The Count Basie Orchestra, featuring Billie Holiday, Elks Hall, 9 until . . .' We'd run behind the truck dancing to the music from the loudspeaker." Tall, slender Solomon was a year out of Jordan High in 1950, and like wide-eyed Buddy Catlett in Seattle, drinking in Central's scenes and sounds: boogie-woogie pianist Pete Johnson and blues singer Joe Turner keeping chickens down by 95th Street, Redd Foxx cracking up the crowd at the Oasis on Western. Black actors who played maids and valets on screen and radio were Central Avenue royalty. Solomon might watch Lillian Randolph, Madame Queen on "Amos and Andy," sweep into Ivie's one evening for dinner with friends, and at dawn see Scatman Crothers stroll out of an after-hours joint like Black Dot McGee's.

Solomon heard about the hot new piano player from Seattle, even jammed with him a few times, but Ray, only a year older, was moving in faster circles. A Swingtime artist with a hit under his belt, Ray was, in his own words, a "jiveass celebrity." Lauderdale took him to the hot spots up and down the avenue, introducing his latest discovery to all and sundry. At KOWL he met dapper Joe Adams, Los Angeles' "Mayor of Melody." Adams soon forgot the routine handshake with the artist, but Ray long remembered the thrill of getting an on-air plug from a top disc jockey like Joe Adams. The newcomer learned how to play the fame game, how to charm others and act charmed himself. When he met Art Tatum, however, his act fell apart, and he stammered like a ten-year-old before the ultimate master of jazz piano. Ray had always felt "too musically divided," as he put it years later, to pour all his energy into playing piano. He wanted to sing and play, to write and arrange. Yet listening to Tatum, Ray regretted his multiple directions; by focusing on the keyboard, Tatum reached pianistic pinnacles he would never climb.

Daytimes Ray hung out at the Swingtime office in a stucco building at 34th and San Pedro, a few blocks west of Central. He flirted with Lauderdale's secretary Loretta, and soon he moved into her cozy apartment in a bungalow court. Loretta's friends considered them married, but for Ray the liaison was more practical than passionate. Something romantic had died in Ray with the end of his first great love affair. Though he later married and stayed married for nearly twenty years, no one woman after Louise ever captured his whole heart and soul. Instead he became a confirmed cocksman, always ready for a new body, a new touch, a new perfume. The intrigue of sex came to fascinate him, its strategies of deceit and desire. Women found Ray intensely attractive, and blindness proved no handicap in bed. He often carried on two, three, or more affairs at once and still responded to the willing ladies whom he met as a traveling entertainer. In Los Angeles Ray Charles began to live as he would for years, a bachelor on the prowl, high on pot and heroin, making music and making love as he pleased. He kept no listed phone and no fixed address, and he became as hard to follow as a tomcat who knows how to cover his tracks.

Lauderdale gave Ray only a few weeks to play in Los Angeles. "Every Day I Have the Blues" was riding high in the charts, and Fulson had already recorded the follow-up, "Blue Shadows." Lauderdale planned to put it out with Ray's "Late in the Evening," and he wanted Fulson to promote the record on tour. Ray could play piano in Lowell's band and do his own featured spot. For $35 a week Ray was game. Ben Waller, a Los Angeles black-music agent, booked Fulson on a zigzag string of one-nighters across the Southwest, and in late June they set off east on Highway 66, Fulson out front in a Roadmaster Buick, Ray and the other fellows behind, jammed into a station wagon with the instruments.

Lowell Fulson, an easygoing twenty-nine-year-old from Oklahoma by way of Oakland, led a burning little blues band that hot dusty summer. Fulson played a loping electric guitar and sang the blues plain and simple, much like the blues Muddy Waters and Howlin' Wolf were playing in Chicago. The band drew good crowds, and as the tour progressed, Waller kept booking new gigs in towns and cities from Arizona to Louisiana: Saturday and Sunday, July 1 and 2, at Joe's Skyline in Oklahoma City, then slowly east to a September weekend in New Orleans. In Texas promoters sometimes added T-Bone Walker and Joe Turner to the bill. Ray loved T-Bone's electric guitar sounds, and playing for Turner was a thrill: he had first heard Big Joe's open-throated roar on Mr. Pit's jukebox back in Jellyroll. Ray started contributing ideas to tighten up the sound, and Fulson soon let him take charge of the music. Though second-billed, Ray got noticed. The Houston *Informer* reported that at the El Dorado "heading the orchestra was a blind piano player." "Have ya noticed how popular that blind pianist, Ray Charles has become?? . . ." Dr. Daddy-O wrote in the "Boogie-Beat Jive" column of New Orleans' *Louisiana Weekly.* "His waxing of 'Late in the Evening Blues' has really started sumpthin'." In October they drove west through Texas, getting back to LA for a gig at the Elks Ballroom on the 29th.

As blues tours went in 1950, Lowell Fulson's summer jaunt was small potatoes. Percy Mayfield and Dinah Washington were circling similar circuits at better clubs and municipal auditoriums. For Ray, however, the tour took him the last big step from local to national musician. RC had watched from the sidelines when Lucky Millinder moved through Orlando; Ray Charles was now one of the fellows moving through. With the first Fulson tour, Ray entered the coast-to-coast commerce in black American music, the arena in which he would live and work for the entire decade, slowly and steadily battling his way up from the bottom to the top of the heap.

It's possible to see, in retrospect, that the black music business in 1950 was a cauldron of art and ambition heating up from a simmer to a boil that would soon make headline news. At the time, however, black music existed as a subculture that the grand culture grandly ignored. White Americans who loved Louis Armstrong and other established black pop and jazz artists knew nothing of the lower rungs where Ray Charles was starting out. For the few whites who noticed them at all, the gigs Ray played with Fulson were no more than multicolored placards tacked to telephone poles announcing strange and probably dangerous goings-on in the black part of town. Black Americans enjoyed the latest jumping band and each new jukebox hit, but they also accepted them as unremarkable events of daily life. This week Lowell Fulson was in town, next week Roy Milton. Few blacks or whites knew or cared much about the network of record men and dj's, agents and promoters, distributors and retailers, hangers-on and hustlers, who got the artists to the clubs and the records to the jukeboxes.

Ray entered this network as a Swingtime recording artist. The sprouting, in cities all over the country, of small companies that recorded and sold black music to black audiences became a running story in *Billboard* after the war. King in Cincinnati and Chess in Chicago, Savoy in Newark and Duke in Houston, Apollo, Atlantic, and Jubilee in New York; every issue seemed to advertise releases by a new independent, or "indy." Swingtime, founded in 1947, was one of six independents in Los Angeles alone, ranking fifth in size below Art Rupe's Specialty and Lew Chudd's Imperial Records; Modern, owned by the Bihari brothers; and Aladdin, owned by the Mesner brothers. Charles Brown recorded for Aladdin, Percy Mayfield for Specialty. B. B. King had just signed with Modern's Memphis subsidiary, RPM, and Fats Domino's first record, "The Fat Man," produced in New Orleans, hit for Imperial in 1950.

Indies sprouted for many reasons. Specialty's Art Rupe was a Jew who loved black music so much, he said, "it brought tears to my eyes." Abe Green began Chicago's National Records to create an outlet for a plastic shellac substitute that he manufactured. Black songwriters Leon and Otis Rene used their royalties from "Sleepytime Down South" to start LA's Exclusive Records; they pressed rainbow-colored discs using melted shellac from old records they bought for a penny. The typical indy founder was a businessman already selling music to Negroes, often the owner of a record store or a string of jukeboxes—Lauderdale started as a record distributor. The major labels—Columbia,

RCA-Victor, Decca, and Capitol—gladly signed black artists who sold well to whites, but they found the "race" market too small and culturally too foreign to pursue. Their ignorance and disdain created opportunity for the indies. From storefront offices in the black communities, independent record men could see that Negroes had become a reachable market. Millions more lived in cities than a decade earlier, and most had more money in their pockets. Negroes liked hot blues with a big-city beat. Come up with a record they could dance and romance to, and they'd snap it up.

Distribution posed the highest hurdle for the indies. Radio could make a record a national hit before an indy could get product to stores in faraway cities. Railroad porters carried cases of records cross-country, and Leonard and Phil Chess sold records from the trunk of their car on trips through the South. Indies often recorded each other's hits to grab sales in their own territory. "Open the Door Richard," Jackie McVea's 1947 novelty tune, hit first on the West Coast on LA's Black & White label, then became an East Coast hit for National by comedian Dusty Fletcher, and still got covered by eight other indies.

The hope of hit-size profits on small-stake investments crowded the indy marketplace. By the lopsided math common in American commerce, the four majors sold 85 percent of the 200 million records Americans bought in 1950, while dozens of indies scrambled to sell the remaining 15 percent. Competition was fierce, the dominant figures shrewd businessmen like Herman Lubinsky of Savoy and King's Syd Nathan, "rough, ignorant guys who knew how to make a buck," in the admiring assessment of a rival. "Don't pay anybody," ran the indies' credo for survival, but when somebody had to be paid, studios and pressing plants were harder to fob off than musicians eager to be stars. Lauderdale never pretended to pay the 2 percent royalty he owed Fulson and Charles, humoring them instead with spot cash, $200 or $500, when he was feeling flush and they were feeling broke. Such off-the-cuff accounting was the rule for the industry.

After the Elks Club gig, the Fulson band laid off in November, Ray making the scene along Central with Jack and his lady friend Betty, and meeting Madeline, a new lady for himself. Swingtime was on a roll. Lauderdale released Lloyd Glenn's "Chica Boo," a Latin-flavored blues that shot up the Rhythm & Blues charts to #1, put out Fulson's "Lonesome Christmas" for the seasonal market, and booked a session for Ray at Universal Recording on November 24.

Ray's big-band record had done less well than "Confession Blues," and Lauderdale planned to try Ray with a trio again, this time, however, with star players. Ray was still imitating Nat Cole, so why not book Oscar Moore on guitar and Johnny Miller on bass, the original members of Cole's trio? Ray loved the idea, even though Moore had the clout to command a $400 fee while he and Miller made do with $82.50. They got four songs down in three hours, and the results prove Ray's progress from the Maxin Trio days. The arrangements are more defined, and Moore earned his extra money, his guitar matching Ray's elegant piano. Yet two of the songs are utterly predictable—"I Wonder Who's Kissing Her Now," the Cole tune of the set, and "Lonely Boy," the Charles Brown. "All to Myself" is so bland and impersonal that the baldly autobiographical lyrics

> *Without a father, without a mother*
> *Without a sister, or a brother*
> *I'm what they call all to myself alone.*

skim by nearly unheard.

On "Baby Let Me Hold Your Hand," however, the best elements of old and new come together. "Baby" is a lighthearted, romantic blues, and Ray opens on celeste, the tinkling instrument setting a playful mood. He sings with a warm tenderness, coming in so close to the microphone that "let me hold your *hand*" becomes an intimate purr. Moore plays a stinging solo, and Ray sings out the happy ending:

> *Baby I'll buy you a diamond ring*
> *Cadillac and everything*
> *I'm gonna buy you a house in style*
> *Then I'll live there forever*
> *With my little wife and child.*

Lauderdale heard a hit in "Baby"'s catchy, ethereal sound, unlike anything else on the market: Cole plus Brown plus a quality uniquely Charles. Lauderdale decided not to rush "Baby" out before the end of the year, but to give himself until January 1951 to mount a campaign, the first step of which was to get Lowell and Ray back on the road. After Thanksgiving the Roadmaster and the station wagon again rolled southeast from LA. "Tennessee Waltz" by Patti Page topped the charts. In faraway Korea, Communist Chinese troops swept south from Manchuria, and the war that should have been "over by Christmas" turned into a bloody stalemate.

On its second outing, the Fulson-Charles tour moved up a notch, playing re-bookings to bigger crowds and new bookings in bigger joints. Lowell's brother Martin had acted as road manager, but in mid-December Lauderdale hired Wilbur J.

Brassfield, formerly Louis Jordan's road manager, and sent him to Kansas City to meet the band. Lauderdale also announced Swingtime's campaign in one of his infrequent ads on *Billboard*'s R&B page. Under the slogan "Swingtime, The Sign of the Best Seller," Lauderdale sent wishes for "A very Merry Xmas and a Happy Prosperous New Year to all our Dealers and Distributors from Swingtime Record Co. and their artists Lowell Fulson, Ray Charles, Lloyd Glenn, Jesse Thomas, Percy Mayfield, Charles Brown, Johnny Moore's 3 Blazers, Jimmy Witherspoon, and Mabel Scott." The list, like many such, was inflated: Lauderdale was selling reissues of Mayfield and Brown, not current releases. No matter; the long list looked good in the narrow ad. In smaller print Lauderdale went on:

> With such guaranteed "hit" makers as Lowell Fulson, Lloyd Glenn, Ray Charles, and new artists like Jesse Thomas and others to be introduced throughout the year, Dealers and Distributors of Swingtime Records can look forward to 1951 as a banner year and watch the Cash Registers ring with Sales!

By the end of December the tour reached east Texas, and on New Year's Day, 1951, Lowell, Ray, and company played the City Auditorium in Houston. *Billboard* reported that Swingtime would soon be releasing "new Ray Charles diskings," and the tour headed up U.S. 75 for a return booking, January 15, at the Empire Room in Dallas.

On the Road
1951-1952

The Empire Room stood at 1710 Hall Street in North Dallas, a low gray wood-frame building with a tall blue neon sign that spelled out EMPIRE in large vertical letters, ROOM small and horizontal beneath. Left of the front door gleamed the plate-glass window of a booking agency; through the door lay the club proper, an open room with a long bar running along the right-hand wall, wooden-back chairs and square tables around a polished dance floor, a low stage at the far end. In January 1951, the Empire Room was in its heyday, a growing concern owned by a shrewd and powerful black man, Howard Lewis. A Dallas native then about fifty, Lewis carried 250 pounds of muscle on a six-foot-one frame; his friendly smile concealed a penetrating glance. Depression years on the bum and war years working the trains as a roving gambler had seasoned Lewis' judgment of men and money, and he returned to Dallas with a bundle won from drunken soldiers. That bundle bought a neighborhood bar, and Lewis used its profits to buy the Rose Room, the city's top black nightclub, on Hall near the corner of Thomas Avenue, a busy hub of cafes and cabstands that a wag once called "the Tigris and Euphrates of black Dallas."

Lewis renamed the Rose Room the Empire Room, and in his hands the club became the center of a vast realm. From the office behind the plate-glass window, Lewis controlled a broad swath of the black music network, Texas east to west, New Mexico, Oklahoma, and Arkansas. Only Don Robey, his archrival in Houston, kept Lewis out of south Texas and Lousiana. Like Robey and similar titans in Atlanta and Chicago, Lewis had the bankroll to buy band dates wholesale, guaranteeing agents like Waller in Los Angeles or Shaw Artists in New York two or three weeks of one-nighters for their acts. Lewis then sold the dates retail to local promoters at clubs, fairgrounds, and municipal auditoriums across the territory. Business was booming; Lewis' eldest son John had just come back to Texas from California to help out. Lewis had booked much of the Fulson-Charles tour the summer before, but the packed Empire Room on January 15 at $1.50 a head proved that this was a band on the move. People liked the contrast of Lowell's gut-bucket blues and Ray's cool blues. The pair returned to the Empire in mid-February, and Lewis began booking spring and summer dates for them all along his circuit.

As the tour was growing, so was the band. They started out this time with three horns—Earl Brown, alto, Lucky Newble, tenor, and Fleming Askew, trumpet—and then added a second trumpet, Billy Brooks, a nice kid from Cincinnati. Wilbur Brassfield told Lauderdale the band needed a bus, and Lauderdale bought a thirty-seat Flexible with a big Buick engine. The bus needed a driver, and Lewis suggested a Dallas cabbie, Jeff Brown, known as a soft-spoken, steady-going guy. "Have you ever driven a bus?" Brassfield asked him. "Yes," said Brown, but he hadn't driven anything bigger than a logging truck back in Henderson, his hometown. The fellows stowed their instruments and bags on the overhead racks, and the Flex started out for the East Coast.

R&B tours seldom made such long trips out of their home territory, but the Fulson-Charles tour got to Philadelphia in late January and played a weekend at the Showboat Musical Bar in the Douglass Hotel. Francis Cauthorn, "Night Shift" columnist for the Philadelphia *Tribune,* noted that he met "Ray Charles, blind pianist extraordinaire," on his first trip to the city, and that Ray said he was "looking round Philly to see what it has to offer in eligible women." From there the bus turned west to Pittsburgh, where Ray insisted on hiring a second tenor player. At the union hall, black Local 471, they found a kid named Stanley Turrentine, only sixteen and a half but good. "I got on that raggedy bus," Turrentine recalled years later. "We headed west into Ohio, and then we turned south and we *stayed* south."

Jack Lauderdale released "Baby Let Me Hold Your Hand" in January, Swingtime's biggest month ever, 103,000 records shipped, double the year before. By the time the band got back to the Empire in mid-February, "Baby" had made it to *Billboard*'s R&B jukebox chart, but just barely: #10 and one of three records tied for the spot. Still, after two years Ray was back on the charts. In good company, too: Ruth Brown's "Teardrops from My Eyes" held the number-one spot against Joe Morris' rapidly rising "Anytime, Anyplace, Anywhere." "Baby" moved up to #8 the next week, and LA disc jockey Hunter Hancock made it his "disc of the week." In March, as the tour played the Sunset Terrace in Indianapolis, "Baby" reached #7 and from this modest high point slowly faded through April to drop off in May.

Its chart numbers are similar, but "Baby Let Me Hold Your Hand" sold many more records, and did much more to establish Ray, than "Confession Blues." Swingtime had grown in a growing market. Ray's name, not "Maxin Trio," was on the label, and he sang "Baby" on tour across the country. Yet the song's low-lying curve through the charts profiles a record the public liked but didn't flip for, one that never pushed its way into contention at the top. Charles Brown's "Black Nights" entered the charts with "Baby," went straight to #1, and stayed there, becoming for Brown a signature song second to "Drifting Blues." "Baby" left Ray still a vague identity in the music marketplace, known but not well known. That spring of 1951 Ray began to puzzle why he was doing well but not better. Imitating Cole and Brown had been his meal ticket since Jacksonville, and he had always taken it as a compliment when people told him, "Ray, your voice is the *spittin' image* of Charles Brown." Now he began to think it would be nice "if people began to recognize *me*, if they'd tell me I sounded like Ray Charles." Yet how could the public know what Ray Charles sounded like when he didn't? That spring Ray began cautious experiments to find out.

In April, as the tour rolled from New Orleans to Atlanta, *Billboard* reported in the "Rhythm and Blues Notes" column that "Shaw Artists signed new management contract with Lynn Hope. Also signed were blues singer Ray Charles, Lowell Fulson, and thrush Joan Shaw." For Ray, eight hundred miles from the Shaw office at 565 Fifth Avenue, New York City, signing with Shaw Artists may have seemed good news but no big deal. He had been signed as a piece of the successful Fulson package. Quite possibly Brassfield told him, "Hey, we've signed with Shaw, we'll have gigs all summer," and Ray said, "All right!" and that was that. Yet in becoming a Shaw artist, Ray took the next big step in his career after signing with Swingtime. Through the next fifteen years Ray moved from this lowest spot on Shaw's roster to company superstar, and he left Shaw only when the agency, and the Shaw family, collapsed.

Shaw Artists was only two years old in 1951, but its founder, William "Billy" Shaw, had a decade's experience in the black music business. A Runyonesque little Napoleon, capable of towering rage and fast-talking charm, Shaw put together Billy Eckstine's big band in 1944 at William Morris, earning himself the title "boy wonder of the booking industry." After a stint at the Gale Agency, owned by brothers Tim and Moe Gale, Shaw hung out his own shingle as Shaw Artists. Jazz artists formed the first core of his roster; Shaw battled to get Charlie Parker gigs and battled with Parker when he missed them. In the 50s Shaw moved into R&B. Among his top acts in 1951: Charles Brown, Amos Milburn, and the Dominoes. Lee Shaw, Billy's wife, managed the office. Their son Milt, a tall, good-looking twenty-one-year-old, worked there too, booking jazz dates. When Milt was still a teenager, Shaw had sent him out as Dizzy Gillespie's band boy; he came back talking hip and shooting heroin.

Along with Joe Glaser, the Gale brothers, and Ben Bart of Universal Attractions, Shaw Artists had expanded circuits established in the 20s and 30s by the Theatre Owners and Bookers Association, wryly known as TOBA: Tough On Black Asses. Each agency worked the same way, offering the artists three-year contracts for live performance only: agents seldom got a piece of record sales, though hits, of course, boosted a live act's value. "We sold artists then as we sell them now," said Dick Alen, a Shaw agent in the 50s and later with William Morris. "You have an artist in St. Louis, so you draw a three-hundred-mile circle on the map, and call everybody you know in that circle. And we knew everybody."

To secure a date, local promoters wired half the artist's fee to the agency, which deducted its 10 percent and held the balance for the artist. The artist picked up the other half at the gig, nearly always in cash, and used it to pay band and travel expenses. Artists on the road stayed in daily touch with New York, getting new dates and directions. Theaters that engaged by the week, the Apollo in New York, the Howard in Washington, the Regal in Chicago, were the cream of Shaw's gigs; one-nighters were the meat and potatoes. "You could spend two weeks moving an artist through Florida," Alen recalled. "There was money all over." Business had been good in 1950 and promised to get better in 1951. "Black music is on the threshold of something big," Shaw told young agent Larry Myers on his first day at work. "You're in on the ground floor, and you'll never regret it."

Now Ray had a New York agent and an LA label: he was connected coast-to-coast. There was food for dreams in that, but as spring turned to summer, 1951, the connection meant, in practical fact, driving mile after mile of American highway in the bus, Jeff Brown at the wheel, from the Sunset Terrace in Indianapolis May 13, down to the Houston Civic Auditorium, up again to the Empire Room and farther north to the Up-Daters Club in Oklahoma City in June. "Amos and Andy" premiered with an all-black cast on national television, and Alan Freed started his Moondog Rock 'n' Roll party on Cleveland radio. The tour drove east to Atlanta, eight months on the road and still rolling.

As a band bus rolls through the big world, it spins itself into a little world all its own. Good-natured Lowell led his world, its population shifting between ten to a dozen fellows and a few girlfriends; Brassfield cracked the whip when it needed cracking. Earl Brown, on the other hand, could always crack everybody up with a silly gag.

Drummer Eddie Piper was a steady guy from LA, Billy Brooks a romantic always in love, and Stanley Turrentine the baby of the band; Lowell kept an older brother's eye on him. Through long afternoons Jeff sat up front at the wheel, and the musicians lounged in the seats behind him, their wardrobe bags hanging over the windows. They played cards and dominoes, slept, talked music, smoked cigarettes, gossiped about girls they knew and guys they had played with, told dirty jokes, nipped at gin bottles, and smelled each other's farts. When they knelt in the center aisle for a noisy crap game, Ray joined in the fun, feeling the dimples on the dice with his fingertips. Yet more often he sat quietly by himself, thinking his own thoughts.

At sunset, when they reached whatever town Brassfield had scratched down from the last phone call with Shaw, Jeff turned the bus to the colored part of town. Near the club or Elks hall where they were booked, there usually stood a small hotel or boardinghouse, most owned by blacks, some by Jews, that catered to traveling black musicians. Pee Wee Crayton's blues band might be stopping there, too, or a gospel group like the Pilgrim Travelers. Gigs lasted from nine to one, divided into an intro set by the band, Lowell, intermission, then a set featuring Ray before Lowell closed the show. After the gig was the time for ladies, serious drinking and/or reefer, a poker game that could last until bus call the next morning, and off again.

In towns and cities the band lived in the black world. Traveling the highways put them face-to-face with Jim Crow: colored rest rooms and colored water fountains, buying food to take out from the kitchen door of restaurants, stopping to relieve themselves by the side of the road. Sometimes segregation was so stupid it was almost funny. One afternoon during a swing along the Carolina coast, the band stopped at Myrtle Beach. Ray jumped in and swam with everybody else until he heard the fellows shouting, "Ray, come back, man, come back." He thought they were telling him he had gone out too far, and swam in. When he got to them, they said they had stopped him just in time before he swam over into the "white side" of the ocean. Sometimes segregation was terrifying. One night out in the country near Natchez, the bus crossed a bridge only one lane wide. The white driver of a car speeding toward the bridge from the other side panicked when he saw the lumbering bus and ran off the road. Jeff pulled over to see if he could help. The driver started yelling that it was Jeff's fault. Minutes later the state police arrived.

"What you doin' 'round here, boy?" the cops asked Jeff. "Everybody off the bus!"

They forced the men, Ray included, to line up, hands above their heads, and shone flashlights in their faces and fired off insulting questions. The older hands knew the only safe response was to say, "Yes, sir," "No, sir," as long as necessary, but young Turrentine, from Pittsburgh, left off a few sirs at first. "Don't you know, boy, it's the law in Mississippi a nigger gotta say 'Yes, sir' to a white man?" screamed one cop.

"Yes, sir," said Stanley, scared out of his wits. "I learned that night that we put our lives in jeopardy going out to play our music," Turrentine recalled years later. "We clung together tight, because our lives depended on each guy watching out for the other."

After the dances Ray and the fellows might jam with other musicians in town, polished jazz veterans from Buddy Johnson's big band or the rough-and-ready blues cats playing behind Little Milton. Sunday mornings Ray often woke up to hear a gospel vocal group rehearsing down the hall, and they always welcomed him to join the harmony. A few times he found himself in the same city with Lionel Hampton's band and got together with his pal Quincy Jones, now playing trumpet with Hampton. One Saturday night when Ray and Lowell were booked in nearby Birmingham, Charles Brown played a dance hall in Bessemer, Alabama. Ray came over to jam, and Clifford Solomon, the kid from LA touring with Charles Brown that summer, never forgot it. "That dance hall had a big old fan down at one end to blow out the smoke, but it was *hot*. Ray and Charles sat at this out-of-tune upright piano, Ray playing the left hand, Charles playing the right, and the people went nuts."

That summer, friendship sprang up between Ray and Jeff Brown. A slender fellow of medium height and coffee-and-cream complexion, Jeff had a calm, intelligent face that, with his rolling gait, conveyed a quiet self-confidence. He was six years older than Ray, but the two country boys from Henderson, Texas, and Greenville, Florida, had much in common. Jeff admired Ray's valiant attempt at independence, but he could see that Ray needed help in little ways. With natural tact, Jeff began to do Ray small favors, checking Ray's show clothes for spots he couldn't see, straightening his money. "Ray could tell coins, but not bills," Jeff recalled. "If he bought something and offered a five, some people'd say the five was a one. So I'd take his money and put the twenties on the bottom, then the tens, fives, and ones, and I'd tell him how many he had of each. Then, if he had six ones, he knew that after six bills, he was down to the fives."

The two talked by the hour. Jeff told Ray about surviving five major battles in Europe during World War II. Ray told Jeff about the Florida band that made him ride on a soda case instead of a seat. He told him how Retha had forced him to wash his own clothes, how she had impressed on him that he had to help himself. Jeff sensed that Ray's ambitious drive had a bitter edge. "Things hadn't come easy for Ray," Jeff remembered. "It was a constant challenge to him to come out on top in any situation. He succeeded in music because music was his gift, but he *worked* on his music."

On the road heroin was hard to find, and Ray had to keep his habit on a tight leash. Only if he planned ahead could he score enough in New Orleans to last the few weeks across the backwoods until he got to St. Louis. That summer in Atlanta he met a teenage saxophone player, David Newman, nicknamed Fathead, who was out on his first tour playing alto with Lloyd Glenn. Fathead was into heroin too, and when Ray asked him for help in scoring, Fathead said sure. He was from Dallas and had good connections there; elsewhere it was catch-as-catch-can. Numerous times, the two pooled their money and got high together, Fathead cooking up Ray's dose and shooting it into his arm.

Ray and Fathead, however, became more than junk buddies. Standoffish Ray felt drawn by Fathead's open, friendly disposition, and Fathead, a skinny kid with a long handsome face, admired Ray's musical ability. The two jammed together when their tour paths crossed, listened to records, and talked about music. "Ray and I clicked as friends and musicians," Newman recalled years later. "I loved the way he played the piano. Ray played jazz, but he liked all kinds of music, gospel and country. I had been strictly into be-bop, taking R&B gigs for the money. Knowing Ray, my appreciation of music opened up, and my playing got bluesier."

The tour rolled into Cleveland for a mid-July week at the Ebony Lounge. In a previous pass through Ohio, Billy Brooks had introduced Ray to a beautician from Columbus named Eileen Williams, a friend of Billy's girlfriend Artelia Ferrell. Ray liked Eileen, and this time he asked her to travel with him to Atlanta. Petite and pretty, Eileen took over caring for Ray, combing his hair and choosing his stage clothes. Artelia, "T" as they called her, came along with Billy, and in Atlanta they got married, which started Eileen and Ray thinking. A week later, on July 31, they too got married before a Fulton County justice of the peace. The four newlyweds took a few days off together and then got back on the bus. The tour swung south to New Orleans and the "beautiful and air-cooled" Club Desire.

With every gig, Ray became more and more the tour's chief musician. Directing a big band was heaven for Ray. He wrote music steadily, dictating to Turrentine arrangements of swing classics like "One O'Clock Jump" and of his own original songs, including the rocking "Kissa Me Baby." He wrote intros and outros, segues and fanfares, and put the band through long rehearsals until they had his music right. In the process Ray transformed the Lowell Fulson Orchestra from a loose blues band into a tight R&B show band.

Lowell, however, was bandleader, not Ray, and no leader likes being eclipsed by his number-two man. Fulson struggled to keep up, but he didn't read music, and big-band precision didn't suit his style. "Ray was the perfectest man you ever saw," Fulson remembered. "Everything had to be *his* way. It got to where I'd just do my little old blues and then get out of there." Fulson resented Ray, but he also recognized the value of his work. "He took young players and whipped them into a band that was *ready*, with the variety to fill a whole night. We got gigs that I couldn't have gotten by myself." Ray demanded one raise after another, and got them, grudgingly, from Brassfield. Lowell needled Ray, teasing him that he sounded too much like Nat Cole, that audiences didn't like imitations. Self-interest on both sides kept things polite, but as summer turned to fall, the easygoing tour had turned awkward.

When the bus got back to LA in late October for a well-deserved month off, Ray bought a '51 Oldsmobile. He had had enough of the bus; when they went out again, he'd ride by himself with a driver. Buying a car was a bold step for a blind man and a sure sign that by this time Ray was by no means broke. He still had the savings account in Greenville, and he was salting away a portion of his tour salary and the odd $500 he got from Lauderdale. In a world where many musicians lived hand-to-mouth and often fell into debt, Ray was managing to keep a little bit ahead. Just as he hadn't told Gossie about his stash in Seattle, now Ray had more money than he let on to the people around him.

Lauderdale booked studio time for Ray that November, and Ray used it to record with Lowell's nine-piece band, his largest ensemble yet: two trumpets, five saxes, bass, drums, and Ray on piano. They got four of his original blues on tape that afternoon: "Kissa Me Baby," "Hey Now," "The Snow Is Falling," and "Misery in My Heart." With a band rehearsed and ready to go, the session was a ball, Eddie Piper kicking the beat and Turrentine and Brooks blowing their hearts out. From the big brassy opening of "Kissa Me Baby" to the rocking rideout of "Misery in My Heart," these four blues capture the young, exuberant band Ray had whipped into shape on the road, the driving R&B that had gotten the people dancing at the clubs all summer.

And they present a new Ray Charles. The June 1950 session with the seven-piece band was the bud; this is the first blossom. Ray shatters the cool shell around his voice, shouting and crooning with the horns, changing vocal texture at will, leaping into falsetto. Within tight big-band discipline, Ray and the rest play with a rollicking freedom, and the charts, though simple, paint dramatic sound colors, staccato brass against legato saxes, lush horn chords under bouncy piano triplets. "The Snow Is Falling" demonstrates the change from the old to the new Ray: he sings the first mournful chorus with a trio à la Charles Brown, then the band enters, the rhythm goes into overdrive, and Ray's voice grows into big shouts and happy howls. Not even mock sadness dilutes the good cheer of "Kissa Me Baby." Ray's got a gal with a "fine brown frame," and all he wants is "Kissa me, baby." "All night long," Earl Brown chimes in in silly harmony, "Love-dovey all of the time." With its Louis Jordan wit and Kansas City riffs, "Kissa Me Baby" is fun, not autobiography, but one lyric—"I'm gonna buy me a house in style for me and my little wife and child"—echoes a similar line in "Baby Let Me Hold Your Hand," suggesting that a wish for home crosscut Ray's wanderlust. Lauderdale picked "Kissa Me Baby" to release in January and sent a "Holiday Greetings" card to distributors that declared: "For 1952, watch Ray Charles on 'KISSA ME BABY.'"

The tour got on the road after Thanksgiving just as it had the year before. Getting his road heroin together made Ray late getting started, and Billy Brooks drove the Oldsmobile across New Mexico at 100 miles an hour to catch up to the others. Besides his clothes, stage outfits, and toiletries, Ray carried a small record player and an assortment of gospel, country, jazz, and blues records. He also kept a fat Braille notebook with the phone numbers of clubs and hotels, promoters and musicians, girlfriends and drug dealers, and a Braille stylus and frame to punch in new numbers as needed. Soon he got a Zenith Trans-Oceanic radio; slow hours riding over land he couldn't see passed more swiftly when he could put on earphones, fiddle with the dials, and listen to the world.

In January 1952, "Cry" by Johnny Ray topped both the Pop and the R&B charts, and the Lowell Fulson tour rolled through Oklahoma, Ray's Oldsmobile darting alongside the bus like a pilot fish by a whale. Eileen got tired of the road and went home to her hairdressing customers in Columbus. As the tour moved south to Memphis, the conflicts of the fall resurfaced and intensified. Brassfield resented Ray's independence in the Olds, and he told Fulson that Ray's drug use set a bad example for junior members of the band. Money was a bigger problem. The band was earning more, $300 a night guaranteed plus a percentage on good nights, and most nights were good nights. Ray demanded and got raises until he was getting $175 a week, but it still wasn't enough. When Brassfield tried to dress him down, Ray told him to go to hell. "Just pay me," Ray said. Once Ray swung at Brassfield, "quick as a snake," Fulson remembered. Jeff and the fellows pulled them apart as they rolled punching and grabbing in the aisle of the bus. Afterward Ray went into a sullen funk, sat by himself, and refused to talk. After a few silent hours, Fulson nudged him on the shoulder.

"You playing possum on me, boy?" he asked.

"I got my hidden secrets," Ray said and pulled away.

Whatever Ray hid among his secrets, two known events converged in February, pushing and pulling his life in new directions. First, the Shaw agency booked the Fulson-Charles tour, billed with the Orioles, on the Northeast theater circuit: the Howard in Washington, the Royal in Baltimore, the Earle in Philadelphia, the Apollo in New York, and then, with the Dominoes, out to the Circle Theatre in Cleveland and on to the Regal in Chicago. This marked a big step up from obscure one-nighters in the vast reaches of Texas.

Second, Jack Lauderdale's lucky streak in the record business ran out. He didn't know then that a two-year decline had begun for Swingtime, one that would end in bankruptcy. But as an experienced record man, Lauderdale knew his problem: no big hits. To survive, an indy needed hits big enough that distributors would pay up over-due accounts to get them; medium hits that distributors didn't have to have always left an indy starved for cash. Lauderdale tried a two-for-one deal to stimulate orders, but advance interest in "Kissa Me Baby" was still so tepid that he put it out in mid-February, a month later than he hoped. *Billboard* picked "Kissa Me" as an R&B "Record to Watch," but listeners picked "Three O'Clock Blues" by B. B. King to buy. In the three years since Seattle, the blind sensation had only half delivered on his promise. Lau-derdale needed to consolidate Swingtime around his core earners, Glenn and Fulson, and he needed money. He put out word that Ray's contract was for sale.

Among the first to hear was Billy Shaw. Shaw needed Ray recording for somebody to keep drawing crowds on the road, and he passed the word to Leonard Chess, Syd Nathan at King, and Herb Abramson and Ahmet Ertegun at Atlantic in New York. Chess and Nathan expressed interest; Abramson and Ertegun acted. Ertegun had liked "Baby Let Me Hold Your Hand" a year before and had been saying ever since, "I want a piano player like that on our label." He talked on the phone with Lauderdale, and they quickly agreed on a price: $2500. Ertegun sent the check, and Ray Charles became an Atlantic recording artist. Like a rookie baseball player being traded, Ray had no voice in the deal-making that swirled around him. He knew the name Atlantic Records, however, and knew he was now signed to a bigger, more successful label. Bad luck for Swingtime had meant good luck for him.

The tour reached New York and, February 29 through the first week of March, Ray played his debut at the Apollo Theatre on 125th Street, "Harlem's High Spot," the top venue in black show business. The Orioles ("Youthful Versatile Leading Quintette") headed the bill, followed by Hal Singer and his band, Lowell Fulson and his band, and then, in tiny type, "Ray Charles, Blind Pianist." The weather was cold but clear, and they had a good time, the fellows marveling at the Apollo's gold-trimmed curtain and cavernous balconies. Jackie "Moms" Mabley was the comedian, and when she did her routine about an old lady looking for a lover boy, they almost wet their pants laugh-ing. Ray couldn't believe the number of people hanging out backstage; as many, it seemed, as the crowd out front in the seats.

One morning Ray got to midtown and Shaw Artists' four-room office on Fifth Av-enue. Lee Shaw welcomed him to the agency with Jewish-motherly warmth, and Milt

Shaw, just Ray's age, made friendly overtures. Billy Shaw sat him down in his private office and told him what he told all new artists: "Kid, anytime the Shaw agency doesn't fulfill its duties toward you, *you* don't need the Shaw agency. But anytime you don't perform for us, *we* don't need you." Shaw's tough talk scared Ray, but he also recognized and liked the brass-tacks honesty that underlay it. Raised on Retha's similarly tough-minded proverbs, Ray understood the challenge of "no quarter asked, no quarter given." In time it would become his own bedrock business credo.

Ray stayed that week at the Braddock Hotel on 126th Street, popular with musicians because its entrance adjoined the Apollo's backstage door. Herb Abramson and Ahmet Ertegun came up to the hotel to meet their latest acquisition, but not much more happened than handshakes all around. They said they were excited to have him at Atlantic, and Ray said he was glad to be there. Abramson and Ertegun were in no hurry to schedule a first session; recording could wait until the next time Ray got to New York.

As "Kissa Me Baby" straggled onto the R&B chart at #10, the tour played Cleveland's Circle Theatre, a week after an Alan Freed "Moondog" concert turned into the first "rock 'n' roll riot." At the Regal in Chicago came the final showdown with Lowell Fulson. Through a winter of growing suspicion, Ray had figured out that Shaw, in booking the tour as a package, was selling Ray as singer and bandleader for far more than Fulson and Brassfield were paying him. That was and is, of course, standard business practice, an employer profiting by paying an employee less than his worth. To twenty-one-year-old Ray, however, it came as a revelation. He felt betrayed, not by Shaw, who was simply charging what the market would bear, but by Lowell and his road manager, who pocketed the difference between his price and his salary. That, as Ray saw it, was cheating. Why should they skim the cream off his crop? Lowell was using him to get classy theater gigs, Ray ranted to Jeff, and he wouldn't take it anymore. On his own he'd get his full price; he'd put together his own band, and Jeff would be his manager and drive the Ray Charles bus. "I'd be glad to," said Jeff, not thinking that the day would ever come.

Anger spurred Ray on, caution held him back. He had a secure gig with Lowell. If he went solo and didn't deliver, Shaw would drop him, and then where would he be? Shaw told him to stay with Lowell. "Kissa Me Baby" got to #8 in April, then disappeared for good, proof to the agency that Ray didn't have a big enough name to draw on his own. Jack Archer, Shaw's assistant, told Lowell to pacify Ray with another raise, but Lowell said he was paying Ray top dollar already. That was the last straw for Ray. Two years playing second fiddle to Lowell Fulson was long enough, and after the Regal, Ray quit the tour.

Fulson felt relieved to see Ray go, yet bore him no ill will. "I can't afford him, but don't you lose him," he told Shaw. "You're gonna be proud of this boy, he's millionaire material." "Forgive and forget," however, was not one of the proverbs Retha had taught her son. Ray nursed his anger for years, telling and retelling the story of how Fulson had cheated him. From time to time the two appeared on the same bills, but Ray kept a polite but impenetrable distance. "Ray may have been naive," a colleague from the mid-50s remembered, "but Lowell had hurt him deeply. When Lowell's career declined and Ray's rose to the heights, Ray could have helped him but he wouldn't."

Ray went back to Columbus, but with his future suddenly uncertain and the prospect of a home and family remote. Eileen, it turned out, had been drinking in his absence, and though he got high every day, Ray didn't like his women to drink, certainly not his wife. This hasty first marriage began to fade away to eventual divorce. Ray moved on to Cincinnati, where bandleader Johnny Otis ran into him on the porch of the Manse Hotel. Otis, on tour with Little Esther, also scouted talent for King Records, and Ray asked him to arrange an audition with Syd Nathan. Maybe Nathan would want to buy his contract from Atlantic and bid up his value. Otis drove Ray over to King's studio on Brewster Avenue, got him set up, and asked Syd into the control booth. Ray played, and Syd made a snap judgment: "Shit, I don't need a poor man's Charles Brown." Ray didn't say a word on the way back, but Otis knew he was deeply disappointed.

Two years on the road, however, had made Ray a seasoned trouper, and he got back to work. Howard Lewis added him to a string of one-nighters with Joe Turner that wound through Houston, Dallas, and Oklahoma City and to Little Rock on June 23. Then trumpeter Joe Morris signed Ray as a piano player and second act for a tour that crawled out to Utah and back through July and August. Ray went south on his own for an early-September weekend at the Royal Peacock Club in Atlanta. That done, he headed to New York and his first recording session at Atlantic Records.

PART III

THE 1950s:
THE ATLANTIC YEARS

Atlantic Records
1952

In the summer of 1947, twenty-one-year-old Tom Dowd had just come back to New York from observing A-bomb tests on Bikini Atoll. The tuba-playing son of a stage manager and an opera soprano, Dowd had been snatched by the war from physics classes at City College of New York and put on the night shift at a Manhattan Project cyclotron. Hands-on experience, however, didn't grant the degrees he needed to work as a full-fledged physicist. Dowd needed a job, any job, and he found one as assistant recording engineer at the Carl Fischer Music Store on West Fifty-seventh Street. An old-line classical music publishing firm, Fischer maintained the studio for students at Carnegie Hall across the street to check their progress by listening to themselves. Dr. Frederick Oetgen, Dowd's Swiss boss, wore a monocle and a white coat, and he liked his recordings as coldly neutral as a laboratory photograph. For Dr. Oetgen, any blur in the sound caused by signal overload was verboten. Watch the dials, he instructed Dowd. Never must the arrows go into the red!

Compared with repairing cyclotrons, recording was a snap, and the first few months on the job were dull for Dowd. That fall, however, James C. Petrillo, boss of the American Federation of Musicians, ordered a recording ban to start January 1, 1948. Suddenly producers from Savoy, Apollo, and other New York–based indies crowded the studio trying to stockpile sides on Charlie Parker and Lionel Hampton, and Dowd found the work getting much more interesting.

Black-music producers found Oetgen's stiff engineering style too prim. They wanted more color in their records, a broader sound palette: intense trebles for the high horns, rich basses for the bass, and pumping left-hand piano riffs. Dowd began to experiment, playing bass sounds alone, then treble sounds. By carefully combining the two, he found ways to widen Oetgen's narrow spectrum, to push deep into the redline and still get a clean recording. Word spread about the kid engineer with the fat sound, and more clients arrived: Dizzy Gillespie, Billy Eckstine, and the Ravens.

Among the new clients in November arrived an unlikely trio: Herb Abramson, an unkempt, dynamic Jew; Jesse Stone, a dapper soft-spoken Negro; and Ahmet Ertegun, a bald and talkative Turk. Abramson, in his mid-twenties and trained as a dentist, produced records for National, Abe Green's indy. Stone, an experienced bandleader in his mid-forties, was Abramson's music man; he wrote songs and charts, coached singers, and hired the backup bands. The two had done well for National, scoring with Dusty Fletcher's version of "Open the Door Richard," but Herb was restive. "Abe Green cares nothing about music," he liked to shout, "he's selling shellac." Finally Herb got up the nerve to quit. "I'm going to start my own label with all black artists," he told Stone. "Come with me!" Abramson and his wife Miriam had the plan for a record company on paper, but, two kids from Brooklyn, they had no capital. Where could they get the money? Perhaps from their exotic friend Ahmet Ertegun.

Herb had known the odd but charming Ertegun for some time. Ahmet and his older brother Nesuhi, sons of a Turkish diplomat, had fallen in love with American jazz when, as boys in London, they heard Duke Ellington on his first triumphal tour of England in 1933. Their father, Munir Ertegun, came to Washington as Turkey's wartime ambassador to America, and the brothers amassed huge record collections and sponsored jazz concerts with the help of their fellow collector in New York, Herb Abramson. After Munir Ertegun died, in 1944, Nesuhi headed out to the West Coast cool-jazz scene, but Ahmet dithered. He was studying international law and had planned to follow his father into government service. "We came from the Turkish landowning class," Ertegun explained years laters. "No one in my family had ever gone into trade. It was considered unseemly."

The love of black music, however, proved too strong a lure. Ahmet dropped out of Georgetown and went to New York to make jazz records. He slept on Herb and

Miriam's sofa in their Greenwich Village apartment, and there they pooled resources. Herb and Miriam put in $2500; Ahmet put in $2500 and borrowed $10,000 from the family dentist, who never seemed concerned about his payments. Now that they had the money, what would they call the company—Uneida Record Co.? Out in California, Nesuhi was working with Pacific Records. They were in New York. They'd name their label Atlantic Records.

"It was a bit like, 'We have a barn, let's put on a show!' " Miriam recalled, "but we were serious." Herb became president, Ahmet vice president, and Miriam bookkeeper and bill collector. They rented a suite in the Jefferson Hotel on Broadway, moved briefly to an office on Eighth Avenue at Forty-eighth Street, and then, more permanently, to a floor above Patsy's restaurant in a grimy brownstone at 234 West Fifty-sixth Street. At night Dowd pushed the desks and chairs back to the walls, and the office became the studio. In 1948 the intrepid band put out records by the Harlemaires, one of Jesse's vocal groups, and Rex Stewart, Duke Ellington's famed trumpeter, but Sticks McGhee won Atlantic its first hit, "Drinkin' Wine Spo-dee-o-dee," in early 1949. Success, as often happened, swamped the boat with pressing plant bills, but a loan from Milt Gabler, their mentor at the Commodore record shop, bailed them out, and Atlantic Records was truly launched.

Ahmet recorded cabaret singers Barbara Carroll and Mabel Mercer and went back to Dixieland with Sidney Bechet, but for Herb and Jesse, this was dabbling. They wanted to fight it out in the contemporary R&B market, and they took Ahmet on trips south to find the sounds that Negroes actually wanted to buy. "We went to juke joints in Atlanta and New Orleans, and we listened," Stone recalled. "I took a metronome to check the tempos. When we came back, I started setting my melodies and bass figures to the bouncy rhythms people down south were dancing to."

Ruth Brown, a former waitress in Philadelphia, gave Atlantic its first R&B smash, "Tear Drops from My Eyes," in the fall of 1950. In 1951 Herb and Ahmet signed the Clovers, a vocal group popular with the emerging black (and white) teenager market, and they opened 1952 by recording Joe Turner's slow rocking "Sweet Sixteen" and signing Ray Charles. The Atlantic team had caught its stride. Jesse's bluesy charts, Dowd's full-sound palette, Herb's rough "get it on wax" approach, and Ahmet's Manhattan polish began to mesh in a distinct style. At the end of the decade pop music fans would talk of the "Atlantic sound," a funky elegance that historian Charlie Gillett described as *"clean* . . . a tight sound [filtered] out of a rough group." By the summer of 1952 the basic elements of that sound were in place.

Paying $2500 for the privilege of recording Ray Charles had been a bold step for the young company, and the team looked forward eagerly to the September session with their newest star. They knew Ray was still imitating Cole and Brown, but they sensed his raw talent, his deep feeling for blues and jazz. Though young, he had years of experience under his belt. He hadn't yet defined his style, but they might be able to help him find it and, in the process, mold their discovery into a big money-earner. What direction would be the best for Ray? They weren't sure.

Ray had spent the summer, meanwhile, on the road with Joe Morris, doing the same job he had done with Lowell: his own solo spot, playing piano in the band, and writing charts as needed. Despite moderate success as a recording artist, Morris was still always strapped for cash, his bus always breaking down. Ray liked the leader and loaned him money a few times to get the tour to the next gig, but studying Morris' operation closely, Ray realized that he wasn't ready to lead a tour himself. Morris' "Anytime, Anyplace" had shot past "Baby Let Me Hold Your Hand"; if Joe Morris could barely keep a band going, Ray Charles didn't have a chance. For the foreseeable future he'd be traveling as a solo artist.

Ray wasn't working every minute that summer. His Seattle pals Traf Hubert and Gerald Brashear, on tour with Cecil Young, ran into him in Columbus, Ohio, and visited him at his boardinghouse. "Ray'd come up a notch in the world," Hubert remembered. "He had a guy chauffeuring him around from gig to gig, had made records, and was getting decent sales." Ray told the fellows he had played the Apollo and hadn't turned the place upside down, but he had gone over. They smoked pot and talked and laughed away the afternoon. "Ray told us about the first time he ever got a blow job, he was seventeen, in Orlando, and a girl singer started kissing his nipples and then kept on going down. Blind, he didn't know what was happening, but he loved it!"

Saturday, September 11, Ray got to 234 West Fifty-sixth Street for the first time. Ever afterward he remembered the address by the numbers, 23456 in a row. Upstairs, Tom Dowd opened the piano and set up four mikes—one for Ray's voice, one for the piano, two for the band. He ran the mike cables through two mixers to an Ampex quarter-inch, one-track portable tape recorder. Jesse Stone had booked a few horn players, Connie Kay on drums, Lloyd Trotman on bass. Within minutes Ray was walking about the studio without hesitation; Ahmet noticed how totally he focused on his work. Ray brought in three of his own blues, and Jesse suggested another by Sam Sweet. That was fine with Herb and Ahmet—just get them done in three hours: after that the musicians went on double union scale. Ray played each song through, and with Jesse's pencil-sketch charts, the session players fell into unforced grooves that fit each tune like a glove. As run-throughs progressed to takes, Dowd set levels for each mike, mixing them on the fly to one track.

The songs displayed, to Ahmet and Herb in the tiny control booth, four different versions of Ray Charles like a salesman's samples: they could take their pick. Three were frankly imitative: cheerful "Roll with My Baby" the Nat Cole of the group, slow and somber "Midnight Hour" the Charles Brown, and "Jumping in the Morning" the Count Basie, Ray singing like Jimmy Rushing against the riffing band. The fourth, "The Sun's Gonna Shine Again," sounded like nothing else. From the wailing trumpet cry that opens it to the somber chords at its close, "The Sun's Gonna Shine Again" paints a stark landscape, red-hot sun, sharp black shadows. The lyric—"When I've done the best I can, and my baby don't understand"—suggests romance, but Ray ad-libs more "Lord"s than "baby"s, and the thudding beat under his piercing shouts gives the track an Old Testament density: Ray a blind prophet crying in the desert, "The sun's gonna shine again!"

Today, the "The Sun's Gonna Shine Again" stands out like a diamond among pearls, the track that takes the next step beyond "Kissa Me Baby," but at the time no one seemed to notice it. Ray left for two weeks at Detroit's Flame Showbar, and Dowd reviewed the tapes, doing a few splices to get a better intro on a better vocal, then presented the edited tracks to Herb and Ahmet. They picked the two safest choices, "Midnight" and "Roll," the Brown and the Cole, as the A- and B-sides of Ray's first release, and told Tom, "Master it!"

Mastering session tapes was a part of Dowd's job as important as getting the music on tape in the first place. By 1952, tape had superseded glass discs as the medium for primary recording because, unlike the discs, tape could be easily edited to eliminate the goofs inevitable in live music. Until the digital 1980s, however, transcribing tape to disc was the next step in the record-making process. Dowd's mastering apparatus combined a screw-arm lathe and a turntable. An aluminum disc coated with cellulose nitrate sat on the turntable; a cutting head hung from the lathe. When Dowd played the edited tapes of "Midnight" and "Roll" and set the disc spinning, electric currents pulsed around the cutting-head magnets, vibrating a sapphire needle held between them. Moved slowly across the disc by the screw-arm, the needle cut a spiral groove in the cellulose, turning Ray's music into wiggles in the groove. This was the acetate, the first record: the master.

When Dowd delivered the master of "Midnight"/"Roll" to MGM Records' pressing plant in Bloomfield, New Jersey, technicians electroplated it with silver and, for rigidity, backed it with copper. On this they cast the "mother," whose ridges corresponded to the master's grooves. The mother bore a second plating called the "mold," and the mold in turn bore steel "stampers" that pressed "biscuits" of hot shellac into records. Ertegun and Abramson asked the MGM plant to press only two or three thousand copies of "Midnight"/"Roll"; since more could be pressed overnight, they never made more than needed to meet immediate demand. The record, Atlantic #976, with its bold red-and-black label, began moving to the sales network of disc jockeys, distributors and jukebox operators, mail-order houses, and mom-and-pop record shops in black neighborhoods all over the country. *Billboard* gave the disc a good review in late October:

> Roll with My Baby: Charles goes to town on this rollicking rhythm opus for a spirited effort. Platter should do right fine in the coin boxes. Midnight: Charles projects this mournful blues effectively for a side that should win some attention.

But the record got ignored. Jesse Stone was sure he saw the problem: "Nobody will accept Ray Charles as Nat 'King' Cole," he told Ertegun and Abramson. "Nat is in a class by himself." Herb wanted to push Ray away from slow ballads into big-beat rockers like those they were cutting with Joe Turner. Ray hadn't learned that you had to pour more energy into a record to grab the listener, he argued. Ahmet agreed but saw the problem differently. "We didn't capture Ray's real soul at that first session because we were using New York studio musicians," he recalled. "They were reading musicians who had contempt for the illiterate bluesmen from the Deep South. Blues and jazz musicians spoke different musical languages, but Ray spoke both languages easily. He was familiar with the blues and its origins, and a jazz musician at ease in a big band—that was very unusual."

Overall, Ray's first outing on the label disappointed the Atlantic team, but not overly so. They knew it might take time to find the key to unlock this complex young musician. In the winter they'd put out the other two sides and see how they fared, and in the spring they'd record Ray again.

Ray returned to New Orleans in mid-December, headlining two weekends at the Pelican Club, packing the club for three shows nightly. "Tears streaked down the eyes of the famous blues shouter Sunday night," reported the *Louisiana Weekly*, "the crowds whistled and cheered." A week later Ray got a spot as an unbilled add-on to a Clovers/Lowell Fulson show in Houston, and the gig put a fittingly irresolute end to the year. Nine months after quitting Lowell, Ray was still playing second fiddle, still teetering on the brink of success, still dodging back and forth between experiment and imitation. He knew what was happening inside him, but he couldn't force the pace. "I was trying to get a pulse," Ray later said, describing this time in his life. "Slowly I began to wean myself [from imitation] and come into my own, but not about to give up what I already had."

Watching Ray Charles grope toward musical maturity can be a frustrating exercise in hindsight. We know where he was headed and wish to hurry him along. Yet Ray, still only twenty-two, could not see his goal, and the powerful music he was finding inside himself frightened him. Native caution warred with native creativity, and as 1953 approached, Ray was still resisting his own becoming, much like a chick who pulls his shell about him even as he pecks it to bits.

10

New Orleans
1953

January 1953, the month Dwight D. Eisenhower became president, Ray Charles spent in Texas. He kept a room at the Green Acres Motel in North Dallas, but home base was Howard Lewis' office at the Empire Room around the corner. Though known as a cold, crafty man, Lewis had taken a liking to the young blues singer, and he kept Ray's schedule packed with one-nighters: a dance in Houston, January 4, with Joe Turner and a dozen dates in San Antonio and Fort Worth before Oklahoma City, January 23. Lewis' son John, a tall, easy-grinning man of thirty-five, drove Ray and looked after him on the road. John Lewis had been a pimp in California before rambling home to Texas, and he knew his way around the shady side of life. Whatever town they were in, he could steer the Olds to the right house on the right street so Ray could score a bag of heroin or a tin of Mexican marijuana. Ray wasn't doing much heroin that winter, but one night in Longview, Lewis had to sit next to him on the bandstand, nudging him and talking to him to keep him from nodding out.

In town after town the routine was the same. The local promoter booked a dance hall or auditorium with its worn-out piano and raggedy speaker system, put up placards, took ads on the radio, and sold tickets in advance. When John and Ray rolled into town, Ray met the fellows he'd play with that night and ran down any particular licks he wanted, but it was all blues, and everybody knew how to fall in. From nine to past midnight the music built to one climax after another, pushing the sweaty dancers over the edge to ecstasy. Cool in the chaos, John watched the door to make sure the promoter wasn't shorting the money. When the audience melted away at one A.M., John paid the band from the wad of bills the promoter had paid him and pocketed the rest to take back to the Empire.

As the Olds rolled across wintertime Texas, Ray told John about his dreams. One day, Ray said, he'd own his own airplane. It sounded far-fetched, but Ray already knew a lot about planes. Once they had to fly down to San Antonio, Lewis' first flight. When the engine sound suddenly changed mid-flight, he panicked. "Don't worry," Ray told him, "the pilot is just feathering his props." A dream closer to home was a band of his own. He was tired of pickup groups, Ray said; only an ensemble that he hand-picked and rehearsed could get the sound he wanted. John encouraged him but knew how unlikely a Ray Charles band was in the near future. "Howard and the promoters didn't have much faith in Ray as a bandleader," Lewis remembered. "They liked him, but he was a junkie. Nobody paid him much mind."

Some nights Ray's buddy Fathead Newman drove the Olds. Fathead had more time on his hands than gigs, and driving Ray earned him a taste of Ray's dope and an occasional chance to sit in with the band. Not every night was fun. Once Houston police pulled the Olds over on no greater charge than suspicion of two young black men in an expensive car. In those days Newman straightened his hair, and the white cops found his "conk" too flashy for their taste. "You blind, boy?" one cop asked Ray. "Well, you better find a way back, because we're taking this other nigger and his fucked-up hairdo down to the station." Leaving Ray by the road to fend for himself, they took Fathead to jail, roughing him up for the hell of it. Ray bailed his pal out in the morning, and the two hightailed it back to Dallas. The experience soured Fathead and Ray on Houston, but deepened their friendship.

Back in New York, Atlantic released a second single from Ray's September session, "Jumping in the Morning"/"The Sun's Gonna Shine Again." *Billboard* noted the unique flavor of "Sun's," calling it "a moody blues sung with feeling," but predicted "Jumping" was the side that "could catch coins." The record, in fact, didn't catch many coins, but enough other Atlantic platters did to make the label a major indy: three of 1952's top ten R&B hits had been on Atlantic, more than any other label; to kick off 1953, the company released Ruth Brown's smash "Mama, He Treats Your Daughter Mean." At the same time the founding team underwent its first major change: the Army, which had paid for Herb's dental training, recalled Lieutenant Abramson back to active duty filling cavities in Germany, and by February Ahmet was looking for someone to fill the hole left by Herb's sudden departure. Jerry Wexler, one of his and

Herb's jazz-buff pals for a decade, came immediately to mind. While they had launched Atlantic, Jerry had become a journalist, coining the term "rhythm & blues" in an essay for the *Saturday Review of Literature*. Herb and Ahmet had earlier offered him a job as Atlantic's chief record plugger, but Jerry had replied that to work with friends, he had to be a full partner. Then Herb and Ahmet hadn't needed a third wheel. Now they did, and Ahmet called Jerry to talk it over.

As Atlantic was growing and changing, so was the pop music business. Eighty-three percent of the discs played on radio were still 78s, *Billboard* reported, but the new 45 and long-playing 33⅓ rpm records were clearly the wave of the future. Americans rushed to buy "hi-fi" phonographs that could play all three speeds, and soon found they never clicked the changer to 78. Adults savored classical music and cast albums on LP; kids snapped up the little 45s on impulse, playing stacks of the latest hits on portable players. *Billboard* also noted a "great increase in radio hours allotted to R&B discs," and a March headline declared: "Six Largest Diskeries Reduce Pops by 37% in 1st Quarter; But C&W, R&B Output Increases." In April, Big Mama Thornton hit big with "Hound Dog," a novelty blues written by Jerry Leiber and Mike Stoller, two twenty-year-old white kids whose mothers still acted as their legal guardians.

A long southern tour with bluesman Little Walter Jacobs wound down in early May, and Ray headed to New York and the 23456 studio for his second Atlantic session. Considering the poor sales of the first two records, Ahmet decided to try a new tack. They wouldn't push for finished tunes; they'd rehearse and experiment instead and record a week later. No sidemen: Ray and Ahmet would feel each other out one on one. Tom suggested they run a tape; they might catch a gem by accident. Fragments of that tape exist, and patched together in sequence, they open a cracked but invaluable window on a dramatic moment: Ray and Ahmet starting the search for Ray's true sound on record. As the tape begins, Ray plays a barrelhouse blues; then he breaks off.

"Man, one of these days I'll know all that junk," he says and pauses. "Have you ever heard this before?" and he drives into a dozen choruses of rocking boogie-woogie, each brilliant, each with its own flavor.

"Yeah, that's good," says Ahmet.

Ray gives Ahmet an illustrated tour of blues piano styles dating back to ragtime, and Ahmet laps it up, amazed at the depth of the young bluesman's knowledge. "That lick, da, da da, what was that," Ahmet cries at one point. "That was . . ." Ray responds, searching for the name. " 'Little Rock Getaway,' " they say together, laughing.

From time to time Ray apologizes for lapses ("I know a lot of those things, but I just gotta sit down and think about them"). His prowess, however, is awesome. Two-fisted chords clang over dark, sinuous bass runs. Discordant right-hand dashes stab into silence. Ray imbues every note with a primitive, even scary, energy. After one gorgeous passage, Ray coughs and stops. "I can't think of nothing, my mind ain't with it today," he says. "If your mind ain't working today, man," responds Ahmet, "I'd like to see you on a day when your mind is with it." Ray laughs, pleased.

As they get down to brass-tacks rehearsal, a few sparks fly. One song may be too short, Ahmet says, and he asks Jesse Stone to write a new verse. Jesse suggests a tenor sax solo to fill the time. "He wants to make it like I can't play better than some sorry tenor solo," Ray cuts in sarcastically. "Tenor solos don't sell the record, though, thank you. I can't stand them things." Yet the sparring between Ray and the control booth relaxes as the session rolls on and strangers become colleagues. Ray lets Ahmet set the tempo on one number, on another he questions Jesse's lyric: "You only got six words there, that way I get off." "Yeah," Jesse agrees. "Try it again." Tom puts an echo effect on Ray's vocal mike. "Cool," says Ray. Late in the session Ahmet sits beside him on the piano bench, and Ray lets him sing his own song, "Mess Around." Ahmet has the time of his life singing over Ray's propulsive piano, his nasal monotone contrasting comically with Ray's full-bodied voice. Ray finishes off with a flurry of be-bop chords and an exultant shout, "Okay, Henry!"

At the session the next Sunday, the afternoon digging for roots paid off. Jesse wrote tight-as-a-tick three-horn charts and added Mickey Baker on guitar. With Ahmet waving encouragement and Tom riding the board, Ray and the fellows started rolling through six songs instead of the usual four. Suddenly, in the middle of "Losing Hand," the booth phone rang. Tom answered it. Someone was calling from Greenville, Florida; was Ray Charles Robinson there? His mother, Mary Jane, had died. Tom told Ahmet, and Ahmet said, "Tell Ray."

Tom went into the studio, chills running up and down his spine, and stood with his hand on the piano. "Ray, I have a bad message for you," he said.

"What is it?" Ray said.

"I just got a call, someone says your mother has passed away." The news didn't hit Ray as a complete surprise; Mary Jane had been ill for months, and he had been paying the doctor bills. Still, Mary Jane dead—the sweets, the hugs she had given him so long ago.

"Do you want to stop recording?" Tom asked.

Ray sat silent for a moment, then replied. "It's too late for me to do anything. Let's continue."

Ray's impassive response scared Tom, but it seemed Ray was right. They had developed too much momentum to stop, and by its end the session became Ray's richest to date, six distinctive songs, hot rhythms and sophisticated lyrics, ranging from the lighthearted "Mess Around" to the achingly romantic "Funny But I Still Love You." "It Shoulda Been Me" paints a wry picture of a poor Joe on a Little Harlem main drag, staring goggle-eyed at the high life:

> *When I got to the corner I saw a sharp cat*
> *With a $300 suit and a $100 hat*
> *He was standing on the sidewalk by a Dynaflow*
> *When a voice within said,*
> *"C'mon Daddy, let's go."*
> *It shoulda been me, with that real fine chick . . .*
> *It shoulda been me, driving that Dynaflow!*

Jesse's arrangements bend with the mood of each song, and Mickey Baker's reverberant guitar swirls around Ray's piano on "Losing Hand" like fog around a streetlight. Ray hasn't completely broken away from his early idols—"Funny But I Still Love You" suggests Charles Brown as "It Shoulda Been Me" hints at Nat Cole—yet his growth is overwhelming his urge to imitate. Never before has he sung with more freedom, his voice bounding from agonized cries to cheerful chuckles. He takes the lead on every track, his piano driving the rhythm section, his phrasing guiding the horns. "Go get it, boy," he shouts on "Mess Around," unleashing the tenor player for a solo, and then, leaping into his own, he cries, "Now let me have it, boys!"

With the session done, Ray went home to Greenville to bury Mary Jane in the cemetery behind the New Zion Baptist Church. He stood over her grave and said good-bye. Two mothers had loved him with all their hearts. Now they both were dead. At twenty-two, he was the only one left of the little family that had lived in the shacks behind Mr. Pit's cafe. At this moment of complete orphanhood, Ray crossed a major threshold in his life. As he headed out for more one-nighters that summer, he finally told himself, "Stop this Nat Cole imitation. . . . Sink, swim, or die."

In New York, Jesse Stone kept reminding everybody how prickly and stubborn Ray had been, how slow to see the light, but like Ray, Ahmet was looking ahead, not back. They had broken through to Ray, uncovered the kernel of his personal style—that's what mattered. Ahmet picked "Mess Around" as the A-side of the next single. Though proud of his song, on the label he hid under a pseudonym, "A. Nugetre," Ertegun backward; still thinking of a diplomatic career, he didn't want his risqué songs to come back to haunt him at the Court of St. James's. On the B-side he put "Funny But I Still Love You." When the bobbysoxers got tired of dancing to "Mess Around," they could flip the record over for some smooching music. Tom pushed the disc into immediate production.

[|||||||||||||]

Jerry Wexler, formerly with the Billboard and more recently director of publicity and promo at Robbins-Feist publishing firms,
has joined Atlantic Records as a partner in the firm. Wexler will
work with Ahmet Ertegun on all phases of the firm's business
including a&r, sales, etc.   *Billboard,* May 30, 1953

During the May sessions, Jerry Wexler had squeezed into a corner of the booth, watching and listening, untypically quiet. No one introduced him to the star, but he studied Ray at work, impressed by the singer's "physical presence: strong, broad-shouldered and barrel-chested." Jerry had come to get a first look at how R&B records got made, because soon enough he'd be making them himself. During the spring, he, Ahmet, Miriam, and Herb had agreed that for an investment of $2000, Jerry would join Atlantic as an active 13 percent owner of the firm.

When bargaining with Ahmet, Jerry had had to conceal his glee. A bright Jewish kid from the shabby side of Manhattan's Washington Heights, young Jerry had read *Studs Lonigan* and dreamed of writing the Great American Novel, smoked pot and gone nuts for jazz. Since the war he had bounced around the fringes of the music business but caught hold of nothing. At thirty-six, he saw his life as "a series of aimless mean-derings." Writing reviews and plugging songs were dead ends, he thought, because they were about what other people were doing. The offer from Atlantic came as a god-send, his chance to do something himself. When he reported for work on June 1, Jerry Wexler had at last found his role in life.

Ahmet and Jerry didn't know then that their partnership was destined to become one of the most creative in pop music history. They did know they liked to work to-gether, Ahmet the Turk floating above the tumult of the casbah, Jerry the Jew diving into it, plugging disc jockeys, schmoozing with distributors, outfoxing the competition. Both omnivorous readers and avid moviegoers, Ahmet and Jerry loved to argue about Art, Life, and everything in between. They felt the irony of intellectuals like themselves fighting it out in R&B's rough-and-tumble world, and they viewed its colorful char-acters with a degree of humorous detachment. Of the two, Jerry was the worrier and Ahmet the epitome of cool, but they shared a passion for black music of all kinds, hear-ing in it a "secret language" of endless fascination. After a long day making and selling records by the Ravens and LaVern Baker, both liked nothing better than to blow some reefer and see in the dawn at a jazz joint in Harlem.

The South was the key to success, Ahmet told Jerry early on. They had to aim their records at a hardworking black man from Opelousas, Louisiana, a fellow tight with what little money he had. But, said Ahmet, "one morning he hears a song on the radio. It's urgent, bluesy, irresistible. . . . He drops everything, jumps in his pickup, and drives twenty-five miles to the first record store he finds. If we can make that kind of music, we can make it in the business." They'd go down south together, and Jerry would see what he was talking about. Black cabdrivers, properly bribed, would take them to the hottest clubs in Atlanta and New Orleans.

Atlantic released "Mess Around"/"Funny" in June, and again *Billboard* gave Ray a rave: "Mess Around" was "a solid waxing," and "Funny But I Still Love You" proved Ray "a first rate chanter of the slow stuff." From quick early sales, Ahmet sensed that they might have a minor hit on their hands this time, not a stiff like the first two. Still, like the others, "Mess"/"Funny" lingered somewhere beneath the charts.

"Indies Get Hotter: Trade Growingly Aware of Small Diskeries' Impact," *Billboard* headlined that summer. Alan Freed expanded his Moondog shows from Cleveland to Akron, and the tide of Ray's travels carried him to New Orleans. New Orleans had noticed Ray on his first tour with Lowell Fulson, and in the two years since, he had built a following there large enough to use the city as a base. Promoter Hosea Hill put bands behind him and sent him out to Thibodaux and Baton Rouge and back the same night. Scoring dope in a port town posed no problem. Ray met a young woman named Rudell and settled in at Foster's Hotel on LaSalle Street, west of the Quarter, where wooden houses crouch under shade trees and the streets curve with the crescent of the river. Ray couldn't see the Mississippi, the iron balconies in the Quarter, or the green streetcars on leafy St. Charles Avenue, but like many others before and since, Ray succumbed for a time to the charm and sensual ease of the old French city.

Near Foster's, at 2836 LaSalle, stood Frank Painia's Dew Drop Inn, the hub of New Orleans' black music scene. A handsome Creole, Painia set the club's flamboyant style; he put his own photo, not the performer's, in his weekly ads. He liked to undercut rivals by taking large parties to their joints, acting bored and announcing, " *We're* off to the 'Drop.' " With hotel rooms (colored only) upstairs and the club open round the clock, musicians could drop in at the Drop and never leave; when their tabs got long, Painia let them sing for their supper. Dawn Patrol, the last show, started at 3 A.M. Drug dealers plied their trade at the Drop's corner booths, drag queens paraded their finery on its stage.

Like Howard Lewis, Painia took Ray under his wing, promising him a weekend in late August and putting him together with a wildman guitar player he managed, Eddie Lee Jones, from Greenwood, Mississippi, who called himself Guitar Slim. Maybe disciplined Ray could tame Guitar Slim enough to get a hit out of him. Ray loved the Dew Drop's red beans and rice, and he got to the club every day. Once a group of fellows watched him stride down the four blocks from Foster's, cross Philip Street, and turn smack into the center of the Drop's front door. As mystified as others had been in Los Angeles and Seattle, they put trumpeter Renald Richard up to ask Ray how he did it. "Easy," said Ray. "I do just like a bat. You notice I wear hard-heeled shoes? I listen to the echo from my heels, and that way I know where there's a wall. When I hear a space, that's the open door."

In mid-August Ahmet and Jerry recorded "Money Honey" with Clyde McPhatter in New York, then flew down to New Orleans. This was their first recording trip together, and Jerry the greenhorn got so drunk at the Drop that Painia put him to bed upstairs, assuring him at breakfast that he was only the second white man ever to sleep in the hotel. That night they had a session with singer Tommy Ridgley at the J&M studio on Rampart Street near Dumaine, and they asked Ray to come in and play some piano.

J&M Recording, popularly known as Cosmo's, was a bare-bones studio, sixteen by eighteen feet, cooled in August by a fifty-pound block of ice and a big fan. Cosmo was Cosimo Matassa, son of Joe Matassa, a Sicilian immigrant who owned a grocery in the Quarter. After the war, Joe and his partner Joe Mancuso linked up a jukebox chain and opened the J&M Record Shop. In the back they installed a studio for folks to make "Happy Birthday" records for their moms, and installed young Cosimo, who had studied chemistry at Tulane, to run it. Like Tom Dowd, Cosimo possessed the blend of musical feel and technical skill that makes fine record engineers, and J&M expanded as word spread about the good $15-an-hour room. After producer Dave Bartholemew brought in Fats Domino to cut "The Fat Man" in 1949, Cosmo's held a small but important spot on the R&B map.

Ahmet and Jerry got a few sides down on Ridgley, nothing too thrilling. Cosimo watched amused as the New Yorkers argued fiercely over details until one would say abruptly, "Yeah, you're right," and they'd push on. When Ray played a hot piano break, Jerry barked, "Don't play like Ray Charles, you're backup." Ray didn't say much but remembered it. With time left over and the band still there, they let Ray bang out a couple of tunes himself, "Feelin' Sad," a funereal blues by Guitar Slim, and Ray's "I Wonder Who," only a trifle less gloomy. On both, Ray weeps his way through the lyrics as horns drone somber chords. Compared with those of the May session, the sides sound unfocused, the overall effect "blues by the yard." Relistening reveals Ray opening his voice in baby steps, exploring how to shade his vocal textures, but at the time, Ahmet and Jerry thought both tunes were too damn slow, though they might be able to use "Feelin' Sad" as a contrasting follow-up to "Mess Around." If they had missed an opportunity, at least they hadn't wasted any time. They'd try again.

The weak session proved to Ray that baby steps weren't big enough, and he pushed himself further and faster into widening his emotional range. "I became myself," he wrote years later of this time in his life. "I opened up the floodgates." After a weekend at the Dew Drop, Ray took off to Houston and a string of one-nighters; when he got back, around the time of his birthday, his friends in New Orleans noticed a change: Ray had started to sound like a gospel singer. "The first time I heard him, I thought he was Charles Brown," trumpeter Wallace Davenport recalled. "Then he started getting into that church thing." Sunday mornings when Earl King passed his room at Foster's, Ray was always listening to gospel music on his radio and reading the big Braille Bible he carried with him. "Ray loved blues singers like Joe Turner, but most of all he loved gospel singers," remembered Renald Richard. "He used to talk all the time about Archie Brownlee, the lead singer with the Five Blind Boys of Mississippi, how much he liked him. Then he started to sound like him, turning his notes, playing with them to work the audience into a frenzy."

"Feelin' Sad," backed by "Heartbreaker," came out in late September, and Atlantic took an ad in *Billboard* to declare it "Tremendous in Dallas, New Orleans, and Houston!" That really meant, unfortunately, that the disc did fairly well where Ray was working and died everywhere else. Ahmet and Jerry were becoming mystified and impatient. They had put out four singles by Ray in a year, and none had caught fire, whereas newcomer Clyde McPhatter's first record, "Money Honey," was leaping up to #1. Where was the hit that would launch Ray Charles?

Ray knew that his career was crawling, and he too was impatient for greater success. Yet unlike Ahmet and Jerry, Ray had no overview on himself. All he could do was keep working, keep playing, keep pressing forward day after day into the darkness as he had always done. What difference did anybody else's opinion from the outside mean? He *knew*, from the *inside*, that his music was growing more powerful by the minute. On Tuesday, October 27, he had a chance to prove it.

The gig began as no big deal: playing piano behind Guitar Slim in a session at Cosmo's. Frank Painia had signed his singer with Art Rupe of Specialty Records and booked Cosmo's to get four songs in the can. Guitar Slim could scratch his way through a fierce blues, but his music was less art than one of a flaming extrovert's many gushing outlets—he came to the session dressed in a lemon-lime-colored suit with a fuzzy felt hat and tie to match. Zoot suits don't write charts, however. The other musicians, looking for someone to tell them what to do, turned to Ray, and Ray took charge.

Slim played Ray the songs he wanted to do: "The Things I Used to Do," "Story of My Life," "Well I Done Got Over It," and "Letter to My Girlfriend." Ray took it from there, quickly dictating horn lines to trumpeter Frank Mitchell and running them down with the group. Cosimo watched him, deeply impressed. "Ray had *au-*

thority. A guy who can't see, rehearsing a big band in a tiny room, and he knew if one cat was playing a wrong note. He could hear everybody at once, the ensemble and every little thing. There was no way he could not be in control."

When it came time to record, Ray's biggest problem was keeping Slim on mike: he liked to wander around the studio as he played his guitar, a long cord trailing back to his amp. Slim kept rushing the beat, trying to pull the band into his excitement, and Ray had to put on the brakes to hold the tempos steady. A few of the songs needed a dozen or more takes, but they got them all down, finishing "The Things I Used to Do" at dawn. Ray, tired but triumphant, shouted "Yeah" in perfect time with the last drumbeat.

It had been a tough night for Ray, riding and guiding Guitar Slim's undisciplined energy, but the tracks they cut capture the contrast between Slim's twisted electric guitar and the velvet gloss of Ray's band. Except for a few fancy endings and one jump-swing piano solo, Ray keeps himself and the fellows in the shadows, letting Slim take the spotlight. The textures—Slim and Ray, folk blues and jazz blues, freedom and control—tug against each other like sandpaper on silk, charging the tracks with crackling musical excitement. Ray's job that night was to frame Slim's picture, not paint it himself. Yet today one can sense Ray in the background listening to and learning from Slim as from the gospel singers, taking courage to reach for the joys, the musical possibilities, of shameless self-expression.

On Halloween, Ray played a dance at the San Jacinto Ballroom that got so noisy, the *Louisiana Weekly* reported, that the police arrested forty-seven "youthful chippies" and seized two guns and "evidence that 'weeds' had been used," and then he headed to the hinterlands with a semi-steady seven-piece band he had assembled that included New Orleans veterans Wallace Davenport on trumpet and Lloyd Lambert on bass. Winding through Mississippi and Alabama became a grind with a few oddball moments, like the night he and T-Bone Walker stayed up playing blackjack at a lady's rooming house in Hattiesburg, Mississippi. As usual, they used cards pinpricked in Braille, and Ray wasn't allowed to deal. "T-Bone had been losing money most of the night," he told an interviewer years later. "Finally, about six o'clock in the morning, he wins this nice little pot. Just then Mrs. Watson comes in, sees all this money on the table, and starts telling us about how sinful we were. She turns to T-Bone and says, 'Especially you, sir, the Lord ain't gonna bless you for taking money from a poor blind man like that.' T-Bone starts shouting, but still saying 'Miss' because T-Bone was a gentleman, 'Miss, this man done take everything I got all night long, and you gonna tell me the Lord ain't gonna bless me? As a matter of fact, the Lord is just now giving me back my breakfast!' "

When Ahmet and Jerry came south again, Ray had rehearsed the band on four original tunes he had arranged himself. Cosmo's, it turned out, was booked solid, but they got a few hours on December 4 at radio station WDSU. This time Ahmet and Jerry stood back and let Ray run the show, and in short order they had four tunes, "Don't You Know," "Nobody Cares," "Ray's Blues," and "Mr. Charles Blues," on tape. From the a cappella howl that opens "Don't You Know" to the be-bop piano solo in "Mr. Charles Blues," Ray's growth since August is obvious. His singing is sexier, more playful. Instead of droning, the horns weave long lines through subtly shifting chords, the tenor sax singing high and light, the baritone plumbing its lowest depths. One can hear three distinct elements—big-band jazz, deep blues, and fervid gospel—coming together in early synthesis, a sound not fully jelled but one that sounds like Ray Charles and nobody else.

Ahmet and Jerry were impressed. This wasn't Ray Charles doing songs they picked for him, fitting in at the end of a Tommy Ridgley session. This was Ray all the way, singing and playing his own compositions, his own arrangements, with his own band. Ruth Brown might be selling more records, but she couldn't do all that. Anyone who could grow as fast as Ray, who could so easily tackle each new stage of musical control, must be a musician of truly unusual powers. The sound he was developing was new, arresting, unique. Could they sell it? They still had tracks in the can they hadn't released. In the new year they'd put out the comedy number from the May session, "It Shoulda Been Me," and see how it fared.

Ray went back to gigging. "The Things I Used to Do" came out to poor reviews but made the charts by the end of the year. On January 1, 1954, Ray played a Friday-night dance, "8 pm until ?" at the Houston Coliseum with T-Bone Walker and Amos Milburn, tickets $1.25 pre-sale, $1.50 at the door. This made the fourth year in a row Ray had seen in the new year in Houston, but this year it didn't seem like the same old same old. Nineteen fifty-four might be a whole new ball game.

The First Band
1954

During that same turn of the year in Houston, a young woman named Della Beatrice Howard was home one afternoon listening to the King Bee Show on radio station WCOH, when the King Bee, dj Clifton Smith, welcomed popular blues singer Ray Charles to the show. In chatting, Ray said he loved gospel music and that one of his favorite groups, the Cecil Shaw Singers, came from right here in Houston. Della Bea knew all about the Cecil Shaw Singers—she sang with them herself. Something in Ray's voice overcame her usual reserve, and she called the station. Would Ray like to meet Cecil Shaw? Yes, he would, but he'd also like to meet the young lady who called. They met a day or two later, and Ray was instantly taken with quiet Della Bea.

Della Beatrice Howard was an attractive woman a year older than Ray, small with smooth dark-brown skin and a little bit plump. She never seemed to raise her voice, and her pretty, round face often shone in a sunny smile. Della Bea and her younger brother James, the only children of a well-respected couple, had grown up in Houston's Third Ward, the most comfortable of the city's three black districts. After graduating from Jack Yates High School, Della Bea joined Cecil Shaw's choir and toured with them for several years. Only the top gospel groups worked as relentlessly as R&B performers, however, and Della Bea centered her hopes and dreams on home and family, not the stage.

"Della Bea didn't smoke, she didn't drink," remembered Herb Miller, a cousin who lived nearby. "She was a good southern girl." When John Lewis met her with Ray, he saw she wasn't flashy like the ladies they met on the road. "Della," he recalled, "was an ordinary woman who carried herself in an ordinary way."

Della Bea's down-to-earth qualities attracted Ray powerfully. He had been singing about a happy home with wife and kids since "Baby Let Me Hold Your Hand," but so far it hadn't worked out. Louise had given birth to a daughter, Evelyn, when she got back to Tampa, and Ray sent money when he could, but as a couple, Louise and he had missed their chance. He and Eileen had already divorced, that hasty first marriage a mistake receding into the past. Now the rising curve of his music gave Ray the confidence to think about putting down roots, about love that would last longer than a night or a few weeks. Ray had found someone sweet in Della Bea, someone he could trust.

Their romance grew more intense with the approach of spring. When he went on the road, Ray didn't manage perfect fidelity, but he did call Della every few days and even carried a typewriter with him in the Olds to write her love letters. Not for nothing had he learned to type at D&B. Between gigs, Ray took a little place in the Fourth Ward, where Della Bea cooked Ray's greens and beans southern style the way he liked them and kept a tidy, economical house. Yet Ray never felt completely at home in hot, humid Houston. He hadn't forgotten the cops busting Fathead for no reason, and remembering his battles with Louise's family, he hoped to get Della away from her many aunts and uncles. They could move to Dallas, he said. Della Bea was reluctant to take such a big step so fast.

"The Things I Used to Do," meanwhile, climbed the R&B charts through January and reached #1 by mid-February. Atlantic released "It Shoulda Been Me," and *Billboard* picked it as a "Record to Watch, Charles' hottest disking to date." Ahmet and Jerry backed up the review with ads on the R&B page for two weeks running, and they soon felt the response. As producer and artist, Ray Charles was finally selling records.

On the first weekend in March, Ray jumped to Los Angeles to play the 5-4 Ballroom, a new club in South Central, with the ever-popular Joe Liggins and his Honeydrippers. Los Angeles had apparently forgotten Ray in the four years since he had lived there. "Ray Charles . . . will be making his first appearance in the Angel City," reported the *Sentinel,* noting that he "has been widely acclaimed throughout the east and south where he has been making record-breaking engagements." Two weeks later *Billboard* reported that "Shoulda" had "broken nationally."

This level of success, Ray thought, might support his own touring band, and in early May a miserable week in Philadelphia fired his determination. Shaw had booked him for a week at Pep's Bar, and the first night was a disaster. The pickup band behind him stumbled through his charts, and when Ray pounded out the riffs he wanted, they couldn't follow him. "Man, I *love* music and I hate to hear it played wrong," Ray recalled years later. "That band was so bad I went back to my hotel and cried." In the morning he called Billy Shaw and told him that unless he could get a decent band, they'd have to cancel the rest of the week. Shaw calmed Ray down and paid for a new band, but for Ray that week was the last straw. He had to have his own band, he told Shaw. Shaw didn't say no, but he didn't say yes. Ray was selling well as a single for $75 to $100 a night. Would anybody pay $300 for him with a group?

One who did buy Ray as a single that spring was John J. "Bubba" Snow Jr., chairman of Clemson College's annual Block C Club dance, the highlight of the South Carolina college's spring calendar, scheduled for Saturday, May 15. Usually the club held the dance in the school gym, but that was being renovated, and Bubba rented the town recreation center in nearby Anderson for $50. Anderson had a "no alcohol, no colored" policy for its brand-new facility, but no one told Bubba. With the hall in hand, Bubba turned to booking the band. Unlike most student bookers, Snow saved his paperwork and his memories, giving us an invaluable snapshot of one of Ray's last solo gigs.

Bubba called Shaw Artists at a number he found in the club files. He couldn't afford Louis Jordan, but his goal was the best black band he could buy, Erskine Hawkins or Buddy Johnson. Bob Astor, Jack Archer's assistant in Shaw's one-nighter department, responded with a telegram on April 2: "Possibility Arranging Paul Hucklebuck Williams Orchestra, featuring Margie Day, and Jimmy Brown plus Five Keys Famous Singing Group May 15. Terms $1000 flat." That sounded good to Bubba, but $1000 was too much. Without the Five Keys the package would cost $700, Astor said, but if Bubba was going to save that much money, why not add the blind piano player Ray Charles for only $100? An R&B fan, Bubba had vaguely heard of Ray Charles and said okay. On April 9, Astor sent a confirming letter:

> As per our phone conversation, I can definitely arrange PAUL "HUCKLEBUCK" WILLIAMS & HIS ORCHESTRA who has four terrific sides coming out on Victor next week plus MARGIE DAY (Decca Records), as an extra added attraction.
> Along with this, we can package RAY CHARLES, the sensational blind singing piano player, who is currently hot with, "IT SHOULD HAVE BEEN ME" (Atlantic Records).

A few days later the contracts arrived with a cover letter for Bubba to sign and return to them with $400, the standard half-fee deposit. Press materials and photos would come under separate cover, and in conclusion, "We sincerely hope that you will enjoy a very successful engagement."

White colleges and fraternities in the South had long booked black bands for dances, but Bubba's call to Shaw also signaled a national trend. That same April, Atlantic started a subsidiary label, Cat Records, to reach the growing white teenage market. White kids "have discovered R&B records and are using them as dance records," Jerry told *Billboard*. At the end of the month, with "Shoulda" #8 on the charts, the trade paper headlined its first "Spotlight on R&B" issue:

Teenagers Demand Music with a Beat;
Spur Rhythm-and-Blues

The teen-age tide has swept down the old barriers which kept music restricted to a segment of the population. . . . The present generation satisfies its hunger for "music with a beat" in the Earl Bostic, Buddy Johnson, Tiny Bradshaw bands, or uses the rhythmic pronounced recordings of the Clovers, Ruth Brown, and others as its dance music.

Jukebox owners in California reported that "popular records take a secondary position to R&B" at teen hangouts. King Records released Hank Ballard's "Work with Me Annie," a sexy blues that white kids played in the basement so their parents wouldn't hear, and Alan Freed planned his first East Coast Moondog concert in Newark on May 1.

Yet kids crossing the color line could create sparks. "You can't have a black band in here," the manager of Anderson's recreation center finally told Bubba. Bubba was dumbfounded but thought quickly. "Fine, then you call Frank Howard and tell him the Block C dance is canceled," he told the manager (Howard was Clemson's legendary football coach). At that threat, the manager wilted. "Okay, okay," he said, "but for God's sakes, don't tell anyone."

"Shoulda" inched its way to #7, Decca Records released "Rock Around the Clock" by Bill Haley and the Comets, and Ray and the Williams orchestra played Atlanta with the Orioles and Dizzy Gillespie, then headed on to Bubba's Block C dance party. In the afternoon, Bubba trucked in tables and chairs, setting them up in a horseshoe around the dance floor. He laid out a buffet table of hors d'oeuvres and ice, but given the nervous manager, liquor had to be "BYOB"—"Bring Your Own Booze." The band bus rolled up on time, and everybody was glad to see that they were a colored group. After a band intro, Ray was announced. Someone helped him out to the piano, where he sang and played three or four songs. Then he played sax on a few more and went off. The students and their dates liked Ray, but his set was short and soon forgotten in the swirl of the evening. After an intermission the band played for dancing, the climax coming as everybody lindy-hopped to Williams' biggest hit:

Do the Hucklebuck,
Do the Hucklebuck,
If you don't know how to do it,
Boy, you're out of luck!

As the dance rolled on, Ray sat backstage by himself, not talking to anyone. Bubba thought he seemed isolated, withdrawn. About one or one-thirty it was over, as big a success as the Shaw office had hoped for. Bubba paid the $400 balance to Williams' road manager, and the bus drove off into the night.

〔ⅢⅢⅢⅢ〕

On the following hot and muggy Monday, May 17, the Supreme Court delivered its long-awaited decision in *Brown* v. *the Board of Education.* Public education must be "available to all on equal terms," wrote Chief Justice Earl Warren for the unanimous court. Separating Negro children from others "solely because of their race, generates a feeling of inferiority . . . that may affect their hearts and minds in a way unlikely ever to be undone." Segregated schools were therefore unconstitutional and must be abolished with "all deliberate speed." News of the Court's decision flashed like lightning across America. The New York *Amsterdam News* called *Brown* "the most important single victory for the American Negro since the emancipation"; the Los Angeles *Sentinel* declared it "a giant step in the direction of complete equality." The lightning lit up storm clouds: the *Amsterdam News* found anger and fear mixed with joy on the streets of Harlem. "It should have been done a long time ago," said Mrs. Edith Connell, owner of a tailor shop. Porter David Coles worried "that violence will result" and predicted "another generation" would pass before integrated schools would function normally.

With his nose pressed to the grindstone of his career, Ray barely saw the lightning flash. Still living in a segregated world, he didn't know, as few did, how the school victory would embolden African-Americans to fight for the right to vote, for fair housing and employment, and how their fight would transform the landscape, the mindscape, of America. In the wake of *Brown,* black Americans from all walks of life began to speak up as never before, writers and musicians, housewives and carpenters, preachers and politicians, expressing themselves in proud, personal voices across the full spectrum of human experience. Ray's voice grew with other growing voices, his music inspiring many who advanced along parallel, connected paths.

"Shoulda" hung in low on the charts through May, fading in early June. "Things" finished its run, and "Sh-boom" by the Chords on Cat broke into the pop charts. Ray moved from one-nighters in the East to one-nighters in the Midwest, playing the Sunset Terrace in Indianapolis, then working his way down to Houston with the Clovers and Guitar Slim at the Civic Auditorium June 20. Back with Della on home ground, Ray began to fight for a band in earnest.

He pestered Billy Shaw with phone calls. "You ain't strong enough," Shaw told him again and again. "Shoulda" had been only a minor hit, not the smash that could make him a dependable draw. He *had* to have his own band, Ray replied. Hadn't Shaw always told him, "If you think pennies, you're gonna make pennies, if you think dollars, you're gonna make dollars"? Still Shaw put him off. Ray went up to Dallas to talk to Howard Lewis, John Lewis arguing on his side. The elder Lewis hemmed and hawed. He too doubted Ray could carry a band, and he knew he was a junkie. Junkies missed dates, stole money, and got in trouble with the law. Ray's habit was his own affair, but from a business point of view heroin was a needless risk.

One afternoon at the Empire, Shaw called Lewis, selling him two weeks of Ruth Brown one-nighters across Texas in July. The only problem: he didn't have a band to back her up. John got the drift of the call and tugged his father's sleeve.

"Let Ray get a band together," he said. "Let him back up Ruth."

Lewis relayed the idea. Shaw saw it would solve his Ruth Brown problem and get Ray off his neck. Plus, it only committed them to a two-week trial that would either launch the band or sink it at a minimal loss. Lewis told Ray: two weeks and we'll see what happens. Ray leapt at the chance. His own orchestra—that dream stretched back to Joe Walker's make-believe ballroom in the dorm at D&B.

Plans make dreams come true. Riding back to Dallas from a final single gig in Austin, Ray talked over his practical needs with John. In that discussion was born Ray Charles, entrepreneur and businessman. First, transportation would be the biggest outlay. He would need two cars, a sedan for himself and a couple of the fellows, a station wagon for the others and the instruments. Ray figured he could cover the down payment on the sedan. Howard Lewis and Shaw said they'd help pay for the station wagon. John Lewis shopped around and bought a '54 two-door Ford and a De Soto Firebird wagon.

One of the fellows would gladly drive the wagon for an extra $5 a week, but Ray needed a road manager to drive the Ford and take care of business. John didn't want the job, he liked working for his father. But, he told Ray, steady-going Jeff Brown was back in Dallas, driving a cab again around Hall and Thomas. Jeff was surprised to hear from Ray after so long, but he said yes. Jeff liked going on the road with bands; this time he'd be manager, as Brassfield had been with Lowell Fulson.

The next question: musicians. Ray figured he needed seven pieces: bass, drums, his own piano as rhythm section, two trumpets, and two saxes—tenor and baritone—three when he filled in on alto. He had put that lineup together briefly in New Orleans, and he knew he could get a big sound with the right players. To be right, a fellow had to be able to sink into the slowest low-down blues with Ray; that was rock bottom. Anybody who couldn't would never fit in. He had to read music, because Ray wanted to write full instrumental charts for his band, and he had to be able to improvise jazz solos over exotic chord changes and blend in big-band harmony.

"Texas cats," Ray told Jeff, "I want me a Texas band." By early July in Dallas, Ray had picked bassist Jimmy Bell, trumpeter Charles "Clanky" Whitely, and tenor saxist A. D. Norris, veterans of many one-nighters with Ray in Buster Smith's bands. Then he and Jeff headed down to Houston. Somebody told Ray that Renald Richard, the trumpet player from New Orleans, was in Houston with Ivory Joe Hunter but looking to quit. Richard had played in a USO big band and toured with Guitar Slim, just the jazz-blues blend Ray was looking for. "Jeff came to see me," Richard remembered. "He offered me more money than Ivory Joe, $35 a night, even though Ivory Joe was hot with 'Since I Lost My Baby.' Jeff said Ray was strong and was gonna make it. I had liked Ray in New Orleans, and Ivory Joe could be kinda nasty, so I said okay, and I gave Ivory Joe my notice."

Louis Dickerson, owner of Houston's Club Matinee, gave the band daytime rehearsal space in the cocktail lounge. "We checked out 'Mess Around' first," recalled Richard. "Then we went through his music, song by song." Jimmy Bell remembered the rehearsals as tough. "I learned that with Ray, the music's gonna be right or not at all. Off the bandstand he's nice, but on the stand he's a horse of a different color." In mid-July, after two weeks of hard work, the band took off to El Paso for the first gig with Ruth Brown.

"Houston to El Paso is a nice little jump," said Jeff dryly, recalling it. "Seven hundred fifty-two miles, to be exact." That little jump lingers in Ray Charles' legend as a bad start to end all bad starts. They loaded the instruments on top of the station wagon, and with Jeff driving the Ford, Renald the De Soto, they headed west on U.S. 90, running late. The De Soto had a top speed of 105 miles an hour, and Renald kept his foot to the floor hour after hour across the desert, Jeff staying behind in case any instruments flew off the top of the wagon. The breakneck pace got them to El Paso on time, but the promoter then told them that Ruth Brown hadn't shown. Without his headliner, he'd postponed the show.

Ruth Brown, coming south from the Apollo, arrived overnight and they did the show the next day. "I wasn't sure this blind piano player could do my music," Ruth Brown remembered, "but he could, and beautifully." Ruth, Ray, and the band were due the very next night in Alexandria, Louisiana—all the way back east to Houston and two hundred miles more, and now they had only one day to get there. The cars rolled out of El Paso right after the gig and pounded back the same way they had come. This time, driving all night and day, they didn't make it. They pulled up at the club just after the promoter had canceled and, swimming against the tide of people leaving, they couldn't even push their way to the door.

As Ray and the fellows were racing back and forth across Texas, Atlantic released "Don't You Know" from the hot New Orleans session. *Billboard* gave the disc a lukewarm review, and sales got off to a slow start. More exciting for Ahmet and Jerry was the battle over "Sh-boom." Cat's original R&B version by the Chords had sold well enough to white kids to edge its way onto the pop charts in early July, but by midmonth a cover version by a white group, the Crew Cuts, climbed past it, reaching #1 in August. Ahmet and Jerry felt robbed of a victory they deserved. The *black* sound of the Chords' "Sh-boom" had sold it to the kids. It was unfair for white groups to copy R&B hits note-for-note and skim the cream off the market. Pop A&R men paid "too much attention" to what goes on in R&B, they complained to *Billboard*, "staying as close to the original R&B arrangements as possible when they cover the tune." Still there was triumph, and profits, in the Chords' original reaching #10 on the pop chart. Even the Crew Cuts' stolen win proved a tide rising in R&B's favor.

With August, Brown went her way, and Ray and the band went theirs, the first gig a week at Gleason's Musical Bar in Cleveland, beginning August 2. "This Charles boy is quite a lad," commented the Cleveland *Call and Post,* noting the change in his career:

> He appeared at Jack's Musical Bar last year and stood the people on their heads . . . and that was before he hit the jackpot with his "It Shoulda Been Me."
>
> Charles plays piano, and that's about all he had with him on the bandstand at Jack's; still he went over big. Backed by his own orchestra the man should be sensational.

From Cleveland the Ford and De Soto rolled west to Los Angeles and a weekend at the 5-4 Ballroom opening for Dinah Washington, the band's biggest gig to date. Fathead Newman was in LA, having moved away from Dallas' drug scene only to fall into the same scene on the coast. When he heard the band was in town, Fathead looked Ray up at the Dunbar Hotel. "He needed a baritone player," Newman recalled years later. "In those days I was playing alto, but I wanted the gig, so I started playing bari." The 5-4 Ballroom gig was a big success. Down-to-earth Dinah invited everybody to hang out at the studio where she was recording with members of Duke Ellington's band. Ray felt in an expansive mood, and he bought a brand-new Selmer alto sax. One afternoon Renald Richard took him to the amusement park in Santa Monica. "How's your nerve today?" asked Renald. "I got as much nerve as you have," said Ray. Renald got tickets to the roller coaster, but as they got on, Ray said, "This is the roller coaster, ain't it?" "How do you know?" asked Renald. "Man, I can *hear!*" Ray answered. *"Ooooooweee,"* he howled when their car hit the first drop. "You better hold on," Renald said laughing. "You live too recklessly for me," Ray shouted back over the wind.

Heroin was the only part of working with Ray that Renald Richard didn't like. With Fathead along, the band suddenly had two junkies, the leader and his best buddy, whose habits, if anything, grew by their being together. A drug dealer followed the band up the coast to Seattle and, as Richard remembered it, made enough money from Ray and Fathead "to drive back in a Cadillac." When Ray was high he could be hard to handle, becoming sometimes withdrawn, sometimes manic, flailing his arms and legs, scratching himself incessantly. When Ray craved his next fix, he could become sullen and irritable, picking squabbles with Fathead, suspecting that his pal was holding out on him, taking more dope for himself. Like Gossie, Renald felt shut out by the two hipsters. With good reason: Ray and Fathead considered heroin a cool secret language that squares like Renald would never understand.

Alan Freed moved his nightly radio Rock 'n' Roll Party from little Cleveland to big 1010 WINS in New York, and the band worked its way east to the Magnolia Ballroom in Atlanta. With every gig the band got tighter, and on days without gigs they rehearsed. Despite their differences, Ray respected Renald's musical ability and made him the band's musical director. Being straw boss, as the fellows called the job, meant $5 extra to act as Ray's top sergeant, running rehearsals and keeping the band on its toes. Through long highway-rolling afternoons Ray worked out arrangements for the band in his head. One day off in the Midwest, he offered Renald another $5 to take the charts down by dictation. "Bring manuscript paper and your pen up to my room," he said. When Renald got there, Ray was lying in bed.

"You ready?" said Ray.

"Yeah," said Renald.

"Okay, let's start with the tenor sax. Begin with an eighth-note A. . . ." From there Ray started spinning out the chart for "Ray's Boogie." Nothing had changed in Ray's method since Tampa, but like dictatees before and after, Renald was deeply impressed. "Ray dictated fast, he knew exactly what he was doing. And he didn't work out the chart in the concert key, the chords as he played them on the piano. No, he'd give me the parts transposed, the trumpet in C if the tune was in B-flat. Do one instrument, on to the next, and I'm writing and writing!" When they finished a complex chart for "In a Little Spanish Town," Renald asked, "Any mistakes in here?" "I don't make mistakes," Ray replied. "I might change something, but you'll never find a wrong note." He called a special three-hour rehearsal to break the new arrangement in, and he was right: no wrong notes and nothing to be changed.

Richard's amazement at Ray's uncanny ability did not fade in time. "There's a story that when Mozart was invited to hear a choir rehearsal, he asked to see the score," Richard said over forty years later. "The choir director said no, but at the next rehearsal Mozart gave the choir director a copy of the score he had written out from memory. I'm not exaggerating: Ray Charles has that kind of mind. If he hears something once, he can dictate every note you played."

As the band built up a book, the gigs started to fall into a format. The fellows opened the show at nine o'clock and played the blues for about a half hour, A.D.'s honking tenor sax stirring up the crowd. Ray came on about 9:30 playing alto sax as the band's fifth horn, and they'd do the jazz charts. Each of the fellows had about twenty tunes in loose ring-binder notebooks. "Okay, we're gonna do number five," Ray would say, and count it off, "One, two . . ." the band jumping in and the jitterbuggers jumping to their feet. Sometime after ten Ray sat at the piano and sang his featured part of the show. After a half-hour break came more of the same. "Ray was so into the music, he didn't spend much time in his dressing room," Newman remembered. "After the break, we'd do two numbers, and he'd come back with his alto for four or five arrangements, then he'd close the show singing."

In early October the faithful Ford and De Soto rolled northwest through Tennessee, Kentucky, and on to Indiana. After many gigs, too excited to sleep, Ray and the fellows pushed on to the next town, driving through the small hours into the dawn. They were good nights, Jeff quiet at the wheel, Ray stretched out on the back seat, smoking cigarettes and reefer, laughing and talking with Fathead or Renald. Ray was always searching for good music on the radio, and when he found a gospel station, that's where he stopped the dial. One such night near South Bend, Richard remembered vividly, a gospel tune came on with a good groove, and they started singing along. "Ray sang something like, 'I got a woman,' and I answered, 'Yeah, she lives across town,' then him, 'She's good to me . . . ,' like that, being silly. But then he said, 'You write songs. Think you could come up with something for that?' I said, 'Hell, yes,' and the next morning, ten o'clock, I was in his room with 'I Got a Woman.' I didn't really write it all that night. I stuck in the bridge, 'never grumbles or fusses,' from another song I had written years back."

Ray liked "I Got a Woman" instantly. The songs he had done gospel-style so far, like "The Sun's Gonna Shine," had the hortatory tones of a preacher in the pulpit. "I Got a Woman" was the preacher at a picnic, lighthearted gospel that converted spiritual joy into sexual delight. Renald's bridge said just what Ray loved about Della Bea:

> *She's there to love me both day and night,*
> *Never grumbles or fusses, always treats me right,*
> *Never running in the streets leaving me alone,*
> *She knows a woman's place is in the home.*

Ray wrote a nice offbeat riff for the band, dramatic stop-times in the bridge, and gave A.D. an eight-bar solo on tenor. As the two-car caravan moved south into Howard Lewis territory for a two-week tour packaged with T-Bone Walker and Lowell Fulson, Ray worked "I Got a Woman" in with the band, brightening its polish, sharpening its punch. Audience response told him he had something.

As the two cars turned east toward Atlanta, Ray worked in three other new songs with the band: "Greenbacks," a funny blues about money by Renald, and two he had written, "Come Back Baby," a bluesy lament, and "Black Jack," inspired by his crazy night with T-Bone. These were ready to record, Ray figured, but Shaw hadn't sent him any gigs near New York. He called Ahmet and Jerry. Could they come down to Atlanta? He'd be at the Royal Peacock the third week of November. Always ready for a trip south, the two producers flew down and took a cab to the club, eager to hear what Ray had put together.

The Peacock was empty in the midafternoon except for Ray and the band already set up on the club stage. The moment Ray heard Ahmet and Jerry walk in, he counted off "I Got a Woman." The band leapt into it, and when they finished, Ray swept them into another tune and then another. Ahmet and Jerry sat astonished as the music poured over them, "an amazing succession of songs," as Jerry remembered ever after. Ray had come so far in the year since they recorded him last. This time he had everything prepared for the session and knew every note to be played by every musician. "It was a real lesson for me to see an artist of his stature at work," Ahmet felt. The power and precision of the music "stunned" Jerry: "I knew something fantastic had happened." Overnight, it seemed, Ray "had hatched . . . Ray was full-fledged, ready for fame."

All they needed now was a place to get the tunes on tape, and through Xenas Sears, an Atlanta R&B dj, Ahmet and Jerry booked studio time the next day, November 18, at WGST, Georgia Tech's radio station. Every hour on the hour they had to stop so an announcer could read the news, and the elderly engineer kept missing Ahmet's frantic cues to adjust the mikes for solos and ensemble passages. Jeff could see that Jerry's anxious stream of suggestions irritated Ray. "He felt pressure from Jerry," Jeff remembered, "squeezing him like a vise." But despite a chaotic atmosphere, they got the four new tunes on wax. Ahmet and Jerry liked the edgy intensity of two slow blues, "Black Jack" and "Come Back Baby," but questioned their commercial appeal. "Greenbacks," with Fathead's hot baritone solo, was a novelty tune as funny as "It Shoulda Been Me." This time the poor sap has enough "Lincolns" and "Jacksons" in his wallet to taste the high life until a floozy disappears with his last "greenback dollar bill, / Just a little piece of paper coated with chlorophyll!"

"I Got a Woman" had hit written all over it. Listening to the playbacks in Atlanta, Ahmet and Jerry let themselves hope they had found Ray's breakthrough smash at last. The record blended elements like a hybrid flower. It had a dancing beat like a jump blues, but it was built on gospel's "rise to glory" chords, and the cheerful lyric, infectiously delivered by Ray, gave that mix a pop music gloss. As a bonus, Ray repeated the title so often that "I got a woman, way over town" might become a singalong line people would plug nickels into the jukeboxes to hear over and over again. "I Got a Woman" was a record for every happy couple in America, black, white, and in between.

In blending gospel and blues in "I Got a Woman," Ray had, for the first of many times, fused two idioms of music. Musical idioms group traditions of music by stylistic, ethnic, geographic, commercial, and cultural similarities. In the African-American community before "I Got a Woman," the blues and gospel idioms lived as close together and as far apart as Saturday night and Sunday morning. Blues singers didn't sing gospel, and gospel singers didn't sing the blues. They appeared in different halls that advertised on different pages of the black newspapers, and they appealed to different, even contrary, aspects of the black American soul. Some bluesmen, and some preachers too, complained that "I Got a Woman" and Ray's later blues-gospel hits joined what God had put asunder. "He mixing the blues with spirituals. I know that's wrong," said Big Bill Broonzy, and Josh White agreed: "How he takes a spiritual and makes it into a love or sex song, it's a kind of sacrilege."

Many musicians switch idioms informally, a wedding-band pianist, for example, playing Bach at the service and boogie-woogie for the reception, but major artists seldom make major contributions to more than one idiom: jazz giant Dizzy Gillespie, for example, played no role in country music. Ray Charles, in contrast, has proved himself uniquely able to transcend idiom and become a master of many, finding the subtlest currents of each and the mighty musical river that runs beneath them all.

Ahmet and Jerry took the tapes back to New York and rushed "I Got a Woman," backed by "Come Back Baby," into production. Maybe they could have it out by Christmas. They knew they had passed a milestone with Ray. It had taken two and a half years, but with a band that Ray had made an extension of himself, they had begun to get the special quality of Ray's music on record. The more Ahmet worked with Ray, the better he liked him. Slowly, he felt, he was getting to know a fascinating man. Ray had acute insights into the people and personal situations around him, Ahmet noticed. He played a mean game of checkers and was a quick mimic. Ray was both totally aware of the music being made around him and totally focused on his own. Unlike many musicians, Ray followed the news on the radio and could talk about what was going on in the world. Above all, Ahmet thought, Ray possessed supreme self-confidence. One night in his Atlanta hotel room, Ray said, "Let's go get some coffee," and he ran down three flights of stairs ahead of Ahmet and Jerry. "You're going to kill yourself," said Ahmet, but Ray said he had memorized the number of steps. Ahmet was still amazed: "Not so much by the physical skill, but because *he was absolutely sure of what he was doing.*"

Ray and the band moved on to East St. Louis, leaving one drummer in Atlanta and picking up Ray's old pal from Orlando, Bill Peeples, to take his place. Then Clanky Whitely left, replaced by Riley "Fats" Webb, another Floridian Ray had known in Jacksonville. Jimmy Bell, too, had had enough by the time they got back to the Royal Peacock in December. The weather was turning cold, and somebody had stolen his winter coat. Roosevelt Sheffield, whom everybody called Whiskey, came in to play bass. After only six months on the road, the band had completely turned over, Ray and Jeff the only veterans left of July's two-way streak across Texas.

That fall back in Houston, Della Bea realized she was pregnant. The doctor said the baby was due in May. On trips home between gigs Ray urged her to go with him to Dallas. Ray wanted the baby and wanted a family with Della. They would get married soon, and Dallas could be their home. With the months passing and her belly beginning to show, Della consented. By the end of the year she and Ray made the move north, took a room at Ray's old stand, the Green Acres Motel, and began to look for a place of their own in South Dallas. On the road, of course, Ray continued affairs with numerous women, but home and the road were worlds he kept separate, a twain that need never meet.

Ahmet and Jerry didn't get "I Got a Woman" out in time for Christmas, but before the New Year they got a few advance pressings to dj's and distributors in southern cities where they knew Ray was strong. In days word filtered back: "I Got a Woman" was taking Durham, Atlanta, Nashville, and other key markets "by storm."

The owners and heads of many R&B firms should be happy with the acceptance of the music with a beat by thousands of teenagers in the North, South, East, and West who have helped zoom the sales of R&B records until the demarcation between R&B and pop wax has almost reached the vanishing point.

Billboard, **January 1955**

VIRTUAL SURRENDER
1955—THE YEAR R&B TOOK OVER
POP FIELD   *Billboard,* **November 1955**

Breakthrough 1955

The quotations above tell the story. The line between R&B and pop music, almost gone at the start, was all gone by the end of 1955, the year that gave birth to rock 'n' roll.

Ray Charles played a part in the process from day one. The January 1 *Billboard* quoted from above gave "I Got a Woman" a rave Spotlight review: "One of the most infectious blues sides to come out on any label since the summer . . . a driving beat and a sensational vocal." Having just finished its best year to date, Atlantic advertised in the same issue, "Look out, 1955, Atlantic is rolling with 3 new hits," including "I Got a Woman" / "Come Back," by "the Great Ray Charles." The next week *Billboard* reported that though deliveries to West Coast cities had been slow, the disc was getting excellent initial reactions in St. Louis, Cincinnati, and Buffalo. Through January "I Got a Woman" rose on regional charts and touched the national R&B chart at #15. Alan Freed started playing it on 1010 WINS with "Ko Ko Mo" by Gene and Eunice and ads for Crawford Clothes, "$3 broadcloth shirts today only $1.68." Elvis Presley, a white kid from Memphis making a name for himself by singing R&B country-style, heard "I Got a Woman" and immediately added it to his act.

That January, Georgia Gibbs covered LaVern Baker's "Tweedle-Dee-Dee" and the Crew Cuts covered "Earth Angel" by the Penguins. In February, as "I Got a Woman" reached #3 on the R&B chart, the Fontane Sisters hit pop #1 with "Hearts of Stone," originally an R&B hit by the Charms, and Alan Freed started his stage shows at the Brooklyn Paramount. In March, as "Woman" peaked at #2, thirteen of the thirty top pop records were either R&B discs or covers of R&B hits, despite, Paul Ackerman wrote in *Billboard*, "the scarcely veiled antagonism of many pop publishers to rhythm and blues."

These were only 1955's opening months. The musical wave that had been gathering since Alan Freed's 1951 Moondog shows in Cleveland grew through the year from a medium-size breaker to a tsunami. Most of the clues we have spotted before 1955 are the kind found by historians after the fact, hints scarcely noticed at the time. In 1955 rock 'n' roll emerged to full public attention as, one by one, its originators—Bo Diddley, Fats Domino, Bill Haley, Chuck Berry, Little Richard, and Ray Charles—came up with records that set the bouncing ball of popular music bouncing in a whole new direction.

What created rock 'n' roll? Ike's optimistic peace-and-prosperity era gave American teenagers more money and time to enjoy themselves, less pressure to grow up and get to work. Flimsy 45 discs and transistor radios ("slightly bigger than a cigarette package," said one early report) became, like hula hoops a few years later, emblems of a disposable "fun" culture shared nationwide. The new frank speech by African-Americans in the public forum also contributed. Bo Diddley stated the new music's social message:

> *I'm a man*
> *I spell it*
> *M — A — N*

and Chuck Berry stated its musical message: "Roll over, Beethoven, and dig these rhythm and blues." White kids liked R&B's rebelliousness, and taking the music as a direct expression of their own feelings, danced to Fats and Chuck with abandon. More than a simple shift in musical taste, rock 'n' roll fused black and white music on a deeper level than jazz had ever reached. For decades to come this black/white music would be the true voice of young America.

Electricity powered rock 'n' roll. Electric guitars became common, not played in the understated jazz tradition of Gossie McKee and Oscar Moore but in Guitar Slim's wildman style. Singers turned up their vocal mikes to top the guitars and, soon enough, the electric basses and pianos. Rock 'n' rollers used electricity boldly, grasping, as older musicians had not, how its invisible energy could expand music's possibilities. They began to explore the rich new timbres of electric instruments, and they used microphones not as quiet ears that overheard acoustic music, but as loudspeakers through which one could speak intimately to millions. "You got your radio turned down too low," Bo Diddley told the world. "Turn it up!"

With "I Got a Woman" Ray Charles entered rock 'n' roll and the national consciousness. At the beginning of 1955, Ray was still unknown to the country at large. Had he gone no further, he would be listed today as a minor blues singer. By the end of the year, Ray had become known to millions of Americans coast to coast, recognized, with Bo and Fats and Chuck and Little Richard, as "one of those crazy rock 'n' rollers."

Ray and the band played through Georgia in January, at Atlanta's Magnolia Ballroom on the 13th with Roy Milton and his Solid Senders, and a week later at the Royal Peacock with Tangula the Exotic Shake Dancer. In February they moved through the Midwest. March took them back to Texas, and Ray went back to Della Bea in Dallas. The baby was due within two months. It hadn't been an easy pregnancy, Della spending lonely weeks in bed at the Green Acres Motel. She didn't want to have her firstborn there; the time had come to find a place to live and get married. Ray was ready and willing. Fathead took them riding through the quiet tree-lined streets of South Dallas looking for a house to rent. At the corner of Eugene and Myrtle, they found one that Della Bea liked: a modest one-story frame house set back on a wide lawn and shaded by a tall live oak tree in the backyard. On Tuesday, April 5, a lady minister, Mrs. T. L. Daubeny of the African Methodist Episcopal Zion Church, united Ray Charles Robinson and Della Beatrice Howard in matrimony, and the newlywed couple moved into their new home. Ray established credit at the Four Seasons grocery across the street. He would be away a lot, he said, but Mrs. Robinson was to have what she needed, and he would settle up regularly.

2642 Eugene Street became Ray's first fixed address since Seattle. Making a home with Della and a baby on the way satisfied deep longings in Ray; "I Got a Woman" painted a Joe-and-Jane romance like his own as an earthly paradise. Yet ambition urged Ray into a life on the road that had by now become a deeply ingrained habit. He loved the freedom of travel, and he refused to give it up, just as he refused to give up drugs and other women. He resolved the conflicting desires by separating them rigorously: he'd have his drawers in the dresser, he told Della Bea in the first days on Eugene Street, and she'd have her drawers. He told her about Louise and Evelyn, and he told his girlfriends that Eugene Street was off-limits, not to call him there. If a letter came by accident, the best thing for Della to do was leave it unopened. "Let's respect each other's privacy," Ray said. "Let's not go looking for trouble." He didn't tell Della about heroin, but she found out soon enough. Della didn't like the drugs and the shadowy presence of other women, but, compliant by nature and loving her husband, she accepted life on his terms.

"Woman" hung high on the charts into mid-April as Ray and the band took off on tour. The De Soto wagon was still limping along, but now Ray rode in a '55 Cadillac Coupe de Ville. Within a few days they stopped for a gig at the Army base at Fort Knox, Kentucky. During a break, a few local musicians approached the fellows in the band with a lovely, dark-skinned lady blues singer in tow. She was Mary Ann Fisher, they said, and she sang at the Orchid Club in Louisville. Could she do a number with the band? "I hadn't really heard of Ray Charles," Mary Ann remembered years later, "but the fellows were pushing me." Ray's tenor player, Donald Wilkerson, said they had an arrangement of "I Got It Bad" in G. That was my key. When I went out there, Ray said, 'Okay, sing, little sister,' like it was a drag for him. Then I hit it off with the audience, and as I finished, Ray said, 'Sing it, little sister!' like now he knew I was good."

After the show Ray told Mary Ann he'd be coming back through Louisville in a month. If she wanted to go on the road, she could sing with them as a featured vocalist. Mary Ann said she'd think it over, but she knew that if Ray came back, she'd go with him.

Ray had new songs to record but barely a moment in the grind of one-nighters to stop and record them. In late April, they had a gig in Miami, and Ahmet and Jerry flew down for a session. They booked time at a radio station after the gig because the gang had to race north to Atlanta, and the session didn't get started until 4 A.M. Ray had been singing for hours and felt tired and hoarse. As they set up for recording, Jerry kept spouting suggestions from the booth. Finally Ray had had enough. He stood up, slammed on the piano keys, and shouted, "If I'm gonna do a session, I'm gonna do it my damn way, or I ain't gonna do it at all."

Jerry capitulated immediately. Against Ray's anger and his musical authority, what else could he do? "From then on, Ray was the boss," Jeff Brown recalled. "Instead of telling Ray how to do his sessions, Jerry and Ahmet asked him what *he* wanted to do." Having become the boss, Ray Charles remained the boss for the rest of his recording career. Others made vital contributions, but his collaborators all agree: Ray's records come out the way Ray wants them, and until he gets them that way, they're not finished.

Many pop singers are incapable of designing the music to surround them, and one may wonder where their work ends and their producer's begins. With Ray Charles, the question need not arise. For better or worse, he is the author accountable for all his records from 1955 onward.

The four tracks they cut that April dawn in Miami—"This Little Girl of Mine," "A Bit of Soul," and two slow blues, "A Fool for You" and "Hard Times"—reveal Ray's total control. Though varied in tempo and feel, they share a concise, concentrated sound, the horns often silent as Ray's piano and bass and drums set an insinuating pulse, the few solos short and sweet. Restraint, however, pays off in climaxes that truly climax. "A Bit of Soul" builds from an easy-rolling piano blues into an out-and-out rocker, the horns blowing twelve-to-a-bar triplets through long four-measure riffs. "This Little Girl of Mine," based on the well-known gospel song "This Little Light of Mine," is the "I Got a Woman" of the set, but this time Ray adds Latin drums and syncopated horns under the gospel chords. The band has become a tool in Ray's hands, and he wields it like a sculptor's chisel, carving forceful works in his first mature style.

The two slow blues, "Hard Times" and "A Fool for You," reveal extraordinary growth in Ray's singing. His pitches still range from bass to falsetto, his textures from whisper to shriek, but now his shadings are subtler, his touch more tender. More than ever before, Ray invests *himself* in his voice, not so much singing to us as letting us into his lonely ruminations. Like an actor, Ray is learning how to use his own emotions to make his art convincing. When he sings in "Hard Times," "My mother told me before she passed away, / Son, don't forget to pray," memories of Retha suffuse his tone and give depth to the brooding monologue. In "Fool for You" Ray drops the mask of the cocksure lover and confesses to abject sexual weakness. "Ever since you were five years old I've been a fool for you," he sings. As he confesses, he asks us to connect our inner voice with his, our experience with his:

> *Did you ever wake up in the morning*
> *Just about the break of day*
> *Reach out and feel the pillow*
> *Where your baby used to lay?*

In these two beautiful blues, Ray Charles begins to emerge as a truly great singer, and his technique begins to serve a formidable goal: opening the souls of his listeners by opening his own. Ahmet and Jerry rushed back to New York with the tapes, awed by the quality of Ray's work. "A Fool for You," they were convinced, was the best record they had ever made.

From Miami, Ray and the band drove to Atlanta and played the City Auditorium, billed below Ruth Brown but above Lowell Fulson at last, then rolled southwest to New Orleans for a gig with Fats Domino. After four months "I Got a Woman" was still #3 on the charts. Ray and the band came back north, picked up Mary Ann Fisher in Fort Knox, and headed to Dayton, Ohio.

Within days Mary Ann and Ray became lovers, and as a mark of status, she rode with him in the Cadillac. That Ray had been married a month before didn't matter; he told her he was single. Ray rehearsed with Mary Ann daytimes, and soon she had a segment of the show, singing blues and late-night ballads like "Black Coffee." Ray also put her with Fathead and Donald Wilkerson to make a vocal trio; more and more he wanted the sound of other voices framing his. Adding Mary Ann meant a step up for Ray. He now had a featured female vocalist just as Hucklebuck Williams had Margie Day at Bubba's show a year before. Work and romance with a touring star was a step up for Mary Ann too. Being orphaned by a lynching and working clubs for ten years in Louisville had toughened Mary Ann Fisher without souring her. She had a ribald tongue and a hearty laugh, and she liked to gamble and drink whiskey with the band. "A black Mae West," one of the fellows called her. By the time they got to Texas, "Fish," as Ray nicknamed her, was one of the troupe.

On May 25, as Ray and the gang played Houston City Auditorium, word came from Eugene Street that Della Bea had had a healthy baby boy. In the morning Jeff drove Ray up to Dallas. Like many fathers, Ray felt scared to hold so fragile a thing as his own newborn son, and he quickly handed him back to Della. They named the baby Ray Charles Robinson Jr. After a few days Ray went back to Mary Ann and his other life on the road.

Through May, as Bo Diddley's "I'm a Man" rose on the charts, "Woman" slid slowly to the bottom, falling off just as Atlantic released "A Fool for You" / "This Little Girl of Mine" the first week in June. "Records like this don't come along often," raved *Billboard;* "Charles, who wields an incredible spell on his live audience, gets much of that commanding quality in these almost gospel-style blues . . . look for a double-barreled hit with this one." Within ten days Ahmet and Jerry felt strong action on the disc in southern cities, Baltimore, Richmond, and Atlanta, the pattern that had launched "I Got a Woman." As *Billboard* had predicted, dj's and store customers took to both sides. Two-sided hits were uncommon in the 50s, largely because record companies filled B-sides with inferior material, figuring that two good songs should sell two records, not one. Ray, however, wasn't creating inferior material, and the public seemed to like Ray happy as well as sad, flipping the disc to suit their mood.

As the Caddy and the De Soto rolled through Texas with T-Bone Walker in June, "Fool" / "Little Girl" moved rapidly to #2 on the R&B charts, challenging but not toppling Fats Domino's "Ain't It a Shame," which clung to #1 week after week. In July, Chess released "Maybellene," Chuck Berry's first record, and it streaked past Ray's disc to reach #1 in August. Without such hot competition, "Fool" / "Little Girl" might have been Ray's first #1 hit. It was still holding at #6, however, as Ray and the band got to the Mambo Club in Wichita, Kansas, in late August. Two hits in a row, and "I Got a Woman," though off the charts, was still on the radio.

After a year together, Ray Charles and his Orchestra had worked life on the road into a groove. "It got to a place where every city you went to was home," Jeff Brown recalled. "We'd see the same people and play in the same places. Most Fridays and Saturdays we had gigs, a few on Sundays, then we'd lay up in a cheap motel waiting for the agency to get us some more jobs." As road manager, Jeff kept in touch with Shaw, picked up the cash from the local promoters at each gig, and paid the fellows every Sunday night. Though not a big man, Jeff had a quiet strength that kept people from messing with him. "I handled a lot of money but came close to being robbed only once, in a club in Los Angeles. It must have been a setup, because I was supposed to come to the club at an exact time to get paid. But I was busy, and an agent went to collect the money for me. Right after they paid him, somebody came in and robbed the office. He got hit across the head, a nice little gash. Then the club said they'd paid him and weren't responsible for the money. Maybe it was pals of theirs, you figure it out."

Riding long miles in the Cadillac, Ray and Jeff discussed the details of running the band. Their motto: "Two heads are better than one." In all their business dealings, Ray told Jeff, he wanted Jeff to play the bad guy, so Ray could play the good guy. It became Jeff's job to chew out the fellows for being drunk on the stand, to get tough with a promoter who was holding out. "I did what was necessary," Jeff said. "Of course, I stayed out of the music. That was Ray's department."

Ray learned to rely on Jeff's honesty, and the trust between them as working partners grew to brotherly affection. Sometimes they said the hell with work. Once in Cleveland, they met twin lady singers, and Ray had one and Jeff had the other. The next night they were supposed to be in Kentucky, but they decided to stay with the twins and skip the gig. Yet for all the camaraderie, Jeff remained Ray's employee, on salary with no percentage, and Jeff noticed a coldness in how Ray dealt with those around him. "Ray held his cards very close to his chest," Jeff recalled. "He wasn't friends with anybody in the band, except maybe Fathead. He always tried to become less and less attached to people. Maybe he wasn't *using* people, because when you pay somebody, then you're not using them, but he only liked people, Shaw, Wexler, everybody, to the extent that they could do something for him."

That summer Ray quarreled with Donald Wilkerson over drugs, and Wilkerson left. Fathead stepped up to tenor sax, glad to take over its juicy solos, and Jay Dennis replaced Fathead on baritone. Dennis used heroin too, and with Whiskey Sheffield, Fathead, and Ray, the band had more junkie members than straight. Jeff called Renald Richard back to give the band some discipline, but there was no chance the hipsters would stop getting high for square Renald. On a swing through Florida the drug problems reached a crisis. One night, Whiskey Sheffield picked up his bass and smashed it into splinters and tangled strings, and Jeff had to front the money for a new instrument. A few days later in Jacksonville one of the musicians nodded out onstage. Renald found Jeff at the door collecting tickets. "Jeff," he said, "so 'n' so is about to pass out." Jeff took him to a white doctor, who looked at him and said, "Get that black son of a bitch out of here, he's full of dope." Jeff kept the man awake with cups of coffee, then took him to the airport, called his wife, and told her he'd be on the next plane.

Despite the problems, Renald found the band more prosperous than the year before and Ray still fun to be with. Some days they'd talk science, and Ray was always up on the latest developments in airplanes, electronics, and transistor technology. Other days they'd take a break from driving and stop beside the road to clown around. Renald would slap Ray's face and run away zigzag. "When I catch you, I'm gonna poke you," Ray would shout, running after him, and Renald would reply, "You gotta catch me first." When Renald stopped, Ray couldn't tell where he was, but the second he moved, Ray was after him. "One of these days," Renald shouted, "I'm gonna stand in front of a tree, and when you get close, jump to the side." "You wouldn't do that," said Ray, and Renald said no, he was only kidding.

In Florida, a promoter they called Chicken invited them out to his ranch. Chicken liked target shooting, and Jeff told him that Ray could shoot a pistol. "He's blind, how can he shoot?" asked Chicken. Whenever they disagreed, Ray and the fellows always said, "I bet you $20." So Jeff said, "I bet you $20 he can hit two out of five cans with a revolver." "That's a bet," said Chicken. They got some empty tomato cans and went out to an open field behind the house. Jeff gave Ray the gun, stood behind him, and threw out the cans. When a can hit the ground, Ray aimed and fired. He hit three out of five.

In September, as the lynching in Mississippi of fourteen-year-old Emmett Till filled the nation's newspapers, "A Fool for You" / "This Little Girl of Mine" slipped off the charts. In October, like clockwork, out came "Greenbacks" / "Black Jack" to another rave *Billboard* review ("plenty of entertainment in his lyrics and lots of sock music out of his fine little band"), and the same prediction: "Charles could have another two-sider with this one." The wandering minstrels got home to Dallas for a few days. Renald met Della Bea and liked her immediately as a "strong, dependable woman." Ray and she, he felt, had a cordial, loving relationship. Now that Ray Jr. was three months old, Ray felt easier holding him and took a father's pride in dandling his firstborn son. On the road people sometimes called Mary Ann "Mrs. Charles," a mistake not worth correcting, but in Dallas Ray kept her away from the real Mrs. Robinson.

While the troupe was touring Texas and Oklahoma with Fats Domino, "Greenback" / "Black Jack" became the predicted two-sided hit. "Most areas do not report a marked preference for one side," *Billboard* reported, "but give indication of general acceptance of the record itself." As Little Richard came out with "Tutti-Frutti," Ray's record reached #8, then inched up to #5. Not as strong as the previous two releases, but strong enough to call it three hits in a row.

On Thursday, November 17, the troupe rolled into Philadelphia to play a dance at the Town Hall Ballroom on Broad Street at Race, a dreary corner just north of city hall. Kae Williams, a popular R&B dj, had booked "Ray Charles & Orch" as his headliner, filling out the "9 until" show with local acts, The Sensations and Princess Margot ("Exotic Queen") among them. Ray and the band didn't know it, but they were entering a city on edge about drugs. For months a special police squad had led so many "dope raids" in the black community that the Philadelphia *Tribune,* the city's black weekly, declared that the raids were unfair to Negroes and that dope was "more than a black problem." The troupe got in too late to stop at a hotel and drove straight to the gig, waiting in the common dressing room through the opening acts. Their first set, the *Tribune* later reported, "really moved the people."

Back in the dressing room, it was time to get high. Ray and Fathead, Whiskey and Jay Dennis kicked everybody out and locked themselves in. The Sensations came off stage and knocked on the door. "You can't come in, my wife is dressing," Ray shouted from inside. Someone told Kae Williams, but when he demanded that they open up, Ray and his buddies still wouldn't unlock the door.

Williams instantly suspected drugs and called the cops. "I had already heard that the police might conduct a raid," he told the *Tribune.* "I knew if I cooperated with the police, there was less likelihood of the six hundred people who attended the dance being embarrassed." In minutes detectives from the special squad slipped unnoticed through the smartly dressed dancers, broke into the dressing room, and arrested Ray and the three others. Bill Peeples had spent his intermission at a table with his relatives from Camden and wandered back at the wrong moment. The cops found cigarette papers and loose marijuana in his pocket, and arrested him too. For good measure they swept

Mary Ann, Tommy Brown, and everybody but Jeff to the police station at 26th and York, where they fingerprinted them and locked them up overnight.

At the magistrate's hearing the next morning, the detectives testified that they had confiscated a burnt spoon, an eye-dropper syringe and needle in an instrument case, and "a quantity of marijuana" hidden in a dressing-room chair. Ray, Fathead, Whiskey, and Jay had "fresh puncture marks on the arms," and a police doctor found the four "positive" for recent narcotic use. Mary Ann and the others were found "negative," but magistrate John P. Daly ordered all nine musicians held on $2000 bail pending trial.

Every junkie's nightmare had come true: Ray was busted. Legend has it that he had been nabbed first in New Orleans in 1953, but even if the legend is true, Ray was then arrested as a nearly anonymous junkie. Now he was a semi-celebrity, a businessman with his whole company behind bars. The *Tribune* ran a front-page picture of the troupe being arraigned, their faces grim in the flashbulb glare, their right hands raised to take the oath. Ray alone kept his head down and his hand only half-raised; behind his dark glasses he was already coolly plotting his escape. The others gave the police their home addresses; Ray gave the address of the Shaw office. He denied all knowledge of heroin. He was blind, he said, and didn't know what they were shooting into him; maybe it was a flu shot. From cash on hand, Jeff bailed Ray out, and, leaving the others behind in jail, the two drove to New York. Jeff got in touch with a lawyer, who found out how much it would take to get the charges dropped. Ray paid the money, and the case disappeared. "That bust was nothing but a shakedown," Jeff said. "Just a question of $6000, I recall. The same thing happened to Billie Holiday in Philly a few months later, and Philly wasn't the only city playing that game."

Mary Ann and the band members had a harder time of it, sitting in jail for a week, annoyed that Ray didn't spring them sooner. The guards watched Fathead and the junkies every day to see if they got sick, but somehow they made it through. Bill Peeples' relatives scraped up $600 for a bribe to get Bill out, then, after they paid it, realized that it was wasted money: the cops dropped the charges against the band as part of the deal with Ray, and they were released. Shaw gave them train tickets to Dallas. They were to go there and wait for Ray.

Ray had to cancel a few late-November dates, and *Jet* ran a gossip column item a few weeks later, but the bust had little other effect on his career. Arrests of blues and jazz musicians for drug and other vice charges were common enough in the 50s for all but the most notorious cases to be forgotten. But rumors of Ray's habit spread on the jazz grapevine, clinging about his name like smoke for years to come. The bust left Ray with a cynical view of the law and a sharpened insight into what money and lawyers can buy. He certainly didn't stop using heroin, nor did Ahmet or Jerry or anyone at Shaw try to talk him out of it or even talk to him about drugs at all. They all knew Ray was a junkie, but the prevailing code of conduct demanded a hands-off, "It's none of my business" attitude.

On November 30, Ray had a record date at Atlantic that he didn't want to cancel, even if he had to do it without his regular band. He brought back Donald Wilkerson on tenor and Joe Bridgewater on trumpet, and Jesse Stone put together the rest of the group from his New York crew. Ray had three originals he wanted to get down, "Hallelujah I Love Her So," "Mary Ann," and "What Would I Do Without You," plus a cover of Henry Glover's "Drown in My Own Tears," a hit for Lula Reed and Sonny Thompson three years before. For that, Ray wanted something new, a female vocal group to back him up. Jesse suggested a group he was grooming, the Cookies, three girls led by growly-voiced Margie Hendricks. The Cookies, all in their teens, were glad to sing behind one of the label's top stars.

The finished tracks reveal, if not the growth spurts of the previous two sessions, a widened emotional range, sounds enlivened with crisscross textures. "Mary Ann," a sexy blues Ray wrote for Fish, is set to a Latin beat, but every few choruses the band leaps into swing rhythm, an alternation that adds to the fun for dancers. "Drown in My Own Tears" has the stately tempo of "Fool for You" but uses sound and silence with even more dramatic precision. Ray lays in perfect piano tinkles between the rock-steady thump of the bass and bass drum, and over the track's long three-plus minutes, the ensemble sound develops a majestic depth. When the Cookies enter at the end, moaning, "Drown in my own tears, drown in my own tears," the tragic image is complete: Ray a modern Oedipus, crying his eyes out before a chorus of lamenting women. "Hallelujah," in contrast, hits the same cheerful note as "I Got a Woman." This time, however, Ray adds a musical joke, singing:

> *If I call her on the telephone*
> *And tell that I'm all alone*
> *By the time I count from one to four,*
> *I hear her . . .*

then the drummer hits four quick beats (*knock knock knock knock*) before Ray finishes, "on my door." Pop music fans love "hooks" like this, and will play a record over and over so they can jump into the music and sing "knock knock knock knock" themselves. Ray even throws in references to his last two hits, singing, "She's my little woman way cross town," as the track fades out, "Baby, I'm a little fool for you."

Ahmet and Jerry were delighted with the results. They had never heard a record with the impact of "Drown in My Own Tears." They'd put that out at the first of the year, and follow it with "Hallelujah I Love Her So." "I Got a Woman" hadn't broken into the pop charts, but they had another chance with "Hallelujah." The two producers realized they had nothing more to teach Ray about making hit records; now he was teaching them. "Ray developed an uncanny feel for structuring a song to grab the audience," Ertegun remembered. "He was becoming a great recording artist before our eyes, an artist fully aware of his medium."

In December, Ray rejoined the band in Dallas, and they played a few weeks on the Howard Lewis circuit before heading out to the West Coast. That month writer Ruth Cage devoted her "Rhythm & Blues" column in *Downbeat* to a glowing description of Ray and his music. The jazz magazine had given "Baby Let Me Hold Your Hand" a brief, lukewarm review back in 1951, but that excepted, Cage's piece marks the first time Ray's name had appeared, and his work been discussed, in anything but the black newspapers and *Billboard.*

Cage began by noting that the Top Ten Revue of R&B stars (Joe Turner, Bill Doggett, Bo Diddley, and others) that had packed Carnegie Hall in October was the first R&B show "to make this fancy scene," a sign of a new "respectful attitude to this music with a beat." The next time R&B played Carnegie Hall, Cage hoped, the "long deserving" Ray Charles would be on the bill. She had recently seen him perform and "realized anew what a fantastic talent this young man is. . . . Whether as a pianist, saxophonist, singer, composer or arranger, he stands octaves above the competition." Jazz critics might consider the blues monotonous, but Cage felt she had been "made sensitive enough by [Ray's] excellence to feel the variety of messages his skill presents." The gospel music that inspired Ray accounted for his "genuineness," and his blues was not a "lackluster imitation of traditional blues—it's for real!" Charles had a single motive powering all his music: "I try to bring out my soul so that people can understand what I am. I want people to feel my soul." At twenty-five, Cage concluded, "Ray Charles is on the threshold of a really great career."

The December *Downbeat* column dates the moment when jazz fans began to notice Ray. Two year-end entertainment reports, published the same month, indicate how high he had pushed himself in the national black music rankings. An Associated Negro Press (ANP) story headlined "1955: Big Year for Top Colored" listed Louis Armstrong as the "World's No. 1 Jazz Box Office attraction," and noted the continuing success of Nat "King" Cole, Count Basie, and Ella Fitzgerald. "The nation went Rock 'n' Roll in '55," reporter Dave Clark went on, singling out "Only You" by the Platters, "Maybellene" by Chuck Berry, and "Ain't That a Shame" by Fats Domino. Ray's name appeared nearly lost in a laundry list of hitmakers that included Ruth Brown, the Drifters, Muddy Waters, Howlin' Wolf, the Spaniels, and the Moonglows. The second report, a *Billboard* poll of R&B disc jockeys gave a nuts-and-bolts picture of Ray's breakthrough year. "I Got a Woman," said the dj's, had been their ninth-most-played record in 1955, and Ray himself their seventh-favorite artist. Strikingly, Ray's three double-sided hits had a cumulative effect greater than these middle rankings indicate: in the "Most-Played" category, Ray placed second only to Johnny Ace and his posthumous hit "Pledging My Love."

Christmas fell on a Sunday that year. Ray, Mary Ann, and the band played the weekend at the 5-4 Ballroom in LA, packed the place to capacity, and got invited back for the first weekend in 1956. Then they headed back to one more grind around Texas for Howard Lewis.

Ray didn't let what anybody else was
doing influence his music. I never
heard him say this guy or that guy
was the guy to beat. He fought
against nobody. Inwardly he may
have, but not openly. He always was
himself.   **Hank Crawford**

Growth to
Genius
1956-1958

My life was what it was. Whatever it
became, I made it so.   **Ray Charles**

It may be said, in admiration, that Ray Charles possesses
a molelike quality in his character, an unusual ability to dig a one-man tunnel into time,
to concentrate on the task at hand, doing what he needs to do, what he wants to do
second by second, month after month. The years 1956, 1957, and 1958 demonstrate the
quality well. Through them Ray Charles plugged away at his music with relentless determination. Three times a year he put out a new single; one finally reached the pop
charts. He recorded his first jazz albums, added the Raelets to his touring act, and honed
his band to a peak of perfection. Della gave birth to a second son, and the family
moved from Dallas to Los Angeles. Ray met two women who attracted him powerfully.
His income increased many times over. Viewed end to beginning, the changes of this
era loom large, but they came in small daily accretions, their net weight pushing Ray
to a second, bigger breakthrough in 1959.

Through these years Ray continued his endless ride across the terrain of America,
east, west, north, and especially south, the two thousand miles and two thousand
towns between Virginia and Texas, New Orleans and St. Louis. In every season and cli-
mate, Jeff at the wheel of a new Cadillac each year, Ray rode across the Carolinas and

red-dirt Georgia, the Mississippi delta and the bayous of Louisiana, hearing the *whump-whump* rhythm of concrete roadbeds, the soothing whir of new macadam, and the dusty sizzle of old dirt roads. He rolled through the hazy heat of southern mornings and the thunderstorms of southern afternoons, and he played deep into sticky southern nights, driving the band, igniting the crowd, his feet splayed and dancing, his head thrown back and sweating, his mouth wide-open singing. Each night the gig came to an end and Ray, on Jeff's arm, came out to the parking lot behind the club, a million bugs batting about the stage-door light. A word with the band, a check on the money, then into the Caddy and off again, Ray blind to the forward-stabbing headlights but hearing the frog chorus chanting through the open windows.

For six, seven, and then eight years Ray had ridden the same highways. To every backroad joint, downtown nightclub, and stately theater in every black community from Boston to Seattle, he came once, twice, a dozen times, hammering out his music and, in the process, forging bonds of trust and affection with the people. Ray was no one-hit Johnny. His records had been in the jukebox for years, some now old favorites. Listeners heard truth in Ray's music, an earthy gospel preached from the heart of conviction, a cry from the soul too compelling to be denied. A growing number of whites listened with intense pleasure to Ray's music, loving and learning from what Ray had to say. His voice, the horns, the rock-steady beat—every sound *spoke*. Like many of his peers riding the same circuit, Ray embraced the joys of life in his music, but few others developed his depth of sympathy for sadness and pain. Ray dug down to the bottom, and no one can dig deeper than that.

In January 1956, the Negro boycott of the Montgomery, Alabama, bus system entered its second month, and the country began to hear the name of the young minister leading it, Martin Luther King Jr. In Nashville, Elvis Presley recorded "I Got a Woman" and "Heartbreak Hotel" at his first session for RCA. Ray, Mary Ann, and the fellows drove to Houston from LA and joined Joe Turner, Charles Brown, and Etta James in a Howard Lewis package tour of Texas. On their own again in February, they played Atlanta's Magnolia Ballroom, then moved north. *Billboard* advised fans to grab the chance to see Ray live in Newark: "Not everyone realizes Charles has a real hip swinging band that can play progressive jazz." "Drown in My Own Tears" came out, and again *Billboard* raved: "Tearful dripping wet shouting blues opus. . . . Looks like money in the bank from the start." "Drown" rose through March to peak at #2, then fell slowly through April for a strong ten-week run. Not as big as "I Got a Woman," but poignant records, by their nature, seldom stir up dance-craze excitement.

The same weeks that "Drown" had its run on the R&B charts, Elvis' "Heartbreak Hotel" and Carl Perkins' "Blue Suede Shoes," on Elvis' original Sun label, rose to the top of the Pop, Country and Western, and R&B charts. "Barriers Being Swept Away in C&W, Pop, and R&B Fields," *Billboard* headlined. "Categories Now Overlap." In rock 'n' roll history, 1956 is the year white kids answered 1955's R&B wave with a wave of their own. Elvis, Carl, Gene Vincent, and many more learned to play R&B hillbilly-style and, by throwing themselves into the music heart and soul, made records as gutsy as the black originals. Nineteen fifty-six was also the year rock 'n' roll became "teen" music, thirteen-year-old Frankie Lymon and the Teenagers showing the way with "Why Do Fools Fall in Love." Henceforth, rock 'n' roll's prime subject would be the joys and agonies of adolescence, and "the kid with 89 cents in his pocket" became the great motivating force of pop music. A mighty force at that: rock 'n' roll's second tidal wave pushed record sales past the $250 million mark and *Billboard* expanded its Honor Roll of Top Ten Songs to a Top Thirty Songs and then to the biggest chart of all, the Top 100 Records.

Through these years, Ray's music grew parallel with rock 'n' roll while remaining independent of its fads. Fats Domino and Chuck Berry played for millions of white kids and sold them as many records; Ray's gigs and record sales stayed largely in the black world. Ten years as a working pro had given Ray a depth of experience that none of the enthusiastic young rock 'n' rollers could match. He knew, and his audience sensed, that his music was more adult than rock 'n' roll, "more difficult," he wrote years later, "for teenagers to relate to. . . . A tune like Little Richard's 'Tutti-Frutti' was fun. Less serious. And kids could identify with it a lot easier than my 'A Fool for You' or 'Drown in My Own Tears.' "

As he moved on from rock 'n' roll, Ray took a big step into jazz, getting to New York in late April for the first in a series of sessions produced by Nesuhi Ertegun. A smaller, quieter man than his younger brother Ahmet, more a musician and less a showman, Nesuhi had come to Atlantic to develop the label's jazz line—he had just signed the Modern Jazz Quartet. Nesuhi wanted to record Ray as a jazz pianist with jazz players. They kept the first session simple, a trio with Oscar Pettiford on bass, Joe Harris on brushed drums, and got four tunes done: "Dawn Ray," an original blues; Gershwin's "The Man I Love"; "Black Coffee"; and "Music Music Music," the "put another nickel in, in the nickelodeon" hit from a few years before. With calm Nesuhi in the booth, Ray relaxed more than he could at the R&B sessions with their hit-making pressure. The trio meshes with easy grace, and Ray plays with dazzling invention, his touch at times tickling lightly, at others slamming deep into the keyboard.

Ray's recording pace was stepping up. From the jazz session, he dashed down to a gig in Atlanta (where James Brown was emerging with his first hit, "Please Please

Please"), then dashed back to New York for an R&B session, Jeff Brown driving straight to the studio and unloading instruments from the station wagon. They got three tunes down, "I Want to Know," "Leave My Woman Alone," and Doc Pomus' striking "Lonely Avenue," with its staccato melody and stark lyrics:

> *My covers feel like lead*
> *My pillow feels like stone*
> *I toss and turn every night*
> *I'm not used to being alone*

Six months before, Ray had held the Cookies to one chorus of "Drown in My Own Tears." This time they sing with and around him on every track, the male-female voices fitting together so naturally that Ray's earlier vocals without a woman's touch sound suddenly naked. In the Cookies—Margie Hendricks, Ethel McRae, and Dorothy Jones—Ray had found the masculine-feminine balance that would give his subsequent music its vigorous unity. He loved the sensual pleasure of singing swathed in feminine harmony. The women's voices act as a foil, freeing him to play with his voice, to dance before them. Ray sensed all he could do with the new sound color, and he wanted to take the three young women on the road. But could he afford to? Taking cautious stock with Jeff, Ray decided he couldn't swing it yet.

After the session, the gang headed to a May 23 gig at the Trianon Room in Indianapolis. "Hallelujah I Love Her So" peaked at #6 over the summer, a bigger hit than its numbers indicate; white kids, having missed "Drown in My Own Tears," heard happy "Hallelujah" as a follow-up to "I Got a Woman." Atlantic, still expanding, moved to larger offices at 137 West Fifty-seventh Street, keeping 23456 as Tom Dowd's studio. Shaw Artists, in contrast, suffered a major blow: Billy Shaw died of a heart attack at home in Brooklyn, June 23, and was buried at Mount Ararat Cemetery in Pinelawn, Long Island. Rumors that the widow and son, Lee and Milt, might sell the business spread and then evaporated. Milt's heroin habit was no secret, but with experienced Jack Archer as vice president and Lee still coming to the office every day, the trade briefly mourned the father ("a straight shooter" and "good friend to the Negro") and began to do business with the son.

The faithful De Soto Firedome finally expired, and Jeff replaced it with an ungainly limousine made in Ohio from a cut-in-half Chevy with an added six-foot midsection. The Weenie, as the fellows soon dubbed the red-and-white monstrosity, was so ugly that fellows in other bands laughed at them. Bill Peeples thought Jeff drove the Weenie too damn fast, and crowded in with the other guys, he got annoyed at Ray riding ahead in a Cadillac. Yet the Weenie carried twelve, had an instrument rack on the roof, and still had room for Ray's new PA system, mikes and stands, cables and speakers that Jeff and the men, for a few extra bucks, set up at each gig. After years of suffering with out-of-tune pianos, Ray bought a Wurlitzer electric, similar to the one he had rented in Seattle; Fathead remembered Ray as the first musician he'd seen taking one on the road.

Renald Richard came back for what he long remembered as "the 'Hallelujah' summer." They played the newly air-conditioned Houston Coliseum on the Fourth of July, stuck around for a gig at the El Dorado July 7, then headed east, playing 9-to-1 dance after 9-to-1 dance on the "chitlin circuit." Howard Lewis' one-nighter trail in Texas and Don Robey's in Louisiana were only two links of this circuit. B. B. Beamon in Atlanta booked Alabama and Georgia, and Ray's shooting buddy Chicken took over in north Florida. In Maryland, Virginia, and the Carolinas, the Caddie and the Weenie rolled through Weinberg territory, organized in the 40s by Ralph Weinberg, now overseen by his son Eli. At Weinberg gigs, they played in dusty tobacco warehouses where the promoter put the band on a flatbed truck and pushed bales of cured leaf against the walls to clear space for the dancers.

The Montgomery bus boycott dragged on, and news of small victories in school integration filled the papers. Ray and the band were working too hard to pay that simmering pot much mind, but for them as for Negroes everywhere, the more Jim Crow's days were numbered, the more galling became its slights. Sick and tired of peeing by the road and eating sandwiches in the cars, Renald and Jeff sometimes ruffled Jim Crow's feathers for the hell of it. "We'd see a white cafe and go in," Richard recalled. " 'What do you boys want?' they'd say. 'Can't you read that sign? We don't serve so 'n' so's here.' Only once, in Texas, did we sit down and eat. If they said we could take something out, we'd say if we couldn't sit here and eat it, we didn't want it. 'Then go on about your business,' they'd say, and that's what we'd do."

Black and white relations were changing faster at the gigs. That summer Carl Perkins toured in a package show with Chuck Berry, Bill Haley, with Bo Diddley. A Houston R&B dance advertised a "Reserved Section for Whites," and everywhere white kids showed up at black dances in larger numbers. Jeff noticed that promoters, who had once cordoned off a corner for whites who came to see black folk dance, started roping off half the floor for white kids who danced too. "It'd be blacks on one side, whites on the other," Jeff remembered. "Then, when the music got really hot, hell, the rope would come down, and they'd all be dancing together."

Heroin was still causing problems in the band—worse, Richard felt, than the summer before. Ray and his junk buddies squabbled constantly. One week Ray would fire Wilkerson and let Fathead step up to tenor; then Fathead would quarrel with him and leave, and Donald would come back. When the buddies divvied up a score, Ray made Mary Ann stay in the room to tell him if the others took too much. Mary Ann hated heroin. More than Della and the women in every town, more than the time in Chicago when Ray hit her so hard Jeff took her to the hospital and she couldn't sing for three days, drugs took the bloom off Mary Ann's romance with Ray. At first he went to another hotel room so she wouldn't see him shoot up. Later he tried to teach her to shoot him up and suggested she try snorting heroin to see how good it felt. She refused on both counts.

The worst time came in Raleigh, North Carolina. "The guys were out of drugs, Ray, Fathead, and Whiskey, all sick," Mary Ann recalled. "They wanted me to fly to New York to buy some for them. I didn't like to fly, I could have gone to prison. Ray wasn't right to make me do it, but I was in love, so I went." In New York, Mary Ann checked into a midtown hotel, knocked on a door at 5 A.M., and gave a man $200. "He gave me a package, and I flew back. A young soldier who sat next to me could tell I was scared, and he said, 'Don't be afraid, Mary Ann.' "

In September, Atlantic released "Lonely Avenue," and it pushed to #6 in October against heavy competition from Bill Doggett's "Honky Tonk" and "In the Still of the Night" by the Five Satins. Elvis' two-sided hit, "Don't Be Cruel" / "Hound Dog" also competed with "Lonely Avenue" on the R&B charts, but his first album, with "I Got a Woman" as one track, sold over a half-million copies, earning Ray and Renald Richard substantial songwriter royalties. As an Atlantic artist, Ray had long since agreed to let Progressive Music, the label's publishing arm, publish his original songs, he and any collaborators getting the standard 50-50 split of whatever income the songs produced. Ray and Renald had done well from Ray's "I Got a Woman," their first checks from Progressive about $1800 each. Smaller but similar checks had been flowing to Ray for "A Fool for You," "Hallelujah," and the rest. Elvis' album made the checks leap to the $8000 range. "I was tickled pink," Richard remembered. "And those checks were payments for just half the year."

Ray, in a word, was prospering, his two-year-old business distinctly in the black. Broadcast Music Inc. (BMI), the corporation that licensed Progressive songs for radio play, had begun to send him a steady flow of checks. His 5 percent artist royalty from Atlantic came less dependably, royalty payments having been a hit-or-miss affair among the indies since Jack Lauderdale's heyday. Atlantic, less perhaps than other labels, reduced what they owed artists by charging inflated fees for recording expenses and other semi-fictitious services. Still, hits like "Drown in My Own Tears" and "Fool for You" earned Ray, as he coyly put it, "a few pennies."

Ray liked doing business, though he felt himself a country boy slowly learning big-city ways. He had already grasped one basic lesson: keep costs low. He ran the band as a tight, even stingy ship, still paying the fellows $30 a night as he played more gigs for better fees. He rejected investments like touring with the Cookies if he feared they might threaten his security. His accountant, Paul Orland of Orland & Chase on West Forty-second Street, kept his books up to date and his taxes paid. Having money brought out the pack rat in Ray. Coming into New York from a run of one-nighters, Jeff might have $10,000 or more in cash stuffed in his briefcase. Ray sent some of it home to Della to put in a Dallas account; the rest he deposited in a variety of New York banks, visiting them with Jeff every few months to make sure the money was still there. He kept his old savings account at the Bank of Greenville, and on passes through his hometown he stopped to make deposits there too. The Greenville account was the deepest of all his cubbyholes, "a secret," said a valet from that era, "between Ray and God."

Ray got so far ahead that he didn't need to draw on the deposit money Shaw held for him, and he let the account pile up for months at a time. After Billy Shaw's death, Milt floundered and income dwindled. Taking a cold look over the books, Lee Shaw realized she needed to borrow money, and she asked Ray for a loan to tide them over. Ray had always liked Lee and said yes. Lee drew on Ray's account until Milt found his feet, and later repaid Ray in full. Improvident R&B artists often borrowed money from canny agents, but this rare instance of an artist-to-agent loan indicates both how close Ray had grown to the Shaws in five years and how unusually strong his financial position had become.

After a week in Cleveland, the Caddy and the Weenie rolled east in November to more sessions with Nesuhi. This time they planned to record the jazz sound of Ray's seven-piece band, hoping to get enough tracks to make Ray's first jazz album. Quincy Jones wrote a half-dozen arrangements, and Ray brought in a few himself. He knew just what he wanted: "An LP that would have a modern feel, but would be simple enough so that any person could grasp my ideas." On the 20th they got an extraordinary six tunes in the can, including "I Surrender Dear" and "Sweet Sixteen Bars," and on the 26th four more, "Doodlin' " and "My Melancholy Baby" among them. Each track is a revelation. The same fellows who put the brimstone under Ray's fiery sermons are now a miniature Basie band, playing sophisticated late-night jazz. Ray's touch is feather light, reminiscent of Erroll Garner, the horns understated, even subdued. On "There's No You" the mood grows lushly romantic, but here as elsewhere Whiskey's walking bass anchors the moonlight to the groove. Until now Fathead had loyally backed up Ray and kept his recorded solos short. Here he steps out front to play stinging be-bop blues. "Doodlin' " may be the masterpiece of the set, an infectious tune by Horace Silver with a muted-trumpet/sweet-sax chart by Jones that became a classic.

The very next day, November 27, the same band returned to the studio and turned out four hot-as-a-pistol R&B sides: "It's All Right," "Ain't That Love," "Get on the Right Track," and "Rockhouse Parts 1 and 2." "Rockhouse" blends jazz and R&B in one of Ray's best instrumental charts: an unsual two-measure rhythm figure for the horns (sharp hits on beats 1 and 4 of the first measure, a whole rest for the second) kicks the beat along with dynamo force. Ray wanted solo tambourine to open "Ain't That Love," but the Cookie asked to do it couldn't catch the lick. Jerry got bold, picked up the tambourine and started playing. "Who's that?" asked Ray.

"It's me," said Jerry.

"You got it, baby." Off Jerry went, setting the tempo with an unaccompanied intro and then hanging on for dear life, worrying every second, "What if I fuck up?" Somehow he made it to the end without missing a beat.

"It's All Right" is sublime. Until now the Cookies have played a rather formal role in Ray's passion plays, distanced from him by their own stoic chant. Here Ray sings his sad lyric, "So many times I sit down to cry," and the women respond caressingly, "It's all right, it's all right." Their voices reach out to Ray, their sympathy helps him accept his sorrows and sing with them, "It's all right, it's all right."

Ahmet, Jerry, and Nesuhi suddenly had more Ray Charles on record than they knew what to do with. They would put out "Ain't That Love" as the January single to keep Ray's R&B side developing. For the jazz Ray, the best new tracks plus a couple from the trio session would make a strong album. To sell that debut album, however, would take careful planning. What they contemplated, thanks to the variety of Ray's talent, was unprecedented: launching an R&B singles artist as a jazz album artist. Atlantic was already preparing a series of LPs, to collect the singles of Joe Turner, Ruth Brown, and their other top R&B stars. Ray's collection album was due to come out with the others in the spring of '57. Why not hold off the jazz album until after the collection had its chance? If that got Ray started with the album audience, older and more likely white than singles buyers, then they could release the jazz album. A second article about Ray appeared in *Downbeat*, writer Dom Cerulli letting Ahmet and Jerry praise Ray for paragraphs: Ray, said Jerry, "can put his finger on the soul part of the blues." Publicity like that would prepare the ground for Ray's coming foray into jazz.

In December the Montgomery bus boycott ended in victory: no more "back of the bus," the courts declared. The gang toured the South, playing a "Big Sunday Night Dance!" at the Labor Union Hall in New Orleans a few days before Christmas, then, just as in the old days, headed to Houston for a Saturday night at the El Dorado, January 5 in the new year.

"Whoever booked us kept us going 'round in circles," Bill Peeples remembered of his years with Ray Charles. "Up from Texas through the Midwest to Chicago, over to New York, down the coast through Virginia—we might do that three times a year." The Caddy and the Weenie wasted no time starting the circle in 1957, heading north from Houston to Detroit's Graystone Ballroom January 28, on to a mid-February dance in Muncie, Indiana, then Cleveland for a week in March. "Ain't That Love" came out to the usual rave ("plenty of sweet agony in his tone"), but climbed only to #11 in a six-week run, a sign that Ray had hit a plateau in the upward curve of his career.

Elvis topped the pop and R&B charts that spring with "All Shook Up," and *Billboard* pointed out that Negroes were no longer the prime target for R&B indies; Atlantic and the others now geared their sales to "both white and black listeners." People in the music business began to notice other changes in pop music. "Until rock 'n' roll, the *song* was the thing," said the other Ray Charles, music director of TV's *Your Hit Parade*. With its cheerful all-white corps of performers singing the ten most popular songs in the country, *Your Hit Parade* had from the early 50s been the heart of mainstream pop. Now the "sound" of the record was becoming a bigger selling factor than the song itself. Viewers, said Charles, "didn't want anybody except Fats Domino doing 'Blueberry Hill,' " and *Your Hit Parade* began to flounder in the ratings.

At the Uptown Theatre in Philadelphia in April, Ray headlined a double bill with Ruth Brown. Brown had passed her peak as a record seller, and Ray, who had labored so long on the lower tiers, was cresting past her. This was the band's first gig in Philly since the bust, and as became customary, police cars escorted the Caddy and the Weenie in and out of town from the Camden bridge. A playboy courting Mary Ann followed the gang on one lap west, hopping from gig to gig in a private plane. He invited Jeff and Ray to fly a couple of legs with him, and Ray was instantly hooked. This was the way to go: not up and down every hill, but over all the hills at once. From that moment Ray became determined to fly to gigs instead of driving whenever possible. He liked the speed and freedom of flying, the mechanical grace of airplanes. Soon Jeff was taking flying lessons, and the fellows complained that they had to sit in the Weenie at godforsaken county airports while Jeff got a couple of hours of instruction.

In May, Atlantic released Ray's new single, "Get on the Right Track," but the disc got a lukewarm *Billboard* review and never touched the charts. The plateau seemed to be turning into a slump. Ray responded by working harder, getting to New York to record four new songs. Once again Tom Dowd was impressed with how tough Ray was on his musicians. "A drill sergeant from the old school! When he said, 'Play!' you better be ready. He might change an arrangement if it didn't work, so he'd shout, 'No, man, can't you remember, play the new lick, not the old one!' He'd play a guy's part for him on the piano, saying, 'Do it again, do it again.' "

The results justified the effort. "That's Enough" and "Talking 'Bout You" have a sexy, self-confident swagger, the ladies responsive to Ray's slightest wish. Ray doesn't sing at all on "What Kind of Man Are You?" but, mysteriously, it is still a Ray Charles record. The Cookies sing, "What kind of man are you?" as Mary Ann asks her own heartsick questions:

> *Why do I love you so?*
> *Why do you love me no more?*
> *Why can't I let you go?*

Their questions go unanswered, Ray responding only with an enigmatic piano fillip at the end of each chorus that could mean anything or nothing at all. Making himself the silent center of the song was exactly Ray's intention, Mary Ann remembered. "He wanted me trying to find out what kind of man could hurt me as he did, but me not being able to find out."

"Swanee River Rock" is Stephen Foster's "Old Folks at Home" done "I Got a Woman" style. Ray romps through the vocal, the ladies set a hand-clapping beat, and Fathead lays a bluesy tenor solo over Ray's gospel piano. The fun of turning a somber old song into a cheerful modern one is obvious on first listening; a second reveals a satisfying "turnabout is fair play": Ray transforming Foster's sentimental slave's lament into a joyful African-American stomp. On third listening, "Swanee River Rock" gives evidence of Ray's emerging grand ambition: to absorb all American music, from its deepest roots to the present day, into his own music. For pop singers, Stephen Foster belonged to the square and distant past; jazzmen looking for songs to jam on seldom reached further back than Irving Berlin and Jerome Kern. In recording rock 'n' roll Foster, Ray declared American music of any era fair game for his devices.

Ray's first album, *Ray Charles,* came out in June, number six in the Rock 'n' Roll series that collected singles by Atlantic's top R&B artists. The first of countless times Atlantic would repackage Ray's tracks, *Ray Charles* opens with his latest, "Ain't That Love," ranges as far back as "Mess Around," and closes with "I Got a Woman." The idea of R&B on albums, however, was still brand-new, and despite a special low price of $3.98 and an attractive gray-green cover, Ray's album, and the whole series, sold only moderately well.

The band, stable through two years, began to change as spring became summer, a turnover due in part to wear and tear. Bill Peeples quit because women and alcohol had made him sick—and because Ray was hiring better players. John Hunt and Milt

Turner, graduates of Tennessee State University, came in on trumpet and drums, and trumpeter Wallace Davenport came up from New Orleans. In the old days around New Orleans, Ray and Davenport had talked as pals. Now Davenport kept his distance. "Hey, Wallace," Ray asked him backstage one day, "why don't you ever talk to me?" "Because you're the bandleader now, Ray," Davenport replied.

Davenport stayed a few weeks; Edgar Willis replaced Whiskey Sheffield on bass, and he would stay with Ray for twenty years. Ray first heard Willis playing with Sonny Stitt and knew instantly he wanted him. A Pittsburgh native, Willis was a tall, slender man with a modest smile; his glasses and his schoolteacher manner soon earned him the nickname "the Peeper." Tom Dowd remembered Willis in the old Atlantic studio, standing in the curve of the piano close to Ray. "Let me hear you, Edgar," Ray would say, "play with me!" And Edgar would follow Ray wherever he went.

Another newcomer who became a trusted veteran joined that summer: Leroy Cooper on baritone sax. A rotund man with a rotund smile who soon won the nickname Hog, Cooper stayed only a few months at first, but with a few breaks, he lasted with Ray into the 1970s. The son of a Dallas bandleader, Leroy Cooper had toured in Ernie Field's territory band out of Tulsa and in army bands before coming back to Dallas in the mid-50s. Fathead sat in with Leroy at the Club Birdland, and when Jay Dennis left, he recommended him to Ray. When Jeff called, Leroy told him he needed cash to settle a few debts before he could leave town. "How much you need?" "Six hundred dollars," said Leroy, and Jeff said okay. "Two hours later here comes Western Union with the money," Leroy remembered years later. "I told my wife, 'I gotta go with this band.' My old baritone was so ragged, wired up with rubber bands, the keys going clack clack clack."

Leroy took the train to Washington, D.C., and met the band rehearsing in the basement of the Charles Hotel. "Ray says to me first thing, 'Can you read?' I tell him I haven't read charts since I'd been in an army band. The guys were watching us and laughing. Ray had 'em put up some syncopated charts, we started, then Ray told everybody to stop, and I kept going. 'Okay,' he said, 'he can read.' " With that Leroy was in, and they set off. Nat Cole's show was on TV that summer; the fellows watched it in cafes on the road. Leroy roomed with Ed Blackwell, one of them booking the hotel room to get a single rate, the other slipping in later. The musicians called that "ghosting," and they all did it: Ray paid nothing for expenses.

In the R&B touring hierarchy, Leroy found, Ray Charles and his Orchestra were just another band. "We played picnics in parks in New Jersey, cinder-block clubs in the backwoods with fish frying in the corner and the people drinking beer by the quart. In the tobacco warehouses people'd be kicking up so much dust in the air dancing, you could hardly breathe." Fathead had seen worse days and worse joints, and for him, the new recruits were one sign of many that things were looking up. Once they had routinely driven four hundred miles between gigs; now it was more like two hundred miles, three hundred miles tops. A few years before, the band might get stuck in Meridian, Mississippi, from Monday to Friday, and Ray would call midweek rehearsals to keep the fellows from wandering off. "Now we were playing four, five nights out of the week. Sometimes the only reason we didn't play every night was we couldn't get there."

Ray, Mary Ann, and the fellows lived a rough-and-ready life on the road. The music they played had a sweaty, funky flavor, and the drinkers and dancers at the clubs responded in kind. Fights often broke out at the dances while they played. Anything could start a brawl, Ray recalled: "Some cat steps on another dude's foot. . . . Some woman comes in and sees another woman dry-fucking her man." In Daytona a man cracked a bottle across a woman's head, and she fell bleeding onstage; in Pittsburgh a cop fired his pistol to calm the crowd and instead started a stampede for the doors. When trouble started, Ray ducked behind the piano, figuring its wood and steel would protect him if anything could.

Bunking together in cheap hotels, crammed together in the Weenie, Mary Ann and the band had no privacy, and nerves often scraped raw. One night in Washington, Fathead, drunk, tried to make Mary Ann get out of "his" seat, and she hit him so hard with her straightening comb that he carried the scar for years. Sometimes forced intimacy made for noisy fun. Gambling in the Weenie, crouching on the floor for all-night games of blackjack, tonk, and poker, $100 to get into the game, a whiskey bottle making the rounds—those were good times. A three-dice crap game they called "4-5-6" got everybody's blood going. Three sixes beat anything; two deuces and an ace crapped you out. When promoters rode with them for a leg, everybody tried to capture the outsider's wad of greenbacks for the band. Ray sometimes rode in the Weenie just to play 4-5-6, throwing himself into the game with the others, laughing and squealing and slapping his thighs. When a die rolled deep under a seat, he'd drop to his knees and grope for it with his long arms, find it, feel the dimples, and, if he was lucky, come up crowing.

None of the fellows knew how much Ray was making from the gigs and his various royalties, but they knew he was cheap with them, and the boss's tight fist with a nickel set off jealousies over money within the band. Everybody had his own deal with Ray, and nobody knew what anybody else got paid. Some remembered getting $25 a night; Fathead got $35. A fellow could earn extra money driving or setting up the PA, but those were privileges that Jeff granted and that Jeff could take away. Jeff also held the band bank. If you got behind, he might loan you money, or he might not. "Jeff had guys he liked," remembered Leroy Cooper. "Advances were a privilege, and I couldn't get nothing from him. One day he'd be in a good mood, and a cat would say, 'Jeff's loaning money today.' Cats would run up whether they needed it or not just to have a few bucks." Beneath the money tension lay another worry: When Jeff was tough on you, was Jeff acting on his own or on a sign from Ray?

Ray got to New York on his own in early September for another jazz session, this one with a small combo featuring Milt Jackson, star vibraphonist of the Modern Jazz Quartet, Atlantic's top jazz group. A few months before, Tom Dowd had been mastering an MJQ album when Ray wandered in, listened, and said, "That Milt Jackson's got soul." Jackson, at the same time, had been telling Nesuhi, "No more of this MJQ Mozart Society shit, I'm gonna play the blues with Ray." Dowd got the piano tuned in the old 23456 studio and waited for Jackson's vibraphones to arrive. "No vibes came," Dowd remembered with a chuckle. "But Milt comes walking in with a guitar on his back and says, 'Where do I plug this thing in?' Then Ray comes in with an alto case and he says, 'I ain't playing piano tonight, I'm playing sax.' "

Ray and Jackson did play gorgeous piano and vibes at the session, but "How Long Blues" remains the most extended example of Ray's sax playing on record. Compared with his singing voice, his sax voice sounds modest, even deferential, yet he mixes ingenious be-bop lines with plaintive cries, and he leaps gleefully into trading fours with Billy Mitchell on tenor. Overall, the ten tracks demonstrate how wide a gap Ray was straddling between jazz and R&B. Playing for a jazz album, he and the combo could stretch out in long laid-back grooves, "Soul Brothers" weighing in at 9:34, "Bags of Blues" at 8:49. The soloists blend like old friends sharing late-night stories, the microphones eavesdropping on their intimate interplay. On "Swanee River Rock," in contrast, the players and singers direct all their energy into the mikes, too busy working the unseen audience to talk to one another. The jazz tracks simmer like a slow-cooking stew; the R&B tracks explode like musical dynamite.

In early September an integration standoff loomed at Central High School in Little Rock, Arkansas, and Jerry Lee Lewis, a professed admirer of Ray's, topped the R&B charts with "Whole Lotta Shakin' Going On." Atlantic released both the first jazz album, *The Great Ray Charles,* and "Swanee River Rock." *The Great Ray Charles,* a mix of the trio and band sessions, got a warm send-off from *Downbeat:* "a wondrously natural sound, a wholesome blues feeling." In the liner notes Ray said four pianists had influenced him when he was starting out: Art Tatum, Bud Powell, King Cole, and Oscar Peterson.

> Tatum and Powell, he says, were instructive technically, while
> Cole and Peterson attracted him for their ability to play with feel-
> ing and still keep a clean, delicately articulated facade. Ray con-

siders "clean playing very important, but he feels that the com-
munication of emotion should be the transcendental interest of
every musician."

Of the single, *Billboard* raved, "a snappy adaptation of the Stephen Foster cleffing with smart staccato choral backing." Ahmet and Jerry saw instant action on the disc, especially with white buyers. Maybe Ray was coming out of his slump.

If so, it was hard to tell on the road. After a mid-September week at the Club Bel-Aire in Chester, Pennsylvania, Ray and the gang joined "The Fantabulous Rock 'n' Roll Show of '57" in Raleigh, North Carolina. Despite its grandiose name, the Fantabulous show was a second-tier R&B package tour that had straggled out of the West Coast in the spring. Mickey and Sylvia topped the bill; Larry Williams, Joe Turner, Bo Diddley, the Del Vikings, and "Ray Charles and his Concert Orchestra" ranked beneath. The Fantabulous Show rolled to Knoxville, Louisville, Chattanooga, and Atlanta through October, the stars traveling in a Scenicruiser, Ray, his band, and everybody else in a battered old Flexible bus. One night Mickey Baker had a fight with Sylvia and quit the show for a week. Fortunately, this was Mickey and Sylvia's first tour, and nobody knew what they looked like. The promoters got a guitar player to play Mickey's part and pretend to sing, while Ray sang Mickey's vocal with a mike between his legs. By such makeshifts the Fantabulous Show limped into Houston and dragged itself north to expire in Indianapolis.

Then, as if by magic, Ray's slump ended. In November, "Swanee River Rock" entered Billboard's Top 100 at #70 and started climbing. Such pop chart success was old hat for Chuck Berry and Fats Domino; for Ray it was historic: the first time he had ever shown up on anything but the R&B charts. Atlantic's experiment in launching Ray as a jazz artist was also paying off. *The Great Ray Charles* began to sell, and so many jazz dj's were playing "Doodlin' " and "Sweet Sixteen Bars" that Ahmet and Jerry decided to put them on an extended-play 45 rpm. By Thanksgiving they could announce in an ad, "Ray Charles EP Selling Like Single."

That Friday, Ray opened at the Apollo—five years after the first tiny billing, "RAY 'Swanee River Rock' CHARLES," topped the bill. As icing on the cake, Ray slipped downtown between shows the first night to appear briefly at a Carnegie Hall jazz concert with Billie Holiday, Dizzy Gillespie, Thelonious Monk, and John Coltrane. Playing the venerable hall didn't make Ray nervous—he had dreamed he would and now he could check it off his list—but appearing with Lady Day impressed him deeply. Holiday was near the end of her career, and Ray found her voice tired and nearly worn out. Still, he realized, "she could make you cry like a child."

People kept dropping by Ray's Apollo dressing room to say hello. Ahmet and Jerry brought jazz arranger Ralph Burns, currently writing charts for Chris Connors' Atlantic albums. Burns loved the hot, tight sound of Ray's little band. Larry Myers came up from the Shaw office. Once the kid of the agency, Myers now booked clubs and theaters and had, in fact, booked this week with the Apollo's Frank Shiffman. Myers found Ray and Jeff playing a fierce, noisy game of dominoes; Ray, winning, was pushing Jeff to play for higher stakes than Jeff felt he could afford. Not much was said about business, but Myers came away impressed. Ray had a class act: "He had a good band, good songs, and a great voice. Put 'em together and they spell M-O-T-H-E-R." Milt Shaw came by too. The fellows liked Milt, a Jewish guy who talked more jive than the black cats. Big good-looking Milt liked to have fun, and hanging out with musicians was the most fun possible. Everybody who wanted got a taste of Milt's dope. Smoke a joint with Milt, and pretty soon everybody was laughing.

"Swanee River Rock" peaked at #42 in December and started a slow fade into the new year. By that time Leroy had had enough. Ray's low pay was bad enough, but it was Jeff's tightness with the side money that broke the Hog's back. "I was one of the guys who couldn't get a dime from Jeff," Cooper remembered. "So when we got to Dallas at the end of '57, I quit the band. Ray was upset. He came out to my house as they were leaving town, asked me to go with them. I should've told him I was leaving because Jeff played favorites, but I just said, 'I'm gonna stay around Dallas.' That's when they got Hank Crawford to take my place."

When he was a high school sax prodigy in Memphis, gigging weekends with Ben Branch's dance band, everyone said that trim, dapper Bennie R. Crawford Jr. looked and sounded just like Hank O'Day, a legendary local saxophonist, and they nicknamed him Hank. Crawford studied theory and composition at Tennessee State University, led the famed Tennessee Collegians big band, and played with his own rock 'n' roll quartet, Little Hank and the Rhythm Kings. When Ray and the band had passed through Nashville in October, Leroy, on the verge of quitting, was out for the night, and Ray needed a baritone player. John Hunt and Milt Turner, both Tennessee State grads, recommended Hank, and he did the gig on a baritone sax borrowed from the band room. With Leroy gone, Jeff called from St. Louis, and Crawford took a bus north along the Mississippi and met the band for his first gig at the Riviera Ballroom on January 10, 1958. Hank was twenty-four. He would stay with Ray for five years and become one of his most trusted lieutenants.

Hank wasn't the only newcomer that January. In a four-day layover after the Riviera gig, the Cookies came out from New York. Ray had proposed the idea to the three young women during the Apollo week, but Dorothy Jones didn't want to go. The group had just come back from an abortive trip to Brazil where scorpions crawled in the hotel rooms and nobody understood English; that taste of the road was enough for Dorothy. But Margie Hendricks and Ethel McRae, tough kids from Harlem, were game for an adventure together. Margie said she knew another girl, Pat Lyles, who could take Dorothy's place. Pat was only sixteen, and before she could go, Ray had to meet her mother and get her permission.

Thus Ray met Mae Mosely Lyles, a small dark-skinned woman, attractive if a bit coarse, and about five years older than he. Mae became in time a major mistress, one might even say Ray's New York wife. Not much happened at their first meeting, but Ray Charles' entrance into her life was a major event for Mae, a door to who knows what that only a fool would leave unopened. Mae Mosely was no fool. She said Pat could go. Through Pat she'd be able to stay in touch with Ray. She had done some singing herself; maybe someday she could sing with Ray Charles too.

Ray began to rehearse Margie, Ethel, and Pat during the St. Louis layover, and when the band moved on to Youngstown, Ohio, they began doing their own spot and backing up Ray just as they had on record. The Cookies added a powerful new element to Ray's performance, but the changes women wrought in the band went far beyond music. The fellows Ray had drafted to sing back up were relieved of duty; they didn't have to hear the other men snicker, "Look at them faggots," behind their backs whenever they stood together at the mike. A new act on the bill meant Shaw could sell a Ray Charles one-nighter for a higher price, but also increased Ray's expenses. Thirteen bodies now crammed the Caddy and the Weenie, fourteen when Jeff's girlfriend Shirley came along. Most of all, tossing three new women among Ray and seven men totally changed the sexual dynamics of the group. As Ray put it, "There was suddenly more perfume in the air."

Thus began an extraordinary aspect of Ray Charles' life: discreet but open polygamy. Like a sultan in his caravan, Ray began to travel surrounded by his wives. Onstage the women provided a feminine counterbalance to his maleness; offstage they provided the available core of his far-flung harem. In time, the Cookies became the Raelets, and generations of Raelets succeeded the original three. As a venerable joke declares, to be a Raelet, a lady must let Ray. With many, many exceptions, the joke is true. From St. Louis onward Ray would sleep with one of his lady singers while seducing a second and going cold and silent on a third, all of it happening at once, in plain view and behind closed doors. The men of the group, of course, eagerly attended any woman Ray ignored, whether for one night or a whole season. The women both thrived on and fended off all the male attention, and they jockeyed with one another for status. With the coming of the Cookies, the air of the Caddy and the Weenie became thick with crisscross sexual tension. Snarling fights and lonely tears entered the daily life of the band.

Pat Lyles wanted Ray, but Ray didn't want her. He wanted Margie Hendricks. Then twenty-three, born in Statesboro, Georgia, short, feisty Marjorie Hendricks had come up to New York as a teenager to live with her big sister Lula in an apartment on West 111th Street. Margie wanted to be a singer and took lessons at a Broadway studio in midtown. Moderate success as a Cookie, however, was a world apart from going on the road with a name R&B band. Lula didn't want Margie to go, but Margie was a spit-fire who was hard to stop, a rough-edged tomboy the fellows nicknamed "Henry." Everybody soon learned that Margie was bisexual, but that, if anything, intensified Margie's appeal for Ray, suggesting exciting possibilities. When Ray felt Margie out, she responded willingly. Ray and Margie began sleeping together regularly, and she took the seat in the Caddy that had once belonged to Mary Ann.

Poor Fish! Mary Ann refused to be merged into the Cookies and jealously guarded her own solo spot, yet her romance with Ray had run its course, and riding in the Wee-nie, not the Cadillac, lowered her status in the band. She took up with Rick Harper, a new trumpet player in the band, but even though Ray had cast her off, he didn't like her sleeping with one of the fellows. She and Ricky felt they might be fired at any minute. Handsome Ricky had a roving eye, and Mary Ann had a hard time keeping him to herself. He also was a junkie, and she found that her trinkets and transistor ra-dios kept disappearing. Life on the road was losing its charm.

"Swanee River Rock" hovered low in the Top 100 through January, and Atlantic released "Talking 'Bout You," Ray's sixteenth Atlantic single, but this one didn't sell. Back in Dallas, Della was pregnant again, the baby due in April. The rented house on Eugene had sufficed for three years, but with a second child on the way, the time had come to move to something bigger, more permanent. Della didn't want to stay in the drafty house through another windy Texas winter, and Ray's touring was slowly be-coming more national than southern. Why not move to Los Angeles, where the weather was good all year round? Ray's accountant, Paul Orland, told him a house would make a good investment for some of his stockpiled cash. He talked it over with Milt Shaw, and Milt flew out to LA to help him look.

Ray and the gang got to New York for a session in late February, only a month after Tom Dowd had bought an Ampex eight-track recorder for the 23456 studio. All the world knows today that multitrack recording allows many sound sources to be recorded separately, each track so well isolated that any may be altered or re-recorded without affecting the others. In 1958, however, eight-track recording was a brand-new art, Atlantic's machine only the second one that Ampex had made (to specifications laid down by guitarist and electronics wizard Les Paul). Eight-track, Dowd found, perfectly suited "stereo" sound, a likewise emerging art, and on a LaVern Baker album he had experimented with spreading voice, piano, horns, and rhythm tracks between the left and right speakers, heightening the illusion that the music surrounds the listener as it does at a club or concert.

Ray may have heard about eight-track recording before the session, but he had had no experience with it, and Tom didn't take the time to explain to him what he was doing with the mikes and dials. At one point during the session, Ray stopped the band because he heard something he didn't like from Edgar Willis' bass. Before he could ask Edgar to play his line again, Tom played back just the bass track over the studio speakers. Ray jumped up like he'd been hit by an electric shock.

"What's that, pardner?" he shouted. "That was just the bass track," Tom said over the intercom, and Ray came running into the control booth. "Lemme see that machine," he said. His hands started flying over the console, and he peppered Tom with questions. "What's this button for, what's this switch do?" Tom walked him through it, putting Ray's hands on a knob and saying, "See, if I do this, it sounds like that." By their next session Ray had started thinking ahead to how to use the eight tracks, telling Dowd, "Tom, can you save me a track?" or "Don't mix the trumpets so loud as you did the other time."

Until now Ray hadn't involved himself in the recording process itself, partly because he was satisfied with Tom's engineering, and partly because, before eight-track, recording was a relatively straightforward technique of capturing live sound. Mixing and overdubbing eight tracks, as Les Paul and now Ray, Tom, and others had grasped, could manipulate live music elements at will, play them up and down against each other to create expressionistic sound pictures. When the recording process began to offer challenges as creative as music itself, recording began to interest Ray Charles. In time he became one of the art's grand masters.

They got five good songs in the can at the February session, Ray finally recording Sy Oliver's "Yes, Indeed," the best-known gospel-pop song before Ray's own fusion of the two idioms. In rocking the Scottish folk song "My Bonnie Lies Over the Ocean," Ray leaps even further into the past than with Foster's "Old Folks at Home." He had sung "My Bonnie" with the kids at Florida D&B and heard "Yes, Indeed" on the radio in the dorm. From now on a major factor in Ray's song selection becomes a process one could summarize as: "I liked this song back in Greenville, St. Augustine, or Tampa. Can I sing it? Yes? Okay, I'll record it my way." "I Had a Dream," on the other hand, is a brand-new blues. The Cookies chant "I had a dream, I had a dream," as Ray confesses to a jealous nightmare:

I dreamed someone else was here with you
Doing all the things I used to do
Please don't let this dream come true,
Tell me I'm not losing you,
Baby, say it was a dream.

In the dream his woman's voice rang in his ears, and he couldn't hold back his tears. He begged her to stay, but she wouldn't listen. Sex drenches "I Had a Dream" as it drenches "What Kind of Man Are You?" but here Ray, not the woman, is love's victim, and he quivers before her, as naked now as he once was cloaked in mystery.

By late February, Ray and Della had found the house they wanted in Los Angeles, a two-story stucco at 3910 Hepburn Avenue between 39th Street and Santa Barbara (now Martin Luther King) Boulevard. On March 6, they bought it from a Mr. and Mrs. Bedford, paying $30,000-plus in cash. Hepburn runs north-south many blocks west of Central Avenue, but during the 50s the South Central neighborhood spread steadily west toward Crenshaw. The Robinson family moved in to find black neighbors on either side, Ella Fitzgerald across the street, and white, Chinese, and Japanese families nearby. The house at 3910 Hepburn marked a big step up from the Dallas house. Like other houses on the well-kept block, it had graceful proportions and, though not large, an affluent presence. A Spanish wall hid a flowery side garden, and a porch and bay window flanked the front door. Inside, a big living room with a piano opened to the right off the entrance hall; the dining room and kitchen were to the left. The cellar became a recreation room, and Ray made a small bedroom upstairs his private office. Della had the house painted a cheerful yellow. The family moved in just before Ray Jr., almost three, had a baby brother, David.

That spring of 1958 "Top 40" programming, a short list of hits played in quick rotation, began to spread in pop radio, and Congress held hearings to investigate "payola," the ancient practice of bribing disc jockeys. After a week in Philadelphia topping a bill with the Moonglows, Ray came to New York in April for a second session with Milt Jackson, and they got another half-dozen limpid jazz-blues on tape, including an instrumental "Hallelujah I Love Her So." In May, English jazz writer Max Jones made Ray the lead item of his column in *Melody Maker,* London's major music newspaper. "Every American I meet seems to be talking about Ray Charles," wrote Jones, but England had barely heard of him. Atlantic had sent Jones Ray's *Rock 'n' Roll* album, and he found "more varied listening than you would expect from an R&B set." Ray's vocal style is "coarse-toned and countrified" but "commands a wide range of effects, not the least of which is an electrifying scream." This is the first known writing on Ray outside the United States, a hint of the worldwide fame to come.

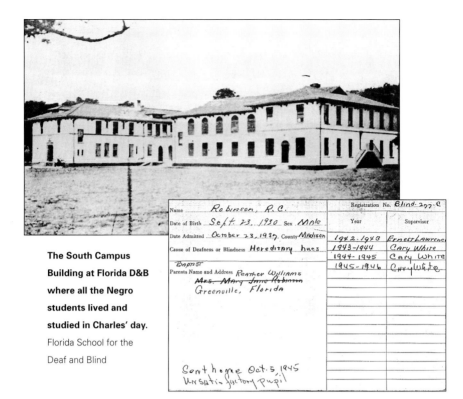

The South Campus
Building at Florida D&B
where all the Negro
students lived and
studied in Charles' day.
Florida School for the
Deaf and Blind

Charles' registration card at Florida D&B, with the date he
entered the school and when he left as an "Unsatisfactory
pupil." Florida School for the Deaf and Blind

Ray and Louise's house
on 24th Avenue in
Seattle. [Inset]: Ray and
Louise listed proudly as
a married couple among
the Robinsons in the
Seattle City Directory,
1948–49. Nick Jahn (inset:
Seattle Public Library)

The earliest known photograph of Ray Charles Robinson, taken at a Seattle radio station late in 1948. Gossie McKee

The first photo of the McSon Trio was undoubtedly taken the same day: Charles on piano, Gossie McKee, guitar, and Milt Garret, bass. Gossie McKee

"Confession Blues" in its
Down Beat Records
sleeve; Charles' first
record. Steve LaVere

Charles' pay receipt for
a recording session on
November 24, 1950.
Steve LaVere

Pianist-arranger Lloyd
Glenn, business manager
Franklin J. Kort, and owner
Jack Lauderdale of Swing
Time Records, ca. 1950.
Showtime Archives, Toronto

The Apollo ad from the
New York *Amsterdam News* for
Charles' first appearance in February 1952.

Schomburg Center

Mary Ann Fisher

Michael Ochs Archive,
Venice, CA

The first four Raelets:
Ethel (Darlene) McRae,
Gwen Berry, Pat Lyles,
Margie Hendricks; 1958.

Kriegsmann/Michael Ochs
Archives, Venice, CA

Charles and the gang at a roller rink, Rochester, New York, in the winter of 1958. Leroy Cooper is to the left of Charles; Hank Crawford and the Cookies, who had just joined the band, are on the right. The Cookies, left to right: Pat Lyles, Margie Hendricks, Darlene McRae, and unidentified. Paul Hoeffler

Charles before a gig on the R&B circuit, circa 1959. Jack Stagler/ Globe Photos

Charles signing his first ABC-Paramount contract with president Sam Clark, December 1959. Michael Ochs Archives, Venice, CA

Charles' longtime bassist Edgar Willis, guitarist Don Peak, and Jeff Brown, Ray's first manager, about 1960. Shirley Brown

Charles at the Palais des Sports, Paris, 1961, with valet Duke Wade. Archive Photo

Charles on the balcony of the Hotel Claridge, the Champs-Élysées at his feet and the Arc de Triomphe over his shoulder, during his triumphal first trip to Paris, in October 1961. When first published in Paris' *Jazz* magazine, the photo carried a banner headline: "Ray Charles Reigns over Paris for Five Days." Archive Photos

This grim photo of Charles under arrest on drug charges, being questioned by Indianapolis police, was taken less than a month after the radiant pictures in Paris. Associated Press

Charles with Frank Sinatra at a recording session in Los Angeles, early 60s. Howard Morehead

Charles investigating a kettle drum on a recording session break in Los Angeles, early 60s.
William Claxton

Charles and the orchestra on Dinah Shore's show, January 1963. Among the players are long-term members Edgar Willis on bass, David "Fathead" Newman closest to Ray in sax section, Hank Crawford beside him, Leroy Cooper at far right; among the trumpets, left to right: Marcus Belgrave, Wallace Davenport, John Hunt, and Phil Guilbeau.
Howard Morehead/Michael Ochs Archives, Venice, CA

The house on Hepburn Avenue in Los Angeles where Ray and Della lived from 1958 to 1964. Michael Lydon

The RPM International Building at 2107 West Washington Boulevard, the office/studio/hideaway that Ray built in 1964. Michael Lydon

Ray, Della, and the boys, David, Robert, and Ray Jr., at Southridge, in Los Angeles, 1966.
Bill Ray/Time Life © Time Inc.

Charles in the cockpit of the Martin, 1966. Bill Ray/Time Life © Time Inc.

Charles and
Aretha Franklin
in the studio at
RPM, during
the taping of a
Coca-Cola
commercial in
the late 60s.
Howard
Morehead

Charles and arranger Sid Feller at the piano in the RPM studio, circa 1970. Howard Morehead

Joe Adams giving last-minute instructions to the band, mid-70s.

Howard Morehead

Charles with Jerry Wexler and Ahmet Ertegun at a ceremonial dinner in the 1970s. Oddly, there are no known photographs of the three men together from their days working together in the 50s.

Globe Photo

Charles rehearsing the band at RPM, mid-70s. Howard Morehead

Charles on his way to the stage in Nanuet, New York, "coffee" mug in hand, mid-70s. Benno Friedman

Charles playing chess at his desk at RPM, mid-70s. Neal Preston

Listening at RPM, mid-70s.
David Ritz

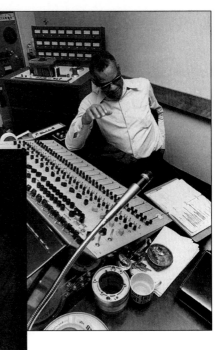

Charles with his two eldest sons, David and Ray Jr., at a banquet, early 80s.
Nate Cutler/Globe Photos

Old friends: Charles and Quincy Jones at a Hollywood dinner party, in the 80s.
John Bartlett/Globe Photos

Charles being congratulated by President Ronald Reagan and Vice-President George Bush, after singing "America the Beautiful" at the Republican Convention, August 1984.
Paul Hosefros/*New York Times*

Charles and company at the Circle Star Theatre, near San Francisco, in December 1972. From left: B. B. King, Ray, John Henderson, Raelets Vernita Moss, Dorothy Berry, Mable John, Susaye Green, and Estella Yarborough. Ellen Mandel

Ray Charles at Hampton, Virginia, Jazz Festival, 1992. Ben Costello

From the Bel-Aire in Chester, Pennsylvania, the Caddy and the Weenie rolled out to Detroit for a week at the Flame Showbar. As time passed, Ray felt himself increasingly attracted to Margie Hendricks. Sexually, Margie was eager and knowing. Unlike Mary Ann, she was willing to try getting high with him. Most of all, Ray felt attracted by Margie's voice, a preternatural match for his own. Mary Ann sang with Billie Holiday's slow burn, but Margie exploded like a gospel singer, the husky growl that rose from deep in her chest conveying the dust of her southern birth, the grit of her northern youth. Margie found learning harmony parts difficult, and Ray gave her extra rehearsal time, the two of them going over the same lines for hours. He found an old blues, "The Right Time," and worked it into a sexy duet. At the dances audiences could feel the sensual chemistry as Ray and Margie agreed, with many a steamy "Baby, baby," that "The night time is the right time to be with the one you love."

After six months, Hank Crawford was still thrilled to be playing with Ray Charles. Studying Ray's arrangements from inside the band, Hank found that Ray voiced his horns like a vocal group. Ray kept his harmonies simple, sticking to major and minor sevenths, a few ninths, but nothing more complex. He stacked his chords in plain 1-3-5-7 verticals, the baritone sax chugging on the roots, the tenor, alto sax, and trumpets chiming the upper intervals. Hank had written for Ben Branch's small band in Memphis and felt an affinity for Ray's style. One day he said to Ray, "I could write for this band." Ray, busy writing charts for his vocal tunes, said okay, try an instrumental. "This was my first chance to prove to him that I could do more than play," Crawford recalled years later. "I wrote a tune I called 'Sherri' for my daughter." As the band headed east from Detroit, Ray listened to Hank's arrangement and liked it. Over July Fourth they'd be making their Newport Jazz Festival debut; he needed some new instrumentals to show the band off to best advantage.

In five years George Wein's Newport Jazz Festival had grown from a sedate affair underwritten by the millionaire colony to a summer gathering of 60,000 jazz buffs from around the world. New names could be made or broken at Newport, and record company executives battled behind the scenes to get their acts good spots on the star-studded bills. Nesuhi Ertegun pulled the right strings to get Ray on the Saturday-night concert and brought along Tom Dowd to record it. "Ray knew this was his initiation into the jazz circuit," Hank Crawford remembered. "He was into it." Duke Ellington, Miles Davis, and John Coltrane wowed the crowds the first two nights, and Ray had his work cut out to match them.

Saturday night was Newport's first "Blues Night," and Joe Turner, Chuck Berry,

Big Maybelle, and Ray drew a huge youthful crowd. Jazz's old guard, however, had long resisted any incursion of R&B into the festival, and the purist-pop dichotomy made the experiment less than a perfect success. A backup band of jazz cats stumbled trying to keep up with Chuck Berry's clanging guitar. Big Maybelle kept snapping her fingers to get the jazz drummer to give her a backbeat she could lean on. Ray started out with jazz, his own blistering "Hot Rod" and Hank's mellow "Sherri," before going on to his R&B hits, "Yes Indeed" and "I'm a Fool for You." He and Margie tore up "The Right Time" as the first encore, and they closed with a long "I Got a Woman," Ray howling wild lines over a one-chord vamp that faded to pianissimo as the crowd went bananas.

"An enjoyable performance," said *Downbeat* neutrally, but *Billboard* reported that "Ray Charles failed to achieve rapport with the audience," because, "for some inexplicable reason, [he] decided to play jazz selections before he played any blues," thereby losing both segments of the audience. When Atlantic released the album, *Ray Charles at Newport,* in the fall, Nesuhi wisely changed the concert order to mix the jazz and R&B tracks, but the energy that leaps from the record belies the criticism. Ray and company played up a storm that 5th of July, and a large and happy crowd went with them all the way. Ray's Newport appearance, many also felt, affected the direction of jazz, his raw blues encouraging the "back to roots" movement of Horace Silver and Cannonball Adderley.

The band headed south. Little Jimmie Scott, a singer with a captivating high voice, had played Atlanta's Royal Peacock the week before Ray and company got there, and he stayed over to hear them. Scott loved the exactness of Ray's diction, his musical common sense. "I could feel Ray listening for the same 'silent instinct' that I do," Scott remembered. "He sang the *thought* of the song." Scott noted how attentively Jeff took care of Ray—"Ray was his child"—and he watched amused as Margie, Mary Ann, and the other girls bustled and fussed to be close to him. "Ray had two songs he played, 'Margie' and 'Mary Ann.' When he sang 'Margie,' she'd stick her chest out and say, 'He's singing my song tonight!' The next night, Mary Ann would say, 'He sang "Mary Ann" for me!'" Ray didn't project a cocky attitude, Scott recalled, but the rooster ruled the roost. "Every girl knew he'd ship her home if she got out of line. To appease him, one girl didn't make big waves about the others."

That summer, as the band headed to LA for an afternoon at the Shrine Auditorium with Sam Cooke, Ray made Hank band director, "straw boss," as the fellows called it. Like Renald Richard before him, Hank began calling rehearsals and leading the band through its forty-five-minute show before Ray came on. Ray didn't shower his new straw boss with compliments, but he knew Hank Crawford was a find, a talented kid who knew his boss's music and had a feeling for his style. With a first lieutenant as good as Hank, Ray could think of realizing the dream of his own big band. "The idea that someday Ray was going from seven pieces to a big band started floating in the wind," Crawford recalled. "Fathead whispered to me, 'Brother Hank, Ray's thinking about getting a big band with you as a music director.' 'Me?' I said. 'I'm the newcomer. Why can't you do it?' But Ray knew I had my degree in arranging, theory, and composition. The other fellows were good players, but nobody else had my credentials."

In September, during a week's run at Washington's Howard Theatre, in came a fourth Cookie, Gwen Berry, a woman so short the fellows nicknamed her Squat. A couple of bisexual women started tagging along with the band, and that led to three-way sex for Ray. These "parties," as he called them, became a passion, long sweaty hours of surprise and pleasure in which he lost himself as both participant and blind voyeur. Ray planned his party nights weeks in advance, slowly feeling out possible participants, sometimes including one of the men. Free-form sexual experience, he learned, was much like a groove in music. One had to be patient, to follow, not push, the flow of action, to let moments come and pass in their own rhythm. Sexual adventure, however, also brought out a streak of malice in Ray. He pestered Jeff's girlfriend Shirley for a week in Pittsburgh, demanding that she party with him. She told Jeff, and he had it out with his boss. Shirley could barely believe what the other girls took from Ray. "Ray could be a mean and selfish man," she remembered. "If you didn't know how to stand up for yourself, he'd try to control you. He had no use for any girl he couldn't get on drugs or get into bed."

In the fall of 1958 the nation went mad for hula hoops. "Chantilly Lace" by the Big Bopper and "Tom Dooley" by the Kingston Trio topped the charts, and after three years of tunneling, Ray began to move up to the surface. In New York a couple of days before Halloween, he and the gang recorded four songs that reveal Ray's sound moving out of the gospel mold and edging into a new era. This time Ray wanted conga under everything. Jerry booked Mongo Santamaria, and his ticka-tack rhythms, with Milt Turner's sting cymbals, give all the tracks a bright Latin bounce. On "Early in the Morning" and "Tell Me How Do You Feel," Ray cushions the horns with the tremulous timbres of electric piano and organ. When Margie and Ray did "The Right Time," the atmosphere thickened with emotion. "This was Ray's first duet, the first time where everything didn't hinge on him," Tom Dowd recalled. "Sometimes Ray and the fellows joked between songs, but not that session. Margie and Ray had heavy chemistry, the energy pushed you back to the wall."

A week later Ahmet and Jerry released "Rockhouse," and *Billboard* gave the single a rousing send-off: "a first class wax for both pop and jazz jocks and it can pull plenty of coin." The next week *Ray Charles at Newport* was released. Critics agreed that Ray sang the blues better than his band played jazz. Still, "a sock album all told," said *Billboard.* "This could be Charles' biggest LP to date." Disc jockeys started playing "The Right Time" from *Newport,* and over Thanksgiving Ahmet and Jerry rushed out the studio version as a single. Which meant that, in December, Ray had a new album and two singles out at once. Competing with himself didn't lessen his appeal. "Rockhouse" hit the R&B charts mid-month, and "The Right Time" ran hard on its heels. "Rockhouse" even entered the Hot 100 at #95 and rose to #79 a week later. Another week and it was gone, but showing up at all indicated Ray's continuing foothold in the pop market. As icing on the cake, Harry Belafonte rode high in the album charts with *Belafonte Sings the Blues,* five of its eleven tracks songs Ray had recorded. Belafonte turned Ray's blues into tinkling Manhattan jazz, weak tea compared with the originals, but the album earned Ray chunky songwriter royalties and introduced him to Belafonte's legions of white fans.

"Ray was zooming." That's how Hank Crawford recalled the end of 1958. "The hard days digging were over, and Ray was coming through." The band had more gigs and bigger audiences, still largely black audiences but getting more mixed all the time. Through the rising excitement of success Ray drove the band even harder. In a five-horn band, as Cooper put it, "there's no place to hide. We had to *listen, listen, listen.* A lot of stuff was never written down. Ray'd say, 'Fellas, put some stuff on this,' and boom, we had it. You had to let Ray set the pace, watch his left shoulder dipping on the big beats, his feet dancing the little ones. On the slow stuff like 'Drown in My Own Tears,' the beat would almost stop, then over would go that shoulder, and we'd *melt* with him."

"If you couldn't play the music right," said Crawford, "Ray'd fire you, no matter whether he had a replacement—you gotta go." Liberal use of the strop kept the band honed to a razor's edge, but spellbound by Ray's fierce dedication, the men willingly worked like dogs for him. The result, said Crawford: "The band was *hot!* We used to burn through our opening set, and when Ray came out, he had to pump to catch up. We had a band full of soloists, John Hunt, Fathead, me, Leroy when he came back in. It was getting to be like when Ellington had Johnny Hodges and Cootie Williams; people started going to hear us as well as Ray."

More success brought more money, and more money bought more heroin. Everybody could see the dealers coming and going, Ray disappearing with Fathead or one of his "doctors." When high, Ray often scratched himself in jerky movements, but he also knew how to project a cool front to the world. The fellows figured most people wouldn't have guessed he did drugs. None sensed that Ray used heroin to escape from pain or for any deep psychological reason. "If he trusted you enough to talk about it, he'd just say, 'I like to get high,' " Crawford said. "I never saw him cry over anything. If he cried, he did it in his heart. He *sang* about being heartbroken, but he was always laughing, gambling, and carrying on."

In December the caravan worked its way west from New York. At a dance in Brownsville, near Pittsburgh, with fifteen minutes left of the gig, Ray realized he had run out of things to play. The crowd was up and excited, but nothing in the book that they hadn't already played seemed to fit the mood. "So I said to the guys," Ray remembered years later, " 'Look, I don't know where I'm going, so y'all follow me.' " He turned to the ladies and said, "Whatever I say, just repeat after me." Ray started a low bouncy bass riff on electric piano, the drummer clicked in on his big cymbal, the band fell into the up-tempo groove, and Ray started singing nonsense choruses, "See that gal with a diamond ring, she knows how to shake that thing." The crowd loved it and, without knowing that the song was being made up on the spot, fell into the improvisatory feeling.

Soon Ray ran out of words and started to moan. The ladies moaned back. The call and response began to crescendo of its own accord, until it sounded like a man and woman losing themselves in lovemaking. Somehow they brought it to a close, the people went nuts, and everybody collapsed exhausted. Offstage, people ran up to Ray and asked where they could buy the record. "What record?" Ray replied. "That last thing you played, it was wild, we loved it." The next night Ray tried it again, and in weeks to come the response grew. People loved the "Unnnh, unnnh" part and began to moan along too. Ray called the song "What'd I Say."

The Caddy rolled on through the southern days and southern nights. At first glance, not much seemed to have changed since 1956. Ray slouched smoking in the back seat, Margie at his side, Jeff at the wheel, Fathead riding shotgun, all talking, joking, and listening to the radio. Yet in faraway France, Ray's first release won the 1958 Grand Prix du Disque; he had become *"une folie"* with Parisian jazz fans. In England, Decca issued an album of Ray's Atlantic jazz, an R&B album was on its way, and the starchy *Jazz Journal* declared that Ray's blues, though marred by "a slightly over-emphasised offbeat," were "the product of a receptive mind and a well-disciplined musical instinct."

Ray and the gang got to New Orleans for New Year's Eve at the city's handsome Municipal Auditorium. Elgin Hychew, the "Dig Me!" columnist in the *Louisiana Weekly,* urged everyone to pay $2 and hear this "classical blues singer and a serious man." In evaluating Ray's place in jazz history, Hychew soared past the *Jazz Journal's* pale praise. "Ray Charles the great blues singer has at last emerged as a fine musician and a rare poet," he wrote, "the sum total of the reaction of his people and a marked spokesman of his time." A new master had arrived:

The great artist uses no effects. Every innuendo is in fine rhythm and is part of Charles' personal story. . . . When his music is happy, it's glorious in the happiness of self-expression. When it is sad, his pleas are the cries of a man in pain, and when they are angry, it is the anger of a multitude. . . . It is his insight, his imagination, and artistry as compared to the musical sterility of a simple entertainer which makes him different and makes him click with the public, all people, all races, all classes, all backgrounds.

The Genius
Moves On
1959

As Dwight Eisenhower approached the end of his White House years, the rock 'n' roll boom was still accelerating. "Flood of Records Hits Peak in 1958," *Billboard* headlined in 1959's first issue. Forty-five singles on two dozen labels had each sold a million-plus copies; the output of LPs had more than doubled. Records had become a mass consumer item, buyable not only in specialty shops but in discount stores and supermarkets. The launching of stereo proceeded full steam ahead and the year to come was anybody's ball game.

Atlantic Records and Ray Charles had barely met when Ike took office, but through the long summer of his peace-and-prosperity years, they had grown apace with the industry. Atlantic had nearly realized the dream of all indies: becoming a major label. The label had "an aura," wrote Charlie Gillett in *Making Tracks*, "felt as soon as the outsider puts his foot on the edge of the music business." Ahmet's custom-tailored vicuna coats and Jerry's gift for schmoozing with reporters contributed to the aura, but its core was records with "strong content, accurate yet still improvised singing, and imaginative accompaniments." Ahmet, Nesuhi, and Jerry recorded pop-rocker Bobby Darin, the cerebral MJQ, and the clowning Coasters, and Atlantic enjoyed a label-wide reputation for excellence. Kids and connoisseurs alike respected the discs with the big black A on the bright red label.

As Atlantic had matured as a company, Ray had matured as a man and a musician. At twenty-eight, his lean body had filled out. His head loomed heavier on his shoulders, and was more likely downcast, than in the lighthearted Seattle days. Ray had become a married man and a father, and he had been leading a band and meeting a weekly payroll through five straight years on the road. He had put out twenty singles on Atlantic, fourteen of them medium to major hits, and four albums, all strong sellers. Two of his original songs, "I Got a Woman" and "Hallelujah I Love Her So," had become oft-covered standards. From R&B Ray had successfully crossed over into jazz; *Downbeat* readers had just voted him top "Male Singer–New Star" by a two-to-one margin. In a business crowded with imitators, Ray had earned a reputation for being unique. Looking back, Tom Dowd could see how Ray had built his sound brick by brick from his blues-and-ballad days: "To his Nat 'King' Cole base, Ray added something from gospel, from R&B, from jazz, giving the public a little of everything. With each new sound, the circle of people who liked what he was doing got wider."

In these seven fat years, Ray and Atlantic had become deeply entwined in each other's success. Ray felt grateful for the freedom Ahmet, Jerry, and Nesuhi had given him to record what he pleased. They, in turn, held Ray in utmost respect and had begun to believe that he was, like Brahms or Tolstoy, a "genius," an artist of mighty ability and capacious insight. Ray and his producers had not become close socially, but deep bonds of trust and friendship had grown from years of sweating together. The backbreaking days of plowing and planting were over, all felt; harvesttime was near at hand. Only one cloud marred the blue skies of 1959: Ray's contract was due for renewal in the fall. Ray could, if he chose, leave Atlantic. Given the long-term success and cordiality of their relationship, however, no one thought that possible.

From New Orleans, the gang drove to the Magnolia in Atlanta, and that January 14 gig became the Fish's last stand. With part of her heart Mary Ann still loved Ray and believed he loved her best, but the sex-and-drugs scene that had started with the Cookies turned her off. After three and a half years, it was time to go home to Louisville. She told Ray she was leaving. "No one leaves *me*," he said, but the black press soon reported that Mary Ann Fisher, "former mainstay with the Ray Charles Singers, recently joined the realm of the freelancers in the theatrical profession."

Reporter Ren Grevatt called from New York during the Magnolia gig to interview

Ray for *Billboard*. In later years wide-ranging interviews with Ray Charles became a staple of the pop music press, but Grevatt's call was among the first, and Ray sounded off volubly on a variety of musical matters. "If I don't feel what I'm doing on a record, then I'd rather forget it," he said. Many singers do what their label tells them to do, but if "they never feel it . . . they don't make a good record." He loved gospel and thought Mahalia Jackson was the greatest, but even in gospel "the artist has to feel it or it's no good." For him, R&B was "genuine, down-to-earth Negro music," and it hurt him when critics called it bad music. Ray dismissed rock 'n' roll as "getting a couple of guitars together with a backbeat," but country music was wonderful: "I think I could do a good job with the right hillbilly song." He allowed that "there's nobody greater than Frank Sinatra," but he didn't know what to say about Elvis except "You can't argue with the public." To sum up:

> If all artists would do what is really right for them and would feel within themselves what they are doing, they would stay up there longer. A new star is born every day, but it's always a question of how long he will shine. A true artist will be around for a long time.

From France came word that disc jockey and jazz writer Frank Tenot had made "Hallelujah I Just Love Her So" a hit on his popular Europe One radio show. "The Right Time" started an eighteen-week run on the R&B charts that peaked at #6, while, underneath it, "Rockhouse" traced a lower eight-week curve. On February 18, Ray and company got to New York to record a new duet with Margie, "Tell the Truth," and "What'd I Say," the sexy blues they had been improvising on the road. "Tell the Truth" burns with the same passionate heat as "The Right Time," but, masterpiece though it is, it stands in the shadow of the session's grand accomplishment, "What'd I Say."

"What'd I Say" didn't feel like a big deal at the time. "We made it like we made all the others," Tom Dowd recalled. "Ray, the gals, and the band live in the small studio, no overdubs. Three or four takes, and it was done. Next!" When the team reviewed the tapes, however, they knew they had something unusual on their hands. The track was over seven and a half minutes long and strangely asymmetrical: Ray hammering fuzzy bass riffs on electric piano for a half-dozen choruses, finally singing a grab bag of blues clichés that tell no story. The horns join him at last, and after building to a climax of "What'd I say" repeated over and over, Ray and the band stop.

Immediately a gaggle of men and women's voices rise in protest. They want the music to keep going, and though pretending he doesn't understand, Ray starts again, this time singing a long "Unnnnh" to which the ladies respond, "Unnnnh." Then a long "Ohhhhh" from Ray, and a long "Ohhhhh" response from the ladies, then faster and faster:

> *"Unnh!"*
> *"Unnh!"*
> *"Oh!"*
> *"Oh!"*

the grunts each time becoming more edged with sexual pleasure until Ray is screaming, the ladies moaning, and the band rocking. Out of the ecstatic tumult come exhortations to "Shake that thing," and the general agreement, "Don't it make you feel all right!"

Atlantic wasn't sure what to do with "What'd I Say." Its driving beat gave the track dance-craze possibilities, but it was too damn long. "There were too many piano instrumentals before the vocal," Dowd remembered. "And girls with yellow dresses, blue, red, and green dresses." Ray's tempo, however, was metronomically exact, and Dowd edited out unwanted choruses and telescoped the track to two three-minute sides of a 45, "What'd I Say, Parts I & II." When they heard Tom's shortened master, Ahmet and Jerry knew they had a record too hot for spring release. Summertime, when kids took their transistor radios and portable record players to the beach, had become the big selling season for rock 'n' roll singles. They'd hold back "What'd I Say" until June and then make it the dance hit of the summer.

In March, Clyde McPhatter's contract with Atlantic ran out, and after a bidding war with Warner Bros. and United Artists, MGM Records won the singer with a contract that guaranteed him $50,000 a year. Losing their principal balladeer to a major label gave Ahmet and Jerry pause. The fight for McPhatter proved that scouts from the majors were cruising the indies to snatch up artists. The same sharks would surely circle again when Ray's contract ran out. Might Ray prove no more loyal than McPhatter, whom Atlantic had also discovered and developed? Not that he had given any sign that he was unhappy. Ray and Nesuhi had started planning a major new album of standards with a big band and strings. With that on the horizon and "What'd I Say" ready for the summer, Ray would never leave the label that made him. In any case, Ray still hadn't broken big-time in the white market; Ahmet and Jerry figured that the majors were interested only in R&B singers who, like McPhatter with "A Lover's Question," had already demonstrated power on the pop charts.

When Ray and the gang played the Skatearena in Indianapolis, on March 30, the

Cookies were no longer the Cookies: the Indianapolis *Recorder* ad promised, "On Same Bill, Those Gorgeous Girls, THE RAELETS." Ray's affair with Margie Hendricks continued hot and heavy, and for months at a time Della and the boys floated far to the side of Ray's life, in touch by phone yet emotionally out of touch. That spring, Margie realized she was pregnant. She and Ray talked it over. Would she get an abortion? She didn't want to, and Ray agreed. They loved each other too much. They'd have the baby, and he would provide for it. For the moment, however, there was no reason for her to stop singing.

In April, Ray got down to brass tacks on the all-American pop album that he and Nesuhi had been plotting, Ray crooning in front of a big band and strings. Strings behind an R&B singer was totally unprecedented, and behind a jazz singer, nearly so; critics still considered Billie Holiday's *Lady in Satin* a questionable experiment. Pop music, however, had long nestled its African elements on the comforting cushion of the European symphony orchestra. For Bing Crosby, Frank Sinatra, Perry Como, Dinah Shore, and many more, singing with a big band "sweetened" by violins was commonplace.

Like every other American, Ray had been hearing these singers all his life, and he loved the sound of voices cresting over surging violins while the drummer swung the beat. Why not try it himself? Ray figured he could sing the pop songs of Berlin and Kern, Gershwin and Arlen as well as anybody—he'd sung many of them at the Skyhaven Club back in Tampa. Quincy Jones began writing big-band charts for one side, and Nesuhi called the best players in New York to surround Ray's band and bring the roster up to eighteen pieces. Looking for an arranger for the string side, Ray asked Nesuhi who wrote the string charts for Chris Connor's recent Atlantic records. Ralph Burns, Nesuhi said. The same Ralph Burns who used to write for Woody Herman's big band? asked Ray. The same, said Nesuhi, and Ray booked him on the spot.

Ralph Burns, a piano whiz from Newton, Massachusetts, had, after fifteen years of arranging for Herman, become a freelancer in New York, writing jazz or classical charts, whatever the occasion demanded. Ray picked seven songs, going back to Irving Berlin's "Alexander's Ragtime Band" and up to Louis Jordan's blues ballad "Don't Let the Sun Catch You Crying." On the road, using his portable recorder and electric piano, Ray taped the songs and sent the tapes to Burns. "The electric piano sounded terrible!" Burns remembered. "Ray talked to me on the tape, gave me the keys. I never used his introductions, but since he couldn't read a lead sheet, I strictly followed his chords." Burns had a cup of coffee and a cigarette and got to work. "An arranger for a singer is like a hairdresser for an actor," he said, to sum up his trade. "He makes a singer sound good. Being a jazz singer, Ray wouldn't sing exactly like the tape, so I wrote him backgrounds he could float over, gave him space so he wasn't locked in." Burns got his score finished and his parts copied before Quincy did, and Nesuhi scheduled a session for May 6, Ray coming east from a gig in Indiana.

The session went off smoothly, Jerry in the booth with Nesuhi, Burns conducting a string-and-woodwind orchestra plus rhythm section. Nesuhi was pleased with the results, Jerry astounded at how tenderly Ray caressed the lyrics. Ray takes no big melodic liberties, and a tentative quality reveals the tracks as Ray's first attempt at pop. Yet on the masterpiece, "Just for a Thrill," and elsewhere, he sings his long lines on well-taken breaths, gliding up to high notes with the assurance of a classically trained baritone. The voice that has sobbed the blues and unleashed gospel screams comes undiminished through the polished pop surface; the rough burr on his legato conveys that this man has ventured further into life and love and music than most pop singers ever dare.

The gang headed south to Atlanta for two concerts, May 28 and 29, promoted by WAOK disc jockey Zenas Sears in Herndon Stadium, a minor-league ballpark. Like San Francisco's "Gentleman George" Oxford and Detroit's Ed "Jack the Bell Boy" MacKenzie, Sears was white but mimicked a black style so well that many listeners thought he was a Negro. The two concerts were to celebrate his fifth year at the station. Roy Hamilton topped the bill, and in support there were Ray, B. B. King, Ruth Brown, and the Drifters. On-and-off rainy, misty weather kept the crowds under 9000, smaller than Sears had hoped, but musically everything jelled. Each act in the long lineup sounded better than the one before, and Ray and company went on next to last. The second night, the crowd gave them a ten-minute standing ovation, and Sears ran on stage, screaming over the applause, "The great Ray Charles, the High Priest, the High Priest!" Then the gang headed to gigs in New Orleans and Baton Rouge.

Nobody told Ray, but Sears had recorded the Atlanta shows with a single mike hung above the stage. He wasn't hoping for a pressable record, only to get snippets to advertise his next show. But Ray's tape sounded so good that he edited together three minutes to send to his buddy Jerry Wexler. The tape arrived at Fifty-seventh Street one sticky June night. Jerry put it on an office machine and heard Fathead's tenor open "The Right Time" with a bolt of zigzag lightning. He jumped to the phone and called Zenas. "Do you have more of this?" he shouted. "Oh," said Zenas, "a couple of hours."

Jerry reached Ray on his way to a riverboat cruise out of Philadelphia, and got his permission to let Tom edit Sears' full tape into an album. Released a year later as *Ray Charles in Person,* it is Ray's first, last, and only unintended album, and one of his best. Given the single mike and a portable recorder, its sound is superb—clear as "glare ice," Jerry said—and its music magnificent. This is Ray Charles *au naturel,* the best document we have of how he and the gang sounded night after night at countless gigs in the

50s. The Newport album sounds nervous in comparison: there Ray was a newcomer in the jazz world. In Atlanta he was at home playing for home folks, and despite its all-out passion and white-hot climaxes, a calm gravity pervades *Ray Charles in Person*. Ray issues brief stage directions from time to time; more often the maestro rules with silent, unquestioned authority. Many songs he expands to four minutes and more, giving "Drown in My Own Tears," the album's magnum opus, over six. Ten years after the show in Herndon Stadium, "rock opera" became a commonplace term indicating that pop music could achieve, on its own terms, the grandeur of *Tosca* or *Rigoletto*. If rock opera be possible, *Ray Charles in Person* is the first: Margie Hendricks an American Carmen, Ray a black Don Giovanni.

From the South, Ray and the band drove back to New York for the big-band side of the studio album. Ray had sent Quincy Jones, as he had sent Burns, tapes of the songs he wanted arranged; unlike Burns' tapes, one of Jones' survives. At dawn one morning that spring, exhausted after riding five hundred miles to get home to LA, Ray sat in his Hepburn den and flipped on a recorder. "Ahh, Quincy, on this first tune, it's A-flat," Ray said, his voice a hoarse, warm whisper, talking to his old friend. "What I'm gonna do is to play a chorus, and you can have me come back in anytime you think it's gonna round out to two minutes and fifty seconds or thereabout, two minutes forty, forty-five seconds. You can write the first sixteen bars and I can come back in on the last sixteen, or the first twenty-four bars and I'll sing the last eight, depending on how you feel. All right? Now, here we go." Ray proceeded to play "It Had to Be You" softly on electric piano in a rolling rhythm, singing the lyric with sweet simplicity, stopping after one chorus. "Okay, now if you can do something with that, you're better than me."

One song took three tries to get right. "I sound pretty bad, but don't fault me for it," he rasped. On others he forgot the words and sang la-la. "Don't worry, I'll have the words when you get the music." Except for the key signatures, Ray gave Jones few instructions, letting his tempos and treatment convey his overall intentions. On "When Your Lover Has Gone" he played high, showy chords to suggest trumpet riffs, and he wanted "Let the Good Times Roll" "loud" and taken at a quick shuffle. "Okay," Ray said at the end, "hoarse voice and all, you got it."

Nesuhi booked the extra players and a big studio on West Forty-eighth Street for Monday afternoon, June 23, but the Friday before, Quincy still hadn't finished his charts. Panicked calls went out to arrangers Ernie Wilkins and Al Cohn, who slaved over the weekend; as the musicians assembled in the studio, messengers were still arriving with the latest revisions and copyists had set up shop in the corners. "I was sweating bullets," Jerry remembered years later. "The most expensive session in Atlantic history, and disorder ruled." Ray was nervous too. For weeks he had been telling the group, "Y'all better stick with me, something big's coming." Trumpeter Marcus Belgrave walked in to find he'd be playing with Clark Terry and Joe Newman, greats from the Ellington and Basie bands. "I was so scared," he remembered, "my hair was sticking up on end."

Gradually the buzzing conversations quieted as they all found their seats. Ray's little band sat in the center, looking over their shoulders at the big band: four trumpets, four trombones, four saxes, two basses, and two drums plus conga. When he opened to the "Alexander's Ragtime Band" chart, Belgrave saw that he had been assigned two eight-bar trumpet solos. "Me solo with Clark Terry right there?" he thought. He turned to Terry and said, "Man, you take this." Terry said okay, but when they got there and he started to play, Ray stopped the band. "Where's Marcus?" he shouted. "That's Marcus' solo, you can't have it, son."

After one run-through, trumpeter Ernie Royal noticed that Jones had given him a high D as the top of a G-seventh chord above an F-seventh, the same double chord RC had shown fifteen-year-old Quincy back in Seattle. "Let's take it higher," suggested Royal. "I'd like to hit my high A."

"I'd like it better," said Ray, "if you hit your high G so we'll have the tonic on top." Amazed that Ray had heard the arrangement in such detail, Royal turned to Jones. "Is that all right, Quince?"

"I ain't gonna tell you wrong, baby," said Ray, and everybody laughed.

On all six tracks they completed that afternoon, one can hear Ray's elation. A dream he'd cherished since Henry Washington's band in Jacksonville had come true at last: he's singing surrounded by the colors and textures of a big band, growly trombones, satiny saxes, high bright horns. Ray and the fellows roar, *tutti fortissimi,* through Louis Jordan's "Let the Good Times Roll"; on "When Your Lover Has Gone," Ray tinkles on piano over the pianissimo pulse of bass, drums, and Freddie Green's guitar, and he sings E. A. Swan's lyric with plainspoken tenderness:

> *When you're alone*
> *Who cares for starlight skies*
> *When you're alone*
> *The magic moonlight dies*
> *At break of dawn there is no sunrise*
> *When your lover has gone.*

Once again, new surroundings don't mold Ray, he molds them. His voice takes center stage, his piano holds the band together. When they had finished for the day and listened to the playbacks, Ray and Nesuhi and Jerry knew the hassles had been worthwhile. These tracks on one side and Ralph Burns' string tracks on the other would make one hell of an album.

With two complete albums in just over a month, this became Ray's most productive recording period ever. And there was more to come. Three days later Ray, the Raelets, and the band came back to the 23456 studio to cut a new single. They rollicked through "Movin' On," by country singer Hank Snow, Ray happy to be singing a hill-billy song, the horns blowing train-whistle riffs behind him. Then, on "I Believe to My Soul," things got sticky.

By now Ray and Tom were regularly using a valuable eight-track option: "over-dubbing," recording several tracks on one take, then rewinding the tape and recording other voices or instruments on the open tracks, creating a stack of tracks that listeners would believe had been recorded at once. That night the ladies couldn't get "I Believe" 's four-part harmony right, and each time they screwed up, they started giggling. Ray, as Jerry remembered it, "got a fig up his ass," and the more they giggled, the more irritated he became. "I don't see what's funny if you're messing up a song," he groused, but that made matters worse. Finally he lashed out, "Forget about it, I'll sing it my damn self."

Open up four tracks one at a time, he told Tom, he'd sing the ladies' parts in falsetto. To Tom and Jerry's amazement, he proceeded to do just that, listening to himself singing the original track on headphones:

> One of these days and it won't be long
> You're gonna look for me and I'll be gone
> Oh, I believe . . .

and then singing the Raelet line, "I believe it, yes, I believe it." Doing this, and achieving, as Ray did, a four-voice blend faultlessly in tune and feminine-sounding, would be a virtuoso turn for any singer, but Jerry remembered that Ray added an extra degree of difficulty. "When most singers overdub harmony parts, they listen to the tracks they've already laid down to guide them. Not Ray. Each time he sang a new line, he listened only to the band and himself singing lead."

As Jeff loaded up the car after the session for a short hop down to Philadelphia, no one noticed the irony so obvious now: they had recorded two songs of farewell and Ray was indeed moving on. Ray, Ahmet, Jerry, and Tom didn't know this would be their last session together, the last time they'd make records as a four-man team. If fate had told them so, they would not have believed her. Who quits when they're ahead? The team was on a roll, their best days still to come.

Atlantic released "What'd I Say, Parts I & II" as Ray and company drove overnight from Philadelphia to Louisville, Kentucky, and continued west to California. *Billboard* gave the single a bland review ("He shouts out in percussive syle. . . . Side two is the same"), and it got off to a slow start. Distributors called Miriam Abramson to complain that the single was too sexy for radio; they wanted to send their orders back. "You're not authorized to ship back," she said. "But we can't sell it because nobody will play it," they replied. She reported the problem to Ahmet and Jerry, and they told Tom, "Do whatever the hell you have to do."

Dowd took out a few "Shake that things," and substituted girls in prim blue dresses doing the Madison for red-dressed gals doing "the boogie all night long," and in July, the new "What'd I Say" took off, entering the Pop chart at #82, starred to indicate strong upward action. *Billboard* now declared it "the strongest pop record that the artist has had to date." A week later "What" leapt to #43. Ray could feel the hit giving his career a tangible boost. At mid-month he and the gang played the 5-4 Ballroom, but at the end of July, as "What" reached #26 Pop and was blasting out of radios everywhere, they played the Hollywood Palladium on Sunset Boulevard for the first time. Fats Domino had played the Palladium often, but for Ray it was still a white club far removed from the world of South Central.

"What'd I Say" fought its way up the charts that summer against heavy competition. Lloyd Price's "Personality" held #1 for most of July, and Dinah Washington's "What a Difference a Day Makes" hovered near the top. Yet by August "What" had pushed up to Pop #15 and #1 R&B, and as Ray and company came east to Philadelphia, the record clawed its way to #6 and held at #2 R&B. Bobby Darin's "Mack the Knife" rocketed past "What" to become Atlantic's biggest single ever, but Ray's record clung to its #6 peak for two more weeks. Only in September did the single begin to fade, dropping off the Pop chart in mid-October and lingering on the R&B listing until November.

One song or another is always topping the hit parade; many come and go and leave little trace behind. "What'd I Say" was a monster with footprints bigger than its numbers. Daringly different, wildly sexy, and fabulously danceable, the record riveted listeners. When "What'd I Say" came on the radio, some turned it off in disgust, but millions turned the volume up to blasting and sang "Unnnh, unnnh, ooooh, ooooh" along with Ray and the Raelets. "What'd I Say" became the life of a million parties, the spark of as many romances, a song to date the summer by. For Ray, it was a breakthrough like "I Got a Woman" four years before but much, much bigger. "What'd I Say" brought Ray Charles to everybody. In faraway Liverpool, Paul McCartney heard "What'd I Say" and chills went up and down his spine: "I knew right then and there I wanted to be involved in that kind of music." "What'd I Say" earned Ray his biggest royalties ever, raised his price on the road, and made a fortune for Atlantic too, contributing mightily to the label's first-ever million-dollar month in gross sales. Everybody was rolling in dough. And at that moment Ray's contract ran out.

On Friday, October 2, 1959, "Ray Charles, His Band & Singers" opened a week at the Apollo, and Larry Myers of the Shaw office came up to Harlem again to say hello to his star client. The sellout crowds and standing ovations that greeted Ray at every show told Myers how much Ray's appeal had grown in two years. "My God," the agent figured, "if he can do this kind of business with the blacks, he can do it with anybody." Soft-spoken but sharp, Myers realized that if he, a regular white guy from Brooklyn, liked Ray's music and admired him for overcoming his blindness, so might the entire white audience. Getting white people to hear Ray could open up a huge market of nightclubs, theaters, TV, radio, and records. Not that Ray was doing badly on the chitlin circuit. Myers knew to the penny how Ray's nightly price had climbed to $1000 and more, and he knew that Ray, Ahmet, Jerry, and Milt were happy with their progress. Yet, Myers believed, they were thinking too small: Ray could be much, much bigger than any of them dreamed. With the self-confidence of many small men, Myers figured he knew how it could be done.

As the band headed to gigs in the Midwest, Myers started selling Milt Shaw on his idea. "First, we have to get him off Atlantic Records," Myers told Shaw. For all its growth, Atlantic was still a black label, and if Ray stayed there, he'd stay stuck in the black world. Ray's contract running out gave them a window of opportunity, and if they acted, Ray (and they) could move into the big white market and earn much, much more money. Milt took some persuading. Atlantic was doing a great job; why rock the boat? At least talk to Ray, Myers said, advise him not to re-sign with Atlantic right away.

Milt spoke to Ray, and Ray took some persuading too. Atlantic was home, just like Shaw Artists was home. "What'd I Say" was still on the charts; and the strings/big-band album was due in a month. They'd told him they were going to call it *The Genius of Ray Charles.* How could he leave Atlantic? Yet the common sense dinned into him by Retha and a decade in the business told Ray there was no need to rush. He could stall Atlantic awhile and see what developed.

Ahmet and Jerry began to get scared. They called Ray constantly on the road. Come to New York or we'll come to you, they said. Let's get the paperwork over with and get back to work. Ahmet flew out to the Midwest twice, contract in hand. When Ray avoided him, he took Jeff to one side and said he'd give him $5000, maybe $10,000, if Ray renewed. Myers meanwhile moved on to phase two, going to the Paramount Building at Forty-third and Broadway and talking to Harry Levine.

Since Frank Sinatra's first heyday, Harry Levine had been the chief booker of live entertainment for the nationwide Paramount Theatre chain. For agents like Larry Myers, he was Mr. Big, and through the 50s Myers had sold Fats Domino and dozens of Shaw acts to Levine for Alan Freed's rock 'n' roll shows at the Brooklyn Paramount. Yet despite Freed's success, live shows in movie theaters were in decline, and the chain's parent corporation, American Broadcasting–Paramount Theatres, shifted Levine to its newest division, ABC-Paramount Records. There Levine's nose for talent might help get the label on its feet.

In 1959 ABC-Paramount Records was just four years old, the youngest major on the block. The label ranked as a major not by age, size, or track record, but by its blue-chip corporate lineage. Its parent, American Broadcasting–Paramount Theatres, had been formed from two earthquakes that shook the highest levels of show business in the early 50s: antitrust decrees that forced motion picture studios to sell their theaters and forced the National Broadcasting Company to sell its Blue Network. Leonard Goldensohn, who had run Paramount Pictures' theater division, bought the chain from the studio and formed an independent company, Paramount Theatres. With the help of powerful Wall Street and Washington connections, Goldensohn then linked Paramount Theatres to the brand-new American Broadcasting Company, formed from the old Blue Network. Hence ABC-Paramount.

For a wealthy corporation, starting a record label doesn't involve the seat-of-the-pants struggle Herb and Ahmet faced in 1947. A board member who had Goldensohn's ear suggested they start a record division. Why not? It would be one more way to market the stars, songs, and styles already attracting people to their theaters and television shows. Looking for a label president, Goldensohn approached Sam Clark, a record distributor in Boston. Clark was interested, if Goldensohn would give him a half-million dollars seed money and 10 percent equity. That posed no problem. Clark sold his business to his partners and joined Harry Levine at the Paramount Building. Of course, neither Clark the stolid businessman nor Levine the dapper talent scout knew how to make records. For that they needed an A&R man, and they hired Sid Feller, a portly arranger who had made his name producing Jackie Gleason's easy-listening albums. Singer Dick Duane had the honor of recording ABC-Paramount's debut release, "Siboney," numbered 9655 for September 6, 1955.

Though born with rock 'n' roll, ABC-Paramount ignored it at first. Clark's mandate was to make the label "another Capitol or Columbia," and his early efforts included a tie-in with Disney and a couple of medium-size hits by Eydie Gorme. After a slow first year, however, Clark consulted Larry Newton, an indy record man whose Derby records Clark had distributed in Boston. How could ABC-Paramount get off the sidelines? Newton, a fast-talking salesman, gave it to Clark straight: to sell records in 1955 you had to get into rock 'n' roll, either black music or white music with the black sound. Clark hired Newton as sales manager, and with his prodding, ABC-Paramount moved into rock 'n' roll, scoring with "A Rose and a Baby Ruth" by George Hamilton IV in 1956 and Paul Anka's "Diana" in 1957. A deal to distribute Philadelphia's Chancellor Records brought the label Frankie Avalon and Fabian, and "Personality" by Lloyd Price, their first major black artist, had reigned at #1 as "What'd I Say" was climbing. When Larry Myers came over to dangle Ray Charles before them, Clark, Levine, and Newton nibbled hungrily at the bait. They wanted Ray Charles, badly.

What could they offer Ray to make him break away from Atlantic—a higher royalty rate, advances, guaranteed annual payments? So could a half-dozen other majors with longer track records and more prestigious artist rosters. They'd have to come up with something special. Larry Newton had a simple but brilliant idea. Everybody in the business knew that Ray wasn't a singer who needed help every step of the way; he really made his own records at Atlantic. Why not offer Ray a contract, not as an artist, but as a producer of his own records?

Newton's idea was breathtakingly original, but not because it meant a major label would be contracting with an independent producer. Big labels often leased masters produced by little labels, and ABC-Paramount had already made such a deal with Bob Marcucci of Philadelphia's Chancellor Records: Chancellor produced Fabian and Frankie Avalon's master tapes, and ABC-Paramount sold the records, keeping 20 percent as a distribution fee and passing 80 percent back to Marcucci. What made Newton's idea original was offering the deal to an artist. Marcucci, not Fabian and Avalon, got the 80 percent. They still got a 5 percent artist royalty or whatever Marcucci deigned to fork over. Newton was suggesting that ABC-Paramount treat Ray as if he were Marcucci, the artist as a businessman-producer. That had never happened before in the record business and has seldom happened since.

Newton's idea intrigued Clark and Levine. They'd have to work out the details, but they outlined enough for an excited Larry Myers to go back to Milt Shaw, and for Shaw in turn to tell Ray that the gentlemen over at ABC-Paramount wanted to meet him. They had a good deal cooking.

Ray Charles has always said, rightly, that the contract with ABC-Paramount came to him unsought, and that before it came he had not planned to leave Atlantic. For all his success, Ray had been, like most performing artists, relatively passive in business, signing any paper Jack Lauderdale put under his nose, and at Atlantic acceding, without deep investigation, to the terms of their contracts. Yet the invitation to a meeting at ABC came like a wake-up call, opening his eyes, slowly at first, to opportunities for himself and his music that even he, ambitious dreamer that he was, had never dreamed possible. "Sure I'd be interested in talking to them," Ray responded to Milt. "My mother always said, you can always talk to people, no harm in talking."

Ray came to the mid-October meeting with Jeff, Milt, and accountant Paul Orland. Meeting Ray for the first time, Newton noticed how restless he seemed, his body twisting back and forth, his hands waving with abandon. After the usual meet-and-greet palaver, Clark made his pitch. Ray would sell many more records on ABC, Clark said, and draw larger crowds at better clubs, white crowds as well as black. But in moving from an indy to a major the question really was: would it help Ray develop his full potential as an artist? They weren't trying to minimize Atlantic's role, but all that Ray had accomplished was now just the foundation of his future.

Clark spelled out ABC-Paramount's offer: the company would finance Ray's recording costs and put out the records, recouping their basic costs before sending Ray a dime. Records that did poorly might earn Ray little or nothing. But once a record got into the black, 75 cents of every dollar would go to Ray, Shaw Artists getting a 10 percent commission for brokering the deal. To show their faith in Ray's chance of success, they would guarantee him $50,000 a year for the three-year life of the contract.

Used to the cash economy of the road, Jeff liked the $1000-a-week guarantee. What got Ray's attention, however, was the 75–25 split. "Seven and a half cents out of every dime is a lot of goddamn money if you luck out," he realized. "They were giving it to me because I'd be producing my own music, but that was no big deal, I was doing that already. This was throwing the rabbit into the briar patch." Yet for the moment Ray's native caution prevailed. He asked Clark to write up the proposal for Shaw's lawyer, Earl Zaidens, to look over, and he felt obligated to give Ahmet and Jerry a chance to match it. Ray also had his own simple but brilliant idea. "Look," he said across the table, "since I'm producing my own music, I want to own my own masters."

Clark's jaw dropped, as did Levine's and Newton's. Give up the ownership of the master recordings? Master tapes were the ultimate source of a company's value, the right to lease them for reissue a source of long-term revenue. No company let its masters go unless bankruptcy forced it to sell off assets lock, stock, and barrel. "We've never done that before," were the first words the stunned Clark could speak, and the others echoed him. "We never do anything like that."

"I understand that, Mr. Clark," said Ray, "but that's what I'd like if I'm gonna produce my own records."

Ray would have accepted the deal as is, but Clark didn't know he was bluffing, and asked for time to think, promising to call with an answer. On their own, Clark and his two lieutenants argued it out: they wanted Ray for himself and as a magnet to attract other R&B and jazz artists. But was signing him worth giving up the precious masters? Clark and Levine weren't sure, but Newton said yes, if they made it eventual ownership: Ray could get the masters back in five years, plenty of time for ABC-Paramount to reap the first harvest. And because Ray was an addict, they should also build in a suspension clause as an extra level of protection. The contract required him to produce twelve tracks a year. If he fell behind, the contract year would keep running until he finished the full dozen.

Ray had no problem accepting the suspension clause; he felt confident that he'd never let heroin get in the way of his music. Nor was five years too long to wait to own the masters if, after that, he'd own them forever. Lawyer Earl Zaidens reviewed the proposal and saw at a glance that it gave Ray the chance to make a fortune. "It's a fabulous deal," he told Ray, "the kind of contract even Sinatra doesn't get."

Ray took the finished proposal to Ahmet and Jerry. If they'd match ABC-Paramount's offer, he'd stay, but he was sure they wouldn't, and they didn't. "We love you, Ray," Ahmet and Jerry blandly told Ray, "but we can't do that."

Ray took off to a gig in Detroit, leaving Ahmet and Jerry, beneath their cool exteriors, incredulous and angry at a betrayal too bitter to comprehend. It must be Jeff's fault, or Milt's. Ray would never leave them of his own accord. *They* had recognized Ray's talent when he was a nobody, a Nat Cole knockoff. *They* had given him the chance to grow, the freedom to record as he wished. Sure, Ray made great records, but *they* had pushed them relentlessly to dj's, distributors, and jazz writers, not just to make a buck for themselves, but out of their passionate belief that Ray's genius deserved to be heard by millions. Now, at the height of their shared success, Ray was stabbing them in the back, abandoning them for a soulless corporate giant. Did Ray think for an instant that Sam Clark cared about black music the way they did? Had that pushy s.o.b. Larry Newton ever sweated out an all-night session at Cosimo's in New Orleans? Never. Did Harry Levine know the difference between Earl Hines and Art Tatum? Of course not.

Ahmet and Jerry thought they'd hear from Ray again; this was just the first round. Meanwhile they fought back, releasing the *Genius* album the first week of November and sending out 3000 promotional EPs to dj's. They took a full-page ad for Ray in *Billboard*, their first ever, plugging "Movin' On," *Genius*, and a new album of hit singles, *What'd I Say. Genius* hit quickly with pop and jazz listeners, and "Movin' On" entered the pop chart at #96, jumped to #68, #55, and then higher.

Yet Thanksgiving came and went, and Atlantic still didn't hear from Ray. A buddy in the business called Ahmet and Jerry; he'd heard that Ray had signed with ABC-Paramount, the contract was already filed at the musicians' union. They called the union, and yes, they were told, Ray had signed a contract with ABC-Paramount. *Billboard* carried a bare-bones story on December 7, "AM-PAR SIGNS RAY CHARLES . . . thus ending an association of several years with Atlantic Records," and a week later gave details of the "exceptional" 75–25 split.

Ray was gone. Ahmet and Jerry took his silent departure as a personal rejection, "emotionally a great blow," Ahmet called it years later. Ray and he had been friends. How could Ray treat him so coldly, never give him a chance to develop a second offer? Looking back, Jerry realized that Ray had always kept his distance; maybe behind those shades was an egotistical bastard who cared about nothing but himself. He lay awake nights until dawn, staring at the ceiling and wondering what would become of the company, his job: "How could we lose Ray Charles and exist? If Ray could go, how the hell will we keep Bobby Darin, the MJQ?" Tom Dowd could hardly believe that a few months after engineering "What'd I Say" and *Genius,* two of the best records of his career, it was all ancient history. Even Miriam Abramson was furious. She had never really liked Ray, she realized. He used to go into the tiny bathroom at the old studio, and the sounds he made, banging around, maybe shooting up, had always disgusted her. Now she'd never forgive him.

Over at Shaw Artists, Lee, Milt, and Larry Myers were cheering too much over their 10 percent of Ray's new deal to shed tears for Atlantic. "Sure Wexler and Ertegun were upset," Myers remembered. "Ray had sold a bunch of records for them. But 'What'd I Say' was still selling, so were the albums, and of course they could keep repackaging the tracks they had, and by now we know how many times they've done that!" The Atlantic line that Ray had been hoodwinked was no more than sour grapes. "I would be glad to convince Ahmet and Jerry that Ray knew all about it," said Myers. "*Nobody* put anything over on Ray."

At this turning point in his life, Ray himself did little crowing or looking back. Nothing, he knew, lasted forever. Forward motion had become an ingrained habit of his life. It took him to places and away from places, into people's lives, out of people's lives. Jacksonville, Orlando, Seattle; Gossie, Mary Ann, and little Bill Peeples—how many more had come and gone, how many more would come and go? The crew at Atlantic had done what they could for him during the time he was with them; now that time was over. He'd never forget their help, and he'd always be proud of the work they had done together. They might collaborate again someday, who could tell? But making records was a business, and in business everybody made the best deal they could make at the time. "Seventy-five cents out of a dollar and owning my own masters, that's why I left Atlantic," Ray recalled years later. Friendship and sentiment had nothing to do with it. He was moving on; it was as simple as that.

In early December, Sam Clark invited Ray, Jeff, Milt, and Larry to an informal get-together at the ABC-Paramount office to celebrate the signing. On the way in Milt Shaw spoke quietly to Sid Feller, about to meet Ray for the first time. "Do me a favor," he said. "Ray is an odd man. He likes to do things his own way, at his own pace." That made sense to Feller, and he had a word with Clark: "Don't push him, okay? Don't ask him when he's going to record. When he's ready, he'll let us know." When Clark introduced Sid to Ray as his new record producer, Feller got an immediate impression of Ray's wariness with strangers. Ray, however, tried to break the ice. He'd be home in LA over Christmas, he said. Could Sid come to California over the holidays to talk and get acquainted? Feller said sure, though he'd miss his wedding anniversary at home. As everyone stood up to shake hands at the end of the meeting, Clark said, "So, Ray, when are you going to the studio and make us some records?" Feller, horrified, looked at Ray and saw his face get stiff. "When I'm ready I'll let you know," Ray said, annoyed. Sid grabbed his head and looked at Clark, his expression saying, "I *told* you to keep your mouth shut."

While the wheeling and dealing went on in New York, life rolled along in the band. Margie went home to Lula's apartment in Harlem to have her baby, and she gave birth to a boy, Charles Wayne, on October 1. Ray paid the bills, and Lula made him promise that he'd support the child, a promise that, in a rough-and-ready way, he kept. During Margie's months off, Mae Mosely came out on the road to replace her. This was Mae's chance, and she made the best of it. In no time, it seemed, Mae became Ray's main woman. Small, dark, and forceful, her black hair crudely straightened, Mae Mosely was "a tough piece of work," as Jeff's girlfriend Shirley remembered her. Like Eileen years before, Mae took care of Ray, did his hair and organized his clothes. She knew how to keep other women away, and she became gatekeeper to Ray's dressing room. Mae wanted to own Ray, Jeff thought. Others had tried and failed, yet Mae attracted Ray more powerfully than most. His time with Margie was coming to an end, his time with Mae beginning.

As always, more money meant more heroin. "Ray had the best," said Hank Crawford. "Big Hoss, Mule, they called it. Ray'd hit up, and it'd look like he was gonna croak over." Jeff hated heroin. What it did to Ray was Ray's business, but heroin created risks for the whole enterprise. Through the fall as the negotiations progressed, Jeff tried to crack down on drugs in the band, fearful that another Philadelphia might make ABC back away. They made it through by luck, not because anybody, including Ray, cleaned up his act.

Yet to many observers, even more amazing than the constant sex-and-drugs antics was how Ray developed a tight family feeling in the touring company. Old-timers and newcomers, the Raelets, the valets and drivers—Ray led them all. Ray's confidence and ambition drove them from gig to gig. As his music moved the crowds in the dark, it moved those working with him every night in the hot bright light of the stage. "He had us spellbound," Hank remembered. "He was a *general!* And blind! He was young, but we followed him as an older person. He was striking a big chord with the world, and we felt it with him."

Leroy Cooper, who hadn't found much work in Dallas, came back in on baritone sax, Ray switched Hank to alto, and the seven-piece band became an eight-piece band. Trumpeter Phil Guilbeau, a spare young man from Lafayette, Louisiana, joined the gang. Guilbeau, soon nicknamed "Bilbo," was a gambler, a drinker, a dignified clown, and a player with piercing-pure tone. Some said Guilbeau sounded like jazz great Clifford Brown, but inside he worried that he was a "flubby," a fellow who made too many mistakes.

Ray first heard Guilbeau playing lead trumpet in the house band at Washington's Howard Theatre and sent Edgar and Leroy to check him out. They approved, and word came a week later: call Ray. "I talked it over with a friend," Guilbeau remembered. "'Ray Charles wants me,' I said. 'You think I'm good enough?' My friend said, 'Man, you can work with anybody.' So I called Ray, and he said . . ." Here in telling his story, Guilbeau got on his feet and began to act out both parts, imitating Ray by slapping his thighs and talking in a raspy whisper. The rite that Guilbeau acted out, Ray played out with dozens of fellows over the years.

"Hey, uh-uh, yeah listen, I want you to come with me," said Ray. "I know what you can do, you fit my band to a T. How much will you need to join my band?"

"Oh, I'm sick of you bandleaders starving us to death on the road," said Phil.

"That's why I'm asking you what you need," said Ray. "I don't want you to come into my band and quit."

"Lemme see," Phil said. "Fathead been with you so long, I don't want more than Fathead. How much is Fathead getting?"

"Damn Fathead!" Ray shot back. "I pay everybody the same, $30 a night."

Thirty a night sounded okay to Phil, but he said, "Thirty on nights you're *working* don't sound like much to me."

"How much will you take, man?"

"Tell you what," said Guilbeau. "Just give me what Fathead makes." Ray said okay, and Phil joined the band. Come pay night three gigs later, there was only ninety dollars in his envelope. The band was deep in North Carolina, and Guilbeau had his hotel bill to pay.

"Shit!" he said. "I'm going home." Jeff saw Phil grabbing his stuff and told him to hold on, Ray wanted to talk to him. Phil waited for twenty minutes.

"You are doggone hard to please," said Ray when he came out. "I told you to tell me how much you want."

"This chump change ain't gonna hold me," said Phil. "I'm leaving before we get so far I can't make it back home."

At which point Ray, to Phil's surprise, changed his tack completely. "I been thinking of putting the band on salary," he said. "How does $175 a week guaranteed sound?"

That was just what the Apollo paid the house band, Phil knew, and, he calculated, it was better than $30 a night, because often Ray had gigs only three or four nights a week. On $175 a week, a fellow could get by without dragging. "Yeah," he told Ray, "that sounds a little better." Ray said he could tell everybody, $175 guaranteed from now on.

A few days later Jeff was pushing the Weenie through gathering dusk, late for a gig, and the gang sat craned forward in their seats, tense about making it to the club on time. Suddenly Phil burst out laughing. John Hunt turned around, scowling. "What are you laughing at?" he asked.

"You all," said Phil. "We don't have to worry no more about getting anywhere on time, we're on *salary* now!"

As soon as the ABC-Paramount deal was signed, Milt Shaw and Larry Myers started looking for better gigs for Ray. A promoter in LA, Hal Zeiger, had big plans. Zeiger said he'd put Ray on at the Palladium, Sunday, January 10, 1960, and he wanted to talk about similar dates in other cities, a concert tour maybe; he hoped to make a lot of money for Ray. That sounded good to Myers. Ray's one-nighter price was already up to $1500, and on the white circuit it would zoom. Ray had taken a big gamble leaving Atlantic, Myers knew, but it was paying off. The agent sometimes observed Ray get quiet around other people, sink into himself. He read steady courage in Ray's silence, and it made him determined to sell Ray even harder and make his gamble pay off even bigger.

Ray, the Raelets, and the band got to LA a few days before Christmas. Seldom home with Della and the boys during the year, Ray tried to make up by being with them on Hepburn over the holidays. But that didn't mean he stopped working. Most days, riding in his purple '59 fishtail Cadillac, Ray picked up Hank Crawford at the Watkins Hotel and brought him over to Hepburn Avenue to take dictation of new charts. "I was like a houseguest," Crawford remembered. "I'd spend the whole day there sitting in their front room writing. Sometimes Ray'd go upstairs and not come back for three or four hours. When he came back, I'd still be there—I was young, I didn't mind! Della fed me in the kitchen, she was a great southern-style cook. When Ray got tired, I'd go back to the hotel, and the next day I'd go write some more. It got to a point where he'd write, I'd write, and nobody would know where he stopped and I began."

Sid Feller got out to LA a few days later, and he too spent several days with Ray at Hepburn. Feller had known little about Ray before he came to ABC-Paramount. "I liked Frank Sinatra, never listened to R&B," Feller remembered. "Ray was an absolutely new experience." Feller had a genial nature and an open mind to match his rounded form, and the first day he and Ray spent hours talking about God, politics, and everything in between. Sid met Della and the boys, and he told them about his wife Gert and their children in New York. The second day they talked about music, and Sid told Ray about scratching out his first arrangement for the Brooklyn Boy Scout band and how he gave up the trumpet when he realized he'd never play like Louis Armstrong. Ray in turn told Sid his plans and ideas. He wanted to do more recordings like the *Genius* album, to come out of little-band R&B and do more pop. Sid soon understood that Ray was going to run his own show.

On the third day, Ray said, "Let's record." From that moment Feller dates a musical collaboration that would last for thirty years. "Not when we met in New York, and not the first day when we talked, but when he said, 'Let's record.' That minute something clicked in Ray. He must have said to himself, 'I'll trust this man.' Ray trusted very few people, but now he believed that I would be honest with him, that I'd do nothing to hurt him and would do the best I could to help him. That day we became friends."

Sid booked time at Hollywood's Capitol Studios for December 29, and Ray brought in the gang and three songs he had arranged with Hank. It turned out to be a weak session. Supervising from the booth, Sid felt nervously aware that he didn't know when and when not to offer suggestions. Capitol had a three- not an eight-track machine, and he could tell that it cramped Ray's style. Of the songs, only "Them That Got" had hit potential. Like Louis Jordan's best songs, "Them That Got" wryly captures the puzzlement of a poor Joe who knows that "them that's got is them that gets," but:

> *If you gotta have something*
> *Before you get something*
> *How you get your first*
> *Is still a mystery to me!*

Ten years before in rainy Seattle, Ray could have put himself in Joe's position with hardly a strain on his imagination. By the end of the 50s, however, he had gotten his first together, even his second and third, and had become one of them that keep on get-ting. He had been picking out new Cadillacs every year for years by feeling the head-lights, the doors, and the dashboard. He had his silk suits and tuxedos custom-made and carried seven with him when he traveled. "I know exactly what I like," he told a *Tan* magazine reporter, "and I know what I want." His success could be attributed to one simple fact: "I work hard."

So it didn't matter that his first ABC session had been a semi-bust. In the 1960s, he'd be starting all over again, with money in his pocket, a major label behind him, and a growing audience eager to hear whatever he had to say. Who would dare put a limit on what he might accomplish in the decade ahead?

PART IV

THE 1960s:
THE ABC YEARS

Georgia on
My Mind
1960

Nineteen sixty marks the beginning of Ray Charles' Midas years, years when, after a decade struggling upward, he reached the top. Through the 1960s Ray Charles circled the globe, and fans of every nation showered him with gold. He began to live as a prince of the modern city, a life not without danger.

Ray's decade opened on January 10 at the Hollywood Palladium, his second gig at the Sunset Strip club and his first booked by Hal Zeiger. "The Most Creative Musical Giant of the Generation!" Zeiger headlined the newspaper ads. "RAY CHARLES and His Orchestra and Entertainers, Playing His Hit Records *in Person!*" The show sold out, and Zeiger began to play a major role in Ray's career. According to one who knew him well, Hal Zeiger was a "hard-hitting guy who loved music and money and managed to make both." Tall, balding, and possessed of a "do it my way" manner, Zeiger had started in show business promoting a show called the Borschtcapades, but he soon saw bigger money in black music. By 1956 he was booking R&B shows in El Monte and sharing an office at Hollywood and Vine with bandleader Johnny Otis. Zeiger's simple but brilliant idea was that he could make a fortune by shaping Ray Charles, king of the black dance halls, into a class act that he could present to integrated audiences in the top theaters and concert halls of any big city in America. For the next four years Zeiger did just that, promoting shows for Ray in dozens of cities, renting the hall, taking out ads in white as well as black newspapers, and bankrolling advance expenses. Zeiger did not immediately become Shaw's prime customer for Ray's talents; Milt and Larry Myers continued selling Ray to the chitlin circuit. But throughout 1960 and for years to come, Zeiger booked the best-paid and most prestigious of Ray's engagements.

Sid Feller brought a tape of the LA session back to New York, and his bosses hated it. Clark, the understated executive, merely frowned and grunted, but Newton, the blustery salesman, exploded. "The worst piece of shit I ever heard in my life," he told Sid. The band was too small, the feeling too bluesy. It might sell down south, but not to the white urban/suburban audience Clark and Levine had in mind. Obligated, however, to release anything Ray submitted unless obscene, they put a good face on their disappointment and took a full-page ad in *Billboard* to declare "pride and pleasure in welcoming Ray Charles, one of today's truly great recording stars," and to announce "what promises to be one of the year's 2-sider successes, 'My Baby' / 'Who You Gonna Love.'" "We pressed 5000 copies," Larry Newton remembers, "and we didn't sell one." To add insult to injury, Atlantic put out "Let the Good Times Roll" from the *Genius* album, and its single touched the Pop chart as ABC's debut single sank like a stone.

Those 5000 records, however, carried a new credit, "Published by Tangerine Music," Ray's new publishing company, named for his favorite fruit, and this credit, in time, far outweighed the single's failure. Atlantic's Progressive Music had published Ray's original music, paying him fifty cents of every dollar earned, for example, by the many cover versions of "Hallelujah I Love Her So." Like Irving Berlin before him, Ray hung out his shingle on Tin Pan Alley; now he'd keep the whole dollar from "My Baby." Tangerine Music moved Ray a big step up the music business food chain: all royalties from record sales and airplay would be paid direct to Tangerine, and anyone who wanted to use Tangerine songs would have to deal with him personally.

Ray and Jeff talked over the new business moves through long afternoons rolling east to Atlanta. Producing and publishing excited Ray. Steady-going Jeff knew how to get cash on the barrelhead from a backwoods promoter at 2 A.M., and he had done okay with Ahmet and Jerry. But the amounts Ray was talking about were bigger and the contracts behind them more complex. Jeff felt out of place in lawyers' offices and corporate boardrooms; he had approved the ABC-Paramount contract without reading the fine print. Jeff was also still on salary, not a percentage, and Ray didn't want to cut his manager in on the record money. "When the question came up, Ray told me I wouldn't get anything from the record deal," Jeff remembered years later. "But he said he'd give me 12 ½ percent of the publishing company." An eighth of the publishing didn't sound like much to Jeff, but he accepted it. When Tangerine affiliated with BMI, Jeff D. Brown was listed as a minority owner. Yet the whole thing remained papers between Ray and the lawyers that Jeff didn't fully understand. Jeff was still Ray's manager, but now Ray was managing without him.

That winter Elvis came back from the army and John F. Kennedy started running for president. *Billboard* reported that in 1959 albums had outsold singles for the first time, 6 million to 4.75 million, and Ray put weeks into planning his first album for ABC-Paramount. *Genius* and the jazz albums had balanced ballads and up-tempo tunes, but otherwise had been arranged in no particular way. Ray wanted to give this album a theme, and he came up with a simple one: place songs. Soon he had a list, "Moonlight in Vermont," "Alabamy Bound," "California, Here I Come," and others in the same vein. Riding in the Caddy, he often broke into Hoagy Carmichael's "Georgia on My Mind." One day his driver said, "Why don't you record that?" and "Georgia" got added to the list. As before, Ray made up demo tapes and sent them to Ralph Burns. Sid scheduled two sessions at the end of March. Ray flew to Detroit after the first to meet the gang for a gig, then flew back to New York with the Raelets for the second.

The first night was a near disaster. Burns had gathered an orchestra of thirty-five and a chorus of twenty voices. Ray was due at nine o'clock. Nine o'clock came and no Ray Charles. Larry Newton paced the booth, sweating the double overtime for the musicians. Sid watched the clock. Ten o'clock. No Ray. At eleven o'clock Ray walked in on Mae's arm, high as a kite. Nobody said a word.

Ray sat down at the piano. Burns got everyone in their places, lifted his baton, and brought it down for the first beat of "Georgia." The orchestra didn't come in. "What's going on?" he whispered, and the violinists pointed at Ray, sitting on the piano bench, oblivious to everything but Mae, who had taken off his shoes and socks, and, on her knees, was scratching his feet with her long painted nails. Larry Newton saw blood coming out of Ray's ankles and couldn't believe his eyes. A long silent moment passed, and then Ray turned to the mike, suddenly ready to work. They did twenty takes of "Georgia," tears at times streaming down Ray's cheeks. Finally he was satisfied, but in the days and months ahead he'd kick himself for details he could have improved. At the second session they got down a rocking "Alabamy Bound," and "Carry Me Back to Old Virginny," done gospel-style like "Swanee River Rock." Sid was struck by how close Ray stuck to the melodies. "For a jazz singer, he took surprisingly few liberties. Ray added his own textures, but if you listen to 'Moon Over Miami,' he's singing the melody as written, not the ad-lib version you'd get from Dinah Washington."

Even Ray couldn't make "New York's My Home" a distinguished song, and somehow the lively "California Here I Come" came out sounding routine. Yet every track had the professional gloss ABC-Paramount was looking for, and Ray's simple album theme worked. The place songs embrace America coast to coast, and Ray sings them with the voice of experience: in ten years on the road he'd been to all these places and many in between. Notably, seven of the twelve songs paint the South, and of these, "Georgia on My Mind" stands out. The song, a classic American pop song, has a blues-inflected melody by Hoagy Carmichael and a lyric by Stuart Gorrell that says much with little:

> *Georgia, Georgia,*
> *A song of you*
> *Comes sweet and clear*
> *As moonlight through the pines.*

Burns' arrangement gives hushed, tremulous support to Ray's vocal; the bass and offbeat guitar create a dreamy dance-band pulse, and Ray packs every note, every syllable, with palpable, personal content. Is Georgia a girl or the singer's native state? Ray makes them one, singing to the land and women who gave him birth, to Georgia and Greenville, to Retha and Mary Jane, to his own lost childhood. Ray invests the lyric with so much of his own life that, by art's mysterious chemistry, he conveys the universal yearning for home, for the road to the past that we can retrace only in our dreams.

Clark and Newton loved the album and titled it *Genius Hits the Road.* They made plans to release it in the summer.

That spring, in cities all over the South, Negro students sat in at white lunch counters in Woolworth 5 & 10 cent stores, singing "We Shall Overcome" and refusing to leave until they were served. In the new decade, Negroes north and south felt a new determination to end Jim Crow once and for all. With leaders like Roy Wilkins, Martin Luther King Jr., and Malcolm X, with the energy of idealistic students, and with the growing sympathy of many whites, the time seemed ripe for "Freedom Now!" As the 60s progressed, the civil rights movement became a "nonviolent" war, fought in Congress and in the streets, with its own celebrated battlefields and honored dead.

Ray, working nonstop, continued to watch the civil rights struggle from the sidelines. The more he heard the news on radio and TV, the more he liked what Reverend King had to say and how he said it. Ray felt a kinship with King, another Southern Baptist, another ambitious black man only one year older than himself. Though no churchgoer, Ray had kept the hard-bitten religious faith instilled by Retha and Jellyroll's tin-roof Baptist church. He played his gospel tapes Sunday mornings, read and reread his Braille Bible, and said the Lord's Prayer most nights before he fell asleep. This core of Ray's character responded to King's eloquent faith. Yet, being perpetually wary and playing his own game to capture world attention, Ray avoided close involvement with King or civil rights politics. "I am an entertainer," he said many times, "a musician, not a politician." For Ray, political benefits were just one-nighters the promoter wanted him to play for free. "Ray hated benefits," Larry Myers remembered. "He'd tell me, 'When the stagehands and the ushers work for nothing, that's when I'll work for nothing.' " As the 60s developed, Ray maintained that distance from the civil rights movement, at the same time that, personally and musically, he contributed to its course.

From a barnstorming tour of the Midwest in April, Ray and the gang got back to New York for a session making singles. This time Ray went back to bare-bones blues: "Sticks and Stones" sounds like an Atlantic track circa 1958. Not what ABC was looking for, but it had "What'd I Say" 's catchy beat, and they got it out mid-May. Atlantic again put out a competitive single, "Just for a Thrill." As the two releases battled on the charts through June, Ray and the gang joined the "Hitmakers of 1960" tour.

Like the "Fantabulous" tour of 1957, "Hitmakers" was a Shaw Artists package, but this time Ray headlined with Ruth Brown, the Drifters, and comedian Redd Foxx in support. A roly-poly jokester named Roy "Duke" Wade worked the tour as Ruth Brown's personal manager. At the Tivoli Theatre in Chicago, Brown told him she wanted the star's dressing room. It was lined with mirrors, and what did Ray need mirrors for? But Ray did want it, and he was the star. Moods turned icy until Jeff talked to Duke and Duke spoke to Brown. She gave way, and harmony was restored. "When the tour ended, Ray said he liked the way I took care of business," Wade remembered, "and he asked me if I'd work for him as his valet. I said okay. I stayed with him for three years, and me and Ray became like brothers."

Only a week after he started, at the Newport Jazz Festival, Duke had his baptism by fire. By this time the festival had become a Fourth of July event that attracted, as well as jazz fans, college kids looking for a boozy good time. As Ray started his set, kids and police were engaged in a pitched bottle-throwing battle outside the stadium. Inside, as Ray built to a climax with "What'd I Say," the audience went crazy. "They were doing the unnh-unnh, oooh-ooohs, it sounded like religious chanting," Duke remembered. "I was standing in the wings, and George Wein was shouting at me, 'Take him off, he's holding a revival meeting out there!' But I let Ray go on, and he played some ballads and cooled everybody off."

From Newport, with stops in Atlantic City, in Chicago, and at the Mambo Club in Wichita, Kansas, the caravan rolled to LA and a month off the road. Ray stayed home on Hepburn Avenue and Della got pregnant. "The Twist" by Chubby Checker held #1 against all comers that summer. Ray had no hit to challenge Checker's, yet he was beginning to saturate the charts with a continuing multi-record presence. *Genius Hits the Road* got off to a good start. Atlantic's *Genius* album had begun an eighty-two-week run on the album charts; *Ray Charles in Person* kept it company for thirty-seven weeks. "Sticks and Stones" squeaked to #2 R&B ahead of Atlantic's "Just for a Thrill," and hit #40 on the Pop chart, which the Atlantic disc didn't reach at all. Another favorable sign: *Downbeat* put Ray on its cover for the first time; the effusive piece painted a sharp picture of Ray smoking:

> [Ray] smokes incessantly, lighting one cigaret after another. He uses a pocket lighter. Usually it lights but sometimes it doesn't. But Ray cannot see the flame when it does, and when the lighter fails, there is a long agonizing moment as you watch him try to light a cigaret without fire.

Like the De Soto before it, the Weenie had at last become an unreliable rattletrap, and Ray took advantage of the long LA layover to junk it. Jeff flew to Ohio and drove back in a brand-new Flexible bus. The Flex gave everybody breathing room for a change and had space for Ray's new Hammond B-3 organ. Buying the Flex soaked up about $20,000 of Ray's burgeoning income as a tax-deductible business expense, and he put $40,000 more into a long-term dream: his first airplane, a used twin-engine, five-passenger Cessna 310, call letters 3657 Delta. Ray's decade of endless driving was over. As the Flex lumbered along the highway carrying the fellows from gig to gig, Ray began to hop the same distances in the Cessna, piloted by Detroiter Tom McGarrity, one of very few black Air Force veterans. Sometimes Mae, Jeff, Duke, or a favored member of the band accompanied them. "Ray loved that little Cessna," Duke Wade remembered. "He'd sit beside Tom, asking questions, feeling the dials, damn near flying the thing. On the ground, he always had his head under the cowling. He knew all its parts."

After a second sellout Zeiger gig at the Hollywood Palladium in August, Ray recorded his second album for ABC. Again he had a simple theme: girl songs, from "Hard-hearted Hannah" to "Sweet Georgia Brown." This time the noted West Coast jazz arranger Marty Paich did the charts, another blend of big-band and string/choral numbers. Like Burns, Paich conducted at the sessions, and again Sid oversaw everything from the booth. This time there were no disasters. In his fourth session with Ray, Sid felt more confident making suggestions. "Do you think it would be better if we tried . . . ?" he'd say. Ray would stiffen warily, saying, "No, I worked it out, forget it." Two takes later, he might try the idea and even keep it. "Ray thought everything through," Sid recalled. "But let's face it, not everything we do in life, even when we think it out, is utter perfection. So I learned how to suggest a solution when something wasn't working. See, we were trying to make the best record possible, not him trying to please me or me please him. With me and Ray, nobody was boss."

The smooth session created a smooth record, *Dedicated to You. Dedicated*'s mood is more romantic than *Genius Hits the Road,* but otherwise the albums are much the same: one theme, half big band, half strings and chorus; strong songs and weak songs, but strong or weak, pop music as polished as it comes. Paich's arrangements give Ray all the brass and velvet any singer could ask for, and Ray responds with one flawless vocal after another, getting raunchy with "Hard-hearted Hannah," then tender with "Nancy with the Laughing Face." Ray colors his voice with burrs and rasps, but his diction is a model of clarity, his long, well-supported vowels cut off with well-articulated consonants:

> . . . *a great symphonic the-e-e-e-e-m*
> *That's Stella by starlight and not a dre-e-e-e-m*

Overall, however, *Dedicated to You* demonstrates how difficult a task Ray had set himself: to make passionate albums in the polished pop mode. Perfect charts perfectly played would not guarantee success. A subtle chemistry was required, a blend of the elements that came together on "Georgia": a lyric and melody dramatic enough for Ray to explore, a mood resonant enough for the orchestra to amplify. On this album, the sex-drenched "Ruby" best finds that empathetic blend, and Ray brings to it the musky knowledge, the ache and whisper, of a thousand liaisons.

▮▮▮▮▮▮▮▮▮

A few days after finishing *Dedicated to You,* Ray and company headed east, on the road again. ABC-Paramount took a big ad in *Billboard* designed to look like a telegram to distributors: "Tremendous reaction two sides from Ray Charles album, *Genius Hits the Road* . . . 'Georgia on My Mind' and 'Carry Me Back to Old Virginny.' Tested in Chicago and San Francisco. Fantastic response." A tag line below read, "Just listen to the Records. Nuff said." The review in the same issue concurred: "Ray Charles packs a powerful emotional wallop on 'Georgia,' with violins and chorus giving backing a big sound. Flip has true gospel feeling."

"Carry Me Back," in fact, was destined to remain an obscure B-side, but "Georgia" began to make its mark in September. As the Cessna and the Flex worked their way, "Georgia" appeared at #9 on the "Bubbling Under" chart. Ray turned the string/voices arrangement into a band chart featuring Fathead on flute, and they started playing it at every show. Coming through Chicago, he and Fathead performed it on *Playboy's Penthouse,* Hugh Hefner's syndicated television show—Ray's TV debut. On September 26, as Ray and company opened two nights at Detroit's Birdland, "Georgia" entered the Hot 100 at #94.

As "Georgia" rose to #59, then #24 and #13, *Ebony,* the *Life* magazine of black America, gave Ray its seal of approval with a long positive article. The first of many such, it told the tale of Greenville and Mr. Pit, D&B and taking off for Seattle. Ray's fans loved his "funk," *Ebony* declared, "that mixture of raw emotional ingredients with which Charles can send the listener to the dizzy heights of joy, or mire him in the pit of despair." Jazz musicians revered Ray as they did Charlie Parker and Billie Holiday: "Ray is the earth," said drummer Chico Hamilton. By now, *Ebony* reported, one-nighters earned Ray $1000 plus a percentage of the gross, a week at a theater up to $10,000, and in 1959 he had grossed "well over $100,000." He had come up "the slow way" to success, said Ray, but that had its advantages: "People see your name on the jukebox and say, 'There's another Ray Charles,' or they walk into a record store and they remember you. . . . Even though you haven't had a smash hit, people are as familiar with you as their own phone number."

"Georgia" broke through to #4 in the first week of November. As the nation elected John F. Kennedy president, Ray and the gang were playing the Howard Theatre in Washington. Frank Tenot, the French jazz journalist who had played Ray's records on the radio, was seeing America for the first time, and he drove from New York to Washington to hear them. On the way south the car radio played "Georgia" at least twice an hour. The desk clerk at the Willard Hotel had never heard of the Howard, and a ticket agent warned Tenot to avoid the "bad neighborhood." A black cabdriver, however, got him there, and when he stepped out, the theater doorman whisked him, the only white patron, to the head of the line and let him in free. Inside he found an ambience that, as he wrote in Paris' *Jazz Magazine,* "couldn't be compared either with Carnegie Hall or with Birdland." Workaday black people filled the theater, as did the heavy smells of buttered popcorn and cheap perfume. Sitting beside him was an enormous woman, "a living portrait of Ma Rainey," who, while dishing out Cokes and ice cream to her ravenous kids, kept a watchful eye on the sharply dressed young blades flirting with her teenage daughter. A Three Stooges movie on the screen got a few laughs, but no one paid much attention until organist Jimmy Smith opened the live show. Through Betty Carter's and the Coasters' sets, excitement built in the theater. The curtain then closed, and to the throbbing beat of a hidden rhythm section, one of the Coasters danced out. "And now, he is here, the man you have been waiting for, he's come here just for you, you know who I'm talking about, yes, the Genius."

"Yeah! Yeah!" came Ray's voice through offstage speakers, and the audience cheered wildly as the curtain opened to reveal the band rocking through "Yes Indeed," enormous Leroy Cooper on baritone sax and *"fidèle"* Edgar Willis on bass. Four Raelets in low-cut green dresses stood swaying around a mike, swinging their bottoms and bosoms.

> . . . behind a tiny electric piano that sounds like a guitar at times,
> sat Ray Charles. His dead eyes and his temples are hidden by
> enormous glasses which are almost a mask. He's dressed in a
> sumptuous tuxedo with silk lapels. He sways from right to left,
> smiles, grimaces rather, moves his legs under him and, keeping
> the music going without losing tempo, he adjusts the volume of
> his voice and his instrument with an amplifier next to his piano.

Ray played all his hits that night, making "Georgia" last six minutes, the audience adding to the music by singing along and clapping on the backbeat. "From time to time," Tenot wrote, "Ray pulls from the bottom of his throat a sombre note that he modulates tragically, moving you in the marrow of your bones."

Afterward Tenot went backstage and talked to Ray. "Ray was excited that someone came to hear him from France," Tenot remembered years later. "He told me his life story, how he worked like a dog to make it all by himself." Tenot told Ray that many French fans loved his blues-gospel-jazz, and that he hoped to promote a Ray Charles concert in Paris. Ray laughed and said, "I'm ready whenever you get it together." The next week Tenot was Nesuhi's guest in the Atlantic studio when John Coltrane recorded *My Favorite Things,* and he went back to France satisfied that he had heard the latest and best in American jazz and R&B.

Then, on November 14, "Georgia on My Mind" pushed out the Drifters' "Save the Last Dance for Me" and reached #1. Eleven years after "Confession Blues," Ray had the most popular record in the country. Elvis was also riding high with "Are You Lonesome Tonight?" and *Billboard* noted Ray's #1 with a short piece linking them: "Ray Charles and Elvis Hit with Sweet Stuff; two pioneers of the rock 'n' roll school are bigger than ever on *Billboard*'s Hot 100, and they're doing it with ballads."

Every week has its number-one hit, and since weeks and hits slip away like falling leaves and fading flowers, one can easily forget the musical challenge involved in coming up with a song, a sound, a few catchy notes that will propel a record to number one. "*Nobody* knows what makes a hit record," Ray Charles has said many times, and it is true. The American public has taken to heart songs and sounds from the entire musical spectrum, and may embrace a tune next week no one could predict today. Ignoring for a moment commercial factors like promotion and payola, what *musical* factors will get a song played on so many radios and record players, sung in so many showers, that it becomes an "air" borne by the breeze to every ear, a sound declared by popular acclaim to be, forever, a sound of that time? "What'd I Say" succeeded as a raucous dance number, all sex and sweat. "Georgia on My Mind" succeeded as a poignant ballad that evokes the universal yearning for home. The words and music of "Georgia," already thirty years old in 1960, look back to times past. The sunset colors of Ray's voice, the strings and chorus, underscore its nostalgic appeal. Millions of listeners surrendered willingly to the force of "Georgia" 's unforced beauty, feeling a bond of sympathy with its unseen singer. For black listeners, this sympathetic bond with Ray was nothing new; they knew "Drown in My Own Tears" and "A Fool for You." The great white audience, however, had known only Ray's happy hits like "I Got a Woman," and now first heard Ray's brooding side. With "Georgia on My Mind" Ray began to plumb not only the black American soul, but the soul of the country.

Clark and Newton, of course, were delighted. "Georgia" was what they had wanted all along; this was the start of the big payoff. The single's success swelled the sales of the album: *Genius Hits the Road* reached the LP chart in mid-October, peaked at #9, and stayed on well into the new year. "Georgia" also helped pull "Ruby," the second release from the album, up to a respectable #28 by December. Atlantic's latest Ray single, "Come Rain or Come Shine," had lasted only two weeks on the Pop chart, and its nine Ray Charles albums all lagged below *Genius Hits the Road.* Larry Newton crowed that they had trounced Ahmet and Jerry once and for all.

What Ray felt about hitting #1 is harder to chart than the charts. All who know him agree: Ray Charles loves to compete and he *loves* to win. "Georgia" at #1 made a sweet victory indeed. Ray loved the growing size and excitement of his audiences, and he loved the growing money for itself and for the plans it made possible. Yet the long battle to the top had imbued Ray with a certain stoicism: he had learned to take good times and bad with a grain of salt. Since he truly didn't know what record would hit, he put his all into all of them and left the rest to fate and the record company. Often Ray was intent either on a new woman or his next fix, or slumped in a heroin rush and not thinking about "Georgia," success, or much of anything at all. Overall, as Hank Crawford put it, "Ray cared and he didn't care about success. Somebody'd tell him a record was number so 'n 'so this week, and he'd say, 'That's nice.' " A number-one record, another dream ticked off, then onward. He was already making new demo tapes to send to Quincy Jones and Ralph Burns for the big-band album coming up.

That fall Ray and company played gigs up and down the East Coast, returning to New York when they had a few days off. The band members, whose salaries had not increased with Ray's earnings, stayed with lady friends or at the Flanders, a musicians' hotel on Seventh Avenue near Times Square that rented hole-in-the-wall rooms for $30 a week. "Lloyd Price's band stayed there, Slide Hampton's," Leroy Cooper remembered. "So many cats practicing, the halls sounded like a studio." Manny's, a good music store, was a block away. Across the street a Greek restaurant offered a bowl of goulash and a roll for a buck that did as well for breakfast as for dinner. They sometimes stopped by Lula Hendricks' big apartment on West 111th Street for plates of greens and beans southern-style. Margie stayed there with her big sister, spending time with baby Charles Wayne, now a one-year-old.

Ray stayed in a suite at the Hotel Theresa, the "Waldorf of Harlem" on 125th Street, but he didn't see much of Margie or little Charles Wayne. That fall in New York were the months of Mae's ascendance. Mae wanted a fur coat, Ray got her a fur coat. Mae wanted to move into Manhattan from Flushing, and Ray rented her a $250-a-month, two-bedroom apartment in a new complex of buildings at Central Park West and Ninety-seventh Street. "How much money do you make?" the rental agent asked Ray. "You'll have to ask Duke," he replied. "Three hundred thousand dollars a year," said Duke. "Are you joking?" she said. He wasn't, and Mae moved in. Duke didn't like Mae much. "Once I saw her wearing Ray's platinum watch, and then she said she lost it, that it must have gone downstairs with the guy who picked up the clothes. So I called down and the only thing they found in Ray's suit was a stick of reefer. The guy brought it up and said, 'You lost your cigarette!' I never said nothing about that watch, didn't even tell Jeff about it. Ray never said anything either, so I figured, it's not my business. She was his woman."

The December *Jazz Magazine* published Frank Tenot's piece. Its observant details and rapturous conclusion—"Ray Charles knows that his voice helps us discover a more powerful light, one that shines deep in a great soul"—stirred increased interest in bringing Ray to France. *Playboy* ran a boxed paragraph and picture of Ray, introducing him to its audience of college-age white kids as "the moaning, moving singer-pianist [who] has a firm lock on what has come to be called 'soul' jazz." For Ray's third ABC-Paramount album, Sid booked time two days after Christmas at a studio in New Jersey.

This time producer Creed Taylor, head of ABC's new jazz label, Impulse, called the Count Basie band, minus the Count, to play Jones' and Burns' charts—they had come a long way, Sid realized, from the little blues session in LA a year before. Ray wanted to play organ for his first time on record, and he also wanted Phil Guilbeau to take the big trumpet solos. When the album came out, titled *Genius + Soul = Jazz*, Guilbeau's name was all over the credits as "Ray Charles' discovery Phillip Guilbeau." The album's success has given Guilbeau a footnote in jazz history, and it's fitting to let "Bilbo" tell the story of how it happened.

"I was in Washington, out of the band at the moment, when Jeff called me from the road," Guilbeau remembered years later.

"Ray wants you in New York," said Jeff.

"When?" said Phil.

"Tomorrow evening."

"Where's the band?"

"Not the band, just you. Six o'clock at Mae's place."

At 5:30 Phil knocked on the door, and Mae opened it. "Oh, Ray, Phil's here," she called into a bedroom, and Ray called back, "Have a seat, Phil, I'll be out in a minute." An hour later Ray appeared on Mae's arm, saying, "Ready to go, get your horn, man."

Where to? Phil didn't know. They took the elevator down to the garage and Mae's bathtub Corvair with the motor in the back. When Ray had offered to buy Mae the car of her choice, the fellows hadn't understood why she asked for a little Corvair, not a Jaguar; then they figured it was to impress Ray that she wasn't greedy. Phil got into the back seat, Ray sitting beside him and saying nothing. Mae drove a long way until Phil was completely lost. "Finally I said, 'What's going on?' Ray says, 'Phil, we're doing a few tracks, and you're gonna play me a few tasty cuts.' "

When they got to the studio, Phil sat on a bench against the wall and looked around. "I say to myself, hey, that's Clark Terry, Marshall Royal, Snooky Young—man, it's the whole Basie band!"

Years later Guilbeau would play in the Basie band, but now he shivered like a greenhorn. "These were hard-hitters. If I said hi to them on the street in New York, they'd pass me by like I was nothing." The studio was cold, and Phil was blowing on his icy trumpet, trying to warm it up, when he heard Quincy Jones say, "Phil, we're waiting on you."

The others had their chart books open. Phil opened his and found it blank but for a big "A" and "B."

"Hot dog," Phil shouted. "What am I supposed to play?"

"I didn't have time to write anything out," said Jones, "but Ray wants you to play the solos."

"How can I blow solos, you don't even have titles on here," said Phil.

"Ray says you can handle it," Jones replied, and Ray chimed in, "Yeah, man, don't worry about it."

Phil was well and truly on the spot, all the more so because, as everybody knew, Bilbo had a big mouth. "I used to go around saying, 'I'm the world's greatest trumpet player,' and calling the other guys flubbies. Guys got annoyed at me. Now I had to put up or shut up."

"Phil, you ready?" said Ray. "If you're ready, Ray, I'm ready," cried Phil, thinking to himself, "My horn is still cold, but hell, now all these guys are gonna hear me play, I'm gonna *blow.*" The other fellows could see the emotions working in his face. "You okay, man?" said one. "Yeah, yeah," said Phil.

"Step over there," said Jones. "Okay, the tune is 'Let's Go,' you blow after Frank Foster." Jones clapped off a driving up-tempo, Roy Haynes exploded on drums, and the band was off, Ray skittering on organ through the crosscutting riffs. Foster ripped off a red-hot solo, and Phil started to lift his trumpet to his lips. Thad Jones put a hand on his arm to say, "Wait, we play one more round before you." As the blaring band rocketed to his entrance, Phil felt a rising confidence. Jones caught his eye and signaled, "Noww—go!"

" 'Whee-ee-ee-a-dee, dah-wee-dah,' I started," Guilbeau remembered years later, the pleasure still fresh. "I'm thinking, 'Boy, you're playing some mean trumpet today.' " When they finished, Jones let out a yelp of relief, and the fellows started shouting, "Ooowee, Ray, where'd you get this guy?" Ray laughed, and Phil thought, "That sucker knows what I can do better than I do."

"What you think, Ray," asked Jones, "you wanna take another one real quick?"

"I was the only one stumbling," said Ray. "Everybody else was cut and dried. Let's go to the next one."

For the rest of the session, Guilbeau kept leaping blind into the music, and the insouciant solos he came up with highlight *Genius + Soul = Jazz,* a ripsnorting album that harks back to the glory days of the big bands. Phil could relax only when, listening to the playbacks, he could hear how good he sounded. Tony Bennett had dropped by the studio and came up to shake Phil's hand. "He was saying, 'Man, can you play that horn, blah blah blah,' and I was thinking, 'Now I'm one of the greats.' " In memory, however, the terrors of the session loomed as large as its triumphs. "The last thing I got to say about Mr. Charles," Guilbeau concluded, "is that the best and worst thing that ever happened to me was the day we made *Genius + Soul = Jazz.*"

After the session everybody flew out to California. Mae had had Ray to herself all fall, and she didn't want him to go. She had just gotten pregnant, she told him; she was his wife now. Ray told her he loved her and promised to come back. Then, despite her tears and threats, he pulled himself away. He got home to the visibly pregnant Della and the two boys on Hepburn for a late and awkward Christmas. Della didn't know exactly what had been going on in New York, but she could tell that much of Ray's heart and mind was elsewhere.

All told, however, 1960 had been a year of triumph for Ray and the team behind him. From ABC-Paramount came a year-end check for nearly $800,000, more money than Ray had seen in one piece in his life. A check for 10 percent of that also arrived at the Shaw agency, making a splash at 565 Fifth Avenue that Larry Myers never forgot. "Shaw had never made $80,000 from an artist's recording contract before, never!" he said years later, still proud of helping to engineer the coup that made it possible. "Mrs. Shaw gave me a Christmas bonus of $7500, and I'll tell you, when you're only making $175 a week, that's one hell of a bonus."

New Highs,
New Lows
1961

Ray's second Midas year began as smoothly as his first. On Sunday, January 1, 1961, Hal Zeiger presented Ray and company at the Hollywood Palladium, Ray's "Exclusive Los Angeles Engagement," said the ads—exclusive, that is, except for another Zeiger date ("By Irresistible Demand!"), January 13 in nearby Pasadena. As "Ruby" fell off the charts and "Them That Got" replaced it, the Flex rolled up the Pacific coast, Ray city-hopping in the Cessna. Jazz writer Ralph J. Gleason caught the gang at Longshoreman's Hall in San Francisco and raved in *Downbeat* that Ray was a "contemporary giant . . . the finest singer of the pop commercial ballad since Louis Armstrong." Gleason also flipped for "fiery" Margie Hendricks and the band's "first-rate soloists," Fathead, Cooper, Guilbeau, and Crawford. From San Francisco the Cessna and Flex continued north to Vancouver, then looped back to Seattle. There cracks began to appear in the golden surface.

Ray never made the Seattle gig. The fellows got to the club and set up, but Ray didn't appear. They played one long set and then a second. The crowd got restless and started booing. Duke looked at Fathead and said, "I'm putting Ray's horn back in the case." The MC came out to say that foggy weather prevented Ray Charles' plane from landing and he wouldn't appear. "The people tore up the place," Wade remembered.

"We got on the bus and got the fuck out of there." The next stop was Tingley Coliseum in Albuquerque, New Mexico, on Saturday the 21st. Again the fellows arrived and set up, but no Ray, and this time the crowd's reponse made the front page of *Variety:*

> The Charles band had been on the stand from 9 pm, but about 11 pm, rumor went around the hall . . . that Charles wasn't going to show up. That resulted in a mad scramble for refunds with lots of pushing and shoving. Private cops on the scene were unable to cope with the situation and called sheriff's deputies, who finally put down the riot.

No one was seriously hurt, but the crowd roughed up promoter Mike London and snatched his money bag. Ray finally arrived after midnight Sunday morning.

The problem, as Jeff, Duke, and the whole inner circle knew, was heroin. "Ray was staying high enough to take the top off the ceiling," Wade remembered. "For hours at a time he could barely function, let alone perform." Hank Crawford started calling him "Dr Pepper," because, as the tonic's slogan suggested, Ray was shooting up every day at "10-2-4." "And at 6 and 8," Crawford added. Ray bought heroin in large quantities, three or four ounces at a time, and each new stash seemed to disappear into his arms faster than the one before it.

From Albuquerque the troupe headed east. Concerned that he hadn't heard about any new recording sessions, Larry Newton sent an assistant to Columbus, Ohio, and he found Ray sprawled semiconscious on a motel carpet. When they got to New York, Ray kept asking Jeff to get him cash—$700, $900, $1000—from the bank and to make up excuses to fool the accountants. That much money slipping between the cracks led to sloppy bookkeeping, which, in certain moods, could set Ray off on suspicious tours of his banks, checking for imaginary thefts.

Not every day was crisis. Ray's life in New York settled into a routine that, for $200 a week, Duke Wade came to enjoy. "I woke his ass up in the morning—first thing, he'd smoke a joint—and I put him to bed at night." Because Ray didn't know when a shirt or suit got spotted, Duke had charge of Ray's clothes. A sharp dresser himself, Duke bought Ray shoes at Saks and took him to a custom tailor on Fifth Avenue for suits and tuxedos. Ray liked to pick out his own fabrics by feel, preferring fine wools and raw silk. Sometimes Ray stayed with Mae, but he also kept a suite at the Sheraton Hotel in midtown. Duke made a pal of the night man, Patrick, who sent up whatever food Ray wanted at any hour. Some nights they'd stay up late smoking pot and laughing and arguing so loud that the people downstairs would call to tell them to pipe down. On quieter nights Ray talked about growing up in Florida, about his mother and how much she liked sweet potato pie, but how a sweet potato pie had killed her.

Mornings after a late breakfast, Ray got down to business. With Duke at his side, he'd stop at his lawyer's office near Carnegie Hall, then cab over to the Shaw office on Fifth. Hal Zeiger was planning Ray's first national tour, a connected series of twenty concerts leading up to Carnegie Hall, Sunday, April 30, and for it Ray wanted to enlarge the band. He'd already been adding players to his eight-piece band at the theater gigs. How much would it cost to keep a big band together? Could he afford to? Those calculations took him crosstown to his accountants, Orland and Chase. When they were done, Ray and Duke hung out at the Automat on Fifty-seventh Street, laughing and talking for hours over pie and coffee.

In February, at a studio in Brooklyn, Ray made his network television debut on the *Kraft Music Hall,* a variety show hosted by Perry Como on Wednesday nights. At the rehearsals, Como and the staff musicians crowded around Ray admiringly, yet on the show Ray performed only in his own segment, taking no part in the songs and sketches shared by Como and guest stars Anne Bancroft and Jimmy Durante. As he had on *Playboy's Penthouse,* Ray seemed nervous and withdrawn, singing "Georgia" softly, playing minimal piano, and working neither the camera nor the studio audience. When he swung into "What'd I Say," the camera pulled back to reveal a bandstand full of white boys and girls singing along and swaying stiffly to the beat. As the song ended, the camera cut back to the three stars.

"Ray Charles, he's really something," said Como.

"A real genius," said Bancroft.

"He studied with me for years," wisecracked Durante.

"Ray Charles and TV Just Do Not Agree," commented the Philadelphia *Tribune,* and a grainy videotape of the show confirms that Ray's network debut was something of a dud.

In early March, Ray and the gang rode the Flex to New Haven for an afternoon concert at Woolsey Hall on the Yale campus. A highlight of the Junior Prom weekend and also advertised to the public, the concert drew a mixed crowd of white college kids and Negroes from Dixwell Avenue, the city's black community. This was a more integrated event than usual for New Haven, and a few policemen stood by looking for the first sign of trouble. The concert got off to a great start, "the band hot as a pistol," remembered Harry Huggins, then a senior at Hillhouse High. "The white kids sat there listening, but the black people started to shout out, 'Yeah, yeah,' and a few couples got up and started dancing. That was enough for the cops. Dancing might lead to a riot!" The police declared the show closed, the music had to stop. Ray didn't understand what was happening, but Duke got him offstage. The Negroes felt robbed of the show they deserved, but the Yalies barely noticed what had happened. "Ray Charles put on a rip-roaring show," reported the 1961 yearbook, "even if he did run out of numbers midway through the second half."

The next stop, the Magnolia in Atlanta, was home territory, where a little cutting loose was taken for granted, but in Augusta, March 15, Ray again ran into the nation-wide battle over integration. Civil rights trouble had arrived late on the campus of Augusta's little Paine College, but that spring it reached full ferment. Eleven students had just been arrested trying to integrate the city's bus system. When student president Silas Norman learned that Ray Charles was coming to town to play a segregated dance, he and his colleagues sent him a telegram. Perhaps Ray didn't know "the conditions under which you will perform here," the telegram read. "The dance floor is only open to whites, and Negroes are allowed only as spectators in an opposite auditorium."

For black entertainers touring the South (and North), playing segregated shows had been a matter of course from the dawn of black show business. Jim Crow ruled in show business as elsewhere: buck the system and you couldn't find work. Only after World War II did whites begin to appreciate jazz and blues in great enough numbers to make "Who sits where?" a pertinent question. In 1951, black Atlantans found they had to enter the civic auditorium by a back entrance to hear Duke Ellington, Sarah Vaughan, and Nat Cole, while white patrons were ushered in the front door and given a choice section to themselves. Protesting loudly, many Negroes tore up their tickets and refused to enter. Why should they take a back seat to hear music by people of their own color? The stars, with their livelihoods to earn, showed little sympathy. Vaughan had her maid tell a reporter it was "terrible," Cole had no comment, and Ellington snapped, "I don't want to discuss it." The show went on.

Shaw Artists and the other black music agencies played their role in the system, and so did Ray. Many times coming out on stage he had whispered to Duke, "How is it tonight?" Duke would glance out over the house and estimate, "Oh, thirty-seventy," meaning 30 percent black, 70 percent white. "Where are they at?" Ray would ask, and Wade would say, "Up and down," meaning the blacks in the balcony, the whites in the orchestra. "I'm getting tired of you telling me this up-and-down shit," Ray would respond. Still, it was business as usual.

Now the students that Ray'd heard about on the radio were challenging him directly. Ray made a snap decision and crossed a major line. "I'm too big for this shit," he said, "I won't play it." That was fine with Jeff and Duke, and the gang got back on the bus. The promoter swore he'd sue Ray for breach of contract. "I don't give a fuck," said Ray, sending a message to the students as they pulled out: "I feel it is the least that I can do to stand behind my principles and help the students in their fight for their

principles." Strong words from one who had just discovered those principles, but Ray
stuck by them. No more segregated gigs, he told Milt Shaw, and Shaw agreed—which
meant that for years most of Ray's southern concerts were on college campuses. The
promoter did sue, Ray lost, and he paid a $757 fine for breach of contract. The story
of Ray's "no" to segregation got wide and appreciative coverage in the black press.
"America's Great High Priest of Jazz," the Pittsburgh *Courier* put it, "dealt his home
state's racial bias a resounding slap in the face."

From Atlanta the band dispersed on a two-week break before the Zeiger tour, and Ray
flew to Los Angeles. There a still-deeper crack zigzagged through the golden surface.
Thursday, March 20, began like many at the Hepburn house, Ray dictating music to
Hank. They had a lot of writing to do: Ray had decided to tour with a big band, and
a big band needed a big book. Della, eight months pregnant, made them lunch. Ray
disappeared a few times into his private den upstairs with a lady heroin dealer who shot
him up; Della acted as if she didn't know what was happening. Each time, after an hour,
Ray came down and continued dictating. He had been up most of the night before but
didn't feel tired.

The dealer came for the last time late in the evening. Hank could hear Ray upstairs,
bumping into the walls. "Hank, I don't think Ray's gonna do anything else today," Della
said, and Hank went back to the Watkins. Soon six-year-old Ray Jr., whose bedroom
was next to Ray's den, kissed his mother good night. "I said I wanted to tell my father
good night," Ray Jr. remembered as a grown man. "She said no, go to bed, she'd tell
Daddy good night for me. She knew he was high and didn't want me to see him like
that." But Ray Jr. sneaked out of his room and knocked on his father's door, a child-
ish impulse that saved Ray Charles' life. "He didn't answer, but I knew he was in there
because I heard him. I opened the door and I saw him jumping around. His shirt was
covered in blood, there was blood on the wall. I yelled down to my mother that Daddy
was bleeding."

Della ran upstairs, but in his flailing Ray had locked the door, and she couldn't get
into the room. She called Hank to come over right away, she needed help. Hank knew
Ray could be hard to handle when stoned, so he asked drummer Milt Turner, a burly
two-hundred-fifty-pounder staying down the hall, to go back to Hepburn with him.
When they got there, Milt threw all his weight on the door and broke it down, and
there was Ray slumped on the floor, his left hand sliced by the sharp edge of a glass-
topped table, a severed artery gushing blood. Della nearly fainted; Hank wrapped Ray's
hand in towels, and Turner walked Ray, almost unconscious, around and around the

kitchen table. Della called the family doctor, Robert Foster. Foster said to bring him to his clinic. They got him there, bleeding all over the Cadillac's upholstery, and Dr. Foster closed the wound. Yet Ray had lost so much blood that he began to have convulsions, and Foster took him to a hospital. With a four-pint transfusion, the immediate crisis passed.

Foster then discovered that Ray had severed a tendon as well as an artery. He sewed the tendon back together, bandaged the hand, and said Ray couldn't use it for six weeks. But the Zeiger tour was only a week away. Ray insisted that he was going on the tour as scheduled. He would play right-hand piano; with the big band behind him, nobody would notice. In case anyone did, Milt Shaw put out the story that Ray had slipped in the bathtub. Foster insisted that he go along. Ray was glad to have him, and with April he pushed into Hal Zeiger's triumphal march to Carnegie Hall with his left hand an unhealed wound. Most pianists would blanch at a month of one-handed concerts, and Ray's doing the tour stands as a prime example of his ability to steam past obstacles that would stop many another in his tracks.

"The Most Creative Musical Giant of this Generation RAY CHARLES and his Augmented Orchestra plus the singing Raelets and Betty Carter," read Zeiger's ads for the tour. For Ray, the proudest words of the billing were "augmented orchestra." Ray had spent his entire life since Jacksonville preparing for this moment: taking a big band on the road just like Count and Duke. He planned on the classic lineup: four trumpets, four trombones, four saxes, plus piano, guitar, and bass in rhythm. Only the trombone section would be brand-new; in the sax and trumpet sections he could blend newcomers with old-timers like Marcus Belgrave and Leroy Cooper. Edgar Willis would still lay down the bottom on bass. As Fathead had hinted, Ray made Hank Crawford musical director. Quincy Jones had just disbanded his big band and sent his mentor a trunkload of charts. With those, plus the small-band charts expanded and Burns' and Paich's string charts reset for brass, Ray had more tunes than he could use. Despite his pride at this big step, the words "augmented orchestra" gave the ever-cautious Ray a line of retreat: if the experiment didn't work, he could "de-augment" the band more quietly than he could fold a boldly announced "big band" that flopped.

From Easter in St. Louis, the tour rolled to Detroit's Masonic Auditorium, where somebody brought out a blind teenage harmonica player called "Little Stevie Wonder." Little Stevie, already recording for fledgling Motown Records, idolized Ray, and Ray let him play on a couple of numbers. Critiquing the Detroit show, Zeiger felt he needed an MC to pull its segments together, to give it "some dignity," he explained to his partner Johnny Otis; somebody who was "well-known, black, and polished." "Get Joe Adams," said Otis. "Who the fuck is Joe Adams?" replied Zeiger. Otis gave him Adams' number, Zeiger called, and Adams flew in to work the rest of the tour.

There in Detroit, eleven years after Jack Lauderdale introduced them, Ray and Joe Adams made their first real contact, beginning a relationship that grew slowly but lasted long. In the mid-60s, Joe Adams became Ray's closest adviser and personal manager; he held the same post over thirty years later. Even the most acute Ray Charles watchers disagree on the role Joe Adams has played in Ray's life, a role best defined by the unfolding events of the decades to come.

Joseph E. Adams was born in Watts in 1924. His father was a wide-awake salesman, later a partner, at Gold's Furniture, the biggest store on Central Avenue, his mother a housewife who kept their roomy house on Bandera Street neat as a pin. At Jordan High School, Adams discovered radio announcing, and he became first a sidekick to Al Jarvis, host of the popular "Make-Believe Ballroom," and then, as the "Mayor of Melody," he hosted his own show on KOWL. By the mid-50s Joe Adams had become a well-known figure in black Los Angeles; Duke Ellington even named a tune for him, "Smada," Adams spelled backward. Tall, slim, and handsome, Adams carried himself with a conscious elegance, his hair flat to his skull in a sleek process, his mustache shaved pencil-thin, his tailoring dapper to a fault. Joe Adams kept his fingers in many pies: a national show on NBC radio (he was "the first Negro coast-to-coast," he liked to boast), as well as syndicated radio shows that he packaged in Las Vegas. The Los Angeles *Sentinel* ran stories on him every week for years: Joe Adams at a club opening or business luncheon, off to a Hawaiian vacation with his wife Emma.

The number and flattering tone of the stories argue the existence of a press agent, yet Adams' claim to celebrity had merit. Most notably, he was a successful character actor with two dozen film credits, one of them a plum: the boxer Husky in Otto Preminger's *Carmen Jones*. In October 1957 he debuted on Broadway in the musical *Jamaica,* a nearly all-black show produced by David Merrick. Adams played Joe Nashua, a Harlem highlife who comes to mythical Pigeon Island like a serpent into Paradise, tempts Savannah (Lena Horne) with dreams of wealth, then loses her to a simple fisherman named Kali (Ricardo Montalban in deep-tan makeup). Critics found the show uneven but agreed that Adams "capably represented an oily scoundrel."

Jamaica closed in early 1959; Adams came back to LA, and, as he remembered years later, "I got bored. So when Hal [Zeiger] called, I figured I'd give this a try." The excitement Ray generated impressed him, as did the lines around the block in every city. Ray, he observed, was a relentless perfectionist, yet as the tour rolled on to Cleveland and Chicago, Adams noticed one gross imperfection Ray couldn't see: the concert hall crews lit the stage brightly from the beginning to the end of each show, making no changes to suit the changing musical moods. Having become fascinated by lighting effects on Broadway, Adams started doing lights for the show, putting blackouts between songs and spotlighting soloists. "I'd pinpoint Ray's face when he was doing

'Georgia,' " Adams recalled. "The audience would grow quiet, and he could sing the ballad, not scream it."

After a few nights, Ray asked to see the MC; Adams thought the boss was going to chew him out. Instead, Ray said he had heard him offstage counting backward during the show; what was he doing? Calling light cues, Adams explained. When fading several lights at once, he'd tell the operator, "Start fading the reds on ten, the greens on seven, and the blues on five," then he'd count slowly, "Ten, nine, eight," down to zero, when the change would be complete.

"I'll be damned," said Ray, slapping his leg. "Why are you doing it?"

"It needed to be done," said Adams, to which Ray replied, "Do you know how great it is for somebody to do what *needs* to be done, and not say, 'It ain't my job' ?"

That was that for the moment, but Adams' ability to take charge impressed Ray. He asked Duke what he thought of Joe Adams, and Duke said he thought Joe was a good businessman and a great disc jockey. Ray began to observe Adams, to listen to his rounded tones and mannered diction, sense the chill politeness that he wore like a courtier's mask. In business, and Ray was doing more and more business, a man as suave as Joe Adams could be very useful.

As the tour wound toward Carnegie Hall in May, life showered Ray with bouquets. The National Association of Recording Arts and Sciences (NARAS) awarded him his first Grammy for "Georgia" as the best pop single of 1960. His new single, "One Mint Julep," an instrumental from *Genius + Soul,* got to #14 on the Pop chart and #1 R&B. He had five albums on the LP chart, the newest, *Dedicated to You,* at a respectable #29. Della gave birth to their third son, Robert, and Ray's hand, though briefly infected, began to heal. Carnegie Hall, however, proved anticlimactic. Both *Variety* and *The New York Times* found the opening forty minutes by "The Original Small Ray Charles Band" too long. The *Times* thought the "lumbering" big band and Ray's "mushy" organ "dimmed the searing electricity that one expects from Mr. Charles." *Variety* complained that Ray didn't start singing until the show was more than half over, even though "it was his vocalizing that really made the fans happy." Still, Zeiger and Ray made good money: $15,000 gross at Carnegie Hall, $220,000 for the whole tour.

Back in Los Angeles in June, Ray and company settled into ten nights at the Zebra Lounge on Central Avenue. The long run became old-home week, Della taking tables for family and friends, and everybody on the LA black-music scene dropping in to see and be seen. Among them came singer-songwriter Percy Mayfield, a glamorous star of R&B's early days, sidelined by a disfiguring car accident in 1952. Ray, who had grown up with Mayfield's music, proposed that he write for Tangerine. Mayfield had a rocker, "Hit the Road Jack," that could feature the Raelets, and "Danger Zone," a mournful blues. Ray liked both and said he wanted more. "Can you write me a song about a woman you do the best you can for, but on the other hand . . ."

"Hold it right there," said Mayfield. "I can use that for your title, 'But on the Other Hand, Baby.' "

"How long will it take you to write it?" asked Ray.

"That's me knocking on your door right now," said Mayfield. The next day he brought Ray the finished version.

Marty Paich, meanwhile, had the charts ready for Ray's third ABC album, duets with Betty Carter, a young singer newly signed to the label. Sid flew out for the sessions. Hangers-on and celebrities, including Frank Sinatra, crowded the studio, but with the speedy professionalism standard for the era, Ray, Carter, the strings, chorus, and big band got twelve songs down in three three-hour sessions. "The musicians were sight-reading," Feller remembered, "but with a couple of rehearsals for interpretation and balance, boom, we had a tune." The long, lush tracks of *Ray Charles and Betty Carter* betray no sign of haste. Carter's kittenish purrs contrast sexily with Ray's husky growls in harmonies that are breathtakingly pure. Their "Baby It's Cold Outside" may be the definitive version of Frank Loesser's witty interlocked lyric:

> **Girl**: *My mother will start to worry*
> **Boy**: *Beautiful, what's your hurry?*
> **Girl**: *And Father will be pacing the floor*
> **Boy**: *Listen to that fireplace roar!*

From LA, Ray and company flew to New York for a week at the Apollo, and they so packed the venerable house that Frank Shiffman held them over for a second week. In New York, Ray was with Mae again. She was due in August, and Ray said he'd support the baby. July Fourth the band had a "Cabaret and Dawn" dance in Atlantic City that didn't start until midnight, and Ray made a snap decision to record in the afternoon. Using the little band and the Raelets, he could knock off a few of Mayfield's tunes and make the gig on time.

That spur-of-the-moment session became one of Ray's boldest, the fellows ad-libbing arrangements, Ray singing and playing with a confident swagger. "You know I'm hot for you, mama," he sighs to open "But on the Other Hand, Baby," setting a mood as steamily intimate as music can get. "Danger Zone" ("Just read your paper and you'll see . . . the world is in an uproar, the danger zone is everywhere") came as close as Ray ever had to commenting on the civil rights headlines from Alabama and Mississippi. Domestic comedy, however, provided the afternoon's high point: "Hit the

Road Jack." Margie is kicking Ray out, no mistake. "I'll be back on my feet someday," begs Ray. "Don't care if you do," growls Margie, " 'cause it's understood, you ain't got no money, you just ain't no good." "Hit the road, Jack," her girlfriends sing in support, their "Don't you come back no more no more" rising triumphantly over the descending bass line. In the control booth, Sid and Larry Newton knew they had a hit on their hands.

From the studio, Ray and the band raced down to Atlantic City, but when the Flex pulled in at four A.M., the 8000 fans, crammed into a hall designed for 5000, were hurling bottles and chairs at one another. It took an hour to push Ray's organ through the mob to the stage. Ray was "unperturbed by the chaos," reported the Philadelphia *Tribune*. "I was at a recording session in New York," he said calmly, "and the fellows were late getting through." Once the music started, all was forgiven, and Ray played encores until 6:30 A.M.

Three days later in Chicago, another crack split the golden surface. Ray wanted to score before the first show at the Regal Theatre, and he, Duke, and Donald Wilkerson headed to the South Side apartment of a dealer named Fifty. "We were inside when the police knocked on the door," Wade remembered. "They didn't know Ray was there, they were after the dealer. Ray took his dental bridge out, stuck his shit in there, and they never found it. Jeff got Ray and me out of jail after four hours. As we left, Donald was calling to Ray, 'Don't forget, come back and get me.' " Ray missed the first two shows, and once again an audience got riled up over a late Ray Charles.

A judge soon dismissed the charges on the grounds of an illegal search, but the black press carried the story widely, the first publicity to link Ray and heroin since Philadelphia six years before. "Charles' fans just couldn't believe that their idol had been arrested on narcotic charges," reported the ANP. "But he was. . . ."

From a gig at Melody Skateland in Indianapolis, Ray, the Raelets, and the old eight-piece band made their biggest leap ever: to the south of France for four days at the Juan-les-Pins International Jazz Festival. None of them had ever been to Europe, and it was wonderful. Ray took Mae, and she basked happily in his reflected glory. They played well: a taped fragment reveals a tremulous "Ruby" and a lush "Lil Darling" played *molto molto lento*. In the first flush of fame, Ray had his name and face on more posters than Count Basie, but when not on stage himself, Ray listened rapt to the Basie band, learning from the master. He also kept getting his heroin. At a press conference, photographer Jean-Pierre Leloir waved to a newsreel cameraman to stop filming when Ray began to scratch himself so freely as to be embarrassing.

Yves Boucher, a teenager from the Paris suburbs, watched the concerts on French television. A few years before, Yves' older brother had brought home a grab bag of American records, Louis Armstrong, *Porgy and Bess,* Elvis Presley, and Pat Boone. "I didn't know the categories of this music with a beat. I just received it and tried to find my way," Boucher recalled. When he heard Ray's "Heartbreaker," he felt he'd been struck by lightning. "The music talked to my whole body. I could barely understand the lyrics, but I didn't care. My friends liked Ray, but none were as mad as I." Yves started coming into Paris to buy records at a little shop on the rue de Rivoli. He decided that he liked Ray's Atlantic R&B better than his smooth ABC pop, so, glued to his TV, he was glad to see Leroy, Hank, and the little band he knew playing oldies like "My Bonnie" and "I Believe to My Soul." The only problem was an announcer who talked over the band: "I was yelling, shut up, I want to hear the music!"

In these four summer days on the Côte d'Azur, Ray put just his toe into the European jazz scene and still made a splash. London's *Melody Maker* declared Ray the star of the show, and the French press declared him the "Golden Youth of Jazz." Agent Henry Goldgrand called Shaw to book return engagements. At first Goldgrand hoped for a full European tour, but that dream dwindled to one night each in Zurich and Lyons, and three in Paris—Friday, October 20, through Sunday the 22nd—at the Palais des Sports, a rough-and-tumble boxing arena near the Porte de Versailles. Tickets to the Palais shows sold so fast that they added concerts Monday and Tuesday.

Ray and company, meanwhile, flew back to America, getting to Detroit's Graystone Ballroom in mid-August. In the hotel after the gig, Ray and Duke heard someone knocking. Duke opened the door, and a young woman said Ray had told her to come up. "Sure he did," said Duke and went back to Ray. "You said a girl could come up?" Duke asked. "I dunno, I might have," said Ray. "What's she look like?" "She's nice," said Duke, and Ray said, "Okay, let her in."

From Detroit they moved on to Memphis, where, only a few months before, the city government had begun allowing promoters who rented the City Auditorium to decide between segregated and integrated seating. So far promoters had stuck with Jim Crow, fearful of offending white patrons. Ray refused to play to a segregated house, so black promoter Sunbeam Mitchell took the risk, and for the first time ever in Memphis, whites and blacks in equal numbers sat peaceably together and the "For Colored Only" signs came down over the rest rooms. Policemen stood everywhere but, crowed the Memphis *World,* "they weren't needed. Old Man Segregation had gone for a swim in the muddy Wolf River." Once again the story spread in the black press and even earned a page-one headline in *Variety:* "Ray Charles Makes History in Memphis; 1st Integrated Show a Social & B.O. Click."

Ray Charles and Betty Carter came out to good reviews, and ABC took a two-page ad in *Billboard* to say of Ray, "He put the soul into jazz, he put the sell into jazz." "I've Got News for You" got to #80 on the Pop chart, and "Hit the Road Jack" came out to instant interest. As Ray and the gang played the Palladium in LA, in New York Mae gave birth to a baby girl, Raenee. Doctors soon realized that Raenee had severe eye problems, which they diagnosed as congenital glaucoma, a defect passed on by Ray as his was passed on to him. Fathering a child who might become blind shocked Ray, but still enamored of his mistress, he undertook to pay the baby's medical expenses, including a full-time nurse.

He couldn't, however, get east right away to visit the baby. Through the first week of September he and the gang rehearsed for their biggest concert ever, "A Salute to Genius," at the Hollywood Bowl. For this, forty-seven people would be on stage: Ray, the fifteen-piece band, a nineteen-piece string section, and a twelve-voice chorus. The night of the concert arrived clear and cool. Leroy Cooper stepped out on stage and, looking out over rows of seats receding up the hillside, realized how far they had come from the days of the tobacco warehouses. Hank, conducting with his back to the audience, stole a few sideways glances and saw Ralph Burns and Quincy Jones listening in the wings. "These guys are ready to step into my spot if I don't do my job," he thought. "I better not fold." To judge by *Downbeat*'s rave review, he didn't. The small-band opener had become "hard-smacking big band jazz," wrote John Tynan, and when Ray came on, "from the first measures of 'Moanin',' he had 'em." Alternating rockers with string-and-chorus ballads, Ray built the musical excitement from peak to peak until, with the opening notes of "What'd I Say," teenagers in the crowd of 6000 went wild:

> Beyond restraint now, they poured into the aisles . . . in a human torrent down the steps from the cheaper sections to the edge of the pool separating audience from stage. Two youths leaped onto the low wall of the pool; a dozen followed. In moments the top of the wall was alive. A line of youths was silhouetted against the lighted water, arms madly waving, bodies jerking in ceaseless motion to the music.

The police moved in cautiously to break up the dancing, but when the music was over, the kids dispersed and "the audience, still agog, moved toward the exits." Popularity had not spoiled Charles, Tynan concluded: "Nothing in the *music* of this magnetic and profoundly moving musician has undergone change or cheapening. Nothing, in fact, has changed—except now the audience is larger."

Monday's *Billboard* brought the news that "Hit the Road Jack" had entered the

Pop chart at #55, starred for "strong upward movement." The single leapt to #22 a week later, and leapt again to #13 as the gang played four days at the Palace on Broadway in Manhattan. Another week and "Hit the Road Jack" reached #4. Then, on October 9, as the gang played a week at Detroit's Fox Theatre with Gloria Lynne and Fabian, Ray had his second #1 hit, this one with the enormous financial advantage of being a Tangerine tune. The disc still held the top spot a week later, then Dion's "Runaround Sue" took over, and Ray's single slid to #4. Most hit records rise to brief, knife-edged peaks, but "Hit the Road Jack" stayed nine weeks in the top ten, its high, flat plateau at the top of the curve indicative of unusual strength.

As yearning for home made "Georgia" a smash hit, down-home humor succeeded for "Hit the Road Jack." Its danceable rhythms and vibrant vocals are indelibly African-American, and the two-minute musical comedy struck the nation's funny bone just as Louis Jordan records had, for a moment obliterating the nation's color barrier. Ray and Margie were funny, period, and whites identified with their Punch-and-Judy brawl just as blacks did with Ralph and Alice on "The Honeymooners." People turned up the car radio to sing along every time "Hit the Road Jack" came on, boys singing, "You're the meanest old woman I ever did see," and girls singing, "Don't you come back no more no more," to each other as joking comments on their own lives.

With "Hit the Road" still at its peak, Ray and the gang took off again for Europe. First Zurich and Lyons, which none of them remembered, then Paris, which none of them ever forgot. In Paris, October 1961, Ray Charles triumphed in a way that few artists live to enjoy. At thirty-one, the full height of his manhood, he stormed and captured the heart of the rose-gray city on the Seine. For old-time jazz lovers like Maurice Cullasz, president of the Jazz Academy, Ray's triumph recalled Louis Armstrong's and Duke Ellington's European debuts in the 1930s. "Ray Charles Reigned Five Days over Paris," headlined *Jazz Magazine* over a photograph of "The King of Paris" relaxing on the balcony of the Claridge Hotel, the Arc de Triomphe behind him, the Champs-Élysées at his feet. Triumph was not too great a word for Ray's success, Frank Tenot wrote, a triumph "made to the measure of the man's genius." On his government clerk's salary Yves Boucher got to only one of the six sold-out shows but, he remembered, "it was extraordinary. There are no words."

Ray won his victory at the Palais des Sports, a cavernous hall with grimy walls and bare wooden seats in a nondescript neighborhood far from the center of the city. Only days before, the police had made the Palais a temporary jail, packing it with thousands of Algerians arrested at a mass demonstration; the right-wing *Paris Presse* sniffed that Ray Charles' "Yeah-yeah" had replaced the Algerians' wailing "You-you" cries. As in America, the big band played a long set before Ray came on, but the Ray-less opening didn't bore the French as it did some Americans. The French loved every second, taking Ray's big band as seriously as Ellington's, looking eagerly for Ray's Johnny Hodges and Harry Carney and finding them in Fathead and Leroy. When Duke led Ray into the spotlights cutting through the smoky haze, and sat him behind the big Hammond organ, the crowd leapt to its feet cheering, and a bluesy trumpet fanfare, "Dweeeeeee, dweeda dweeda," kicked off "Let the Good Times Roll."

A terrible echo distorted the sound in the cheap seats under the rafters where Yves Boucher sat, yet he and everyone leaned forward to catch every note. The music sent ripples of excitement through the crowd, and occasional cries rang out, but more often the audience sat silent until the end of each song set off explosions of wild applause. Compared with the records, everything sounded bigger, the rhythms hotter, the soloists freer, the sound colors splashed more vividly. Once-smooth "Georgia" had been "gospelized," Ray singing it with as many squeals and screams as he ever gave "Drown in My Own Tears." Each show built to a grand climax with "What'd I Say," Ray leading 6000 happy voices through the unnnh-unnnh—oooh-ooohs, and ended in a tumultuous standing ovation as Duke led Ray, bowing, slowly out of the spotlights.

Offstage, journalists crowded around Ray. The blues was "the greatest expression of Negro America," he told them. And no record company chose his material: "I will sing anything I like." They also eagerly questioned the band, devouring each fresh tidbit of information: trombonist Keg Johnson had played with Louis Armstrong, alto saxist Rudy Powell studied with Benny Carter's teacher. The fellows loved the attention; back in the States jazz writers didn't pay them much mind. Some reporters complained it was hard to get to Ray through his "retinue," i.e., Jeff and Duke, and for some it was. Frank Tenot, Maurice Cullasz, and a few ladies found it easy, Ray hanging out with them affably through lazy afternoons at the Claridge and after the show at Mimi's, a bistro near the Palais. With the legendary Harlem hipster Mezz Mezzrow in Paris dealing drugs, Ray had no problem staying high. Cullasz, who had first smoked pot with Satchmo, bought some for the two of them, but the gamin who delivered it smoked most of it on the way. Tenot found Ray an exciting, electric person to be with, funny, warmhearted, and brilliant. Cullasz felt Ray Charles' pride in himself as a black man.

There may be fifty million reasons why the French fell for Ray Charles: because they love to adopt American artists; because Ray's name, like Sidney Bechet's, sounded French; or because, as Cullasz put it, "Ray had charisma, and what works on Americans works on the French." Hank Crawford thought the French felt a mystique in Ray's blindness. "They couldn't believe all this music coming from a blind boy." Tenot felt that the blues was the heart of Ray's appeal: "True blues had been slow to get to Europe. We knew jazz blues, Louis, Duke, and Count, and we knew folk blues like Big Bill Broonzy. Ray brought modern R&B to France." Cullasz, in contrast, stressed the appeal of Ray's gospel: "We felt the intensity of his spiritual feeling. Ray's music is really gospel, even when he's singing about sex." Yet when Cullasz asked Ray if he would ever record true gospel, Ray said no. "My mother said you can't serve two masters, and I sing rhythm and blues." *Jazz Magazine* concluded that, however one heard him, Ray's music had a "grandeur savage and refined, charged with brutal beauties and wise subtleties," and bade "Le Génie" a reverential au revoir:

> This time, *c'est fini;* the curtain falls again on an empty stage. A
> fragile silhouette cut by the spotlights. . . . Ray Charles says
> farewell to the crowd of his friends. No one wants to let him go.
> But he will return.

Ray's foreign triumph did not go unnoticed in America. "Ray Charles Wows Crix, Audiences in Four Capacity Shows at Paris Arena," headlined *Variety.* "Charles now looms a bigtime international performing and platter name."

┌┤┠┤┠┤┠┤┠┤┐

From this peak Ray plunged into deep trouble. Back in America, where "Hit the Road Jack" still held at #6, Shaw booked the group, now a twenty-two-person entourage, for six weeks of one-nighters that started in Troy, New York, on November 3, winding up in Denver by mid-December. Larry Myers got them a spot on *The Ed Sullivan Show* on November 18; they'd fly back to New York for that. Ten days into the tour, the Cessna and Flex arrived in Indianapolis, Ray checking into the downtown Sheraton-Lincoln Hotel, the fellows into the old black Claypool. In his room Ray got a call from a man he didn't know who offered to sell him drugs. Ray told him to come over and, when he did, bought pot from him and a dozen $3 capsules of heroin.

Late Monday afternoon everybody rode the Flex an hour east to Anderson, Indiana, for a "Big Concert" at the New High Gym, played it, and rode back to Indianapolis. Duke got Ray to his room, then he and Hank took off to catch Aretha Franklin at the Pink Poodle. Duke knew Aretha from her father C. L. Franklin's gospel show. At nine A.M., Ray woke up to a knock on the door that became a steady pounding. "Who is it?" he asked. "Western Union," came the reply. Groggy with sleep and in his underwear, Ray didn't think to say a cautious, "Slip it under the door." Instead he opened up.

Immediately two detectives from the Indianapolis police rushed in, acting on a tip from the anonymous dealer. They searched the room, and in the bathroom medicine chest they found what they were looking for: a syringe, hypodermic needles, the heroin capsules—now empty but for a white powder residue—and a cold-cream jar filled with marijuana. The narcs pulled up Ray's sleeves and saw the scars of repeated injections on his arms, the worst "tracks" they had ever seen. They hustled him to police headquarters, fingerprinted him, and charged him with violation of the 1935 narcotics acts and with being a common drug addict. While they had their celebrity prisoner, the police let the press and photographers in on the questioning.

Perhaps it was the combination of shocks—the jolt of the rough awakening, the cops' pushy speed, the knowledge that they had caught him red-handed—but that morning in police custody, Ray Charles broke down in public as he never had before and never would again. He sat on a bench in the city jail, looking disturbed and lonely, as one reporter noted, crying softly at first, then losing control of himself. The reporters asked him how he got started on narcotics. "I started using stuff when I was sixteen," Ray said in short, broken sentences. "When I first started in show business." Then he broke off and began to cry again. "I don't know what to do about my wife and kids. I've got a month's work to do, and I have to do it."

He maundered into self-pity and age-old junkie excuses. "I really need help. Nobody can lick this thing by themselves. I'd like to go to Lexington [Kentucky's famed narcotics hospital]. It might do me some good. I guess I've always wanted to go, but it was easier the other way. A guy who lives in the dark has to have something to keep going." He wasn't the only star to use heroin. "Believe me, there are a lot of bigger guys than me who are hooked a lot worse." Ray raved at the fink who turned him in. "Whoever he was, it was a dirty trick for him to pull." A reporter asked if he'd like to see children using narcotics. Ray started crying again and said, "It's a rotten business."

The worst lasted only a few hours. Jeff and a lawyer got Ray released until the arraignment the next morning by posting a $1250 cash bond and by pleading that Ray had an engagement that night in Evansville, over two hundred miles away. Leaving police headquarters, Ray covered his head with his overcoat to ward off photographers. At the Claypool, Leroy Cooper woke up, turned on the radio, and heard the news: Ray Charles busted. He hustled out into the hall and found the other fellows milling about. They had just heard too. A minute later Ray came walking in with Jeff, free on bail.

Backstage that night at the Evansville Coliseum, Ray was still in an agitated mood. "Charles jumped, apparently uncontrollably, up and down on the floor, much like a child skipping rope," the Evansville *Courier* wrote. "Occasionally he bent his knees and almost squatted. He said it was caused by nerves and lack of sleep." As the reporters watched, however, Ray began to pull himself together, answering their questions more curtly. No, he didn't know how much he had spent on drugs. "That's like asking how much you spend for cigarettes." He'd been misquoted; he hadn't been an addict since sixteen. "It ain't been that long, not near that long." What would he say to the judge the next morning? "I'll deny everything, and you can quote me."

Word of the arrest spread quickly, far beyond the black press. Evening papers and news shows ran detailed stories, and overnight the police got press inquiries from all over the country and Europe. When Ray and Jeff arrived at municipal court Wednesday morning, fans, reporters, and TV and radio crews jammed the halls outside the courtroom and caused a big enough commotion inside that Judge Ernie S. Burke threatened to clear the court. After a brief hearing, Judge Burke dropped the "common addict" charge, set January 4 as the trial date on the possession charges, and released Ray on $1000 bond. Ray left hurriedly, saying to reporters, "I don't feel up to answering questions about my life or this event," then flying to Nashville with Jeff in the Cessna, rejoining the gang who arrived in the Flex direct from Evansville.

Back in New York Milt Shaw and Larry Myers tried to control the damage. No, Myers told the New York *Post,* Ray had never been "in serious trouble" before. Ed Sullivan called Myers and said they'd have to postpone Ray's Sunday appearance. Myers argued with Sullivan, saying, "Come on, the guy is out on bail, he isn't guilty yet." But Sullivan didn't want anybody on the show who was in trouble with the law. Myers called Ray and told him the disappointing news; he took it stoically. In Nashville, Tennessee State, Hank Crawford's alma mater, wanted to cancel Ray's gig at a homecoming concert. Dozens of calls flashed back and forth to Shaw until the promoter rented the Nashville State Fair Coliseum so the show could go on. The coliseum held 3500 people, more than TSU's hall, and *Variety* reported that Ray was "grinning broadly" as he performed to ovations from the sellout crowd. He refused, however, to discuss the arrest with newsmen.

As the tour continued, the problems continued. Nervous promoters asked Shaw for telegrams guaranteeing Ray's appearance; the New Orleans promoter printed his in the *Louisiana Weekly* to quell rumors: "Ray Charles and His Entire Unit of 20 Artists will definitely appear as contracted in New Orleans on December 1st. . . . He is playing and has played all contracted dates up to the present time." Southern Methodist University called to cancel its December 8 concert. "He's still under charge for possession of narcotics," said an SMU official. "Until it's cleared up we cannot sponsor his appearance here." For Shaw Artists Ray and his drug arrests were becoming a pain in the neck. Writer Nat Hentoff, doing a magazine profile of Ray, came to the office in December and heard that Ray had been out of touch for days. "Be nice to him when he calls," an agent said to Milt Shaw, "he's frightened."

"The hell he is," said Shaw. "I know him. He's embarrassed. If he had some of the frigging humility he had five years ago when I started him, he wouldn't be in this jackpot. And listen! Cancel those Philadelphia bookings for him. Throw them in the toilet. That's all I need now, another pinch on top of this."

Ray was a newcomer to the white press, and there the story of his arrest died as a three-day wonder. The black press had been following him for a decade, and there the story lingered through December. In a widely syndicated series, "The Genius and Heartbreak of Singer Ray Charles," Chicago *Defender* reporter Bob Hunter blended the Indianapolis news with familiar biography into a sympathetic but penetrating portrait of Ray's predicament. The hardships of his childhood had left a "deep sense of hurt" that "spills forth with untamed fury" in his music, Hunter declared. Sadly, trying to dull the hurt with heroin had made Ray an addict, and now he faced the possibility of prison. Because he was rich, Ray might be able to beat the rap if he promised to take the cure, but, Hunter asked, "can a sixteen-year-old habit be broken so easily?" He hoped so but saw a well-known downhill cycle emerging:

> Of late Ray has been flirting with one of deterioration's main companions—unreliability. When Charles Parker . . . and Lady Day began showing up late for sets, and sometimes missing them altogether, the obvious end was in sight. Many people feel that this is precisely the situation with Baby Ray.

The Indianapolis arrest turned Ray's addiction from an open secret to a known fact, beginning a game of cat and mouse between Ray and the police that lasted years. In city after city detectives showed up backstage, for no reason, just checking, then disappeared after a word and handshake with Jeff. The game was subtle and not one-sided. "The cops wanted to bust Ray, but they loved him too," Hank Crawford remembered. "There were times when they had him, but they put the squeeze on him instead. Partly they figured, Ray's blind, somebody's got to be shooting him up, and that's who they were really after." Traveling as a celebrity with a retinue gave Ray a degree of protection. Most days he "got his taste" at the hotel before the gig, then afterward again in his room. "If they ain't gonna break down my door to get me, they ain't gonna get me," he told Duke.

After the first shock wore off, the arrest left Ray more cynical than ever about the law. Cops hounded poor junkies and left rich dealers alone; that was "kicking the weak and protecting the strong," Ray figured. Nobody had the right to tell him what he could or couldn't put in his body, and he had no intention of changing his ways. Luckily he had money. "Just like you can buy grades of silk, you can buy grades of law," Ray wrote years later, discussing the arrest. "Good lawyers, like good doctors, don't come cheap . . . Your chances of surviving the crisis start improving at the first sign of those new green bills." An Indianapolis lawyer told Jeff that $6000 ought to do it. The cops had entered by a ruse and without a warrant; that was illegal search. Ray would have to appear in court in January, but the case would never go to trial. The miserable morning in November began to recede.

By Christmas, "Hit the Road Jack" was falling fast, but "Unchain My Heart" climbed swiftly to #15 on the way to a #9 peak. Ray got back home for the holidays on Hepburn Avenue and, like any long-absent father, felt awkward at first with his children. Christmas Eve he went down to the basement to put together a bike for six-year-old Ray Jr. The next morning the boy was overjoyed to find the bike under the tree, but puzzled to see the handlebars on backward. Ray Jr. was beginning to understand that his daddy wasn't like most daddies. He wasn't home very much, and when he was, he barely talked to him or his brothers. And he had such a strange way of moving, wiggling and slapping himself all the time. Ray Jr. asked his mother about it, and Della said that's just the way Daddy was.

As usual Hank took a room at the Watkins and came over every day to write charts for Ray's next single, "At the Club," and a funny new Percy Mayfield tune, "Hide nor Hair." Ray also started working on his next album—his idea this time, country songs. He called Sid and asked him to get together forty country hits from the last twenty years. Feller hadn't known that Ray loved country music, and Clark and Newton were frankly dubious, but Ray insisted. Sid put a call out to Nashville publishers, and from the tapes they sent in, he picked forty and sent them to California. Ray listened to them and began selecting the dozen he liked best.

On New Year's Eve Ray and company played the Los Angeles Sports Arena for Hal Zeiger, an ending so like the year's beginning at the Palladium that 1961, with all its ups and downs, must have seemed a mirage. Yet when they finished the gig at 2 A.M., it had become 1962.

I Can't Stop
Loving You
1962-1963

It took two trips to Indianapolis to get the drug bust over with. On January 9, 1962, in a courtroom packed with fans, Ray sat silent and sunken into himself, squeezing his hands between his knees, as his lawyer attacked the police for entering the hotel room on false pretenses and without a proper warrant. Three weeks later he stood beside Jeff in a five-minute session as Judge Burke ruled the police search illegal and dismissed the charges. Though a celebrity, Burke said, Ray Charles "had the same constitutional rights as any other citizen." From the hearing, with one "no comment" to the press, Ray flew to New York for the first country album sessions.

Two Midas years had made Ray a rich man. In 1961, Ray Charles Enterprises grossed a conservatively estimated $1.5 million, up fifty percent from the year before. Despite the expenses of carrying a big band, touring at $5000 per one-nighter turned a profit; that income was dwarfed by the singer, songwriter, and publisher royalty checks from ABC, Atlantic, and BMI, which, less minimal office expenses, came in as pure gravy. Not that Ray waited patiently for money owed him. When Atlantic got behind in its payments, Ray sent lawyer Earl Zaidens after Ahmet and Jerry. Zaidens got as far as serving papers before Atlantic coughed up $50,000. Then Zaidens saw the other side of Ray Charles. Ray had been paying Zaidens a retainer for "services exclu-sive of litigation," but the lawyer felt that, as litigator, he was entitled to a third of the Atlantic settlement. Ray balked; he thought the retainer was enough. "If you take a third," he said, "you'll no longer be my attorney." "So be it," said Zaidens, and that ended their relationship.

Ray bought a few toys with his newfound riches, among them a sleek Corvette that Duke drove while Ray shifted the gears. Yet the man who had starved as a boy in Or-lando took money too seriously to be satisfied with toys. Wealth inspired Ray to take up the adult game of making money. He had come to love the cut and thrust of fight-ing it out as an independent entrepreneur, and he proved himself a quick study of busi-ness forms and language. "If I used a bit of legal terminology, like 'debenture,' " Newton recalled, "Ray would jump on it. 'What does that mean?' he'd ask. After I explained, he'd say, 'Oh, that's a great word, I like that word.' "

Two years of profits had left Ray awash in cash, and for him as for other lucky en-trepreneurs, the question arose: where to put it? Bank accounts were safe—several of Ray's New York accounts climbed to $100,000 and more—yet bank accounts, Ray learned, are more subject to taxes and the whittling effect of inflation than many in-vestments. As 1962 began, Ray was looking into more adventurous outlets for his money.

In this search Joe Adams proved indispensable. A year after coming aboard, Adams was still around, emceeing, doing the lights and other odd but inventive jobs like de-signing new outfits for the Raelets. Ray had watched Adams closely, and Adams had passed all the tests. He and Ray hadn't signed any piece of paper, but by early 1962 Adams had become an employee a cut above the rest. Joe Adams wasn't afraid of any-body, white or black, and he didn't hesitate to chew out those he deemed incompetent. Joe and Ray had fierce arguments, and Joe, unlike anyone else in the entourage, could hold his own and sometimes win. Adams had also been well-to-do for a decade; he had a portfolio of investments and Los Angeles properties. He began to advise Ray on his investments, recommending apartment houses and, later, a ranch in northern Califor-nia. Ray flew often enough, Joe said; why not buy a travel agency? Ray thought that was an excellent idea; they could even buy a big plane for the band.

That winter Ray had long discussions with Clark and Newton about starting his own label, Tangerine Records, and here too Joe proved invaluable. After two years, ABC-Paramount felt well satisfied with its bargain in signing Ray. He was making money for the company hand over fist, and, as the executives hoped, his presence had attracted other black artists. They had just signed jazz great John Coltrane and Curtis Mayfield, whose group, the Impressions, had "Gypsy Woman" high on the charts. Since ABC prided itself on being "the label of labels," with Impulse, Chancellor, and Westminster already under their wing, giving their biggest star his own label was an easy concession. For Ray, owning a label meant taking another big step up the music business food chain. Asked years later why he wanted to own a record company, Ray laughed. "That's like me asking you why you want to own your own car. Why do people want their own anything? It was natural. I am a musician, and I was saying to myself, 'I see what the record companies are doing. I don't know if I'll be successful at it, but I'd like to try.' " How hard could it be? Find artists and songs for them to sing; get them arranged and recorded, press a few thousand discs and get them out there—he could do for others what he was already doing for himself. Music, Ray figured, was his best investment: use the money he made from music to expand his control of the music-making process.

Music publishing and investing are basically paperwork businesses, and the label so far was no more than a name, Tangerine Record Corporation, and a logo, a big T with a small RC entwined around its stem. A big band, in contrast, is an unwieldy matter of men and matériel, and running his was the biggest practical problem that Ray faced every day. The "augmented band" had become permanent, the small band a thing of the past. Now sixteen musicians and four singers, all of them artists and some of them loose-livers, had to be shepherded from airports to hotels to stages to airports on time day after day. Their tuxedos and dresses had to be cleaned and pressed, the library of their chart books kept in order. Instruments, luggage, and stage equipment could not be lost despite continual transit. Every Sunday everyone had to be paid. The days when Ray and the band barnstormed as buddies across Texas were long gone: he had become a millionaire, they were still hardworking musicians paying their own room and board out of decent but low salaries. Ray often flew to gigs, meeting the group, who had humped on the bus, at the side of the stage. Ray was merciless about getting the music right onstage, but Jeff had the job of keeping the fellows in line offstage. Even in the small-band days Ray had thought Jeff too soft, but now that the band had doubled its size, he became more and more impatient with Jeff's down-home style. Joe, on the other hand, had an endless vocabulary of superior stares and sarcastic remarks that stung the men like whips. He was the martinet Ray had always wanted, a manager willing to play bad cop to his good cop. It was still too soon to remove Jeff from running the band, but through 1962 that possibility grew.

No one around Ray was glad to see Joe's increasing influence on the boss. Hal Zeiger made it clear that he preferred Jeff by adding, "Entire production under the supervision of Jeff D. Brown," as a tag line to his newspaper ads. "I wouldn't say I welcomed Joe to the family," said Larry Myers. "I saw nothing wrong with Jeff." The fellows couldn't stand Joe. Hank thought he was two-faced: "One minute he'd be laughing with you, the next cussing you out." Jeff's girlfriend Shirley found Joe's manner slick and insinuating; he seemed jealous of anyone closer to Ray than he was. Jeff, the one most threatened by Joe's rise, took it more philosophically than the others. "Ray liked Joe because Joe had the same cold attitude as Ray," he remembered. "Naturally we didn't agree, but if that was what Ray was going to do, that was that."

By 1962, Ray's growing business had him flying so frequently between New York and LA that he became what later decades called "bicoastal." Ray Charles Enterprises had its office at 100 West Forty-second Street; Shaw, ABC, his accountants, lawyers, principal bank accounts, and registered corporations were also in New York. Los Angeles was Della and home and family, and, because of Joe Adams' influence, a secondary business center. New York was also Mae, though that link was weakening. "Mae got pushy," Wade remembered. "She wanted to be Della, but nobody was gonna be Della Bea." Once Della came to Chicago to bring Ray his winter clothes and stayed with him at an uptown hotel. Mae flew out to Chicago and checked in to a downtown hotel. "Shit," Ray told Duke, "Mae's downtown. I don't know what the hell to do." Duke went downtown, talked to Mae, and got her to go back to New York.

With these currents moving above and below the surface, Ray got to New York the first week of February to record the country album. In two sessions they got down six tracks with the big band, charts by Gerald Wilson and Gil Fuller, then Ray flew out to LA and laid down six strings-and-voices tracks arranged by Marty Paich—the two sessions cost $22,000, *Billboard* reported. Sid Feller had become a convert to Ray's country music experiment. "I hadn't known what the hell he was talking about, then, boom, it worked," Feller remembered. "Ray understood country music. He loved the simple plaintive lyrics, and he felt that giving the music a lush treatment would make it different." Clark and Newton remained skeptical. "Who wants country music from Ray Charles?" they asked each other. Then Ray sent in the tape. "We put it on the machine," Newton recalled, "and we went out of our minds. It was the greatest."

Awkwardly but accurately named, *Modern Sounds in Country and Western Music* is an extraordinary work of art. Its dozen tunes run the Nashville gamut from the traditional "Careless Love" to the rock 'n' roll "Bye Bye Love"; from Hank Williams' classic "Hey Good Lookin' " to the unknown "I Can't Stop Loving You," the B-side of a Don Gibson flop from 1958. Big-band tracks alternate with string-and-voice tracks, but for all the jazz and symphonic effects, the heart of every arrangement is a simply strummed guitar. Ray's bluesy melismas wring every tear out of the country weepers, all the poetry out of their monosyllabic lyrics:

> *Born to lose, I've lived my life in vain*
> *Every dream has only brought me pain*
> *All my life I've always been so blue*
> *Born to lose, and now I'm losing you.*

On "I Can't Stop Loving You" Ray uses a device that became a trademark: letting the chorus lead the lyric, his solo voice following:

> **Chorus:** *They say that time . . .*
> **Ray:** *. . . they say that time . . .*
> **Chorus:** *. . . heals a broken heart . . .*
> **Ray:** *. . . heals a broken heart*
> **Chorus:** *. . . but time has stood still . . .*
> **Ray:** *. . . time has stood still . . .*
> **Chorus:** *. . . since we've been apart . . .*
> **Ray:** *. . . since we've been apart.*

Following the chorus gives Ray a roving independence over the musical flow. No longer the singer fixed in the spotlight, he cruises in and around the music as if on wings, the Greek chorus no longer commenting on him, but he commenting on the chorus.

Though an experiment, *Modern Sounds* is, from the razzmatazz opening of "Bye Bye Love," American music comfortable as an old shoe. Ray neither parodies nor jazzes hillbilly; he sings it his way, expanding country's sound spectrum without distorting its essential shades. The naturalness of Ray's blend obscures the fact that *Modern Sounds* marks his boldest leap yet over the barriers of idiom. Invading white country music, a musical world proud of its redneck roots, was something pop-jazz singers didn't do: you had to *be* country to sing country in 1962. Yet Ray had been country since he'd heard the Grand Ole Opry in Greenville and gigged with the Playboys in Tampa. More surprising than Ray's singing country is how long this element of his music had lain dormant. After *Modern Sounds* it lay dormant no longer. In time country music became a primary pigment on Ray's palette—and on pop music's palette: *Modern Sounds* did much to introduce country music to city listeners and to show Nashville producers how to color their music to reach a wider audience.

By the end of February, Ray and Clark and Newton were ready to announce the formation of Tangerine Records. ABC threw a lavish press party at the Waldorf-Astoria, and Ray, with Joe at his side, announced he would direct Tangerine as the label's A&R man. He was looking for "a variety of musical categories," Ray said, and he promised "important name artists" as well as unknowns. ABC would distribute Tangerine records; the first release would be out in a couple of months. No, he wouldn't be recording for Tangerine himself; he had re-signed with ABC-Paramount for three years on the same terms. The *Billboard* reporter present noted in his story that record labels for stars were unusual but no longer unknown: Frank Sinatra had just founded Reprise and Sam Cooke SAR.

That spring was the heyday of the Twist, Chubby Checker, and Joey Dee. Atlantic put out an album of Ray's rockers called *Do the Twist!*, with instructions and diagrams showing squares how to swing their hips; the repackaged LP rose to #11 on the album chart and stayed there a year. Joe Adams took time off in March to play a psychiatrist in *The Manchurian Candidate*. In April, as Ray and company moved through New Jersey, ABC released *Modern Sounds*.

From day one the company shipped albums as fast as they could press them. Not only the album was hot. Disc jockeys started playing "I Can't Stop Loving You," and Larry Newton started getting calls from distributors and jukebox operators crying for the release of a single. No one, including Ray, had thought the Gibson song would hit. "You can tell what I thought of it," said Feller, "by the weak position I gave it on the album, second to last on side two. Yet that's the song the public picked." Clark and Newton called Ray to ask his permission to put out the single. He was reluctant. His latest single, "At the Club," had climbed to #50 in four weeks and was still rising; why compete against himself?

Then, on Thursday afternoon, April 19, a distributor called from Philadelphia. Tab Hunter had covered "I Can't Stop Loving You" on Dot Records, he said. Dj's were already playing it, and if ABC didn't get a single out, Tab Hunter would have the hit. Ray had gone back to LA from a week at the Apollo, and Clark and Newton reached him on Hepburn Avenue. "Now we have to put the single out," they said, and Ray agreed. He had heard Tab Hunter's record, a note-for-note copy of his own, down to the cracks he put into his voice on purpose, and he wanted to crush the imitation. There was only one problem: the album track of the song was over four minutes long, and a single couldn't be over two and a half. Ray thought for a moment and said, "Put Sid on the phone."

That Thursday was the first night of Passover. Sid was hoping to leave early to join Gert and the children at his mother's seder in Brooklyn, but he got on the phone and talked it over with Ray. What could they cut out of the full-length track? Ray picked his cuts; Sid said okay and went straight to Bell Sound Studio, at Fifty-fourth and Broadway, where the tapes were stored.

When Sid ran the master tape, however, he realized that the instrumentation before and after Ray's cuts didn't match: at one end there were strings, at the other no strings. He tried cutting a different section. It worked, and he did it. Nobody, not even Ray, ever noticed the difference, and Sid never told him. Before sending out the edit for pressing as a single, Sid made a couple dozen acetates that Newton rushed out for major dj's to play over the weekend. Sid got to the seder late, but he had saved the day. "If Tab Hunter's record had gotten any more head start," he recalled, "Ray's record would have been lost. Even though Hunter was copying us, people would have thought we were copying him. But once those acetates got to the dj's Friday morning, Tab Hunter was finished."

ABC took out a full-page ad in the April 28 *Billboard* to announce that "from the Nation's Hottest Selling Album, Ray Charles releases the smash single of our time, 'I Can't Stop Loving You.'" A week later, as Ray played Cleveland on the second Zeiger tour, the single entered the pop chart at #78; *Modern Sounds* stood at #50 on the album chart. In Philadelphia, the touring group could feel the rising tide of excitement. When they got to Convention Hall, the place was packed with 12,000 people, the largest crowd that veteran ushers could remember. Duke walked Ray out on stage, and the noise the people made, he remembered, "was like launching a rocket from Cape Canaveral, an ovation like I never heard in my life. 'What the fuck?' Ray said to me, and I said, 'Man, there's 20,000 people out here,' and he said, 'Get out of here!'"

Ray was on a roll. The tour got to New York, and *Modern Sounds* jumped to #10, "Can't Stop" from #52 to #21. This year *Variety* loved Ray's Carnegie Hall show. Hank Crawford's band opening was now "driving and sophisticated," and Ray's fourteen-song set "carefully laid out to build dramatic impact"; songs from his "recent country and western album received the most enthusiastic response." The album and single kept rising, and the gang took off for three weeks in Europe. For nine nights in May, Ray and company played to SRO crowds at the Olympia, Paris' great vaudeville theater, and the French received him more rapturously, if possible, than they had seven months before. "I'd have walked from Orléans to hear Ray Charles," a fan told *Jazz Magazine,* which wrote that Armstrong and Bechet had *"le magnétisme personnel,"* but Ray had their power "four times over." One saw "couples in their sixties and children of eleven shouting back their 'Yeah' with everybody else." Ray was beginning to feel at home abroad. Maurice Cullasz had him to dinner, and he devoured the French dishes Cullasz's wife Vanette prepared, especially her *bouche à la reine*. The fellows were less adventurous. Ahmet Ertegun took them to the newly opened Le Drugstore, but the fried egg on top of Drugstore hamburgers turned their American stomachs. Finally they found a soul food restaurant in Montparnasse.

As *Modern Sounds* reached #5 and "Can't Stop" #4 in America, the gang left Paris for Brussels, where the crowd stood in the rain for hours, and on to the Sportspalast in Berlin, where Hitler once spoke. That night they were magnificent, playing ballsy jazz with utmost swagger. During "The Danger Zone," when all the lights went out except for one spotlight on Ray, the music sounded so ominous that Duke Wade got an eerie feeling, "like Hitler was there his damn self." Duke had ordered wiener schnitzel before the show, wrapped it up in towels, and put it on the hotel room radiators. "When we come back we'll eat the hell out of this," he told Ray. But as a result of Cold War tensions caused by the new Berlin Wall, the air corridors closed at midnight, and they took off right after the show and never did get back to their wiener schnitzel.

Ray was back in Paris, asleep at the Claridge, when Sam Clark called in the first week of June. Duke answered. Tell Ray to come home, Clark said; "I Can't Stop Loving You" is #1. Duke woke Ray up. "Sam's on the phone," he said. "You gotta get your ass back to the States."

"Why?" said Ray.

" 'Cause you got a number-one hit over there."

"Get the fuck outta here."

"No," said Duke, "you talk to him." Ray took the phone. Orders for forty, fifty, and sixty thousand "Can't Stop" were coming from Dallas, Miami, and Atlanta, and sales of the single had passed 700,000 on the way to a million. *Modern Sounds* was cruising to half a million units and more. Three years, three #1 hits, and this one, from what Sam was saying, far bigger than the others; a monster, a steamroller. Sam was right: it was time to go home.

"I Can't Stop Loving You" ruled at #1 for five long weeks that golden summer of 1962, dipping to #3 in July and only beginning to slide in August, dropping off in September after eighteen weeks on the charts. The single also topped the R&B and Easy Listening charts for weeks, though, curiously, it never made the country chart. *Modern Sounds,* meanwhile, held #1 on the album chart for fourteen weeks and stayed on for two years. Ray's country music experiment had turned out to be a phenomenal success, and "I Can't Stop Loving You" the kind of pop music event that happens only two or three times a decade. Ray Charles' hymn of undying devotion saturated the airwaves of America that summer and soon the airwaves of the world. By early 1963 Japanese women began to greet Americans by singing, "I can't stop loving you," then bursting into giggles.

Why was "I Can't Stop Loving You" so popular? It doesn't have "Georgia" 's subtle shadings or "Hit the Road Jack" 's comic bounce. It does have folk-song strength— a major-scale melody marching up and down over three simple chords—and it has operatic grandeur, a baritone backed by chorus and orchestra. Ray sings his overwhelming love for an unnamed "you," and because the lyrics and mood don't specify romance, "you" could be a friend, a child, a parent, any listener who responds, "Ray can't stop loving *me!*" The music builds to a climax at the last line of the verse:

But time has stood still since we've been apart . . .

and in the brief pause before the refrain, the music propels us to drop our reserve, take a big breath, and join Ray and all the other voices singing:

I can't stop lo-o-o-oving you!

Starting out to rake the hay of that sunny summer, Ray had a surprise for the fellows. "We're going to the airport," he said after a gig a few nights down the road. The band boarded the Flex not thinking much, but when the driver bypassed the passenger terminal and pulled up to the commercial hangar, they started wondering what was up. "This is your new plane," said Ray, and then they got their first glimpse of the 44-seat, two-engine Martin 404 he had just bought from American Airlines for half a million dollars. The men and women climbed the aluminum steps into the sleek, silver plane, and looked goggle-eyed at the rows of plush seats, the lounge, galley, and spic-and-span toilets. "Stewardesses served us drinks and food," remembered Leroy Cooper. "The cats started crying, 'Bring me a scotch, no, a martini, if you please.' After a week, Ray being Ray, the stewardesses were gone, and the Raelets had the job."

In the Martin, Ray and company set off hopscotching across America. From the Southwest they flew east to Asbury Park for the Fourth of July, on to Chicago, Dallas, and New Orleans, then back to LA for the Shrine Auditorium on July 27. Every show was a sellout. "I Can't Stop Loving You" reached one and a half million sold, and *Modern Sounds* became ABC's first million-selling album. ABC released one *Greatest Hits* album, and Atlantic released two, *The Ray Charles Story Vol. I and II*. "Born to Lose," "Can't Stop" 's B-side, had its own run on the charts, and then "You Don't Know Me" started a quick climb to #2 in early September. Ray had become, for the moment but by a wide margin, the most popular figure in American pop music. " 'I Can't Stop Loving You' was the record that changed everything," as Duke Wade put it. "The money got better, everything got better."

Between gigs Ray flew back to LA to work on an album with Louis Jordan, whom he had signed as Tangerine's first artist. According to Jordan's wife, Ray had "wined and dined" Jordan to get him and felt proud to have his onetime idol on Tangerine. It was a sentimental choice—Jordan had long since passed his peak—but Ray and Jordan were both optimistic and eager to finish his album. Ray was also producing albums with Percy Mayfield and Little Jimmie Scott. Many a morning Scott and Mayfield came over to the house on Hepburn, picking songs and keys with Ray at the living room piano. Gerald Wilson and Marty Paich, both writing arrangements for Ray's follow-up country album, might stop by to pick up Ray's taped sketches or drop off finished charts.

Della always had something good on the stove, and a workaday informality prevailed. One evening when Ray and Della had to go out, Gerald Wilson gladly baby-sat the three boys for a few hours. Scott sensed how important Della was to Ray: "Della had to put up with Margie and Mae having babies by him, but she was Ray's *home* wife."

Yet even at home Ray was restless. A reporter from *Melody Maker* found him splashing with Ray Jr. in the pool while Della sat inside with David watching a Western on TV. First Ray talked bitterly about his own struggle to succeed: "When you grow up in the southern states of America where anyone colored is treated like dirt, you either grow to accept it or become determined to find something better—even if it kills you." Then he felt like going for a drive, and Jeff drove them out to the beach in a white convertible, Ray chain-smoking and talking knowledgeably about the British hit parade. At the beach he ran up and down the sand at top speed, plunging into the surf. That night Ray led them on a high-speed round of nightclubs. "Sometimes ten minutes of the floor show was enough before Ray became fidgety. He'd sit uncomfortably, bounce on the balls of his feet, and have yet another cigarette." At three A.M. Ray decided he wanted to fly to San Francisco, but the reporter had had enough, and he left Ray and Jeff arguing about where they'd have breakfast in San Francisco.

Pumped up by success, Ray seemed to career from crisis to triumph to new crisis. In Portland, Oregon, that August Ray got so stoned that two of the band members had to walk him around backstage and feed him coffee to keep him awake enough to perform. The gang flew south, playing Atlanta, Memphis, and Tulsa, Oklahoma. After the Tulsa show, Ray and his valet took off for the airport. Jeff and the band, following in a bus, stopped for a bite to eat at a drive-in restaurant. No colored, they were told. When they put up a stink, four police cars arrived to investigate a "racial disturbance," and they had to take out cold cuts from a Git 'n' Go food store across the street—this just weeks before James Meredith registered at Ole Miss amid nightlong riots. By the 31st they had hopped back east to Harlem's Hotel Theresa and rehearsals for *Modern Sounds in Country and Western Music Volume Two.*

Just as with the first *Modern Sounds,* Ray and Sid recorded *Modern Sounds Vol. Two* on both coasts, the big-band tracks in New York September 5 and Marty Paich's strings and voices a few days later in LA. The LA sessions went smoothly, but in New York Ray got high and needed Mae, sitting beside him, to feed him lyrics that otherwise drifted away. Ray also didn't like one of Wilson's charts, and with Sid and all the musicians standing around looking at one another, he took two hours to dictate a complete rewrite. No fault marred the finished product; Ray was in fine voice, and on "No Letter Today" and "Midnight" he overdubbed a second vocal to sing light, true harmony with himself. Yet like many sequels, *Modern Sounds Vol. Two* suffers by comparison with the breakthrough work it followed, and Ray achieves nothing like the majesty of "Can't

Stop" or the knife-edged pain of "You Don't Know Me." Clark and Newton, however, knew the market was hungry for more country-Ray, and they rushed it out. *Modern Sounds Vol. Two* hit the charts in November, peaked at #2, and stayed on for sixty-seven weeks.

In November, a year after the bust, they played Indianapolis again, this time without incident. ABC released "You Are My Sunshine" from *Modern Sounds Vol. Two,* and the single rose rapidly on the charts. After Thanksgiving, Ray and company opened one of their biggest gigs ever, ten nights at the Latin Casino in Cherry Hill, New Jersey, just across the river from Philadelphia. An 1800-seat nightclub that dated back to the big-band glory days, the Latin Casino booked its performers from the first rank of entertainers, white and black: Dean Martin, Ella Fitzgerald, and Patti Page. Larry Myers had gotten Ray top dollar, $25,000 plus a percentage, but the gig was even more valuable as a showcase. "Club owners all over the country," noted the Philadelphia *Tribune,* "will be watching to see how the nitery's customers will react to Ray." The first night was ragged, the band straggling late onto the stage and the sound badly balanced, but the problems were fixed by the second night, and the run turned out to be a smashing success. Capacity crowds filled the club for every show, the people clapping in rhythm from the moment the music started. Milt Shaw and Myers came down from New York, and Mae, presiding at a reserved table, was introduced to one and all as "Mrs. Charles."

"You Are My Sunshine" peaked at #7, and its composer, Governor Jimmie Davis of Louisiana, planned an elaborate award ceremony for Ray at a New Orleans concert in December. Fog enshrouded the city airport that night, however, and the Martin landed at Baton Rouge. Davis sent a state police motorcycle escort to rush the gang eighty miles south to New Orleans. Ray still had to get high, and he disappeared with Fathead into the airport bathroom. "Man, we gotta get the fuck out of here," Duke half-whispered through the stall door.

"I ain't ready, I ain't ready," Ray kept saying.

Duke went outside and stood guard, keeping everybody out of the bathroom but trying to look casual before the dozens of troopers milling about the airport lobby. Finally Ray was ready, but despite the motorcycles and their sirens, they got to the Loyola Field House three hours late. The integrated crowd, "New Orleans' first fully all-American audience," said the Louisiana *Weekly,* had waited patiently and erupted with joy when the band arrived. Governor Davis gave Ray the award, and the Martin took the gang home to LA for the holidays.

At a Christmas party, Duke Wade recognized a pretty, light-skinned young woman as Sandra Jean Betts, a college student Ray had met in Dayton, Ohio, two years before. Then she had been eighteen and with her aunt; now she was on her own, working as a receptionist. Ray had never forgotten her, Duke said, and he took her number. Ray called the next day and invited her to his concert at the Shrine that night. "Afterwards I went backstage," Betts later told a reporter, "and he asked me to go out with him. I had to turn him down because I was living at a residence for young women and I had to be in by one A.M." But Sandra Jean came New Year's Eve as his special guest to a concert in Long Beach, and soon she was ensconced at the Olympian Motor Hotel, the same motel Ray used for Mae when she came out to LA. For the moment Ray was infatuated. He told Sandra Jean he wanted to teach her how to be a woman, that he loved her and would divorce his wife for her.

ABC sent Ray a year-end accounting of his earnings for 1962: $1.6 million dollars. Through three Midas years Ray's touch had grown ever more golden.

A few days into 1963 Ray and the gang taped the *Dinah Shore Show.* The afternoon at NBC's LA television studios was a ball, and not just because it paid $15,000. Shore and the staff welcomed everybody warmly, showed them to large, clean dressing rooms, and gave them plenty of rehearsal time on a classy black-and-white set. "The Piano" was the theme of the show, Liberace the other featured guest. Ray sang "You Don't Know Me" and they rocked out with "What'd I Say," the cameras drifting slowly around the bandstand. Everybody sounded and looked first-rate; this was Ray's best TV exposure to date. At the finale all the guests sang "Zip-a-Dee-Doo-Dah," and Dinah put a friendly hand on Ray's shoulder. A white woman touching a black man was an unusual sight on television at the time, and when the show aired, a wave of approval rippled through the black press: "Dinah Shore and Ray Charles on TV is a sight Klansmen hate to see," commented the Philadelphia *Tribune.*

That done, the band went on vacation and everyone dispersed. Ray stayed in LA, Duke and Hank bunking at the Watkins to be nearby. Touring from spring to the new year, then wintering in LA had become a strong rhythm in Ray's life. It made sense: a natural lull in gigs followed the holidays, and Ray had had two terrifying experiences with winter flying: when they were coming in to Oklahoma City, ice coated the Cessna's wings and windshield; in Newark, they came out of low cloud cover on top of a runway full of planes. The first time, a circle of ice melted in the windshield big enough for pilot McGarrity to eyeball his way in. The second time, the pilot managed to zoom the plane up again into the soup and straggle over to Idlewild. On the ground, Ray screamed at Jeff and McGarrity: they must never, *never* take him up in weather like that again. Jeff didn't like being chewed out, but he knew the rules of the road: "You'll have a lot of narrow escapes no matter what, but the less chances you take, the better." Not touring in winter cut the risk of flying to a minimum Ray could accept.

Ray's LA winter days began in the late morning, when he went over the mail with Duke in his upstairs den. One day in the pile of song tapes that people sent in, Duke found a taped letter from Mae. Ray said put it on. "I know you don't wanna hear this," Mae's voice began. "I sure the fuck don't," said Ray. "Take it off and throw it in the wastebasket." Another day Duke opened a brown envelope filled with charts returned by Atlantic Records. Stuck in the middle, almost as if Atlantic had hoped Ray wouldn't find it, was a check. "You got a check here from Atlantic," said Duke. "How much?" asked Ray. "Thirty thousand." "Okay, give it to Della Bea."

Afternoons were for business. Tangerine Records took time. Ray had Lula Reed, singer of the original "Drown in My Own Tears," on the label, newcomer Terrell Prude, and a promising young group, the Vocals. Louis Jordan's album *Hallelujah—Louis Jordan Is Back!* came out. Jordan hoped the release would trigger a comeback; when it dive-bombed, he blamed Ray. "Ray must have just signed me up as a tax deduction," Jordan told jazz writer Leonard Feather, complaining that Ray lost interest once the records were made. "The jockeys played them, but if you went into a store you couldn't find them." Jordan criticized Ray unfairly. Compared with Jordan's greatest hits, *Hallelujah*'s tracks have none of the vitality that had made Jordan famous. Louis Jordan continued as a lively stage performer for years, but as a recording artist he was ancient history. If any label could have brought him back, little Tangerine didn't stand a chance. At least Ray got Jordan's album out: Jimmie Scott's album, *Falling in Love Is Wonderful,* never appeared. Scott had recorded for Savoy, a Newark-based indy owned by Herman Lubinsky. When Lubinsky heard about the Tangerine album, he declared that Scott still belonged to Savoy. Scott insisted that Lubinsky was bluffing, but Clark and Newton and Adams all advised Ray not to tangle up Tangerine's first album in a dogfight. Ray took their advice. Running a record company, he was learning, was tougher than it looked.

Evenings Ray spent with Sandra Jean in motels, where he registered under false names, and at a hideaway apartment he rented. They made love and lay around watching TV by the hour. Sandra found it amazing how Ray could follow a show's story by the sounds, always knowing if the characters were inside or outside, in a car or airplane. "Ray, look at that," she'd say, pointing at the screen, and Ray would say, "I see, I see." Some nights they club-hopped with Duke. One night at the 5-4 Ballroom, they took a big table, buying drinks for all. When it came time to pay the check, Ray and Duke discovered they didn't have a dime in their pockets. Ray being Ray, the club owner smiled and said don't worry, it's on the house. Out in the car, Ray and Duke laughed themselves silly.

Most mornings Ray got back to Hepburn by dawn. Della, of course, knew about

Ray's womanizing, but she and Ray seldom fought, and she didn't demand that he stay home. Della just continued, quietly looking after the boys and the house, playing cards with her circle of lady friends. Sometimes Duke took her to the movies. Duke figured Della was the best thing that had ever happened to Ray: "Della Bea had access to all the money in the world, and she clipped coupons for groceries."

Ray's LA winter stretched comfortably through February into March. The longer he stayed, the more Ray wanted to end his bicoastal years and center himself on the West Coast. He talked it over with Joe Adams. He'd need to move his corporations to California. A lot of paperwork, said Adams, but it could be done. Money from "I Can't Stop Loving You" was still pouring in, and Adams urged Ray to buy a house. Prime residential property in Los Angeles was a solid investment, he argued; Ray had outgrown Hepburn Avenue and deserved a house worthy of his status. Della and the kids liked the idea of a big new house; more important to Ray was a "foundation," a building that could house Ray Charles Enterprises, everything under one roof, with offices for the companies and a studio where Ray could rehearse and record anytime he felt like it. Adams set about scouting home and business properties.

In late March, as the band gathered for the spring tour, the Beatles topped the English charts with "Please, Please Me," but no one in America had heard of them. Hardly anybody had heard of Bob Dylan, the new hotshot on New York's folk scene, but Motown was a hot new label, launching one artist after another: Mary Wells, Marvin Gaye, the Supremes. Little Stevie Wonder put out his first album, *A Tribute to Uncle Ray*, his eleven-year-old voice piping Ray's barrel-chested originals. *Billboard* declared Ray the number-one recording artist of 1962, "I Can't Stop Loving You" the top-selling single, and *Modern Sounds* the top-selling album, but now, a year later, Ray was in a mini-slump: "Don't Set Me Free" didn't make much noise, and "Take These Chains from My Heart" peaked at #8. Sandra Jean missed her March period, and Ray sent her to Dr. Foster. If she was pregnant, Ray said, he would take care of her. Then he and the gang flew off in the Martin.

As the tour began in April, Ray was pissed at Hal Zeiger; no one remembers why. He got to his hotel in Cleveland and told Duke to tell "motherfucking Hal Zeiger" that he was still in California.

"The man'll have a heart attack," said Duke.

"Damn him," said Ray.

Backstage at the Music Hall, Duke started saying noisily, "That son of a bitch, where can he be?"

"You mean Ray?" asked Zeiger.

"He told me he was taking off from California to get here on time," said Duke.

"You mean he ain't here?"

"I don't know where the fuck he is, Hal," said Duke. "I'm tired of him doing this shit."

With a crowd of 10,000 in the hall and the band already playing its warm-up set, Zeiger started to sweat. Duke watched, laughing to himself, as Mae slipped Ray into his dressing room. When he finally emerged ready to play, the shocked look on Zeiger's face told Duke that Ray had gotten his revenge.

As the Martin flew south for a swing around the old Texas circuit, a major change became clear: Joe Adams, with Ray's approval, began to assert authority over the day-to-day running of the band. The move clearly invaded Jeff's traditional territory, and everybody watched to see how he would react, hoping for a fight. Jeff disappointed them by beating a slow retreat and watching his back every step of the way. Jeff could read the handwriting on the wall as well as anyone, and if truth be told, he was getting a little tired of working for Ray Charles.

Much, and little, had changed for Jeff Brown in the decade since the Lowell Fulson tours. He had prospered with Ray. As manager to a star, Jeff stood in a good spot to make side deals with promoters, hustlers, and anyone else who wanted to do business with Ray Charles. As the band's banker, he made a few dollars from loans to the fellows, many of whom needed—"just this week"—a piece of next week's salary. Yet, as he rose with the rising tide, Jeff had never pushed his luck, remaining the steady-going Texan he had always been. The huge leap in Ray's income had bypassed him completely. Ray paid him a yearly salary of $15,000, but Jeff didn't get regular payments from his percentage of Tangerine Music. Milt Shaw and Hal Zeiger thought it unfair that the guy who had been with Ray from day one was still earning at the 50s R&B level while they and Ray had struck pop gold in the 60s. But Ray wanted Jeff to get what he paid him and no more; like the band members, Jeff was his employee, and that was that. Zeiger and Shaw responded, quietly, by cutting Jeff in on a share of their loot. When the Shaw agency got its 10 percent of the ABC royalties, Milt often sent a check to Jeff; after each tour Hal Zeiger gave him generous bonuses. Jeff was building a house in his hometown of Henderson and looking into an investment he liked, a bowling alley in Houston. If that worked out, maybe he could finally get off the road.

For the band, everything changed when Joe Adams started cracking down. Jeff's good-old-boy style had cushioned the no-nonsense basics of life in the band, and they respected his authority. "Jeff would come out telling you what Ray told him to say," Hank Crawford remembered, "but from Jeff, we could laugh it off. We'd be mad, but we knew it was just Jeff following orders. With Joe, it became a dictatorship." Joe Adams didn't like musicians, and musicians didn't like him. He barked commands in a tone that got the fellows' backs up; they felt a streak of malice under his bland hauteur. Ray had long ago set up a system of fines for lateness, sloppy dress, and drunkenness, but where Jeff gave the men room to maneuver, Joe enforced every rule to the letter. Even Hank got stung for $50 one night: he'd worn ankle-high boots on stage instead of standard dress shoes. Ray often came off stage shouting that he'd fire this or that s.o.b. Jeff tended to tell Ray to think it over, he'd talk to them; Joe was more likely to agree: fire him, musicians came a dime a dozen.

In two years, however, by hook or by crook, Ray had whipped his big band into an ensemble comparable with any in jazz history. The first outfit, 1961 to 1963, was a band of players, each a personality. Phil Guilbeau liked to flip into the stratosphere, while Wallace Davenport's steady lead trumpet held the whole section to a knife-keen edge. Two old-timers, Henderson Chambers and Keg Johnson, anchored Ray's trombones; Chambers had played with Count Basie, and everyone, even Ray, called him "Mr. Chambers." Audiences, and Ray, loved to hear Donald Wilkerson and Fathead's tenor battles, Hank's greased lightning on alto, and Leroy laying down a baritone bottom you could sit on. By this time mainstays like Edgar Willis had blended with newcomers like Texan tenor saxist James Clay into one superbly responsive unit. The band knew how to follow Ray through driving up-tempos and, even harder, through what the fellows called Ray's "death tempo."

"Ray could play so slow and sing so laid-back, there was no way to count to keep your place," explained Leroy Cooper. "If you counted, you'd always end up ahead of him, which he hated! To catch Ray's feeling, you had to *watch* Ray, not take your eyes off him, his left foot, his left shoulder, his hands." With a band this trustworthy, Ray could begin a slow song like "Drown in My Own Tears" with a meandering piano solo, the band listening, silent. When he got to the opening line, he could sing, "It . . . brings . . . a . . ." as an out-of-time howl, take a big breath, the band breathing with him, then sing "tear" on a huge downbeat, the band melting into harmony behind him. Playing well, however, did not often earn compliments. When new fellows asked Leroy, "You think Ray likes my playing?" Cooper responded, "When he don't like it, you'll hear from him."

For the third year in a row, Zeiger's spring tour wended its way across the country to sold-out afternoon and evening concerts at Carnegie Hall. A reporter from *Time* came to Carnegie Hall and found Ray "the best blues singer around," but also "haunted by narcotics . . . a man in trouble with himself." April's *Ebony,* in contrast, painted a glowing picture of Ray's success in a long article, "Blues Becomes Big Business." Ray had become more than "a soulful musician . . . lamenting 'Georgia,' " *Ebony* declared. He was an uncommonly astute singer who had parlayed his voice into a "multimillion-dollar, national enterprise" that hired Negroes in all the top positions. Everyone at Ray Charles Enterprises had two or three jobs to fill, and nobody worked harder than Ray.

"For every hour he spends as an entertainer," an associate told *Ebony,* "he spends ten as a businessman."

After one-nighters in Syracuse and Quebec, Ray and company took off again for Europe, the Palais des Beaux Arts in Brussels first this time, then Amsterdam, and on to their debut in England. Throughout the American tour Sandra Jean had called Ray nearly every day, and she kept calling him overseas, running up a $1400 phone bill. She was definitely pregnant, she said, the baby due in October. Ray tried to reassure her and even spoke to her mother in Dayton: he loved Sandra, he would take care of the baby. But a pregnant girlfriend couldn't promise the footloose sex that Ray was after, and he began to lose interest in the romance. Sandra Jean found it harder and harder to get through to him at his hotels, and she began to worry about her future. She resolved to confront him when he came back in June.

"The Genius Hits Britain," *Melody Maker* headlined as Ray and the gang flew into London. Two years of delay had worked Ray's English fans to a fever pitch, and his debut became a major cultural event, stirring up a frenzy of articles in the jazz and daily press. The Sunday *Times* ran a long profile by Nat Hentoff that recapped Ray's biography and declared "raw, undiluted passion" as the core of his power. "In his music [Ray] is so vividly, vulnerably *present* that he personifies the root human condition," wrote Hentoff, going on to quote James Baldwin on Ray's art:

> The blues and spirituals are all about . . . the ability to look at things as they are and survive your losses, or not even survive them—to know your losses are coming. Charles sings a kind of universal blues. It is not self-pity, however, which you hear in him, but compassion.

Fans gladly paid scalpers twelve pounds for thirteen-shilling tickets to the Sunday-night show May 12 at the Astoria Cinema in Finsbury Park. As Duke led Ray on stage, the crowd of 3200 roared so loud the *Melody Maker* reporter feared the building might fall down. Ray's shoulders looked too big for his legs, and he moved stiffly, yet when he sang, "it all came out in the voice," a voice that turned "Without a Song" into "a ten minute blues, with the audience waiting on every amplified breath." The crowd left the theater rubber-legged, and the reporter sat down to write still punch-drunk from the music: "A sane train of thought tangles to spaghetti when you try to frame a fragment of that glorious hour and ten minutes when Ray cast a fine mesh net of emotions to ensnare his first British audience."

On to Birmingham and Manchester, a long hop to Geneva, then a short hop to Paris for a sold-out week at the Olympia, French fans embracing Ray as an old friend.

One spot of trouble came when Ray heard that Frank Tenot was giving free tickets to the fellows for their lady friends. Ray sent angry word through Joe Adams: no free tickets for the band. Tenot didn't understand why Ray cared: he was earning a flat fee, and a few free tickets took no money out of his pocket. But Ray was adamant. He didn't want the band getting any extras, and unless Tenot stopped, he wouldn't play the next show. Tenot stopped. Another night the manager of the Claridge called. Drug dealers coming and going from Fathead's room were disturbing the other guests; could M. Tenot have a word with M. Newman? Tenot had that word and the week ended smoothly.

When Ray arrived in LA, Sandra Jean called and called until she got through, but his cool first words on the phone, "Hi, sweetheart," told her it was over. Dr. Foster would continue taking care of her and would deliver the baby, Ray said, but he refused to pay her phone bill, and he was vague about money in the future. Then he took off again to Boston for a week at Blinstrub's in early July. Ray's new single, "Without Love," labored up the charts. Sandra Jean had melted when Ray had played the old Clyde McPhatter weeper for her in the winter. Now she hated hearing the song on the radio; it seemed all too true. She found a lawyer, Peter J. Kaplanis, and told him her tale. Kaplanis thought a paternity suit against Ray Charles had definite potential.

After five years with Ray, Hank Crawford quit the band in July. With three albums out under his own name on Atlantic, he figured it was time to take a shot at a solo career. Ray and Hank had no hard words, but under the surface, Joe Adams was a reason for the split. "I could see the recognizable band slipping," Crawford recalled. "Joe didn't want anybody who was going to distract from Ray Charles." Hank told Duke he was leaving, and Duke said he was getting ready to go too; he had gotten married, a baby was on the way, and his wife wanted him to settle down. Soon the two had a plan: Duke would manage Hank out of the Shaw office and launch him on the R&B circuits Ray had circled so long. Crawford put together an eight-piece band, largely composed of Ray's veterans, and by August they were rolling their way across Texas and Louisiana.

Hank and Duke felt a wrench leaving Ray. "Everybody who had been through the small-band days was like *this*," Duke said, interlacing his fingers and squeezing his palms together. Hank looked back proudly to nights sharing the stage with Ellington and Basie and to his own role in building the band. "I'm not boasting, but I was the cat after Quincy. Ray's had a lot of bandleaders, but I'm the only one who stood out front conducting." More than music, Hank had learned discipline. "If you're in Ray's band, *you will be disciplined.* You're gonna take his shit, and he can dish it out too, he's a General Patton. It's his way or you go, and I left, never went back. You think you can go back, but you can't."

Edgar Willis stepped up to bandleader and a series of alto players stepped in and out of Hank's shoes, but Crawford's departure broke the unity of Ray's first big band. A long second era began, in which, around a dwindling number of mainstays, new men came and went with the tide, sometimes for better, sometimes for worse. When the band seemed too full of strangers, Ray tried to lure back old-timers like Marcus Belgrave. "I'd only been gone a few months when Ray started calling, preaching at me for hours," Belgrave remembered. " 'What you mean you want to stay home?' he'd say, 'You need to be out in the world, you gotta play for the people to make your mark.' I'd tell him I wasn't getting enough money, I had a family. 'I got a family too,' he'd shout." The sheer force of Ray's personality almost bowled Belgrave over, but he had found steady session work at Motown in Detroit and he refused.

Duke's departure mattered less than Hank's, but Ray liked Duke and hated breaking in new valets. Duke had hired a young fellow named Cash Williams to sell the programs, and he told Ray that Williams would make a good replacement.

"What's his name?" asked Ray.

"Cash," said Duke.

"He got any money?" asked Ray.

"No," said Duke.

"Then what the fuck you call him Cash for?"

Ray flew to New York for two album sessions July 10 and 13, 1963. As Ray outlined it to Sid, his theme this time was more subtle than anything he had tried before: painting the portrait of a complex emotion, "soul." He asked Sid to gather songs about "people with the blues, black people who were poor, held back by society," and from Sid's submissions Ray picked ten. Marty Paich and Benny Carter wrote most of the charts, but Ray pleasantly surprised Sid by asking him, for the first time, to write several arrangements himself, the beginning of a long, fruitful collaboration. Only one incident marred the sessions. Ray had a cold on top of his heroin high, and as the Jack Halloran singers sang a long introduction to "Ol' Man River," he kept nodding out. "I knew we'd never get it," Sid remembered, "so I found a way we could start the singers four bars before Ray came in, and we got it. Ray's voice was cracking because he was sick, but it sounds deliberate, a cry coming out of his voice in just the right places."

They named the album *Ingredients in a Recipe of Soul,* and it is one of Ray's finest, musical meat-and-potatoes blended in a blues-jazz-C&W-R&B-and-pop stew. Country songs lie cheek-by-jowl with Broadway warhorses, chick-a-boom rhythms lope under syncopated horns, and Ray's cocktail piano ripples over solemn *amen* endings.

Ingredients blurs the once-clear division between string/voice and big-band tracks; "Born to Be Blue" opens with strings, switches to big-band and back to strings, as an oboe wails a poignant countermelody. On *Ingredients* for the first time Ray and Sid laid the songs out in a dramatic sequence, Ray playing a character going through a plotted sequence of emotions. He starts flat broke in "Busted." Asking his brother for a loan only makes things worse:

> *My brother said, "There ain't a thing I can do,*
> *My wife and my kids are all down with the flu,*
> *And I was just thinking of calling on you,*
> *Cause I'm busted."*

Ray doesn't know where to turn in "Where Can I Go?" and figures he must be "Born to Be Blue." As he struggles to survive, Ray envies "That Lucky Old Sun" who's got it easy "rolling through heaven all day"; then "Ol' Man River" teaches him a more patient acceptance of his lot. The sun has set as side two begins, and a bluesy guitar picks "In the Evening." Ray is "A Stranger in Town," feeling "Ol' Man Time" stealing away his youth. In "Over the Rainbow" he glimpses the dawn of hope, and with his faith newly fired, he marches into the grand finale, "You'll Never Walk Alone." *Ingredients* may be enjoyed simply as a collection of songs, but Ray's dramatic subtext, subtle enough to be missed, does unite the album's disparate styles. On *Ingredients'* release in August, *Billboard* praised its "soulful songs of loneliness and loss," getting a piece, at least, of Ray's intention.

The caravan stayed east through July until an early-August concert with Nina Simone at Forest Hills Stadium. One night they played an NAACP dinner in New Jersey, Ray picking up an award for his "outstanding musical contributions," and on another they rode the bus to the Concord Hotel in the Catskills. They got to the Concord too late for Ray to get to his hotel room for a fix, and he had his current "doctor" shoot him up just inside the bus door, in view of curious passersby. Minutes later, walking along a corridor to the dressing room, Ray ran his hand along the red flocked-velvet wallpaper. "Sure looks like a nice place," he said.

Leroy Cooper bunked at the Flanders during the eastern sojourn. At first he was stone broke. He had dropped and cracked his sax mouthpiece; new ones cost $35 at Manny's, and he had $50 in the world. As he stood on the sidewalk trying to decide what to do, a pal told him that a $1000 tax refund check was waiting for him at the Shaw office. That turned Leroy's life around, and when the money from the *Ingredients* sessions came in, it was party time at the Flanders. One night he and Edgar Willis were whooping it up with four Broadway chorus girls when they heard a knock on the door. They opened up, and there stood their wives paying a surprise visit. "Who are these bats?" demanded Mrs. Willis, marching in. Then, as Cooper remembered wistfully, "the chicks had to start putting on their shoes."

▌▐▌▐▌▐▌▐▌▐▌

On August 9, in Los Angeles Superior Court, attorney Peter J. Kaplanis filed Sandra Jean Betts' complaint against "Ray Charles, also known as Ray Charles Robinson" to "establish paternity . . . and provide support" of the minor child due to be born out of wedlock in October. The child, Sandra Jean declared, would need $1100 monthly, broken down into $300 for rent, $150 for food, and similar sums for clothes, doctor's bills, insurance, and "incidentals." Kaplanis, in addition, asked for his legal fees and court costs. Judge Roger Pfaff ordered Ray to appear at a show-cause hearing September 3. Encouraged by Kaplanis, the black press made the story front-page news. "Ray Charles is a first class Casanova who finds them, fools them, and forgets them," the lawyer told the Philadelphia *Tribune.* To the *Sentinel,* he hinted broadly that he was willing to deal: "Miss Betts is very sorry she had to resort to the courts. . . . If we had a chance to sit down together, I'm sure we could work something out."

Kaplanis had misjudged his man. "It's very hard to threaten me," Ray often said of himself. Women and lawyers didn't tell him what he could or couldn't do. The suit was nothing but legal blackmail, and Ray Charles couldn't be blackmailed. Whatever the cost in bad publicity and embarrassment to Della, he wouldn't budge. If Sandra Jean hadn't been greedy, he would have taken care of her. Now she'd have to fight for every penny. As the summer tour moved to the West Coast, San Francisco and Seattle, Ray told Joe Adams to "No comment" the press, and he told his lawyer, James Reese, to stonewall in court. Reese, accordingly, answered the complaint in late August, declaring that the defendant was "at present engaged in an appearance in Canada," and that he denied "each and every allegation": he was not the father of "said expectant child," and the plaintiff was not as poor as she said she was. Ray, therefore, "should not be legally compelled to contribute such support," and the complaint should be dismissed.

Sandra Jean and her lawyer would not disappear that easily. On September 3, opposing counsel met in Judge Pfaff's chambers, with Joe Adams and Della ("demurely attired in a pink dress and white gloves," said the *Sentinel*) present to lend Ray silent support. Reese said that Ray had agreed to take a blood test but asked that the trial be put off until January; he had a full fall schedule of long-contracted appearances all over the country. Kaplanis insisted that Ray be deposed in LA immediately, but Reese introduced a list of fifty gigs from mid-September to the end of December: a tour of

Brazil followed by twenty-eight cities in seventeen states—everywhere but Los Angeles. That settled it: Judge Pfaff set January 13, 1964, as the date for a jury trial.

The *Saturday Evening Post,* meanwhile, carried a long article that balanced the dark and bright sides of Ray seen by *Time* and *Ebony* in the spring. Ray was both a nervous chain-smoker, wrote reporter Al Aronowitz, and a confident leader whose simple "All right, children" could snap his band to full attention; a great "Negro folk figure" and a businessman who had grossed "over two million dollars in 1962." Ray was also a man in hiding, drug addiction his "secret torture." In jazz argot sunglasses are "shades," Aronowitz explained to the *Post*'s huge Middle American audience; on Ray, "the shades are always drawn." Americans, perhaps, could not see the real Ray, but they continued to like what they heard. *Ingredients* reached #2 on the album chart, and the single "Busted" climbed through September to #4. Ray's mini-slump was over, but by this time hits and misses mattered less to Ray than they would to a less seasoned artist. Music Operators of America, the jukebox industry association, had just voted him "most consistent supplier of good records" in the business.

Joe Adams had been searching since the winter for the Robinson family's new home, and for land where Ray could build his "foundation." By the summer he had found good prospects in both categories; in September they made their decisions, and Joe got down to the paperwork. For their home, Ray and Della paid $100,000 for three open lots on a hillcrest in View Park, a wealthy residential development in the rolling Baldwin Hills. View Park had been all-white when built in the 1950s, only a few miles southwest of Hepburn Avenue yet a world apart. Adams had been one of the first Negroes to buy there a decade later, but his house stood on a lower slope. The Robinsons' lots, grouped as 4863 Southridge Avenue, had a sweeping view east over downtown Los Angeles. Under Joe's general direction, architects designed a large multiwinged house that would be the biggest in the neighborhood. Ray Jr., now eight, didn't want to leave his pals on Hepburn, but Della looked forward to shopping for furniture and decorations.

On September 6, 1963, "Ray C. Robinson and Della B. Robinson, husband and wife as joint tenants," bought from Ernest and Cora Warren, for $52,000, 2107 West Washington Boulevard, two lots a few blocks east of Western Avenue and just north of the Santa Monica Freeway. The lots looked as anonymous as any hundred feet along a Los Angeles boulevard can look: an out-of-business gas station and a small house set in a shabby but respectable Negro neighborhood. Yet if any of Ray Charles' actions deserve a drumroll and a trumpet fanfare, buying 2107 West Washington Boulevard stands among them. This anonymous three-eighths of an acre became in time Ray's true home on earth. The building he built there, its offices, recording studio, and bachelor pad, became his castle, his fortress, his faraway island; the place where he could work and play and live and love and be by himself whenever he pleased. For the next thirty years and more, no matter how often and far he wandered, Ray always came home to 2107 West Washington Boulevard. With one night off between gigs on the East Coast, he'd fly home to 2107 just, as a longtime associate put it, "to touch the walls."

With two buildings to build, Ray pushed Joe to start the studio and office building first. The house could wait until next year, but Ray wanted the ground broken on West Washington as soon as possible. Bulldozers soon demolished the old buildings, and for an estimated $400,000, Greve & O'Rourke, licensed contractors, began building an unadorned two-story box, one hundred and twelve feet long and fifty feet wide, surrounded by a parking lot.

On September 30, Dr. Foster delivered Sandra Betts of a five-pound baby girl. Blood tests of Ray, Sandra Jean, and newborn Sheila revealed that "paternity is possible." Ray, crisscrossing the South in the Martin, didn't retreat an inch; he would still go to trial in January. In New Orleans snapping police dogs panicked the overflowing black crowd, numerous people getting knocked down and trampled. Ray blew up when he heard about it, shouting that he wasn't coming back to New Orleans until the cops stopped treating all Negroes like rioters. In Tampa a lawyer handed Ray a subpoena demanding increased support for thirteen-year-old Evelyn. Louise Mitchell, now married to a Mr. Green, had read about Sandra Jean and Ray's $1-million-plus yearly income, but her imitation case did not turn bitter. Ray still had a soft spot for his first love. After he promised to send more money and to invite Evelyn to visit in LA, Louise dropped her suit.

After early-November gigs in New York and Kentucky, Ray flew to LA for a few days off. He was in the car headed to the airport to fly back east when news came that President Kennedy had been assassinated in Dallas. Ray rejoined the band at the Latin Casino in Cherry Hill, he, the ladies, and the fellows as shocked and saddened as the rest of the nation.

As the welded-steel frame of Ray's office building began to rise in Los Angeles, Jeff Brown launched his business, the Big J Bowling Lanes, in Houston. Located in the sprawl along the East Texas Freeway, the Big J was a classy place, sporting a coffee shop and a party room with pink and gray carpeting and furniture to match. It got off to a booming start with an integrated clientele. Jeff installed a cousin as his manager, but he still needed to drop off the tour for days at a time to look after his new concern. In his absences, Joe Adams roused Ray's suspicions with a few well-timed questions. Where did Jeff Brown get the money to build a bowling alley? Could he have been stealing from Ray?

Jeff's stake in the Big J had, in fact, not been great: AMF, the bowling supply company, leased him the equipment, and the bonuses from Milt Shaw and Hal Zeiger, plus a small bank loan, had done the rest, about $20,000. Yet, once aroused by Adams, Ray went on the warpath. He ordered Paul Orland to search years back through the books for signs of theft. He set up an afternoon at his New York lawyer's office and called in Duke, Larry Myers, and others, questioning them in detail about Jeff and money: what had they seen, what did they know? Myers stayed firm under the interrogation. He said he liked Jeff and knew him to be honest to the penny. Duke said he didn't know much, that he liked Jeff *and* Joe; privately he thought Joe was behind the fuss. When Ray found out how much Milt Shaw had given Jeff, he became bitterly angry and nearly quit the agency. Shaw, known for his impulsive generosity, figured that he could do as he pleased with his own share, but Ray figured differently: if Milt didn't want the money that he got from the sweat of *Ray's* brow, he should give it back to *Ray,* who had earned it in the first place. The dispute with Milt cooled off, but Ray's distrust of Jeff froze solid. Jeff had stolen from him, Ray was sure of it. Why? "Greed," he concluded.

Once Ray had made that decision, Jeff was history, the only question how and when to get rid of him. Ray didn't say a word to Jeff, however, and when the tour came through Houston in mid-December, all was apparently friendly. The Raelets and a few of the fellows bowled at the Big J, and Jeff got their pictures into the Houston *Informer.* Larry Newton, on the other hand, heard enough of Ray's rage to become convinced that Jeff, whom he had always liked, was really "a motherfucking piece of shit" who had taken Ray for all he was worth.

To the end of his life Jeff Brown insisted that he never stole money from Ray Charles. "I wish I had," he said years later, "because I deserved more from Ray than I ever got." Visible fact supports his argument—Ray remained wealthy and Jeff never became well-to-do—as does a core of agreement among many people in Ray Charles' orbit at the time. Brown may have dipped a few thousand out of the cash flowing through his hands; he may have cut side deals he never told Ray about. That he did more is unlikely. Jeff instead had the misfortune of getting pinned down by twin beams of unfriendly fire: Joe weeding out a rival, Ray needing an excuse to drop the manager he had once considered "a second brother."

Jeff could feel the growing coldness from Ray, but he had long known his boss's icy side, and as the '63 season wound down, he planned to be back on the tour when they started up again in the spring. Renald Richard, Ray's first bandleader, was still in touch with both Jeff and Ray. Watching the silent battle from the sidelines, he could see better than Jeff that Ray's "iron curtain" was coming down. "With Ray," Richard recalled, "if you do him wrong, he'll hug you, smile at you, pretend that you're still his best friend, but inside he's thinking, 'You did me wrong, and I'm gonna slice you for it.' And he will get back at you somehow."

As Ray and the gang got back to California at Christmas, a year-end issue of *Billboard* reported that, after nine years of growth, all record sales had dipped in 1963, for the first time since the birth of rock 'n' roll. Industry spokesmen worried aloud that the 50s boom had finally tailed off. Would anything come along to replace it? Ray's sales had dipped too. In 1962, he'd been the top seller of singles; now he was fourth after the Beach Boys, Dion, and the Four Seasons.

Still, Ray was the fifth-biggest album artist after Peter, Paul and Mary, Andy Williams, Joan Baez, and the Kingston Trio, and among American singers of international stature, he ranked seventeenth. Elvis ran away from the pack with his total of seventeen #1 hits; the next closest was Perry Como with five. Ray joined the Everly Brothers, Tony Bennett, Pat Boone, and a handful of others with three. The numbers and the names of his peers make an important point: Ray had grown far beyond his R&B roots and become an all-American pop star. His pop hits still became R&B hits, but more as a reflection of their pop success than because of special appeal to the Negro market. At the black dance halls where Ray had once reigned, B. B. King and James Brown now ruled. Ray had graduated to the integrated concert circuit, playing halls one week where Nat Cole, Duke Ellington, or Ella Fitzgerald had played the week before.

Ray was determined to go from strength to strength in 1964. Milt Shaw took out a full-page ad in the same year-end *Billboard* to announce that from April 15 to May 3 Ray would make his usual concert tour of the United States, capped at Carnegie Hall. Then he'd fly to Dublin to star in a feature film, *Ballad in Blue,* and from July to September, for the first time, Ray and the gang would circle the globe: Denmark, Sweden, Belgium, Holland, France, Italy, Greece, Australia, Japan, Hong Kong, and Hawaii. The ad gave Ray a little balloon to say hello to his fans and friends in the business. "Thanks all," he wrote, "for a Wonderful Year."

Ray might better have wished good luck to himself in the year to come. By the end of 1964, he would need all he could get.

Busted in Boston 1964

Ray's winter in LA turned out to be not the idyll of the year before, but an ordeal to be survived, and, such being the fickle nature of romance, the same woman provided both the pleasure and the pain. At 9:45 Monday morning, January 13, 1964, Ray, in a dark suit and tie, sat at the defendant's table as Judge A. Scott opened the *Betts v. Robinson* paternity trial in Los Angeles Superior Court. Questioned by Kaplanis, Sandra Jean Betts told her sad story of dreams and broken promises. Sandra's mother came out from Ohio to testify that Ray had told her on the phone that Sandra Jean was carrying his baby. Kaplanis even brought three-month-old Sheila into court and had her held near Ray's face for the jury to look for a resemblance. Through the long hours of the six-day trial Ray sat and listened, his face expressionless and his body so still that reporters wondered if he slept. On the stand, he admitted that he and Sandra Jean had been intimate, and that he had spoken to her mother. Had he ever told Sandra Jean he loved her? Kaplanis asked. "I could very well have told her that," said Ray. "I had just met her."

While Kaplanis painted Sandra Jean as an innocent betrayed, James Reese, Ray's lawyer, painted her as a floozy who had dated several men the previous winter, including one who took her down to Nogales, Mexico, on a "business trip." Yet the jury needed only an hour to decide that "Ray Charles Robinson is the father of Sheila Jean Robinson." Judge Scott ordered Ray to pay $400-a-month support and $7500 in fees to Kaplanis. Sandra Jean burst into tears at the good news; Ray was stoic in defeat. "The jury said I'll have to pay, so I'll have to pay," he told the Los Angeles *Sentinel.* "As far as I'm concerned 100 percent of the evidence is in my favor. I'll be supporting a child I have no faith or belief is mine."

Ray toughed it out in public, but the trial wounded private Della Bea to the core. As long as she remained Mrs. Ray Charles Robinson to the world, Della could stand Ray's girlfriends coming and going behind closed doors. Now anyone could read the humiliating facts of their hollow marriage in the *Sentinel,* and even in the *Informer* back home in Houston. Sandra Jean testified that Ray had told her, "I swear to you that I love you and my unborn child more than I love Ray Jr." Could he have said it? Could he have meant it? Quiet Della didn't say much, but inside she felt sick with grief and rage, and the air in the house on Hepburn became thick with distrust.

Nothing stopped Ray from working. Before, during, and after the trial, Ray started Percy Mayfield's excellent *My Jug and I* album and completed his own *Sweet and Sour Tears.* The album began with a call to Sid asking him to comb the catalogs for cry songs, and Sid came up with a dozen classics, "Cry Me a River" and "Willow, Weep for Me" among them. *Sweet and Sour Tears* returns to the clear strings/big-band division of his early ABC albums, and compared with the complex drama of *Ingredients in a Recipe for Soul* six months before, *Tears* seems a little Johnny-One-Note. Yet the pop style born on the *Genius* album has had five years to grow, and Ray handles its raw materials with enormous authority. The jaunty jazz of "I Cried for You," the slapping country backbeat of "No One to Cry To"—all the musical textures of the album sound utterly natural, the right rhythm and resonance always in the right place. Ray has subtler colors on his palette than he did in the stark days of "Drown in My Own Tears," but the same jagged burr that once rasped through R&B horns now rips through soaring violins like a rusty knife through a gossamer veil.

Ray was not the only American to begin the year on a somber note; in the winter after Kennedy's death the whole country came down with a bad case of the blues. With February the Beatles arrived, and their cheerful smiles dosed the country like a spring tonic and chased those blues away. As one can trace the birth of rock 'n' roll in *Billboard* 1955, so too one can trace the musical tidal wave called the Beatles in *Billboard* 1964. "I Want to Hold Your Hand" entered the charts in January at #45; three months later the Fab Four stacked up "Can't Buy Me Love," "Twist and Shout," "She Loves You," "I Want to Hold Your Hand," and "Please Please Me" at #1, #2, #3, #4, and #5, an unprecedented and never duplicated achievement. Louis Armstrong knocked the Beatles out of #1 with "Hello Dolly" in May, but the Beatles soon returned with the

Rolling Stones, the Animals, and the Dave Clark Five, an invasion that radically changed the substance and style of American popular music.

Three decades later, the British Invasion remains a remarkable event, both for the musical originality of its leaders and for their dedication to the blues, R&B, and rock 'n' roll roots from which their music sprang. The British Invasion echoed the rock 'n' roll boom ten years before; British teenagers reamplified the wild sounds they heard coming from America and hurled them back across the Atlantic. Through the decades, American pop/jazz groups had toured and sold countless records abroad, and British, French, and Italian musicians had adapted American sounds and rhythms to native tastes. Yet until the British invasion, Americans preferred domestic pop music to foreign imitations. The Beatles and their buddies changed all that, and British-American pop ignited a mid-60s boom as loud as the mid-50s boom it echoed.

One effect of the British Invasion was to render many American pop singers instantly out of date. Ray, like Frank, Ella, Nat, and even Elvis, became, for the moment, one of the old-timers shoved aside by the guitar-strumming moptops. ABC put out five Ray Charles singles in 1964; two inched to highs of #38 and #40, the rest rose and sank in the depths of the Hot 100's lower fifty. Like his colleagues, Ray wasn't overjoyed to see the invaders snatch away his fans. He wouldn't buy a Beatles record himself, Ray told reporters at the height of Beatlemania, though he did allow, echoing his comments on Elvis years before, that "they must have something. The public can't be wrong if the public buys their records." The year of the Beatles' triumph marked Ray's second year of decline from his "I Can't Stop Loving You" peak. Most pop performers reach only one such career peak, and in 1964 it appeared possible that Ray had climbed his mountain and was sliding to the lower slopes of success.

At thirty-four, however, Ray was still too young and tough to go quietly into pop music obscurity. His current records might be generating a weak response, but the response to his past work was growing steadily. Much to Ahmet and Jerry's delight, Ray's Atlantic sides continued to sell, and many who rushed to see Ray Charles live in 1964 did so, not excited by *Sweet and Sour Tears* or the dive-bombing singles, but because they had just heard "The Right Time" on *Ray Charles in Person* or "What'd I Say" on *The Twist.*

Ray's popular past, unfortunately, competed with his present. In the liner notes for *The Ray Charles Story Vols. One and Two,* which introduced Ray to many young mid-60s listeners, Jerry Wexler declared Ray the peer of Duke Ellington, and just as if he were Picasso, divided his Atlantic years into four glorious periods: "West Coast," "New Orleans," "Gospel," and "Ballads & Strings." Yet, still bitter at Ray's defection, Wexler peppered his praise with criticism of his success in the 1960s. Strings-and-voices made Ray's sound "palatable" for those "who weren't quite ready for the unvarnished Charles

brand of musical truth," Wexler wrote. "In Europe as well as in certain listening segments of this country, there is a marked preference for the early, seven-piece, hard-
hitting gospel style." Wexler had once schmoozed music journalists in Ray's favor; he
now spread subtle disparagement, and an opinion critical of Ray's ABC years caught
on widely. Ray's recent recordings have not been "as earthily idiomatic as his initial hits,"
Nat Hentoff wrote. *Time* brooded over Ray's "willingness to sing valueless songs," and
his best new tracks, according to *Downbeat,* summoned up "remembrances of Charles'
past glories"; the rest was "unworthy material . . . a memorial to the shifting pragma-
tism of the recording industry." The sniping added up to one sum judgment: Ray had
sold out. In place by the mid-60s, the "Atlantic Ray good, ABC Ray bad" critical formula proved remarkably persistent, dogging Ray through the 70s and 80s and closing
many ears to his later masterworks.

As Ray's LA winter wore to a close, a steel skeleton rose over the foundation at 2107 West
Washington, and over the skeleton spread a windowless cream-colored stucco skin. The
building would not be ready before touring began, but one night Joe took Ray on a tour
of the still-rough second floor. Ray walked everywhere, feeling the width of doors, the
length of corridors, the size of the studio space in the rear. When they came back out
to the street, policemen were waiting for them with flashlights and questions: who were
they, what were they doing? Ray said he was Ray Charles, owner of the building. The
cops didn't recognize or believe him: how did a blind black guy get the money to own
a building? "I work for a living, every day of the week," Ray replied. The cops took that
reply as uppity enough to deserve a trip to the station house for a few hours. Ironically,
only weeks later the *Sentinel* listed Ray among the "Thirty-seven Richest Negroes" in
Los Angeles. Tradition declared most Negroes poor, the article stated, but "there have
always been wealthy Negroes," and LA had "a sizable clan . . . rolling in riches." Archi-
tects, attorneys, and bank presidents joined such stars as Sammy Davis Jr. on the list.
"According to an executive of his firm," said the *Sentinel,* undoubtedly quoting Joe
Adams, "Ray Charles . . . has grossed upwards of $4 million annually."

The fourth Hal Zeiger spring tour worked its way east through late April, selling
out two shows at Carnegie Hall on May 2. Still in New York the next week, Ray and
the gang knocked off *Have a Smile with Me.* When Leroy Cooper saw the titles on the
charts, "Two Ton Tessie" and "The Man with the Weird Beard," he looked at Fathead
and rolled his eyes—what was Ray up to now? Plainly, an album of comedy songs, the
opposite of *Sweet and Sour Tears.* The band whoops through the loose arrangements,
the trombones blowing farts on "The Thing." "I Never See Maggie Alone" evokes the

innocent days of flivvers and front-porch swings: Maggie's "mother, her father and her big fat brother" pop up whenever Ray and Maggie start to spoon. A lighthearted vulgarity imbues *Smile*—on "Two Ton Tessie" Ray hee-haws happily about a gal so fat "the boys play tennis on her double chin"—but the album also reveals Ray's steady purpose: this "happy" brick gets mortared in beside the "sad" brick and the place, women, and country bricks in the wall of his album-making style.

From the sessions, the gang flew off to Ireland for the filming of *Ballad in Blue* and the world tour to follow. Paul Henreid, an actor best known for playing Ingrid Bergman's husband in *Casablanca,* directed *Ballad in Blue* (sometimes titled *Light out of Darkness* or *Blues for Lovers*). Producer Alexander Salkind gave Henreid a bare-bones budget, so he planned to shoot the film in cheap Dublin instead of London and Paris, where the story supposedly took place. The prospect of acting scared Ray, but he'd be playing himself and that, he figured, would make it easier. He also liked the story about helping a blind English boy overcoming his handicap, and Joe Adams, playing Ray's valet, had the experience to guide his boss through the filming.

The month in Dublin was an oddball experience, but by and large Ray and the gang enjoyed it. Rita, a Finnish journalist Ray had met in Paris, came to Dublin and joined him at the Intercontinental Hotel. The fellows found cheaper lodging, Leroy settling into a cozy furnished flat for a few Irish pounds a week. His landlady, Mrs. Hanrahan, invited him downstairs to watch the telly in the evenings over a cup of "tay." They worked five days a week at the Ardmore Studios, with tea breaks and an hour off for lunch. At six Edgar Willis led the way to the pub.

Yet the film shoot wasn't all cakes and ale. Ray had lines to learn and scenes to rehearse, but after the band numbers were filmed, they got bored waiting around for the slow-paced Irish crew. Drugs were scarce in Dublin, and though James Clay slipped over to London a few times to score, Ray, Fathead, and the other junkies in the band lived through the six weeks on the nervous edge of withdrawal. Calling her mother in New York, Pat Lyles let it slip that Ray had a girl with him, and Mae caught a plane to Dublin and tried to break in on Ray and Rita. Ray sent Jeff to get her a room in another hotel, and in bitter exile, Mae ordered the whole menu from room service to stick Ray with a big bill, then didn't eat a thing. Calls flashed back and forth, but Ray refused to leave his new girlfriend. Jeff eventually convinced Mae that she'd better go back to New York, and she left in a cold fury. Mae had been angry with Ray before; this time she stayed angry.

This oddball time in Dublin created a film just as odd. *Ballad in Blue* has crisp black-and-white photography, six hot songs by Ray and the gang, and Leroy mugging in a party scene and saying, "The trouble with this cake is, it's delicious and I'm on a diet!" Nor is the story implausible: Ray meets eight-year-old David (Piers Bishop) and his attractive mother Peggy (Dawn Adams) when he visits an English school for the blind. David is learning to accept blindness, but Peggy is overly protective, and through the film Ray teaches her the lesson Retha taught him: "David must make it on his own." Despite good intentions, however, *Ballad in Blue* is stiffly written, acted, and filmed. The script makes Ray a plaster saint full of pious maxims, and in his dramatic scenes, he sits motionless waiting for his cue and then tonelessly recites the line he'd memorized from the Braille script. Only at the climax, when Ray lets his body shake and his arms wave as they do in real life, does his natural dynamism animate the screen. "Don't protect him, let him find his own way in the world," he tells Peggy, his brow knotted with feeling. "If you lose your courage now, you'll *cripple* the boy for life." In that moment Ray truly "plays himself," and the savage emphasis he lays on "cripple" opens a quick window on his unending struggle to minimize his own handicap.

After a few last scenes shot in London, *Ballad in Blue* wrapped in late June, and Ray and the gang set off around the world. In Hamburg they packed the legendary Star Club, and in Copenhagen 15,000 fans crammed the Tivoli Gardens, where the Beatles had drawn only 12,000 a few weeks before. During the week at the Paris Olympia an era came to an end: Ray fired Margie Hendricks. For years Margie had been drifting in and out of an affair with trumpeter John Hunt, and drifting in and not out of drugs. Always a prima donna who carried and constantly combed an endless supply of elaborate wigs, Margie sassed the boss once too often, and suddenly Ray had had enough. Joe Adams gave Margie her ticket home, and they finished the tour with three Raelets. Margie's departure—to a decade in which she spiraled downward until her death in 1973—ended a historic partnership. Ray sang with many other women later in his career, but none matched him in tone and texture, or challenged him in emotional intensity, as did the immortal Marjorie Hendricks.

Adams flew back to LA from Rome to supervise the finishing touches at 2107 West Washington and the ground-breaking on Southridge, while Ray and the gang headed to Australia and the Far East. By this time European concerts were old hat, but Ray looked forward to the Far East. "It'll be nice to go there and see how my music is going down, enjoy the trip, and pick up one or two dollars on the side," he quipped to reporters in London. Deeper down he knew he was surpassing his own wildest dreams. "If you had told me in 1952 that one day I'd be flying to Singapore and Sydney for gigs," he wrote years later, "I'd have said, 'Baby, I may be blind but I ain't dumb; I'll be lucky to keep working the chitlin circuit.'"

Audiences down under received them rapturously, but Ray and the other junkies in the band had more than music on their minds. Touring in strange countries posed an anxious riddle: was it better to carry your dope through customs and risk a major bust, or to travel clean and risk withdrawal if you couldn't score when you got there?

Going into Tokyo was the scariest; everyone had heard that Japan was tough on drugs. Ray decided he'd be safest from search if he traveled alone, and he told Jeff to take the band into Tokyo without him. When they got off the plane, Jeff faced a battery of flash-bulbs and reporters' questions: where was Ray, where was Ray? Sweating buckets, Jeff said over and over that Ray was delayed, but he'd be on time for the concerts. Which he was, much to Jeff's relief. Compared with Tokyo, Hong Kong was an all-night drugstore, and Ray and Fathead raced off the plane to do what they had to do.

When the tour re-entered the States in Hawaii, customs officials, aware of Ray's reputation, searched the band's luggage carefully, turning up nothing on Ray but find-ing in Fathead's bag bottles of an opium cough syrup he had bought in Hong Kong. A 1950s marijuana arrest meant that, by law, Fathead had to register as a drug offender whenever he went abroad. Few drug users did register, but the law remained a techni-cality that cops could slap on a suspect when a bigger charge might not stick—which is just what happened. "We're letting you go," Hawaiian customs told Fathead, "but we're filing against you for failure to register." A mere cloudlet of trouble, but in ret-rospect, a summer warning of the stormy fall to come.

During the gang's four months away, three civil rights workers were murdered in Philadelphia, Mississippi. In odd counterbalance, President Johnson pushed Kennedy's Civil Rights Bill through Congress, guaranteeing all Americans the right to "work, eat, and travel side by side in their own country." "White Only" and "Colored Only" signs began coming down all across the South. On the fall tour, for the first time ever, Ray and his band, B. B. King and James Brown and their bands, and other Negro trav-elers would begin eating and staying where they pleased from Maine to California.

When Ray got home in August, Joe Adams gave him and Della a tour of the two properties. The Southridge lots were bustling with activity. Workmen had leveled the hillside for a patio around a piano-shaped pool, and carpenters framed walls on a foun-dation that enclosed 6500 square feet. A white brick fireplace rose up through what Joe said would be a dramatic two-story living room. Della thought the house lovely, but almost too grand. And 2107 West Washington was ready to occupy. Joe and Ray had agreed on the floor plan: two large connected offices at the front of the building, one for each of them; a studio in the rear as large as the two offices together; and the space in between divided into a dozen small rooms for the divisions of Ray Charles Enter-prises. Joe was busily selecting colors and fabrics for the carpets and furniture, but the offices were still vacant, the recording studio still bare of equipment. There wouldn't be time to move in before they'd be off again on tour.

Jeff Brown got his first full look at the new building in September. As soon as he got up the stairs to the second floor, he saw Joe's and Ray's big offices and the cubby-hole they had allotted him. It felt, he remembered years later, "like a slap in the face."

He confronted Ray angrily, but Ray didn't budge. "That's the way I want it," he said, adding that he still hoped Jeff would sell the bowling alley, move to California with his family, and continue overseeing the band on the road. Joe stood in the background, smiling his agreement. As Ray spoke, Jeff realized that his words were hollow. Ray didn't want him around anymore; offering the tiny office was a way to fire him without firing him. His dozen years with Ray had just come to a dead end. No, said Jeff; he'd do the fall tour as planned, but then he'd go back to Houston and the bowling alley. It was high time he started taking care of his own business; he'd had more than enough of taking care of Ray Charles.

The fall tour began auspiciously with a Zeiger gig at the Shrine in LA. Sid came out to record it and caught a great show, as the album *Ray Charles Live in Concert* reveals. Lillian Fort, Margie's replacement as lead Raelet, sounded tentative, but Fathead was red hot that night, and Ray ripped off a hair-raising piano solo on "Swing a Little Taste." The audience went predictably nuts at the finale, "What'd I Say," but earlier in the show Ray had, more subtly, held the crowd in the palm of his hand with his voice, piano, and hushed rhythm section through a six-minute version of "Makin' Whoopee"—he'd added it to the act as a droll comment on his own woman troubles:

> *I don't make much money,*
> *About five thousand per*
> *And some judge who thinks he's funny*
> *Says I gotta give six to her!*

After two nights in New Orleans, the Martin flew into trouble in Dallas. The band came off from its opening segment to find rumors spreading that Internal Revenue had seized the ticket money because the promoter owed a fortune in back taxes. Ray refused to go on until his fee was guaranteed. The promoter hemmed and hawed, intermission stretched to an hour and a half, and the crowd got restive. Finally someone took the mike and announced, "There will be no more show. Ray Charles has not been paid. . . . If I were you, I would make a run for the box office and get my money back." That pushed the people over the edge, and they stormed the box office, breaking windows and overturning tables. A flying soda bottle knocked a cop unconscious; other cops with drawn guns dragged him away from the mob. Ray and the gang, meanwhile, slipped out a rear entrance to the bus. "We had to lay on the floor while they drove us out,"

Leroy Cooper remembered. "People were throwing rocks at us, and I lay there thinking, 'This is my hometown, and we're leaving it like bandits.'"

They flew out of the South and into the Northeast. Most nights, once at cruising
altitude, pilot Tom McGarrity switched the Martin to autopilot, a device that picked
up radio beams broadcast from beacons across the country. When the plane stayed on
course, the beams hummed in synch, but if it strayed, the beams went out of synch, creating the "wah-wah" familiar to anyone who's tuned guitar or violin strings. Autopilot
set allowable limits to the "wah-wah" and nudged the plane back on course whenever
it approached them. The device, however, had a manual override, and many nights as
they flew to the dawn, Ray, revved up after the gigs and unable to sleep, told Tom to
kill the autopilot, he'd do it himself. As the gang quit their card games, yawned, curled
up under blankets, and fell asleep, Ray sat in the cockpit, headphones over his ears, listening to the hum of the beam tones, easing the stick right or left at the first whisper
of a wah-wah. Fatigue and the day's drugs left him spent but mellow. High above the
clouds, the day and its hassles, the concert and the crowds, Joe and Jeff, Della and the
kids, Mae and her threats, Sandra Jean and her lawyers, all dropped far, far away. Ray
let himself slip into a realm of pure sound, quietly proud that twenty-five people
trusted him to guide them safely in the big plane, blind through the night.

They played Cleveland and flew to Montreal, played Montreal and flew to Boston,
and there Ray fell heavily to earth. It was bitter cold at 2:10 A.M. Saturday morning, October 31, when the Martin landed at Boston's Logan Airport. Everybody shivered off the
plane and onto the waiting bus that whisked them through the Sumner Tunnel to the
city proper. At the hotel the gang dispersed to their rooms, off until the gig that night
at the Back Bay Theatre, an old movie palace trying stage shows to stay alive.

Once in his room, Ray realized that he had left his drugs on the plane. He had
nothing for a taste before bed, nothing to get high with before the show. There was
nothing to be done but go back to the plane and get it. Others in Ray's position might
have sent a valet for the dope, but Ray had long before decided that he took care of his
own stash: no one carried for him unless they also carried for themselves. He roused his
current chauffeur, aptly named Clarence Driver, and they drove back to the airport.

A private plane full of Negroes showing up in the wee hours had been a notable
event for the customs officers on duty, Joseph J. Lally and Arthur Fitzgerald, and they
had noted it fully. Like most cops, they knew Ray's reputation and his arrest record.
They checked their departmental bulletins and found that David Newman Jr., one of
the guys they'd just passed through passport inspection, was listed as "a person required to register." When Ray and Driver drove into the parking lot again at 5:30 in the
morning for no apparent reason, Lally and Fitzgerald suspected something was up.

They watched Ray, wrapped in a heavy overcoat, enter the plane on Driver's arm. Lights went on, stayed on for twenty minutes and went out again; then the two men deplaned and started walking through the commercial terminal to the car.

Lally and Fitzgerald stepped up, stopped Ray and Driver, and asked them to enter the customs office. They'd been watching the plane, they said. Hadn't Ray just come back from Canada? Yes, he had. Why had he gone back to the plane? To get a book, Ray said. They said they thought he'd gone back to get some drugs. "So if you don't mind, we'd like to see that overcoat."

For a split second it seemed funny to Ray. *"If I didn't mind?"* Of course he minded! Lally and Fitzgerald searched the coat pockets and came up with just what Ray knew they'd find: a Lowery's pepper jar full of pot, his hypodermic needle and burnt spoon, and, in a little bag, a day's supply of heroin that he had just scooped from the three-ounce stash he kept on the Martin. What's this? they asked. "It's soda for my stomach," said Ray.

The agents couldn't prove on the spot that the white powder was heroin, but they knew pot when they smelled it and took Ray before their boss, customs agent Robert Bishop. Bishop promptly arrested Ray for possessing marijuana without paying the proper federal tax. By midmorning, in the custody of the U.S. attorney, Ray appeared before U.S. commissioner Peter J. Nelligan. Nelligan scheduled a hearing for the following Friday and released Ray on his own recognizance. Ray got back to his hotel by midafternoon, free to play the show that night.

Inside, Ray was furious with himself: caught again, dead to rights. Being in and out in a few hours made it seem like Indianapolis, but Ray knew in his gut that this bust was different. These weren't city cops and city justice for sale at a price. This was the Feds, the *United States of America* v. *Ray Charles,* and that worked out to 180 million to one against, long odds for a percentage player like Ray. The charge could turn out worse than simple possession. Customs had impounded the Martin, and they'd surely find the stash on the plane. Maybe they'd charge him with smuggling; losing on a charge like that could mean doing real time in prison. That thought was unendurable. Ray was in the worst trouble of his life, and he knew it.

Yet on the outside Ray kept his cool. They played the Boston show before the news got out. No one in the Back Bay crowd sensed anything wrong, but a few who knew Ray's music well felt a special edge that night. Then the Boston Sunday papers carried the story on page one, and throughout the week it spread to the world. The Indianapolis *Recorder* put the blunt facts in eight words: "Ray Charles Faces 40 Years on Dope Rap."

The Boston bust threw Ray's world into havoc. College bookers started calling Shaw Artists to cancel, and Milt and Larry Myers in turn canceled dates the gang couldn't make without the Martin. Ray didn't care. He didn't feel much like playing in public. Not play in public? Hal Zeiger didn't like the sound of that. Mae begged Ray to stay in New York; Della wanted him to come home. Joe thought LA was a good idea too. Larry Newton felt glad, one more time, that ABC had built the suspension-for-no-delivery clause into Ray's contract. Deeper than that, Newton couldn't understand why a guy with so much talent could risk it all for drugs. Ray didn't seem unhappy; he took drugs because he liked to and the hell with anybody. But if drugs meant losing his whole career? Newton really didn't understand it.

Jeff watched the whole brouhaha as if from afar. He was going back to Houston and his bowling alley; Joe would have to take care of Ray through this one. Joe had won and he had lost, but Jeff figured being bitter wouldn't help. He wrote Ray a letter of res-ignation, explaining that he knew Ray's business had grown out of his range. "All I ever brought to Ray was my honesty," Brown remembered years later. "If Ray didn't want that, I was no use to him anymore."

Ray's attorneys pled Ray's busy calendar and got the preliminary hearing postponed twice. On November 24, however, Ray had to take his medicine, and it wasn't sweet. Lally testified to the facts of the arrest; a chemist testified that the herb and powder seized had indeed been marijuana and heroin. Nelligan found probable cause for the charge and held the case, Docket 9-5409, over for trial in the U.S. District Court. The only good news: Nelligan continued bail, and when the gavel came down, Ray was still free to go.

The gang played the Brooklyn Academy of Music on November 28, the last major gig in the East, and Ray made up his mind. He'd go to LA and stay there; he wouldn't tour in 1965. He had too much to think about to be gigging nine months of the year; there was plenty of work he could do in the new building. Take time off and you'll lose your audience, Zeiger shouted, but Ray was immovable. He told the fellows the band was disbanded, and they were off until further notice. They took it with a shrug and went their separate ways, Fathead back to Dallas and his own legal woes, Leroy to playing strip clubs in Washington, D.C. Mae took Ray's decision to mean he'd never come back to New York; he was abandoning her and baby Raenee at last. She found herself a lawyer. The summer Ray took her to Juan-les-Pins as his best girl seemed a long time ago.

Ray went home to Hepburn Avenue. The boys were excited about moving to the new house on the hill; Della hoped it would help put the past behind them. Ray had been back only a few days when the news spread like wildfire: Sam Cooke was dead, shot at a sleazy motel on Figueroa. A sad day for the many fans of Cooke, a handsome singer still growing as an artist, and for Ray a chilling one. Walks on the wild side held dangers. He had just been busted, Cooke had just been shot. Might one of his women, one of his drug dealers, shoot him? Cooke's funeral became a huge event, 5000 people surrounding the packed Mount Sinai Baptist Church. When Ray entered, the crowd craned their necks for a better look. He was led past the bier and then to the mike. Tears streaming from his eyes, Ray told the people Cooke was "a marvelous man and my good friend." The crowd stirred, wanting more.

"What do you want me to do?" Ray asked.

"Sing, Ray, sing!" they responded. Someone led Ray to the piano, and he sang "The Angels Keep Watching Over Me," his voice cracking with feeling, the congregation singing on the chorus.

A few days later came yet another shock: Nat "King" Cole had lung cancer. Mrs. Shaw was in the hospital with cancer too, and Milt was going crazy with worry. It seemed no one was safe anymore.

One afternoon the phone rang. It was Tom Dowd, in town for an audio engineers' convention, calling to say hello—the best news Ray had had in weeks. "Come over, come over," Ray said excitedly. "The studio stuff has come, I need you to tell me what I'm doing wrong." Dowd came over to the new building and found a four-track board, mikes, and cables half in and half out of their cartons.

Ray and Tom attacked the hodge podge of equipment together, and they fell quickly into their old working groove, sitting side by side and saying only a few words: "This will go here, that'll go there, okay?" The goal was a place where Ray could work comfortably. Tom tried to think like Ray, putting everything possible within arm's reach. He could scoot to the rest on a wheeled chair. They established a "normal," a basic position for the knobs that Ray could always get back to, no matter how they got twisted. After a few dry runs, Ray knew it was perfect.

"Tom Dowd built my first studio," Ray has declared in years since, giving Dowd more credit than Dowd felt he deserved. Ray felt grateful for more than Tom's practical help. Focusing with his old partner on step-by-step technical problems, Ray could block out the worries that swarmed about his head like gnats, waiting only for an idle moment to assail him. Yet work as he might, Ray couldn't hide from the fact that he was in big trouble with no easy way out. The decision not to tour had given him time to think, but it had also broken his unbreakable routine. Moving from city to city, gig to gig, the daily obligation to be here at this o'clock and there at that o'clock, had structured his life since his first road trip with Lowell Fulson. Now he had shaken it off. No New Year's Eve gig at the Palladium capped 1964, and 1965 stretched ahead, a blank and empty year.

I'm heading to the roundhouse, they
can't corner me there.

Ray Charles

The Year Off
1965

Ray got back to New York sooner than he had expected. Lee Shaw died on January 5, 1965, and was buried beside Billy at Mount Ararat Cemetery on Long Island. Ray wore a yarmulke at the funeral and sat beside Milt, who was devastated by his mother's death. The two men left the cemetery together, and Larry Myers watched them stagger across the street, both so stoned they could have been killed and not known it. Ray flew back to work in LA, but Milt didn't pull out of his grief. He stayed high night after night, coming into the office for a few foggy hours in the afternoon looking sickly and pale. Milt called Ray in California to maunder about his problems, but Ray was losing patience with him. He had problems of his own, and a business to run just like Milt. If Milt didn't take better care of his business, he was going to lose it. Ray didn't plan on losing his.

"Cry" came out as the year's first single, trudged to #58, and then disappeared. Blustery Larry Newton replaced stolid Sam Clark as president of ABC-Paramount; Newton's star had risen with Ray and the other black artists he had signed, B. B. King, Curtis Mayfield, and John Coltrane. The new label president knew his star artist was in trouble. Drugs had always been the big question with Ray, busts always the wrong answer. Could he slip out of this one as he had slipped out before? Newton had never talked to Ray about drugs, and he didn't know how to start. "So I tell him, 'Get straight!' So what?" he figured. "Addicts change when *they* want to change." Anyway, Ray had sold millions of records for ABC on heroin; maybe he wouldn't sound so good straight. Newton felt he knew Ray "better than I know my ten fingers and toes"; but how close could he be to someone who suspected him all the time? Everything he told Ray, Ray checked with Joe, and everything Joe told Ray, he checked with Newton. Ray's contract was up in the spring, and making a new deal with Ray Charles might take forever. Still, Newton knew he'd sign him again. Sinatra kept bouncing back, so would Ray. ABC had enjoyed fat years with Ray; they'd weather this lean one together.

After seven years on Hepburn Avenue, the Robinson family moved to their new house on Southridge, a home they felt proud of but not quite comfortable in. Close-cropped ornamental trees guarded the tall front door of the house. Inside, cold opulence à la Joe Adams reigned. A white marble foyer opened onto a white marble staircase that led down to a huge living room with a white marble fireplace and windows that stretched from the white-carpeted floor to the white cathedral ceiling. Della put down strips of plastic to protect the snowy wall-to-wall, and the family spent most of their time in an informal den and ate their meals in the kitchen. Ray installed his office and tinkering room in one wing of the basement. The boys loved splashing in the piano-shaped swimming pool, and they put up a basketball net in the tennis court.

Otherwise the news was all bad. Nat "King" Cole died, Malcolm X got shot to death, and Mae filed a petition in New York's Family Court asking Ray for $2000 a month in support of Raenee. Because Ray no longer lived in New York, the case got transferred to Los Angeles and began to wend its way to trial. A second paternity suit piled on top of the drug bust: somone else might have settled with Mae to clear his plate, but not Ray. He'd bulldog it through as he had with Sandra Jean. All that was small potatoes compared with the big bad news: on February 26, a Federal grand jury sitting in Boston returned a criminal indictment against Ray Charles on four narcotics charges: two for possessing 3.17 ounces of heroin and 588 grains of marijuana, and two for bringing the heroin and marijuana into the country "contrary to law." Ray's attorneys were given a month to respond with Ray's plea. What would he do?

First, he'd get to work. The million and one details of settling into 2107 West Washington provided Ray a welcome respite from worry. Vice president Joe Adams thought a sign announcing "Ray Charles Enterprises" to the passing public was not a good idea, so president Ray Charles decided on the "RPM International Building," RPM for "revolutions per minute," a common recording term, and for the three businesses the building housed: recording, publishing, and management. The little offices along the corridors filled up with staff and secretaries handling the paperwork for Tangerine Records, Tangerine Music, and Racer Personal Management. Arranger Onzy

Matthews, a young Texan who had worked with Lou Rawls, moved into an office next to bookkeeper Ethel Rubin. Modest Miss Rubin seemed never to make a mistake, and Ray thought he had finally found a money person he could trust. Meeting a payroll of a dozen employees was a challenge Ray welcomed. With his corporations and his team under one roof at last, he felt truly launched as an independent businessman. "Ray Charles Moves Base to West Coast," *Billboard* informed the trade; for over three decades that base did not move an inch.

Ray also threw himself into recording in the big gray room at the back of the building, sparsely furnished with mikes and cables and a Steinway grand. After years of sessions booked long in advance and on the clock, Ray loved the luxury of having a studio waiting for him night and day, where he could work like a painter in his atelier, stacking up canvas after canvas. Before RPM, Ray had been notorious for getting to sessions late; at RPM he was on time to the minute, and everybody else had to be punctual too. When they weren't, Joe Adams was there to chew them out. *Country and Western Meets Rhythm and Blues* collects Ray's first work at RPM, and it's a grab bag. Gems abound—Sid Feller's lovely chart for "Please Forgive and Forget" and a ripsnorting "Blue Moon of Kentucky"—but Ray was too busy experimenting in the new studio, and too distracted by legal problems, to settle on an overall theme. He was not so distracted, however, that he forgot the bottom line: five of the twelve tracks are Tangerine songs.

In March, when his recording contract ran out, Ray and Joe flew to New York to negotiate a new one. Flanked by lawyers and accountants, they met Newton and his lawyers and accountants in a corporate conference room. Its long oak table was soon covered with full ashtrays, empty coffee cups, and briefcases spilling papers. Ray sat quietly as Joe, unruffled by the fray, dueled for him. Rebates given dealers during the phase-out of mono for stereo was the nub of the problem. Joe claimed that ABC owed Ray $200,000, and ABC's accountants said no, that was Ray's share of the rebate that he had to pay as owner of the masters.

Newton listened to the haggling as long as he could stand it, then he took Ray by the arm and led him into the executive bathroom. "This could go on forever," he told him as the door closed behind them. "I hate lawyers, I hate accountants. What do you need to sign?"

"What do you think is fair?" asked Ray.

"How about a hundred thousand?"

"You got a deal." They shook hands and came out smiling. Joe Adams and the lawyers and accountants took the news openmouthed. Suddenly they had nothing to do.

From New York Ray flew to Boston, to appear on March 26 in U.S. Federal District Court. At the brief hearing he spoke only two words: "Not guilty." Judge George Sweeney continued Ray's $1000 bail and gave his lawyers twenty days to file further pleas, but Ray could feel himself being backed into a corner. If convicted on all four charges, he faced a maximum of sixty years in prison and $40,000 in fines. Federal prosecutors pushed for a summer trial, Ray's lawyers bargained for delays. If Ray would name his dealers, the Feds suggested, that might help. Ray refused; no dealer ever made him buy dope, and he wouldn't bring down someone else to save his own skin. What would kicking heroin do for his chances? Ray's lawyers asked. It couldn't hurt, replied the Feds, but they'd have the right to check him to prove he was clean.

Irritations buzzed about Ray's head through April and May. A single, "Without a Song," came out and died. Mae had her well-publicized day in court; again Ray lost a paternity suit, and again the tension between Ray and Della reached the breaking point. Instead of sending a Welcome Wagon, a few hundred of the Robinsons' white neighbors signed a petition declaring the Southridge house a "monstrous dwelling" that cut off their views. But one worry above all nagged at Ray, demanding an answer: Heroin, heroin, what to do about heroin?

For the moment Ray kept shooting up, but change stirred in his spirit. As in the summer after Retha died, Ray dove deep into himself. Who was he? Where was he headed? Forces within him rose to the surface, ideas, memories, and fears, yet the swirl of emotions did not shut down his mind. Ray had few illusions about the bind he was in. He believed he had a right to heroin, to hell with the law; but the law wouldn't go to hell, he would. If by hook or by crook he beat this bust, there would be another and another and another after that. Billie Holiday and Charlie Parker stared Ray in the face, stark examples of what clinging to heroin could do to his future. Look at Fathead: his little scrape in Hawaii had been switched to Texas, and Texas judges didn't like black men who did drugs. Fathead might be doing hard time soon.

Ray didn't think he'd survive prison. Maybe he could survive life inside, but the thought of all he'd be denied—no women, no touring, no business, no records, no music!—would kill him. Heroin or music, that's what it came down to: heroin or music? It would be crazy—worse, it would be *stupid* to throw away music for a drug. Music had given him all he had, music held all he hoped for. But could he kick? Ray had gotten deep enough into withdrawal a few times to know it was no picnic. Junkie lore said kicking cold turkey meant three days of pure hell, then it got better. "I can stand almost anything for three days," he knew of himself. "Especially if I see the purpose right there before me. All I got to do is continue to breathe and I'll make it over." That's how he had made it through his days in court: hunker down and hold out. He'd make himself a rock, he wouldn't budge. He'd call the devil's bluff, and he'd win.

The climax of his decision came one night in late May. Ray Jr., just turned ten, had won a Little League award, and Mom and Dad planned to go to the presentation dinner. Then Quincy Jones called. He wanted Ray to sing the title song for *The Cincin-*

nati Kid, a Steve McQueen film he was scoring. It turned out that he had booked an orchestra and studio for the night of the banquet. Ray asked him to reschedule, and Jones did. The dinner committee then changed its date to the night of the new session, and Ray didn't think he could ask for a second change; he'd have to leave the dinner before Ray Jr.'s moment of glory. The boy burst into tears as his father got up to go, and Ray walked out on his valet's arm, his son's cries in his ears, feeling everyone's eyes on him. At the studio that night and for days after, the sound of little Ray's sobs stayed with Ray. He had never been a demonstrative dad, seldom home, and when there, too busy for man-to-man talks with his oldest boy. Still, Ray Jr.'s misery reached him. "This kid really loves me," Ray realized. If he went to prison, the other kids at school might tease Ray Jr., "Your old man's nothing but a jailbird." Clinging to heroin would mean losing, along with his music and freewheeling life, his son's love and respect. That did it. Ray walked into Joe's office one day in June. "I intend to check myself into a hospital," he said. "I ain't ever gonna mess with heroin again."

"You don't have to tell me that, Ray," Adams replied.

"I'm not talking to be talking," said Ray. "I'm telling you what's gonna happen."

It didn't happen right way. Cautious Ray wanted to kick under a doctor's care. His lawyers insisted that Dr. Foster wouldn't do; Ray needed a doctor with the credentials to convince the court that he had truly quit and that the cure would stick. Discreet inquiry soon yielded the name of Dr. Frederick Hacker.

Friedrich J. Hacker had been a medical student in Vienna when the Nazis invaded Austria in 1938. A Jew, he fled first to Switzerland, then to America, spending the war years as a psychiatrist-psychoanalyst at the Menninger Clinic in Topeka, Kansas. After the war, Hacker moved to Los Angeles, joined the Hollywood émigré community, and soon had a flourishing celebrity practice. Silver-haired and dapper, "a social lion who loved famous people," in the words of a longtime colleague, Hacker was also a respected therapist whose method went beyond classic Freudian analysis. "Hacker was a psychiatrist the way Perry Mason was a lawyer," recalled the colleague. "He didn't stay in his office. He'd find an alcoholic patient in a bar, confront him, and drive him home."

When they met at Hacker's Beverly Hills clinic, Ray said he had no interest in going through formal analysis. Hacker didn't push for it, but he did suggest that Ray could wean himself off heroin gradually, taking other drugs to ease withdrawal. No, said Ray; he'd kick cold turkey. He just needed a hospital for safety and privacy. Hacker had the perfect place, St. Francis Hospital in Lynwood, a drab corner of southeastern LA. He had recently opened a second clinic at the hospital, and he could easily get Ray admitted. When it came time for court, he'd be glad to testify for Ray as an expert witness; he knew the legal-psychiatric ropes inside out.

Through June and into July Ray delayed the fateful day. Rumors spread. "Why all the hush-hush about blind singer Ray Charles' reported illness?" a *Sentinel* gossip columnist wondered. "His business office has refused announcements about his condition to the Negro press. We can only say, 'people need people.' " Ray cleaned up his desk. One final detail: advertising in the *Sentinel* that, "starting next week," RPM, a "modern and flexible studio, with editing, mixing, mono and stereo facilities," was available around-the-clock, rate cards on request. Ray might be entering hell, but the studio could make a few bucks in his absence.

On the afternoon of Monday, July 26, valet Vernon Troupe drove Ray to the hospital. They rolled across flat miles of Watts, little houses baking in the sun, and through miles of scrap-metal junkyards, the steel belly of Los Angeles where the city digested its own waste as food. Beyond the junkyards lay Lynwood and, on wide Imperial Boulevard, the anonymous cream-colored buildings of St. Francis Hospital. In Los Angeles terms, Ray had gone to Siberia. Nobody but Philip Marlowe could track him here.

Dr. Hacker took Ray inside to Room 127 in "1 South," the twenty-bed psychiatric ward. Ray refused the tranquilizers he was offered. Vernon left. Evening drew on as Ray lay on his bed and waited for withdrawal to come on. It took its time. He had some dinner. He napped. In the long hours before dawn, the first waves of nausea arrived. Ray began to puke, and he puked and puked until there was nothing in his gut. He felt as if he was vomiting pure poison, and the experience, he wrote, was "bitter—bitter as gall." For two days, waves of nausea and diarrhea passed over Ray. "My body stunk," he later wrote. "My sweat stunk. Everything about me stunk."

Through the third and fourth days the storm of spasms calmed. Though still queasy, Ray could hold down a few crackers crumbled into soup. He was past the crisis; now came the long haul. He dozed afternoons and paced nights alone in his room trying to focus on the future, all the work he'd begin when he got out. The old blues, "Going Down Slow," went through his mind, the dying boy sobbing to his mother that he "won't be home no more." Now he understood the song; he could record that.

At RPM, Joe Adams stonewalled reporters, as did Milt Shaw in New York, but the black press had a piece of the story in a week, and in two weeks the *Sentinel* put Ray's room number on page one. Other papers printed wild speculation: Ray was on the "critical list" with "cancer" or an "incurable disease." Two court dates came up, Sandra Jean again and the Feds in Boston. Hacker brushed both aside: Ray had been hospitalized for "depressive anxiety," a serious condition "greatly aggravated by excitement"; Ray couldn't stand the strain of a trial for at least nine weeks.

In Siberia all that was far away. Ray slept and played cards with the nurses on the late shift. Three times a week he had sit-and-talk sessions with Hacker. Ray's prickly intelligence intrigued the doctor. Ray resisted his questions and tried to keep the subject to music or politics, yet over weeks, a healing bond grew up between therapist and patient. Ray told Hacker about George's drowning and about going blind, the lonely first days at D&B and Retha's death. "Ray Charles," Hacker told his brother one night over a glass of wine, "had a very hard childhood."

Slowly Ray came out of his cocoon. Della visited, bringing home-cooked food. Ray started calling the office, talking figures with Joe and charts with Onzy Matthews. Larry Newton called; *Country and Western Meets Rhythm and Blues* was out with its funny cover: two Rays shaking hands, one in cowboy duds, the other in a purple tuxedo. Watts exploded in riot, and Vernon Troupe drove Ray's Corvette through fierce rock-and-bottle battles, carrying messages for his boss and sometimes smuggling in a little reefer. When Hacker got wind of it, he had Ray's room searched. Ray blew up and threatened to check himself out. Joe came back from a business trip to New York and calmed Ray down. The nurses didn't search Ray's room again.

September came and went. Used to doing what he liked when and how he liked, Ray got bored in confinement. He was glad he had kicked, but he resented being backed into it. "I don't get in other folks' business," he growled at Vernon, "and I don't like folks in my business." Hacker appeased him by letting him out for visits to lady friends and, a good player himself, taught Ray the rudimentary moves of chess. Another patient played, and he and Ray, both insomniacs, battled deep into the night, the novice Ray feeling the pieces before and after every move, seeing their positions and possibilities in his mind's eye. Night after night he lost, but with the doggedness of an avid beginner, he wrested some crumb of knowledge from every defeat, and could boast at least that the fellow never beat him the same way twice.

Chess came to Ray as love at first sight. The dominoes and checkers he had played with Jeff dropped away as child's play; card games lost their appeal. Ray loved chess, because, as he explained years later, "there's no luck in it. With cards, no matter how well you play, you ain't gonna win unless the cards fall for you. But in chess, it's *my brain against yours!* We start with the same pieces in the same places, the only advantage, if you call it that, is that one player moves first. You've got to outwit, out-think, and out-maneuver the other person, and he's thinking how to outwit you." From the hospital onward Ray always kept a chessboard at hand, and in time he became a superb player. Had he not been blind, Ray, with his athletic figure and competitive drive, would surely have played basketball, tennis, or golf. Yet Ray's affinity for chess went beyond the love of a game. In chess he found the perfect metaphor for how he already saw the world. Attack and retreat, hide and dare, plan five moves ahead. Ray Charles had been playing chess long before he knew a pawn from a bishop.

In October Ray started to record again, coming in to RPM evenings, working with a band Onzy Matthews had put together and with Sid and strings. These tracks became *Crying Time,* one of Ray's true masterpieces, the self-portrait of an artist in a season of despair. *Crying Time* has a theme, intense sadness, yet for the first time, Ray didn't choose his theme; it chose him. Every track, every note, bears the scars of experience. "I've lost everything, I have no friend," Ray cries on "No Use Crying," and Billy Preston's organ screams in pain. A bluesy electric guitar crackles throughout, Sid's strings ache with regret. In "Let's Go Get Stoned" Ray sings about booze, not drugs, but it's still a noisy thumb of his nose at the authorities who made him kick. On Percy Mayfield's "You're in for a Big Surprise," he vents bitter anger at the hurt of being black in white America: "I call you Mister, I shine your shoes, You're laughing while I sing the blues."

"My heart's in trouble," "You treat me just like dirt," "It's too late to cry"—harsh lyrics leap like daggers from every song. Ray exits laughing a hollow laugh that he hurls in our faces:

> You've got a great big problem,
> You've got a great big problem
> Yes, you've got a great big problem,
> And there's nothing that you can do!

At each session, as Ray sang and heartbreaking music filled the long gray room, Sid felt, in a way he never forgot, the contrast between the passion in Ray's music and his dispassionate approach to making it. "Ray and I had worked out the charts weeks before, and Ray didn't change a note. Take after take, he'd sob and crack his voice in the same places. When we talked about music, we talked quarter notes and eighth rests, not hearts and flowers. Ray never talked about feelings at all."

In the high-stakes chess game with the Feds, a major court date loomed before Thanksgiving in Boston. For weeks Ray's lawyers bargained with the prosecutors. Ray had kicked; if he pled guilty, what could he expect? The Feds refused to make a deal. They wouldn't throw the book at him, but they wanted him to do time; three ounces was a lot of heroin to fly in from Canada. When he and Joe left LA, Ray thought prison was a "distinct possibility." They stopped in New York and met Hacker at a hotel; Joe went over the doctor's testimony with him in detail. On November 22, Ray stood before Judge Sweeney in Federal Court, and this time he said one word: "Guilty."

"This man has been in previous trouble with narcotics," said defense attorney Paul J. Redmond, playing it straight. "And at no time has he done anything, prior to this arrest, to endeavor to help himself." This time, however, he had, and Redmond introduced Hacker (with a six-page résumé of his degrees and publications) to tell the story of Ray's cure. Ray Charles had been his patient since June, Hacker testified, and had come through supervised withdrawal. Hacker believed that Ray was a man of strong willpower who desired to kick heroin for good. To incarcerate Ray Charles would ruin his career and ruin him as a person, but if freed, Hacker felt confident, Ray would continue his cure. The U.S. attorney acknowledged Ray's attempt to kick, but argued that he shouldn't be let off scot-free. Two years in prison and a $10,000 fine was a reasonable minimum punishment for his crime.

With that, Ray's fate lay in the hands of Judge Sweeney, but the judge decided that he wouldn't decide right away. "The best test for withdrawal from drugs is time," Sweeney declared. If Ray would waive his right to an immediate sentence, he would continue the case for a year with the provision that the "defendant will report to Government doctors for examination at such times as are designated by the Court." Ray readily agreed: no sentence today meant he was free today and would still be free tomorrow. If he could stay off heroin, and he was sure he could, an exam by the court's doctors would only be a few days' hassle. And if he came up clean on the exam, the chance that he'd ever do time dropped to nil. It had taken thirteen months, a year off the road, and the wrenching experience of withdrawal, but the worst of the Boston bust was behind him at last.

Ray flew back to LA elated. He had his future back, his work, his family, his music. Much as he thanked his lawyers and Judge Sweeney, Ray thanked Frederick Hacker most of all, a gratitude that did not fade with time. He continued seeing Hacker in informal therapy sessions that tapered off into friendship. After Hacker died in 1989, Ray told an Austrian magazine, "Dr. Hacker saved my life."

Word that Ray had kicked spread on the band grapevine. Hank Crawford heard that he had "walked in and out in two weeks, cool as a cucumber." Ray knew kicking had been tougher than that, but once it was over, he didn't feel any change for better or worse in his mental or physical state. He simply didn't crave a fix every morning. Yet Vernon Troupe noticed a "night and day" difference for the better. "There had been something pitiful about Ray when he got stoned," the valet recalled. "It was like being with a stranger. He knew me but only as my function, a tool that got him from one place to another. The warmth that I got afterward, the kidding and joking, the *person*, were not there in the heroin days."

A week after the Boston court date, Ray strolled into Hollywood's Moulin Rouge theater for *The TNT Show,* a concert filmed as a rock 'n' roll movie. Reporters badgered him with questions about the hospital, and he brushed them off with a grin: "Man, I'm tired and I've been trying to get a little rest." Record producer Phil Spector put together an eclectic bill for *TNT*—Ray, the Byrds, Joan Baez, Bo Diddley, Ike and Tina Turner, among others—and in brilliant black-and-white photography, he captured the diverse energies pulsing through mid-60s pop music. Previously Ray had looked nervous on camera, but here, delighted to be performing again, he's as exuberant as a kid out of school for the summer. "What'd I Say" opens the film, setting a pounding pace for all that follows. The camera bounces with Ray's beat, frequently cutting from the stage to the screaming kids, nearly all white but responding to the music like a Saturday-night crowd at the Apollo. After segments by Petula Clark and the Lovin' Spoonful, Ray came back to sing "Georgia" and "Let the Good Times Roll." As they started "Good Times," somebody goofed and the band stopped. "Who you waitin' on?" Ray shouts to general laughter; then they leap into the tune together:

> *Hey, everybody, Ray Charles is in town,*
> *I got a dollar and a quarter, I'm raring to clown*
> *But don't let no female play me cheap*
> *I got fifty cents more than I'm gonna keep.*
> *Let the good times roll!*

Through December the RPM building hummed with activity and plans for the upcoming year. Ray wanted to play as many gigs as possible, let the world know he was back. Joe had an idea: why not take a twelve-piece band on the road? Fewer musicians meant fewer problems, and of course, cheaper. Always ready to save a dollar, Ray thought it was worth a try, and Onzy Matthews started writing new twelve-piece charts for the top tunes in Ray's book, doing his best to keep the signature sounds and phrases of the originals. "Crying Time," the single, entered the charts at #92, but a week later it had jumped twelve notches and the week after that another twenty: a strong single at last.

Ray invited Larry Newton to California in December to hear the new album. Newton came to dinner at Southridge and found Ray underneath a car in the driveway fixing a noisy muffler. Once he washed up, Ray gave his guest a tour of the house, and Newton oohed and aahed over the magnificent living room and the piano-shaped pool with a keyboard of black-and-white tiles. Like Vernon, Newton noticed a big change for the better in Ray; he was easier to talk to and get along with. Newton was sure that if Ray stayed off drugs, they could rebuild his career. Della cooked a delicious meal; then Ray took him to RPM and played him a tape of *Crying Time*. Listening to it, Newton felt tears come into his eyes. "I love it, Ray," he said. "This is going to number one."

Just before the holidays, a reporter caught up with Della at a supermarket. Ordinarily, Della never said a word to the press, but now, bubbling over with happiness, she couldn't help herself. Yes, Ray had been discharged from the hospital, but no, she wouldn't give any details of his treatment. That was all in the past now and didn't matter. "My husband is at home and he is looking healthier than ever," she said. "It's going to be a real Merry Christmas for us."

20

Coming Back
1966-1967

Back in July 1965, Sid Feller had decided to leave ABC
and had moved with Gert and the kids to Los Angeles. Gert found them a home in the
San Fernando Valley, and Sid found work arranging music for television. Ray invited
them to dinner one night at Southridge. Sid no longer produced Ray's records, but Ray
continued giving him songs to arrange, and 2107 West Washington became one of Sid's
landmarks as he learned his way on and off the freeways. It was a busy place, Percy Mayfield going over new tunes with Ray on the office piano, the Four Tops stopping by with
Stevie Wonder to say respectful hellos. Ike and Tina Turner might be rehearsing in the
studio, or Quincy Jones recording a Chrysler radio commercial. Tenor sax player Clifford Solomon, who had known Ray since his first days in LA, played for Quincy, and
one day Ray heard him blowing a riff. "Is that you out there, Sol?" he asked. "Yeah,
RC," said Clifford and they had a laughing reunion.

The blind R&B star Sid met in 1959 had come a long way in seven years. "Before
Ray came to ABC, he made a living," he said to Gert. "Now he's a rich man." Larry
Newton told Sid that to keep his taxes low, Ray spent only his performing and investment income and let his record royalties accumulate at ABC. He had even figured out
how to build RPM with no capital outlay: a $300,000 loan from ABC, which he was

paying back, painlessly, by having ABC withhold a small percentage of the influx to his treasure trove. With heroin behind him, in his own building with his own staff, Ray could grow in any direction he pleased. "Ray's gone to the tippy top," said Sid. "He's become an industry giant."

Joe Adams had played a major role in Ray's success. The two men often erupted in noisy quarrels, but the working bond between them had underlying strength. "Nei ther Joe nor Ray gave an inch," Sid recalled, "but when they got through yelling, they'd made another coup." Larry Newton said Joe was "riding a good horse." The job held more than money for Adams. As Ray Charles' manager, he was a wealthy man's stew ard, a servant endowed with his master's power. Anything and everything lay within Joe's scope: hiring and firing, negotiating contracts, driving the bus, picking the fab rics for Ray's tuxedos, decorating (and redecorating) RPM's reception area, designing album covers, and engineering in the studio. He often worked seven days a week; he liked the challenge of coming into the office not knowing if he'd be there all day or catching a midday plane to New York. He was even studying for his pilot's license to fly the Cessna and the Martin. "I'm not gifted," Joe liked to explain, "but I get things done." By doing so much, Joe saved Ray Charles Enterprises money and allowed the boss, who hated delegating authority, to deal with one invaluable sub-boss rather than a half-dozen expendables. Secretaries often didn't know whom to take their orders from, Joe or Ray, but they knew for sure that nobody at RPM gave orders but the two men at the top.

Joe made a good executive salary, and power of attorney gave him the heady abil ity to spend Ray's money. Yet like Jeff before him, Joe remained an employee and Ray the sole owner of Ray Charles Enterprises. "No partners!" was Ray's inflexible motto; he wanted the freedom, he often said, "to burn the damn place down if I want to, and hurt nobody but myself." Ethel Rubin became Ray's day-to-day watchdog over his manager. After a busy day at the office, Ray might call Miss Rubin at home and ask her, casually amid minor details, "How many checks did Joe sign today?"

As 1966 began, Joe and Ray had one major task: to bring Ray back from the black hole of the year off. There was no use kidding themselves: Ray had lost ground in pop music's fast-moving marketplace. Motown's growing galaxy of stars—the Supremes, the Miracles, Stevie Wonder, and Marvin Gaye—and a dozen white British and American groups had taken over the top of the charts, all of the new hitmakers a decade younger than Ray. One group, the Mamas and Papas, had replaced Ray as ABC's top-selling artist. Luckily, the single "Crying Time" reached #6, Ray's biggest hit in two years, and *Crying Time* the album was climbing toward an eventual #15. Ray pushed ahead on a new album, *Ray's Moods,* an eclectic mix of country, comedy, and old chestnuts— something, he hoped, for everyone.

Strong product gave Ray a fighting chance at a comeback, but Larry Newton argued that only a positive press campaign could offset the year of negative publicity. The trade needed to be reassured that Ray's friends in the business stood behind him; the public needed the bust and the cure presented in a way they could sympathize with, even admire. Newton hired New York public relations man Dick Gersh to lobby *Life* magazine for a major profile and to line up ads and puff pieces for a Ray Charles tribute in *Billboard*. Joe hired the LA press agents Hanson and Schwam to pepper the press with items on Ray. The account got assigned to Bob Abrams, a kid from Brooklyn who had drifted into show business as a pal of Eddie Fisher's. Abrams got his items on the phone from Joe; Ray didn't want to meet him or reporters at all. Ray kept himself aloof from the press campaign, and he refused to speak out against heroin or to say that he regretted his years of addiction. "When I was doing it, I was doing it because I wanted to," Ray said. Other than that, he refused to discuss the subject.

Getting back on the road was what mattered to Ray. "I must get back in front of the people," he told Milt Shaw. To get the Martin back, Ray Charles Enterprises had to deposit $90,000 with the Commissioner of Customs, yet touring was worth any cost. Even paying for a full band: when it came to it, Ray realized he loved the big band too much to scrimp by with a band of twelve, and he scrapped Onzy's twelve-piece charts (Onzy had to sue Ray through the musicians' union to get paid for them). Of the old-timers, only Leroy Cooper and Edgar Willis returned; Fathead was doing nine months at the Federal pen in Sigaville, Texas, and couldn't make it. Yet strong soloists sat in every section: high-note specialist Bill King among the trumpets, be-bopper Curtis Amy on tenor sax, and on guitar, Oklahoma bluesman Tony Mathews. Three new Raelets, Alexandra Brown, Clydie King, and Merry Clayton, joined old-timer Gwen Berry. Ray wanted a clean band, and Joe hired an ex-policeman to screen the new members for drugs. As March came in, everybody came out to Southridge for a big dinner, then they dug into rehearsal at RPM; as March went out, they were packing the Latin Casino in New Jersey.

The Martin had hopscotched out to Las Vegas by late April for a week at the Thunderbird. There, after the last show, a U.S. marshal approached Ray and told him he had twenty-four hours to get to Boston for the court-ordered heroin check. Short notice, but since Ray knew he was clean, he flew east with the marshal as if going on vacation. From Boston they drove out to suburban Waverly and red brick McLean Hospital, well-known as the asylum where Boston Brahmins discreetly stowed insane relatives. After joking his way through a psychiatric interview, Ray went to bed. In the middle of the night, he woke up, shivering cold. He instantly suspected that the doctors had ordered the heat turned off to intensify the chills of withdrawal, and he stomped out to the nurses' station. "If I catch pneumonia," he told the head nurse, "I'm gonna sue this joint so bad everyone is going to be working for me. . . . Dig?" He stomped back to his room. In a few minutes he felt the heat come on and dropped back to sleep.

For three days doctors tested him head to toe, and Ray amused himself by flirting with the nurses and playing the piano. On April 28 they pronounced him clean; until his sentencing session in the fall, he was free to go. Now the gang could get back to touring and earning in earnest: over the next weekend—Friday at Rensselaer Polytech in Troy, New York, Saturday at Carnegie Hall, and Sunday at Symphony Hall, Newark—they grossed $68,000.

"Nineteen sixty-six was dynamite," remembered Harold Patton, a band boy on his first tour. "Ray was running full-throttle that year, a guy with something to prove. We crisscrossed the country, hitting every watering hole there was to hit." Audiences packed the concert halls, and the music press gave Ray a warm welcome. "Ray Charles is back in the big band saddle," *Downbeat* announced, and Ralph Gleason declared that Ray's "enforced lay-off hasn't hurt him one little bit. . . . He still creates that unique emotional spell."

"Fired with vitality," one of the fellows described Ray to a reporter that spring, and his energy proved contagious. "Let's Go Get Stoned" came out in May and climbed through the summer to #31. A brazen sentiment for a man still facing sentence on drug charges, and a raucous dance record played at a million parties, "Stoned" followed "Rainy Day Women #12 & 35," Bob Dylan's smash with its "Everybody must get stoned!" hook. The resonance between the songs connected Ray to the new waves cresting in pop music, and the two hits together acted as an anything-goes overture to the emerging psychedelic era.

On Monday, June 12, two days after Ray headlined a Yankee Stadium concert with the Byrds and the Beach Boys, came shocking news: Milt Shaw had been found in his Park Avenue apartment, dead of an overdose of heroin at thirty-nine. Once again Ray rode in a procession of black limousines out to Mount Ararat Cemetery. Had he not kicked, Milt might have been attending *his* funeral. With Milt buried beside his parents, the Shaw family was wiped out. Larry Myers would always remember Milt as a man "generous to a fault, who negotiated deals so everybody made money." Yet the sad truth of his last spring, Myers added, was that "Milt couldn't function." His life spinning out of control, Milt had sold Shaw Artists to Don Soviero, a fast-talking hotelman from Massachusetts. Myers and many other agents left, taking artists with them. Ray moved on, first to Ruth Bowen at Queen Booking, and soon Shaw Artists, after twenty years in business, went bankrupt and disappeared.

In July out came the article in *Life*. Entitled "Music Soaring in a Darkened World . . . The Comeback of Ray Charles," the seven-page spread was everything Larry Newton had hoped for, approval from America's mightiest magazine. Ten photographs showed many sides of Ray: on stage and in the studio, with Della and the boys on Southridge, playing chess and flying in his plane. Writer Thomas Thompson told Ray's story as a triumph of courage over hardship, and elicited a ringing endorsement from Frank Sinatra: "Ray Charles is the only genius in our business." His descriptions of Ray's music were turgid—Ray sang like a "Roto-Rooter drilling through the sorrow and heartbreak that clog up the private man"—but Thompson let Ray define "soul" in music with a few well-chosen words:

> Soul is when you take a song and make it part of you—a part that's so true, so real, people think it must have happened to you. . . . It's like electricity; we don't really know what it is, do we? But it's a force that can light a room. Soul is like electricity, like a spirit, a drive, a power.

Underneath the comeback gloss, however, Thompson found Ray that spring still edgy in the first months off heroin, bursting into tears at the memory of his brother George's death. He haunted his "colorless and cold" office deep into one night, chain-smoking and noodling Bach, Chopin, and eerie blues on the piano. Finally Ray felt his Braille watch. It was time to go home to Della and the boys, and he called the valet sprawled fast asleep on the sofa.

It was raining cats and dogs as the Martin flew into Cleveland's Lakeside Airport for a mid-August gig at Leo's Casino. Ben Strong, an old Navy pilot, made three passes at the runway and had to pull up each time. "Can't you put it in?" Ray asked him. "I can put it in if you bear with me," said Strong. Ray said, "Put it in."

"The fourth time we made it," remembered Harold Patton. "Ben set that son of a bitch down in the rain, he was one hell of a pilot." Patton, an unusually bright fellow in his mid-thirties, had left a $500-a-week job in LA for Ray's $125 for the fun of travel and to search for first editions by African-American authors at used-book stores in every city. Patton was finding that touring with Ray was a nonstop scramble: on the plane, off the plane, set up for the gig, break down from the gig, from Cleveland to New York to the Camden County Music Fair near Philadelphia for Labor Day weekend. His $125 didn't go far. Joe told him if he kept the equipment in his room, they'd pay his hotel, so he started stacking the bandstands beside his bed in rooms so small, he joked, "you had to go out in the hall to change your mind."

Joe Adams was Patton's immediate boss, and he impressed the newcomer with the polished style he set for the tour. "If you can't go first-class," Joe liked to say, "stay at home." Patton told him the old cardboard equipment boxes had worn out, and Joe okayed three custom-made aluminum cases, two for the bandstands and the music, one for mutes, cups, tambourines, and other odds and ends. Patton next told Joe it was rough organizing the baggage when everybody had their own suitcase, some of them wrecks held together with string. Joe agreed and ordered two dozen Samsonite bags, gray for the men and red for the Raelets. Patton numbered the bags and Joe presented them to the gang, announcing that from now on only these could be used for personal possessions; for that privilege $21 each would be deducted from their pay.

As cool fall drew on, Ray continued hot. "I Choose to Sing the Blues," a single that *Billboard* rightfully called a "wild rocker," climbed as high as "Let's Go Get Stoned." Out on the road trumpet players and drummers came and went, but the new Ray Charles orchestra had jelled, as Patton put it, into "one hell of a band." Tony Mathews, the new guitar player, got nervous in the up-tempo jazz numbers, but came alive on the blues, igniting the crowd with a burning solo on "Honky Tonk." Merry Clayton, a teenager they nicknamed Baby Sister, brought a Margie Hendricks–like intensity back to the Raelets. "Believe me," remembered Mathews, "Baby Sister could *sing.*" *Variety* noted the band's "hard-biting swing" and found Ray "in superlative form." Robert Shelton in *The New York Times* called one concert "deeply moving" and praised the "instrument that is Ray Charles' voice." Patton had his own meter for how well the tour was going: "At first, if the guy selling programs sold 300 programs, it was a damn good show. Then he started hitting 350, even 400."

The Martin flew to Florida in September. At the Tampa concert Evelyn, now a pretty, dark-brown-skinned teenager, sat beside her daddy on the piano bench. *Ballad in Blue* came out and got panned ("fairly interesting," allowed the *Amsterdam News*). In October, the gang played Philadelphia and *Billboard* put out the issue with a special section on Ray, seventeen pages titled "A Touch of Genius."

Billboard often ran such pat-on-the-back sections as frankly commercial ventures, paid for with ads bought by the tributee's friends—in Ray's case ABC, Atlantic, European promoter Henry Goldgrand, the Righteous Brothers, Southland Record distributors in El Paso, Texas, and many more. Here no mention of drugs or Ray's childhood intruded among the photographs of Ray smiling with Larry Newton and Sid Feller, Dinah Shore and Liberace. Headlines like "An Artist with Unerring Vision" ran over stories that declared, straight-faced, "Ray is universally liked by others in the music business." Yet the long discography, thirty albums and twice that many singles, spoke louder than the flattery, and frequent mention of his grosses—$750,000 for live shows so far in 1966—reminded all concerned that there was still money to be made with Ray Charles.

Life in July, *Billboard* in October: Larry Newton felt the two prongs of the press campaign had worked to good effect on public and industry opinion. On November 22 the question became, How would they play in Federal Court? From a three-day gig in Chicago, Ray flew to Boston for the sentencing deferred a year before. He didn't know what to expect. Judge Sweeney, who had given him the chance to prove himself, had died in October, and the case had been transferred to Judge Charles Wyzanski, who, Ray had heard, was "a real hard-ass." Hacker again pleaded the success of Ray's cure, then a surprise set off a hopeful commotion in the courtroom. Judge Sweeney, Wyzanski announced, knowing he was ill, had dictated a sealed memorandum of his intentions in Ray's case. Wyzanski proceeded to read the memorandum into the record. If Ray had been caught using drugs, Sweeney planned to throw the book at him; if he was clean, he would have given him a lenient two years' probation and a fine of $10,000. Wyzanski tried to stiffen Sweeney's intent, making the sentence four years' probation and adding a five-year suspended sentence, but Ray knew that was paperwork. By kicking heroin for good, he had worked the Boston bust down to a slap on the wrist.

Ray paid the $10,000 fine by check and flew to New York to meet the gang for a handful of college gigs. From there the Martin took them all down to New Orleans and out to LA and the end of the season. As the group scattered in every direction, Ray took a few days off around the holidays with Della and the boys on Southridge. He had passed through one year of private hell, another running the public gauntlet, and he had emerged unscathed, his bond with his audience still strong. Drugs and legal troubles could now disappear into the dismissible past, and he and Joe would make damn sure they never reappeared. From now on nothing would interfere with music making. He began working on a new album with Sid.

▯▮▮▯▮▮▯▮▮▯

A ritual began that winter of 1967, one that lasted years and that became a high point of Ray's LA week: Sunday chess matches at Southridge with a shifting circle of male buddies. Trombonist Fred Murrell was a regular; so were Della's cousin Herb Miller and Billy Brooks, Ray's pal since the days when they ran down to Atlanta with T and Eileen and got married. Ray had learned chess quickly in his first year of play, and his blood was up to test himself against worthy opponents. The fellows started at ten in the morning and often played to midnight. Della served food and drinks and kept the kids out of the way. As the afternoon wore on, Ray's den became thick with smoke and laughter, the mood of the tussling men reminiscent, in a grown-up way, of rambunctious nights in the dorm at Florida D&B.

As Ray debated his next move, he bounced in his chair, his fingers flying over the board, feeling the flat tops of the white pieces, the pointed tops of the black, standing on dark squares raised a quarter-inch over the light. "Uh-huh, uh-huh," he'd say in a steady stream of gab. "I see what you're doing, but you ain't gonna do it. I'm gonna move this knight here to king four. Now you stew in your own gravy!" And he'd rear back in his chair laughing, his mouth wide open, his arms waving, his hands slapping his thighs and chest. Billy Brooks found Ray a formidable adversary, as strong on attack as on defense. "Except he likes you to make the first move, and then counterpunch," Brooks explained. "He likes to devil you with his pawns and to get rid of your knights—their odd movement is the hardest for him to keep track of in his mind."

Ray and his pals played "Rise and Shine," the loser getting up, the winner staying for the next game. To keep the rotation going, they set tight time limits for each move. Ray adored playing chess under time pressure; even talking about it made him as animated as if he were playing. "Speed chess, that'll get your ass up," he laughed. "It's like the twenty-four-second rule in basketball: not only do you have to think, you have to think *fast*. If you truly analyze every possibility, or *most* of them, that might take you a while, but now you gotta run that shit through your head like lightning."

Everybody lost sometimes, Ray less than most. When Ray did hear "checkmate," his disbelief was comically obvious: his face a grimace of annoyance and disappointment, his fingers darting one last hopeless time over the board before folding in defeat. When he won, he'd crow like a rooster, "Damn, man, don't you know how to play? Now get everybody a round of drinks, you're the waiter now!" Then he'd turn to his new opponent with a savage grin. "I beat *him,* and he beat *you,* so what do you think is gonna happen now?"

By ten o'clock Monday morning Ray was back at work at RPM. Tangerine Records was limping along, a slow second to Dunhill among ABC's sub-labels. The company's best bet, the Vocals, slipped away and, produced by others, became the Fifth Dimension with an emerging smash, "Up, Up, and Away." Racer Management, on the other hand, had signed Billy Preston, a kid with a big smile and a heavenly voice, who could play the hell out of the organ and was a show-stopping dancer to boot. Quincy Jones came over to record Ray singing "In the Heat of the Night," the theme song for a film starring Sidney Poitier and Rod Steiger. In other good news, Larry Newton told Ray that ABC was planning a "giant promotion" to launch *A Man and His Soul,* a double greatest-hits album with a twelve-page booklet of photographs and a rapturous appreciation of Ray by jazz writer Stanley Dance.

Ray got to work on a new album, *Ray Charles Invites You to Listen*. This time Ray asked Sid to write all the arrangements, and through January the two men worked side by side at the studio piano, Ray leading Sid through the ten songs he had picked, Sid noting everything down. Two of the charts called for a standard big band; the rest needed fourteen strings, eight brass, guitar, bass, and drums. At the string session, Sid conducted the orchestra and, through the control booth window, Joe Adams engineered at the board. On one track, the strings played alone, and Sid knew their sound would bleed into the brass' microphones. So he told Joe to fade the brass pot to zero and wait until he signaled. As the moment approached, Sid waved frantically, "Bring up the brass, bring up the brass," but Joe came in late. Ever after Sid could hear a slight "whoosh" on the track as Joe's twist of the knob caught up with the music.

No one but Sid would be able to hear a blemish on *Ray Charles Invites You to Listen*. From the hushed strings that open it to the discordant strings at its close, *Listen* is a splendid recording. Four magnificent standards, "She's Funny That Way," "How Deep Is the Ocean," "I'll Be Seeing You," and "Love Walked In," would be enough to make the album memorable, but in addition, Ray sings throughout in a high sustained falsetto, an experiment that he tried, he said, "for no other reason than self-satisfaction." One reviewer found the falsetto "grating and most unpleasant," others thought it had an unearthly, feminine beauty. To sing at such high pitches, Ray focuses his voice, crisping every consonant, hissing every sibilant; his focus compels the focused listening that he wants from us. Sid's strings add eloquent tone textures perfectly matched to Ray's voice and piano. At the end of "How Deep Is the Ocean," a piano run falls faster and faster from the treble to the bass, and the cellos thrash like waves in a squall.

Ray also experimented in putting Barbra Streisand's "People" and the Beatles' "Yesterday" on *Listen*. When older artists record hits by younger artists, they risk revealing themselves as fogeys trying to be kids. Ray's covers soar over such dangers. Building from a soft trombone vamp to a blaring Las Vegas finale, his "People" outdoes Streisand in schmaltz and, good-humoredly, parodies her as well. The Beatles' "Yesterday" has the charm of youth, Ray's the weight of age. He gives his voice an edge so hoarse that "Yesterday" comes out "Yeshh-terday." When Sid heard Ray developing the voice in their work sessions, he thought Ray had a cold, then realized it was intentional. "Ray was putting on a deliberate sound to speak for the character he was trying to create."

The '67 tour kicked off with a benefit aboard the aircraft carrier *Constellation*, docked in San Diego Harbor and bound for Vietnam. Ray and the gang played three hours for

3000 sailors and their families, and Joe milked it for all the publicity it was worth. In mid-April, they took off for Europe, Ray's first tour abroad since '64. Norman Granz handled the gang's European bookings, and they packed first-class venues, the Royal Festival Hall in London, in Paris the Salle Pleyel.

In Vienna, Ray stayed in a vast cream-and-gilt suite at the Imperial Hotel. Dr. Hacker was in Vienna with his wife Stasi on holiday, and he brought a small party of friends to meet Ray in his suite after the concert. Among them was an unstable young heroin addict, the daughter of an American millionaire who had begged Hacker to take her to Europe. Ray played for a moment, then sat on a sofa beside the young woman. Hacker's friends watched over their drinks as Ray progressed from flirting to serious seduction; through double doors in the shadowed bedroom stood a large white-canopied bed. The woman responded warmly, and as the party began to break up, Ray spoke a few words in Hacker's ear—would it be all right if he, if she. . . ? Hacker thought not. Both Ray and the woman were his patients, and Ray was leaving in the morning. The doctor walked the woman up and down the hotel corridor, his arm around her shoulders, urging her to go no farther. She didn't. Ray called the next day from Switzerland, but Hacker's patient remained one woman who slipped away.

Ray and the gang got back to America in early May, played Carnegie Hall, then flew to California for a run of one-nighters. In this year, unlike '66, critics at home and abroad hurled brickbats. *Jazz Journal* found the London show "prosaic, almost corny," and even loyal *Jazz Magazine* in Paris worried about Ray's "sugar-sweet ballads and syrupy violins." "The Ray Charles show cheats the public," Ralph Gleason wrote in the New York *Post*. The big band was "boring," and Joe Adams' "interminable flowery" intros threatened to drown Ray in "a sea of flattery." More annoying than bad reviews was a gossip item in *Jet*. What Ray once paid for heroin, said *Jet,* he was now paying to cops who shook him down with phony drug charges. Ray blew up. He had just told *Downbeat* in no uncertain terms that he was sick of reporters harping on his drug problems, and now this libel. He'd sue, Ray told Joe; they had to put a stop to it.

Joe agreed, but he knew that stars of Ray's magnitude didn't wait for attacks to defend themselves in the press. Stars fought bad publicity with good publicity. Ray needed a thick armor of awards, keys to cities, and stamps of approval to make him invulnerable to the slings and arrows of the gossip columnists. Only inside the shell of a public Ray Charles could the private Ray live as he pleased. Joe had already arranged that Ray become national chairman of the Sickle Cell Research Foundation, and he pulled strings to have Los Angeles city councilman Tom Bradley (later LA's first black mayor) declare June 8 "Ray Charles Day." Ray came to City Hall, flashbulbs flashed, and he received a florid proclamation commending him for "his many artistic, civic, and commercial achievements." Della, looking chic in a suit, pearls, and white gloves, stood at his side as Ray accepted "one of the highest honors I've ever received." A few weeks later, the gang played Constitution Hall in Washington, D.C., and Joe began angling for a congressman to read a laudatory resolution about Ray on the floor of the House of Representatives.

Ray Charles Invites You to Listen came out, but the album the world listened to that summer was the Beatles' *Sgt. Pepper's Lonely Hearts Club Band*. *Sgt. Pepper's* excellence, ambition, and originality spoke for themselves; they also trumpeted a new era in popular music. This was the summer of the Monterey Pop Festival, Jimi Hendrix, Janis Joplin, and "psychedelic" San Francisco. Bob Dylan, the Beach Boys, and the Rolling Stones had discovered electric music as a potent medium. Audiences began to respond to their messages, and pop music began to receive a new level of attention, to be enjoyed as something more than America's aural wallpaper.

Similar, related changes stirred black music. After languishing for years on Columbia, Aretha Franklin had emerged on Atlantic as a singer of awesome power, her first smash, "I Never Loved a Man," quickly followed by a second, "Respect." The public gathered her music and that of James Brown, Otis Redding, Wilson Pickett, and Curtis Mayfield under one name, "soul music." Most universally, "soul" meant music performed as a true expression of a person's inmost being. More specifically, it meant a fervid, gospel/blues that sprang from a people conscious of a common heritage, music bursting with pride in being African-American.

The new generation of black and white musicians adored Ray Charles. Rockers considered "I Got a Woman" an early shot fired in the rock 'n' roll revolution, and soul singers bowed to him as their "spiritual father." Since he shared Baptist and chitlin circuit roots with the young black singers, Ray felt a close kinship to soul music, much of which copied his horns-and-rhythm Atlantic sound. Aretha, he said, was his "one and only sister," and soul music "the way black folk sing when they leave themselves alone." Yet the youngsters, black and white, were also competitors trying to push Ray to the sidelines of the music marketplace. "There are a lot of artists coming up, and they're bad too," Ray told a reporter, "bad" meaning good in current slang. "The challenge is to keep up with the public." "Yesterday" had been Ray's first attempt to connect with the new audience, and he convinced Larry Newton to release it as a single. "Eleanor Rigby," a more mysterious Lennon-McCartney song, also intrigued Ray. He'd tackle that next.

In Houston, meanwhile, Jeff Brown's Big J bowling alley was sinking fast. Accountants from AMF found relatives on the payroll and the books a mess. Jeff should close down, they said, and reopen in three weeks. Debts tightening on him like a vise, Jeff went to the Small Business Administration and to a black bank. The bank said it would lend him $18,000 if Ray Charles co-signed the note. Jeff called Ray, and Ray said to send him the papers. Jeff sent them and waited. At the mention of Ray Charles' name, his creditors waited too. One week, two weeks, three weeks, no papers came back from LA. Finally Ray's pilot Tom McGarrity flew in with a message. "Are you waiting for Ray to co-sign that loan?" he asked Jeff. "He's never going to sign." AMF took out the bowling equipment, and Jeff turned the Big J into a ballroom. For a time the club became a minor stop on the chitlin circuit—Margie Hendricks played there a few times on her downward spiral—but soon enough the Big J closed its doors, and Jeff went out on the road again, this time managing the soul singers Sam and Dave.

At busy RPM Jeff Brown had become ancient history. Among the office staff only Vernon Troupe remembered him. Ray and Joe were looking ahead, not back. They had two major fall debuts to prepare for, the first, three weeks at Harrah's in Reno. Despite a few minor Las Vegas gigs, Ray hadn't broken into the lucrative Nevada casino circuit. This was his chance, and Joe Adams put on the dog for opening night, inviting a *Sentinel* reporter, Eunice Pye, along in the Martin and getting picked up in a Rolls-Royce at the Reno airport. At the afternoon rehearsal, Billy Preston had everybody in stitches doing impressions of the boss. Joe remained cool in the flurry, becoming, wrote the wide-eyed Pye, "mother, father, trouble-shooter, overseer, and goodness knows what else to this gang." They just had time to grab sandwiches while dressing, but when the curtain rose at 8:15, everybody was looking "fresh as a new day." From the packed first show Ray's run grew into a smash success that, *Variety* reported, fully "justifies the advance ballyhoo." The Ray Charles show—the band, the Raelets, Billy Preston, and Ray—clocked in at precisely seventy minutes, "each minute programmed for full values . . . architected for variety in moods and tempi." Ray's "total involvement" with the music and the twice-nightly queues waiting outside to get in convinced *Variety* that "Charles is a good bet for an encore outing at Harrah's." Indeed he was; in years ahead Ray would play Harrah's and other Reno and Las Vegas venues dozens and dozens of times.

"Yesterday" came out in October and climbed to #25, Ray's "*Yesh*-terday" becoming a sing-along hook. Fans young and old enjoyed Ray doing a Beatles song so well, and a delighted Paul McCartney and John Lennon wired him, "Ray Charles' genius goes on and on. We love you heart and soul." Less spontaneously, Rep. Charles S. Joelson of New Jersey delivered the arranged congressional resolution commending Ray for his "charitable and professional achievements." In November, Ray and the gang taped "Crying Time" for "The Nashville Sound," a segment of NBC's *Kraft Music Hall.* Ray was in a jovial mood at rehearsal, teasing the sax players for running out of breath on a legato passage: "It's a little long, isn't it, baby? You gotta quit smoking so much." A reporter asked him about hard times with drugs, and Ray brushed him off. "I'm always having hard times," he said, laughing. "But I learned from them . . . what was absolutely meaningful and what was just material." Anyway, Ray said emphatically, *"I just want to make every day count, minimize my troubles and . . . be what I am."*

Leaving the band in New York, Ray flew back to LA to get the new album started. Tangerine's growing stable of songwriters—Percy Mayfield, Jimmy Holiday, and Dee Ervin—had come up with a half-dozen good songs, and Ray worked them up with arrangers Rene Hall and Oliver Nelson, saving "Eleanor Rigby" and "Am I Blue?" for Sid. He kept at it until the last minute, flying back to New York Thanksgiving morning and landing only a few hours before show time at the Copacabana, his second big debut of the fall.

Jules Podell's Copa, tucked off Fifth Avenue on East Sixtieth Street, was a class joint favored by the silk-suit-and-shoulder-holster set. Ray's drug busts had long made him ineligible for the cabaret card he needed to play Manhattan's swanky rooms, but the regulations had recently been eased, and Ray had gotten his card. Stars at the Copa usually worked with the house band and the famous "Copa Girl" dance line; for these two weeks, Podell turned the whole night over to the Ray Charles Show '67, paying a $50,000 guarantee for two shows nightly, three on the weekends. Just as in Reno, the show went off like clockwork. *Variety* worried that Ray was too bluesy for the Copa crowd, the *Times* that he'd become too polished, but the club was jammed every night. Pearl Bailey came by, and so did football star Joe Namath with a big party; columnist Walter Winchell was spotted dancing in the aisles.

Arlette Kotchounian, a photographer from Paris, came to New York during Ray's run at the Copa. A classic Left Bank bohemian, small, dark, and a heavy smoker, Kotchounian had translated the lyrics of a starkly beautiful song, "Il Est Mort le Soleil" ("The Sun Died"), that a singer friend had recorded. She brought the record with her and pushed her way into meeting Ray at his hotel. Ray liked "The Sun Died," was intrigued by Arlette, and soon had her, most willingly, in bed. This was not to be a one-night stand. Arlette had a scrappy streak in her character that Ray liked, and the meeting began a relationship that lasted for years.

The Martin flew everybody back to LA for the holidays and the end of another tour. Three years after the bust and two after withdrawal, Ray's grand crisis had receded into the past, its public and private wounds healed. He had hit a steadier, longer stride in his life that could still carry him far. New surges of ambition coursed through him. He had new women to meet, new gigs and new chess games to play, more to do than he had time for. He threw himself into the new album. He'd call it *Portrait of Ray.* "The Sun Died" would be its centerpiece, he told Sid. For that he wanted a big production number, some really gorgeous music.

> Our organization is like a big wheel.
> I'm the axle and the members of my
> firm the spokes. The wheel can be
> no stronger than each individual
> spoke, no stronger than the axle
> which supports the spokes.
>
> **Ray Charles**

Rolling Onward
1968-1969

As the 1960s drew to a close, the wheel of Ray Charles Enterprises rolled onward in a groove grown smooth through use and time. By dint of musical excellence and longevity, Ray had become acclaimed worldwide as a star of the first magnitude, and his wheel regularly harvested that acclaim and brought it back to RPM as so much hay to the barn. Protected by the public Ray Charles, the private Ray worked with and loved the men and women who nourished him. These, the spokes of his wheel, became a cast of characters that remained stable well into the next decade.

▐▌▐▌▐▌▐▌▐▌▐▌▐▌

"The Great One," Joe Adams told the *Sentinel* in January 1968, would relax in LA for the winter and "then resume another busy schedule." Not that Ray was idle. He and the gang played another benefit in San Diego for Vietnam-bound sailors, and Ray taped guest spots on the Jonathan Winters and Andy Williams TV shows. At the Williams taping, the cast of Rowan and Martin's popular *Laugh-In* crowded over from a studio next door to watch Ray at work. *Playboy* elected Ray into its Jazz Hall of Fame, at thirty-seven the youngest member ever, and the President's Council on the Arts and Humanities commended him for his "many charitable performances." On the other hand, Ray's latest single, "That's a Lie," died, as did Tangerine's latest, a Clydie King cover of "Ode to Billy Joe."

That winter Ray finished *Portrait of Ray*, a free-form collage of ten songs, everything from a snappy jazz waltz to a moody blues. After so many one-theme albums, *Portrait's* variety is refreshing but a bit diffuse—Ray seems to be reaching for a no-theme theme still beyond his grasp. *Portrait's* elements, however, are excellent. "The Sun Died" turned out to be the big number Ray hoped for, his stark cries of "The sun died!" knifing through Sid's tender strings. On "Eleanor Rigby," Ray puts himself shoulder to shoulder with Father MacKenzie and "all the lonely people," but on "Understanding," he preaches a mock sermon on love that reveals an ugly side of his self-portrait. He understands, Ray says, that if he doesn't keep his woman in furs and pretty clothes, she'll find a man who will; and she understands that she better not let him catch her, because if he does—

> I'm gonna go downtown to the hardware store and buy myself a double-bladed axe handle, come back, square off, and believe me, her soul better belong to God because her head's gonna belong to me!

Portrait came out to moderate success in March, and Ray rehearsed the gang for the tour. The season was to kick off at New Jersey's Latin Casino, but Thursday, April 4, the night before the opening, a sniper assassinated Martin Luther King in Memphis.

Vernon Troupe heard the news and called Ray. With millions around the world, Ray felt stunned and saddened. He had just seen King at a banquet in Beverly Hills that Quincy Jones had dragged him to, and had told King, as he always did, that he'd help raise money, but he wouldn't march—"When folks start throwing bricks, I wouldn't know where to run!"—and they had both laughed. The Ray Charles Show '68 opened Friday night, but over the weekend Ray decided to go to the funeral. The nightclub closed Monday, and he flew with Joe to Atlanta. On the muggy Tuesday morning, they joined the flood of mourners who walked west from the Ebenezer Baptist Church to Morehouse College, following the mule-drawn wagon that carried King's coffin. Marchers took turns guiding Ray's steps along the way, and for a distance he led the people in singing the spiritual "Amen." Then he and Joe flew back to Philadelphia, and that night the gang was back at work.

Ray's wheel rolled on through the spring, thirty-one cities in fifty-six days, getting back in June for six nights at Melodyland in Anaheim. "Black" replaced "Negro" as the accepted term for African-Americans in common parlance that summer, and the wheel rolled out again: the Chicago Opera House, JFK Stadium in Philadelphia, and a whole Sunday afternoon at the Newport Jazz Festival. "Ray has charisma and he knows what to do with it," *Downbeat* reported. "He made us cry, he made us laugh . . . he made us glad to be alive."

Back in LA, Ray taped an "essay on music" for *Of Black America,* a CBS special focusing on black achievement. Over a montage of himself onstage and in the studio, and film clips of black American life, Ray talked thoughtfully about his music and its roots. Black music is "loose," said Ray, "you play what you feel." It began with rhythm—"black people could always find something to tap a beat on"—and with the blues, music that "belonged to the black man." "Cleaning up the music" to reach the white audience was fine, but it was important not to lose the black "heart and soul." The secret of getting that black feeling across was investing lyrics with a double meaning.

> You sing about the woman, but you are really also talking about all the kicking around you've had, the humiliations that you've had, the throwing out of doors you've had, the hunger that you've had. You *think* about all these things, but you're still *singing* about that woman.

Ray signed with William Morris that summer, and as a debut engagement the agency booked the show into LA's top nightspot, the Coconut Grove at the Ambassador Hotel. Opening night was a black-tie benefit for the Sickle Cell Anemia Foundation; Della came in a feather boa and long white gloves and gave her husband a good-luck kiss on the cheek for the photographers. Joe, emceeing, had so many celebrities to introduce that the show stretched to over two hours, yet the "What'd I Say" finale still earned a wild sing-along, clap-along, standing ovation.

During the run, however, tempers flared backstage. After two years, the Raelets were fed up with Ray's pay and Joe's rules. Three hundred fifty dollars a week with no per diem for room and board wasn't enough, argued Gwen Berry, the veteran of the group; a $50 fine if they were one minute late was outrageous. After the last show on Saturday, a shouting match broke out. Ray fired Berry, and the others, Merry Clayton, Clydie King, and Alexandra Brown, quit in sympathy. If the singers hoped Joe or Ray would beg them to return, they were mistaken. "It is unfortunate that we had to lose the girls," Joe told the press. "They were pretty, qualified, and certainly talented. But of course the Raelets will go on. The name is ours, and already we have replacements." By the Monday closer Ray had thrown together a trio of local background singers, and by the next gig, Mr. D's in San Francisco, he had assembled a new group of Raelets, among them a pretty and petite teenage soprano from New York named Susaye Green.

The doted-upon daughter of singers Allen and Vivian Green, Susaye grew up in St. Albans, Queens, a well-to-do black neighborhood; Lena Horne and Count Basie lived nearby. On stage since childhood, Susaye graduated from New York's High School of the Performing Arts and was singing in the Catskills and at the Apollo when her parents split up. "We're going to Hollywood," Mrs. Green told her daughter, and off they went. In LA Mrs. Green looked up an old friend, singer-songwriter Dee Ervin, and he invited the ladies to stop by RPM and meet his boss. They did, and Ray accompanied Susaye on "My Funny Valentine." He liked Susaye's clear high voice, and when it turned out he needed new Raelets, he asked the ladies back. Mrs. Green sat down with Ray in his office. "My child has never been away from me, Mr. Charles," she said. "I promise to take care of her, Miss Vivian," Ray replied, and with that Mrs. Green entrusted him with her eighteen-year-old darling.

Opening night at Mr. D's, a mob joint on San Francisco's Broadway strip, Susaye sang "Funny Valentine" again, her knees shaking in fear. Duke Ellington came backstage to speak to Ray afterward and bowed her a flirtatious compliment. From San Francisco, the Martin flew east to the Sugar Shack in Boston and a week at the Apollo in September, and wide-eyed Susaye was launched into the world of Ray Charles.

"I was *different,* that's the first thing I realized," Green remembered years later. "Music was something I had studied; I knew how to hit high notes so the people would applaud. Now I was exposed to raw, Baptist-church emotion. We didn't get polite applause, we got people shouting, 'Sing, girl, sing!' Seeing Ray reach into that well of intensity every night was *overwhelming.*"

The band adopted Susaye as a baby sister, listening to her chatter about the Beatles and her favorite Motown groups, hugging her when she got homesick. With the other new Raelets, Barbara Terrault and Stella Yarborough, her relations were more wary. Susaye saw them as grown women, more used than she to life's rough-and-ready; they saw her as a pushy little princess who acted innocent to win Ray's favor. If that was her plan, it worked. Ray gave Susaye a featured solo spot and, delighted by her ripe figure and her bubbly enthusiasm for pleasure, soon made her his first lady of the moment. Susaye fell head over heels in love. "I was eighteen, Ray was thirty-eight, but he became the first real love of my life," she recalled. "I knew he was married, but times were changing for women, and I felt free to take what I wanted. This may sound coldhearted, but when you're eighteen years old, you don't care about your man's wife. On the road, I was Ray's woman."

Ventriloquist Aaron Williams and his dummy Freddy joined the troupe in Wild-wood, New Jersey, as an opening act. His first night was Ray's birthday, and the fellows chipped in for a cake and threw the boss a party after the show. Williams was thrilled to have steady work; he'd quit his day job as a printer only a few months before. Between gigs Ray flew back to LA to start work on *I'm All Yours, Baby,* his next album with Sid. A new single died, but a series of Coca-Cola commercials he'd cut at RPM with Aretha Franklin began to air, and millions of listeners turned up their radios to hear the King and Queen of Soul assure the world that "things go better with Coke!"

As Ray's wheel rolled through Europe and the American Midwest in the fall, the only squeak to be heard came from the Raelets. The three young women, all new to the road, squabbled incessantly. The Raelets needed a leader, Ray realized, a matron who could keep the girls out of one another's hair. The best candidate for the job was Mable John, a blues singer from Detroit. Mable John, however, was not a dewy-eyed teenager like Susaye, but a mature, confident woman, and to win her, Ray needed to mount a major campaign.

The oldest of ten children, Mable John had grown up on the Motor City's North Side, she and her siblings coached by their parents to sing gospel songs and act out Bible stories. Younger brother Willie was the first to go into show business, and as Little Willie John, he became a major R&B star in the 50s, "Fever" his biggest hit. Mable, the family's business brain, managed Willie's bookings, then began her own career with Berry Gordy in Motown's earliest days. Willie's life, sadly, took a wrong turn: convicted of manslaughter, he died in prison in May 1968. Devastated, Mable stopped performing for six months, then put on a memorial concert in November. Knowing Ray from crisscrossings on the road, she asked him to take an ad in the souvenir program. "You know how I felt about your brother," he responded and took a full page. Two weeks later Ray called from the Regal in Chicago. "John, I need a lead singer for the Raelets," he said. "Could you find me somebody?"

Guessing that Ray wanted her to volunteer, Mable fenced. "You're the Genius," she replied. "I don't know who I'd recommend to sing with you."

"Promise me you'll look," Ray said, and hung up, abruptly, as always. Over the next month he called again and again, finally making a direct offer. "I like your voice, John, I'd like to have you with me. Not just as lead singer but to take charge of the girls. Would you like the job?"

"I don't know," said Mable.

"Think about it," said Ray. The next time he called, as soon as Mable said hello, Ray started singing one of her songs. "You know my material?" she asked, flattered.

"I know everything about you," Ray said. He was headed to New York for a second run at the Copa. Could he send his plane to Detroit to pick her up?

"I don't fly private planes," said Mable. "People with private planes cut corners on the servicing."

"Eastern Airlines services my plane," he replied, nettled. "And if your luck is that bad, don't take a bath. You'll slip in the damn tub and kill yourself."

"Well, call me when you get to New York," said Mable, softening her tone. "I'll let you know my answer then." She consulted friends in the business, and a promoter who had known Ray for years advised her to take the job. "Ray Charles is cheap," he said, "but he's honest. Whatever he promises you, you won't get a dime more, but you'll never get a penny less." When Ray called again, Mable told him what she'd need: extra pay, her own distinctive gown, her songs added to the band book, and full authority over the Raelets—all for a one-season trial. "Fine," said Ray. "And remember, you won't be working for me, you'll be working with me." On that note, Mable took the job; she'd start when the band reassembled in March. Joe Adams heard about Mable's deal and hit the ceiling. "You've never given that to anybody," he said. "But that's what I'm giving her," Ray replied.

▮▮▮▮▮▮▮▮

In January 1969, Ray and Joe flew to Miami for ABC's yearly sales conference, a strategic attempt to keep the company's attention despite declining sales. Three years after his last top-ten single, and four since an album had broken into the top half of the charts, Ray was in danger of becoming a label has-been: ABC had conspicuously left him and Tangerine out of a year-end omnibus ad in *Billboard*. Larry Newton thought Ray had peaked, and instead of investing to boost his sales, ABC was spending $25 million dollars to buy up rack-jobbers, wholesalers who stocked record racks at Sears, Woolworth, and discount outlets. "Businesses last longer than acts," Newton said in explaining the move to the trade press; selling Columbia, RCA, and Atlantic records on the racks gave ABC a hedge against the diminishing returns of aging stars. Ray fought back with his own spirited pitch to the conference. He had two albums coming out, he announced, *I'm All Yours, Baby,* and *Ray Charles Doing His Thing.* As for Tangerine, its failures may have been due to himself and Joe, who could operate the label only "when time allowed." Now they were appointing Ron Granger, an experienced record promoter, to run Tangerine full-time, and Tangerine "would increase its recording activities in 1969."

Through the winter in LA, Ray finished two new albums, which, when released in the spring, proved to come from opposite ends of Ray's musical spectrum. The first, *I'm All Yours, Baby,* drips romance, Sid's gauzy strings gift-wrapping old ballads, including "Indian Love Call," which Ray had heard Jeanette MacDonald and Nelson

Eddy sing when he was a kid. As its liner notes promise, *I'm All Yours* creates "an elegant backdrop for any romance," but with no big-band brass, no comedy, and every track *molto lento,* the album dives into and drowns in its own mush.

Ray Charles Doing His Thing, in contrast, is one of Ray's funniest, funkiest albums, an R&B jumper with a Saturday-night-at-the-Apollo sound: scratchy electric guitar, lean, mean horns, and bounding electric bass. *I'm All Yours'* songs are by the noblest names in Tin Pan Alley—Rodgers and Hart, Razaf and Blake; *Doing His Thing's* songs are by the unknown Jimmy Lewis. A lean, scrappy fellow from Itta Bena, Mississippi, Lewis came out to LA in the mid-fifties and had hustled a living in the music business ever since, scoring a minor hit on his own and singing second tenor with the Drifters. Ray heard him singing song demos, at $15 a song, for Tangerine writer Jimmy Holiday and, liking his raw style, asked to hear his original songs. Lewis brought thirty into the office. "I sat there thinking he's not going to like any of them," Lewis remembered. "But he listened and said, 'Tell you what, we're going to do a whole album of your tunes.' "

The Genius and the journeyman proved to have a genuine chemistry. Lewis fleshed out a hook that Ray came up with: "The same thing that can make you laugh can make you cry"; the result, Ray figured, was better than what he could have done himself. Lewis' lyrics border on the pedestrian, but his down-home humor appealed to Ray's country-bred funny bone. In Jimmy Lewis' world, a guy can "get his nose opened" by the wrong woman: "My mama told me I should let you go, but there's something about you that Mama don't know." On "If It Wasn't for Bad Luck," Ray and Jimmy jive back and forth like two cats on the corner. "I ain't done nothing wrong," Ray complains, "so tell me why am I doing two years' probation?" "I don't know," replies Jimmy, "I'm on probation myself."

A dozen of the guys from the '68 band came back in '69, and Ray spent most of his rehearsal time with the new Raelets. He kept Susaye and Stella from the group thrown together in August, added Mable, and auditioned a dozen women for the fourth spot before Susaye recommended a distant cousin, Vernita Moss. Roly-poly Vernita had been singing all her life, first in church, then at background sessions. When Susaye called, gigs had been scarce, and she was working at a beauty parlor. The idea of singing for the Genius terrified her, but encouraged by her mother, Vernita got to RPM and, when her moment came, jumped into a boisterous "When the Saints Go Marching In." "You're *good,*" Ray said and offered her the job. "I was shocked," she recalled. "But the salary sounded like big money to me, so I packed up my stuff at the beauty shop and told 'em, 'I'm gone, y'all, I'm gonna sing with Ray Charles!' "

Ray put the ladies through their paces. Susaye, he said, would be the top soprano, Stella alto, Mable contralto, and Vernita what she called "female bass." He played their parts on the piano, saying, "This is what I want you to sing, Sister Vernita, and for you, Sister Stella . . ." As lead singer, Mable set the group's phrasing, attacks, and cut offs, and Ray kept them in rehearsal until he got a four-voice blend that sounded like one voice. Then choreographer Lon Fontaine drilled them in matching intricate steps and hand gestures; Mable found it hell dancing and singing at the same time. Rehearsal days often stretched to twelve hours and more. Vernita's feet hurt her, and when Stella got bored, she sometimes wandered off, but brisk, confident Mable kept the ladies on the mark. Don't sit down, she told them; standing seems harder, but it keeps your energy up. Ray didn't allow the women to be daunted by the task, and he brooked no complaints. "You only become good by doing," he told them. "You can't do something for an hour and compete with someone who does it all the time."

The wheel rolled out in April: a week in Miami Beach, college dates in Texas, and a dip down to the El Camino Real, a nightclub in Mexico City packed with millionaires and their lady friends who paid $200 to get in and three times that on champagne. As the Martin flew east in May to Carnegie Hall and west again to the Frontier in Las Vegas in June, Mable John began to get a handle on her new job. The music was wonderful, fresh every night, but the music took only one hour a day. As mother figure to three young women, she had her hands full the other twenty-three. Mable saw to it that the girls woke up and got their bags packed and to the lobby on time, and that they were stageside and ready to sing with their gowns cleaned and pressed, their hair and makeup impeccable. Then she led them out into the lights.

Each girl was different. Susaye became her favorite, "a happy-go-lucky child," John recalled, "but brilliant, knew her music backwards and forwards." Mable and Susaye became close, going shopping together and staying up late at night talking. Vernita was a crybaby, apt to burst into tears when she got overtired or when her stage shoes pinched. "And every shoe pinched Vernita!" Mable recalled. "Stella was the strange one, from a small town in Texas, not as naive as she looked. If something was bothering her, she might walk off or have a tantrum. I was the only one who could talk to her."

Mable laid down her ground rules from day one. "Raelets may have squabbled before I got here," she told her three charges, "but the only squabbling you all do will be with me. No girl will cuss out another girl, there will be no drunken girls. You will behave in a ladylike manner. If there's ever a choice between you and Ray Charles, don't expect me to lean toward you. He's paying me, and I will never go against Ray Charles."

Ray, in turn, backed up Mable's judgment to the hilt. "Did you talk to your leader?" he'd say if a Raelet complained to him. One rule applied to everybody: "You don't have to love everybody, and you don't have to be with anybody offstage you don't want to be with, but *onstage* we're giving a show, and I don't care how you feel, how you don't feel, or if your mama died. Do your job pleasantly, or take the night off and we'll dock your pay." One blowup that spring got Ray's attention. Before a show, her feet already swollen, Vernita spotted a chair. She didn't dare sit down—that was forbidden because it crushed the gowns—but for a moment she rested one knee on the seat. The road manager, Mr. Briggs, threatened to fine her. "I got mad," Vernita recalled, "and I called him a sick old man. For that I got 'the operation,' a serious talk with Mr. Charles."

"I understand that you called Mr. Briggs a sick old man," Ray said. "How would you like it if you were old and sick, and a young person said that to you? Sister Vernita, here or at a beauty shop, someone will always be telling you what to do, and you have to learn how to accept it."

The lecture hurt but taught a lesson that, Vernita said years later, "my hand to Jesus, I apply to my life today. I wanted the job, so I learned how to keep my mouth shut and not hurt people's feelings." With that hurdle passed, Vernita began to enjoy herself, throwing herself into the music, striking up a romance with sax player Andy Ennis. She didn't care to smoke weed with the fellows, but she liked the noisy crap games—in the Martin they still played the old 4-5-6 game once played in the Weenie. One night Vernita ended up a thousand dollars ahead. Another night, as the action raged fast and furious in the plane's center aisle, Phil Guilbeau jumped up yelling, "Somebody open a window, it's getting hot in here!"

Being in love with Ray made life as a Raelet a more complex matter for Susaye. In a year together, Susaye's romance with Ray had deepened. Ray enjoyed Susaye's innocent, playful personality, the way she made him take her out to silly places like the zoo. He bought her jewelry, and she was sure he cared for her. Susaye knew she was crazy about him. She loved the way that he held his cigarette, the way he bit his bottom lip like a ten-year-old kid. Yet Ray continued his many affairs, a fact that she woke up to slowly and painfully. His code of respect demanded that he tell Susaye nothing, but from time to time she saw Vernon conducting other women to his room, and in merciless flashes of jealousy, she glimpsed all that Ray concealed from her. She felt the other women mocking her, cruelly pleased to see the little princess brought low, and she'd rush to Mable for the comfort of a good cry. A few unbroken days of love and laughter with Ray would make her happy again, but Susaye still sensed depths in her lover she didn't understand. Many nights she woke up and felt Ray thrashing in his sleep, his body stirred by troubling dreams, shaken by running currents that never let him rest.

Before going on tour in the spring, Ray had hired a new recording engineer, David Braithwaite, a onetime apprentice of Tom Dowd's at Atlantic, now with years at Motown under his belt. Braithwaite found RPM's four-track equipment woefully out-of-date. When he got back to LA in August, Ray had a chance to sit down and discuss the problem. There was no way to upgrade the old board, Braithwaite said; they should make the big change to eight-track. Ray asked dozens of questions, letting the engineer know that his new boss, though blind, was a gadget man who knew his stuff. Then he gave him an $80,000 budget to do the job. When the gang flew to Europe in September, Braithwaite gutted Dowd's original console and built a new board from custom components that he assembled by hand. Braithwaite's goal was the clean, colorful sound he had learned at Motown, and with four equalizers and four echo effects on each track, he felt he achieved it—despite, and not because of, Ray's daily calls from Europe nagging him on his progress.

Ray took Della and Joe Adams took his wife Emma to London for the first leg of the European tour; Victor Lowndes threw them a party at the Playboy Club. When Della flew home, Ray went back to Susaye and his other ladies. At the afternoon rehearsal in Royal Festival Hall, Ray complained, as he always did, about the hall's acoustics. "I don't care who you shout at," Harold Patton told him. "This place is still gonna sound like the Holland Tunnel." By this time, Patton figured, Ray should know that being a pro means making the best of any situation, but Ray kept on with his sour grousing.

French fans packed the Salle Pleyel for a week in early October; *Jazz Magazine* found the band dull but Ray's music always new: "He seems to rediscover himself with each note, each sigh, each strangled silence." In Berlin Ray had just stepped out on stage when he realized he had to go to the bathroom. After one number, he stood up and whispered to Andy Ennis, and Andy waved to the valet to lead Ray off; the band played their "pee number" until Ray got back. "Glad we're going home, glad we're going home," Stella sang as they flew back across the Atlantic. In New York Ray taped a guest spot on the Bill Cosby show, and then they all flew out to the West Coast for November gigs in San Diego and LA. Braithwaite had the new console ready, and Ray spent hours at the board, his fingers darting from knob to knob. Sid was writing charts for a new country album that they'd record on the eight-track; Ray was itching to get down to it.

The wheel had rolled home one more time, and with it the 1960s rolled to a close—a momentous decade for popular music, and a momentous decade for Ray Charles. In these years his music spread to its full palette and reached around the

ROLLING ONWARD 1968-1969 **283**

world. He had three #1 hits in a row, got busted and put down heroin, achieved great wealth, and built a house and place of business. What would the next decade bring? The 1970s might be tough. Ray's record sales had been declining for years. The last four singles had flopped, and the two new albums, *I'm All Yours Baby* and *Doing His Thing,* had both sold dismally. Ray blamed Larry Newton for neglecting him; Newton replied he couldn't sell records nobody wanted to buy. In December nerves got raw. Bob Abrams sent out press releases announcing that after nineteen albums and forty-four singles, Ray Charles was leaving ABC. He'd continue recording, *Billboard* and *Variety* dutifully reported, "but without the big pressure of certain recording commitments." The bluff worked. Larry Newton poured golden oil on the waters, and Ray calmed down and stayed put.

It was, however, a battle won, and not the war. To keep his place in pop music's endless competition would mean, Ray knew, an uphill struggle on a slope steepening with every passing year. Yet he faced the future with a certain confidence. William Morris still had as many gigs for him as he could play. Besides the new country album, he had a half-dozen album ideas simmering in the back of his brain. Billy Preston wouldn't be back in 1970—he'd become a star on his own—but Ray still had a good team: bright rookies like Braithwaite, old dependables like Edgar Willis and Leroy Cooper. Over the holidays, Mable John wrote Ray that her first year with him had been a pleasure, thanks to his "well-organized organization," and that she'd be glad to come back. Ray re-signed her in an instant. Approaching forty, Ray was beginning to enter a second maturity as an artist: past the storms of youth but still at the height of his powers, and with well-worn tools in his hands.

PART V

THE 1970s:
THE INVISIBLE YEARS

22

Volcanic Messages Early 1970s

From the late 1960s onward, these became words that Ray Charles lived by. Once he had his big wheel back in the groove after the Boston bust and the year off, Ray reached cruising speed. No scandal marred and no hit blessed his 1970s, but Ray continued to work, not as obscurely as the mole of yore, but with the same steadfast purpose. He recorded at RPM, piling up track after track after track. He played concert after concert, anywhere and anytime anybody came up with the money. He circled the globe dozens of times, and traveled millions of miles. He appeared on television and won awards, made love with women and ran his business, and he maintained these patterns with little outward variation through the entire 1970s and 1980s and into the 1990s.

In the first of these decades, as his hair turned gray and his face and voice developed new crags and depths, Ray Charles became invisible. Far more famous than he had been in the heady days of "What'd I Say," he was also far more familiar. Listeners around the world felt they knew Ray Charles, had grasped the essential qualities of his music and public self. Many already owned a half-dozen of Ray's albums, and anyone could hear his hits in random but frequent radio play or catch him by chance on television. If one missed him at a festival in the summer, it didn't matter: he'd be back in the winter at a hotel downtown. Ray was simply there, one of many vibrations swirling in the sense-surround of the electric media, heard everywhere with so little effort that, like the birds and footsteps in the street, he was both heard and not heard at the same time.

This is not an uncommon fate among twentieth-century popular artists. Once performers like Marlene Dietrich, Cary Grant, and Frank Sinatra discover a public responsive to what they do, they keep doing their best to get that response for as long as they can. Such stars attempt a kind of time-defying life, exerting all their control to make the difference between one year and the next as imperceptible as possible. Yet if their careers last more than a decade, few escape a doldrums when, in spite or perhaps because of the limelight, they seem to disappear from the public eye. While it lasts, artists can do little about invisibility except to survive, keep working, and hope that the accretion of many small changes will someday make the audience see them from a fresh perspective.

In the winter of 1970 Ray sent the Raelets to the El Camino Real in Mexico City for a two-month gig on their own. The ladies made a big hit, but Vernita got tired of the men whistling and calling, *"Buenas noches, chiquitas,"* at them. "Lord, if I hear *buenas* one more *noches,*" she told Mable, "I'm gonna go crazy." Ray, meanwhile, flew to New York for an NAACP benefit at Madison Square Garden, to London for a television show with Tom Jones, and to Nashville for a similar guest spot with Johnny Cash. In a long interview with *Playboy,* he refused to rehash his drug history ("Jesus Christ couldn't get me to say another word on the subject"), but spoke out acidly on race. Being blind was easy compared to being black in America, Ray declared. "The greatest handicap I've had—and still have—is my color." It made him angry that it took "ten housing laws and thirty tanks" for a black family to buy a home in a white suburb. More calmly, Ray said he had thought about what he could do if he ever had to land his own plane. Since "staying level, knowing my altitude, and keeping the right airspeed" were crucial, he'd break the glass over the horizon, altitude, and airspeed gauges with his cigarette lighter, feel the dials, then call the tower to tell them his plan.

> I'd climb to 12,000 or 13,000 feet and practice landing by slow-
> ing the plane down and dipping it . . . all the time feeling the

gauges to see what was really happening. Once I felt I had practiced enough, I'd attempt to land. I might tear off a wing or
something, but I think I'd come out alive.

Ray's feud with ABC continued to simmer. As the label celebrated its fifteenth
birthday, Larry Newton switched to the parent corporation's film division; Jay Lasker,
the head of Dunhill, ABC's most profitable subsidiary, replaced him as president and
moved the company headquarters to Los Angeles. For Ray, Sam Clark and Larry Newton in New York were the real ABC, and Lasker's rise, based on Dunhill's success selling folk rock, only reminded him of Tangerine's failure to sell R&B. For Lasker, Ray
was a label old-timer whose rugged independence had taken him out of the mainstream. Ray needed an outside producer, Lasker said, and should do concept albums
like Ella Fitzgerald's successful songbooks: why not "Ray Charles Sings and Plays the
Beatles"? Lasker's suggestions infuriated Ray. "Nobody's ever going to tell me what to
record," he yelled at Larry Newton. Newton sympathized, but he also heard the other
side of the story from Lasker. "Maybe Jay's right, Ray," he told his aging star. "You ain't
selling shit, and you know it."

As usual, Ray steamed on, and that winter he broke in his new eight-track board
with two superb and very different albums, *My Kind of Jazz* and *Love Country Style.*
Ray's *Kind of Jazz* turned out to be, not surprisingly, blues à la Basie, and *Love Country Style* romance à la Nashville. Except for humming a few vocal overdubs on the
slinky "Booty Butt," Ray did the jazz album the old way, everyone playing at once. On
Love Country Style, however, Ray began, more often than not, to sing and play the piano
after the basic tracks were down. Which meant, first, that during the basic session he
could sit in the control room beside David Braithwaite and assist in the engineering;
and second, that he could take all the time he wanted to record his own vocals. Both
had musical advantages that Ray explored eagerly; he also found a way to use the second as a ploy in seduction.

Ruth Robinson, a beautiful young woman with luminous, copper-toned skin,
had recently come to work at RPM as Dee Ervin's assistant. One morning, accidentally
on purpose, Ruth was standing at the top of the stairs when Ray came bounding up
from his private side door, and they chatted for some time, Ray holding her hand just
above the wrist, enjoying the soft Kentucky twang in her voice. Later that day Ervin
said Ray wanted to see her in the studio, and she went back to find him and Braithwaite listening to Ray's latest overdub. "I'm gonna play something for you," Ray said.
"Tell me if you can understand the words."

Ruth listened, told Ray what she heard, and left. Over the next few weeks he
often asked her to the studio for further listenings: had his slurring and sliding the vocal

muffled its meaning? Flattered that the Genius valued her opinion, Ruth barely noticed that this was Ray's mating dance, a way to bring her close to him. On "Ring of Fire," Ray whispered sexy ad-libs over the ending vamp; those, he said, were just for her. One late afternoon in his office, Ray made his intentions clear. Ruth didn't resist, but as he drew her to the couch, she stopped him. "What do I look like to you?" she asked.

"Well, you're five-four, you weigh 120 pounds, you've got hair down past your waist and great legs," said Ray.

"How do you know all that?" asked Ruth.

"I know how tall you are by where your voice is coming from," he replied. "I can tell how much you weigh from holding your arm. I know you've got long hair because you wear silk blouses, and I can hear it brush against your back. As for your legs, the fellows in the band are always saying how good you look in short skirts!"

Like Susaye and others before her, Ruth Robinson fell deeply in love with Ray. She knew he was married—Ray's valet joked that Della was "the wife-in-law"—but she didn't know at first that she had joined a harem. "Love made me faithful to him, so I thought it would make him faithful to me. God, what I did know?" she said with a laugh years later. She found Ray a sensuous man and a practiced lover, but there was more to their relationship than sex. Men had often chased Ruth for her looks; Ray was interested in what she knew and thought. He encouraged her ambitions to write songs and to be a journalist. They often talked at the office deep into the night, and Ruth found herself fascinated by Ray's restless intellect, his keen interest in every subject under the sun, from politics to hydroponic gardening.

Early in their intimacy, Ray asked Ruth to make his "coffee," and he told her the exact recipe to follow. A Boston University beer mug lived on his desk—Evelyn had given it to her dad when she studied nursing at BU. Ruth was to lay a foundation of sugar in the bottom of the mug and then fill it halfway up with coffee, the rest of the way with Bols gin, and stir. "Sounds nasty!" she said. "It's not nasty to me," Ray replied, and when Ruth tried it herself, with cream and less gin, she liked it. "Careful of the Bols, it's lethal," he told her. Without ever getting obviously drunk, Ray sipped his laced coffee from morning to night, replenishing the gin from an ample supply of brown crocks in a closet. Everyone in the office kept up the fiction that Ray was just drinking coffee, but since putting down heroin, Ruth soon realized, Ray had found its replacement in a steady habit of all-day drinking.

Fathead Newman came back to the band for the 1970 season. He had no trouble fitting in, nor did two new stellar trumpeters, Johnny Coles and Blue Mitchell. The tour began mid-April at the Sugar Shack in Boston, moved to Bill Graham's Fillmore East in New York (with Dizzy Gillespie), and headed west to Harrah's in Lake Tahoe by the end of the month. Like the De Soto, the Weenie, and the Flex before it, the Martin earned its honorable retirement, and Ray bought, for $400,000, a British-made Viscount turbojet with four Rolls-Royce engines. Joe designed a new interior for the plane—a stateroom for Ray, a lounge and thirty-five oversize seats for the gang—and to protect his extravagance, he strictly forbade smoking, drinking, or eating while on board. The fellows grumbled at the rules but liked the Viscount's stately pace and smooth landings. The Buzzard, as they soon dubbed the plane, carried them around the country all summer.

After October in Europe, they flew to South America, starting in Argentina and working north. When they got to Caracas it was December and cold. Instead of installing heaters to warm up the dressing rooms, the promoters brought in jugs of rum. Blue Mitchell and Phil Guilbeau got plastered and, against band rules, started cursing in front of the Raelets. Hearing the ruckus, Ray came out of his room just as Blue called Phil a "motherfucking liar."

"Who said that?" Ray asked angrily. "Blue Mitchell," said the loyal valet. "I'm sick of this, get me Joe Adams," said Ray. When Adams came in, Ray turned to Mitchell. "Blue, I told you about cussing, I ain't gonna tell you again. Joe, send his ass home."

"We're going home the day after tomorrow," said Joe.

"I don't give a damn, send his ass home," said Ray.

"It'll cost $2000," said Joe. That took the wind out of Ray's sails.

"Dammit, Blue, why can't you do right?" Ray cried. The gang stood about looking at one another, then tiptoed out, laughing behind their hands.

Whenever possible between gigs, even if he'd have less than a full day on the ground, Ray flew to LA. Della and the boys on Southridge often didn't know he'd come back. He'd stay with Ruth at RPM, where she cooked him southern-style pork chops; they'd only leave the building to make midnight runs to a favorite donut shop on nearby Western Avenue. More than Ruth's charms, however, drew Ray to LA; he came to work.

In the early 1960s, Ray had made his albums in two or three sessions, each scheduled weeks in advance. By the early 1970s, for Ray and the entire pop-music industry, recording had evolved into a nearly continuous process of adding overdubs to basic tracks, the finished record a collage constructed of bits and pieces from dozens of sessions. On Ray's early records, Fathead Newman played his tenor solos on the fly; in the 70s Ray might call in Clifford Solomon to blow four tenor solos over prerecorded tracks, and then build the final solo from all four. Background singers sang response phrases weeks before Ray sang the call, and he overdubbed his own voice ad-lib, singing harmony with himself and the chorus, talking to the audience in playful asides. From the 70s onward, it becomes difficult to say exactly when Ray made his albums; he often worked on several at once, pushing dozens of tracks through varying stages of development, assembling them into albums as he saw fit.

Ray began the album-making process by calling Sid Feller from Paris or Peoria and setting a date for him to come to RPM to go over a few tunes. Portable cassette recorders became popular in the early 70s, and Sid began bringing one to the sessions. He erased most of the tapes by using them for something else, yet eight survived in scratched, dusty cases with titles like "Ray Charles original lay-out" scribbled on faded labels. They are treasures, blind films, one could call them, of Ray at work during a most fruitful period of his career, the making of two great masterpieces, *Volcanic Action of My Soul* and *A Message from the People.*

To see the films, one must picture lean Ray and rotund Sid seated beside each other at a black Steinway grand in the beige-walled studio. By this time, Sid and Ray had been working together for over ten years. The family man and the lone wolf had never become pals socially, but a musical bond deeper than many friendships connected them. Feller tried years later to explain their closeness by saying, "No human being feels for me, and I feel for no one, the way Ray and I feel for each other." Sid and Ray stuck to business at the piano, but their cheerful out-of-tune mooing of still-forming melodies attests to the trust and affection between them.

" 'There'll Be No Peace Without All Men as One,' in B-flat," Ray begins one typical segment. He and Sid count off slowly together, "One, two three four *one*— " Ray starts to play and goofs. Sid clicks the tape off and then on again. Ray goofs again. "You're terrible," says Sid. "I get messed up when I get here," says Ray, but when he plays to demonstrate, it works. "I got it now," he says, and he sings "boh-boh-boh" sotto voce where he doesn't know the words, calling out "Everybody!" to indicate where the chorus will enter. Sid comes in ahhhing a counterline on the bridge. By the end Ray is singing with passion over big piano chords. Sid checks his stopwatch. "Four-oh-five," he says.

"Good," Ray says. "One thing I didn't mention, Sid. When we finish, we ought to slow up, a fast slowness from the tempo I'm singing."

"In other words," Sid says, "where the brass come in . . ."

"Right."

". . . will get slower, then I'll ritard the ending more."

"Right."

Sometimes Ray gives brisk commands: "Voices here," "No, the intro stays the same." At others he says, "I ain't gonna tell you what to write, Sid," or admits, "I don't know what I'm gonna sing, that's the truth." Occasionally they call a sound something vague like "pretty" or "cryable"; more often they deal only with the musical nitty-gritty: "You can play a scale B-flat to E-flat when they're holding that G-flat." Sid readily admires Ray's ideas—"You went to an F chord at the end, wild!"—and Ray returns the compliment. "Yeah! Put that shit in, don't forget," Ray shouts when Sid sings a neat mirroring phrase. "Okay, baby," says Sid, pleased. Sid calls one chord "a roving fifth," and that amuses Ray no end. "Oh! Is that what you call it? A roving fifth!"

"I just made it up," says Sid, "I swear to God."

"That's good, Sid," says Ray. "A roving fifth, I'm gonna remember that."

Ray sips his coffee as they work. A valet comes in to remind him of appointments; Ray puts him off. They struggle to spice up the bland "Take Me Home, Country Roads." "You know those songs there ain't much you can do with?" moans Ray. "This is one of them." Sid shrugs. "So what are you going to do?" When Ray tries to play a tape on the console, Sid holds his cigarette to give him a free hand, but as Ray feels about the machine, he becomes annoyed with himself. "Can't understand why it did that." He rewinds the tape and plays it. "Sure sounds bad." The music stops again. "What the hell? . . ."

"We had a lot of false starts, remember," says Sid.

"Right," says Ray, "but the way I'm knocking around, I can't get it. . . . Ohhhh!" he says, relieved as he solves the snafu. "There's the right way to do something and the wrong way."

"The cockamamie way," says Sid, laughing.

"I want to do it *right,*" says Ray.

When the process moved to the recording stage, David Braithwaite became Ray's chief colleague. This was a spikier relationship because Ray wanted to be the engineer himself. He shamelessly picked Braithwaite's brain with needling, argumentative questions—"But Dave, didn't you say, theoretically . . ."—to make the engineer, in defending himself, teach what Ray wanted to learn. Braithwaite showed Ray the Motown method of sticking tape strips along the sliders to mark volume adjustments; Ray stuck spare strips on his chin so he could always find them. Soon Ray was sitting at the dials and sending Braithwaite out to the studio to move microphones an inch or two to the right or left. "I was a second engineer working for Ray," Braithwaite remembered. "You couldn't be first with Ray around."

Ray allowed no one but musicians, arrangers, and Braithwaite in the studio during sessions. If Ray didn't like what he heard, he could tongue-lash musicians until they were too scared to play. Not even old friends like Quincy Jones escaped. Once Jones was conducting thirty musicians through one of his charts when Ray called a sudden halt. No, no, that wasn't what he wanted, and he started dictating new parts. Jones threw his hands up in disbelief and then retired to a corner where he doodled in a notebook, smoked cigarettes, and drank coffee for the next hour. "Ray can be a pain in the neck," Sid admitted to David. "If you didn't like him, you'd leave him." The trouble was, the men agreed ruefully, they liked him. Ray could be funny and charming too, and many sessions ran smooth as silk. Glen Campbell and Jerry Reed came by one night to lay down mandolin and guitar overdubs on *Volcanic Action*. They openly idolized the Genius, and Ray, flattered to the top of his bent, had a grand time showing them the studio and goofing off between takes. Nights like that they'd end up sitting around and shooting the breeze, playing a few noisy hands of poker.

When the process got to his vocals, Ray really got picky. Sometimes he brought a mike into the booth so he could sing *and* keep his hands on the dials. If he sang "oohh," he'd stop and say, "No, I want 'ohh-*huh*-oh,' " and he'd sing it again. Braithwaite became adept at "punching," opening and closing the vocal track for a few beats so Ray could insert tiny improvements. "How's that, Dave?" Ray would say, and Braithwaite, zeroing in on the effect Ray was after, would reply, "No, Ray, not quite, you want . . ." or "Yeah, Ray, you got it!"

Mixing the final tracks could take even longer. At Motown, Berry Gordy had often let Braithwaite try a mix, and if it sounded good, Gordy would shout, "Dyn-o-mite!" and use it. Ray thought he had to do everything himself to be able to say, "I did it," and he'd sit at the board for hours making minute adjustments to treble and bass settings, adding echo effects and subtracting echo effects. Braithwaite enjoyed staying with Ray at first, but he didn't get paid by the hour, and his wife complained that he never got home before midnight. "I came to think of myself as a baby-sitter," Braithwaite remembered. "Ray had friends, but he was sightless—what was he going to do, go to a movie? He had no place else to be, so he'd stay there, mixing one song, *every* song, for seventeen hours. Sometimes he'd get through, and say, "I was just fooling around, Dave, let's come back tomorrow and do it again."

Nineteen seventy-one, Joe Adams declared, would be celebrated as "Ray Charles' 25th Anniversary in Show Business," and he instructed Bob Abrams to feature the fact in all his press releases. Two unusual events kicked off Ray's banner year, the first a February premiere in Houston of "Black Requiem," a work written and conducted by Quincy Jones, with the city's Symphony Orchestra and the Prairie View College Chorale. The music blended slave songs, spirituals, and jazz, and Ray sang/read a text woven from the words of W. E. B. DuBois, Malcolm X, and Martin Luther King Jr. A capacity crowd gave the two hundred performers a roaring, standing ovation, yet on listening to the tapes, Ray decided that the college chorale lacked the oomph of a true gospel choir, and "Black Requiem" has never been released.

The second event, in contrast, came about by accident but helped spark a best-selling album. Jerry Wexler had booked Aretha Franklin into San Francisco's Fillmore West for a March weekend to make a live album, and he invited Ray to stop by. Ray came, and Aretha got him on stage to join her singing "Spirit in the Dark." Ray didn't know the song, but he told himself, "Since I'm here, we might as well fake it the best we can." He and the band struggled to find each other for a few choruses, but after he worked the song into a two-chord vamp, he and Aretha got wailing and the whole house started rocking. When Wexler listened to the tapes, "Spirit in the Dark" did sound messy, but he redid the horns, cut out the worst goofs, and sent an acetate to Ray for approval. Ray hated how unprepared he sounded. He played it for Ruth, and she laughed at him. "I can hear you trying to catch up," she teased. "You don't have a clue!" But the track did catch a rough magic, and once Wexler offered generous financial inducements, Ray gave his approval, and *Aretha: Live at Fillmore West* became a smash hit.

In April, as the gang set off around the country in the Buzzard, Tangerine Records proudly released *Volcanic Action of My Soul.* The long hours in the studio paid off in what may be Ray's most beautiful album. Since *Ray's Moods,* Ray had been searching for his "no theme" theme, and with *Volcanic Action* he found it. No stated concept holds *Volcanic Action's* songs together, yet they cohere, each song a movement in a musical whole. Sonorous cellolike tones predominate on *Volcanic Action,* and Ray's sound colors, like Rembrandt's golden-brown palette, convey a profound insight into the human spirit, a knowledge of life tempered by sympathy, patience, and sensual vigor—the qualities of a true master.

"Another dream," Ray sings to open the album, and *Volcanic Action* is like a dream. Sounds glide past one another, evoke moods, and then disappear. On "Wichita Lineman," a pedal steel guitar gleams like railroad tracks in moonlight. Piano notes in George Harrison's "Something" splash like pebbles in a pool. Most of *Volcanic's* songs are love songs, but Ray goes beyond sexual passion to sing about life itself, mysterious, evanescent, bittersweet. Lonesome "Down in the Valley" is a song for the campfire when the night's music is in all ears—"Hang your head over and hear the wind blow," sighs the chorus, and Ray moans like trees in a summer storm. "The Three Bells" tells of little Jimmy Brown, born, married, and buried to the ringing of chapel bells in a village deep in the valley. As the last lonely bell rings, Ray cries, "Farewell, Jimmy, we all loved you, son." A choir sings the climax, "May his soul find its salvation in that great eternal love," and Ray adds a quiet spoken coda: "Jimmy, you were a friend of mine. I'm sorry, Jimmy."

Volcanic Action entered the LP charts at #150 in late May, climbing through the summer to a peak at #52. In June, Florida A&M, Ray's old stomping ground in Talla-hassee, honored him as "a distinguished musician and astute businessman." Veteran bass trombonist Henry Coker left during an August week with the Supremes at the Mill Run Theatre in Chicago, and was replaced by a twenty-three-year-old recruit, Dana Hughes. One of Ray's first white players, Hughes had worked with Don Ellis' big band, and he found playing Ray's R&B-pop "a piece of cake" compared with struggling with time signatures like 7/4 in Ellis' book. On the other hand, the tattered charts he inherited from Coker were a mess of cuts and corrections, and Hughes didn't play the unread-able bars until he had a chance to study them with Leroy Cooper.

In September ABC put out *A 25th Anniversary in Show Business Salute to Ray Charles,* a double album, one record of the Atlantic years, the other ABC and Tanger-ine. Saluting Ray's longevity, however, had the disadvantage of reminding everyone how old he was. *Billboard* had started calling Ray a "revival show," and a fan told the *Sen-tinel,* "I can't even remember when there wasn't a Ray Charles."

In October they took off for another grand tour of Europe. At La Scala, the au-dience stood up cheering at the end of a brilliant show and didn't let the gang leave the stage for half an hour. When Ray and Susaye finally got into the limousine, a crowd sur-rounded them, screaming, "Ray, Ray," for another forty minutes before they could pull away. In Dusseldorf, Stella Yarborough wandered off once too often, and Ray sent to LA for Dorothy Berry. Dorothy had the low alto Ray loved, and he had asked her to join before. Then she was married to Richard Berry, composer of "Louie Louie," and opening for Tina Turner on the chitlin circuit, and she said no. Two years later, her mar-riage broken up and her career stalled, she said yes. "I went for six weeks," Berry re-called. "Then Ray said, 'Miss D, I need you to go to Japan with me.' I was making enough to send money home to my sister taking care of my kids in LA, so I stayed."

The Japanese tour wound up in Tokyo, and the gang flew home to LA the week before Christmas. Fathead Newman left to go with Herbie Mann at double Ray's salary. "I couldn't refuse Herbie's offer," Newman recalled. "Ray sent me a ticket in the spring, but I returned it, saying this time I wasn't coming back." Except on a few special oc-casions, Fathead never did come back. Two decades after they met, the two pals from Texas went separate ways.

***

Ray settled into RPM for a winter of work as 1972 began. He liked being the patriarch of Ray Charles Enterprises, but being responsible for his brood weighed heavily on his shoulders. No matter how much money he made, Leroy Cooper observed, Ray always felt, "I have to go to work, so you all can have something to eat." He roamed the building with a big ring of keys in his pocket, checking up on everything and everybody. His valets lived at his beck and call twenty-four hours a day, seven days a week. Secretaries came and went monthly. Ray held his employees to a high standard and himself to higher one. Once he spilled his sticky-sweet coffee on the console and was furious with himself. Braithwaite tried to tell him anyone might have done it. "If *you* spill, that's okay," Ray replied. "I'm supposed to know better."

Ray's ceaseless drive made RPM a volatile place to work, and Joe Adams did all he could to exacerbate the tension. "The roaring lion of Ray Charles Enterprises," as Mable John called Adams, liked to stride through the office in his perfect suits and his white patent-leather shoes like a marquis through a French court, berating one underling, smiling blandly at another. Yet he in turn was intimidated by his boss. Ray could wake up Adams at three o'clock in the morning, say "Come, Joe," and Joe would jump to do whatever Ray wanted. Whenever an employee tried to tell Ray, "Well, Joe said . . ." Ray would respond, " '*Joe* said'? *I* pay Joe Adams." If a booking agent called with a gig for Ray, Joe couldn't say yes without asking Ray. Then if Ray responded, "Goddammit, Joe, I told you I don't want to work at that place," Joe would go back to the phone and tell the agent in his haughtiest manner, "I will not have Ray Charles come to your sleazy joint."

Yet in ten years together, a durable bond had grown up between artist and manager. Only Ray and Joe knew where all the money was, where all the bodies were buried. Joe's picky style guaranteed the tight ship that Ray demanded from his crew, and he never shrank from his job as hatchet man. "Everybody needs a Joe Adams," Ray sometimes said with a sour laugh, and he had come to depend on his. "Nobody was going to separate Ray and Joe Adams," Braithwaite remembered. "Joe made sure that no one did. I was close to Ray, working with him in the studio to all hours of the day and night, and Joe was always popping in, jealous as a woman."

Ethel Rubin, the bookkeeper in charge of payroll, royalties, and residuals, ranked third in charge at RPM. Tall and straight, her hair beginning to gray, Miss Rubin ("Mama" in Ray's good moods) knew how to stand up to Joe, but she idolized Ray, and when he yelled at her, it hurt. One day a Raelet came to Joe to get a check. Joe told Miss Rubin to write the check; she did and then told Ray. Ray went into a tirade. "What? Don't you *ever* spend any of my money before you come to me!" Miss Rubin broke into tears, and Joe sidled away. Soon after, she quit, and the books quickly got out of hand. Ray rode out to her house and begged her to come back. After months of cajoling, Miss Rubin returned to the helm.

David Braithwaite found his escape from RPM's cantankerous atmosphere: drinking Ray's gin-coffee-sugar mix. "He was high half the time, so I started getting a hit of gin in the morning to get on the same page. Then we started getting along." Soon everybody was nipping at the Bols, and Ray put a lock on the closet door, adding a new key to his ring.

[|||||||||||||]

In the midst of this day-to-day tumult, Ray finished *A Message from the People*. If *Volcanic* is Ray's great "themeless" album, *Message* is his great theme album, a political statement he had been mulling over for years. Ray's message is well worth listening to, incisive and heartfelt, and he speaks in the eloquent American musical language he'd been assembling all his life, a language drawn from every strain of American music, from every inch of its soil.

Ray worked hard on *Message,* gathering songs and going over them with Sid, Quincy, and newcomer Mike Post. His idea, he explained, was to record music "that you might call a little militant, saying some of the wrong things that were happening in the country." He'd start with the Negro national anthem, "Lift Every Voice and Sing," "to make sure the people got on the right side," and go on to songs like Stevie Wonder's "Heaven Help Us All" and Dee Ervin's poignant "Seems Like I Gotta Do Wrong" that painted "some negative things" about America. Yet Ray didn't want anyone to misunderstand: he loved America, "the most beautiful country in the world," and to show its "good things," he'd put on songs like "Take Me Home, Country Roads" and "Every Saturday Night," and close with "America the Beautiful." Every detail of the record mattered. Ray argued with Ruth about the lyrics of "America" until she called the public library and typed out the correct version in Braille. He knew just what he wanted for the cover: himself with children of all races, looking upward at the faces of Abraham Lincoln, Martin Luther King, John and Robert Kennedy. Al Willis, a Los Angeles musician and artist, painted the cover and gave Ray shoes with laces. Ruth told him Ray never wore shoelace shoes, and Willis painted them out.

"I got something in my bones, makes me want to shout hallelujah," Ray sings as *Message* begins. Soon he and a mighty chorus are lifting their voices to declare, "May we stand forever true to our God and to our native land." Ray goes on to paint vignettes of loners, a homeless child, a frightened soldier, and he howls their misery—"Nobody sees me walking . . . I gotta do wrong before they notice me." In "Hey, Mister Congressman" Ray tells the powers that be that they'd better listen to the people: "Don't you hear 'em, don't you hear 'em? . . . I feel sorry for you if you don't! . . . Rich or poor, a man is still a man." The music drives on to a boogaloo beat. Ray is angry. "I'm trying to tell you something, man."

He's still mad as side two begins. "Look what they done to my song, Ma," Ray sings. "What is it, son?" a woman's voice asks. "They put it in a plastic bag, shaked it all upside down . . . drivin' me insane." But as the song ends, Ray vows that he's "gonna keep on working on the building, Mama, just like you told me." "Country Roads" is a one-man hollering match, Ray's overdubbed voice singing the melody, harmonizing with the chorus, and calling for listeners to sing along, "Country roads, take me home, take me home, country roads." "I like that!" Ray shouts on one track; "Me too!" he replies on another.

Message closes with "America the Beautiful," arranged by Quincy Jones. Snare drums and bugles open. "Now when I was in school we used to sing it like this," Ray says and then, at a slow rocking tempo, he lauds America's skies, mountains, and fruited plains. "I'm talking about *America,* sweet America, God done shed his grace on thee, he did, he crowned thy good, yes he did, with brotherhood, from sea to shining sea. Oh, I wish I had somebody to help me sing this." A chorus joins him in swelling majesty. "I love you, America," Ray sings. The record ends with a final "Thank you, Lord," from Ray, and a roll of kettledrums.

The Buzzard flapped out on tour in April and flapped back to Los Angeles for a week at the Coconut Grove in late May. Della came opening night, looking glamorous in a jeweled lavender dress and blond wig. She brought the boys, and Ray sang "Happy Birthday" to Ray Jr., turning seventeen. It made a cozy item for the gossip columns, but Ray and Della's marriage, long a hollow shell, had thinned to the cracking point. Quiet Della Bea had put up with a lot since the happy years in the little house in Dallas. She still loved Ray, and she loved the three slender, handsome sons she'd raised. She felt proud of her position as Ray's legal wife, proud of the grand house on Southridge that she had slowly grown into and made hers. And Ray's authority still cowed her. "It's got to be 51-49 in marriage," he often said. "And I'm the fifty-one as long as I'm out there making a living." Yet through years of lonely nights, jealous rage had smoldered in Della like a fire in a coal mine. She and Ray seldom spoke anymore except in common places, and knife-edged resentments sliced through their silences. Della saw a lawyer about a separation. A judge suggested a marriage counselor, and Ray submitted unwillingly to a few sessions. The marriage dragged on, not dead but dying.

The plainest diagnosis pointed to Ray's endless pursuit of other women. Ray knew his sexual hungers hurt Della, but he felt no shame. "One rooster, many hens," he often crowed, and he liked to tell Ruth about Solomon and his concubines in the Bible. Ray knew that many men like himself, modern princes with the money and charisma to attract beautiful women, acted just as he did. So would most men, he figured, if given the chance. The chance had been given to him, and he was not about to pass it up.

In the early 70s, Ray assembled a harem of such variety and delight that, when officially in LA, he seldom got back to Southridge by the six A.M. curfew that Della set to maintain a last vestige of respect. Susaye was his first lady on the road, Ruth in LA, but they shared him with Norma, a radio executive who moved from New York to LA to be close by, with Arlette in Paris and another French flame who lived in a distant suburb, with Dorothy and Stella among the Raelets, and with assorted newcomers, old-timers, and occasionals along the way. Ray punched the names and numbers of his women into a thick leather address book that he had stitched himself, drawing on his old D&B handicraft skills. As many a working day ended, Ray took out the book and made his calls to plan the night ahead, shading his voice to each woman in the tones of their unique intimacy.

Arlette was Ray's bohemian intellectual, a cynical spice just right for Europe. Norma was his homebody; she quit her job and took an apartment in West Los Angeles where Ray was always welcome. Susaye was Ray's good girl, and her love for him, she knew, was in part that of a daughter looking for a father. Sometimes she sat and watched Ray in adoration, laughing inside at his determined, little-boy trot into the darkness ahead. Ruth was Ray's bad girl, good for hot sex and sophisticated talk. Determined to carve out a career on her own, Ruth quit Tangerine and kept their affair a secret. She also tried to keep a lid on her emotions, yet she learned Braille to write him gushy love letters.

Susaye and Ruth saw Ray from different angles. Susaye thought he had a wonderful sense of humor and loved to be with people; Ruth found his laugh sardonic and thought he liked best to be alone. Ruth played him smooth Commodore records, and he liked them; Susaye played him rough Jimi Hendrix, and he shook his head to say, "We don't have to play that anymore." Susaye sensed a tender soul deep inside Ray, a man with feelings easily bruised, a spirit seldom depressed but often sad. Ruth liked to argue with Ray about politics and the Bible, and she marveled at his stubborn refusal to admit defeat in debate. Ray showered Susaye with expensive, romantic gifts; similar gestures to Ruth, given their saltier affair, would have been faintly ridiculous.

For all their differences, both women found Ray intensely compatible and fun to be with, and both believed he loved them. He told both about Retha and George and his struggles coming up, and both sensed that he saw his own life as a lonely battle. Yet the scars of that battle, they came to realize, closed Ray off from complete openness in love. "There's a piece missing in his heart that he fills with music, not with other human beings," Susaye tried to explain years later. "He put up walls to keep people out, didn't share his real feelings with anyone." Ruth thought he wanted to keep her in "a little box": "I can talk about this and can do that with Ruth, but no, Ruth, don't you come out of that little box and come over here."

As each woke from infatuation, Susaye and Ruth reacted differently. Susaye still hoped for one true love, her dream since childhood, and realizing that Ray would never fulfill it hurt her deeply. Again and again in hotel lobbies, Susaye recognized women—"I know her, I've seen her before"—and each flash inflicted its own stab of pain. If she challenged Ray, he'd tell her the truth, but after a few such brutal sessions, she thought, "Do I want to know the truth? How many times can my heart break?" When it dawned on Ruth that she was one of many, she accepted the fact realistically. "I decided I wasn't going to waste away," she remembered. "I'd have another guy or two who Ray wouldn't know about."

Tomcat that he was, Ray did exude a feral coldness on his midnight prowls. Ruth put it bluntly: "As long as he can get it up, Ray will go with any woman who gives him great sex and great talk." Yet Ray also touched responsive chords in each woman's nature, attaching them to him deeply. Arlette saw Ray five or six times a year, but he became the most important man in her life. Susaye broke off with her mother when Mrs. Green said she hadn't groomed her darling daughter to be one of Ray's string. Ruth's men-on-the-side system worked for her, and she stayed with Ray for twenty years. Yet when it came to a choice between herself and Norma as to who would be Ray's second wife, Ruth let Norma have the job. "Much as I was in love with him, I declined. I was trying to find out who I was, and that wasn't standing in his shadow."

Like Mary Ann Fisher, Mae Lyles, Sheila Betts, and others before and since, Ray's women of the 70s were left with a mystery: Did Ray love them? "It's possible that he loved each of us or some of us or none of us," Ruth Robinson speculated. "I don't know. I *thought* that he loved me, I believed it for a long time. And I still don't know that it's *not* true."

▐▌▐▌▐▌▐▌▐▌

The tour rolled on through the summer to Yankee Stadium, and dozens of county fairs. *Message from the People* came out and, oddly, peaked at #52 just like *Volcanic Action*. Ray put out a single of "America the Beautiful," but it flopped. In September Ray met for a few minutes with President Nixon in the Oval Office; they talked, as arranged, about the need for sickle-cell anemia research. Meeting the president was "a gas," Ray told the LA *Sentinel,* then added, "I'm *not* for the man." Tangerine released *Through the Eyes of Love,* a lush album that pales in comparison with its two predecessors, yet glows at one sublime moment, a violin following Ray up to a last high note on "Someone to Watch

Over Me," and at a silly one, Ray drunk at the end of "Rainy Night in Georgia." He'll crawl into a boxcar and hold his girl's picture close, he sings, then starts mumbling: "I'm just sitting here trying to finish off this half-pint . . . ish rainin' all over the worl' . . . Aw, shut off that rain."

When the gang flew back from Europe in November, a few gigs had fallen through, and Ray laid the band off for a week with no notice and no pay. Trumpeter Tony Farrell and a few men sued Ray through LA's AFM Local 47, asking for full pay for the week and two weeks' severance. Ray won the first round, they won the appeal. Ray appealed the appeal and lost, and they rushed to the bank with their checks, fearful that Ray might close the account rather than cough up the money. Union trouble, however, was a routine annoyance for Ray Charles Enterprises, and as Ray and the gang flew north to San Francisco for a week at the Circle Star in late November, Ray's big wheel was rolling along with the polished smoothness that had become its customary motion.

23

Georgia, ohhhhhh Georgia . . .
No peace I find
Just an old sweet song . . .

Life on
the Road
Mid-1970s

Ray, bathed in light, sweat gleaming on his brow, sang "Georgia on My Mind" on opening night, Tuesday, November 28, 1972, at the Circle Star Theater. In the dozen years since it topped the charts, "Georgia" had become a signature song for Ray, yet his countless remeditations on the theme had barely altered how he sang it. His body still rocked side to side to the slow pulse tempo, and in his voice, once again, moonlight glimmered silver-blue through the pines.

In the dark lower half of the stage the band sat silent, except for Edgar Willis and John Perrett laying down hushed bass and brushed drums. Andy Ennis put his tenor sax in its stand and picked up his flute. The dog-eared chart on his stand dictated that, at the repeat of "other arms reach out to me," when Ray held his note on "arms," Ennis was to play an echoing phrase, as Fathead had first done, and play it again when Ray held "me." That night Ennis began to play just as Ray sang "ar—" Immediately Ray's head swiveled from his mike in Ennis' direction.

"You came in too early," he shout-whispered. "Reach out to me," he sang. Again Ennis came in ahead, and again Ray's head snapped around. "Andy, you're coming in too damn early." Ray was pissed. As the band brought the song to a showy close, Ray ducked his head one more time to say, for the record, "You were startin' too early, man."

Ray, the band, ventriloquist Aaron Williams and his dummy Freddy, plus special guest B. B. King, were all booked Tuesday through Sunday at the Circle Star, a theater-in-the-round in San Carlos, thirty miles down the peninsula from San Francisco. Through the months between the Watergate break-in and President Nixon's reelection, Ray and company had played dozens of similar concert stages across America and Europe. From the Circle Star they were headed south to the nearly identical Valley Music Theatre in suburban Los Angeles.

San Francisco's Thanksgiving-to-Christmas season was in full swing. At the Opera House that week, Artur Rubinstein played Chopin, Gwendolyn Jones sang *Lucia di Lammermoor* with Luciano Pavarotti, and Seiji Ozawa conducted Mahler's Eighth Symphony. A touring company of *Man of La Mancha* had settled into a long run at the Corcoran Theatre, and Lou Rawls worked the Fairmont Hotel's Venetian Room on Nob Hill. The Circle Star held a middle-to-high rank on this entertainment spectrum, filling its thirty-five hundred seats by offering the same talent that headlined across the Sierras at Tahoe and Reno. Jack Benny and Marlene Dietrich pulled in white suburbanites; Woody Allen, Ella Fitzgerald, and the Supremes pulled in college kids and blacks.

The theater building, a bland monument to urban sprawl, stood in the middle of parking lots. To the east, past a fence and a littered weed patch, traffic roared on the Bay Shore Freeway; to the west, traffic crawled on the El Camino Real, the old highway now a strip of gas stations and fast-food restaurants. Dressed-up crowds entered the Circle Star on a red carpet through an elegant red-and-gold lobby. Many had dinner before the show in the Grillroom Restaurant or stopped for a cocktail in the lounge. When the show began, the theater's sound and lighting systems created a glossy professional ambience, and the slow circling of the stage became magical.

Ray flew into San Francisco airport opening night and rode ten miles south on the freeway, getting to the Circle Star about eight. Inside, B. B. King was opening the show—still a good hour and a half before Ray would go on himself. The night was damp and cold. Bob Taylor, Ray's valet, drove up in a yellow Toronado, parked, and then walked around to the passenger side to open the door. Ray stepped out, reached into the back seat for a black woolly overcoat, slipped it over his shoulders, and stood and stretched. On his feet, Ray looked like a light-heavyweight boxer, broad shoulders, narrow hips and legs. He turned back to the car, fumbled for the button to lock the door, then slammed it shut and rocked back on his heels. Taylor gave Ray his arm and they walked up a short ramp to the door, Ray slightly stooped, his head hanging forward, each step a cautious feeling out into the unseen territory ahead.

Taylor led Ray through the metal door and down the smoky, fluorescent-lit con-
fusion of the backstage corridor. Aluminum laundry carts (neatly stenciled "Ray Charles
Enterprises, Los Angeles, Calif, USA") lined both walls; on top of one rested Leroy
Cooper's huge baritone sax. Cooper himself, Santa Claus in a black tuxedo, stood filling a dressing room door, chatting with sax player Don Garcia. Bleets and blaats
sounded from horn players warming up their lips. Susaye Green, tiny and pert and a
little late, slipped past Ray and Taylor, a wardrobe bag over her arm, her breasts swinging freely beneath a pink silk T-shirt. "Hi, Ray," she said breezily. "All right, darling,"
said Ray. Taylor and Ray stepped into the star's dressing room and closed the door behind them.

Onstage, B.B. had the crowd roaring with laughter at his "I gave you seven children, and now you want to give them back!" Freddy, Aaron's wooden wise guy, said he
didn't care that Nixon had been elected: "Shee-it, man, I'm black and I'm poor, I'm
gonna catch hell either way!" The band did fifteen minutes of ripsnorting jazz and the
Raelets laid hot Baptist blues on the people. Then came the moment everyone was waiting for. "Ladies and gentlemen," Joe Adams' disembodied voice announced in mellow
tones, "The Geeenius, 1972 . . . Ray Charles!"

Whoops of primed, expectant delight greeted Ray as he stepped up to the stage,
his left arm linked with Taylor's, his right hand high in salute. Taylor took him to the
corner of the Fender electric piano; its keyboard made an L with that of the black baby
grand. The band played a brassy fanfare and Ray, resplendent in a bright blue tuxedo,
reached out to the audience with both arms, a big smile on his face. With pauses to indicate he was trying to get everyone into his embrace, he wrapped both arms tight
around his body, bowed low, rose, and loosed his arms to wave again. The cheering
started to fade, and Ray sat on the padded leather piano stool and began to play.

His fingers hit the keys with a bounce, a growl ending in a yelp sprang from his
throat, and his feet and legs started a dance that didn't stop for an hour and a half. Ray
played against the beat, the band clapped on it. Three bluesy chords. Clap clap. A dashing run in the right hand over heavy chords in the left. Clap clap. When he felt settled
on stage and in touch with the fellows, Ray waved the groove to a close and set off instantly into a fast-paced "Marie (The Dawn Is Breaking)," an Irving Berlin tune usually dripping with nostalgia, but in Ray's hands rippingly immediate.

The show flowed on. An up-tempo rocker came to a big finish, and in the sudden
silence Ray began noodling ruminatively on the piano. What tune was he introducing
and when would he start? Only Edgar Willis seemed to know. He looked intently at
Ray, his left hand in position on the neck of his electric bass, then nodded at the fellows. They understood the nod and got themselves ready. Ray played on, the chords
coming closer together, more rumbling. Willis' right hand started a slow descent to the

strings. At the instant he plucked, the band melted in, and the song began. "Georgia, oooh, Georgia. . ."

In the mid-70s, a week at the Circle Star was a good gig for Ray. To generate a cash flow steady enough to cover the daily nut of Ray Charles Enterprises, Ray and Joe Adams often took less than top dollar and top billing. Ray performed in noisy Reno lounges in these years and made long hops to isolated one-nighters. Life on the road was nothing new for Ray, but touring took on added importance because, as a recording artist, he remained stuck in a long slump.

Through the Eyes of Love reached a peak of #186 on the album charts as 1973 began, a fitting symbol of Ray's low ebb. *Volcanic Action of My Soul* and *Message from the People* had done better than that, but they had still sold only in the 200,000 range. To the press, Ray bluffed. "Who else is still in the charts after twenty-six years?" he asked *Billboard,* and he told *Rolling Stone* that he had "maintained sales figures between 300,000 and 800,000 per album through the years." Yet he knew the score as well as anyone: 200,000-and-under was the shallows of the big time. Million-sellers like Carole King's *Tapestry,* Curtis Mayfield's *Superfly, Exile on Main Street* by the Rolling Stones, and Marvin Gaye's *What's Going On?* were the albums that fans were rushing out to buy. Ray wasn't in contention.

Continuing bad reviews contributed to Ray's slump. "It's sort of 'in' these days to be down on Ray Charles," *Downbeat* opened its notice of *Volcanic Action.* Jon Landau spelled out the negative line in his *Rolling Stone* review of *Message from the People:*

> . . . it's been one long slide downhill since he left Atlantic in 1961. His fling with C&W was obviously commercially inspired, but at least it was often musically inspired as well. Not so his return to R&B in the mid-Sixties. His material, arrangements, and style in general seemed too far out of touch with contemporary trends. . . . He has coasted continually without ever progressing beyond the style and sound that made him famous.

Almost to his own surprise, Landau went on to call *Message* "a strangely haunting and beautiful album with a hidden universal quality," but critical sniping ("too bland in too many places," "vapid," "poor taste in picking the tunes") still set a dismissive tone that dampened public interest in Ray's new work.

Low sales led, as they always do, to trouble with the label. Ray's feud with Jay

Lasker had never cooled off, and after *Through the Eyes of Love* dive-bombed, Lasker decided that Ray Charles was expendable. Ray was more than ready to go, but where to? He flew to New York for a meeting with his old mentors, Sam Clark and Larry Newton. Clark, now a senior executive in the parent corporation, told him not to worry about Jay Lasker. The top brass were getting fed up with Lasker; every month, it seemed, he was suing or getting sued by somebody. Moreover, ABC was beginning to doubt the wisdom of owning a record label. Television profits dwarfed record profits, and they depended on the federal broadcasting license, a gift of the government and the corporation's ultimate golden goose. Ever since "Eve of Destruction" in 1965, board members had harrumphed that peaceniks on the label could threaten the license. After Nixon's reelection, ABC executives felt increasing pressure to sell the label. Ray was lucky to be leaving a sinking ship.

Like Clark, Newton had been out of the record division for years, but old indy hustler that he was, he felt a tug to get back in the game. If he got a major label to sign Ray, he'd earn a healthy fee for himself. Sam Clark suggested that since Ray was starting fresh, he should drop Tangerine and rename his label: "You'll be doing different types of music, trying to reach different people, why don't you name your company Crossover?" Ray liked the idea. Newton started shopping, and Ray went back on the road.

Through each winter Joe Adams and two secretaries put together the nuts and bolts of the new tour, booked gigs with agents and promoters, signed contracts, and kept track of the money. Bob Abrams sent out pictures and press releases to the media wherever the tour was booked and connected Ray with local reporters for phone interviews. In February, after name-by-name okays from Ray, out went "the letter" to the band. All the fellows signed year-to-year contracts; only when the letter arrived from Ray asking if they were available did they know they still had the gig. "Leroy's got the job as long as he wants it," Ray liked to say; but even trusty old-timers sometimes waited deep into the spring for letters that never came. Auditions and recommendations filled empty slots, and by mid-March Ray had his band together for about two weeks of rehearsal at RPM, more or less depending on the number of new faces.

Come departure day in early April, the gang gathered in the RPM parking lot. Joe handed out the numbered suitcases, the only bag allowed (not counting instrument cases) with a weight limit of forty pounds. If someone's bag was overweight, he had to shed a few shirts or slacks, which Joe always said would be returned, but which were seldom seen again. Into the bus they climbed, and laughing and calling across the seats, they rode to Long Beach airport. Everybody felt a tingle of excitement on boarding the Buzzard. Aaron Williams roamed about shooting home movies. Phil Guilbeau clowned in one of Vernita's wigs, Mable looked trim in a tailored suit and matching shoes, Ray carried his chessboard, a game in progress, from the bus to the plane. As the pilot brought the engines up to speed on the runway, Ray sat in the copilot's seat and announced over the intercom, "Strap yourselves in, children. We'll be flying at 12,000 feet with good weather ahead, so sit back and enjoy the flight." Which, in 1973, was a hop to San Jose for a gig with George Shearing.

Once Ray's wheel got rolling, everybody had a job to do. Some complained that working for Ray felt like serving in the Marines, and with good reason: Ray divided authority in his ranks along military lines for the purpose of carrying out, to the letter, the wishes of Ray Charles, Supreme Commander of the Allied Forces. When Joe came along, with his sharp eyes and barking voice, he became Ray's lieutenant-general. Ray always backed Joe up on minor band matters; for the fellows the day-to-day rule was "Joe's way or the highway."

Beneath Joe was the road manager, the tour's personnel transport sergeant, responsible for getting everybody to and from the gig and making sure that long-reserved hotel rooms hadn't disappeared in a weekend rush. The road manager also carried "the briefcase," the band's traveling office of payroll checks, tickets, and contracts; this sign of Ray's trust hung a mantle of power over the road manager's shoulders. The road manager knew the band's business before the band did; he might joke with a fellow whom he was already, at Ray's request, making calls to replace. The first road manager of the 70s, Don Briggs, was a grouchy, ill old man nobody liked. Briggs collapsed on-stage in Turin, Italy, after a show; when the group heard the news, a ripple of applause ran around the dressing room. Fred Murrell, a former trombone player with the band, followed Briggs, and easygoing Murrell quickly became a favorite. Ray liked him as a chess opponent, and the men thought of him as one of them, risen in rank but his heart still with his pals in the trenches.

Another musician followed Murrell, but the case of Edgar Willis was more poignant. After almost twenty years of faithful service, the gentlemanly, modest Edgar Willis had become a dinosaur in the band. He switched from acoustic to electric bass in the early 70s, but he never fully adjusted to the new sound and feel. Ray's young drummers found it hard to get in synch with Edgar, and Ray retired him. Used to the road and with few prospects elsewhere, Willis hung on for a few years as road manager. Those, like Mable, who saw into his character, knew Willis' kind heart, but Joe Adams treated him as a gofer, and the younger men suspected him of being a yes-man quick to tattle to the boss.

The stage manager was supply sergeant, responsible for movement of tour matériel, and Harold Patton was still on the job (and still collecting his African-American first editions). Harold got to the auditorium first, carrying the bandstands and music, the drum kit, the organ, and Ray's electric piano. He put the right chart book on the right stand, gave the light cues to the lighting man, and did a sound check with the engineer. Getting the right level on Ray's mike was "a bitch," Patton remembered. "We'd fly in an hour before we hit, his ears would pop halfway through the concert, and he'd scream we'd turned the volume up three db's. Or he'd back off the mike to get a soft effect, the soundman would perk his mike up, and when Ray came back in, his voice would blare out, then he'd yell about that."

From top to bottom of this man's army the watchword was just what it had been in Hank Crawford's day: *discipline.* Do your job and you had no problem; don't do your job and you had problems. Joe checked your appearance: missing bow tie, $50 fine; wrong socks, $50 fine. Ray listened to your music. "When I tell you what I want you to sing," he reminded the Raelets again and again, "you sing it that way, word for word, sound for sound, until I tell you different."

Ray Charles Enterprises ran by the clock. "Bus leaves at 6 A.M." printed on an itinerary meant the bus was gone at 6:01. Ray timed every segment of the show. In later years when Aaron Williams opened for Sammy Davis Jr., and he asked how much time he could take, Davis always replied, "Do your thing!" Ray, in contrast, told him, "Give me ten and two," a ten-minute set with two minutes leeway. Most important, the Ray Charles show always started on time. "If the contract said we started at eight o'clock," recalled Williams, "Joe was there beside me watching that second hand go around. When it hit straight up, boom, I'd be out there."

Because he often flew back to LA between gigs, the Supreme Commander lived semi-independent of the band, yet Ray's road routine was as strict as the band's and as well organized for his own convenience. From both RPM and Southridge he had short drives to LA's international airport, and the moment he was ready to go, the valet hopped to bring the car to the door. At LAX Ray knew his way around like the experienced traveler he was. He flew first-class, the valet carrying on, and not checking, the baggage in order to speed up deplaning at their destination.

When possible, and it often was, Ray stayed in the same suite at the same hotel, the room booked from the day before to make sure it would be ready when he got there. In a new room, Ray checked all the exits, then took small steps back and forth, whistling a tune under his breath to measure its size: so many bars this way, so many bars that. In the pantry Ray wanted fresh fruit, fresh milk, and hot coffee. With a country boy's suspicion of city water, Ray never drank from the tap: "Anybody who drinks the water in this country is going to die," he often said. "More than anything," recalled longtime valet Vernon Troupe, "Ray wanted his rest, to be bright-eyed and bushy-tailed at showtime. No calls to his room; it took an earth-shattering emergency for me to wake him up." While Ray slept, the valet tipped his way to a first-name basis with desk clerks and room-service waiters to ensure that Mr. Charles got what he wanted when he wanted it.

In the dressing room before a show, star and valet went through an unvarying ritual. Ray got into his dress slacks and shirt while the valet made up a mug of his gin-and-coffee. Then the valet handed him the coffee and a cigarette, Kools without a filter, and helped Ray on with his dinner jacket. Ray kept sipping the coffee and smoking until the moment the valet led him to the stage. After the show the valet stayed with Ray until he was back in his room, which in Las Vegas could be 2:30 or 3 A.M. The valet checked that Ray had at least thirty cigarettes to carry him overnight, then went to his own room, where, before he could sleep, he called the car service, the airline, and the next hotel to make sure that everything was set for the morning.

As the 70s rolled on, turnover in the band continued, bringing in, most notably, a new generation of young white musicians. "There's a few *white* faces down in the hole now," Aaron's smart-ass Freddy liked to point out, but white or black, the group got along in comradely fashion, nobody bothering much about race. Still, there were differences. "When the Buzzard landed somewhere on a hot day," Leroy Cooper remembered, "all the white boys took off their shirts and headed for the sun, and all the brothers headed for the shade—and the Coke machine!"

Brooklyn-born trumpeter Tony Horowitz joined in the spring of 1973. A child prodigy who turned pro at eleven, Horowitz, at twenty-eight, had just gotten divorced and wanted to get away from LA. At the audition, he played a tough passage as a favor for the auditioner beside him, and Ray hired the other fellow to play first and Horowitz to play second trumpet. When Ray found out he'd been fooled, he switched them. Edgar Willis said the lesson was "Never cover for anybody." A good chess player, Horowitz quickly became pals with Ray. Landing in Little Rock that summer, Ray told the gang a joke that bordered on anti-Semitic. Horowitz had a comeback ready: "You better be careful, Ray." "Why?" asked Ray. " 'Cause we're in Little Rock, and maybe nobody told you, but you're black." Everyone fell silent, but Ray roared with laughter. Horowitz, nicknamed "Sweetie-pie," wasn't so popular with the fellows, however. "He liked to showboat playing high notes," Leroy Cooper recalled. "If you heard him bragging to girls in the bar, you'd think that before Sweetie-pie came along, they didn't have no trumpets."

Fathead and James Clay knew twenty-nine-year-old trombonist Ken Tussing from Dallas, and they recommended him to Ray. When the call came in June '73, Tussing was paying his dues playing Dixieland at a Fort Worth amusement park. His first gig with Ray was a Kool Jazz Festival concert in the Houston Astrodome. "There were

70,000 people in the stadium," Tussing recalled. "I'd barely looked at the book and I was scared to death." "You did a good job," said Ray on the bus back to the hotel. "If you want to come with us, the pay's three-fifty a week and all the bus and plane you can handle." "Fine with me," said Tussing, and he was off and running: Dallas, Memphis, Detroit, and then Europe for six weeks with Count Basie and Oscar Peterson. One night in Germany, stagehands set up three pianos backstage, and Tussing stood awestruck as the three masters jammed on an uproarious blues.

Larry Newton, meanwhile, swung his deal: English Decca Records (London Records in America), agreed to underwrite Crossover with a half-million-dollar advance and a yearly stipend to cover Ray's studio expenses. Decca's chairman, Sir Edward Lewis, threw a party when Ray got to London in October, and Newton, Crossover's new president, flew over to attend. On paper, Crossover was a label like Tangerine—Ray could sign and record other artists—but in fact, Decca was interested only in Crossover records by Ray Charles. Ray realized that his dream of running a record company with an artist roster had died with Tangerine, and it hurt. "I loved Tangerine," he said years later. "But to run a label, especially a small label, you have to keep your hands in it. I was spread too thin, but I wasn't about to give up my own music or going on the road. At least Tangerine didn't lose any money, and figuring in all I learned, I'd say we came out ahead."

Leaving ABC ended a fourteen-year era in Ray's recording career and cut his link to a major American corporation; Ray Charles Enterprises was on its own as never before. One day a truck showed up at RPM with hundreds of cartons filled with reels and reels of Ray's ABC tapes, outtakes as well as masters, even Sid Feller's work sheets. Ray stored them in a fireproof vault he had built on the ground floor of RPM. ABC also handed over $2 million in accumulated royalties it had been holding for him ever since "Georgia." The legal device had helped Ray defer much of his income tax; now he owed the government nearly half the total. Ray winced as he paid $1 million to the IRS, but he paid it to the penny.

And he got down to work on *Come Live with Me,* his first Crossover release. Larry Newton came out to RPM that fall and heard Ray mixing the title track, a big, country-flavored ballad. Excited to be chasing hits again, Newton flipped. He'd rush it out as a single, he said; it'd be as big as "I Can't Stop Loving You." Again and again he asked David Braithwaite to play the tape, and each time as Ray's voice filled the room, Newton started shouting, "Number One, Number One!"

Split into a ballad A-side and an R&B B-side, *Come Live with Me* lacks the mysterious unity of *Volcanic Action,* yet it contains similarly strong tracks of the generous four-to-five-minute length that had become one of Ray's trademarks. "He never tried to limit his material to radio-play length," recalled Sid Feller, who again had long piano-bench sessions with Ray before writing the charts. "He wanted to tell the story no matter how long it took." By now Ray's vocal style is so naturally and uniquely his own that only careful listening reveals how he weaves seamless passion from an overdubbed vocabulary of grunts, whoops, "heh-heh"s, and "baby, baby"s. Few, however, listened carefully or otherwise to *Come Live with Me* upon release in '74. The single Newton had such high hopes for peaked at #82, and the album never reached the charts, Ray's first vocal album to miss since the 50s. Not that the public disliked *Come Live with Me;* they never heard it. Without ABC's native marketing clout and after Ray's five-year slump, Newton had to beg distributors to order product. Many of the albums he did ship came back as unsold returns.

In the concert halls, however, Ray was still a hot ticket, and in April the Ray Charles Show '74 assembled again in the RPM parking lot for another nine months on the road. Clifford Solomon was a new face that year, but he'd known Ray since his earliest days in LA. Ray called him looking for an alto player. "How about me?" asked Clifford. "You play tenor," said Ray. "I play *saxophone,"* said Clifford, and after a week trial in Portland, Oregon, he signed on for the first of twelve years. In August Ray had had enough of his drummer, and tenor player James Clay recommended John Bryant, a young white Texan whom he'd jammed with at Woodman's Auditorium in South Dallas. Bryant flew up to Denver and by chance passed his predecessor in the hotel lobby. "It didn't work out for me," said the departing drummer, with a long face. "Anything can happen," Bryant replied awkwardly, thinking, "That could be me tomorrow." From Denver the Buzzard flew to Hartford, Connecticut, for a week with Gladys Knight and the Pips. The second night of the gig, President Nixon resigned.

Despite the constant turnover, Ray got a single sound by organizing the band with the same clarity he used to organize his staff. Ray's model was the Count Basie Orchestra, and except for the addition of the Raelets, Ray's big band varied in no essential way from the classic American ensemble that evolved in the 1930s.

The players set up in four sections: the rhythm section grouped around the drums, the sax, trombone, and trumpet sections sitting in three rows. The bandleader could be from any section; but he was usually a saxophone player because, sitting in the front row, he could easily step out front to conduct as needed. Leroy Cooper, well respected for his unflappable cool, held the post through the mid-70s. Off stage Leroy acted as a buffer between Ray and the band, absorbing gripes from either side, but his primary authority sprang from his deep knowledge of what Ray wanted onstage. Each night, half an hour before curtain, Leroy went to Ray's dressing room, and Ray gave him the "menu," or show rundown. Every tune had a number that both knew by heart, and that's how Ray dictated them: "We'll do 239 [which was "Georgia,"], 64, 147 . . ." Including the band and the Raelets' tunes as well as Ray's, the menu might have twenty-five numbers—often long sequences of the same numbers in the same order. Leroy wrote the menu down, using carbon paper to make copies for the four section leaders.

The section leaders—the pianist for the rhythm section, the first trumpet, the trombone, and the sax in the brass sections—recopied the menu and handed it out to the others. Ten minutes before curtain came the call, "All on." Everybody took a seat onstage, put the chart book in that night's order, and tuned up to the middle A that pianist Ernie Vantrease struck on Ray's piano. Leroy counted off the tempo for the first tune, and the show began.

Where each player sat had a purpose. Stationing Willis' bass and Cooper's baritone sax at opposite sides of the band gave Ray low-tone anchors at either end. The brass section leaders sat in the center of each row. Each section followed its leader, but the trombone and sax leaders followed the first trumpet, who, from his high seat, set the breathing, phrasing, and dynamics for all the brass. The first trumpeter, in turn, followed the drummer. "The drummer and the lead trumpet must be one," recalled Horowitz from his experience at the post. "When that happens, the horns harmonize the rhythm, and you get the drive *and* precision that make a big band great."

The drummer, in his turn, followed Ray, and that, scarred veterans groaningly relate, was no easy task. John Bryant found in his book a mass of notations, scribbled in a dozen different hands, of Ray's specific wishes: a kick with the horns *here* on the bass drum, *there* on the snare, and when to go from brushes to sticks on a cymbal. Once Bryant tried a new lick on "What'd I Say." Ray jumped as if he'd been struck, and turned and yelled in Bryant's direction. Bryant couldn't hear what he said, but he ducked quickly back to basics. Afterward Ray called Bryant into his dressing room. "Honey, don't change the beat on 'What'd I Say,' " Ray said in friendly but firm warning. "It's written in stone, it's the right beat. Since it ain't broke, don't try and fix it."

Ray warred constantly with his drummers over "time," the steadiness of the beat to the set tempo. In pop music, time is the drummer's responsibility; the job requires asserting one's inner clock against anyone in the band who wanders. This seldom comes to a contest of wills among good musicians, but Ray asserted primacy over the drummer with his inflexible rule, "My time is the right time." One night he took Bryant aside to tell him emphatically, "Stay with *me!* Forget those sixteen other guys. What counts is you and me being together. You stay with me, the rest of them will be with us."

Staying with Ray, Bryant learned, felt "like riding a galloping horse—I couldn't take my eyes off him for a second." Bryant watched Ray's shoulders rocking side to side, his left foot slapping the stage on the big downbeats, his dancing hands, his twisting back—even Ray's knees communicated little offbeats. Watching wasn't always enough. "Sometimes he'd give the downbeat with his left foot and wouldn't want me to go with him. Other times I'd better be with that left foot, or there'd be hell to pay." Instinct got Bryant through many such moments, but Ray didn't want his troops relying on their instincts. *"His* instinct had to rule the day. To test us, he'd pull up a new chart in rehearsal and tell me something very specific: 'Here you go boom-kick on the bass drum, and ta-da-da on the high hat.' Three weeks later he'd call that tune, and as those bars rolled closer, I'd sense him listening: would I remember or would I fall into his trap?"

The Raelets lived as a linked but distinct unit in the band organization, and a degree of tension existed between the ladies and the gentlemen. The band felt that the Raelets didn't work as hard (fifteen minutes in an hour show) and got better treatment (their own dressing room). But the Raelets felt they paid their dues just like the others. "Maybe we didn't work as much stage time, but we rehearsed more with Ray," Vernita explained. "He'd rehearse us for hours, and if we complained we were hungry, he'd say, 'If you ate breakfast, you wouldn't be hungry all day.' We'd reply, 'We did eat breakfast, and we're *still* hungry!' "

Mable John—"Mother Superior," Henry Coker called her—continued to run the Raelets with a firm, fair hand. "With Mable, we were ladies no matter what," Dorothy Berry remembered. "If we were foggy from no sleep getting off the plane, we'd wear wigs and shades, but we looked decent." Vernita was still dancing onstage to ease her aching feet, Stella Yarborough was still strange. Upset by a phone call to a boyfriend, she smashed a glass shower door in a dressing room and wouldn't stop screaming. The theater crew thought they should call an ambulance, but Ray said no, and Mable put her arms around her, got her to her room, and sat with her all night. Susaye Green quit a few months into the '73 tour to sing and write songs with Stevie Wonder. Susaye continued to see Ray romantically, but instead of cooking midnight dinners for him at the Berlin Hilton, she gave him scrambled eggs at dawn in LA. A series of singers—Madeline Quebec, Cynthia Scott, and others—filled Susaye's spot without quite filling her shoes.

Joe Adams supervised the Raelets as he did the band, but while he and the fellows were always at sword points, Joe achieved a "one of the girls" intimacy with the Raelets. He could be picky, endlessly adjusting the ladies' hair at a photo shoot. And he could be mean, yelling at Vernita, "Don't you *ever* come out of your room without your makeup!" Yet Mable admired his high professional standards. "Joe was strict because he wanted Ray Charles and everyone with him to look good. I respected what he was trying to achieve," Mable said. Joe and Mable had fun shopping all over the world for fabrics to make the Raelets' gowns. "Don't you love these colors?" he'd ask her, oohing and aahing over bolts of brightly colored silk. At Mr. Blackwell's, his favorite designer, Joe helped with the fittings and could, without giving offense, put his hand inside one of the ladies' gowns and say, "You must *pull* your bust into the cup, like this, to get the right look." Men weren't allowed in the dressing room when the Raelets were in their bras and panties, but if Joe knocked, the ladies would say, "It's just Mr. Adams," and let him in.

Harold Patton handled the Raelets' gowns on the road and found Joe's Mr. Blackwell dresses both expensive to maintain—$35 apiece for dry cleaning—and dowdy compared with the styles set by Cher and Tina Turner. For a Carol Burnett TV show, the Raelets wore swirling pink and yellow chiffon gowns by Bob Mackie, Cher's designer. The ladies loved the dresses, and, to say thanks for the fun they'd had working together, Burnett said they could keep them. Then came disappointment: "You can wear them onstage," Joe said, "but since she gave them to you as Raelets, they belong to Ray Charles Enterprises."

▐▐▐▐▐▐▐▐▐▐▐

The 1974 tour continued through Mexico, where everybody came down with diarrhea. A sax player rushed offstage one night, didn't make it to the bathroom, and came back on stage in the only fresh pair of pants he could find, which ended inches above his socks. When Vernita saw him looking so silly, she burst out laughing in the middle of a song. Ray didn't know what was going on, and no one told him. In September they made up a date in New York's Central Park canceled in August because of a bomb scare, then spent the fall at Fairmont hotels in Dallas, New Orleans, and San Francisco. Going for high notes, Tony Horowitz blew his lip out, a blister appearing that looked to a frightened Tony "like a headlight on an old Chevrolet." Ray was sorry to see him go, but a doctor said it would be months before he could play again, so Tony left.

They didn't tour Europe in '74, and Ray found time to bring the band back to LA to record a third *My Kind of Jazz* album and a few tracks for the new vocal album, *Renaissance*. David Braithwaite had converted the RPM studio from eight to sixteen tracks, but after five years he was fed up with serving the Genius. Low pay was one reason; another was what felt to Braithwaite like a continuing lack of respect. "Ray was like a pilot of a plane in trouble," Braithwaite recalled. "You try to help him and he shouts, 'Leave me alone, can't you see I'm flying this plane?' " After one Friday-night fight, the two men walked silently down the back stairs to the parking lot. "I'm in the book," said Braithwaite, and he drove off. Monday morning, he didn't show up. For weeks Ray complained to his lady friend Norma, "I've got nobody to help me now," but he wouldn't call for fear of losing face. Norma tried to patch up the quarrel, but Braithwaite had gone to work for Bell Telephone, and though he was tempted, his wife wouldn't let him go back. Ray hired Bob Gratts, another ex–Motown engineer, and as 1974 became 1975, he pushed ahead to finish *Renaissance*.

Renaissance is an apt name for a vital album. Twenty years after *Billboard* reported on a new "electronic synthesizer" that could imitate any sound from "a piano to a hillbilly band," "synths" were widely used, their infinite spectrum of new timbres exciting adventuresome players. Stevie Wonder brought the latest models to RPM for Ray to experiment on, and Ray enjoyed them just as he had enjoyed his Wurlitzer electric piano back in Seattle. On *Renaissance,* Ray recorded with synthesizers for the first time, and they instantly modernized his sound. Pulsing, guitarlike wah-wahs on "My God and I" echo Jimi Hendrix; the ominous synths that rumble under his steamy version of Wonder's "Living for the City" suggest tracks by Sly Stone and Marvin Gaye. Songs by contemporary writers, Randy Newman's sarcastic "Sail Away" and Joe Raposo's tender "(It Ain't Easy) Being Green," also helped bring Ray up-to-date. Old-timer though he was, Ray proved with *Renaissance* that he could still crest pop music's latest waves.

With few exceptions, however, no one was listening. *Renaissance* sold better than *Come Live with Me*—it reached the charts for three weeks and peaked at #178—but Ray's plight as a hit maker had gone beyond a slump. He was firmly parked on the bench, watching the game from the sidelines. Decca was disappointed in its deal with Ray and began to doubt that it would renew Crossover's contract.

▐▌▐▐▌▐▌▐▌▐▐▌▌

After a break-in show at LA's Music Center, the gang gathered for the '75 tour, the first leg to Europe. "I know you're gonna want to buy cameras and gifts while we're over there," Edgar Willis, now the road manager, told the fellows. "So I'm loaning anybody who wants $500, but let's do it now, because I don't want you pestering me overseas." He got, as usual, numerous takers. Having a wad of American greenbacks in one's pocket was a comforting feeling in countries where the natives were friendly but the languages unspeakable, the food inedible, and the money a joke. European hotels were either cramped and smelly or vast and drafty. In one German monstrosity, James Clay unhooked a tapestry from a corridor wall to wrap himself in for warmth. At breakfast he told everybody, "I found out where they store the blankets!"

Everywhere, however, the entourage was greeted with respect, the music with rapturous applause. At an outdoor concert in Le Havre, John Bryant could feel the band clicking, and he let himself go into the music as never before. Afterward Ray's valet told

Bryant the boss wanted to see him. Remembering the lecture about "What'd I Say," Bryant entered the dressing room nervously. "Have a seat, John," said Ray. Bryant sat down on a little two-seat bench. Ray sat on it too, squeezing Bryant against a wall and giving him no chance to escape. "John . . ." said Ray. Bryant had no idea what was coming next. "I really liked the way you played tonight. I always want to hear you play that way." Then he gave the dumbfounded drummer a raise.

Back in the United States, the tour fell into its regular cycle, the apex of which was the golden moment in Ray's room at six P.M. every Sunday when they got paid. Willis handed Ray the checks, drawn on Chase Manhattan Bank, and he handed them on with a brief word: "Ah, Ernie, how you doing, everything all right?" For newcomers this might be their only offstage contact with Ray for weeks at a time. Some Sunday nights, however, Phil Guilbeau got the old 4-5-6 game going in the aisle of the Buzzard, and soon Ray and everybody were on their knees or hanging over the seats, whooping over each roll of the dice. If Ray won, it was tough luck for the rest: he gladly scooped up the money that he had just paid out.

The "hippie" wave in pop culture swept through the band, the blacks growing their hair into bushy Afros, the whites sporting ponytails and beards, and everybody stashing a few joints in instrument cases. In the Buzzard, no longer brand-new, some of the gang got careless, slopping food and drink on the seats. A few fellows even refused to bathe until everybody started holding their noses and complaining. None of this suited Joe's fastidious style, and he fought back with new and newly enforced rules: No pot, no food, and no drinking on the plane; no ragged blue jeans and T-shirts anywhere, anytime. Lest the old rule of being in the theater a half hour before curtain be scoffed at in the lax new era, Joe stationed the road manager at the door with a stopwatch. Anybody not there at seven-thirty on the dot got a fifty-dollar fine.

Yet two decades after rock 'n' roll had supposedly killed the big bands, the Ray Charles Orchestra was not a lone survivor. Count Basie, Lionel Hampton, Woody Herman, Buddy Rich, and others still had big bands on the road, playing the same clubs, concert halls, and festivals as Ray and the gang. Many of the older fellows hopped between one ensemble and another, and for youngsters like John Bryant, working for Ray was a conscious choice between various big bands who would have been glad to have them. Playing for Ray had two big advantages: Ray, a singing star, paid better than nonsinging leaders, and Ray had a plane, while the other bands humped by bus. On the other hand, the jazz bands offered more challenging charts and more featured solos than Ray's star-centered pop. "To play with Ray, you had to be good enough to play with Count Basie," Bryant explained, "but Count Basie spoke through his band; Ray's band *served* Ray. He was the focus."

Ray's better pay in the mid-70s meant $500 a week—more and steadier than most of the group could have made from gigging in their hometowns. Bachelors, like room-mates Bryant and Tussing, found Ray's pay good-to-lavish; married fellows like Tony Mathews found it a squeeze. The kicker for everybody was that, aside from transportation, Ray Charles Enterprises paid no expenses; the band members sprang for their own room and board. This cut Ray's costs and paperwork, yet sometimes left the fellows on the street at midnight, stuck with either paying the tab at the fancy hotel where Ray and Joe stayed or hunting up someplace cheaper. The solution was the rooming list. If someone signed up, the company would reserve him a room for the first night at Ray and Joe's hotel; the next day he could go to the Econolodge down the road.

The system worked reasonably well, and with the old standbys of staying with relatives and ghosting extra sleepers into a room, the fellows and ladies got by. Yet many in the entourage felt undercurrents of meanness from the two chiefs of Ray Charles Enterprises that soured day-to-day life on the road. Joe openly scorned musicians as riff-raff; a hotel clerk once showed one of the fellows a letter from him that said, in effect: Don't give rooms to the band, they have a reputation for stealing. Ray projected a distant, disdainful attitude to the band members, "like we were cattle," one put it. He could be cheap for no reason. If a promoter laid out a dressing room buffet, Ray always had it taken away. "Honey, if you give it to them once," he'd say, "they're gonna expect it every time." Once a hotel in Acapulco gave the band complimentary rooms and service, and the gang had a grand time lying on the beach, drinking margaritas from coconut shells. Then Edgar Willis told Ray about it, and he called a band meeting. "Everybody knows you don't get shit for free out here with me," Ray lectured the group; on their next paychecks, they found themselves docked for hotel fees on those days.

The older men had worn life on the road down to a livable nub. They neither complained nor enthused, and after the gigs they took it easy in their rooms, eating fried chicken out of buckets, drinking Jack Daniel's, smoking cigarettes, and watching TV. The young men, in contrast, complained about everything, loved the music, and after the gigs headed out to the local blues and jazz clubs to sit in, meet girls, and tell them, "Hi, I play with Ray Charles." Yet the younger fellows respected the veterans and learned from them. "Leroy had seen it from top to bottom," Bryant remembered. "Whatever Leroy said went." Ken Tussing sat next to Count Basie alumnus Henry Coker, nicknamed "Big Nasty." "Henry didn't say much, but that's where I got my education, in music and in dealing with life, how to conduct myself with other people," Tussing said.

If one liked the life, there was a lot to like: days and nights of camaraderie, the sparkling music, and silly moments like the time plump Vernita got stuck on a tiny French elevator with heavyweights Leroy Cooper and Joe Rendozzo. "Don't worry,

Sister Vernita," cried Joe as the elevator creaked up to the *sixième étage,* "we're drunk and we don't care!" Little sayings and gags ran through the gang, goosed along by jokers like Leroy. For years, if he came into a room where a fellow and lady happened to be together, Leroy would say, "Oh, 'scuse me, 'scuse me!" with a ribald wink, and that was enough to throw everyone into stitches of laughter.

Sex loomed large among the pleasures of the road. Between Ray, the Raelets, and the band (not to speak of local liaisons along the way), there existed a rolling sexual dynamic that stopped short of free love but embraced crisscross and serial fidelities. Ray was the dynamic's primary instigator. The men called him "The Creeper" for the way he felt his way along the walls of hotel corridors from one lady's room to another. When a new Raelet joined the tour, Ray would call her room, pretend he had dialed the wrong number, but then say, "Since I got you on the phone, why don't you come up? We can talk about a few things." Most ladies knew what to expect, and few refused. "Brother Ray has sex appeal, that's all there is to it," said Dorothy Berry. "He loves women and women love him. For one thing, Ray is *built,* and he's handsome, energetic, and a delight to be with."

Countless nights on the road Ray ended up, mellowed by gin and a well-rolled joint, in bed with one of the ladies. Yet he was so busy with so many that even his favorites were often alone. Ken Tussing had an arrangement with one lady for nights she wasn't with Ray. If she was free, she'd call him up and ask, "Whatcha doing?" "Just mowin' the lawn," he'd reply, meaning that he was free too and would leave his door open for her. Had Ray found out that he was "tampering with the goodies," as the fellows called it, Tussing figured he would have lost his job. "Ray was clever," remembered Leroy Cooper. "If one of his ladies didn't answer her phone, he'd call different guys' rooms early in the morning and say, real fast, 'Hey, lemme speak to Betty!' You're bleary, so you hand the phone to her, and he starts yelling, 'What the hell you doing in his room?' "

Sex on the road could have a sour side. Ray made his advances on one new lady singer, and she rebuffed him in no uncertain terms. Soon the rumor spread through the band that she was a lesbian. The truth of that remained in doubt, but it was soon obvious to everybody that Ray disliked her. One night she sang a note off-key. Ray stopped the whole band and told her over the mike exactly what she had done wrong. He made the band play the passage over and over, shouting, "Repeat, repeat!" at the poor woman, who turned red and teary, too humiliated and confused to know what to do. People in the audience looked at one another in disbelief; a few of the fellows started snickering. A trumpeter (who wished to remain nameless) sat frozen in his seat, disgusted by Ray's cruelty and by his own inability to break stage etiquette and protest on her behalf. The singer was from Houston, and just before the band played there, Ray fired her to keep her from having a triumph in her hometown. The trumpeter found an excuse to give his notice soon after.

⊞⊞⊞⊞⊞

As the '75 tour rolled on through the summer, John Bryant quit, feeling that he had learned what he'd come to learn. When Bryant went to Ray's room to give notice, he found him in his boxer shorts, looking softer without his dark glasses. "John, I just gave you a raise," Ray protested, taken aback by Bryant's decision. But when he realized Bryant wouldn't change his mind, he turned cold. "As I left," Bryant recalled, "I sensed Ray thinking, 'Shit, another drummer out the door, now I gotta get a new one and break him in.' But he'd done it before, and he wasn't going to cry about me long."

After an early-fall swing through the South, the gang took off across the Pacific to Japan, Singapore, Australia, and New Zealand. One concert became an album, *Live in Japan,* and that night they were magnificent, playing big-band jazz as hot and loose as it gets. On "Am I Blue" Johnny Coles wrapped filigree trumpet lines around Ray's voice with a sublime tenderness. "Johnny Coles, ladies and gentlemen," Ray said at the end, moved to tears. "It's all right, Johnny." They extended the bluesy "Feel So Bad" into an endless vamp, the band laying down long, sinuous riffs, and Ray preaching and screeching above them, growling and howling like a banshee, like an angel, like a man possessed by music. The driving beat pushed the normally reserved Japanese over the edge, and they started clapping on the backbeat. "Now, that's it!" Ray whooped, laughing. "That's soul music! Keep it going, I *like* it!"

They got home in December. Clifford Solomon opened his front door, and his dog Sniper started growling: Clifford had been gone so long, poor Sniper had forgotten his master. On New Year's Eve, the gang got together for a party at Harold Patton's house in Studio City, gathering in a big room lined floor-to-ceiling with his precious first editions. Toasting 1976, Leroy Cooper felt a familiar pang. "For nine months, I'd been getting a musical charge from hearing Ray," he recalled years later. "Sitting there night after night, hearing him sing, sometimes I'd be in tears and never let anybody know. Now I was headed back to Washington for the winter, and I'd get this sick feeling that I was going to be away from all that music for three long months to the spring."

24

Divorce
and Decline
Late 1970s

By the beginning of 1976, Ray and Della's marriage had at long last died. Ray stopped coming home to Southridge and took an apartment near Wilshire, west of downtown. Della, tired of trial separations and trying to talk it over, decided to talk to a lawyer about a divorce. As usual in stressful times, Ray kept busy. In January he made a "Soul of America" commercial for McDonald's, keyed to America's Bicentennial. In February ice skaters on the U.S. team danced to his "America" at the Olympics, televised to wide acclaim. This was the first sign that the dud of 1972 might have a life of its own. Ray instantly re-released the single and decided to feature "America" in his stage act. In March he won a Grammy, his tenth, for "Living for the City," proof that the industry, if not the public, was listening to his new work.

With April came sessions for a double album of *Porgy and Bess* produced by Norman Granz. Granz had recorded Gershwin's opera with Louis Armstrong and Ella Fitzgerald in the 50s and hoped to make a 70s equivalent. When he asked Ray to sing Porgy, Ray said yes and suggested Gladys Knight to sing Bess. Knight was at a career peak with her hit "Midnight Train to Georgia." Granz asked Art Cass of Buddah Records to release Knight to sing on the RCA album, and Cass was willing until Ray made his usual demand to own the masters. Cass wouldn't allow that, so Granz signed

British jazz singer Cleo Laine. Ray approved Laine—she had, he thought, the technical skill for the difficult role—but not getting his first choice soured him on the project. Through four days of recording, Granz found Ray unprepared and inattentive, forgetting entrances and lyrics. The two men had angry words but steamed ahead; an eighty-piece orchestra could not be canceled for a spat. Laine, thrilled to have a big American gig, stood in awe of Ray and tried too hard to do everything right. Ray dominated their duets, demanding retakes until he felt satisfied; Laine had to accept that take, no matter how she felt about it. The lavish boxed set came out in the fall and got respectful reviews, but *Porgy and Bess* sold poorly, the public sensing the lack of chemistry that made the ambitious album miss its mark.

The gang played a free show in a Los Angeles women's prison as a tour warm-up, then they boarded the Buzzard bound for Carnegie Hall on April 30. There they debuted what Harold Patton called "the 'America' bit": at the song's climax, Ray asked the audience, "Won't somebody help me sing this song?" The lights came up in the house, a huge American flag unfurled above the stage, and audiences, without fail, leapt to their feet and sang along, "America, America, God shed his grace on thee." The show bowled over critic Whitney Balliett. "Ray Charles is the noblest jazz singer since Billie Holiday," Balliett raved in *The New Yorker,* "a magic man, a hypnotist." "America," "Eleanor Rigby," "What'd I Say"—it didn't matter what Ray sang; what mattered was "the pine sap diction, the pained hoarseness, the guttural asides, the spidery staccato spray of notes."

On May 14, the day Ray and the gang flew to Baltimore for a show with Bob Hope on Preakness weekend, Della had her papers ready and, after twenty-one years of marriage, filed for divorce. In her petition, Della B. Robinson, "homemaker," declared that she had zero income and two minor children at home: eighteen-year-old David and fifteen-year-old Robert (Ray Jr., almost twenty-one, was living at and going to community college in Pasadena). In "Exhibit A" she listed twenty-four items of property "subject to disposition by the court," i.e., everything that Ray owned that she knew about: the Southridge house, 2107 West Washington, and the house on Hepburn, which they had never sold; commercial property in Lomita, two apartment houses in Los Angeles, "all outstanding shares" of Ray Charles Enterprises and its subsidiaries, Tangerine and Crossover Records, Tangerine Music, RPM Inc., Racer Music, and Racer Personal Management; also miscellaneous automobiles, certificates of deposit, copyrights, and master recordings; and a final item that reveals how well Della knew her husband's secretive nature: "Additional community property in the possession of the respondent, the exact nature and extent of which is unknown to the petitioner at this time."

Della also asked for $500-a-month child support for the youngest, Robert, and $7600 a month for herself. Her lawyer, E. Robert Lemkin of Santa Ana, wanted

$25,000 plus $5000 for court costs. Judge Nancy Watson ordered Ray to respond in court on June 7 and to bring with him his state and Federal tax returns and "all bank books, bank statements, canceled checks, and other documents of every kind."

Like many in his shoes, Ray stalled. A process server came to RPM three times but got stonewalled; "Respondent was not available," he wrote in his report, "and no one would say when he would be available." Ray's lawyer appeared in court on June 7 with no financial records. The judge granted a continuance until June 21 but issued a bench warrant for Ethel Rubin, "Custodian of Records of Tangerine Music." By then Ray did have his reply ready, a twelve-page "Respondent's Summary of the Case," prepared by attorney Herbert Hafif, but bearing Ray's mark from first to last. Ray's reply must be read with two or more grains of salt. He was both an angry, soon-to-be ex-husband eager to downplay his assets, and a businessman who knew how to make money while, for IRS purposes, minimizing his taxable income. Ray points proudly, for example, to paying $1 million tax from ABC's $2 million in 1973, but the $1 million he kept he doesn't mention—that has disappeared into what Della called the "additional community property . . . unknown to the petitioner." Its biases allowed for, however, Ray's reply provides a rare look into his finances, and it paints the worried self-portrait of an artist battling to maintain his place in a shrinking market.

"Ray Charles' name still enjoys instant and national recognition," the statement declared in its first paragraph, "but the prominence of his name conceals financial problems." From a peak in the mid-60s, Ray's taxable income had steadily declined to $137,000 in 1970 before plummeting to $11,000 in 1975. No one in the Robinson family seemed to realize that their income "consists entirely of Ray Charles' earnings"; they "continued to spend as if the respondent's peak earnings were still being enjoyed." To pay for their extravagance, Ray had been depleting savings accounts and endangering the community assets. So far in 1976, Ray figured he had earned about $12,000 a month, but with family expenses averaging $15,000, he was running a deficit.

Della, of course, was to blame. She knew that "her husband's earnings have fallen sharply in recent years." Her claims—$550 per month for clothes, $335 a month for Robert's orthodonture—were "far in excess of reasonable," "incredible," and "absurd." Della wanted $400 a month for auto payments when she "has not purchased an auto—and has no idea what a new one costs." The crowning insult: "Mrs. Robinson claims she requires $1000 per month for two full-time maids because paraphrenitis, 'adhesions,' keep her from doing housework—yet she *bowls* two nights a week!"

The long list of Ray's corporations should not make anyone think the respondent was wealthy, Ray's official response continued. Ray Charles Enterprises oversaw his touring, but "the tour rarely generates any income whatever." Tangerine Records had become "a wholly inactive concern," and Crossover Records was in debt, never having sold enough records to earn back Decca's advance. Racer Management "was and is an abject failure," and the commercial property and apartment buildings ran at a loss. Only publishing royalties provided steady income, but Tangerine Music, which had earned $39,000 in 1970, took in only $13,000 in 1974. The reason for the decline? "Ray Charles has passed his financial zenith as the musical public's tastes have changed from rhythm and blues to easy rock and mood music."

The judge heard both sides, held the case over for trial, and found temporary middle ground between the warring parties: $500-a-month child support; $3500 for Della, and she could stay in the house at Southridge. There, for the moment, the matter rested, while in private Della and Ray and the lawyers hammered out their separate futures. Significantly, not a word about the divorce got into the press, and days after the hearing, the B'nai B'rith gave Ray its "Man of the Year" award at a splashy benefit at the Beverly Wilshire Hotel. The public relations shell that Joe and Ray had created in the late 60s withstood its first major test.

After a summer swing through Europe, the gang got back to LA by September, and as they played Nevada and the West Coast, Ray began another self-portrait, this one more reflective. In the spring a jazz journalist from Dallas, David Ritz, had peppered RPM with phone calls and Braille telegrams. A former academic and an ardent Ray Charles fan, Ritz wanted to write Ray's autobiography as the "as told to" writer. Slowly Ritz made his way past Joe's initial rebuffs, and when Ray heard about the project, it intrigued him. He had sketched his life many times in interviews, but he had never thought of taking the time to dig into memory and tell all that he knew of his own story. "Would I be hurting myself?" he asked himself. "Would I be hurting anyone else? Did I really have anything to hide? . . ." Answering no to his doubts, Ray decided to go ahead. He was a hard man to catch, he warned Ritz, but he wanted to be caught. "It'll get done," Ray assured him. "*Gonna* get done. And if we do it good, well, it'll be a motherfucker."

Ritz and Ray began meeting two or three times a week at RPM, talking in the studio long past midnight, the tape machines humming in the background like faraway surf. Ritz was interested in Ray's music, but a veteran of Freudian analysis, he also wanted to dig below the surface into intimate psychosexual material. At first Ray found it hard to talk about himself, but soon they began to click. One early revelation: Ray had been fusing the memories of Retha and Mary Jane in his mind for years. "Ray kept talking about his mama," Ritz recalled. "But I said I kept getting the feeling of two characters, a tough mama and a gentle mama." "Let me give that some thought," Ray replied. A week later he called Ritz: he had realized that the mama who disciplined him and the mother who gave him candy were two different women.

Ritz traveled with the band—"David lived the life," remembered Leroy Cooper—

and sat silent in a corner at recording sessions. Ray could turn from Ritz with a curt "I'm not ready for you," or sink into silences Ritz didn't dare break, yet Ray let the writer into his life. Ritz heard Ray sweet-talking his lady friends on the phone: "Oh, yes, sugar . . . it was very beautiful the other night . . . you got that right . . . have mercy, Jesus!" When Ray's pot dealer came over, Ritz saw Ray crumble the weed between his fingers and smell it for potency, then weigh it on a scale with Braille numbers to make sure he got full weight. A pot smoker himself at the time, Ritz admired the thick joints Ray rolled, yet he couldn't keep up Ray's smoking pace, and Ray's gin-and-coffee floored him.

Their deal was straightforward: Ray and Ritz would divide author's royalties 60–40, and with the bigger share went total control: not a word would go into the final draft that Ray didn't approve. Yet Ritz's questions and interests influenced the course of their conversations. He went to Greenville and St. Augustine to see the places Ray described; he interviewed Quincy Jones and others for stories to jog Ray's memory. Ray, on the other hand, told Ritz not to go to Seattle, and he didn't want him to talk to Jeff Brown or Della. Ray also agreed with Ritz that only the two of them and the editor at Prentice-Hall should read the manuscript before publication. That cut Joe Adams out of the loop, souring him on the project, but the co-authors pushed on as 1976 drew to a close, Ritz coming home many nights at dawn with hours of tapes to transcribe.

The tour made a last swing through the South before heading up to Lincoln Center in December. One night in Birmingham, Alabama, Mable John heard a voice on-stage saying, "Mable, go home." She looked around, thinking the other ladies must have heard it too, but when she realized they'd heard nothing, she knew that it must be a call from the Lord. She called Susaye Green to tell her, and Susaye replied, "Mayberry, you're losing your mind." But the call grew stronger, and when she was sure, Mable told Ray that this would be her last tour. Ray knew better than to try to change her mind. Supporting herself by managing a group of music-publishing companies, Mable went to Crenshaw Christian Center School, and in time she earned her doctorate and started a mission to feed and shelter the homeless in Los Angeles. Through the decades, she stayed in close touch with Ray, going to him often for business advice. Whenever Mable presented an idea to Ray, he'd play devil's advocate. "What's your plan B?" he'd ask. "Remember, John, you got to have a plan B, because plan A don't always work."

"There comes a point in nearly every artist's career," a wise old record executive once said, "when he or she stops selling records. They may still be great, but the market moves past them." By 1977 Ray had reached that point. He recorded through the winter as usual, but for the first time in thirty years, he had no record company eager for his work. Decca was no longer interested; Larry Newton thought there was nothing more he could do. Ray had to go shopping, and it wasn't easy. Hitless for a decade, Ray had come close, in the days of disco and David Bowie, to becoming an anachronism— though Donna Summer's sexy moans on her smash "Love to Love You Baby" strongly recalled "What'd I Say."

Ray, of course, breathed defiance at the world. He had nothing to learn from groups like the Rolling Stones, he told *Downbeat*'s Pete Welding in a long, angry interview; he understood rock perfectly, but it was not "my kind of thing." Young players "don't take the time to really learn their instruments," he said, and Top 40 radio was "sterile . . . what you're going to hear all day is basically the playlist. . . . That's sick." He was willing to try synthesizers to keep up, but always and forever, "I'm still me." No, an artist couldn't ignore commercial pressure, but "the point is not to let it control you. You must control it." Nobody, he said for the hundredth time, knew what record would become a hit:

> What you do know is that you put your all into it. And as long
> as you do that, if you're really honest with yourself . . . I don't
> give a shit what happens. You can't do *no* more! So there ain't
> no point in worrying about trying to keep up with what you did
> last year.

In shopping for a label, Ray spoke early on with Ahmet Ertegun and Jerry Wexler. They were still at Atlantic, but the feisty 50s indy could scarcely be recognized in the 70s corporate giant. Atlantic had scored spectacular success with the white pop-rock of Eric Clapton, the Rolling Stones, and Led Zeppelin, and had been bought by Warner Bros. in a deal that made the two producers multimillionaires. Now Atlantic had offices at Rockefeller Center; Ahmet was there, Jerry had his base in Miami. The three men felt one another out. Ray sweet-talked. Atlantic had always been his favorite company, he told them, they had been so good to him. Ahmet and Jerry were tempted. They knew Ray's recent track record, yet they still admired Ray and felt a nostalgia for the closeness they once shared. Jerry hoped Ray would come south to Muscle Shoals, Alabama, where he was producing R&B based on Ray's small-band style. "I got my own ideas, cousin," Ray replied abruptly, and after that he dealt with Ahmet. When they got down to brass tacks, Ahmet found Ray had learned a lot in twenty years. Ray would own the masters and Crossover would get its logo on the jacket with Atlantic's; those points were non-negotiable. After debating every nickel allowed for promotion and distributor returns, Ray signed a multi-album deal. Ahmet wanted to hear tracks as soon as possible.

Through the winter, Ray taped a variety of TV shows, flying to London for a special with Cleo Laine and doing the Mike Douglas and Dinah Shore shows in LA. These were a few in a stream of television appearances—*Hollywood Squares, Cher, Midnight Special,* and *Sesame Street*—that, in sum, made Ray one star in the galaxy of electric media performers known to some degree by everyone in the culture. One could debate whether Ray was more or less famous than Mary Tyler Moore, but he certainly held an honored place in the late-70s galaxy, a veteran who had moved the public many times. One was always glad when "Hit the Road Jack" came on the radio, and if Ray were on Johnny Carson, that night one might stay up a little later to catch him. Ray's media omnipresence didn't make the public buy his new records, but it sold tickets on the road, kept his old hits earning money, and cushioned him against the knocks of every day. "I wish I had a command of language sufficient to describe how it makes you feel inside to know that you have people all over the world who really love what you do," Ray told Welding in the same interview, "especially as long as I've been in this. So you know it's not an overnight thing that's going to fade."

〔ㅣㅣㅣㅣㅣㅣㅣㅣㅣㅣ〕

At a benefit show in March 1977 at the Dorothy Chandler Pavilion attended by Jacqueline Kennedy Onassis, a young man ran up from the audience to center stage and hugged Ray forcibly, knocking off his glasses and rumpling his clothes. Ray's valet dragged the man away as he yelled, "You will *see,* you will *see!*" Though the man said later he had been trying to cure him with his "healing hands," Ray had taken it as a surprise attack, and backstage he was visibly distraught, pacing about and talking volubly. He almost expected this kind of thing in some funky club, he said in nervous bursts, but never at a high-society benefit! It would take more than one scary night, however, to put Ray off performing, and in April the tour began again.

Ray had a new Buzzard for the gang this year, and Joe again went to town designing the cabin interior. Now *absolutely* no food and drink were allowed on board—except for Ray, who had a hot plate in his quarters to warm up his favorite tomato soup. Dorothy Berry became the new leader of the Raelets, but Ray lost Leroy Cooper after twenty years. Over the winter, Leroy got a job playing soprano sax in a Dixieland group at Disney World and moved with his wife Clemmie to Orlando—a move that Cooper later credited with saving his life. "I was drinking out there, chain-smoking cigars, and my weight was up," he said. "Now I don't smoke, don't drink, and my weight is down. Some of my best friends never stopped, and they've passed away." Andy Ennis became leader briefly. When he and Ray differed over a Raelet named Linda, Clifford Solomon stepped up to the post, where he remained for a decade.

By the end of April, as the tour played through the South, Ray and Della reached financial agreement on their divorce. In essence, Della would get the Southridge house, $380,000 in cash and $3500 a month support, $500 a month for Robert, plus a $150,000 trust fund for all three boys, and she could keep her 1971 Cadillac Eldorado. Ray would get the RPM building, the apartment houses and commercial property, and everything else. All the corporations would still be solely Ray's, and so would be all earnings and increase in wealth from that day forward. The agreement left Della well off for life, yet like many homebody wives of self-made men, she took the proffered plush sofa and gave away half-interest in a moneymaking machine. In June they got their interlocutory decree; six months after that, Ray and Della were no longer man and wife.

After the divorce, Ray's awards and gold albums disappeared from the grand staircase at Southridge, leaving faded patches on the plaster. Della kept bowling and kept running the house and family. Little Robert was still a kid hunting for snakes in the bushes near the house, but David, the middle son, had grown away from his sports-league pals and toward a wilder crowd; Della worried about him. She converted Ray's old den and an entertainment room into a makeshift apartment for Ray Jr. to live in with his girlfriend, pretty Duana Chenier. Ray Jr. was getting C's in his business courses at Whittier College, and Ray kept him on a short allowance—he took Duana to McDonald's on their first date with coupons that Della gave him. Ray Jr. wanted to work for his dad, but father and son seldom saw each other, and fought when they did. Then young Ray would complain to Duana that his father was cold and selfish and that he'd never work for him. Duana didn't care that her boyfriend was Ray Charles' son; she wanted her Ray to call himself Ray Robinson and make it on his own. Yet despite many disappointments, he kept calling himself Ray Charles Jr. and hoping that Ray and Joe would give him something important to do.

Ray's extracurricular family was also growing. Arlette Kotchounian bore him a son, Vincent, and a second French lady friend had given him a daughter a few years before that—the two women had no knowledge of each other's existence. In Tampa, Evelyn, now twenty-seven, had become a nurse but still liked expensive gifts from her daddy. Once when Ray was performing in Florida, he called Larry Newton with an emergency: he needed $10,000 right away. "Why?" Newton asked. "Help me, Larry," said Ray, "I gotta get my kid a car." Newton called Paramount's Jacksonville office, they issued Ray a check, and Evelyn got her car.

In the spring, Ray sent in the tracks for *True to Life,* the first Atlantic album of the new era, and Ahmet didn't like them. Both the songs and Ray's big-band/strings sound seemed fatally old-fashioned in a market dominated by the disco craze. Only the cover of Johnny Nash's reggae hit, "I Can See Clearly Now," had a chance, Ahmet said; Ray should drop three or four tracks and work up new ones with contemporary pop producers like Curtis Mayfield or Philadelphia's Kenny Gamble and Leon Huff. Ray had no intention of agreeing but said fine, with a proviso: "The producer must send me the songs, and if I like them, I'll give him the keys I want to sing them in, and he'll do the rest." "We want you to work with the producer," Ahmet replied. If he did, Ray argued, he'd end up producing it himself. When the young producers begged off ("I grew up on you. How am I going to tell you what to sing?" one told Ray), Ahmet gave up and released *True to Life* as Ray turned it in.

True to Life is a magnificent album, yet Ertegun had a point: in the era of "The Hustle," it was an anomalous disc. Ray was clearly trying to be commercial, and he included something for every taste: a soaring anthem, "Be My Love," and a comic blues, "Game Number Nine"; a Beatles classic, "Let It Be," and a Gershwin classic, "How Long Has This Been Going On." Yet the subtle flavors of *True to Life*'s long, rich tracks reveal an artist creating beauty on his own terms, pleasing the public, he hopes, but pleasing himself first. And they reveal Ray digging ever deeper into American music. He transforms "Oh, What a Beautiful Morning" from a revered classic into a hot jazz waltz at the same time that, with unsurpassed delicacy, he brings out the inner harmony of Richard Rodgers' melody and Oscar Hammerstein's lyric. "The sounds of the earth are like music," Ray intones with utmost conviction. "The sounds of the earth are like music."

When the gang got back to LA from a gig at New York's Belmont Racetrack in September, David Ritz had digested endless transcripts into the first hundred pages of the autobiography. He delivered them, typed in Braille, to his co-author, then watched nervously as Ray ran his fingers over the bumps, grunting from time to time, "Oh yeah?" or "Hmm, don't think so." Ritz, Ray said as gently as he could, had gotten the facts right but the tone wrong. For weeks, they went over the text word for word, Ray pointing out what he did and didn't like. Ritz had worked chronologically, but Ray said no: "When I'm hot on some subject, let me go, even if it's out of order." Ray wanted to tell his life as he saw it, and Ritz didn't push him to make his memory jibe with other accounts or with the calendar. On the other hand, Ray began to understand what Ritz meant by a "literary voice," a lyric interpretation of his speaking voice. "Oh, this is how we're doing it? Great!" Ritz recalled him saying. "Then he'd point out an awkward phrase, suggest a new metaphor. He played with the rhythm of his speech and tremendously improved the text."

Yet when Ritz turned in the manuscript, entitled *Brother Ray,* its four-letter words and frankness about drugs shocked the Prentice-Hall editors, and they rejected it unless drastically revised. Ritz felt *Brother Ray's* raw qualities suited its subject, and Ray agreed. "Stick to your guns," he told Ritz, "I ain't taking nothing out." Ritz' agent succeeded in reselling the book to Dial Press for publication in 1978.

In October Ray and the gang left for a long Asian tour. *True to Life* came out and, boosted by Atlantic/WB's blanket distribution, got to #78, better than any album since *Message from the People.* In November Ray made an effective TV appearance on *Saturday Night Live.* Then just two years old and with its bright first cast, John Belushi, Dan Aykroyd, Bill Murray, and Gilda Radner, SNL had captured a huge youthful audience for its madcap satires. Belushi and Aykroyd, two R&B fans, convinced producer Lorne Michaels to ask Ray to be a musical guest. When he did, Ray responded, "I've been watching your show, but I don't just want to be on it, I want to be the host."

Michaels agreed, and the result became one of the best shows in SNL's annals. Ray was relaxed and witty throughout, and he worked his way with aplomb through the skits, most of them blind jokes that managed to be funny. *"They* think," Ray whispered to the audience at one point about Belushi and Murray, "that *I* think that I'm in Carnegie Hall." Ray reunited his 50s little band for the show, and there on a stage stood Phil Guilbeau, Marcus Belgrave, Hank Crawford, Fathead Newman, and Leroy Cooper, laying it down hot and smooth through a medley of Ray's Atlantic hits. The longest skit was set in the mid-50s, Ray an R&B singer with a great song he wanted to record. No, said his manager, a white group has to record it first, and the cast sang "What'd I Say" as the Young Caucasians, a smiley-face group of white teenagers, their melodies and movements stiff and sexless. Then Ray, the Raelets, and the fellows played it with the funk that made it famous. "Sorry, Ray," said Garrett Morris, playing Ray's manager. "That'll never make it."

The gang played Avery Fisher Hall on December 19 on a bill with Milt Jackson. Ray and Milt did a duet on "Merry Christmas" as an encore, the crowd loved it, and the tour wound to a close.

At RPM, meanwhile, Ray's studio board had grown to twenty-four tracks, and in the winter of 1978 Ray used them all to record his next Atlantic album, *Love and Peace.* This time Ray tried for the disco sound, and long after the session musicians had gone home, Ray labored on the tapes with engineer Bob Gratts. Compared with noisy David Braithwaite, Gratts was a quiet fellow, and he and Ray spent hour after painstaking hour lifting horn tracks that Ray liked from one take and synching them with the rhythm track he liked on another take. To capture disco's swirl of timbres, Ray overlaid synthesizer tracks many layers deep, but their electronic edge still made him nervous. "Bring it down, bring it down!" he kept telling Gratts as they mixed. "Damn, that synth sound cuts through everything." Work as he might, Ray could not bring *Love and Peace*'s weak songs to life, and the album remains Ray's dullest, forgettable first to last. Tangerine Music owned a piece of five of the tunes, but it's unlikely the copyrights earned much money. Ahmet accepted the album reluctantly, and on release in the fall, it sank like a stone.

Not surprisingly: *Saturday Night Fever* by the Bee Gees set pop music's pace in 1978, and *Love and Peace* had about one-tenth of that album's snap and sparkle. Current stars had been outselling Ray for years, but for his music to be duller than the current hits was something new. In the last years of the 70s, the forward drive of confidence that had carried Ray through decades of ups and downs seemed finally to falter. Professional as always, Ray kept plugging, and the general public saw the same Ray Charles; yet those around him noticed a change. The restless anger that had always marked the man entered a new, more bitter phase.

The divorce played a role in this turn in Ray's life, as did his approaching fiftieth birthday; memories stirred up by *Brother Ray* may have contributed as well. A major factor was the frustration at being stuck on the sidelines of a game he had once dominated. Ray still longed for hits; as far as he was concerned, any track could be the next "I Can't Stop Loving You." Yet release after release died at birth. Touring had always been tedious, but playing half-empty Holiday Inns became a grating, unbearable bore. As '78 began, the United High Blood Pressure Foundation "roasted" Ray to raise money, but on the night of the show, the Coconut Grove was embarrassingly empty. The celebrities carried on undaunted—Stevie Wonder said Ray had everything except good looks, "but that's just another blind man's opinion"—yet the low turnout nettled Ray. "I just want to say to the ones who are not here," Ray said when it came his turn to speak, "we were trying to tell you, but you weren't here to hear us."

In May, the tour reached the Chateau De Ville, a pretentious supper club in Framingham, Massachusetts. The white middle-aged audience sat politely on their hands opening night while, onstage and over the mike, Ray chewed out the band and the club's soundmen for numerous goofs. The next day a reporter from Boston's *Real Paper* found Ray in a volatile mood, lurching from one emotion to another. He knew record companies were looking for Ray Charles imitators, Ray said, singers "a little lighter than me" who, though "only half as good," could earn "twice the bread." Was it hard to keep going, the reporter asked. "That's right," Ray replied. "There's times when all you have left between you and madness or even death is a kind of empty will." He would not let himself become bitter; that would be "self-defeating." But:

> I ain't no fool. I'm gonna let you know that I know what's hap-
> pened to me. . . . Don't think just 'cause you see me smilin' that
> I'm out of tune. If you listen close you'll know that I'm alert to
> what's been done to me, you'll hear the dark note, and if you're
> very alert, you'll pay it some mind.

Harold Patton watched Ray grow more irritable and demanding onstage and off. "We'd get down to the bus at 6 A.M.," Patton recalled. "Then we'd wait two hours for Ray because he was the boss and he didn't give a shit." Tony Mathews thought Ray was becoming "cold and dead inside." Another fellow called him "almost friendly, like a caged eagle." Valet Vernon Troupe defended his boss' surliness. "Ray's just the kind of person, you shove him in the corner, and he'll cut off his nose to spite his face." Ray had always been touchy about the band asking for raises; now, with alimony payments due every month, Ray lashed out at anyone who dared bring up it. "Do you realize I have fifty people I have to pay every week, twenty-five on the road, twenty-five back in the office?" he shouted one night at Johnny Coles. "I don't have money to throw away! Ain't gonna be no lilies of the field around me!"

The atmosphere in the band got so tense that fellows started "coming and going like a revolving door," Clifford Solomon recalled. Solomon—"Little Jack Daniel's," Aaron Williams called him—had grown into the job of bandleader, earning the respect and affection once accorded Leroy Cooper. Yet in these more trying times, he was caught between two stools: begging fellows who wanted to quit to hang on until he could replace them, and trying to talk some common sense and compassion into Ray. "Every time a guy leaves, RC, you gotta pay to fly somebody else in," Solomon argued in his quiet voice. "You gotta buy him a new uniform, check him out, and rehearse him. Every new guy is costing you time and money." Ray reacted by blaming Joe—"God-dammit, Joe, leave the guys alone, let Sol deal with 'em"—but little changed.

Ray's women sensed his deepening anger. Arlette Kotchounian thought that Ray had started to play "like a robot." Susaye felt Ray's problem was that he didn't know how to top himself. "What are your dreams? What do you have left to desire?" she asked him. "I don't have any dreams," he replied. With Ruth, Ray sometimes exploded about old losses, telling her how Milt Shaw and Jeff Brown had robbed him. In one mood, he'd be pissed that Frank Sinatra made more money than he did, in another declare that if he had been stronger, he could've pulled his brother George out of the washtub. "Ray was bitter about everything," Robinson recalled. "Especially about being blind. He'd deny it, but he felt trapped by blindness. With sight, he figured, he could have been a lawyer, an engineer, or become a bigger star."

As music business pros themselves, Ruth and Susaye worried that Ray, angry at being ignored, would isolate himself from current trends. They watched how quickly Stevie Wonder adapted to changes in pop style, how Quincy Jones worked the party circuit to line up clients—he had just signed to produce Michael Jackson. Ray was the opposite. He never went to parties, and he played his Billie Holiday and Oscar Peterson records over and over. "He listened only to what pleased him." Susaye said. "And that meant Ray got caught in a time warp." Ruth begged him to let Lionel Richie of the Commodores, on top with "Three Times a Lady," produce him. Richie was eager for the job, but Ray didn't know or care who Lionel Richie was. He wasn't interested.

Brother Ray came out in the fall of 1978, and its positive reviews and strong sales provided an upbeat note in the general gloom. *Brother Ray* is a major and essentially truthful self-portrait, Ray's voice jumping out of the text in a lively, salty fashion. Music, unsurprisingly, emerges as the great passion of his life. In the course of roaming over his past, Ray often pauses to list his inspirations (Artie Shaw, Hank Williams, Muddy Waters, Charlie Parker, Aretha Franklin, etc., etc.), a catalog that paints its own portrait of his musical roots. Ray also admits that he's a tightfisted businessman, and despite saying he's a "shy" man who insists on privacy, he strides into frank descriptions of his sex life. "Half the fun of fucking is watching a woman have an orgasm," he comments at one point; feeling two women making love at his "parties" had given him memories that he wouldn't trade "for a truckload of solid gold."

With a handful of mistakes—the Philadelphia bust, for example, came in '55, not '58—*Brother Ray* also contains minor airbrushing. Ray either doesn't know or hides that Retha had been Bailey and Mary Jane's ward—much about his earliest years, he writes, "remains mysterious." He makes his trek to Seattle from Tampa seem more heroic than it was by not mentioning that Gossie McKee had preceded him and prepared the way. The most revealing of Ray's biases is that *Brother Ray* has only one fully fleshed character: Brother Ray. Retha and Mary Jane are drawn in fair detail, and Fathead Newman and Quincy Jones are sketched, but Ahmet and Jerry, Jeff Brown, Larry Newton, Sid Feller, Leroy Cooper, and many more remain names of people who serve Ray, then disappear. One of the neglected minor characters, Joe Adams, read the book and summoned Ritz to his office. "I work for the man for twenty-five years, and that's all he has to say about me?" he shouted, hurling his copy against the wall. Ritz could only reply that *Brother Ray* came out the way Ray wanted it.

In Paris that November, a young French fan propelled himself into Ray's life, a fan whose enthusiastic devotion would have, in time, a rejuvenating effect on Ray's career. Jean-Pierre Grosz, a locksmith by trade, dabbled in the music business, and listening one day to a demo by a friend, Robert Fitoussi, he had an inspiration: Ray Charles could sing this song, and he, Jean-Pierre Grosz, would get it to him when he played La Salle Gaveau. Grosz knew that Ray stayed in Paris at either the Hilton or the George V. This time, he'd stay at the Hilton, Grosz figured: it was ten minutes closer to the gig. At the Hilton, Grosz passed himself off as a record company executive and installed a stereo system in Ray's suite, stocked the bar with Ray's favorite liquors, and left a note in Braille: "Welcome to Paris, Jean-Pierre."

At Orly, Grosz talked his way past airport security and milling TV crews and grabbed Ray's arm as soon as he touched the ground. "I hate to bother you, Mr. Charles," he said, "but I love your music, and I think my friend's music could fit your trip." "You got a tape?" asked Ray. Grosz gave him the demo, and Ray sped off in the limo. At the Hilton the room service waiters had gone on strike, so Grosz sat at the switchboard, and when Ray called down for breakfast, he dashed to a three-star delicatessen for platters of fresh fruit and sandwiches. At the Salle Gaveau, Grosz sent in his name and Ray came out to speak to him. "What are you doing, man?" asked Ray. "The food, the liquor, the stereo, it's too much! I just wanted to thank you." With that Ray turned around and disappeared.

Three days later Grosz was asleep when the phone rang. It was Ray's valet, Ron Boyd, calling from the George V.

"I thought you were in Germany," said Grosz.

"Ray woke up early this morning," said Boyd, "and told me, 'I'm going to Paris to see Jean-Pierre.' So get your ass over here." Grosz and Fitoussi rushed unshaven to the hotel. "What's on your mind?" Ray asked them over coffee.

"I know that your voice and Robert's will go perfectly together," said Grosz. "I hear a duet between the two of you."

"Can you and Robert be in my studio in Los Angeles on January second?" "What time?" said Grosz. "Come around ten o'clock in the morning," said Ray.

Two days into 1979, at ten on the dot, Grosz and Fitoussi got to RPM, and they started going through the songs with Ray. Fitoussi's high-pitched voice and Ray's raspy voice sounded good together, but after a few days, a call came from Paris saying that Fitoussi's mother had died. That stopped Grosz's project cold, yet he hung on in LA and, at the end of the month, invited Ray to a birthday party he threw for himself. Ray came and stayed for hours. As the party waned, Grosz cornered him on a sofa. "I'm talking to you as a fan," he said. "I don't understand why you struggle in the studio to engineer and mix everything. Why not let other people do it, people that you trust? Then you could come in and do what you want to do without spending days and nights on the buttons."

"I don't do that, Jean-Pierre," Ray replied, "because I never found anybody who could do it for me."

"Ray, I would like to do it for you one day," said Grosz.

"Okay," said Ray, "One day we'll do it together." Shortly afterward Grosz went back to Paris. He stayed in touch with Ray, but their friendship for the time being became dormant.

One of Fitoussi's songs, "Just Because," did get on *Ain't It So,* Ray's third Atlantic album. Ray again closeted himself in the studio with Bob Gratts, endlessly tinkering with his vocals and the mix until the moment—and Gratts never knew when it would be—that Ray called each track done. This time Ray's finicky precision paid off: *Ain't It So* returns from *Love and Peace*'s disco disaster to Ray's unique blend of songs and sounds both old and new. "Some Enchanted Evening," like *True to Life*'s "Oh, What a Beautiful Morning," stands as the album's masterpiece, Ray transforming the beloved classic from a romantic ballad into an irresistible rocker. Like the best of Ray's "themeless" albums, *Ain't It So* coheres despite its variety. While enjoying each song on its own, one can follow Ray and his woman from first meeting on "Some Enchanted Evening," through a half-dozen ups and downs to the happy ending, "Turn Out the Light and Love Me Tonight."

In March, the Georgia House of Representatives proclaimed "Georgia on My Mind" the state song and invited Ray to sing it at the capitol in Atlanta. Recognition from the state where he had been born unnoticed fifty years before moved Ray deeply, and the thunderous standing ovation from the packed chamber did much to perk up his spirits. *Ain't It So,* on the other hand, died ("uninspired selection of material," said *Billboard*). "I'm Ray Charles," he raged at Bob Gratts. "Who cares what they write in the paper? What matters is, the people working in the kitchen of the places I play, *they* like me."

Rudy Johnson, a tenor player with Gene Ammon's fat sound, came into the band when they hit the road in April. He found a band of five black guys, twelve white, but still no white Raelets; "they just don't have that sound," Dorothy Berry told him with a laugh. Rudy the rookie was thrilled to be touring through the States, Europe, and the Far East, yet for Ray and the veterans, '79 on the road was another dispiriting grind. Ray's audience was getting as gray as he was, and they didn't go out as much as they used to; one night in Memphis, seventy people showed up for the late show. Rock's huge electric sound systems made Ray's concert setup seem old-fashioned. Ray wanted one mike for his voice, one for the piano, and two for the Raelets; no more. "Even in coliseums, the band was never miked," recalled one of the fellows. "You could hear his voice and the piano, but the band sounded so thin, we felt we were playing for ourselves."

Harold Patton had survived thirteen years of good times and bad on the road with Ray, but as the decade dwindled to its close, he was ready to quit. Ray's shows, he thought, had become routine. Night after night they played the same songs in the same sequence. Sometimes Ray forgot the list and turned to the bass player to ask, "What the fuck am I singing next?" A few times he played the same song twice, the fellows looking at one another sideways but not saying a word.

The atmosphere in the band, Patton felt, had passed beyond nasty to mean. In Italy, a police team searched the gang for drugs. Fortunately, they found only Tony Mathews' vitamin pills and left as suddenly as they had come. Afterward, Johnny Coles was furious. "I know some of you motherfuckers are carrying," he announced in deadly tones, "but if anybody tries to hide their stash in my pocket, I'll kill him."

"Johnny, you're kidding," said Patton.

"Try me," said Coles.

Patton put in his notice effective the Monday after Thanksgiving. The band had a gig in Houston over Thanksgiving weekend, flying there from LA. Joe Adams told him that since Ray paid on Sunday, that would be his last day of work, so he couldn't fly back on the Buzzard on Monday.

"Bullshit," said Patton, but Ray supported Joe's position: only employees of Ray Charles Enterprises could fly on its plane. Patton figured that if he quit on the spot, he'd lose three days' pay, but the airfare back from Houston would cost that much. "I'm gone," he told Adams, taking his suitcase off the bus.

"What about your notice?" said Adams.

"Are you out of your mind?" Patton shouted in reply. "You think I'm gonna go to Texas, then spend my own money to come back when you guys are flying back Monday? No! Fuck you! That's why I'm leaving. You guys have stopped being a family." Patton stayed in Los Angeles and found a job at a company that made surfboards with sails. He needed quiet time, he realized, time to rest and lick his wounds.

The 1970s had been a punishing decade for Ray too, and he might have been wise to take a break to renew his spirit and repair defenses. To stop and rest, however, was not in the man's nature, and as always, Ray pushed onward. Dan Aykroyd and John Belushi asked him to play a cameo role in their new movie, *The Blues Brothers;* shooting began in December. In the winter he had a new album to make; Joe Adams was already mapping out the 1980 tour. For good or ill, the 70s were history; by hook or by crook, Ray was determined to make his mark on the clean slate of the 1980s.

PART VI

THE 1980s:
THE LONG COMEBACK

25

You have to ask yourself, "Why was I born? Was it just to die?" When you get down to the bottom line, that's the question. The important thing is to make the best of your life, to try to contribute something. You don't gain anything by giving up.

Ray Charles

Nashville
Early 1980s

At the beginning of the 1980s, Ray Charles had sunk to the lowest point of his mature career, his invisibility as complete as it would get. Pop music had passed into the hands of stars twenty or thirty years younger than he; many of their fans hadn't been born when "I Can't Stop Loving You" ruled the airwaves. Through the 80s, Ray had few hits, and his touring year shrank from nine to six months or less. His hair turned totally gray and his face became ever more creased and craggy. Yet in this decade Ray also staged an extraordinary comeback, and by its end, he had emerged from his lean years and become one of the electric media's most resonant icons, an artist known and loved for so long by so many that he seemed to preside over all of pop music as its wise grandpapa.

Ray succeeded in his comeback drive, first, because he refused to accept defeat; and second, because he diversified. Ray increased his television appearances in the 80s, sang duets with younger stars, started performing with symphony orchestras, and made a concerted effort to conquer country music—as well as continuing the record/road pattern that had defined his career since 1950. Ray's comeback also succeeded because in everything he did, he enriched his work with human content, never ceasing his quest to capture and convey the inmost essence of the music.

Shooting *The Blues Brothers* turned out to be an enjoyable few days on Chicago's South Side. Belushi and Aykroyd, big fans of Ray's, put him at ease on the set, and he romped through his bit as Ray of Ray's Music Exchange, from whom the two comedians, as black-hatted, black-suited, and black-shaded Jake and Elwood, buy instruments for their band. While they bargain, a little boy sneaks in to shoplift a guitar; blind Ray picks up his pistol and fires a warning shot inches above the kid's head. Jake and Elwood tell Ray he's trying to sell them a broken-down electric piano; his demonstration that it works fine becomes "Shake a Tail Feather," a dance number that gets the whole neighborhood kicking up its heels. Belushi and Aykroyd's car-chase comedy surrounds a heartfelt tribute to R&B; John Lee Hooker, James Brown, and Aretha Franklin also get flattering cameos. *The Blues Brothers* became enormously popular and continued Ray's introduction, begun on *Saturday Night Live,* to the younger generation as an older cat who is still cooler than cool.

That winter of 1980 Ray finished *At It Again,* his fourth album on Atlantic. A good if not great disc, *At It Again* appeared and disappeared like its predecessors. Ahmet was ready to call it quits, and so was Ray. He might like what he was doing on wax, but the fact was inescapable: nobody was interested. To rewin the mass record market, Ray realized, he needed a new plan.

Putting that pot on a back burner for the moment, Ray started something new: concerts with symphony orchestras. He had done a few such gigs in the 70s, one with the Los Angeles Philharmonic conducted by Zubin Mehta, but as the 80s began, he asked Sid to begin converting his record charts into a full concert program for a string and woodwind orchestra. Sid threw together a "cockamamie" assortment of tunes for a rushed debut in Atlanta, but he soon had a smooth selection—"Georgia," "Being Green," "For Mama," and the centerpiece, "America"—that for the first time allowed Ray to create onstage the cushioned sound of so many of his records. In May, Ray performed with the Boston Pops conducted by John Williams; PBS broadcast the concert that summer as an "Evening at Pops," and Ray's symphony venture was launched.

In years to come, Ray played countless of these "string gigs" in the winter off-season and spotted throughout the year with established city orchestras or freelance ensembles gathered by local music contractors. Many were private affairs, corporate conventions and the like, held at resort hotels; Leroy Cooper played clarinet among the woodwinds at dozens of string gigs in and around Orlando. Joe Adams loved string gigs because they required only five people (Ray, Sid to conduct, and a guitar, bass, and drums rhythm section), making the logistics much simpler than those of the big band. At $50,000 a performance, they also proved highly profitable. Ray found switching from horns to strings an enjoyable change of pace. "The feelings, the grooves, *are* different," he said in explanation. "You can't turn a jazz band into a symphony or a symphony into a jazz band. But I'm a *musician,* and whatever I'm playing, country, blues, jazz, or classical, I adapt myself to the mode that I'm dealing with at the time."

Sid, nearing retirement age, found he enjoyed touring as Ray's conductor—the jokes backstage before going on, the rush of performing for a crowd, and coming off with Ray, both dripping wet in their tuxedos, and sharing sloppy hugs. He watched Ray chew out many an orchestra when they were slow on the uptake, but he and Ray had angry words at only one out of hundreds of gigs. Ray had requested a change in the orchestral phrasing to match a singing change. At rehearsal, Sid forgot and, conducting the passage as written, drowned out Ray's vocal. "No, Sid, *no!*" Ray shouted, waving everybody to stop. The sixty-odd orchestra players sat holding their breaths. "I got so mad," Sid recalled, "I almost walked off stage. Then I realized that if I walked, I'd destroy a whole concert. Even if Ray could've replaced me, the new guy wouldn't know what the hell he was doing. The next time we tried, I realized what I was doing wrong, and it came out sweet as honey."

In September 1980, Ray turned fifty. A sobering birthday for any man, it marked for Ray the turning point between decline and comeback. On the road, business was still slow, but at least getting no worse. When the gang played Dallas' Longhorn Ballroom earlier that year, Ray had asked for a sing-along from the sparse crowd, and so few joined in that he complained, "You're talking so much, you didn't hear what I was saying." The Dallas *Morning News* reviewer was outraged. "Look, folks," she wanted to shout, "this is RAY CHARLES! How many times do you get to hear the Genius?" When they came back to Dallas in '81, however, a playful Ray got the crowd on its feet singing and clapping along on an impromptu "Deep in the Heart of Texas." "Yeah, yeah, I'm feeling good tonight," he said, chuckling, between shows.

Ray Jr. married Duana Chenier in a huge wedding at St. Bernadette's Church in Baldwin Hills, the reception at Southridge. Della and Duana's parents planned everything; Ray, on tour in Europe, flew in for the ceremony and immediately flew back to the tour. The young couple settled into the apartment in the Southridge house; a year later they had their first daughter, Erin, and Ray became a grandfather. That didn't mean that his harem days were over. Norma's place was home when he wanted to go there, and Ruth and others still made themselves available. Susaye, however, had flown the coop, sure at last that Ray would never love her as she hoped. Singing with the Supremes in London, she met a chic salesgirl in a dress shop. One of Ray's records came on the background music. "Oh, don't you love Ray Charles?" said the girl. "The way she said 'Oh,' " Susaye remembered, "I knew she'd been with Ray. 'Yes, I used to work for him,' I said. 'I love him,' she said. The sadness in her voice, I had *lived* that."

At RPM, business was quiet. Bob Gratts quit and David Braithwaite came back to help out part-time, but there wasn't much for an engineer to do. Ray didn't record an album in the winter of '81, the first such gap in sixteen years. He didn't have a contract with a label, and he wasn't sure what to record. But he had noted hints pointing out his next direction. The fall before, he had done so well on an episode of *Hee Haw,* the country-music variety show, that host Buck Owens teased him, "You keep hangin' around here, and you'll get on steady." A duet with Clint Eastwood, "Beers to You," from the movie *Any Which Way You Can,* reached #50 on the country charts. In the spring he played at the Grand Ole Opry with Loretta Lynn, and the country crowd gave him a stomping and hollering ovation. The conservative swing in the nation's mood also suggested that the time was ripe for a move to America's musical heartland. Yet ever-cautious Ray took the rest of 1981, the first year of Ronald Reagan's New Morning for America, to decide on his new direction: he would record country music—not the big-band country of *Modern Sounds* twenty years before, but authentic country music aimed squarely at the country market. Ray decided to conquer Nashville.

"Nashville," geographically, means an old tree-shaded neighborhood of family homes, half a mile long and a few city blocks wide, that sits on a low bluff overlooking the city's downtown. There in the 30s and 40s gathered Ernest Tubb, Red Foley, and dozens of pickers and singers (and their publishers, record labels, and studios) who made the music white country folk loved, and who toured the nation coast-to-coast but hurried back to Nashville every Saturday night to play at the Grand Ole Opry. Through the 50s, 60s, and 70s, Eddy Arnold and Chet Atkins, Kitty Wells and Loretta Lynn, Johnny Cash and Willie Nelson helped Nashville grow. Ray's *Modern Sounds* brought new listeners to country music; so did Bob Dylan's *Nashville Skyline.* Modern office buildings replaced many of the old houses, and Music Row kept stretching farther south along 16th Street. By the 80s, the Nashville Sound had become one of pop music's most important strands and very big business indeed.

Unlike pop and rock fans, country-music fans were known for their loyalty to old-timers, and Ray eyed Nashville as a possible pasture for his old age. Nashville also posed an intriguing musical challenge. Could Ray make country music from the inside, slip into the idiom as into a new skin, both lose himself in it and make it his own? And if he could, would it sell? Given his dismal pop sales in the 70s, Ray figured he had nothing to lose. With a certain cold-blooded efficiency he set out to relaunch himself in late midcareer as a country recording artist.

Ray put out word of his new direction, and in February 1982, a scout reported that Rick Blackburn, youthful head of CBS Records' country division, was a big fan and would love to talk to him. Ray began flying to Nashville every few weeks, staying at the Spence Manor at 16th and Division and walking unnoticed with his valet the few blocks down Music Row to CBS's low tan building. Negotiations, often interrupted by Ray's touring schedule, took seven months. Blackburn knew that taking on Ray was "an irregular signing," yet focus-group research backed up his instinct that Ray was favorably "recognizable by the country-music consumer." He found Ray a "damn good street attorney" who refused to let real lawyers enter their talks. In August *Variety* headlined: "Ray Charles to Do C&W Disk for CBS."

Ray had already started work at RPM, gathering songs and lining up guitar players. By October, he knew the new album would be "so different," he told an interviewer, "that I can assure you it's gonna shock a lot of people." After taking the tapes to Nashville for "sweetening" overdubs by Music City's top session players, he handed in ten finished tracks in November. Blackburn rushed out the sentimental "Born to Love Me" in December as the first single—it climbed to #20 on the country chart—and in January 1983 released the album *Wish You Were Here Tonight*. Corporate backscratching gave Ray's country debut gold-plated publicity: CBS Records got him top billing at the Country Music Association's 25th Anniversary Concert in Washington, President and Nancy Reagan in attendance; CBS-TV broadcast the show in April.

CBS's marketing clout also got *Wish You Were Here Tonight* reviewed in publications as diverse as *USA Today* and *The Village Voice* (the Atlantic albums had gotten so little press that many critics thought this was Ray's first release in four years). With few exceptions, the album got panned—"amateurish," "incredibly dull," "sterile museum piece"—and not without reason. Weak songs, dragging tempos, and Ray's calculated copying of commercial country music push much of *Wish You Were Here* into the bland Kenny Rogers–John Denver spectrum. Yet with multi-overdubs of his own voice, Ray builds the Bellamy Brothers' "Let Your Love Flow" into a whooping rocker, and for "3/4 Time" he puts on an "aw shucks" tone to paint the portrait of a laid-back Nashville cat.

> I write what I feel
> And don't care if the damn thing don't rhyme,
> Just give me a C chord and play it in 3/4 time.

Wish You Were Here Tonight sold "fair to middling," according to one CBS executive, and "3/4 Time" became a moderate hit. Overall, Ray was pleased with the album as a good first try. Brushing off his critics ("A lot of people . . . aren't used to my recording flat-out country music," he told *USA Today*), he pushed undaunted into his second Nashville effort, *Do I Ever Cross Your Mind?*

|||||||||||||

Country music clubs like Gilley's in Houston joined the mix of dinner theaters and concert halls on the '83 tour. Ray had been out with the gang for only a month, however, when he began to suffer from strange sensations in his left ear. He heard a rough shoosh-shoosh sound with every breath, and when he talked or sang, his voice sounded abnormally loud. With one ear not working correctly, his navigation system was thrown off; he found it harder to gauge his way along corridors. He kept performing, and audiences and most of the band never knew anything was wrong. Ray did tell Clifford Solomon that he was hearing a constant echo, "sounds within sounds." Solomon said maybe it was just water in his ear, but the symptoms didn't go away through June and July. Could he be going deaf? If he held his breath for a moment and listened, Ray felt sure he could hear as well as always, but the prospect of silence as well as blackness— life without music!—terrified him. "I'm too old to be Helen Keller," he told Ruth Robinson. Knowing how stoically Ray faced ordinary worries, Ruth realized that his saying anything meant that Ray felt tortured by fear.

One doctor in LA did nothing; then Ray saw James Gould, a New York ear-nose-and-throat specialist well known for treating opera singers. Gould diagnosed "abnormally patent eustachian tubes" and for continuing treatment referred him to Jack Pulec, a Los Angeles ear specialist who had written on the condition. When he examined Ray in August, Pulec could see Ray's left eardrum flapping in and out, but he reassured Ray that he was not losing his hearing. His left eustachian tube was simply gaping open, and the strange sounds were "autophony," Ray's throat sounds coming up the normally closed tube to his ear. To alleviate Ray's symptoms, Pulec made an opening through his left eardrum and put in a ventilating tube, or "button." When Ray was on the road in September and the ear got infected, a Memphis doctor placed him on antibiotics and ear drops. When Pulec saw him again in October, the infection was drying up, and Ray reported his sound symptoms much reduced. Pulec predicted he would have no further problems, but the episode had shaken Ray to his roots. Only as fall turned to winter did the shadow of fear begin to fade.

Worried about his hearing and still driving the country music launch, Ray had no time and a short temper for the guys in the band. The 1983 tour became the most grueling in memory. Ray cussed out soundmen as never before, and even shamed a bass player so cruelly before a hometown crowd that after the show he didn't dare face his relatives. Joe Adams installed a new road manager—"One snake hiring another," the group said—who played all the angles, lending money at high interest and wangling free hotel rooms for himself instead of group rates for the band. By now the Buzzard seemed slow compared with commercial jets; long hours on the plane sagged into deadly boredom. On two trips in Europe, the bus rattled endlessly along narrow, twisty roads, and they got to many gigs with barely time for a tuna fish sandwich backstage.

The tour wore hardest on guitarist Eugene Ross, nicknamed "Big Bubba," a four-hundred-pound Texas bluesman who drank, carried a knife, and had a wooden leg. Big Bubba was always hungry; the tour never stopped long enough for what Bubba called a real meal. His wooden leg gave him trouble sitting cramped on the bus; it also meant he had a hard time attracting women. As the tour ground on, Bubba got more and more discontented. Night after night Ray yelled that his guitar was too loud, and the nagging made him angry. Bubba tried to talk to Ray, but the road manager brushed him off. His anger simmered. Just because nobody opposed Ray didn't mean he was always right, Bubba figured. Somebody needed to teach Ray a lesson in humanity, to tell him, "What you're doing is wrong. You've got to treat people like human beings."

Back from the second European trip, the gang played a gig in Omaha the night before Thanksgiving. Ray flew to Los Angeles on the holiday, leaving the fellows in a dumpy hotel in Omaha's deserted downtown. The company did buy them dinner, but when Bubba looked down at his plate at a skimpy portion of canned turkey, he dropped his knife and fork. "Ray's got $40 million," he announced, "and he doesn't have the decency to give us a real turkey dinner." At the next stop, the Sahara Hotel in Las Vegas, Bubba came into the band room the first night and slapped his guitar case on a shelf where James Polk had stashed a couple of drinks, knocking them over. "What's wrong with you, man?" asked Polk. "I've been pissed off all day at fucking Ray Charles," said Bubba. "If he says one thing to me tonight, I'm gonna tell him to kiss my ass."

As the show began, bassist Roger Heyns, as he often did, turned on a cassette recorder to tape the show. The band was blaring through "Busted," Ray singing, "Cotton is down to a quarter pound, and I'm busted," when Bubba's guitar started to come through too loud. Ray turned to him and said, "Cut it out." That was the last straw.

"Fuck you!" Bubba cried, leaping to his feet and stomping in rage. The band came to a ragged halt. From the sax section, Clifford Solomon signaled Bubba to quiet down, but Bubba ignored him. The audience sat in shocked silence.

"Get the man off the stage," Ray said firmly over the mike.

"*You* get me off the stage, you dog," Bubba shouted. The audience chuckled, and Ray changed his tack. "It's okay, he's just drunk, bless his heart."

"You dog!"

"I love you."

"You're a dog!"

Ray lost patience. "Will somebody come up and get the man off the stage? We're supposed to have security here. I want somebody to *get the man off the stage!*"

Uniformed guards came up but stopped, confused. Clifford finally caught Bubba's eye. "C'mon Bubba, give me a break," he said, and Bubba went off.

"Now play the song, guys," said Ray. The fellows hit the riff right where they had left off, and the audience cheered, glad the show was back on track. The outburst had lasted a minute.

"You're a hero," Phil Guilbeau told Bubba in the dressing room, slapping him on the back, but late that night Clifford found him packing his bags, much deflated. "I fucked up, didn't I?" he asked. Clifford couldn't deny it, so he made comforting noises. The next night when he went in to get the list, Clifford thought Ray would be furious. Instead, he laughed it off, even said he'd pay Bubba's salary for the rest of the week and buy his ticket home to Texas. "You guys shoulda chipped in and bought Bubba some pussy," Ray told his bandleader. "The man's crazy, but he sure could play!"

The end of the season came three days later and Ray decided, better late than never, to try mending fences. He asked the band to stay in the dressing room a few minutes after the last show—a meeting that Roger Heyns also taped.

"Where's Solomon?" asked Ray, walking in. Downstairs, said somebody. "I said I wanted everybody here," Ray groused. As they waited, Ray heard a television on in the corner. "You got a TV up here?" he asked. "I shoulda come up to watch the Cowboys. How much you lose, Rudy?"

"Nothing," said Rudy Johnson in a droll voice. "I don't bet on nothing but myself, and I'm suspect." That got a nervous laugh.

Clifford came into the room. "C'mon, Cap'n," Ray said sarcastically. "You gotta be the last one, goddammit, gotta make your grand entrance." Then he started talking in a quick, flat tone, and the fellows fell silent.

"Listen, darlings," Ray said. "I want to take two minutes of your *precious* time, to tell you I am *more* than pleased with this year's performance. We all know it wasn't perfect, but what is? I think we got 88 percent that we can be proud of. The 12 percent we didn't get right, we ought to be able to cure 10 percent of that next year and only be 2 percent behind, understand? You cats really played for me, and I want you to go home understanding that I really appreciate what went down, *musically,* this year. I can't deal with the bullshit . . ." A murmur went through the room—was he referring to Bubba? ". . . but the *music* was excellent. I talk to the newspaper and television people, they ain't *all* gonna be lying, and they tell me they like the band. Sometimes we raise hell, and you guys think, 'How come?' But believe me, it pays off with the people *we* deal with that *you* don't deal with. Promoters tell me, 'You know, Mr. Charles, most artists never start on time,' but I say, 'Other artists ain't *me.*'

"So I'm through, I'm gonna shut up, I just wanted to tell you that. You all take care of yourself over the holidays—don't get yourself juiced and run into nobody and kill yourselves."

"Merry Christmas, bro," a fellow called out amid relieved laughter.

"We got a bonus in the check?" Johnny Coles piped up.

"What?" Ray asked.

"A bonus," said Coles.

"If you can tell me where I'm gonna get it from, John," Ray shot back. "You're lucky I kept the band working. Bonus, my ass! I wish somebody would give *me* a fucking bonus."

On that note, Ray left the room. In the sudden quiet, somebody mimicked Ray: "You all made me a lot of money last year. I want to thank you very much. Now I got $80 million instead of $79 million." It got a muffled laugh.

▯▮▯▮▮▯▮▯▮▮

Through the roughest months of '83—the year Michael Jackson's *Thriller* sold 25 million copies—Ray never stopped recording. He finished the basic tracks for *Do I Ever Cross Your Mind* at RPM in late summer and again took them to Nashville for sweetening. The second country album marked a huge step forward from the first. Ray sounds much more at home in the idiom, and the instrumental backup has more spunk and color. Yet Ray knew, and Blackburn agreed, that to get the true country sound, he needed to work in Nashville with a Nashville producer. It didn't take much looking to come up with the right man: Billy Sherrill.

The dark, handsome son of an Alabama preacher, Billy Sherrill had been Columbia's top Nashville A&R man since 1968, when he produced "Stand by Your Man" for Tammy Wynette. He had also discovered the teenage sensation Tanya Tucker and revived the career of old-timer George Jones, one of Ray's favorite singers. Sherrill liked a rich recorded sound—big rhythm section, background singers, layers of overdubs— and his success had helped turn Nashville toward pop-influenced "suburban" country music, a style *Modern Sounds* had helped begin. Like Ray, Sherrill approached record making with professional precision. "I look at this whole music scene as a cold, calculating, scientific operation," he told reporters, and he had a simple formula for success: "Go into the studio with a hit song." Yet like every other pro, Sherrill had to admit that what made hits escaped analysis. A hit had to have "emotion, happiness or sadness, love or hate," but beyond that all was mystery: "It's like seeing a chick and you flip over her, you don't know why."

Ray proposed an album of duets, a project on his mind for years: he had signed with Columbia in large part to sing with George Jones, Johnny Cash, and Willie Nelson. A duet album would mean musical fun for him and a "my friend Ray" introduction from his partners to their fans. Sherrill liked the idea and sent out a call for songs to Nashville's top writers, and came up, fortunately, with tunes Ray liked. "A lot of producers think I should do a song because they like it," Ray said a decade later. "It don't work like that. *I* got to like it. Billy Sherrill put the guys on the case and came up with songs that I enjoyed doing." Ray and his new producer finished a comedy tune with George Jones, "We Didn't See a Thing," at a couple of sessions in October, and in February '84 they got down to work on the rest.

Nashville cats pride themselves on being blasé about recording with the superstars who drop into town. Ray Charles created a stir without breaking anybody's routine. For veteran session pianist Bobby Wood, working with Ray began with a call to come to Eleven-Eleven Sound Studios, an old house on 17th Avenue with a fine brick arch over the front door. There he found a handful of top players: Pete Drake on pedal steel, Terry McMillan on harmonica, and drummer Kenny Malone. They were all fans—Wood had been romancing his future wife when "I Can't Stop Loving You" was a hit. One guitar player told Ray he had driven a hundred miles to get the guitar he needed to play with Ray Charles. Ray told Ruth about it on the phone, and she heard in his voice how much he loved soaking up the hero worship.

With Sherrill in the booth, Ray and the cats fell to work with a will; only a few sessions got tense. Once Ray pestered Pete Drake to play a four-bar melody just the way he heard it. Sherrill told him Drake was a slide, not a melody player, but Ray bugged Drake for an hour until he got a piece of what he wanted. "I thought Pete was gonna leave the world on us," Wood remembered. Ray liked jazzy chords from the background keyboards, flat-nines and the like. Whenever he heard them, Sherrill jumped on the talkback mike: "Get those Chinese licks out of there." When Sherrill noticed Ray dragging the tempo, he told him so. No way, Ray insisted, drummer Kenny Malone was rushing the beat. Everyone knew that Malone, an old Navy drummer, had the strictest time in Nashville. Sherrill put a metronome on Ray and the metronome didn't lie: Ray was slowing down. Once Ray heard it, he admitted it, and Sherrill rose in his estimation.

Scheduling the vocal sessions was tough—Ray insisted on singing with his partners live in the studio—but doing them was a ball. Merle Haggard, Ricky Skaggs, and the others got a kick out of matching vocal wits with the Genius, and the Genius got a kick out of it too. One early-spring morning Ray and Sherrill flew to Willie Nelson's

Texas ranch to record "Seven Spanish Angels." More than the other singers, Nelson had long emulated Ray's pop-ballad style, and Ray had long respected the bluesy grit in Nelson's voice. The two felt an instant chemistry that found its way into the song, a haunting tale of the old Southwest. Afterward, they sat down to play a noisy game of chess.

After string overdubs in May, *Friendship* was finished, and it turned out a masterpiece. Sherrill and the Nashville singers and players blow so much fresh air into Ray's music that albums all the way back to *True to Life* seem stale in comparison. In his third try, Ray achieves his goal, genuine country music at its lively, humorous best. The cats play up a storm, and the songs, both ballads and foot-stompers, are tailor-made to the singers. Male camaraderie becomes *Friendship's* informal theme. Ray commiserates, as buddies do, with Mickey Gilley on "It Ain't Gonna Worry My Mind" and, at the album's comic high point, runs into George Jones doing some late-night prowling on "We Didn't See a Thing." The two old tomcats are all winks and grins as they get their stories straight:

> **George:** *Don't forget Ray, I was down in Atlanta*
> **Ray:** *Don't forget, George, I was working late*
> **George:** *You know it's always good to see you*
> **Ray:** *Good to see you too*
> **George:** *But I didn't see you*
> **Ray:** *You didn't see me*
> **George and Ray:** *We didn't see a thing!*

Rick Blackburn was delighted with *Friendship* and scheduled it for release in July. "We Didn't See a Thing" had already reached a highly respectable #6 on the country chart, and more hot tracks could be peeled off the album as singles.

The day-to-day tenor of Ray's life, meanwhile, remained remarkably constant. Though still a man of volatile moods, Ray felt more at ease with himself after fifty than he had before. "Contentment has come to me over the past few years," he told a reporter. "It's part of my maturity." His ear problems seemed gone, but feeling that he'd had a narrow escape, Ray took a position on Dr. Pulec's EAR Foundation board. Work remained the core of his life. As Ray began a Christmas album in the studio that summer, Joe still lorded over all from his front office, keeping a manicured finger in every pie. Ray and Joe's relationship continued to fascinate onlookers. "Strange Siamese twins," one longtime observer called them. Ethel Rubin began her third decade reigning over the books, and Bob Abrams was still sending out press releases and piloting the often reluctant Ray through press interviews and TV talk shows—Johnny Carson was the only show he really enjoyed doing.

The road rolled on. "It's like Mohammed and the mountain," Ray always answered when asked why he toured so much. "The people won't come to me, so I go to them." Ray often traveled on his own and, embarrassed that people might see him spilling food, nearly always ate in his room. After thirteen go-rounds, Dorothy Berry was exhausted. Her unruly teenage son, living with her sister in LA, needed her too. When Dorothy told Ray she was leaving, he chewed her out, but she sang her last gig in Eureka, California, and Stella Yarborough took charge of the ever-squabbling, ever-younger Raelets. Johnny Coles, after years of grumbling, called it quits. Jeff Kaye, a young trumpet player from Chicago, replaced him, boarding the Buzzard in Boston and playing his first gig in Bakersfield. After a week, Kaye confessed to the boss that he'd never be able to fill Coles' shoes. Ray said not to worry, he was doing well and would improve. A few weeks later, playing before 25,000 people in Turkey, Kaye realized Ray had been right: he was playing better than he'd ever played in his life.

In his private life, Ray kept going his quirky, cranky way. The harem changed more slowly than in days of yore, but the love of women, many women, continued to absorb much of Ray's time and energy. On tour in Europe he thought nothing of flying to Paris for a rendezvous between one-nighters in Germany. During Las Vegas gigs, several women would wait for him on various floors of the hotel, happy for brief visits. Ray still had a home with Norma in LA, but his romance with Ruth Robinson turned tempestuous. In one noisy quarrel, he shoved Ruth and she shoved him back. He fell, yelped in pain, and came up holding a badly sprained finger. "You deserve it, you son of a bitch" was her first angry thought, but then she caught herself: "My God, I've broken Ray Charles' hand. He'll never play the piano again."

Time had dulled the pain of divorce. Della herself had gentlemen friends, yet Ray was still patriarch of the Robinson family. Little Bobby had turned out to be an earnest young man who hoped to be a preacher. The two older sons were having a harder time. David, the second son, had gotten deeply involved in drugs, including the hallucinogen PCP, and had frightened the family at Southridge with his outbursts. On successive days in April 1983, he sexually assaulted two women at gunpoint. Arrested, he pled guilty to two counts of rape and was sentenced to eleven years in prison. A son and a brother in prison was traumatic for the whole family, but it hurt Della more than the others. She had struggled for years, with little help from Ray, to keep her boys on the straight and narrow path. Had she failed? When Della and Ray visited David at Vacaville State Prison, Ray showed little emotion; but every time, it seemed, Della's heart broke anew.

Ray Jr., at thirty, was still trying to find his feet. He worked for a time at a mortgage bank in Newport Beach, then tried selling insurance on commission. He and Duana had another baby on the way but spent long nights at Southridge in arguments. Della sided with Ray Jr., and that made Duana furious. When she threatened to leave, Della offered the young couple the house on Hepburn that the family still owned. But Ray Jr. didn't want to move; the responsibility frightened him. He clung to the idea that someday he was going to be his dad's right-hand man, and got angry when his father refused to back him in business ventures. He talked it over with his big half sister Evelyn, and she agreed: Ray was selfish with his kids. "He's going to die a lonely old man," Ray Jr. liked to say. "He'll be all by himself because he's so stingy with everybody."

The heart of the problem, several onlookers felt, was that Ray, fatherless himself, had no idea how to be a father. Blindness and constant travel had kept him from watching his children grow up; the pursuit of women had long provided an escape from the pains and joys of family life. Ray seemed awkward with his three sons. He might have helped Ray Jr. get started in the music business, for example, by pulling a few strings to land him a job at ABC or Atlantic. Instead, Ray did little but say no to Ray Jr., and that blunder always started the same old arguments. Ray was disappointed in his children. A realist above all, he knew that none would ever match him in intellect, talent, or ambition. Could Ray Jr. be entrusted with Ray Charles Enterprises? Ray doubted it. His ingrained secretiveness kept him from preparing his heirs for the wealth they might inherit. "Ray kept the same distance from his boys that he kept from his women, from his male buddies," one onlooker observed. "To be a true friend, you have to invest time with a person, to exchange feelings, to give of yourself. Ray doesn't do that."

In 1984, Ray's gigs became more mixed than ever. Within a few summer weeks, he and the gang played with George Jones in Missouri, Sarah Vaughan in Kansas, and Glen Campbell in Las Vegas. In this mix, the Republican National Convention in Dallas stood out above the rest. Recrowning Ronald Reagan after his triumphal first term, the Republicans needed a grand finale to follow Thursday night's acceptance speech. The Democrats were crying that Reagan's New Morning excluded blacks and rolled back civil rights, stole from the poor, and gave to the rich. What better symbol of a grandly united USA could Republicans pick than Ray Charles singing "America the Beautiful"? Ray's agent at William Morris got the call and passed the offer on to Ray. August 23, Dallas? He was free, the money was right, and he did it, singing and playing piano to a taped orchestral background. A reverential silence held the convention hall while Ray sang of "brotherhood from sea to shining sea." When he finished, the floor became a tumult of American flags, and Ray, Reagan, and Vice President Bush shared a smiling three-way embrace for the crowd and the television cameras.

Though he seldom discussed politics in public, Ray had gone on record as a Hubert Humphrey Democrat in the 70s, and many old fans were surprised to see a Martin Luther King supporter singing for the president who opposed making King's birthday a national holiday. Had Ray Charles, for a buck, lent his name and his music to a cynical illusion of national togetherness? About the same time, anti-apartheid critics began pointing out that Ray had performed in South Africa. Had he become that rare bird, a black conservative?

Close observers felt that, with increasing wealth, Ray had moved to the right—"I found a reactionary streak to his character," said one, "the 'I made mine, you make yours' attitude of the self-made man"—yet the criticism stung Ray, and he responded angrily. Playing the Republican convention had been just one more gig, he said. "The Democrats wanted me to do the same thing, but they didn't want to pay." Appearing with Reagan didn't mean he endorsed him; he had also met Nixon, and that didn't mean he endorsed him. As for South Africa: he had played there long before entertainers began boycotting the Afrikaner regime, and his audiences there had been more integrated than many he could remember a few years back in the American South: "I was one of the first . . . getting sued for *not* playing segregated audiences." Black singers, himself included, still got paid less than white singers in America. "The money, honey, that's still not equal," he told *US* magazine the summer of the convention. "I ain't never gonna make the money that a Sinatra makes, or a Mick Jagger, or even a Dean Martin." For Ray, the bottom line was plain: "I'm a person who plays music, and I'll take my music anywhere in the world people want to hear it. I haven't gone to Russia, but if the president of Russia would like me to, I'd be very happy to go."

Wherever Ray stood on the political spectrum, playing "America the Beautiful" on national television at a national ritual marked a profound moment in Ray's music and in his relationship with his audience. Through the years since *Message from the People*, Ray's "America" had grown from an overlooked album track into an anthem that conveyed to millions a rugged, determined love of the country and its highest ideals. In responding to Ray singing "America," listeners implicitly recognized that after forty years of crisscrossing the land and playing songs from every native idiom, Ray Charles had reached his goal, the heart of American music. Singing from that heart, Ray had found a way to speak soul-to-soul with Americans of every creed and color.

Dashing back to RPM between gigs that fall, Ray tried to get his Christmas album done in time for the shopping season, but he didn't make it. No matter; Columbia would have plenty of time to get it out for next Christmas. *Friendship* got off to a slow start, but "Rock and Roll Shoes," the second single from the album, reached #14. The third, "Seven Spanish Angels," came out in November. Something about the tale of a doomed gunfighter and his girl, scored for guitars and Tex-Mex trumpets, caught at the public ear. Willie Nelson had sold many more records than Ray in the 80s, and Ray was riding his coattails in the marketplace, not vice versa. Yet more than each singer's contribution, the rapport between the two wise old-timers propelled the single up the country chart. If sales kept up the way they started, "Seven Spanish Angels" could go all the way to #1 in '85.

26

Medals
and Honors
Late 1980s

Nineteen eighty-five got off to a busy and varied start for Ray Charles; five years of comeback had brought him a long way. "Seven Spanish Angels" climbed through the winter to reach #1 on the country chart in March, a stunning triumph for Ray's Nashville campaign and noted as such by journals as diverse as *Jet* and *USA Today.* Columbia released the single on video. After Michael Jackson's success with the *Thriller* videos, pop singers had to make similar short films to stay in the game; this was Ray's first, singing with Willie at the piano of an Old West saloon. *Friendship* also got to #1 on the country album chart and stayed in the top ten until the summer. In addition to the standard vinyl LP, Columbia released the album as a CD, marking Ray's entry into the digital technology that had sparked a mid-80s revolution in the electric media.

That wasn't all. One night in late January, Ray got together at an LA studio with Harry Belafonte, Bob Dylan, Diana Ross, Bruce Springsteen, and forty other world-famous pop singers to sing "We Are the World," a folk anthem that proclaims each person connected to everyone else on earth. The stars sang gratis, the proceeds from record sales to go to famine relief in Africa. The night of the recording was a chummy affair, younger stars introducing themselves to Ray awkwardly at first. "I know who you are," he told Billy Joel, putting Joel on cloud nine for weeks. The singers serenaded Harry Belafonte with a silly "Day-O," Ray joining in the fun, until Quincy Jones good-naturedly herded them into a chorus to sing with the prerecorded track. To bring him out of the ensemble as a revered elder, Jones assigned Ray a solo spot at the end of the song, and Ray came back to record it a few days later, punching out his lyrics in Braille while telling Jones he wanted to get it in one take. He did, writhing bowlegged before the mike and howling his lines: "There's a choice we're making, we're saving our own lives, it's true we make a better day, just you and me." Despite its staged sincerity, "We Are the World" remains a powerful record that reveals pop music's belief in itself as a moral voice in the post–Dylan/Beatles era. Its immense success—four weeks at #1— reveals the size of the audience that took that voice seriously.

Within days of this countercultural event, Ray came through the media from the Establishment angle, singing "America the Beautiful" at Ronald Reagan's second inaugural gala. Dozens of actors and comedians, singers and dancers did brief turns before the crowd and an enthroned president and First Lady, building a slow momentum to the grand finale. The lights dimmed, and Frank Sinatra intoned a reverent introduction and led Ray to the piano amid tumultuous applause. The Beach Boys, Dean Martin, Jimmy Stewart, and Donna Summer drifted from the wings to gather around him. By the end the performers, the audience, and millions at home before their TV sets all sang along in a coast-to-coast chorus. More than ever, Ray seemed to have become the singer who sang for every American.

After finishing up *Spirit of Christmas,* a light but enjoyable album, Ray got on the road with the gang once more. They replaced Dolly Parton on a Chicago bill in May, played the Kool Jazz Festival at Lincoln Center in June, spent the summer in Europe, and got back to the Hollywood Bowl for a concert with B. B. King in late August. Then a long era in the touring days of the Ray Charles Orchestra came crashing to a close.

Early in October at a Kentucky airport, a wing of the Buzzard clipped a tree while taxiing before takeoff. Pilot Gordon Smith, an American Indian everyone respected, stopped the plane, and after much yelling in the cockpit, Ray got on the intercom mike. "We might have hit a branch," he announced. "There may be a hole in the wing, so we're not going to take any chances of flying tonight." The band figured the company would fly them commercially to Miami, the next stop, but when they got back to the airport, Ray had already taken off on a commercial flight, and road manager Carl Hunter and his brother Joe were taping up the wing with duct tape. "All on," said Hunter, and a bit apprehensively the guys boarded the Buzzard, gulping as they looked through the windows at the tape fluttering in the wind.

Flying north again from Miami, Clifford Solomon noticed a thunderstorm that seemed to be following them. The next day, Saturday, October 19, at about 3:30 in the afternoon, they approached Bloomington, Indiana, heading to a college concert with B. J. Thomas. The Bloomington tower told Smith it was pouring rain at the airport and suggested they land in Indianapolis. The gig, however, was a "touch and go"—they planned to fly on to Washington, D.C., right after the show—and Ray figured driving the hundred miles back and forth from Indianapolis was too much of a pain in the neck. Land in Bloomington, he told Smith, and went back to his private compartment and a chess game with Al Jackson, a newcomer on baritone sax. The fellows and ladies chatted and smoked as usual. When Smith brought the plane through the low ceiling, he found himself halfway down the runway. The landing was smooth, but when he put on the brakes, the wheels wouldn't grip on the slick tarmac.

"Damn," Clifford Solomon said to no one in particular, "seems like we're going awfully fast." Suddenly the wheels made a boogedie-boogedie sound, running over the rough gravel at the end of the runway. "I guess we're going to slow down now," said trumpeter Jeff Kaye. But then there came an eerie moment of silence, broken only by somebody's "What the hell?" as the Buzzard glided over a twenty-five-foot drop, crunch landed, and skidded one hundred fifty feet on its belly through a muddy cornfield. Clifford felt his spine jam up into his skull as if he had been dropped from a building. The fuselage cracked open just forward of the wing, and when he looked up, rain splashed on his glasses.

Ray's glasses flew off in the crash, and he got thrown to the floor, but when he picked himself up, nothing felt broken. "Everybody off," Smith yelled through the intercom. "The plane could blow." Carl and Joe Hunter kicked open window exits, and Ray and the gang crawled out into the chill drizzle. Sinking ankle deep in the mud, they stood about in shock, talking in nervous bursts, broken cornstalks scratching their legs.

"Smell those fumes?" Clifford said. "Nobody light a cigarette." Someone said Smith was trapped, Carl and Joe couldn't pull him out. They heard sirens in the distance, then ambulances screeched to the edge of the tarmac and medics scrambled down the bank with stretchers. They gingerly tugged Smith out of the cockpit and carried him and Clifford to the ambulances and on to the hospital. There the worst seemed behind them. Ray had escaped unscathed, a few fellows had bumps and bruises, and Clifford's and the pilot's injuries were not life-threatening. Nurses put Clifford to bed and gave him painkillers, and he floated away watching the World Series on TV. Others headed into town and brought back girls and a few bottles. An all-night party broke out in the hospital lobby. Jeff Kaye passed out drunk, and the nurses put him to bed.

Sunday was quiet. On Monday, Ray flew out, and Joe Adams flew in from LA to get the gang on a chartered bus to the gig in Washington, rescheduled for Tuesday. The fellows asked the driver to turn the seats around so Clifford could recline and, still suffering themselves with scraped knees and twisted ankles, made themselves comfortable with pillows and blankets for the long ride ahead. When Joe Adams saw what they were doing, he started shouting, "No no no! Put that stuff back the way it was."

Trombonist Dana Hughes blew up. "You lowlife!" he shouted. "People aren't in damn plane crashes every day. You should be glad we're all alive, but you come on growling bullshit, being your old dog-ass self."

Adams challenged Hughes to step off the bus and fight. Hughes thought twice and fell silent. The ride to Washington was tense. Ray and Joe, the fellows figured, were scared that everybody was going to sue them. Except for the Bloomington paper and a few back-page items, they never saw anything about the crash in the newspapers. One fellow suggested Ray's being with CBS might have kept the story off the TV news. None of the fellows did sue Ray Charles Enterprises. Clifford's back took months to heal. When he filed a claim for disability insurance, Joe and Ray hemmed and hawed until Clifford got an attorney. "Then they offered pitiful sums of money, and we finally settled," Solomon recalled. "Adams had the X-rays, all the medical proof, but Ray couldn't see it, and he convinced Ray that I was playing games."

For the rest of the season, the gang traveled on commercial airlines. Ray looked into a new plane but found his new insurance rates prohibitive. Two years later Joe bought and custom-designed a fancy black touring bus. That, plus scheduled flights as needed, carried the gang gig to gig through the next decade and more. Twenty-five years after he bought his beloved Cessna, Ray's private flying days were over.

The Genius expanded his celebrity presence on television in 1986, playing himself on an episode of *Who's the Boss,* singing "Georgia" under the titles of *Designing Women,* and flirting with Madonna on Johnny Carson's show. The tide of his medals and honors began to rise. In January, he was inducted with Chuck Berry, Little Richard, and Elvis as a founding member of the Rock and Roll Hall of Fame. In April, the Florida legislature presented him with a laudatory proclamation in Braille. "It's a wonderful thing to come back to where it all began," said Ray in thanks. Then he got back to work, flying to Nashville to finish his first solo album with Sherrill, *From the Pages of My Mind.* Ray was his ornery self in the studio. On one tune, a drummer had a simple quarter-note beat on bass drum. "Wait, wait, wait, baby," Ray yelled after two beats, "you're not getting me here," pointing his thumb at his heart. Five takes later Ray was still bitching and moaning, and the drummer swore he'd never play for Ray Charles again. All such blemishes got buried in the mix, and *From the Pages of My Mind* turned out to be a mellow album filled with quiet treasures, country music at its most relaxed and re-flective. Having reached this apex, however, Ray's Nashville kick came to a sudden end. The next album he planned would be all R&B, and he'd do it in LA.

In the midst of work and success, Ray hadn't forgotten the scare his ear troubles had given him three years before, and after characteristically long thought, he decided to act. In May he called Dr. Pulec and said he wanted to discuss creating a Robinson Foundation for Hearing Disorders. Surprised to hear from him, Pulec invited Ray to his home in Pacific Palisades. He came and they talked in the living room for two hours, the longest Pulec would ever see Ray sit still. "He always had his wrist alarm set for a ten- or twenty-minute meeting," Pulec recalled. "This time he had nothing like that. He brought a tape recorder, set it up, and said, 'I want to know what we can do for hear-ing.' "

Pulec responded with dozens of ideas. Ray asked pointed, practical questions: what were the problems, were they soluble, and how much would it cost? He most wanted to help children hear who couldn't hear, and the talk turned to ideas for im-proving the cochlear implant, a device just beginning to restore hearing to the pro-foundly deaf. They could analyze the elements of speech, Pulec suggested, and, by working backward, design an implant that heard speech more effectively. Or if they could find a way to measure the cochlear nerve, they could learn how to skew the im-plant's signal and take advantage of a weak nerve's remaining strength. Ray said to try anything that might work, and he came up with $250,000 for the first year and the pledge of more to come. Pulec hired a pair of Ph.D.'s in auditory physiology and soon had two laboratories up and running.

Ray's fifty-sixth birthday came and went, and life rolled on for this restless man in the dark, life still fueled by coffee and gin and pot, life still bringing its mix of every-day good and bad. On the home front, Ray Jr. and Duana got divorced. Having seen his son's independent efforts fail, Ray finally gave him a desk and a salary at RPM. Ray Jr. had grand ideas for movies, TV shows, and CDs, but Joe Adams nipped each one in the bud. Ray didn't protect Ray Jr. from Joe, and the son still felt kept out of his fa-ther's inner circle. On the road, only women, savage games of chess, and that precious hour of music before the people enlivened the endless hours of travel. With the Buz-zard gone, Ray traveled more than ever as a lone wolf, sleeping or reading his Braille *Reader's Digest* on the plane, meeting the crew and the band only at the gig. He got a backstage walkie-talkie to stay in second-to-second command of his little army. The younger fellows stood in awe of the living legend. "We didn't dare tell him when his fly was down," trombonist Charlie Shofner recalled. Shofner played softly for his first few weeks in the band, hoping Ray wouldn't hear him. After five months, he asked to speak to the boss. Carl Hunter stepped into Ray's dressing room; Shofner could hear him through the door.

"Mr. C, Charlie Shofner wants to see you."

"Who the fuck is that?" said Ray. When Shofner explained that he didn't want more money, just to say hi, Ray welcomed him in with a big hug.

From the Pages of My Mind sold fairly well, but badly compared with *Friendship,* and Ray's instinct told him it was time to head back to pop. The problem was: which pop? Pop music had split into a dozen different categories and markets, and he felt unfamiliar with newer styles and sounds. Synthesizers he found "useful" but "boring": "I can only hear about three records of synthesizers and . . . I can't stand any more." Rap music he disdained as one-chord, nonmelodic garbage. He knew what jazz, blues, and country music were, he told a jazz journalist. "But I get lost with all these different rocks. If you were to say, 'Ray, what is your definition of punk rock?' I couldn't tell you if my life depended on it."

Still, Ray had an ear out for pop possibilities, and when Quincy Jones mentioned that his pal Phil Ramone was producing Billy Joel, Ray responded, "I'd be happy to do something with Billy." Joel instantly set about composing a duet. What could he write that would intrigue Ray? The music came easily, a bluesy ballad with jazzy chords. "Then came the crisis," Joel recalled. "The lyric. I'm Jewish from Levittown, what do Ray and I have in common? I know, the piano, the mistress we wrap our arms around. I wrote the song at night with the lights turned out." He sent a cassette of "Baby Grand" to Ray and soon got a call. "It's clever," Ray said in an upbeat tone. "Let's do it." Ramone warned Joel that Ray's mood might change—"You gotta walk on eggs with him"—but that didn't prepare the songwriter for what happened.

Joel got to Evergreen Studio in the San Fernando Valley at eleven in the morning to find the most expensive session he'd ever underwritten: two grand pianos, a string orchestra, a dozen of LA's top studio players, and a video crew trailing cables everywhere. But no Ray. Joel's manager pulled him aside. Ray had sent word that he wasn't coming until he had a check well into six figures: no pay, no play. Joel felt he'd been set up and sucker-punched. Suddenly singing with Ray Charles didn't seem like so much fun.

Phil Ramone shrugged and said he wasn't surprised. Holding up Billy Joel was standard business procedure for Ray. The country boy in Ray liked cash; only money down really got his attention. Moreover, he'd long been convinced that white singers made more money than black. Again and again he told interviewers that his color had kept him from the big bucks. "I don't know what Sinatra gets, and I'm not going to tell you what I get," Ray told a reporter in the mid-80s. "But if he gets $150,000 a night,

I couldn't even carry his slop bucket in my moneymaking." Hearing him voice the same bitter complaint in private, Ruth Robinson realized that whether Ray in fact did or didn't earn less than his white colleagues, what mattered was that he *believed* he earned less. When a young, white, million-selling singer like Joel was drooling to sing with him, Ray saw a chance to get back a bit of his own, and he took it without compunction. Joel's manager tried to haggle, but by two in the afternoon Ray had his check and walked into the studio.

The tension dissipated into the work. They recorded from the first try, Joel's piano blocking out the song's skeleton, Ray's putting flesh on its bones. Though they barely spoke, Joel heard Ray speaking a strong musical language, controlling the discussion. Again and again they finished takes that Joel thought were perfect and Ray said, "Let's do another." Everyone in the studio followed Ray, his inner clock, his dancing feet, his sudden laughter. Only by late afternoon did they manage to get a track Ray would accept. They did vocals on the second day, Ray pacing about his isolation booth sipping from a spiked soda can, reading the lyric in Braille. He chuckled over the line "They say nobody's gonna play it on the radio." Joel started off singing so timidly that Ramone called him into the booth. "Do you like the song?" he asked. "Yeah," said Joel. "Then sing it, man! Ray's only going to be here a little longer." After that Joel relaxed, singing better with every take. They got it in ten, did an extra to back it up, then Ray smiled and said, "That's soup."

"Baby Grand" became a poignant track on Joel's *The Bridge*. As a single, it fell into the Adult Contemporary pop slot and reached a brief #3—more radio play, perhaps, than the lyric predicted. For Joel, "Baby Grand" remained one of his proudest recordings and an unforgettable experience. "Ray was the teacher, I was the student," Joel recalled a decade later. "What I learned was to let the music lead me, to go with the music at all costs."

The '86 touring season rolled without incident from Northampton, Massachusetts, to Midland, Texas, to Europe in June and July. Not all were thrilled with what they heard. "Perfunctory," said *Downbeat* of the Northampton show, and "totally unprepared," reported the LA *Times* of a gig in Long Beach. A Sherman Oaks woman saw the gang at a suburban theater and wrote the *Times* to complain: "Charles was on stage for a total of 35 minutes, 10 of which were taken up by two songs from his backup singers. What a disappointment."

What mattered the sniping? In August came word that Ray, along with Lucille Ball, Yehudi Menuhin, Antony Tudor, Jessica Tandy, and Hume Cronyn, had been picked to receive the Kennedy Center Honors Medal, America's most distinguished award for the arts. This bow from the highest created quite a stir at RPM. Ray wasn't sure he wanted to go, but Joe Adams assured him that he *had* to. The ceremonies began Saturday night, December 6, with a black-tie dinner at the State Department. Secretary of State George Shultz, smiling through the Iran-contra scandal, played host to the honorees and to *le tout* Washington, who, said a columnist, had stirred up a "social shuffle" to bag "the hottest tickets in the nation." Ray stayed close to Quincy Jones in the crush at the White House reception Sunday afternoon, but at the gala performance that night in the Kennedy Center, he sat back with a grin and lapped up the volleys of laughter and applause that greeted telling moments in the film clip of his life. "I'm overjoyed," he burst out. "I can feel it, I can hear it." Stevie Wonder sang a medley of Ray's greatest hits, and the climax, a chorus of kids from Florida D&B singing "America the Beautiful," brought tears to many eyes in the house. Awards already covered the walls of his office at RPM, but this honor, like Georgia making "Georgia" the state song, moved Ray deeply. "You feel you've come a long way," he told an interviewer soon afterward. "You think of what it was like wearing short pants and going barefoot, and what problems the South used to have."

Ray got back to Washington in April 1987 with Dr. Pulec and other ear specialists, lobbying a Senate Health and Human Services subcommittee for a bigger hearing research budget. Of a problem so close to his own deepest fears, Ray spoke with greater than usual pith. "My eyes are my handicap, but my ears are my opportunity," he told the committee. "My ears tell me 99 percent of what I need to know about my world. To lose my hearing would be like death." The senators were impressed, even a bit starstruck, to meet the Genius. Senator Conte of Rhode Island invited him, the doctors, and their wives to a private lunch in the Capitol, an elegant but informal affair that Ray, usually shy in unfamiliar company, thoroughly enjoyed.

The road unrolled through another summer. In Charleston, West Virginia, the crowd shouted, "Turn it up, turn it up," when they couldn't hear the unamplified band, and Ray cut the show fifteen minutes short. At a gig in Houston he shouted at the soundmen about the miking: "It stinks, and I'm trying to be nice about it. Can't you hear that humming? Are you deaf?" A new valet came on board, Dave Simmons, a big athletic guy from Pontiac, Michigan, who had worked for Marvin Gaye. Joe Adams hired Simmons when Ray was in Europe, and told him nothing more than, "You'll be Mr. Charles' personal assistant." When Simmons met his boss, he was struck by how much smaller Ray seemed in person than he had imagined. "He was tiny!" Simmons recalled. "Broad shoulders, but this little waist."

Ray kept in constant motion, and he said Simmons must stick to him like a burr, never be out of earshot. He showed the new valet how to make his gin-and-coffee mug and told him to have refills ready at a moment's notice. He took him back to the studio, and said, "Pay attention while we're in the studio, David, pay attention." He showed him how to set up the mikes and to watch the gauges while he sang, not to let the arrows sit in the red. Simmons drove Ray wherever he wanted to go, to business appointments, to Norma's apartment and elsewhere. About women, Ray swore his valet to silence: "There's some things I wouldn't want my *mama* to hear about, understand?" Simmons understood. The weekend came, and Simmons said, "So long, I'll see you Monday."

"Oh, no," said Ray. "This job is seven days a week, twenty-four hours a day. You're never off."

Nobody had told Simmons that; but being single, he gulped once and said, "Okay, let's go." Ray explained the routine: gigs came in to Joe through Don Fishel at William Morris; Sue at the travel agency booked flights to get Ray into a city no later than noon the day of the concert. A bite to eat, then Ray wanted to sleep. Simmons was to wake him up two hours before show time with a fresh mug, and he'd get up and shave. Simmons would pick out the tux for the night and get him to the gig and walk him on-stage. "The first time I walked between him and the audience," Simmons recalled. "Ray freaked, shouting, 'Don't you *ever* get between me and my audience!' "

The next morning they flew off again. Ray never checked his baggage, and Simmons staggered under the load: Ray's stage-clothes bag, his day-clothes bag, and "a bag bigger than a bed," as he remembered it, for the tape recorder that Ray took everywhere on the chance he might want to sketch a midnight idea in his room. Simmons never saw Ray use the machine, but he was never willing to leave it behind. "I was a pack mule! Bags over my shoulders, him on my arm, and we always seemed to be at the farthest gate, Gate 59, never Gate 1 or Gate 2. And I couldn't be fumbling and stumbling, because Ray didn't wait for nothing. If the limo wasn't there, we were in a cab and gone. Go, go, go—jet lag couldn't catch up with us!"

When Simmons drove rental cars, Ray could never get anywhere fast enough, asking "Are we there yet?" so often that Simmons wanted to scream, "Man, I'm gonna leave you under a tree in the middle of Massachusetts and drive back to California myself." Mostly, though, they had fun. Riding at night, Ray played cassettes, new demos from Stevie Wonder and Billy Preston or old favorites by Aretha, Donny Hathaway, and Barbra Streisand. He might ask Simmons, "How does this sound?" and sing something he was working on. "We were always laughing," Simmons recalled. "When Ray cracked up, he'd kick his feet up, lay back on the seat whooping, and I'd end up with his feet in my lap." Upon pulling into a city's sprawl strip, Simmons' first job was to find a Denny's—Ray loved the chicken-fried steak. Denny's had a reputation of being hostile to blacks, but there or elsewhere, Simmons never encountered any racial problem. "Everybody treated Ray like royalty. I was the man who was with The Man."

Ray's pace didn't slow down in the fall. He opened the opera season in Houston with a string concert and appeared on TV in a *Super Dave Show* and a two-hour *Salute to Las Vegas.* "Mess Around" got used under a car chase scene in the John Candy comedy *Planes, Trains and Automobiles.* A repackaging label brought out a two-CD set of Ray's greatest hits: in the switch from LPs to CDs, Ray began to reap the long-term advantage of owning his own masters. Forty years after cutting "Confession Blues" in rainy Seattle, he received a well-deserved Lifetime Achievement Award from the National Academy of Recording Arts and Sciences. Ray also let his fifty-seventh birthday be turned into a gala at the Hotel Bel Air to benefit Dr. Pulec's Ear International Foundation. The birthday parties became a yearly event, but turned out not to be effective fund-raisers—one year, tickets first priced at $500 sold at $250—and Ray begged off after three. He was getting older, he told Pulec, and he got bored sitting through the banquet and speeches. After hours of cocktail chitchat, he needed to let fly a few "motherfuckers" to relieve the pressure of acting polite.

As the tour of Europe approached, Clifford Solomon felt a lump on his neck. From a gig in Idaho he flew to Los Angeles for a biopsy, then took off with the gang for France. When they got back to New York, Clifford called his doctor, and she said the lump was a cancer that must be removed immediately. After surgery and radiation, Clifford got home two days before Thanksgiving and recuperated through the winter of 1988. The cancer had been successfully arrested, but the hospital bills posed a devastating financial threat to his family. Ray called Clifford a few times to say hello, but Ray Charles Enterprises did nothing to help out the bandleader with ten years' service; the company carried insurance only for RPM officeworkers, not band members. A benefit concert sponsored by Local 47 saved the Solomons.

In the spring Clifford went to Japan with Ray for a short tour to test his strength. He found playing no problem, but he was still too weak to carry his suitcase between one-nighters. He decided he had to leave the band, and he went with Johnny Otis, playing weeklong hotel gigs where he could rest in his room when he got tired. Ray let him go without a word, a slight that modest Clifford attempted to downplay. "My illness was severe and Ray could have done more," was the most he would say in criticism years later, "but I don't hold that against him."

Nineteen eighty-eight began with Ray putting the finishing touches on the R&B album *Just Between Us,* and a splendid album it turned out to be. The names on the credits— Doc Pomus, Milt Jackson, Percy Mayfield, Ralph Burns, Marty Paich—tell the story: Ray reveling in his past, going back to sounds and styles as comfortable as old shoes.

He touches every base, country in "Over the Top," rocking guitar blues on "Too Hard to Love You," and a tender ballad with Gladys Knight, "I Wish I'd Never Loved You at All." For the first time in years, Ray got the big band into RPM to record, and laying out Ray's own creamy horn lines on "Stranger in My Own Hometown," the fellows didn't let him down. Not everything looks backward: Ray uses velvety violins behind his keyboard solos as he did in Sid Feller's heyday, but now he's not playing piano but synths that chime like tubular bells. Ray saves the album high point for last: "Save the Bones for Henry Jones ('cause Henry don't eat no meat)." "Save the Bones" is a delicious old chestnut, and Ray and straight man Lou Rawls jive in front of the band like zoot suit blades cracking up an Apollo crowd in 1948.

Such ease, however, was not so easy in the making. For one track Ray brought in Percy Heath, famed bassist of the Modern Jazz Quartet. Ray hummed the lick he wanted Heath to play, but somehow Heath couldn't get it right. "Try this," Ray said, and when that didn't work, Ray suggested something else. For all his experience, Heath started trembling and then froze. Finally Ray said, disgusted, "I'll do it myself on synth." Simmons drove Heath to the airport. "Tell Ray I'm sorry I couldn't get it the way he wanted," he said, almost in tears. "He doesn't have to pay me." When Simmons got back to RPM, he told Ray. "Goddamn right I ain't gonna pay him!" exploded Ray. "Damn Percy Heath!"

Two notable events got Ray to New York in May. The first was the 100th birthday salute to Irving Berlin at Carnegie Hall with an all-star cast, including Shirley MacLaine, Tony Bennett, and Marilyn Horne. For his segment, Ray sent Simmons down to RPM's fireproof vault to unearth the charts for "How Deep Is the Ocean" and "What'll I Do." Peering at the long shelves of music folders and tape reels, Simmons felt like he was deep in the Smithsonian. The show itself was well-nigh perfect, Ray resplendent in a bright blue silk jacket. "I love a Berlin song the way an actor loves a good script," he said, then sang the two ballads with unsurpassed poignancy, slipping into a heavenly falsetto on "How Deep" that held the house breathless.

The next two nights Ray spent at Lincoln Center with the New York City Ballet. Dancer and choreographer Peter Martins had long been begging Ray to reassemble the small band for a ballet featuring classic hits Martins had loved growing up in Denmark. Ray stalled him. What did dance-hall R&B have to do with ballet? When Martins enlisted Ahmet Ertegun to argue on his side, Ray agreed, bringing back Fathead, Phil Guilbeau, and Hank Crawford and weaving "I Got a Woman," "Georgia," "Hit the Road Jack," and others into "A Fool for You," a forty-minute piece for dancers, band, and orchestra. Once into rehearsal, Ray loved the work. The only problem came when Joe Adams, left out on the sidelines, magnified a technical glitch into a reason to dress down Martins in condescending tones. Furious at being embarrassed by his manager, Ray told Adams in icy tones, "You can take your stuff and go." Dave Simmons thought Joe was truly fired, but he learned that such blowups were commonplace. Sellout crowds at Lincoln Center cheered "A Fool for You" mightily, PBS filmed it, and Martins booked Ray to repeat the program the following year. Critics liked the music better than the ballet: the Raelets, said *The Village Voice,* had "more rhythm than the hapless dancers."

The touring season got under way in late May—a little later each year, it seemed. Cinemax filmed the gang in Rome with Little Richard, Bo Diddley, and Fats Domino for a "Legends of Rock 'n' Roll" cable TV show, and *Parade* magazine held a promotion: "Write Ray Charles if you want 'America the Beautiful' to replace 'The Star-Spangled Banner' as the national anthem." At Ray's fifty-eighth-birthday party, the California Raisins serenaded the honoree, much to the crowd's delight: a currently popular TV commercial featured Ray as a cartoon raisin, singing "I Heard It Through the Grapevine." *Just Between Us* died upon release, and Columbia, wanting country music from Ray, not R&B, decided that the relationship had been lovely but had to come to an end. Ray was a freelancer once more.

Another good thing came to an end: Ray's eighteen-year affair with Ruth Robinson. All had been peaceable between the lovers, Ruth still seeing other men, when in stepped accident. One Tuesday night as Ruth dropped a boyfriend off at LA airport, Ray and his valet walked in front of her car. She knew instantly that the valet would tell Ray whom he had seen, and she decided that Ray had better hear it directly from her. The valet took Ray to a seat and went off to the airline ticket counter. Ruth approached casually and asked, "Where are you going?"

Ray knew that Ruth usually worked late at the *Hollywood Reporter* on Tuesdays and showed his surprise. "What are you doing here?"

"I'm dropping off a friend."

"Oh," said Ray. Ruth's boyfriend Bill came over and she introduced the two men, who, it turned out, were both flying to Atlanta. On the plane they chatted, and Bill told Ray, "I'm going to marry that girl." When they got off the plane in Atlanta, both called Ruth within seconds of each other. Bill had been thrilled to meet Ray, but Ray said nothing about Bill, just that he'd arrived safely. Long experience had taught him to avoid asking women unnecessary questions, and until Bill, he hadn't had to face the fact that Ruth saw other men. Now he did. A few weeks passed before he asked, "Who's this guy that's gonna marry you?"

"There's no guy who's gonna marry me," Ruth replied. "He can't marry me unless I marry him back, right? And you know I'm not doing that."

"Okay," said Ray. "I'm not whimpering and hollering."

And with that, their romance ended. Ruth would have gladly kept it going, staying available to Ray no matter what else was going on in her life; but without the illusion that Ruth was waiting only for him, Ray didn't want her and he stopped calling. Ruth felt hurt, but like Ray, she didn't whimper and went on with her life.

Ray moved on to other women. As he took his boss on late-night runs across LA, Simmons' job was to help reinforce in each woman the belief that though Ray might be busy or might have to run, she was his one and only. As the 80s became the 90s, Ray ventured less often beyond his familiar harem, scared, quite reasonably, of AIDS. "I feel sorry for young people today," he told Simmons ruefully. "We had it where you could get you some before the show, get you some in the middle of the show, and get you some at the end of the show!" When Susaye Green warned him, as an old friend, about the danger of unprotected sex, Ray smiled and ducked the issue. "Oh, I ain't doin' nothing. If I did half the things that people say I did . . ."

In the winter of 1989, as in so many winters past, Ray began a new album. With no advance from a label, he made low cost a primary objective. Jimmy Lewis, as always, had been peppering him with song demos, and the latest batch had a sound Ray liked. "Who's the band?" he asked Lewis. One man, said Lewis, Charles Richard Cason, an arranger-keyboardist who specialized in creating entire tracks—guitars, strings, horns, hand claps, and drums—using synthesizers and sound samplers. Curious, Ray invited Cason to RPM and as an audition asked him to overdub bass and horn parts on old tracks. Ray liked the results, and started working with him on an album, starting with Lewis' comedy rap "Child Support, Alimony." With a few tracks in the can, Ray started shopping for a label.

After a benefit for the Lighthouse for the Blind, the tour rolled out again. In Europe, Simmons toured the coliseum in Rome and the canals of Venice when Ray was sleeping before show time. Only in the Alps did he feel sorry for Ray—all this beauty and the boss couldn't see it. Ray and Simmons flew first-class to Australia for a string gig, the drummer, bass player, and guitar player in coach. Arriving in Sydney, they flew four hours in a small plane and two more in a helicopter to a millionaire's estate in the outback, where four thousand people sat on grass as smooth as a golf green and listened to Ray with the Australian Symphony Orchestra. After the gig, they immediately reversed direction and flew back to LA.

For all the tedium of travel, the music was still magnificent. "Ray would do things with his voice so gorgeous that I'd think he would do them again, but no, just that one time!" recalled sax player Rudy Johnson. "When Ray sang 'For Mama' for the French, just him and the piano, you could hear a pin drop. He *drained* the people." Ray never relaxed the musical discipline for an instant. If Al Jackson, the new bandleader, counted the fellows off too fast one night on a jazz piece before Ray's entrance, he'd surely hear about it at intermission. "No, man, no," Ray would tell him. "That's not the tempo we do 'Our Suite' at." Then he'd start thumping his chest with both palms to a steady beat, the sound echoing in the cinder-block corridor. "*This* is the tempo for 'Our Suite.' "

Jean-Pierre Grosz, meanwhile, had become the manager of singer Dee Dee Bridgewater and built her into a major jazz act in Europe. A smart next move, Grosz figured, would be a duet with Ray. He got Dee Dee booked as Ray's opening act at the Palais des Sports in '89 and asked Ray to hear her. "You know I love duets," said Jean-Pierre. "I think you and her and a good song . . ." "No problem," said Ray. "Find the song." Grosz called a dozen songwriters and explained how to write for Ray Charles: "Ray doesn't like abstract songs, forget pink flying elephants. The song has to be *real.*" Songwriters Ronnie Bird and Pierre Papadiamandis came up with "Til the Next Somewhere," a bittersweet ballad of two singers and their love affair on the road. "That's perfect," said Ray, and when finished, the record fulfilled the song's promise: two rough, rich voices blending in a pop-Puccini tearjerker that builds from harps pianissimo to a honking sax climax, then ebbs away.

"Til the Next Somewhere" became a #1 hit all over Europe—though never released in the States—and Ray came back numerous times to do the duet with Dee Dee on TV. When an airline foulup kept him from getting to the Sanremo Festival by scheduled flight, Ray chartered a Boeing 737 from London to Nice, flew through a storm over the Gulf of Gascony, and made the gig. After one Belgian TV show, Grosz and Ray got to bed at four A.M. and got up at six for an eight A.M. flight. In the car to the airport both were groggy, but on the plane, Ray bent down to his bag and pulled out his chessboard. "Jean-Pierre," he said, "let's play chess."

"You must be kidding," said Jean-Pierre. "We slept two hours, we haven't had coffee."

"Your head has to be working all the time, Jean-Pierre," said Ray. "Don't become lazy, son—play!" And they did.

Ray's label shopping took him through the Cahuenga Pass to Warner Bros. in Burbank. Mo Ostin, WB Records' longtime president, wanted his shot at working with the Genius. Ray found Ostin, like Ahmet Ertegun, an old pro he could trust, and once WB ceded ownership of the masters, he signed a contract and pushed ahead on the album with Jimmy Lewis and Rich Cason. Joe Adams too had a fish on the line: Pepsi-Cola. Talks with Pepsi and ad agency executives from BBD&O were developing toward a series of TV ads starring Ray. He'd be endorsing Diet Pepsi, but instead of making him give a standard spiel, they planned to film him in low-key comic moments. Pepsi was also negotiating with quarterback Joe Montana to play Ray's buddy in a series of spots for the 1990 Super Bowl, commercials guaranteed to warm the hearts of every regular Joe in America.

Another decade was coming to an end. In the new year, Ray would turn sixty. His hair had turned totally white, and coming through airports, slightly stooped on Simmons' arm, he had begun to look old. People stopped to stare at the famous figure suddenly in view—"Look, there's Ray Charles!"—and when Simmons got him seated to wait for the flight, they gathered around to say hello.

RC Robinson had come a long way from Greenville, Florida. He was a wealthy and powerful man and had been one for thirty years. Once the Federal government had forced him to give up heroin; now the president called him on his birthday. Ray lived life as he pleased, music his only master. "I'm the kind of guy," he told a reporter, "I conform when it suits me, and when it doesn't suit me, I don't." Ray's body-shaking laughter and primal self-confidence could make him exhilarating company, yet he could wound friends with a curt, dismissive word. A lover, a battler, a still-prolific artist—in the late prime of his life, Ray Charles Robinson had become one of those willful few of whom one can truly say, they bestride the earth.

Hints of this complex energy emanated from the blind man in the airport. A few fans held back, made timid by Ray's sudden changes of expression, his flailing body, even by the wide grins and "God bless you, darling" that he dispensed like holy water on all. Many more, however, approached Ray readily as one who had many times touched their hearts with music, an old friend whom they had never met but already loved. If Simmons took off to get himself a snack, he'd return to find Ray's seat surrounded, four rows deep, kids in the front, Ray bending forward to catch their stammered hellos and answer their questions. "At first I thought he'd mind, but he loved it," recalled Simmons. "He'd only get upset if people didn't come up to him. Kids knew him from *Sesame Street,* black folks knew him from the blues, and the white folks knew him from all that country-and-western. Everybody knew Ray, everywhere in the world."

PART VII

THE 1990s:
THE GRAND MASTER

**Ray at a jazz festival
in Holland, 1990.**

Tad Hershorn

No Time to
Waste Time
1990s

On the last Sunday of January 1990, at Super Bowl XXIV, the San Francisco 49ers defeated the Denver Broncos, 55–10, a triumph engineered with dazzling skill by quarterback Joe Montana, making him for the moment the most famous and admired athlete in America. The 49ers' victory came as good news for Ray Charles because, in commercial breaks worth $700,000 per thirty seconds, Pepsi-Cola began running the Ray-and-Joe buddy ads. Montana's golden charm contrasted nicely with Ray's dark, rambunctious style in the simply filmed spots, and millions of Super Bowl viewers got a kick out of the good-natured sparring that sweetened the commercial message: "Diet Pepsi—you got the right one, baby."

Future generations may well chuckle at the "cola wars" that raged on American supermarket shelves and TV screens in the early 1990s: two soft-drink superpowers, Coke and Pepsi, battling to win the heart of the public by trumpeting minor changes in flavor as major shifts in taste. Yet the cola wars gave Ray's long comeback a final boost over the top. Surveys proved the first series of ads to be liked and well remembered, and Pepsi began to plan a more elaborate campaign featuring Ray in '91. At a time of slow record and royalty income, the Pepsi connection was a big deal for Ray Charles Enterprises, bringing in a seven-figure influx of cash. In RPM's office politics, landing Pepsi greatly redounded to Joe Adams' credit, cementing the relationship between artist and manager even more tightly as they began their fourth decade together.

The landmark age of sixty approached, and Ray continued working as if the numbers meant nothing. "If I didn't know how old I was," he told reporters, "I'd think I was in my mid-thirties. Music to me is my blood, it's my breathing, it's my everything. . . . And I'm going to do it until God himself says, 'Brother Ray, you've been a good horse, but now I'm going to put you out to pasture.' " Others didn't have his constitution. Sid Feller, seventy-four and suffering from angina, retired from conducting, and he and Gert moved to a retirement community in Camarillo, California. Sid and Ray occasionally chatted on the phone, and Joe Adams sent a box of steaks every Christmas, but Ray found it hard to believe that Sid didn't keep going till the last breath. "How can you just stop making music?" he said often when Sid's name came up. "I'll never understand it."

Victor Vanacore, a trim New Haven native and Berklee College of Music grad, replaced Sid as Ray's string conductor. Vanacore was a complete pro in the specialized field of conducting strings for pop; his résumé included long stints with the Jackson Five, Johnny Mathis, and Barry Manilow. Joe Adams called him in one Wednesday to ask if he could do Athens, Georgia, with Ray Friday night. "How do you know I'm going to work for you?" Vanacore asked. "We'll find out Friday night," Joe replied. Vanacore met Ray briefly, but the Genius was standoffish, asking no questions, making no suggestions. "This man doesn't know the meaning of nervous," Vanacore thought. "He'll pull this gig off no matter what. A good conductor is just icing on the cake."

At rehearsal the afternoon of the gig, Vanacore finally got the music and a song list. He opened the conductor's book to find Sid's sketches—three pages, for example, on "You Can't Take That Away from Me," but no chord symbols, lyrics, or melody. The basic key was F major, Vanacore saw; glancing ahead, he saw a bunch of B-naturals and figured, "Aha, that's the bridge going into A minor." He raised his baton, thinking, "This is my audition?" But Vanacore found, as the music began, that he barely needed the score. If he caught enough of the written time-values to keep his hands going right, he could get everything else he needed from watching Ray's body sway in time with the chord changes. They finished the tune. Ray said, "Okay, next one," and Vanacore knew he had passed his audition.

The first year Vanacore did ten string gigs with Ray; in the mid-90s the total grew to sixty, diminishing later to about twenty a year. Like Sid before him, Vanacore became orchestra librarian, finding the charts in RPM's vault and putting them together into books according to the song list he got from Ray. Sometimes he faxed the orchestras one tricky violin part in advance; otherwise the books traveled in wheeled suitcases that the road manager never let out of his sight. Working with new players at nearly every gig, Vanacore developed rehearsal rules: be animated, say little, neither bully the players nor beg them, add a dash of humor. He urged the classical players to phrase jazz style, to *lean* into the notes instead of playing them straight up and down. "Two minutes of rehearsal would tell me if they were stilted or not," Vanacore explained. "If so, we had to live with it. The performance would be stiff, but we'd be gone in the morning."

Most challenging was conducting the orchestra through the long passages of "For Mama," "Yesterday," and "Be My Love" that Ray played rubato. As rock-steady rhythm, "the groove" is a glory of African music, rubato is a glory of European music. Music played rubato can stretch and squeeze in time just as it can swell and sink in volume. Operas, symphonies, and chamber music scores are filled with fermatas that slow down and accelerandos that rush the tempo to suit surges in the musical/emotional flow. "Ray's rubato, no matter how slow, always had a pulse, beats pushing us along," Vanacore said, "but they're floating beats. I *float* the orchestra, waiting for him to breathe, start a new phrase. When everyone's breathing together, Ray leading, me following— sometimes me leading and Ray following!—it's like two people dancing. For that hour, we're one."

Once, after Vanacore had gotten the orchestra going, Ray hit the wrong button on his synth and got a sound he didn't like. He kept playing while fumbling for the right button, but Vanacore cut off the orchestra and signaled them to go back to the top and wait for Ray to get his sound and fake his way back to an opening. When he did, Vanacore gently wafted his fifty-plus players back in and the audience never noticed a thing. Afterward in the dressing room, Ray laughed and said, "I gotta give you some skin, man! How did you do it? Once you waved the orchestra out, I *knew* you were waiting on me!" Moments like that Vanacore recalled as pure magic: "It's something that you can't talk about, a gift, an insight. I can't explain it and Ray can't either."

Unlike Stevie Wonder, who rotated four or five valets, Ray worked one until he burned out. As the gang gathered to take to the road in the spring of '90, Dave Simmons was tired. Not that Ray was mean—Simmons felt close to him, "a wise uncle I didn't want to disappoint," but the sheer mileage he logged carrying bags had worn him down, as had Joe Adams' nit-picking interference. Once Adams tried to make Simmons pay for his room, and Simmons told him, "Okay, and *you* explain to Ray why he's at the $500-a-night hotel and I'm a mile away at Motel 6." In public Ray always backed Joe up, but privately he told Simmons, "David, don't even worry about Joe. I don't know how his wife stands him." For months after he quit, Simmons still heard Ray's urgent "David!" in his sleep. Vernon Troupe came back to help Ray and found that not much had changed. "When he gets his sleep and everything's going exactly how he wants it, Ray is the kindest person in the world, but . . . !"

California, Las Vegas, and Phoenix on the way to the East Coast, then European jazz festivals in June and July—the road held few surprises. American crowds seemed bigger that summer because of the Pepsi ads, and "I'll Be Good to You," Ray's sizzling duet with Chaka Khan that had hit big in the discos over the winter. Black veterans like Ernie Vantrease, Rudy Johnson, and James Clay were now outnumbered in the band by young white players—"Konservatory Kids," *Downbeat* called them—who cared more for the credit "Toured with Ray Charles" than the money. After his sixtieth-birthday party, the last EAR benefit, Ray played a week with the gang at the Blue Note in New York, then took off around the world with B. B. King and a "Superband" of jazz stars, including Harry "Sweets" Edison and Ray Brown, while the fellows took a break until November.

Working with Jimmy Lewis and Rich Cason, Ray had assembled an album's worth of material, and he turned it in to Mo Ostin as his first WB album, *Would You Believe?* Ostin was taken aback at the appearance of finished tracks into which he'd had no input, and his A&R staff were disappointed in, and even suspicious of, Ray's submission. The tracks sounded boring, unfinished, and so cheaply produced as to be nearly unreleasable. Could Ray be turning in a grab bag of demos to snatch up a recording advance scaled to a much more expensive production? Ostin called Ray to a meeting to tell him to put this album aside and do another. With Ray sitting across the table, however, no one dared say it that bluntly. Someone aired tentative criticisms, and Ray rebuffed them angrily. Weak material? Hell, no! Ray *believed* in *Would You Believe?*; there were two or three hits on it at least. "Ellie My Love" had just been #1 in Japan! Ostin talked Ray into letting WB producer Richard Perry redo a few tracks, but after hearing fifteen seconds of the first, Ray stopped the tape, shouting, "No one is going to touch my work." WB decided to release *Would You Believe?* as is. If that was the price of doing business with Ray Charles, so be it. This album could be quietly let die; the second one would be the major album.

Like much of the work Ray turned in to Atlantic in the late 70s, *Would You Believe?* is better than the record company realized. Ray sticks to his traditional territory—blues, ballads, and comedy—but the synthesized sounds and drum machine beats give off a sizzling contemporary heat. "Child Support, Alimony" is funky, funny rap—"She's eating steak, I'm eating baloney," Ray complains; a sympathetic buddy murmurs, "The witch"—and he sings up a storm on "Let's Get Back to Where We Left Off," a sexy duet with soul singer Peggy Scott. Still, the WB executives had a point. *Would You*

Believe? lacks focus; it burbles on from track to track, stumbling over a few duds, without ever reaching a high point or creating an overall impression. After its release in September, Ray complained bitterly that WB didn't promote the album, though the label did get Ray a spot on Johnny Carson to sing "Ellie My Love." *Would You Believe?* sold under 50,000 copies—"went into the toilet," as one executive put it—and even the secretaries at WB knew that the top brass considered Ray Charles a difficult man to deal with.

On Super Bowl Sunday, 1991, Diet Pepsi introduced the second series of Ray Charles commercials, the famous "Uh-huh" campaign that ran on television for over two years. The ads now had a bouncy R&B jingle with the hook "You've got the right one, baby, uh-huh," and came in two basic versions. In the first, Ray sits at the piano playing the jingle with three lovely young ladies at his side. "You know I just love this new Diet Pepsi song," he says to them, "but do you think it's caught on yet?" With that, a montage begins of African villagers chanting, "You've got the right one, baby, uh-huh," African-Americans wailing it in a country church, Buddhists intoning it, and geishas singsonging it. In the second, titled "Audition," a punk rocker, a flamenco guitarist, an Austrian accordionist, comedian Jerry Lewis, and a dog all try singing the "Uh-huh" song, but, it turns out, only Ray can do it with proper panache. Both ads are colorful little films, and apart from the obvious sales pitch, make two implicit points: Ray's music is universal, and even on a silly tune like the "Uh-huh" song, no one does it better than Ray.

The "Uh-huh" commercials made a splash in the airwaves as few such ephemera do. *The New York Times* called the jingle "infectiously cheerful," and *Time* named the ad number one in its Top Ten TV ads of 1991. In 1992 Pepsi added $50 million to the campaign's budget, marketed a line of "Uh-huh" T-shirts, and sponsored promotional appearances by Ray and the gang at shopping malls around the country. Like "Brusha, brusha, brusha" in the 50s and "Where's the beef?" in the 80s, "You've got the right one, baby" became a 90s catchphrase, and Ray Charles became more than ever the ubiquitous Grandpa of Pop.

The success of the "Uh-huh" campaign surprised Ray, Joe, and everyone else at RPM. "Let's be honest," said one longtime Ray-watcher, "Pepsi saved Ray's ass." Why did this silliness click, when the albums Ray labored on rolled over and died? There was no way of telling, but the money was certain, as was the surge of fame. On gigs, the fellows felt a new brightness in the audiences' response to Ray. Pepsi made him less an oldtimer and more a hip star of the 90s. In airports the crush of well-wishers grew deeper, and children often recognized Ray before their parents did. "Hey, Ray," passersby sang out, big grins on their faces, "you got the right one, baby, uh-huh!" "You can see why they're calling it my biggest hit," Ray told reporters, but he also downplayed the splash so that it wouldn't swamp his other accomplishments. "My thing goes way beyond the Pepsi commercial," he said. "The commercial was good for both of us, but I wouldn't call it the biggest thing in my career."

Ray's sixty-first birthday celebration came at a "Ray Charles—50 Years in Music" concert on September 19 at the Pasadena Civic Auditorium, filmed for broadcast on the Fox network in October. Both the concert and the TV special turned out to be glossy, varied shows with superb music from Ray and his guests: Stevie Wonder, Willie Nelson, Gladys Knight, and many more, including Paul McCartney on videotape from London. Ray was in top form, singing a blistering "Living for the City" with Stevie, an uproarious "Busted" with Willie, and a rhapsodically tender "Just for a Thrill" all by himself. "I am overwhelmed," Ray said when the time came for a few words. "You all could have gone somewhere else tonight!" Again the climax came with all the stars crowding around Ray to sing "America the Beautiful."

Experienced television producers put the "50 Years" show together, but Ray Charles Jr. worked with them as producer at the RPM end. He did a good job through two years of details and delays, and the big night marked a high point for Ray Jr. at his father's company. In the concert program he gave special thanks to "My Dad—for your love, the opportunity to achieve, and for believing in me." Yet this isolated success didn't lead to a promotion for almost forty-year-old Ray Jr. His frustration fanned a destructive cocaine habit. For weeks at a time the family didn't know where he was. Della worried endlessly.

The Robinson family had grown apart. Della sold the house on Southridge, and the family no longer had a center. David came out of prison, married, and started a quiet new life. Little Bobby turned thirty, moved to San Diego, and became pastor of a small church. Ray kept only in distant touch with them. Della still baked him cakes and sent them to his office on his birthday and holidays, but on more substantive matters, Joe often blocked her access to Ray. "I can't do anything without getting it past Joe," she complained. "He's the gatekeeper." *People* magazine published photos of Ray playing with his granddaughters Erin and Blair, but this was a contrived photo opportunity, not usual practice. The girls often asked Duana, "How come we don't see Grandfather?" (This was their name for Ray, more formal than the intimate "Grandpa" they bestowed on Duana's dad.) Duana found it hard to explain.

[IIIIIIIIIII]

In January 1992, PBS aired *Ray Charles: The Genius of Soul,* an excellent one-hour biography in its American Masters series. While including stage footage going back to the mid-50s, the film digs well below Ray's showbiz façade. Film clips of the Old South suggest the poverty from which he sprang, and newspaper montages from the drug bust days suggest the crises he lived through. One fascinating segment shows Ray shaving with his dark glasses off, his face looking relaxed and vulnerable. In another, he's laughing wildly backstage about some poor guy who "had to pay for pussy!" Only a few months before, Atlantic had released a three-CD box entitled *Ray Charles: The Birth of Soul,* which contained, in chronological order and with notes of session dates and sidemen, all fifty-seven of Ray's Atlantic R&B singles. The CD box received well-deserved raves, and it and the PBS documentary marked a new stage in Ray's critical canonization. Music writers who had once bewailed Ray's decline into saccharine pop now praised him as a visionary. "The paradigm for black pop music today," *The New York Times* opined in a review of the CD set, "owes its being to the radical discoveries of Ray Charles."

The '92 tour rolled on like so many before it. Ray finally gave Jeff Kaye a featured trumpet solo, sixteen bars on "Just for a Thrill," and after eight years, Kaye figured, now he had a chance to equal Johnny Coles' "Am I Blue." Playing the solo became a moment Kaye hoped for every night and treasured when it came. "Ray would be concentrating on me one hundred percent. If I changed what I played, he'd go with it. We hardly ever talked off stage, but onstage we had a musical conversation without saying a word. We got to be like a married couple, knowing what the other person was going to say before he said it."

Working with Ray was less fun for Shantih Mathews, a twenty-year-old guitarist in his first year on the road. The son of Tony Mathews, who played guitar with Ray in the 60s and 70s, Shantih took the job over his father's objections. "They don't treat you like a human out there," Mathews told his son. "I went out because I had to, but you can finish college, get your degree." Shantih went anyway but developed pneumonia in Japan at the end of the season. When they gathered at the Tokyo airport to fly back to New York for holiday gigs, Shantih couldn't walk. The airport doctor put him on intravenous fluids and into a hospital bed.

"Get up, let's go, the plane is leaving," Joe Hunter told Shantih. When that didn't work, Joe Adams came in and told him, "Stop acting like a goddamn baby." Shantih still couldn't get up, and the gang flew off, leaving him no ticket. Shantih called home, and Mathews told him to use his credit card and come as soon as he could. Mathews and his wife picked Shantih up at LA airport with a wheelchair and took him to the UCLA hospital, where he began to recover. Several of the fellows called to say they were sorry about what Ray had done. Clifford Solomon suggested that maybe Ray didn't know about it; Mathews should call RPM, Ray might reimburse Shantih's airfare. Mathews did call, but Ray instantly got on the defensive.

"I didn't leave Shantih in Japan," Ray told Mathews. "I had a ticket for him, he just didn't want to get on the plane."

Shantih had been in the hopsital with an IV in his arm, Mathews said.

"I can't make nobody get on no plane," Ray exploded. "He didn't want to get on the plane." As Mathews had often seen on the road, Ray let his anger build to a frenzy until he was ranting that black people should stick together instead of always believing the worst of each other. "I should never have answered this phone call," Ray concluded. "I got all these people out on the road, and if every time somebody says they're sick I gotta pay their plane ticket, man, I just can't do no shit like that." And he slammed down the phone.

Encouraged by his father, Shantih sued Ray through the musicians' union, but he lost. Mathews cornered a union official. "Here's a kid," he said. "He joins your union, and his first time on the road, Ray Charles runs off and leaves him in Japan. But you listen to Joe Adams telling you that Shantih was just a homesick boy on the road. If you can't stand up to Joe Adams and Ray Charles for one of your own members, you're a failure as a human being." But they were words in the wind. Shantih appealed and lost again.

By 1992 Dee Dee Bridgewater and Jean-Pierre Grosz had professional differences and split up. With time on his hands, Grosz went to Ray. "You saw what we did with the duet," he said. "Now how about a whole album?" "You got it," said Ray. "Start." At first they planned that Grosz would produce the album with his own money and own the masters, but after a few months Ray asked, "If you don't mind, and only if it doesn't bother you, could we change one thing? I'll own the tapes. All you have to do is send me the drawings."

"Send me the drawings"—in Ray's shorthand that meant the bills, and Grosz could tell that Ray didn't expect to be opposed. "No, I don't mind," he said. "It's your life, your music." Thereafter Grosz did an accounting every six months, sent Ray a bill, and a week later had the money in his Paris bank. Grosz whipped his songwriters into action and every few months presented Ray with the best demos. "This one yes, this one no, this one maybe," Ray would comment. When he said yes, he'd sketch it on the piano and say, "Jean-Pierre, do that one in A-flat." Grosz then lined up lyricists and arrangers, putting them in competition with one another. A few complained, but Grosz told them, "If I don't like your song, you get nothing; if I do, Ray Charles is going to sing it. You want to take the risk?" The better writers, he found, liked the challenge. Soon he was booking studios and hiring musicians. As Grosz finished the instrumental tracks, Ray sang to them, then Grosz took them back to Paris for mixing.

More than a year into the work, Grosz learned that his father was dying of lung cancer. He called Ray from his apartment in Montparnasse and told him that he didn't know what to do. "Jean-Pierre, you love your father, don't you?" asked Ray.

"Of course I do," said Grosz.

"So, if you can afford it, stop everything, stay with your father until his last day. Don't worry about the album, just be with your father." Grosz did stop everything, and he long felt grateful for Ray's thoughtfulness. "Most people in this business don't care about your personal problems," he said. "You hear all kinds of bullshit about Ray, but what I've *lived* with him, that's where you see a man, a real friend."

Ray, meanwhile, started another album in '92, the second album for Warner Bros. Two years had healed the scars of *Would You Believe?*, and this time Ray agreed to make the album the label wanted. Mo Ostin put Benny Medina, head of WB's black-music division, in charge of the project, but realizing that he couldn't bring it off on his own, Medina asked Richard Perry to work with Ray as the hands-on producer. Perry had made a specialty of designing comeback albums for artists who had passed their peak, and he had scored notable successes with Fats Domino, Barbra Streisand, and Diana Ross. Some thought that with Perry producing Ray, ego clashes were inevitable—"Richard thinks he's a bigger star than his artists," said one WB insider—but Perry was eager to work with the Genius. "If I could work with Barbra Streisand," he told Medina, "I can work with Ray Charles."

At their first meetings, Perry felt Ray bristle at working with an outside producer. "He's been independent so long, he's painted himself into a corner," Perry thought. "He almost doesn't want success." Perry pushed ahead, choosing songs and taking demos over to RPM, from which Ray approved a pop-R&B-gospel blend that included two well-known tunes, "A Song for You" by Leon Russell and "Still Crazy After All These Years" by Paul Simon. Ray gave Perry his keys, but on several he didn't take time to let his voice truly settle. After the charts were done in one key, Ray called to say, "Rich, sorry, but I made a mistake. . . ."

When recording began, Ray came to only one instrumental session and declared that he'd do his vocals at RPM; he didn't want Perry there. Perry sent the backing tapes over and heard nothing until an abrupt call: "I've got the first three tracks done. Send someone to pick them up." When he listened, Perry found that Ray had given him only one vocal track. Usually he asked singers to record a half-dozen vocals, from which he'd create a composite; even Barbra Streisand gave him two or three. Perry didn't like many of the liberties Ray took with melody, and he begged him for new vocals. Ray refused. "I tried to find the nicest way to tell him things," Perry recalled. "But no one's ever gonna tell Ray Charles how to sing."

Ray had his own grievances. Whenever he called, it seemed, Perry was out of town and nobody at WB could find him. Perry came to meetings three hours late, and he was always behind in finishing tracks. Ray was furious at what he deemed signal disrespect. "If you're gonna produce me, you gotta be there for me," he complained to Medina. "Quincy Jones, Billy Sherrill, they were always there whenever I needed. That's professionalism, the way it should be." Medina did little but pass Ray's nagging on to Perry, and the producer, now dodging flak from two directions, finished the album, *My World*, feeling that he had left blood on every track.

In January 1993, Ray sang "America the Beautiful" for President Clinton's inaugural gala at the Lincoln Memorial. That October, at a White House dinner during the Somalia crisis, the new president awarded him, Arthur Miller, and Billy Wilder the National Medal of Arts. In between, at Radio City in July, the gang played a superb set, yet made a striking contrast with the opening act. The first group played electric guitars, keyboards and bass, congas, and variety percussion on a stage tangled with wires, creating a thick electronic texture, which, though of no particular interest, did sound like the music on the radio and the '93 charts. When Ray's seventeen-piece brass band came out, sitting in the traditional three rows and leafing through the thick books on their stands, they made a stage picture that hadn't changed since Benny Goodman played the Palomar Ballroom. When they played, with no mikes, the lush big band sounded like a museum piece—jazz gorgeously played, but no longer the music of the day. That sense persisted until Ray came on. Then the power of his singing—and his slippery-slidy synth solos—made the music as fresh and intense as music can be.

When released early in '93, *My World* bore the marks of the struggle between Ray and Richard Perry; indeed, it's nearly split in two by them. Ray's vocals and Perry's tracks exist side by side, in tune but seldom in harmony. Without Ray's guidance, the instrumentals often become strident; the session pianist lacks the magical touch that Ray's playing bestows on all his other records. Ray's singing, on the other hand, is magnificent, richer in range and understanding than ever. When he digs into the lyrics, Ray sings with conviction born of experience, and *My World* comes alive.

> *I've been so many places in my life and time,*
> *I've sung a lot of songs, I've made some bad rhymes,*
> *I've acted out my life on stages,*
> *With ten thousand people watching,*
> *But we're alone and I'm singing this song to you*

Ray ends with "Still Crazy," his favorite song on the album. "I'm a fool for you," he sings over a swinging R&B vamp. "I done lost my mind . . . You got me by your little finger—heh-heh—and I ain't lyin'!"

My World was reviewed widely and well as a major statement by a major artist. Ray's "tattered and cracked" voice balances "knowledge of pain" with "reserves of strength," said *The New York Times*. Sensing a hit, Ostin pushed his staff into an elaborate marketing plan with a busy publicity schedule for Ray. When project coordinator Carolyn Baker laid it out for Ray, however, Ray explained, with a bitter edge, that he wasn't naive about the press. Newspapers hadn't written about him until his name made *them* money. Yes, he'd support the album, but he had his own ground rules: he'd do a video, interviews at RPM, Jay Leno and Arsenio Hall on TV, and that was it. When Ray did the *Tonight Show*, Leno cut him down to one song and put him on last. Ray was furious. Johnny Carson, he raged, had always let him do what he damn pleased. Arsenio Hall, in contrast, was fun, and cracked him up with a joke about the Pepsi Uh-huh girls—"Ray, if you got the right one, can I have the one on the left?" What WB executives noticed, however, was that Ray spoke scornfully of hip-hop music, and that he and Hall talked about the bad old days of segregation and how great Art Tatum was. This was not the hip, modern Ray WB wanted to project.

The artist-label friction slowed *My World*'s sales. Instead of a million-selling "Album of the Year" that would reposition Ray in the pop marketplace, Ostin and Perry got a frustrating *succès d'estime*, which, despite the raves and a Grammy nomination for "A Song for You," crawled slowly toward a fewer-than-200,000-copy net sale. Most disappointing, WB discovered that Ray had lost his hold on the black record-buying market. His tried-and-true black fans were well into middle age and not dashing out to Tower Records to snatch up CDs by Ray or by anybody. WB's black music division couldn't get "A Song for You" played on stations dominated by the youthful hip-hop styles. They tried a couple of the up-tempo contemporary tracks, but the word still came back: "Black radio is not interested in Ray Charles. He's ancient history."

As *My World* petered out in the marketplace, Richard Perry wanted to try again. Ray, he felt, was beginning to trust him. A third album, however, was not to be. Mo Ostin got caught in a palace coup at WB; the corporate moneymen declared him "soft on artists" and made Ray a prime example of the unprofitable pets he coddled. Ostin lost and left WB. Without him, Ray didn't want to stay, and the new top brass willingly let him go. Only Carolyn Baker shed any tears. "He made me mad sometimes," she said, looking back, "but he's a genius and he's allowed to be cranky. Artists think nobody understands them, and honestly, nobody does."

Freelance again. Each time Ray had become label-less in the post-ABC years, he had landed on his feet. Now, after long stints at Atlantic, Columbia, and Warner Bros., where could he go? What other major would sign him when everybody knew his track record? Who still believed the Genius had another "I Can't Stop Loving You" in him? For the moment, no one did, and Ray went back to work on the album with Jean-Pierre Grosz.

The Pepsi campaign finally went off the air in 1994. "A Song for You" did win a Grammy for Best R&B vocal, but as usual Ray didn't go to the awards. On the road in Dallas, his "performance never rose above workmanlike," according to the Fort Worth *Star-Telegram;* in New York the *Times* said, "Mr. Charles moved many audience members to tears." In little Moorhead, Minnesota, on the South Dakota border, Ray played an ill-starred symphony gig. The day was windy and cold, and in the long delay as the orchestra set up, it began to rain and the crowd started streaming to their cars. When Ray came on, he twice asked to have his keyboard moved farther under the stage shelter, but nothing helped. "It was a miserable performance," remembered a fan who was there. "Ray's voice was off, there was little rapport between him and the orchestra." "Well, that's it," Ray said a few bars into "Georgia," and he headed offstage. A few diehards hung around to see if he'd come back, but he never returned.

Ray and Grosz threw themselves body and soul into the new album, tapes flying between Paris and LA as the two perfectionists polished and repolished every track. Ray and Grosz both were using forty-eight-track digital recording consoles, which, by offering infinite choices, encouraged as many experiments. Fortunately, a few tracks fell easily into the pocket. When he heard Grosz's track for the mysterious ballad "Angelina," Ray said, "We've struck oil." After marathon mixing sessions in February 1995, artist and producer declared themselves finished. "To produce an album, made-to-measure, for a star I have loved for years," Grosz recalled, "has been a major achievement of my life."

Strong Love Affair, as they titled the album, stands among Ray's most compelling masterpieces. Despite its handful of sexy rockers, an elegiac mood suffuses *Strong Love Affair.* Ray's voice is beginning to show its age, its rich/rough tones undiminished in strength but mellowed in texture. A lyric to a singer is like a script to an actor, Ray had said years before. Here he interprets his scripts with the depth and precision of a grand master, of Chaplin in *Limelight,* Olivier in *King Lear.* Ray knows both passion—"Who can make you tremble the way I do?"—and dispassion—"I don't play games because I make the rules." He often looks inward—"All along you made me feel this useless guilt"—and more often looks back—"I hear the rain on the windowpane, and it brings back memories."

Grosz's blend of live and synthesized instruments frame Ray as delicately as Sid Feller's strings and oboes did thirty years before, yet Grosz contributes Gallic flavors of his own, moods as bittersweet as black coffee in a Left Bank bistro. "Angelina," *Strong Love Affair*'s *chef d'oeuvre*, opens with the sound of waves breaking softly on shore, a mournful organ, and scattered notes on electric piano. "Angelina, why did you have to go—ahh, baby," Ray sings, his voice more intimate with the mike, with the listener, than ever before. He kept watch over Angelina as she fell ill and often heard her weep, yet she never let him hold her until the day before she died. A gorgeous electric guitar solo expresses the inexpressible, and then Ray returns, with the sound of the waves, to cry a last heartbroken farewell to "my angel in the sky."

Grosz had no trouble placing *Strong Love Affair* with Gala Records in Italy, the label that had done well with the Ray–Dee Dee Bridgewater duet. Yet when he began shopping for an American label, he got the runaround. From flattering but painful rejections, Grosz learned that Ray was "too big in reputation, and too small in sales." A label could sign him only as a major artist, but by the numbers, Ray was, and long had been, a minor artist. "It seemed incredible," Grosz recalled, "but in America, Ray had become a dinosaur." He confessed his disappointment to Ray, but Ray told him not to worry. He would do some shopping around himself.

Ray Jr. came back to RPM from drug rehabilitation with a new project: a "Ray Charles: My Early Years" booklet and a greatest hits CD that he could sell at concerts. Ray okayed and put up the money for the project, but he told Ray Jr. that he had better hustle until he paid back every damn penny. The 1995 season got under way with April's New Orleans Jazz Festival. The regular band hadn't reassembled, so Carl Hunter called old-timers like Phil Guilbeau and Marcus Belgrave to fill some of the empty seats. Clifford Solomon was skeptical until Hunter said Leroy Cooper was coming. "The Hog?" said Clifford. "Okay, I'll make it!" The gig felt like old home week, and everybody, Ray included, had a ball.

One morning that spring Ray woke up with a pain in his back. An internist checked him for kidney stones and put him in the hospital overnight, but found nothing wrong. Ray went on to do a gig in Reno, still in discomfort. "Didn't it hurt you?" the doctor asked him at his next visit. "When I start playing," Ray said, "I forget about it." Otherwise, Ray found himself in vigorous health as he approached sixty-five, as exuberant, vulgar, and opinionated as ever. "The doctor says I got the blood pressure of an eighteen-year-old," he boasted. Trim and muscular himself, Ray had no patience for younger men who let themselves get overweight. When he heard trombonist Charlie

Shofner had put on a few pounds, Ray took him by the shoulders and gave him the "Dr. Ray" treatment. "Why do you like to eat?" he asked, his face inches away from Shofner's. "I like the taste," said Charlie. "Me too!" Ray shouted. "But I eat until I'm full, then I go away from the table, and since I was eighteen, I've weighed between 165 and 171 pounds. You try eating and getting away from the table, and come and see me in eight weeks."

Ray let none of his crew forget that he was the hub of the wheel. The road was still Ray Charles University for the group, and the boss could still call a tune they hadn't played for months and then bitch if it wasn't letter-perfect. When promoters gave them free hotel rooms, they kept mum. "If Ray hears about it," said one veteran, "he goes apeshit." At RPM, Ray still patrolled the corridors daily, making sure that his castle was secure. One morning after an LA gig, Ray stomped into Joe's office asking why the side door to the building had been left unlocked. "It's not a door you can forget to lock," he explained petulantly. "You have to unlock it with a key, and I want to know who did it." The janitor, maybe, said Joe, acting unconcerned. "I don't want it to happen again, *ever!*" said Ray, stomping out again.

Ray had no better luck label-shopping than Grosz until he talked to Quincy Jones. Ray and Quincy—"Sixty-nine" and "Seventy," they nicknamed each other—were still close a half-century after their youthful meeting in rainy Seattle. "My true brother," Ray called his old friend, and the two men had weathered years of working, talking, and drinking together as comrades. Ray could scream at Quincy "hard enough to take the enamel off his teeth," said an associate, but Quincy bore with him patiently. Afterward, Ray would make amends by showing up at Quincy's house in Bel Air bearing expensive gifts, once a gold-and-diamond medallion with "50 Years" engraved on the back. Always more adroit at playing the LA music biz game than Ray, Jones could see that his old mentor needed shelter, and he offered to sign him for his own Qwest label—carte blanche, Ray could record what he pleased.

When Jones' A&R man Mike Stradford heard that Ray was coming to Qwest, he began collecting material in hopes of producing an album with Ray. Then Jones gave him the news: just as WB had taken *Would You Believe?* in '90, Qwest (a WB subsidiary) would have to take *Strong Love Affair* in '95. Off the record, Jones admitted that he thought the album weak, both commercially and musically, but he felt obligated by friendship: Ray Charles could not be left out in the cold, label-less in America. They'd put out *Strong Love Affair* and do the best they could with it.

Launching *Strong Love Affair* fell to Stradford. He listened once and didn't like the album, put it aside, listened again, and still didn't like it. The tracks sounded unfocused to him, ridiculously out of touch with contemporary pop. "Ray's playing baseball," he thought, "and everybody else is playing football." His personal taste aside, the A&R

man couldn't see any way to market *Strong Love Affair.* Its style and substance were way over the heads of record-buying kids, yet it was far too pungent for Adult Contemporary, the only radio slot it might conceivably fit. Stradford also had a tough time dealing with Ray Charles Enterprises. Ray insisted the album come out for the Christmas shopping season, but repeated calls and faxes from Qwest to schedule a photo session for the CD cover went unanswered. When Stradford finally reached Ray to tell him that they'd missed the holiday production deadline, Ray went through the roof. "Why didn't you motherfuckers call me?" he shouted in a volley of enraged cursing. Stradford replied that he'd funneled everything through Joe Adams, as Ray had told him to do. "That's bullshit, Mike," said Ray. "You *know* you should have called *me.*"

"All in all," Stradford told Quincy Jones, "I won't say *Strong Love Affair* is gonna stiff, but if it's got a large commercial upside, I don't see it."

The road rolled on at a killing pace. Ray got to New York at the end of August 1995 for an appearance on *Good Morning America,* played Atlantic City over Labor Day weekend, flew back to LA for a couple of nights, and then took the red-eye back to New York to open three nights at Tramps, a rock club on Twenty-first Street near Fifth Avenue. He got a few hours' sleep at the Mayfair Hotel, then a limousine picked him up to take him to a *Sesame Street* taping. He got back to the hotel for a nap before the gig.

"RAY-DIANT LEGEND," headlined the New York *Post,* plugging the run at Tramps. Club owner Terry Dunne had been determined to book the great Ray Charles for the club's twentieth anniversary. How much will it take? he asked Ray. Ray named a figure he thought Dunne would never come up with ($200,000, rumor had it); Dunne, an impulsive Irishman, met the demand and, despite a jammed Saturday night, probably lost money. Yet the risk paid off in red-hot music, the club's low ceiling and whooping crowd fanning a bluesy fire out of the gang. Ray sang "A Song for You," "Oh, What a Beautiful Morning," and other songs of his recent vintage, but when they steamed into a sizzling "I Believe to My Soul," one could believe that Margie, Ethel, and Gwen were singing the refrain, "I believe it, yes, I believe it!" and that the big band had become Ray's old six-piece outfit rocking a Texas dance hall on the Howard Lewis circuit. "I *like* this place," Ray shouted the last night. "We love you, Ray," cried a lady in the crowd, and everybody laughed.

After Tramps, Ray flew back to LA. The band bus, an elegant black monster that lived off-duty in a steel cage in the RPM parking lot, carried the rhythm section to a string gig in Moline, Illinois. Ray and Victor Vanacore flew into Moline on their own; from there Joe Adams drove the bus to Chicago while the driver slept, then flew to LA while the rested driver drove the bus back to New York. From LA a day later Ray, Joe, and Vanacore flew east for another string gig, a private event for a Manhattan investment bank. Then the band rejoined Ray and Joe to fly to Argentina and Brazil. From the last gig in Rio, the gang flew back to LA for a week off, and Carl Hunter got the uniforms dry-cleaned and repaired equipment. The bus then came out of its cage again and carried everybody to Las Vegas for a week at Caesars Palace.

Ray seemed to be going on all eight cylinders, but Joe, six years older, was beginning to feel the strain. Time had put silver in his polished hair and etched little lines around his eyes. Why was he, at seventy-one, flying around the world, herding musicians, checking details? He certainly didn't need the money. Ray and Joe had spoken a few times about getting someone, maybe a couple of people, to replace him. Ray could see the sense of it. The problem was, who could take Joe's place? Another problem: despite what he said, Joe had no intention of quitting. He liked the speed and glitter of life around Ray Charles. Like any couple of such long standing, Ray and Joe were bound together by stout cords of time and habit, by secrets that only the two of them shared, what had really happened when, who was there, and how much money changed hands. If Joe resisted going, he could be hard to dislodge. In public Joe maintained that he was ready to go anytime a replacement was found. "When I started with Ray, I figured I'd do it for a week, a couple of months," he told a reporter. "And I'm still ready to go. I think Ray's gonna outlast me, but if he were through tomorrow, I'd beat him to the door."

A sense of age suffused the end of the year. In November Ray sang "Old Man River" for Frank Sinatra at the singer's eightieth birthday concert at the Shrine in LA. In December, as usual, the gang flew to a bitter-cold Japan. At the end of the two weeks, everybody was exhausted; sax player Rudy Johnson, now a twenty-year veteran, was suffering from congestive heart disease and could only sleep, restlessly, sitting up in a chair. Sad news came from Tampa: Louise, his first love, had died of a stroke. Ray put a message on tape and sent it to be played in the church. Just a year before, the city of Tampa had given him an award. He'd flown down with Norma and introduced her to Louise and Evelyn, even Manzy Harris, the drummer from the old Skyhaven Club. They'd had a grand time talking and laughing over lunch. Yet now Louise was gone, gone like the Simmons sisters and the cabstand at Central and Short Emery, gone like the lovers' first little house across the bridge in West Tampa. "I feel sometimes like I'm lost in a dark forest with huge trees," Ray told a close friend. "And behind every tree there are ghosts."

> Ain't nobody gonna ask me when it's time for me to go. So I figure, it ain't my decision. When it comes to that, whatever is gonna be is gonna be. While you're here, you just try to shift the odds in your favor as much as you can. But that's all you can do.
>
> **Ray Charles**

Epilogue

Ray continued at the same driving pace into 1996, flying in January to Brazil, Berlin, and Barbados, and on to Atlantic City for a Sunday-night string gig at the Trump Taj Mahal. That night, in a black-box arena as huge and cold as an airplane hangar, he played a fifty-minute show, mixing oldies ("Georgia") and newies ("A Song for You") with a few standards he'd never recorded, "The Good Life" and "Let's Get Away from It All." Victor Vanacore led the sixty-odd players through Ray's drag-time pauses in Jacques Brel's poignant "If You Go Away (Ne Me Quitte Pas)." For several bluesy tunes, the strings sat silent and Ray and his long-term trio, drummer Tommy Turre, guitarist Kenny Carr, and bassist Curtis Ohlson, played red-hot jazz; on the jumping "All I Ever Need Is You," Ray even knocked off a tantalizingly brief sax solo. Then all hands got back to work for the finale, "America the Beautiful," Ray howling, Vanacore churning energy out of the strings, the stage awash in red, blue, and white light, everyone singing along. In the shadows at the back of the hall, Joe Adams passed discreetly among the soundmen, dispensing folded bills and nods of thanks. At a table near the exit, Ray Jr. did a brisk business selling brochures and CDs to eager fans. Ray flew back to LA; next stop, Kansas City.

Qwest released *Strong Love Affair* to scattered and mixed reviews. *Time* praised Ray as "one smokin' senior citizen," but noted his "sometimes awkward" efforts to stay current. The Los Angeles *Times* called the album's up-tempo numbers "Vegas-esque" and "overwrought," but liked the "timeless quality" of "elegant slowburners" like "Angelina." Qwest paid for a promotional video to send to entertainment news programs. Ray went on *The Late Show with David Letterman* to plug *Strong Love Affair,* but like Leno, Letterman bounced him to the last few minutes of the hour.

These were efforts far too meager to give *Strong Love Affair* a chance of success. In the mid-90s, pop music had become a global phenomenon even bigger than the "worldwide symphony" Barry Manilow had sung of in "I Write the Songs" a decade before. Transformed into digital bits and bytes, music old and new flooded the airwaves from every corner and culture of the earth, creating a sonic ocean in which nearly every living human swam, willy-nilly. Commerce divided the pop music ocean into dozens of market-size seas, the largest of them youthful, yet the whole was also connected by the many listeners who enjoyed dipping into dozens of its styles and flavors. Despite its size, the ocean could respond to lightning-fast changes in fashion, like crazes for Gregorian chant or opera classics sung by three celebrated tenors. Because of its size, the ocean promised huge profits to those who could conquer it; often it seemed that only pop's most strident sounds could rise above the clanging competition to be heard.

In this ocean of music, made by Tupac Shakur, Cecilia Bartoli, Wynton Marsalis, Andrew Lloyd Webber, and Nine Inch Nails, *Strong Love Affair* drowned without making a ripple. Sales crawled slowly to 15,000 copies, and the album soon joined *Come Live with Me* and *Love and Peace* among the ranks of Ray's least-listened-to works. Though not surprised, Jones and Mike Stradford at Qwest were disappointed. Even the top brass at WB, Qwest's parent label, hoped the old man had another hit in him, one to cap his career as "Hello Dolly" had capped Louis Armstrong's. Yet how to get it? Maybe they could get a song by Ray under the titles of a big romantic movie; that could reconnect Ray to the mass audience. The right song, a hot producer, classy marketing—wishful thinking was easy, but nobody had a plan of action.

Ray was disappointed too. He still hungered for hits; Jean-Pierre Grosz knew just how much from dozens of late-night talks and from Ray's undiminished passion for perfection in the studio. Yet for Ray, at sixty-six, making music as he and he alone saw fit ran far deeper than habit. What he played today summed up all the music he had ever played, marked how far he had come in a lifetime voyaging solo into sound. Tomorrow, God willing, he would go one day further. Ray could no more change his music to make hits than Albert Einstein could have announced that E didn't equal mc^2 to get a better job at a bigger university. Ray didn't care what anybody else was doing in music, just as he didn't care what anybody wrote about him. "I am *not* anybody else, I am *me,"* he said often, stabbing his chest proudly with his thumb in a most character-istic gesture. "I love *me."*

To this defiant loner, the flop of "Angelina" didn't mean he couldn't sing it; Ray had a band chart written of the song for the '96 tour. The gang got on the road in June, later than ever, but by August they were rolling across the South, Atlanta to Shreveport; into the Northeast, Boston to New York; then, by way of Peoria and Kansas City, back to the Hollywood Bowl in September. Ray put "Angelina" on the menu for most shows. Audiences had clearly never heard it before and seemed barely to get it the first time through, but they listened in respectful silence and applauded warmly at the end, moved by a sense of its dramatic depth.

Between an October trip to South America and the December trip to Japan, the fellows had a six-week, unpaid hiatus that took them by surprise. Was Ray sick or tired, they asked one another; were promoters cutting back or offering too little money? "The rhythm section worked year-round, either band or string gigs," said trombonist Charlie Shofner. "But for the rest of us, it became about four months' work, hardly a steady gig anymore."

Aside from marketplace vagaries, gigs were down and business slow at Ray Charles Enterprises because, after thirty years, Ray's big wheel had worn its groove into a rut. Joe and Ray had grown old in harness, become "the two crankies of West Washington Boulevard," as an associate called them, her annoyance mixed with affection. Their business practices had calcified. Joe booked gigs where he had booked gigs before; if a promoter died or a booker got fired, that gig might be gone forever. MTV sent a fax to the office offering Ray a spot on its Unplugged series. Appearances on Unplugged had given Tony Bennett a new career with the youthful audience, but neither Joe nor Ray had ever heard of the show, and the fax went unanswered. In Paris, Frank Tenot had tapes of Ray's French concerts from the 60s that he wanted to release on CD; months went by and he couldn't get past the RPM switchboard, because Ray spent hours in the studio mixing tracks and not taking phone calls. Ray Jr. said the company should start a Ray Charles website on the Internet. They did—http://www.ray-charles.com/—but only after months of stormy meetings and pointless argument.

Early in 1997, Ray realized changes must be made. He needed a younger manager, for the present and for the future, for his own old age and after his death. Jean-Pierre Grosz seemed the best, even the only possible candidate: a showbiz pro and a loyal fan and friend. The two men discussed it at length in Paris. "It's pathetic," Ray said. "I have no one to take care of my business." Joe was too old and Ray Jr. was too naive, but he needed someone. Would Grosz do it, move to Los Angeles and take over Joe's job? Grosz was hesitant, not sure that he wanted to move his family to LA, and quite sure that Joe already disliked him intensely as a potential rival. Ray and he were still friends after twenty years largely because Grosz had always steered as clear of Joe as possible and had vociferously denied any interest in managing Ray's affairs. Yet the job held intriguing challenges. "Where would my office be?" he asked Ray. "Why, Joe's office, of course," said Ray. On the strength of that, Grosz went to LA in the early spring to see if he could make it work. If he could, then he'd move his family.

The first bad news came the day Grosz arrived: Joe was still ensconced in his second-floor front office with its elegant gray color scheme, glass-topped desk, black leather sofa, and a TV console showing the views of security cameras spotted about the property. While Grosz waited, Ray went in to ask Joe to move out and let Grosz move in. "Over my dead body!" replied Joe, and Ray came back to Grosz and explained shamefacedly that he couldn't kick Joe out of the office he'd been in since the building was built. To work in one of the small second-floor offices would have been a major loss of face, so Grosz moved into an empty room on the ground floor, neutral in the RPM pecking order. Joe delayed getting it furnished, then insisted that he, not Grosz, must decorate it down to the desk lamps and pictures on the walls.

Despite Joe's opposition, Grosz pushed ahead into long meetings with Ray to outline his ideas. If he was going to be Ray's new manager, he said, he wanted to change things from top to bottom. The show had to be revamped, for one thing; "Ray-with-band" and "Ray-with-strings" were frozen formats that had to go. A new, open-format show could include the band and strings *and* Ray playing solo piano, Ray with a trio, Ray with the little R&B band, even Ray talking to the audience one-on-one. No more flashy tuxedo jackets; Ray could wear something more informal yet more dignified. Plus they'd have to get and maintain their own sound system; no first-class act still relied, as Ray did, on the mikes and speakers provided by the hall. No wonder Ray complained about squeals and hums all the time!

Ray liked Grosz's ideas, but none of them was destined to come to pass. Joe Adams won the war. A skilled infighter who had fended off rivals before, Joe threw up roadblocks before Grosz in all directions, cast doubt on every new project, questioned costs, and withheld information. It took a major showdown, Ray yelling and shouting, for Grosz to see something as simple as the list of upcoming bookings. Joe spread the word among his contacts to talk only to him, not to Grosz. Many of them then called Grosz to ask what was going on, who was in charge. For Grosz, the tension became hellish. With Ray, Joe played it cool. He was ready to leave anytime, he said, and when he did, Ray could have fifty accountants go over the books of every corporation, every investment, and every deal, and they'd find them accurate down to the penny. With each pointed reminder of his own honesty, the steward sent his boss an implicit message: We've made millions together, you can trust me.

Ray surrendered, not simply to Joe's guerrilla tactics, but to force of habit as well. Ray *liked* routine, and he was unwilling or unable to change. Minimizing variables had long been a principal way he overcame his handicap and coped with his complex life. For example: a small room at RPM served as Ray's wardrobe room. Along one wall stood drawers for socks and underwear; from bars along three walls hung Ray's outfits. Each hanger held a matched jacket, slacks, and shirt combination, ranging from quiet daywear to gaudy brocade tuxedos for the stage. Every hanger had a number: the brown, beige, and green outfits odd numbers; the grays, blacks, and blues even numbers. Beneath the clothes were dozens of pairs of shoes, most made by Bally, in long neat rows; the brown shoes had a straight line scratched on the sole under the instep, the black shoes a cross. The system had been in place for over thirty years. By simply telling his valet, "Bring me number eight," and running his finger over his shoe sole, Ray could be sure, sight unseen, that he was wearing appropriate clothes in coordinated colors.

A man of such dogged habit is unlikely to learn new tricks in his late sixties, and Ray did not. Sensing that Ray felt disappointed in himself, Grosz accepted defeat gracefully and went back to Paris, proud at least of the spring's tangible accomplishment, a superb gospel version of John Lennon's "Imagine," done for a French bank commercial. He and Ray continued as friends and colleagues, and life at RPM returned to status quo. June came and with it the tour: a magnificent, slow-building show at Avery Fisher Hall in New York, July Fourth in Philadelphia, Europe, then, just like the year before, August in the Northeast.

As Ray pushed onward, so did those who had shared paths with him for a time along the way. His childhood playmate Elesta Pritchett, after raising five children, went to college, taught in Greenville's integrated school system, and even served as the town's mayor. As they once dreamed, Joe Walker did become a sports broadcaster and Paul Behn did teach at Florida D&B. Gossie McKee became a ship's steward on a Pacific cruise line and an avid golfer onshore. After his wife, actress Lillian Randolph, died, Gossie lived quietly in Los Angeles, not far from but never in touch with Ray at RPM. On the other hand, Billy Brooks, who'd run down to Atlanta with Ray and Artelia and Eileen to get married, was still a close friend. Brooks lived in Amsterdam, and when Ray was in Europe, he often flew in for a game of chess.

Lowell Fulson was still playing the blues in the mid-90s and sharing a house in California with Percy Mayfield's widow Tina; she continued to get regular royalty checks from Tangerine Music for "Hit the Road Jack" and a half-dozen other songs. Renald

Richard lived comfortably in upstate New York, his checks for "I Got a Woman" getting bigger year by year. Jeff Brown had a tougher time. After leaving Sam and Dave, Jeff became a chauffeur in New York, driving his own limo from the Wellington Hotel on West Fifty-fifth Street. He and Shirley lived quietly nearby in a small apartment. Managing Ray Charles remained the high point of Jeff's life, and bitterness at being dropped lingered beneath his gentle demeanor. "I wish I *had* taken money from the blind motherfucker," Jeff said. "I was his eyes and his legs, and he *owed* me." Jeff Brown died of stomach cancer in June, 1996. When Mary Ann Fisher got the news, she came east from Louisville and stayed with Shirley for a few weeks. The two women stayed up night after night talking over old times.

Many others had died too: Margie Hendricks in 1973, Edgar Willis in 1993, and tenor player James Clay in 1995, the latest of the fellows to die of heroin, the old scourge of the Ray Charles band. Yet many more were alive and kicking. Sid Feller, feeling much better after heart surgery, came backstage after a concert, and he and Ray fell to kissing and hugging in a most affectionate reunion. When Mable John earned her doctorate of divinity, she stopped by RPM, and Ethel Rubin and the office staff crowded around her to offer congratulations. Ray hung back, laughing. "Oh, don't touch me," he said. "This is the devil and God meeting!" Susaye Green, after years in London, came back to LA. Though married and mother of a ten-year-old son, Susaye sometimes heard a song or a news story and thought, "I'll tell Ray . . . ," before catching herself.

Fathead Newman lived near Woodstock, New York, getting into the city for occasional club and recording gigs. Leroy Cooper was still playing at Disney World, at times with his neighbor, Phil Guilbeau. Like old-timers everywhere, Ray's old gang thought the band had gone downhill since their day. "The girls today don't stay long enough to get the sound we had," said Dorothy Berry. Solomon had heard that the current leader was lazy and uninvolved with his men. "If a fellow had a problem when I was the 'Cap'n,' we'd go have a beer and discuss it. Now the leader says, 'I don't know nothing, man, it's between you all,' and heads for the racetrack."

Yet when old-timers got a chance to come back, they grabbed it. After twenty years out of the band, John Bryant played a string gig in Hartford, subbing for Pete Turre, who was getting married. "I got backstage, and Ray and I started going over old names, Henry Coker, Johnny Coles. Trying to keep from being left out, Joe kept saying, 'Now, *when* were you in the band?' Onstage, I realized how much better a musician I had become. As a kid with Ray, I'd been so *literal.* Now I could listen to the music and actually play with him in the moment." Once Leroy Cooper rode with Ray in a stretch limousine from the airport to a private string gig in Palm Beach. "Dig this!" said the

Hog as they rolled along a boulevard of bougainvillea-covered mansions, escorted by motorcycle police. "Sure beats riding in the Weenie with the Philadelphia cops following us across the Camden bridge." "Damn if it don't," said Ray, and they burst out laughing so hard they cried.

|ʜ|ʜʜ|ʜ|ʜʜ|

After thirty-five years, the RPM International building still looked trim and freshly painted. Visitors entered the parking lot through a gleaming metal gate, walked into the spic-and-span lobby through tall glass doors, then climbed a dramatic floating staircase to a black-and-white-carpeted-reception area, highlighted by polished silver lamps with crimson shades. Through frosted glass doors at either side of reception lay the workrooms of Ray Charles Enterprises. There, as always when he was in LA, Ray padded back and forth along the corridor between the studio and his comfortably cluttered office. He kept busy taking care of day-to-day business, recording new songs, and answering his e-mail with brief notes that he signed, whimsically, "the robin." One afternoon Dr. Pulec brought over a little boy from Florida who had received a cochlear implant paid for by Ray's foundation. Ray played a nursery rhyme on a keyboard, and his face lit up as the once deaf boy responded to the music and, giggling, played a few notes of his own.

Big news came in October 1997. Rhino Records, a major reissuing label, released a five-CD set, *Ray Charles: Genius and Soul,* a massive, meticulously produced retrospective of a hundred two tracks spanning his career, from "Confession Blues" to "Still Crazy After All These Years." This grandest of all greatest-hits albums had been long delayed by Ray's caution (and by his insistence on a seven-figure advance), but once they had a deal, he was delighted, and he eagerly took part in selecting tracks and telling stories for the album's glossy booklet.

Yet looking back couldn't take precedence over looking ahead. Bob Abrams had to beg Ray to take an hour off from recording for a magazine photo shoot one morning—*Esquire* was planning a piece on the reissue. As the photo crew set up lights and umbrellas in the studio, Ray kept working in the control booth. He threaded a reel of tape onto the digital recording console, and as it played, he paced back and forth, listening and thumping his chest with his thumb in time to the beat. The lyric leaking through the booth window sounded like "Baby, you know I'm lovin' you." Ray played and rewound the same few feet of tape again and again, making minute adjustments to the sound.

At the tick of eleven, Ray stopped and came out of the booth. He looked like a vigorous old man, his gray hair standing out in sparse clumps on his broad brown head, his posture bent. He made his way through the gaggle of press people like a wise old elephant snuffling newcomers to the watering hole. The photographer wasn't quite ready, so Ray sat at the grand piano and played "Laura" softly, his fingers tentative, inquisitive on the keys. For forty minutes, humming to himself and bantering with the photographer ("Smile? Nobody smiles all the goddamn time!"), he sat and submitted to turning his head this way and that while the camera clicked, taking pictures he'd never see. One flash of the bright lights blew a building circuit, and the room went dark. Ray didn't notice, but when he heard a crewman say, "We just tripped a circuit breaker. Where's the power box?" he reared back assertively.

"Circuit breakers?" he said. *"I'm* the one who knows that, babe. Lemme see what you're talking about. Alex!"

The valet helped him through the tangle of wires and camera equipment into the control booth. There Ray unlocked a utility closet door, felt inside for the metal junction box, and opened it, his fingers flying over the switches. One was out of place. He flipped it back in line with the others and the lights came on. The photo crew stared at one another amazed, then Ray trundled back into the room and the shoot continued.

At noon sharp, Ray said his thanks all around and went back into the booth. In a few moments the same few bars of music began leaking out into the studio, and Ray was again pacing around the console, thumping his chest to the beat, playing and rewinding the tape. "Baby, you know I'm lovin' you . . . Baby, you know I'm lovin' you . . . Baby, you know I'm lovin' you."

▮▮▮▮▮▮▮▮▮

"I never wanted to be famous, but I always wanted to be great," Ray said throughout his career. Whatever more he would achieve in his remaining years, he had long since reached this lifetime goal. His place in music history is assured: Ray Charles stands beside Louis Armstrong, Duke Ellington, and a handful of others among the presiding geniuses of twentieth-century popular music. Five decades of Ray's music pulse in the electric airwaves, music touching millions, soul to soul, every day.

Ray Charles' greatness as a musician began with the abundant musical gifts RC Robinson was given at birth, yet those gifts grew only because, boy and man, Ray labored to perfect them. Endless practice made him a jazz pianist of major importance, a superb arranger, and a songwriter who wrote his own breakthrough songs. Unusual intelligence helped him master the many crafts of record making and run a successful business in a competitive marketplace. Dogged determination made him board and deboard countless trains, cars, buses, and airplanes, and walk in and out of countless halls and hotels—all to bring his music to the people.

Ray's greatness springs, on the grandest scale, from his total immersion in the musical currents of his time. Listening in the dark, he soaked up sounds and styles from every idiom, and from them wrought a personal idiom more vital than many of its sources. His more intimate greatness lies in his singing voice. Critics have found much to fault Ray for, yet few complain about his singing. What a voice! No other singer in pop comes close to his breadth of vocal shadings—falsetto, scream, talk, whisper, croon, laugh, howl, giggle, sob—or his freedom in changing and blending those colors to convey every flicker of evanescent emotion.

What will make Ray's greatness endure is his skill as a record maker, a painter with music. Music's first electric century is also the first in which sound itself became a graphic art, the era when musicians learned to preserve the sound of music as a mark in a medium long after the moment of making it was gone. Like a painter who works pigment onto canvas in painting after painting in his studio, so did Ray work sound onto plastic in record after record at his beloved RPM, painting a broad range of emotions with a bold palette of colors: the bloodred-purples of sexual love, the glorious golds of gospel music, blues in every shade from raw to refined, even the etched, regret-filled grays of Paris in the rain.

For a painter in sound, blindness posed no handicap to greatness. "You don't have to *see* life," Ray said once. "You have to *observe* life." Ray Charles' sound paintings ring with truth and vibrate with sympathy. We respond to them because, as we listen, we sense unmistakably that this man knows what it feels like to live, and that he sings to share that knowledge. We can hear the depth of his understanding in the smallest quaver in his tone. Though his subject is often heartbreak and hopeless yearning, his humanity comes as balm to the spirit.

Experiencing one of Ray's sound paintings is, curiously, not unlike experiencing a great visual painting. Standing before a Rembrandt portrait, we are captured by the eyes. A quality of feeling, of silent sympathy, reaches us eloquently through time. Who is this person looking through those eyes? Is he the sad-faced burgher or Rembrandt himself? Are these eyes alive? If not, how could they move us so, speak to us so intimately, say so plainly: I am alive as you are alive. Life is a mystery to me as it is to you. We live, we feel, we try, we fail, we love, we die.

This presence of the artist provides the spark of all immortal art. "I am with you, and I know how it is," wrote Walt Whitman to future generations from Brooklyn Bridge. "Me too," sang Ray to future generations on *Volcanic Action of My Soul.* Many have felt, and many will always feel, the presence of the man in the music of Ray Charles. Who is this Ray who comes so close to our ears, who enters so swiftly, so pleasingly, so lastingly into our hearts? Someone different to each of us, but someone surely *with us*—not as substantially, perhaps, as in the flesh, yet by art's magic, vibrantly focused in spirit.

Like many practitioners of this magic, Ray never professed to understand its furthest mysteries. All he could do was to pour himself into making music to the fullest extent of his powers, and that he did day after day all his life. The rest was up to his listeners. "People come up to me in airports and tell me they love records I didn't know anybody ever heard," he said, sitting back one morning in his office at RPM, a chessboard at his elbow, his coffee mug in his hand. "A lady the other day said, 'Oh, Mr. Charles, you remember that song "Cry" you did?' I thought everybody had forgotten that one! But it shows you, *people will listen to the music if it's good.* And that's always been my thing: I try to play good music. I'm glad that people love good music, because it makes me happy to make people happy. We play 'Georgia' anywhere in the world, and strangely enough, the people love it. I don't know *why* they love it, but they do."

Acknowledgments

Biographers follow paths through the past. Without guides to point out the trail overgrown by time, we would soon be lost. To my guides I owe heartfelt thanks. More than any other source, their stories, told in long, generous interviews, give this book what flavor it has of what life was like. Those listed below told me all they knew, pointed me to others who might know more, and as often as not, took me into the kitchen for a cup of coffee and a piece of pie. Thank you.

For aid above and beyond the call of duty, thanks to: Bob Abrams, publicist for Ray Charles Enterprises; David Ritz, author of *Brother Ray;* Joel Dufour and his Ray Charles archive in Paris; Ray Baradat and his R&B archive in Tulare, California; Mable John, former lead Raelet, now a minister in Los Angeles; Clifford and Maki Solomon and their flower garden in Los Angeles; and Ellen Mandel—without her loving encouragement, this book would never have come to be.

In Florida, Greenville and nearby: Jacob Bemby, Shirley Hutto, Gertrude and Willie Reddick, Beatrice Williams, Elesta Pritchett, Clarreatha Norris, Bessie Brown, Larry King, Mary Clemmons, Joe Bea, Joe S. and Patricia Reams; in Tallahassee: Hampton Hollins, Curtis King, and Daisy Smith; in Jacksonville: Lena Mae Thompson, Alexander Perry, Matthew McCoy, Paul Behn, the Clara White Mission; in St. Augustine: Mary Jane Dillon, Otis Knowles, Henry White, and Fred Thompson; in Orlando: A. J. Kleckly, Willie Lawrence, Bill Peeples, Leroy and Clemmie Cooper, Phil Guilbeau, Jesse Stone, Bill Allred; in Sarasota: Jerry Wexler; in Tampa: Evelyn Robinson, Manzy Harris; in Miami, Tom Dowd; in Fort Lauderdale, Larry Newton.

In Seattle: Traf Hubert, Buddy Catlett, Floyd Standifer, Jabo Ward, Paul de Barros, and Melody Jones. In New York: Ahmet Ertegun, Larry Myers, Irving Siders, Miriam Bienstock, Jeff Brown, Shirley Brown, Dr. John Wilson Espy, Billy Joel, David Newman, Renald Richard, Sid-

399

ney Seidenberg, Jimmie Scott, Lula Hendricks, Henry Alter, Earl Zaidens, Gordon Anderson, Ted Fox, Richard Gersh, Duke Wade, Hank Crawford, David Sanjek, Al Aronowitz, Tom Michaels, Rich Look, George Newill, and Elliot Paul.

In Los Angeles: Gossie D. McKee, Ken Tussing, Sid Feller, Jeff Kaye, Vernita Moss, Vernon Troupe, Harold Patton, David Simmons, Jimmy Lewis, Richard Cason, Ruth Robinson, Aaron Williams, Ray Robinson Jr., Victor Vanacore, Ralph Burns, Gerald Wilson, Carolyn Baker, Georgia Bergman, Joe Adams, Tina Mayfield, Lowell Fulson, Dana Hughes, Vera Tussing, Jack McVea, Johnny Otis, Rudy Johnson, Dorothy Berry Durr, Richard Perry, Gerald Wilson, Herb Miller, David Braithwaite, Bob Gratts, Susaye Green Coton, Roger Spotts, Duana Chenier, Tony Mathews, Peggy Scott, Mike Stradford, Hannes Hacker, Matthew Lait, and Charlie Shofner.

In Dallas: John Bryant, Jimmy Bell, John Lewis, Angus Wynne III, Tony Horowitz, Onzy Matthews. In Detroit: Marcus Belgrave. In New Orleans: Cosimo Matassa, Fred Kemp, Earl King, Tad Jones, Wallace Davenport, Ramsay MacLean, Charles Neville, Frederick Sheppard, and Boyd Raeburn.

In Nashville: Ernest Vantrease, Margie Hunt, Jim Rooney, Bobby Wood, Troy Seales, Rick Blackburn, Kenny Malone, and Ronnie Pugh. In Washington, D.C.: Stanley Turrentine. In Boston: Stanley Toseski of the Federal Records Center. In Louisville, Kentucky: Mary Ann Fisher. In Columbus, Ohio: Artelia Ferrell.

In Paris: Maurice and Vanette Cullasz, Jean-Pierre Grosz, Jean-Pierre Leloir, Arlette Kotchounian, and Frank Tenot. In Amsterdam: Billy Brooks. In Japan: Musaharu Yoshioka.

Thank you to the New York Public Library, in particular the helpful staffs of the Schomburg Center for Research in Black Culture, the Library of the Performing Arts, and the Reading Room of the Main Branch; the public libraries of Greenville, Jacksonville, Orlando, Tampa, Seattle, Los Angeles, Houston, Dallas, New Orleans, and Boston; the Institute for Jazz Studies in the Dana Library at Rutgers, the Hogan Jazz Archive in the Howard-Tilton Memorial Library at Tulane University, the Museum of Television and Radio in New York, the archive at Nashville's Country Music Foundation.

For research help, Tim Schuller in Dallas; Mayer Vishner, Elisa DeCarlo, Jeff Shames, and Val Ciptak in New York; and Ray Whitehouse in England. For help in transcribing interviews, Stasha Hughes. Special thanks to Ilene Bellovin for excellent work curating the photographs, and to Caroline Trefler for doing the paperwork.

Thanks to Ray Charles for several wide-ranging interviews, for living a life well worth relating, and for years and years of musical pleasure.

Thanks to my mother, Alice Joyce Lydon, for her love.

Thanks to all my family and friends who got earfuls along the way; Peter and Alexandra Guralnick for reading the manuscript and making many excellent suggestions; my agent, Lane Zachary; my editors, Nicholas Weinstock and David Highfill; Bill Rothman and Kitty Morgan for primal encouragement; the Third Street Music School Settlement; the Lighthouse for the Blind; Peter and Norma for Berkeley stopovers; Penny and Sandy Liu; Clara Rodriguez and Brian Smith; Howie Harris, Harry Huggins, Jim Payne, Zick Rubin, Margaret and Santo, JP and Jean Fonseca, and many, many more.

Source Notes

In researching *Ray Charles: Man and Music,* I traveled to Greenville, Tallahassee, St. Augustine, Jacksonville, Orlando, Tampa, Seattle, Los Angeles several times, Dallas, Houston, New Orleans, Nashville, and Paris between 1994 and 1997. The descriptions of these cities, New York, and other locales in the book are based on my direct observation, conversations with natives, and local histories and directories.

Quotations with living witnesses *not* cited here come from my interviews with the people quoted. At various times, when it seemed important, I did cite those quotations. Quotations from secondary sources are cited.

Nearly all of the dates and places of gigs Ray Charles played in the 1950s and 60s come from advertisements in microfilmed copies of black community newspapers consulted at the Schomburg Center in New York. The newspapers are listed in the Bibliography.

All books cited in the Source Notes without full bibliographic information are listed in the Bibliography. For example, the often cited *Brother Ray* was first published by Dial in 1978 and later issued as a paperback by Da Capo in 1992.

"RC interview" in the notes refers to my interviews with Ray Charles.

PART I **YOUTH**

1 . GREENVILLE

3. "I was born": *Brother Ray,* p. 8. **5.** "limbo": Theodore Dreiser, *The Bulwark,* p. 9, New York: Doubleday & Co., 1946. **6.** deeper roots of the Robinson family: No Margaret or Bailey Robinson is mentioned in the 1920 U.S. census in Greenville. A Margaret and Baily Robinson are mentioned together in the 1920 census in Albany, Georgia, but both appear to be too young to be Ray's grandmother and grandfather. When the 1930 census records are opened, more light may be shed on the Robinson family history. **6.** "What she doin' ": Zora Neale Hurston, *Their Eyes Were Watching God*, pp. 1–2, New York: Harper & Row, 1990. **7.** "Lighting up": *Brother Ray*, p. 7. **8.** "normal kid": Radio interview with Rogers Steffens, 1985. **8.** "The man": *Brother Ray*, p. 9, and other interviews. **8.** "Oh no, son": *My Early Years, 1930–1960*, by RC, unpaginated promotional book, 1995. **8.** "That's it": *Brother Ray*, p. 9. **10.** "I understand": Ibid., p. 16. **10.** "not as bad": *My Early Years*; "I was never": *Brother Ray*, p. 15. **11.** "Mama": Ibid., p. 18.

2. ST. AUGUSTINE

13. October 23: date on RC Robinson enrollment card at Florida D&B. **13.** Historical sketch of Florida D&B from pamphlets published by school. **15.** Braille primers: *Brother Ray*, p. 23. **15.** "Foots": *Life*, 7/29/66. **17.** relay races: Ibid. **17.** Ray retaliates: *Brother Ray*, pp. 38–39. **18.** "great musician": Ibid., p. 35. **18.** Ray on classics: RC interview. **18.** "to learn two bars": *Ebony*, 9/60. **19.** "Romance in the Dark": *Brother Ray*, pp. 53–54. **19.** Retha quotes: New York *Post*, 11/18/67. **21.** first sexual experience: *Brother Ray*, p. 54.

3. THE DEATH OF RETHA ROBINSON

23. "Nothing had hit me": Ibid., p. 57. **24.** "I sat alone": Ibid., pp. 59–60. **24.** "Son, you know" and following: *My Early Years*. **24.** "Your mama": *Brother Ray*, p. 61. **24.** "I howled": Ibid., p. 61. **24.** "two greatest tragedies": *My Early Years*. **25.** Fred Thompson a carpenter: RC interview.

PART II **APPRENTICE**

4. JACKSONVILLE

29. The 1942 issue of *Crisis* and the "Jacksonville City Report," Jacksonville Public Library, Florida State Research Division. **36.** "Me and Bing Crosby": Louis Jordan interview with author, 1973. **37.** Brown "closely reproduced": Haskins, *Nat "King" Cole*, p. 47. **37.** Lovey Herman: *Brother Ray*, p. 71. **38.** Soda crate: Jeff Brown interview.

5. ORLANDO AND TAMPA

39. York band breakup: Orlando *Times'* James Clark interview with RC, 4/14/91. **40.** $3 rent: Ibid. **40.** "Sorry, my ass": Bill Peeples interview. **41.** broken glass: story told by RC in many interviews. **41.** "If the man": Clark interview. **42.** "a whole new arena": *Brother Ray*, p. 77. **43.** "Shorty's Got to Go": *Billboard*, 6/21/47. **43.** only white guy: Irv Siders interview; he was Millinder's road manager at the time. **43.** RC believed: Steffens radio interview. **43.** "Ain't good enough": *Brother Ray*, p. 79. **43.** RC's self-appraisal: Steffens radio interview. **44.** "Let's go to Tampa": Clark interview. **44.** Central Avenue description: from *Black Tampa: Roots of a People*, Otis R. Anthony, at Tampa Public Library. **45.** Recording session snippet: from May 1953 Atlantic session tape given author by Jerry Wexler. **46.** Mitchell family background: interview with Evelyn Robinson. **46.** Miami and room in West Tampa: *Brother Ray*, p. 91. **47.** Telegraphone and history of wire recorders: from *Encyclopedia of Recorded Sound in the United States*, edited by Guy A. Marco, Garland Publishers, 1993; also from June and May 1947 issues of *Audio Engineering*.

6. SEATTLE

51. RC in Seattle: Many details drawn from Paul de Barros' excellent book *Jackson Street After Hours;* also from interviews with Gossie McKee and the Seattle musicians named in the chapter and the Acknowledgments. **52.** "RED MIGHT": Seattle *Post-Intelligencer,* 3/14/48. **53.** "walk-up flats" and subsequent quotations from the "Homeboy" chapter of *The Autobiography of Malcolm X*, by Malcolm X with Alex Haley, New York: Random House, 1964. **54.** dining room set: *Brother Ray,* p. 102; kerosene heater, *My Early Years.* **56.** Quincy Jones "couldn't figure": *Jackson Street After Dark,* p. 108. **57.** Louise's miscarriage: *Brother Ray,* pp. 102–3. **57.** RC using heroin: Ibid., pp. 108–11. **58.** McVea meets RC: Jackie McVea interview. **58.** Lauderdale description and offer: from Lowell Fulson, Gossie McKee interviews and *Brother Ray,* pp. 100–101. **59.** "Confession Blues" on charts: *Billboard,* spring 1949. **60.** "I was in hog heaven": *Brother Ray,* p. 101. **60.** Down Beat contract: given author by Gossie McKee. **61.** "One of these nights": *Jackson Street After Hours,* p. 157. **61.** "People give you their bread": Ibid., p. 167. **62.** romance over with Louise: *Brother Ray,* p. 106.

7. LOS ANGELES

63. "Th' Ego Song": lyric by Lloyd Glenn. **63.** double scale: liner notes on Ebony CD, *Ray Charles: Birth of a Legend.* **63.** "I'll Do Anything for You": lyric by Betty T. Hall. **64.** "GROWING": Los Angeles *Sentinel,* 6/1/50. **64.** 216,000 souls: from Lein and Shiesl, *20th Century Los Angeles.* **64.** picture of Central Avenue: from Clifford Solomon and Johnny Otis interviews; also Otis' book, *Up Side Your Head!,* and newspaper sources. **65.** "jiveass celebrity": *Brother Ray,* p. 118. **65.** RC's feeling for Tatum: Ibid., p. 117. **65.** considered married: from Helen Dance, *The T-Bone Walker Story,* p. 203. **66.** $35 a week: *Brother Ray,* p. 119. **66.** "heading the orchestra": *Houston Informer,* 10/21/50; "Have ya noticed": *Louisiana Weekly,* 10/14/50. **67.** "it brought tears": Daniel Wolff, *You Send Me,* p. 74. **67.** Exclusive rainbow records: Haskins, p. 37. **68.** "Open the Door Richard": Ibid., p. 28. **68.** 200 million records, 85 percent: these figures are a composite of several conflicting sources. **68.** "rough, ignorant guys": Gillet, *Making Tracks,* p. 23. **68.** "Don't pay anybody": Arnold Shaw, *Honkers and Shouters,* pp. 226–27. **69.** "All to Myself": lyric by Ray Charles Robinson. **69.** "Baby Let Me Hold Your Hand": lyric by Ray Charles Robinson. **69–70.** Brassfield hired: Los Angeles *Sentinel,* 12/14/50. **70.** Swingtime ad: *Billboard,* 12/23/50. **70.** "new Ray Charles diskings": *Billboard,* 1/6/51.

8. ON THE ROAD

71. Howard Lewis: portrait drawn from interview with his son, John Lewis; also RC interview, and Jeff Brown, David Newman, and Angus Wynne interviews. **72.** Cauthorn column: Philadelphia *Tribune,* 1/27/51. **72.** Swingtime's biggest month: Ebony CD liner notes. **72.** "Baby" chart history: *Billboard,* 2/51 and 3/51. **73.** "if people began": *Brother Ray,* pp. 127–28. **73.** Shaw Artists and Billy Shaw: portrait drawn from interviews with former Shaw agents Larry Myers, Dick Alen, and Irving Siders; also Dizzy Gillespie, *To Be or Not to Bop,* and Ross Russell, *Bird Lives.* **75.** swimming incident: *Brother Ray,* p. 125 **75.** bus on bridge: Stanley Turrentine interview; also interview with Earl Brown by Joe Matthews for a Regional Oral History Project, contributed by David Ritz. **77.** Heroin and David Newman: This and much of the drug-related information comes from off-the-record comments by many interviewees, most of whom wanted to say as little as possible to spare the feelings of others. **77.** RC's first marriage: Fulton County marriage certificate; also interviews with Billy Brooks, Artelia Ferrell, and Jeff Brown. **79.** "Holiday Greetings": Ebony CD booklet. **79.** Zenith Trans-Oceanic radio: *Brother Ray,* p. 129. **79.** tension in Fulson band: from interviews with Fulson, Jeff Brown, Stanley Turrentine. **79.** theater tour: *Billboard* and black newspapers. **80.** Swingtime decline: Ebony CD notes and *Billboard,* Jan./Feb. 1952. **80.** "Record to Watch": *Billboard,* 2/16/52. **80.** $2500: the most common of several figures given by Ertegun and others. **81.** Billy Shaw lecture: RC interview; similar story in *Brother Ray.* **81.** "Kissa Me" on R&B chart: *Billboard,* 3/22/52. **81.** RC leaving Fulson: drawn from interviews with Fulson, Renald Richard, David Newman, and *Brother Ray,* pp. 128–30. **82.** breakup with Eileen: *Brother Ray,* pp. 130–31; Eileen Williams died in the mid-1980s, still a respected beautician in Columbus' black community. **82.** Joe Turner tour: *Billboard,* 4/26/52

PART III **THE 1950: THE ATLANTIC YEARS**

9. ATLANTIC RECORDS

87. "*clean...*": Gillet, *Making Tracks,* p. 6; the sketch of Atlantic's birth is a composite of many sources, including interviews with Jesse Stone, Ahmet Ertegun, Tom Dowd, Miriam Abramson, *Billboard,* the Ruppli discography, and *Making Tracks.* **89.** Mastering: from interview with Tom Dowd. **89–90.** "Midnight"/"Roll" note and review: *Billboard,* 10/11, 10/18/52. **90.** "I was trying": *Brother Ray,* p. 128.

10. NEW ORLEANS

93. Houston arrest: *Brother Ray,* p. 146; also David Newman interview. **93.** "Sun" review: *Billboard,* 1/31/53. **93.** Atlantic hits: *Billboard,* 1/10/53; "Mama" smash: *Billboard,* 2/7/53. **93.** Herb to Germany: *Billboard,* 2/7/53. **94.** Wexler invented term "rhythm & blues": *Making Tracks,* p. 62. **94.** Wexler, Ertegun, and Atlantic: drawn from interviews with Ertegun and Wexler, from *Making Tracks;* also Wexler's autobiography, *Rhythm and the Blues;* and many other sources over three decades. **94.** "great increase in... R&B": *Billboard,* 2/28/53; "Six Largest Diskeries": *Billboard,* 3/31/53. **95.** Death of Mary Jane: Tom Dowd interview; also *Brother Ray,* pp. 158–59. **96.** "Stop this Nat Cole": *My Early Years.* **97.** "physical presence": *Rhythm and the Blues,* p. 104. **97.** 13 percent owner: Ibid., p. 80. **97.** "secret language": Ibid., p. 76. **98.** "one morning": Ibid., pp. 78–79. **98.** "Mess Around" review: *Billboard,* 6/27/53. **98.** "Indies Get Hotter": *Billboard,* 6/20/53. **98.** Painia and Dew Drop: portrait drawn from RC interview, and interviews with Cosimo Matassa, Earl King, Ramsay MacLean, other New Orleans musicians, and books on New Orleans jazz listed in Bibliography. **99.** Wexler stays at Dew Drop: *Rhythm and the Blues,* p. 94; the first white guest was the eccentric stage cowboy Lash Larue. **100.** "I became myself": *Brother Ray,* p. 148; career crawling: Ibid., p. 140. **101.** raid on San Jacinto: *Louisiana Weekly,* 11/7/53. **101.** New Orleans band: lineup from Atlantic CD, *Birth of Soul,* confirmed by Wallace Davenport interview. **101.** T-Bone Walker story: Steffens radio interview.

11. THE FIRST BAND

103. Della Bea Howard: the portrait of Della Bea and the early days of her romance with RC is drawn from interviews with David Newman, John Lewis, and Herb Miller, and *Brother Ray,* pp. 145–47. **104.** "Things" on chart and "Shoulda" review: *Billboard,* 1/16, 1/30, 2/13/54. **104.** first LA appearance: LA *Sentinel,* 3/4/54. **104.** "broken nationally": *Billboard,* 3/20/54. **104.** Philadelphia gig: Whitney Balliett, *American Singers,* p. 69; Pep's Bar: *Billboard.* **105.** Clemson story: from papers donated by and interview with John J. "Bubba" Snow. **106.** Cat Records and following April trends and quotations: *Billboard,* 4/10, 4/17, 4/24/54. **106.** "Shoulda" #7 and "Rock Around the Clock": *Billboard,* 5/15/54. **107.** School integration reactions: NY *Amsterdam News,* 5/22/54; LA *Sentinel,* 5/20/54. **108.** "You ain't strong": Peter Guralnick, *Sweet Soul Music,* p. 62. **108.** "If you think pennies": RC interview. **108.** Ray starts band: this picture is drawn from interviews with John Lewis, David Newman, Renald Richard, Jeff Brown, and RC; also *Brother Ray, Sweet Soul Music,* and RC chapter of *American Singers.* **110.** "Don't You Know" review: *Billboard,* 7/17/54 **110.** "Sh-boom" story: *Billboard,* 8/8/54. **110.** "He appeared at Jack's": Cleveland *Call* *and Post,* 7/31/54. **112.** "I Got a Woman" genesis: Arnold Shaw, in *The Rockin' 50s,* says that "I Got a Woman" is based on "Jesus Is All the World to Me." Because Renald Richard left Ray's band before the song was recorded, he was not at first properly credited; some record labels list RC alone as the songwriter. Richard, however, straightened that out with Atlantic, and he has for many years earned a substantial income from his royalties. **113.** Ahmet and Jerry reaction: Atlantic CD *Birth of Soul* liner notes, and liner notes to Atlantic LP, *The Ray Charles Story, Vol. Two.* **114.** Broonzy quote: liner notes Atlantic LP *Ray Charles at Newport;* Josh White quote: *Billboard,* 6/29/59. **116.** "by storm": *Billboard,* 1/8/55.

12. BREAKTHROUGH

117. *Billboard,* quotations: *Billboard,* 1/1/55, 11/12/55. **117.** deliveries to West Coast: *Billboard,* 1/8/55. **118.** Alan Freed on WINS: tape at Museum of Television and Radio. **118.** Elvis sings "I Got a Woman"; Guralnick, *Last Train to Memphis,* p. 162. **118.** "scarcely veiled": *Billboard,* 3/26/55. **118.** "slightly bigger": *Billboard,* 12/25/54. **119.** Date and details of RC and Della Bea's wedding: Marriage certificate, Dallas County, Texas, archives. Picture of the couple settling down in Dallas from interviews with John Lewis, David Newman, Jeff Brown, Leroy Cooper; also *Brother Ray,* pp. 158–61. **121.** best record: Atlantic press release. **122.** "Records like this": *Billboard,* 6/4/55. **122.** strong action in southern cities: *Billboard,* 6/18/55. **124.** "plenty of entertainment": *Billboard,* 10/1/55. **125.** "Greenback" reports: *Billboard,* 10/15, 10/29, 11/5/55. **125.** Philadelphia bust: composite drawn from Philadelphia *Tribune,* 11/15, 11/19, 11/22/55, and interviews with Jeff Brown, Mary Ann Fisher, Bill Peeples, David Newman, and Philadelphia native Bob Levin; "flu shot": Chicago *Defender,* 12/2/61. **126.** *Jet* gossip item: *Jet,* 12/8/55. **128.** *Downbeat* story: *Downbeat,* 12/14/55. **128.** ANP entertainment report: Indianapolis *Recorder,* 1/7/56. **128.** R&B dj poll: *Billboard,* 11/12/55.

13. GROWTH TO GENIUS

130. "My life was": *Brother Ray,* p. 161. **131.** Elvis records "I Got a Woman": *Last Train to Memphis,* p. 238. **131.** "Not everyone": *Billboard,* 1/28/56. **131.** "Drown" review: *Billboard,* 2/11/55. **132.** "kid with 89 cents": *Billboard,* 2/4/56. **132.** "A tune like . . . 'Tutti-Frutti' ": *Brother Ray,* p. 177. **133.** Billy Shaw death: *Billboard,* 7/7, 7/14/56. **134.** "Reserved Section": Houston *Informer,* 10/56. **135.** "Lonely Avenue" #6: *Billboard,* 9/15/56. **135.** Atlantic and indy royalties: How Atlantic and other record companies reduced royalties owed artists is well described in Ruth Brown's autobiography, *Miss Rhythm.* Brown and others, after a long struggle, forced Atlantic and other labels to pay artists retroactively and to make large donations to the Rhythm and Blues Foundation as a token payment to the many artists long underpaid. **135.** "a few pennies": *Brother Ray,* p. 163. **136.** RC loan to Shaw: mentioned in *Brother Ray,* confirmed in RC interview. **136.** "An LP . . . modern feel": liner notes of the LP *The Great Ray Charles.* **137.** Jerry playing tambourine: from Wexler interview; also in *Rhythm and the Blues.* **137.** Cerulli article: *Downbeat,* 1/28/56. **138.** "sound" of the record: *Billboard,* 3/9, 3/23/55; "They didn't want anybody but Fats Domino": *The Rockin 50s,* p. 71. **138.** Jeff's flying lessons: LA *Sentinel,* 6/9/57; also several interviews. **139.** Rock 'n' Roll album: *Billboard,* 6/10/57. **141.** "Some cat": *Brother Ray,* p. 156. **142.** "wondrously natural sound": *Downbeat,* 10/57. **142.** "Tatum and Powell . . .": liner notes for the LP *The Great Ray Charles.* **143.** "a snappy adaptation": *Billboard,* 9/9/57. **143.** "RC EP Selling": *Billboard,* 11/28/57. **143.** Carnegie Hall concert: *Brother Ray,* p. 186. **145.** Cookies in Brazil: *Kansas City Call,* 11/22/57. **145.** "more perfume": *Brother Ray,* p. 170. **146.** Milt Shaw helped look: *Billboard,* 1/6/58. **148.** March 6: Los Angeles county archives; $30,000: Jeff Brown interview. **148.** payola hearings: *Billboard,* 3/58. **148.** Jones column: *Melody Maker,* 5/24/58. **150.** "Ray Charles failed": *Billboard,* 7/14/58. **152.** "sock album": *Billboard,* 12/8/58. **153.** Birth of "What'd I Say": from booklet with Atlantic CD set, *The Birth of Soul;* also *Brother Ray,* pp. 190–91, and *Sweet Soul Music.* **153.** Elgin Hychew column: *Louisiana Weekly,* 12/6/58.

14. THE GENIUS MOVES ON

155. "Flood of Records": *Billboard,* 1/5/59. **155.** "an aura" about Atlantic and following: *Making Tracks,* pp. 3–4. **156.** "Male Singer–New Star": *Downbeat,* 7/58. **156.** Mary Ann Fisher leaves RC: Fisher interview and ANP story in black press. Fisher later moved to New York and sang at Harlem's Club Baby Grand, and still later moved back to Louisville, where she sang for years, billing herself as "Former Featured Vocalist with RC." **157.** Grevatt interview: *Billboard,* 2/2/59. **158.** Clyde McPhatter–MGM deal: *Billboard,* 3/2/59. **159.** Raelet: The name has also been spelled "Raelett" and "Raelette." **159.** Margie pregnant: *Brother Ray,* p. 124. **161.** RC's tape for Quincy Jones: courtesy Dufour archive. **161.** "I was sweating bullets": *Rhythm and the Blues,* p. 121; also *Making Tracks,* pp. 135–38. **163.** RC singing Raelet parts: Wexler interview; also Steffens radio interview. **164.** "He shouts out": *Billboard,* 6/15/59. **164.** "What'd I Say" on charts: *Billboard,* 7/6, 7/13, 7/20, 7/20/59. **164.** Paul Mc-Cartney quotation: clipping in Houston library. **165.** Atlantic million-dollar July: *Billboard,* 8/24/59. **166.** ABC Records: the portrait of ABC-Paramount Records and RC's switch to the label is drawn from interviews with Larry Newton, Larry Myers, RC, Jerry Wexler, Ahmet Ertegun, Jeff Brown, and other newspaper and trade-paper research. **168.** "Sure I'd be interested": RC interview. **168.** "Seven and a half cents": RC interview. **169.** 3000 EPs and ad: *Billboard,* 11/2/59; full-page ad: *Billboard,* 11/19/59. **170.** Ray's emotions at leaving Atlantic: RC interview and *Brother Ray.* **171.** Margie's baby born: Lula Hendricks interview. **175.** *Tan* interview: *Tan,* 12/59.

PART IV THE 1960s: THE ABC YEARS

15. GEORGIA ON MY MIND

179. Zeiger portrait: *Billboard,* 8/4/56; also Joe Adams and Johnny Otis interviews and *Upside Your Head.* **180.** full-page ad: *Billboard,* 2/15/60. **181.** albums outsell singles: *Billboard,* 2/15/60. **181.** RC's ideas to improve "Georgia": *Ebony,* 4/63. **183.** "not a politician": *Melody Maker,* 5/25/63, and many other sources. **183.** Ruth Brown and RC in Chicago: *Miss Rhythm,* and Duke Wade interview. **184.** *Genius* album statistics: Joel Whitburn Album Chart book, based on *Billboard.* **184.** "Sticks and Stones" chart positions: *Billboard,* 5 and 6/60. **184.** "smokes incessantly": *Downbeat,* 7/7/60. **184.** $40,000 for Cessna: *Ebony,* 9/60; call letters, Duke Wade; purchase noted in FAA records, Oklahoma City. **186.** *Playboy's Penthouse* show: viewed at Museum of Television and Radio, NYC. **186.** *Ebony* article: *Ebony,* 9/60. **186.** Tenot article: *Jazz Magazine* (Paris), 12/60, translated by Ellen Mandel; also Frank Tenot interview. **187.** "RC and Elvis": *Billboard,* 11/14/60. **188.** "Georgia" chart positions: *Billboard,* 11 and 12/60; "nine albums": ad in *Downbeat,* 9/1/60. **189.** *Playboy* quotation: *Playboy,* 12/60.

16. NEW HIGHS, NEW LOWS

193. "Ruby" off, "Them" on: *Billboard,* 1/16/61. **193.** Gleason review: *Downbeat,* 3/16/61. **194.** Albuquerque story: *Variety,* 2/1/61. **194.** Heroin, three to four ounces: *Brother Ray,* p. 182. **194.** RC's clothing: Duke Wade interview and *Brother Ray.* **195.** Como show: viewed at Museum of Television and Radio; "Ray and TV": Philadelphia *Tribune,* 3/7/61. **196.** Yale yearbook: Yale *Banner,* 1961; writer Peter Guralnick remembers the same thing happening that spring at Boston's Jordan Hall. **196.** 1951 Atlanta concert: *New Jersey Afro American,* 11/3/51. **196.** Paine College story: Pittsburgh *Courier,* 4/1/61. **197.** hand-cutting episode: from interviews with Ray Charles Jr. and Hank Crawford; also *Brother Ray,* pp. 201–2. **198.** Slip in bathtub story: Philadelphia *Tribune,* 4/11/61. **198.** Stevie Wonder in Detroit: Duke Wade interview; also *Brother Ray.* **199.** *Jamaica* details and reviews: clipping file, Lincoln Center Library; "oily scoundrel": *New Yorker* review. **199.** Light-change story: Joe Adams interview. **200.** Carnegie Hall reviews: *Variety,* 5/3/61, and *New York Times,* 5/1/61. **201–02.** Percy Mayfield quotations:

Living Blues, Spring 1981 (#50). **202.** Atlantic City gig: Philadelphia *Tribune,* 7/8/61. **202.** Chicago bust: ANP story in Cleveland *Call and Post,* 7/22/61, and other papers of nearby date. Also Duke Wade interview. **202.** Juan-les-Pins music: tape from Dufour archive. **203.** star of the show: *Melody Maker,* 7/22/61; "Golden Youth": *Jazz Magazine,* 10/61. **203.** Goldgrand and European tour: *Melody Maker,* 9/2/61. **203.** integrated Memphis gig: Memphis *World,* 8/26/61; *Variety,* 8/23/61. **204.** Raenee and RC support: court papers filed in County of New York, 8/2/65, in child support suit brought by Mae Saunders against RC. **204.** Hollywood Bowl: *Downbeat,* 12/7/61. **205.** RC in Paris: sources include interviews with Maurice Cullasz, Frank Tenot, Duke Wade, and Hank Crawford; also *Jazz Magazine,* 12/61; *Melody Maker,* 10/21, 10/28/61; and *Variety,* 11/1/61. **207.** Indianapolis bust: from Wade and Cooper interviews; also Indianapolis *Times,* 11/14/61, and Indianapolis *Recorder,* Evansville *Press,* Evansville *Courier,* and New York *Post* about the same date; also *Brother Ray,* pp. 198–99. **209.** Aftermath of Indianapolis bust: Larry Myers and Hank Crawford interviews; *Louisiana Weekly,* 11/25/61; *Variety,* 11/22, 11/29/61. **209.** Hentoff article: *Show Business Illustrated,* 3/62. **210.** Hunter series: Chicago *Defender,* 11/25, 12/2, 12/9/61. **210.** RC's reaction to bust: *Brother Ray,* pp. 199–201. **211.** Ray Jr.'s bike: Ray Charles Jr. interview.

17. I CAN'T STOP LOVING YOU

212. "had the same": Indianapolis *Recorder,* 2/3/62; RC's posture: photo in Philadelphia *Tribune,* 1/3/62. **212.** "$1.5 million": LA *Sentinel,* 3/9/62, and author's conclusion. **213.** Atlantic suit: Earl Zaidens interview. **213.** "Gypsy Woman": *Billboard,* 1/6/61; Coltrane at ABC: *Billboard,* 4/28/61. **214.** RC and record company: RC interview. **215.** "I Can't Stop Loving You," B-side: *Billboard,* 2/3/58. **216.** Tangerine press party: New York *Amsterdam News,* 3/10/62, and *Billboard,* 3/17/62. **217.** #11: *Billboard,* 3/10/62; "year": *Billboard,* 62/63. **217.** Adams filming: *Louisiana Weekly,* 10/20/62. **217.** RC wanting to crush Tab Hunter: *Downbeat,* 9/12/63. **218.** #50 and #10, #52 and #21: *Billboard,* 5/5, 5/12/62. **218.** Paris shows: *Jazz Magazine,* 7/62. **218.** #5 and #4: *Billboard,* 5/26/62. **218.** Berlin concert: from RC Berlin CD (Pablo Records). **219.** "Can't Stop" figures: *Billboard,* 4/28, 5/19, 5/26/62. **219.** Japanese women: Christopher Lydon in Japan in early 1963. **220.** Martin 404 price: New York *Amsterdam News,* 5/19/62. **220.** one and a half million sold: *Billboard,* 6/16/62; ABC's first million-selling: liner notes, *Modern Sounds Vol. Two.* **220.** "You Don't Know Me" #2: *Billboard,* 9/62. **220.** "wined and dined": John Chilton, *Let the Good Times Roll: The Story of Louis Jordan and His Music,* pp. 215–19. **221.** *Melody Maker* story: *Melody Maker,* 7/28/62. **221.** RC stoned in Portland: letter from Rich Look, eyewitness. **221.** Tulsa incident: Philadelphia *Tribune,* 9/8/62. **221.** Hotel Theresa: *Amsterdam News,* 9/62. **221.** Mae feeding lyrics: Leroy Cooper interview. **222.** *Modern Sounds Vol. Two* on charts: Whitburn, Top Pop Albums. **222.** Mae as "Mrs. Charles": Philadelphia *Tribune,* 5/18/65. **223.** Olympian motel: LA County Superior Court records; same as Mae: Philadelphia *Tribune,* 5/22/65. **223.** $1.6 million: Larry Newton interview, confirmed by Jeff Brown and Larry Myers. **223.** two winter flights: *Brother Ray,* pp. 214–15, and Jeff Brown interview. **224.** Louis Jordan's album: *Let the Good Times Roll,* p. 218; Jimmy Scott album: Jimmy Scott interview. **224.** false names: Philadelphia *Tribune,* 1/21/64. **224.** watching TV: *Sepia,* 12/63. **225.** Wonder album: *Billboard,* 3/2/63; tape of album courtesy Ray Baradat. **225.** *Modern Sounds* a top-selling album: *Michigan Chronicle,* 1/12/63. **226.** Jeff Brown and money: the picture of Jeff Brown's and RC's money problems is drawn from many interviews: RC, Jeff Brown, Shirley Brown, Joe Adams, Leroy Cooper, Duke Wade, Larry Myers, Renald Richard and others. Many of these disagreed with one another or felt they had only partial knowledge. This is a construct based on considered evaluation of the evidence. **227.** *Time* quotes: *Time,* 5/10/63. **227.** *Ebony* quotes: *Ebony,* 4/63. **228.** Hentoff article: London *Sunday Times,* 5/12/63. **228.** *Melody Maker* reports: *Melody Maker,* 5/11, 5/18/63. **229.** Blinstrub's: *Billboard,* 7/6/63. **231.** "soulful songs": *Billboard,* 8/23/63. **231.** NAACP award: New York *Amsterdam News,* 7/27/63. **231.** RC at Concord Hotel: Al Aronowitz interview. **232.** $1100: these and other figures, facts, and quotations drawn from files in the archives of the Los Angeles County Superior Court. **232.** "Casanova": Philadelphia *Tribune,* 8/20/63. **232.** "Miss Betts": LA

Sentinel, 8/15/63. **232.** RC on paternity suits: *Brother Ray,* pp. 231–36. **232.** "demurely attired": LA *Sentinel,* 9/5/63. **233.** *Saturday Evening Post* article: *Saturday Evening Post,* 8/27/63. **233.** MOA award: *Billboard,* 9/14/63. **233.** 4863 Southridge information: from LA County Building and Safety Division archives; $100,000: LA *Sentinel,* 5/29/65. **233.** 2107 West Washington Blvd. information: LA County archives; $400,000: California *Eagle,* 11/28/63. **234.** more Betts paternity suit: Philadelphia *Tribune,* 10/1/63; "paternity is possible": LA Superior Court archives. **234.** New Orleans police dogs: Philadelphia *Tribune,* 11/5/63. **234.** Louise's suit: Philadelphia *Tribune,* 10/22/63. **234.** Big J bowling: Houston *Informer,* 11/9, 12/28/63; also Jeff Bown, Shirley Brown, and Renald Richard interviews. **235.** "Greed": RC interview; "second brother": RC interview. **236.** year-end *Billboard: Billboard,* 12/28/63.

18. BUSTED IN BOSTON

237. 1964 paternity suit: information from LA Superior Court archive; also news reports in LA *Sentinel,* Philadelphia *Tribune,* New York *Amsterdam News,* and Cleveland *Call and Post,* 1/64. **238.** Trial hurt Della: *Brother Ray,* pp. 283–84. **238.** Beatles chart figures: *Billboard,* 1/18, 4/4/64; the Beatles held #1 from 2/1 to 5/9/64. **239.** RC on Beatles: *Melody Maker,* 6/13/64. **240.** Wexler notes: from liner notes to *The Ray Charles Story* LPs. **240.** critical quotations: Nat Hentoff, London *Sunday Times,* 5/12/63; *Time,* 5/10/63; *Jazz Monthly,* 7/63; *Downbeat,* 1/3/63. **240.** cops at 2107 West Washington: *Brother Ray,* p. 249. **240.** LA's wealthy Negroes: LA *Sentinel,* 4/23/64. **241.** acting scared RC: *Melody Maker,* 6/13/64. **241.** drugs in Ireland: from interview with James Clay by Tim Schuller, in *Coda* (undated) provided by Schuller. **241.** *Ballad in Blue:* viewed on videotape, courtesy Ray Baradat collection. **242.** Tivoli crowd: *Billboard,* 8/8/64. **242.** Margie leaves: Philadelphia *Tribune,* 5/22/65; wigs: interview by Valerie Wilmer in *Second Shift* (England), Summer 1993. **242.** RC on world tour: *Melody Maker,* 6/13/64; *Brother Ray,* p. 282. **243.** President Johnson quotation: New York *Amsterdam News,* 1/11/64; "most sweeping": Indianapolis *Recorder,* 7/4/64. **243.** Southridge details: LA County Building and Safety Division records; also Duana Chenier interview. **244.** Dallas riot: Dallas *Morning News,* 9/29/64, and Leroy Cooper interview; also reported in *Variety,* LA *Sentinel,* and *Sepia.* **246.** Boston bust: this picture is a composite of many sources: Federal Court records on file at the Federal Records Center in Waltham, Massachusetts; *Brother Ray,* p. 252 and following; stories in the Boston *Herald,* 11/64 and following; the black press; and numerous interviews. **246.** special edge: Elliot Paul interview. **247.** Sam Cooke death and funeral: LA *Sentinel,* 12/64; also *You Send Me,* p. 332. **248.** Nat Cole's cancer: Haskins, p. 166.

19. THE YEAR OFF

249. "I'm heading": interview with Ruth Robinson; she said it was one of RC's most frequent expressions. **249.** Lee Shaw death: date from Mt. Ararat cemetery; details from Larry Myers interview. **250.** Mae's paternity suit: from LA County Superior Court archives and the black press, principally the LA *Sentinel.* **250.** Federal indictment: from Federal Records Center, Waltham. **251.** "RC Moves Base": *Billboard,* 4/15/65. **251.** RC pleads not guilty: details drawn from Federal Records, the black press, and *Brother Ray.* **252.** "monstrous dwelling": LA *Sentinel,* 5/29/65. **252.** RC wouldn't survive prison: from interview with RC in Austrian newspaper, contributed by Henry Alter. **252.** "I can stand": *Brother Ray,* p. 257. **252.** Little League dinner and RC's decision: Ibid., pp. 254–55. **253.** Frederick Hacker: portrait drawn from interviews with Henry Alter, Hacker's friend and onetime business manager; with Hannes Hacker, Hacker's brother; and clippings from Austrian newspapers contributed by Henry Alter. **254.** "Why all the hush-hush": LA *Sentinel,* 7/12/65. **254.** renting RPM: LA *Sentinel,* 7/8/65. **254.** July 26: LA County Superior Court archives. **254.** "bitter" and following: *Brother Ray,* p. 257. **254.** "critical list" and following: Philadelphia *Tribune,* 9/18/65. **254.** Hacker dismisses: LA County Superior Court archives. **256.** "distinct possibility": *Brother Ray,* p. 261. **257.** "This man has": *Life,* 7/29/66. **257.** court details: Federal Records Center; also *New York Times,*

11/23/65. **257.** "Dr. Hacker saved my life": Austrian magazine clipping from Henry Alter. **258.** "Man, I'm tired": LA *Sentinel,* 12/2/65. **259.** "My husband is home": Indianapolis *Recorder,* 12/18/65.

20. COMING BACK

261. "No partners!": David Braithwaite interview; RC's attitude confirmed by others. **261.** "Crying Time" #6: *Billboard,* 2/19/66; "Crying Time" #15: *Billboard,* 3/12/66. **262.** "When I was doing it": *Downbeat,* 11/30/67. **262.** "I must get back": *Billboard,* 10/15/66. **262.** $90,000 for Martin: Federal Records archive. **262.** RC at McLean: *Brother Ray,* p. 263–64; also Federal Records archive. **263.** $68,000 gross: *Billboard,* 5/28/66. **263.** RC "back in . . . saddle": *Downbeat,* 5/6/66; Gleason column: New York *Post,* 5/8/66. **263.** "Fired with vitality": Indianapolis *Recorder,* 3/5/66. **264.** "only genius" and following: *Life,* 7/29/66. **265.** "wild rocker": *Billboard,* 8/20/66. **265.** "hard-biting swing": *Variety,* 8/31/66; "deeply moving": *New York Times,* 8/29/66. **265.** "fairly interesting": New York *Amsterdam News,* 10/1/66. **266.** November hearing: Federal Records archive; also *Brother Ray,* pp. 265–66. **266.** Boston bust and $10,000 check: Federal Records archive; the next item in the court papers dates from four years later, one handwritten line discharging RC from probation. **267.** chess games: RC interview; also interviews with Billy Brooks, Roger Spotts, Herb Miller, Jimmy Lewis, and Renald Richard. **267.** "giant promotion": *Billboard,* 1/4/67. **268.** "for no other reason": *Billboard,* 6/24/67. **268.** "grating . . . unpleasant": *Downbeat,* 8/67. **269.** Vienna story: Henry Alter interview. **269.** "prosaic": *Jazz Journal,* 6/67; "sugar-sweet": *Jazz Magazine,* 6/67. **269.** "RC show cheats": New York *Post,* 1/24/67. **269.** *Jet* item: *Jet,* 5/18/67. **269.** RC had told *Downbeat*: spring interview published in *Downbeat,* 11/30/67. **269.** RC Day details: LA *Sentinel,* 6/15/67. **270.** "spiritual father": *Billboard,* 6/3/67. **270.** "one and only sister" and "the way black folk": *Brother Ray,* p. 269. **270.** "There are a lot": *Sepia,* 6/67. **271.** Eunice Pye report: LA *Sentinel,* 9/28/67. **271.** "justifies the . . . ballyhoo" and following: *Variety,* 9/26/67. **271.** Lennon-McCartney telegram: *Downbeat,* 4/4/68. **271.** Joelson resolution: LA *Sentinel,* 11/12/67. **271–72.** "I'm always having hard times": New York *Post,* 11/18/67. **272.** RC at Copa: details from *Billboard,* 12/2/67; *Variety,* 11/29/67; *New York Times,* 11/30/67, and New York *Post* and *Daily News* about that date.

21. ROLLING ONWARD

273. "like a big wheel:" RC said virtually the same words to *Billboard,* 10/15/66, and to *Sepia,* 6/67; this is a composite. **273–74.** relax and "then resume": LA *Sentinel,* 1/11/68; *Playboy* Hall of Fame, LA *Sentinel,* 1/23/68; President's Council citation: *Downbeat,* 2/4/68. **274.** RC at King funeral: *New York Times,* New York *Post,* LA *Sentinel,* Atlanta *Constitution,* early April 1968; also Vernon Troupe interview. **275.** *Of Black America*: viewed at Museum of Television and Radio. **275.** Raelets quit: LA *Sentinel,* 8/1/68. **278.** omnibus ad: *Billboard,* 12/7/68. **278.** "Businesses last longer": *Billboard,* 5/10/69. **278.** Tangerine and Ron Granger: *Billboard,* 1/18, 4/12/69. **282.** Della and Emma to London: LA *Sentinel,* 10/2/69. **282.** "He seems to rediscover": *Jazz Magazine,* 11/69. **283.** "but without the big pressure": LA *Sentinel,* 12/4/69; RC's threat to leave ABC also reported in *Billboard,* 12/6/69, and *Variety,* 12/3/69.

PART V THE 1970s: THE INVISIBLE YEARS

22. VOLCANIC MESSAGES

287. "I don't think the day": *Sepia,* 6/67. **288.** *Playboy* interview: *Playboy,* 3/70. **289.** "RC Sings and Plays the Beatles": *Billboard,* 2/21/70. **290–91.** 1970 tour dates: LA *Sentinel,* 4/16/70. **291.** $400,000 for Viscount: Joe Adams interview. **294.** RC on "Black Requiem": RC interview; other details: LA *Sentinel,* 3/4/71. **295.** "Since I'm here": *Crescendo* (England), 11/71. **296.** "I can't even remember": LA *Sen-*

tinel, 3/20/71; "revival show": *Billboard,* 5/2/70. **298.** RC on *A Message from the People:* Steffens radio interview. **299.** Della at Coconut Grove: LA *Sentinel,* 6/1/72. **299.** "51-49 in marriage": LA *Sentinel,* 8/13/70. **299.** RC and Della's dying marriage: *Brother Ray,* pp. 283–85. **299.** "One rooster, many hens" and RC's feelings about sex: *Brother Ray,* pp. 230–32; also Ruth Robinson and Susaye Green interviews. **301.** RC meets Nixon: LA *Sentinel,* 9/28/72.

23. LIFE ON THE ROAD

303. RC at Circle Star: portions of this description have been adapted from author's book, *Boogie Lightning.* **306.** "Who else . . .": *Billboard,* 5/26/73; "maintained sales figures" and other details: *Rolling Stone,* 1/73. **306.** "It's sort of 'in' ": *Downbeat,* 9/16/71. **306.** Landau review: *Rolling Stone,* 7/72. **306.** "too bland": in reviews of RC by Landau and others in *Rolling Stone* and *Downbeat,* 1971–73. **307.** Lasker suing and sued: *Billboard,* many issues, 1973. **307.** End of ABC Records: ABC limped along through 1978, then ABC-Paramount sold the label to MCA for a reported $30 million, a "fire-sale price," according to industry insiders. **311.** RC pays taxes: *Brother Ray,* pp. 290–91; $2 million and $1 million: from *Robinson* v. *Robinson* divorce papers, LA County Superior Court archives. **316.** "electronic synthesizer": *Billboard,* 5/7/55; Stevie Wonder gives synth to RC: *Rolling Stone,* 7/13/95.

24. DIVORCE AND DECLINE

321. McDonald's ad: LA *Sentinel,* 1/15/76; Grammy: LA *Sentinel,* 3/4/76. **321.** *Porgy and Bess* album: RC interview; also *Brother Ray* and David Ritz interview. **322.** prison show: LA *Sentinel,* 2/22/76; also *Billboard.* **322.** RC "noblest jazz singer": *The New Yorker,* 7/5/76. **322.** RC and Della's divorce: drawn from records of *Robinson* v. *Robinson* in LA County Superior Court archives. **324.** *Brother Ray* details: from introduction and afterword of *Brother Ray;* also interview with David Ritz and from "Being with Ray," Ritz's article about writing the book, published in *Essence,* 8/78. **326.** Welding interview: *Downbeat,* 5/5/77. **326–27.** re-signing with Atlantic: from RC, Wexler, and Ertegun interviews. **327.** RC's TV shows: LA *Sentinel,* various dates, 1977. **327.** man hugs RC onstage: LA *Sentinel,* 3/3/77; also David Ritz interview. **328.** further divorce details: from LA County Superior Court archives. **329.** RC and Atlantic's reaction to *True to Life:* RC, Ertegun, and Wexler interviews; also *Rolling Stone,* 2/9/78. **331.** Half-empty Holiday Inns: Harold Patton interview; also Memphis *Commercial Appeal,* 5/20/77. **331.** *Real Paper* interview: *Real Paper,* 8/19/78. **333.** "Half the fun of fucking": *Brother Ray,* pp. 244–45. **333.** "remains mysterious": Ibid., p. 5. **335.** "uninspired selection": *Billboard,* 10/27/79.

PART VI THE 1980s: THE LONG COMEBACK

25. NASHVILLE

341. "You have to ask": LA *Times,* 2/28/80. **343.** "Look, folks": Dallas *Morning News,* 11/12/80; "Yeah, yeah": Dallas *Morning News,* 12/4/81. **344.** RC on *Hee Haw: Denver Post,* 12/6/80. **345.** "recognizable by the country-music consumer": Nashville *Banner,* 1/2/83; "RC to Do C&W": *Variety,* 8/4/82. **345.** "so different . . . it's gonna shock": Pittsburgh *Press,* 10/28/82. **345.** "amateurish": Saginaw *News,* 2/5/83; "incredibly dull": *Rolling Stone;* "sterile museum piece": *Village Voice,* 6/28/83. **346.** "A lot of people": *USA Today,* 4/10/83. **346.** RC's ear problems and treatment: Dr. Pulec interview. **347.** Roger Heyn's tape: the "You Dog" and "Bonus My Ass" tapes, long circulated among RC buffs, were given to the author by trombonist Dana Hughes; here they have been abridged but not otherwise changed; other details added from interviews with Clifford Solomon and Eugene Ross. **349.** Billy Sherrill: portrait drawn from interviews in Nashville and a profile published by the Nashville Entertainment Association in April 1986. **350.** "A lot of producers": RC interview. **351.** "Contentment has come": Boston *Globe,* 4/27/83. **352.**

David Robinson crime: LA Municipal Court records. **354.** "The Democrats wanted me": *Today* with Bryant Gumbel, 1991, viewed on tape from Costello archive. **354.** RC on South Africa: Steffens radio interview; also *Jet,* 12/9/85, and *US* magazine, 7/30/84; also the source of "money, honey" quotation.

26. MEDALS AND HONORS

356. RC's country #1 noted: *USA Today,* 3/22/85; *Jet,* 4/8/85. **356.** "We Are the World": details from film of session viewed at Museum of Television and Radio; similarly for inaugural gala mentioned below. **358.** Crash of the Buzzard: details drawn from interviews with Clifford Solomon, Jeff Kaye, and Rudy Johnson; also accounts in the Bloomington *Herald-Telephone,* 9/20/85, and following. **359.** RC on TV: shows viewed at Museum of Television and Radio. **359.** Florida award: *LA Times,* 4/17/86. **359.** "Wait, wait": *Modern Drummer,* 7/96. **360.** backstage walkie-talkie: *Esquire,* 5/86. **361.** RC on synthesizers and punk rock: *Jazz Forum* (Poland), 3/85; Ray on rap: many interviews. **361.** "what Sinatra gets": *USA Today,* 11/1/85. **362.** "perfunctory": *Downbeat,* 3/86; "totally unprepared": LA *Times,* 5/19/86; "RC was on stage": LA *Times,* 8/24/86. **362–63.** Kennedy Center Honors: details drawn from Bob Abrams interview; also LA *Times,* 12/9/86; "I'm overjoyed": *New York Times,* 12/8/86; "You feel you've come": LA *Times,* 12/24/86. **363.** "My eyes . . . My ears": *Jet,* 5/18/87. **363.** "Turn it up": Houston *Chronicle,* 9/3/87; "It stinks": Houston *Post,* 10/3/87. **365.** tickets for RC gala: LA *Times,* 9/7/87. **366.** Irving Berlin 100th Birthday show: viewed at Museum of Television and Radio. **366.** Martins' NYC Ballet: quotations and details drawn from interviews with David Simmons, David Ritz, and Ahmet Ertegun; also *New York Times,* 5/13/88; *Dance Review,* Winter, 1990; *Village Voice,* 6/86. **367.** *Parade* promotion: *Parade,* 8/7/88. **370, 373.** Pepsi ads: viewed at Museum of Television and Radio. **373.** "I'm the kind of guy": interview in *Crescendo* (England), 11/71.

PART VII THE 1990s: THE GRAND MASTER

27. NO TIME TO WASTE TIME

374. "If I didn't know": this quotation is a composite from three sources: the LA *Times,* 5/28/89, the *Wall Street Journal,* 8/22/89, and *Downbeat,* 1/89; RC expressed the same thought in dozens of interviews. **374.** "How can you": RC interview. **377.** under 50,000 copies sold: from Soundscan, a company that compiles sales figures for the music industry. **377.** Pepsi ads: viewed at Museum of Television and Radio. **377.** "infectiously cheerful": *New York Times,* 2/4/94; best ad: *Time,* 1/6/92. **377.** $50 million: *Forbes,* 3/21/92; other details: *New York Times,* 2/4/92, and *Brother Ray* epilogue. **377–78.** "You can see": *Brother Ray* epilogue; "my thing goes": Montreal *Gazette,* 8/7/93. **378.** "My Dad": concert program for RC, "50 Years in Music," 9/19/91. **378.** *People* photos: *People,* 11/19/91. **379.** "The paradigm for black pop music": *New York Times,* 12/15/91. **382.** "If you're gonna produce me": RC interview. **383.** "tattered and cracked": *New York Times,* 4/4/93. **383.** Arsenio Hall show: viewed courtesy of Costello archive. **383.** *My World* sales: Soundscan reported 189,000 copies sold through fall 1997. **384.** "performance never rose above": Fort Worth *Star-Telegram,* 4/21/94; "moved many": *New York Times,* 7/1/94. **384.** "miserable" Moorhead show: letter from eyewitness John K. Johnson. **388.** "When I started with Ray": Joe Adams interview.

EPILOGUE

389. "Ain't nobody gonna ask": *Offbeat* (New Orleans), 5/95. **390.** "sometimes awkward": *Time,* 2/5/96; "Vegas-esque": LA *Times,* 2/4/96. **390.** 15,000 copies: Soundscan.

Bibliography

BOOKS

Anthony, Otis R. *Black Tampa: The Roots of a People.* Tampa: The Black History Project, 1979.

Balliett, Whitney. *American Singers.* New York: Oxford University Press, 1988.

Berry, Jason, Jonathan Foose, and Tad Jones. *Up from the Cradle of Jazz: New Orleans Music Since World War II.* New York: Da Capo, 1992. First published Athens: University of Georgia Press, 1986.

Branch, Taylor. *Parting the Waters: America in the King Years.* New York: Simon & Schuster, 1988.

Britt, Stan. *Dexter Gordon: A Musical Biography.* New York: Da Capo, 1989. First published, as *Long Tall Dexter,* London: Quartet Books, 1989.

Broven, John. *Walking to New Orleans.* Bexhill-on-Sea, Sussex: Blues Unlimited, n.d.

Brown, Ruth, and Andrew Yule. *Miss Rhythm: The Autobiography of Ruth Brown, Rhythm & Blues Legend.* New York: Donald I. Fine, 1996.

Charles, Ray, and David Ritz. *Brother Ray.* New York: Da Capo, 1992. First published New York: Dial, 1978.

Chilton, John. *Let the Good Times Roll: The Story of Louis Jordan and His Music.* Ann Arbor: University of Michigan Press, 1992.

Dance, Helen Oakley. *Stormy Monday: The T-Bone Walker Story.* New York: Da Capo, 1987. First published Baton Rouge: Louisiana State University Press, 1987.

de Barros, Paul. *Jackson Street After Hours: The Roots of Jazz in Seattle.* Photographs by Eduardo Calderon. Seattle: Sasquatch Books, 1993.

Floyd, Samuel A., Jr. *The Power of Black Music.* New York: Oxford University Press, 1995.

Gillespie, Dizzy, with Al Fraser. *To Be or Not . . . to Bop.* New York: Doubleday, 1979.

Gillett, Charlie. *Making Tracks: The Story of Atlantic Records*. London: Souvenir Books, 1988.

———. *The Sound of the City*. New York: Pantheon Books, 1970.

Gioia, Ted. *West Coast Jazz, 1945–1960*. New York: Oxford University Press, 1992.

Gordy, Berry. *To Be Loved: The Music, the Magic, the Memories of Motown*. New York: Warner Books, 1994.

Guralnick, Peter. *Sweet Soul Music*. New York: Harper & Row, 1986.

———. *Last Train to Memphis: The Rise of Elvis Presley*. New York: Little, Brown, 1994.

Hannush, Jeff. *I Hear You Knocking: The Sound of New Orleans Rhythm and Blues*. Ville Platte, LA: Swallow, 1985.

Haskins, James, and Kathleen Benson. *Nat King Cole*. New York: Stein and Day, 1984.

Heilburt, Anthony. *The Gospel Sound: Good News and Bad Times*. New York: Limelight Editions, 1987.

Hirshey, Gerri. *Nowhere to Run: The Story of Soul Music*. New York: Times Books, 1984.

James, Etta, and David Ritz. *Rage to Survive: The Etta James Story*. New York: Villard Books, 1995.

Klein, Norman M., and Martin J. Schiesl, eds. *20th Century Los Angeles: Power, Promotion, and Social Conflict*. Claremont, California: Regina Books, 1968.

Lomax, John, III. *Nashville: Music City USA*. New York: Harry N. Abrams, 1985.

Lydon, Michael. *Boogie Lightning*. New York: Da Capo, 1980. First published New York: Dial, 1974.

———. *Rock Folk*. New York: Citadel, 1990. First published New York: Dial, 1971.

Miles, Betty T., Daniel J., and Martin J. *The Miles Chart Display, Volume I, The Top 100, 1955–1970*. Boulder, Colorado: Convex Industries, 1971.

Millard, Andre. *America on Record: A History of Recorded Sound*. New York: Cambridge University Press, 1995.

Mingus, Charles. *Beneath the Underdog*. New York: Alfred A. Knopf, 1971.

Otis, Johnny. *Upside Your Head! Rhythm and Blues on Central Avenue*. Hanover: Wesleyan University Press, 1993.

Palmer, Robert. *Deep Blues*. New York: Penguin, 1982.

Ruppli, Michel. *Atlantic Records: A Discography, Vol 1*. Westport, Connecticut, and London: Greenwood Press, 1979.

Russell, Ross. *Bird Lives!* New York: Charterhouse Books, 1973.

Sanjek, Russell, and David Sanjek. *American Popular Music Business in the 20th Century*. New York: Oxford University Press, 1991.

Sawyer, Charles. *The Arrival of B. B. King*. New York: Da Capo, 1982. First published New York: Doubleday, 1980.

Shaw, Arnold. *The World of Soul: Black America's Contribution to the Pop Music Scene*. New York: Cowles Book Co., 1970.

———. *Honkers and Shouters: The Golden Years of Rhythm and Blues*. New York: Collier, 1978.

———. *The Rockin' 50s*. New York: Da Capo, 1987. First published New York: Hawthorn Books, 1974.

Smith, W. O. *Sideman: The Long Gig of W. O. Smith.* Nashville: Rutledge Hill Press, 1991.

Wade, Dorothy, and Justine Picardie. *Music Man: Ahmet Ertegun, Atlantic Records, and the Triumph of Rock 'n' Roll.* New York: W. W. Norton & Co., 1990.

Wexler, Jerry, and David Ritz. *Rhythm and the Blues: A Life in American Music.* New York: Alfred A. Knopf, 1993.

Whitburn, Joel. *Top Pop Albums 1955–1992.* Menomonee Falls, Wisconsin: Record Research Inc., 1988.

———. *Top Rhythm & Blues Singles 1942–1988.* Menomonee Falls, Wisconsin: Record Research Inc., 1988.

———. *Top Pop Singles 1955–1990.* Menomonee Falls, Wisconsin: Record Research Inc., n.d.

White, Charles. *The Life and Times of Little Richard.* New York: Da Capo, 1994. First published New York: Harmony Books, 1984.

White, George R. *Bo Diddley: Living Legend.* London: Castle Communications, 1995.

Wilder, Alec. *American Popular Song: The Great Innovators 1900–1950.* New York and London: Oxford University Press, 1990.

Wolff, Daniel, with S. R. Crain, Clifton White, and G. David Tenenbaum. *You Send Me: The Life and Times of Sam Cooke.* New York: William Morrow, 1995.

PERIODICALS

Downbeat, Rolling Stone, Living Blues, Jazz Magazine (Paris), *Melody Maker* (London), *Variety,* with special thanks to *Billboard,* whose issues, read week by week, provide an unfurling history of pop music's facts and fads.

Time, Life, People, Newsweek, Life, The Saturday Evening Post, The New Yorker, with special thanks to the magazines of Johnson Publications, *Ebony, Sepia, Jet,* and *Tan.*

My eternal gratitude to the many excellent African-American newspapers that covered Ray Charles long before the white press found him newsworthy: the Atlanta *Daily World,* Cleveland *Call and Post,* New York *Amsterdam News,* New Orleans *Louisiana Weekly,* Dallas *Express,* Los Angeles *California Eagle* and *Sentinel,* Pittsburgh *Courier,* Norfolk, Va., *Journal and Guide,* Richmond, Va., *Afro-American,* Chicago *Defender,* Oklahoma City's *Black Dispatch,* Houston *Informer,* Philadelphia *Tribune,* Detroit's *Michigan Chronicle,* Kansas City *Call,* Newark *New Jersey Afro American,* and Washington, D.C., *Afro-American*—read, in large part, on microfilm at the Schomburg Center for Research in Black Culture.

Discography

A discography of Ray Charles is not easy to compile. His recorded output is enormous, sixty-five albums and six hundred songs at least, not to mention a wealth of material still in his vaults. Ray's recordings also span a half-century, and his audience circles the globe. His work has been issued and reissued in every format and on dozens of labels. Many early session dates can't be fixed because they were casual enough that no one noted the day. In the 1970s and after, Ray, like most musicians, made his records over weeks and months, so session dates don't apply. Ray also resisted the trend in the 60s and later to list the musicians who played on his records.

This discography attempts to guide a listener through the basic story, annotated with items of interest. Those interested may go on to: Michel Ruppli's *Atlantic Records: A Discography;* Bruyninckx's *Seventy Years of Recorded Jazz;* the discography in the Da Capo (1991) edition of *Brother Ray;* and Joel Dufour's *Ray Charles Discography,* compiled with the help of Kurt Mohr, François Postif, Marcel Chauvard, Alan Leeds, and Michel Ruppli. The best one-stop introduction to Ray's entire body of recording is ***Ray Charles: Genius & Soul*** (Rhino R2 72859), a five-CD set that includes a hundred two tracks recorded between 1949 and 1993.

Ray Charles' body of work is panoramic, and to be seen must be divided into eras. Song titles that follow are in boldface, album titles in boldface italic.

ERA I: SWINGTIME 1949–1952

This era is superbly documented in ***Ray Charles: The Birth of a Legend*** (Ebony CD 8001/2), which contains, in chronological order, all the forty-one songs that Ray recorded for the Down Beat/Swingtime label in the first four years of his career.

I Love You, I Love You and **Confession Blues** are the first, recorded with the original McSon Trio, Gossie McKee, guitar, Milt Garret, bass, in Seattle in the winter of 1948–49. As Down Beat #171, these two sides entered the *Billboard* chart April 9, 1949. That spring the trio recorded seven more songs in Seattle, including Gossie's **Rocking Chair Blues;** in the fall Ray and Gossie went to Los Angeles for the first time and recorded a half-dozen songs with Tiny Webb, guitar, and Ralph Hamilton, bass, a slow **How Long Blues** the standout of the group.

By May 1950, Ray was in Los Angeles on his own, and on the 26th, he recorded four songs with an eight-piece band, including his first comedy tune, **I'll Do Anything for You—But Work.** In November, he recorded with guitarist Oscar Moore and bassist Johnny Miller of Nat "King" Cole's original trio, and they cut Ray's first hit, **Baby Let Me Hold Your Hand.** Ray came back from his second tour with Lowell Fulson in November 1951, and cut four sides with the ten-piece band he had been grooming all summer. The standout here is the rocker **Kissa Me Baby (All Night Long).**

Then come the mysterious **St. Pete's Blues, Why Did You Go, I'm Wondering and Wondering,** and **Walkin' and Talkin',** which Ray claims he recorded on a wire recorder in Tampa before he went to Seattle. He may well have, but the tracks also could have been recorded in Florida in '51 or '52 while Ray was on tour. At that time Swingtime was going under, and Ray may have cut these sides for Henry Stone of Sittin' In With Records, producer and artist concocting the wire recorder story to cover the breach of contract. In any case, Ray did own a wire recorder, and these tracks are extraordinary music.

Ray's Down Beat/Swingtime records have appeared on an endless assortment of labels, American and foreign, in many different combinations and often adulterated.

ERA II: ATLANTIC 1952–1959

In these seven years Ray grew from journeyman to Genius, and he created a body of work on record unmatched for passion and raw beauty. Ray's Atlantic records are widely available in many forms. They may be divided into his R&B work and his jazz work because of the musical differences and because Atlantic considered them separate streams of Ray's music to be sold to separate markets.

R&B: Ray's R&B sides are best presented in a magnificent three-CD set, *Ray Charles: The Birth of Soul* (Atlantic 7 82310), that presents all the tracks in chronological order. An accompanying booklet gives complete session dates and personnel listings.

Ray first recorded for Atlantic on September 11, 1952, in New York, cutting the stark **The Sun's Gonna Shine Again,** among more imitative songs. A second session, in May 1953, captured the comedy **It Shoulda Been Me** and Ahmet Ertegun's rocker, **Mess Around.** That August Ray cut two sides in New Orleans as an add-on to a Tommy Ridgley session, and in December he got down four more, including the early masterpiece **Don't You Know.** A year later, November 18, 1954, Ray made his big breakthrough: his own band doing his own arrangements of his own songs: **Black Jack; Greenbacks; Come Back, Baby;** and his first big hit, **I Got a Woman.** In April 1955 Ray cut the immortal **A Fool for You** at a late-night session in Miami. In November he recorded **Hallelujah I Love Her So,** his second hit to cross over into the white market, and **Drown in My Own Tears,** for the first time using the Cookies, the three-woman singing group, starring Margie Hendricks, which became the Raelets.

Through 1956, '57, and '58 Ray continued recording about every six months, turning out gem after gem and perfecting his small-band–Raelets sound: **Lonely Avenue** and **Rockhouse** in '56; **Swanee River Rock** and **What Kind of Man Are You?,** featuring Mary Ann Fisher, in '57; **Yes Indeed, My Bonnie,** and **The Right Time,** a red-hot duet with Margie Hendricks, in '58. On February 18, 1959, Ray put down his first monster hit, **What'd I Say;** in May, Xenas Sears caught a glorious live show in Atlanta that became the album *Ray Charles in Person;* in June, Ray cut his last two Atlantic tracks, **I Believe to My Soul,** on which he sings the Raelets' parts, and **I'm Movin' On,** his first country song and his song of farewell to the label.

JAZZ: Ray began recording jazz at Atlantic on April 30, 1956, with an easygoing trio session accompanied by Oscar Pettiford, bass, and Joe Harris, drums. They did four tunes, including **The Man I Love** and **Black Coffee.** In November, mixed in with several R&B sessions, Ray used his regular band to get down a fistful of superb instrumentals, among them Horace Silver's **Doodlin'** and **Sweet Sixteen Bars.** These and a few of the trio tracks became Ray's first jazz album, *The Great Ray Charles.*

In September '57, Ray had the first of several sessions with vibraphonist Milt Jackson, Ray playing sax on a few tracks, and Jackson guitar. These sides became the well-known jazz albums *Soul Brothers* and *Soul Meeting. Ray Charles at Newport,* from the jazz festival in July 1958, blends R&B and jazz—for Ray, the two streams are truly one.

In May and June of '59, the same months as *In Person* and *Movin' On,* Ray recorded with strings and a big band, the tracks collected on the album *The Genius of Ray Charles.* A magnificent work of art on its own terms, this album also marks Ray's entry into pop music, a direction he developed at ABC in the 60s.

ERA III: ABC-PARAMOUNT 1959–1969

Ray first recorded for ABC-Paramount, Sid Feller producing, in Los Angeles, December 29, 1959. Ray and Sid were looking for R&B singles, and they came up with **Them That Got.** At ABC, however, Ray's primary recording medium became the album, an LP of five or six songs a side, each song three to six minutes long. At the end of March 1960, in New York, Ray recorded his first ABC album, *Genius Hits the Road*—from which **Georgia on My Mind** became a #1 hit—and began the new era.

Through a series of experiments, Ray began to develop the album into an expressive musical form. His approach at first was plain: pick a single unifying theme. *Hits the Road* was all place songs, like **Georgia.** The second album, *Dedicated to You,* also '60, was all songs to ladies, of which **Ruby** was the smoky standout and became a single hit. The title announces the theme of the third, *Genius + Soul = Jazz,* a blend of R&B and jazz recorded at Christmas '60 with Quincy Jones at the helm. The next album, cut in June '61, was a duet, *Ray Charles and Betty Carter.* To demonstrate that he could still make a hot R&B single, Ray and the gang cut Percy Mayfield's **Hit the Road Jack** a month later, and it bounded to #1 in the fall.

Ray recorded his fifth ABC album in February '62, and it announced an enormous leap in his music: *Modern Sounds in Country and Western. Modern Sounds* became the most popular of all of Ray's albums, and it contains his biggest hit, **I Can't Stop Loving You.** For the rest of the decade, Ray continued to record one or two albums a year, after '64 all of them recorded at Ray's own RPM studio. Sometimes the themes are obvious, like *Modern Sounds in Country and Western Vol. 2* or the back-to-back *Sweet and Sour Tears* and *Have a Smile with Me* in '64.

Yet after *Ingredients in a Recipe of Soul* in '63, the titles and contents of Ray's albums point less often to one clear theme and more often to a group of songs arranged like a collage, a gathering of emotions that adhere because Ray says they do. *Ingredients* turns out to have an implied story line of black American life from the blues of **Busted** to the glory of **You'll Never Walk Alone,** but *Ray's Moods* in '66, *Ray Charles Invites You to Listen* in '67, and *A Portrait of Ray* in '68—to put their themes into words would be difficult.

Not that every album was themeless. *Crying Time,* recorded in '65, the year Ray kicked heroin, is a wrenching portrait of that dark period in his life. *I'm All Yours Baby* in '69 is mushy love songs, and *Doing His Thing* from the same year is R&B songs by Jimmy Lewis. With *Love Country Style* in '70, Ray returned to country.

While experimenting with the album form—and recording so many gorgeous songs that any list would be too brief (**That Lucky Old Sun, Eleanor Rigby, Together Again . . .**)—Ray was increasingly blending musical styles. Early albums of the era usually separate big-band and string orchestra tracks; later albums blend the two until it's hard to tell which is which. In sum, Ray created an enormously varied but utterly personal musical language in album form, a language that drew from every stream of American music and that conveyed cogent musical messages forty minutes long.

Along with the five-CD set, Rhino has reissued many of Ray's ABC albums.

ERA IV: TANGERINE/CROSSOVER 1970–1977

Ray's albums began bearing the logo of Tangerine Records, Ray's own label, beside ABC's logo in 1968. As his sales declined in the 70s, and ABC became less friendly to his efforts, the Tangerine logo got larger, a sure sign of the Genius' defiant self-reliance.

Ray poured everything he had learned about album making into his first two works of the new decade. *Volcanic Action of My Soul* in '71 is a themeless album, a masterpiece of gold and shadow. *A Message from the People* in '72 is a theme album, an eloquent political statement from a proud African-American; Ray pulls no punches yet affirms the deep love he feels for his native land. His **America the Beautiful** from *Message* became in time beloved by millions who felt instinctively that with it, Ray had reached the heart of American music.

Through the Eyes of Love, a quietly lovely album from late '72, was Ray's last on Tangerine. He left ABC and, funded by Decca Records, began Crossover Records. Crossover released the romantic **Come Live with Me** in '74 and the sizzling-hot *Renaissance* in '75. The dates make it plain that Ray's productive pace was slowing down, in large part because of slow sales. Fine as they were, these albums reached a very small audience.

ERA V: FREELANCE YEARS 1977–1990s

When Crossover did not pan out as an investment, Decca dropped Ray, and he henceforth became a freelance artist in the record marketplace, signing with a label for a few albums, then moving on. First he went back to Atlantic and in '77 produced *True to Life,* a tender masterpiece, its high point a transcendent **Oh, What a Beautiful Morning.** The next three Atlantic albums— *Love and Peace, Ain't It So,* and *Brother Ray Is at It Again*—are less successful, marred by weak songs and disco sounds. By 1980 Ray had become old hat. To get back into the game, he needed to find a new approach.

He found it: country music. In 1982 Ray signed with Columbia Records' Nashville division with the avowed purpose of conquering the country market. He began recording at RPM, but the first album, *Wish You Were Here Tonight,* released in '83, sounds too coldly calculating to be genuine country music. *Do I Ever Cross Your Mind?*, from '84, also done at RPM, is warmer, but not until Ray went to Nashville and let himself be produced by Billy Sherrill did he succeed in making true country music. In '85, *Friendship,* an album of ripsnortin' duets with a dozen fine country singers, hit #1 on the C&W charts, and **Seven Spanish Angels,** the duet with Willie Nelson, became a #1 country single. If *Friendship* is Ray's Nashville commercial peak, *From the Pages of My Mind* in '86 was his Nashville artistic peak, but with it Ray's country experiment ended. His last Columbia album, *Just Between Us,* in '88, was knockout R&B, the standout track **Save the Bones for Henry Jones,** a hilarious duet with Lou Rawls.

Warner Bros. signed Ray in '89, but WB didn't like the first album he gave them, the synthesized *Would You Believe?*, which he'd made on the cheap at RPM. For the second, the label put him with producer Richard Perry, and that marriage (not made in heaven) produced *My World* in '93, a flawed album that includes two fine tunes, **A Song for You** and **Still Crazy After All These Years. A Song for You** won a Grammy, making Ray a bigger presence in the pop marketplace than he had been in years, but WB had hoped for more and let him go. Ray had already started another album with his French friend and fan Jean-Pierre Grosz. Working together long-distance between LA and Paris, they finished *Strong Love Affair* in '95, the first album of Ray's old age, a wise, sensuous album built with bittersweet courage. *Strong Love Affair* came out first in Italy. Until his old friend Quincy Jones took Ray in at his Qwest label, Ray had been unable to find an American label ready to release his work.

To this grand line of Ray's work there are, of course, endless addenda: *Ray Charles Introduces David "Fathead" Newman* on Atlantic in '59, the *My Kind of Jazz* series on Tangerine from the 70s; *Porgy and Bess* in '76; the Christmas album *Spirit of Christmas* in '85; the many greatest-hits and retrospective albums; Ray's appearances on other artists' albums, Billy Joel's *The Bridge,* for example; uncollected and nearly forgotten singles; a variety of live-performance videos; plus treasures from the RPM vaults that the world has yet to hear.

Index

About the Author

Michael Lydon, a founding editor at *Rolling Stone,* has been writing about pop music for thirty years. The author of *Rock Folk, Boogie Lightning,* and *Writing and Life,* he has written for numerous publications, including *The New York Times, The Atlantic Monthly,* and *The Village Voice.* Lydon is also a professional musician and lives in New York City with his wife, composer Ellen Mandel.

Song Permissions

Chapter 4 "Choo Choo Ch'Boogie," words and music by Vaughn Horton, Denver Darling, and Milton Gabler. Copyright © 1945 (Renewed) RYTVOC, Inc. All rights reserved. Used by permission. **Chapter 10** "It Shoulda Been Me" by Memphis Curtis. Copyright © 1954 (Renewed) Chappell & Co. All rights reserved. Used by permission. WARNER BROS. PUBLICATIONS U.S. INC., Miami, FL 33014. **Chapter 12** "The Hucklebuck" by Roy Alfred & Andy Gibson. Copyright © 1949 by Bienstock Publishing Co., Jerry Leiber Music, Mike Stoller Music, and Seven Eight Nine Music Assocs. Rights for World excluding U.S. controlled by Music Sales Corp. (ASCAP) Copyright renewed. All rights reserved. Used by permission. • "I Got a Woman" by Ray Charles & Renald Richard. Copyright © 1954 (Renewed) Unichappell Music Inc. & Mijac Music. All rights administered by Unichappell Music. All rights reserved. Used by permission. WARNER BROS. PUBLICATIONS U.S. INC., Miami, FL 33014. **Chapter 13** "Hard Times No One Knows" by Ray Charles. Copyright © 1959 (Renewed) Unichappell Music. All rights reserved. Used by permission. WARNER BROS. PUBLICATIONS U.S. INC., Miami, FL 33014. • "Fool for You" by Ray Charles. Copyright © 1962 (Renewed) Unichappell Music. All rights reserved. Used by permission. WARNER BROS. PUBLICATIONS U.S. INC., Miami, FL 33014. • "Hallelujah I Love Her So" by Ray Charles. Copyright © 1956 (Renewed) Unichappell Music. All rights reserved. Used by permission. WARNER BROS. PUBLICATIONS U.S. INC., Miami, FL 33014. • "Lonely Avenue" by Doc Pomus. Copyright © 1956 (Renewed) Unichappell Music. All rights reserved. Used by permission. WARNER BROS. PUBLICATIONS U.S. INC., Miami, FL 33014. • "What Kind of Man Are You" by Ray Charles. Copyright © 1958 (Renewed) Unichappell Music. All rights reserved. Used by permission. WARNER BROS. PUBLICATIONS U.S. INC., Miami, FL 33014. • "I Had a Dream" by Ricky Harper & Ray Charles. Copyright © 1958 (Renewed) Unichappell Music. All rights reserved. Used by permission. WARNER BROS. PUBLICATIONS U.S. INC., Miami, FL 33014. **Chapter 14** "When Your Lover Has Gone" by E. A. Swan. Copyright © 1931 (Renewed) Warner Bros. Inc. All rights reserved. Used by permission. WARNER BROS. PUBLICATIONS U.S. INC., Miami, FL 33014. "I Believe to My Soul" by Ray Charles. Copyright © 1959 (Renewed) Unichappell Music. All rights reserved. Used by permission. WARNER BROS. PUBLICATIONS U.S. INC., Miami, FL